Early Church Records

of

Lebanon County, Pennsylvania

F. Edward Wright

HERITAGE BOOKS
2019

HERITAGE BOOKS

AN IMPRINT OF HERITAGE BOOKS, INC.

Books, CDs, and more—Worldwide

For our listing of thousands of titles see our website
at
www.HeritageBooks.com

Published 2019 by
HERITAGE BOOKS, INC.
Publishing Division
5810 Ruatan Street
Berwyn Heights, Md. 20740

International Standard Book Number
Paperbound: 978-1-58549-388-3

CONTENTS

INTRODUCTION

Material for this Introduction was taken from two main sources. 1) *Pastors and People, Volume I: Pastors and Congregations*. By Charles H. Glatfelter. Breinigsville: The Pennsylvania German Society, 1980. Cited as Glatfelter; and 2) *History Of The Counties Of Dauphin And Lebanon In The Commonwealth Of Pennsylvania: Biographical And Genealogical*. By William Henry Egle, M.D., M.A. Philadelphia: Everts & Peck, 1883. Cited as Egle.

Researchers may also be interested in the following sources:

Cemetery Map of Lebanon Co., PA, pub. by the Lebanon County
    Historical Society, 924 Cumberland St., Lebanon, PA 17042.
    Reviewed in *Our Name's The Game* 11 (11) 1.

Lebanon County was established in February 1813, when it was cut off from Dauphin County, which in turn had been taken in 1785 from Lancaster County. Settlers began arriving in present-day Lebanon County in the 1730s, coming into the county from the south and the east. The Scotch-Irish settled in the southwestern portion of the county. By the 1740s, most of the population was German.

Pennsylvania churches were often named in several ways: the same church might have a name that reflected a geographical reference, a name of one of the Apostles or other religious leaders, and the name taken from one of the founders. To avoid confusion, the names used are, for the most part, the names as given in Glatfelter.

Repositories mentioned in the text include:
    ERHS: Evangelical and Reformed Historical Society, Lancaster, PA.
    LAC: Lutheran Archives Center at Philadelphia, Lutheran
Theological Seminary, Philadelphia, PA.
    LTC: Lutheran Theological Seminary (either at Gettysburg or at
Philadelphia).
    RCR Reformed Church Records.

THE CHURCHES

LUTHERAN AND REFORMED

BINDNAGEL'S
North Londonderry Township.

The Lutheran congregation dates from the 1730s.

Lutheran Pastors: Casper Stoever, until his death in 1779; Frederick Melsheimer, 1779-c1784; Casper Hoerner, 1787-c.1794; George Lochman, c1795

The Lutheran congregation is known as Bindnagel's, two miles north of Palmyra.

Sources:
Records of Bindnagle Church, near Palmyra... By E.W.S. Parthemore, comp. Harrisburg: 1866.
"The Bindnagel Church," by John W. Early, *Lebanon County Historical Society Papers* 1 (1898): 57-70.
Egle published early marriages, baptisms, and tombstone inscriptions (Egle, pp. 221-222).

CAMPBELLTOWN

The Lutheran congregation is first mentioned in the synod minutes of 1794. Its records cover the years 1794-1889.

Lutheran Pastors: George Lochman, 1794

The Reformed congregation is now called Salem United Church of Christ. It probably dates from the time of the Lutheran congregation, but is first definitely mentioned in 1820. There are no early records for the Reformed congregation.

Sources:
Lutheran Register, on MF at the LAC, Philadelphia.
Notes and Queries, Annual Volume 1898 (1899). By William H. H. Egle, pp. 132-135, 137-140, 147-151.

FREDERICKSBURG (also called STUMPTOWN and NEWTOWN)

The Lutheran congregation was mentioned in a deed of 1766, about the time the church was built.

Lutheran Pastors: Casper Stoever; Peter Mischler; Emanuel Schultze, 1774-1783; William Kurtz, 1783-1799

The Reformed congregation probably dates from about 1766, as it used the same building as the Lutherans. The congregation was considered to be a successor to the one at Swatara.

Reformed Pastors: Conrad Bucher, 1770-1780; William Runkel, 1780-1784; Lewis Lupp, 1785-1798

Both congregations are known as St. John's, and both are located in Fredericksburg.

Sources:
Lutheran Register, for "Stumpstown," was begun in 1774; the translation is at the Lutheran Theological Seminary in Gettysburg.

GRUBBEN
South Lebanon Township

Salem Lutheran Church may date from as early as 1747. (Egle gives c.1733/5 as the date).

Lutheran Pastors: John Casper Stoever; Frederick Augustus Muhlenberg, 1773-1775; William Kurtz, 1775-1794; George Lochman, 1794-1815

The Reformed congregation probably dates from the same time.

Reformed Pastors: Conrad Templeman, c.1750-1759; John Waldschmidt, c.1760

Sources:
Lebanon County Historical Society Papers 11 (1936): 32-34.
Egle published some early baptisms and marriages, but states that the
first regular, well preserved, register was begun by Muhlenberg on
1 May 1773. He also published inscriptions from two old cemeteries
attached to the church (Egle, pp. 139-141).

HEIDELBERGTOWN (or SCHAEFFERSTOWN)
Heidelberg Township

Both Lutheran and Reformed congregations (the latter possibly now
called St. Paul's United Church of Christ) began shortly after the town
was laid out in 1758 (Glatfelter). However, Egle states the congregatio
may have started around 1720, but the church was built in 1765. The
Lutheran Register was begun in 1763. The Reformed Register dates
from 1765.

Lutheran Pastors: John Casper Stoever; Nicholas Kurtz, c.1766-1770;
Frederick Muhlenberg, 1770-1773; Emanuel Schulze, 1775-1809
(Glatfelter), or Samuel Schultz, 1765-1810 (Egle, p. 201); Theophilus
Engelland; Peter Mischler

Reformed Pastors: Jacob Zufall, 1768-1769; William Hendel, 1769-1782;
William Runkel, 1783-1784; Andrew Loretz, 1785-1786; Daniel Wagner,
1786-1793; Lewis Lupp, 1793-1798

The Lutheran congregation is St. Luke's, East Main St.,
Schaefferstown.
The Reformed congregation is St. Paul's, Main St., Schaefferstown.

Sources:
Lutheran Register; translation at the Lutheran Theological Seminary in
Gettysburg.
Reformed Church Records 19, Evangelical and Reformed Historical
Society, Lancaster, PA.
History of St. Paul's United Church of Christ...Schaefferstown, PA
(1965).
Egle published early tombstone inscriptions (Egle, p. 202).

JONESTOWN

A Union Lutheran and Reformed Church was built c.1765 when trustees for both congregations were named in a deed. In 1792 the Lutherans built their own church. The Lutheran Register began in 1779.

Lutheran Pastors: Casper Stoever to 1779; Frederick Meischeimer, 1779-1785; William Kurtz, 1787-1793; George Lochman, 1793

The Reformed congregation was a successor to the Swatara congregation, and used their register.

The Lutheran congregation is Zion, Market and South King Streets, Jonestown.
The Reformed is St. John's United Church of Christ, West Market St., Jonestown.

Reformed Pastors: Frederick Casimir Miller, 1762-1768; Jacob Zufall, c1769; Conrad Bucher, 1770-1780; William Runkel, 1781-1784; Lewis Lupp, 1785-1798

Sources:
Lutheran Register; translation at the Lutheran Theological Seminary, Gettysburg.
Reformed Church Register 17, Evangelical and Reformed Historical Society, Lancaster, PA.
Centennial History of Lebanon Classis... . By Thomas S. Stein, comp. Lebanon: 1920. (See pp. 280-286).

KIMMERLING'S, QUITOPAHILLA (QUITTAPAHILLA)
Lebanon Township

The Reformed congregation (now St. Jacob's United Church of Christ) dates from 1750 if not earlier. The Register was started in 1752 by Conrad Templeman.

Reformed Pastors: Conrad Templeman, c1755; William Stoy, 1756; Henry Decker, 1756-1763; Jacob Zufall, 1765-1769; William Hendel,

1770-1773; Conrad Bucher, 1773-1780; William Runkel, 1782-1784; Lewis Lupp, 1786-1797

The congregation is St. Jacob's United Church of Christ, two miles east of Lebanon.

Sources:
Reformed Church Register 19, Evangelical and Reformed Historical Society, Lancaster, PA.
The History of St. Jacob's (Kimmerling's) Church. 1970.

LEBANON

The Lutheran congregation was organized soon after the town began (it was laid out in 1761). Its register begins in 1773.

Lutheran Pastors: John Casper Stoever, c1762-1779; Frederick Muhlenberg, 1771-1773; Emanuel Schultze, c.1774-1780; and William Kurtz, c.1775-c.1780, and 1781-1794.

The Reformed (or "Dutch Presbyterian") congregation got its first deed in 1760 and a second deed in 1765. Its register begins in 1764.

Reformed Pastors: Frederick Casimir Miller, c.1762-1766; Conrad Bucher, c.1769-1780; William Runkel, 1781-1784; Andrew Loretz, 1785-1786; and Lewis Lupp, 1786-1798.

The Lutheran congregation is Salem, 119 North Eighth Street, Lebanon.
The Reformed congregation is Tabor United Church of Christ, Tenth and Walnut Sts., Lebanon.

Sources:
RCR 20, ERHS, Lancaster.
Old Salem in Lebanon... . By Theodore E. Schmauk. Lebanon, 1898.
First (Tabor) Reformed Church: History of Pastors and Congregations, 1760-1935. By William J. Hinke and William D. Happel. 1935

MILLBACH
Millcreek Township

Millbach Reformed Church, Mill Creek Twp., was organized in 1747. The Lutheran congregation does not, as has been stated elsewhere, date from 1747. Milbach was a Union Church from 1853 to 1964/7.

Reformed Pastors: Conrad Templeman, c.1745-1752; William Stoy, 1753-1754; Frederick Casimir Miller; Jacob Zufall, 1765-1767; William Hendel, 1769-1782; and William Hendel, Jr., 1793-1822.

The Reformed congregation is St. Paul's United Church of Christ, two miles east of Newmanstown.

Sources:
Reformed Church Review 9 (1905):533-534
RCR 17, ERHS, Lancaster, PA
The Reformed Church in Pennsylvania. Lancaster: 1902, pp. 178-181.
Egle published early tombstones (Egle, p. 214).

MOUNT JOY
South Londonderry Township

The Lutheran congregation was organized in 1771 at which time it was in Mount Joy Township, from which it took its name. The Register was begun in 1774.

Lutheran Pastors: Peter Mischler; Michael Enderlein, 1774-1778; Daniel Schroeter, 1778-1782; Frederick Melsheimer, 1783-1786; William Kurtz, 1787-1788; and Peter Bentz, c.1709-1801.

The congregation is now called Trinity, located some two miles south of Colebrook.

Sources:
A Church of Many Names: The Story of Trinity Lutheran Church, Colebrook, Pennsylvania. By Frederick S. Weiser. Colebrook: 1971.

QUITOPAHILLA (QUITTAPAHILLA), HILL
North Annvile Township

Hill Lutheran and Reformed Church, North Annville Twp, was built in 1733. The first definite reference to a Lutheran congregation was in 1743. The first clear reference to a Reformed congregation was in 1740.

Lutheran Pastors: John Casper Stoever, 1733-1779; Frederick Melsheimer, 1794-1784; and Casper Hoerner, 1787-c.1794

The Lutheran congregation is Hill Church, one mile north of Cleona. The Reformed is Hill United Church of Christ, Hill Church Road, Cleona.

Sources:
Lutheran Register, Translation, LTS, Gettysburg.
RCR 17, ERHS, Lancaster.
Egle published early tombstone inscriptions (Egle, pp. 225-227).

SWATARA
Bethel Township

The Reformed congregation was established in the late 1730s. There may have also been a Lutheran congregation, but there is no proof as to its existence. The book for the Register for the Reformed Church was purchased in 1751 but contains some 107 baptisms said to have been performed between 1740 and 1756.

Reformed Pastors: Conrad Templeman, v.1740-1743, 1746-1756; Henry Decker, 1757-1760; and Frederick Casimir Miller, 1762-1768.

Sources:
RCR 17, ERHS, Lanncaster.
"Two Dead and Lost Churches of the Swatara," by E. Grumbine, *Lebanon County Historical Society Papers* 1 (1901): 291-304.

TOLPEHILL, LITTLE SWATARA, SWATARA, BETHEL
Bethel Township

The Reformed congregation dates from the early 1750s. The Register contains several baptisms in 1750, with no subsequent entries until 1770.

Reformed Pastors: William Stoy, 1752 and 1756; Conrad Templeman, 1753-1756; Frederick Casimir Miller; Jacob Zufall, 1765-1767, 1769; William Hendel, 1769-1782; William Runkel, 1782-1784; Andrew Loretz, 1785-1786; Daniel Wagner, 1786-1793; and William Hendel, Jr., from 1793.

The congregation is now St. Paul's United Church of Christ, Hamlin.

Sources:
RCR 19, ERHS, Lancaster.
Pennsylvania State Reports 191. New York: 1899, 306-314.

TULPEHOCKEN, LITTLE TULPEHOCKEN
(originally) Tulpehocken, (now) Jackson Township

The Reformed congregation was mentioned by Philip Boehm in 1738. The Register was begun in 1748.

Reformed Pastors: Dominicus Bartholomae, 1748-1751; William Stoy, 1752-1756; John Waldschmidt, 1756-1758; William Otterbein, 1758-1760; Jacob Zufall, 1765-1767; William Hendel, 1768-1782; Andrew Loretz, 1785-1786; and Daniel Wagner, 1786-1793.

The congregation is now Tulpehocken Trinity United Church of Christ, Richland.

Sources:
RCR 18, ERHS, Lancaster.

WALMER'S
(originally) Hanover, (now) Union Township.

The Reformed congregation dates from c.1772. No records from the
18th Century have survived.

Salem and Walmer's within the Indiantown Gap Military
Reservation still comprise a union church, with a Cooperative Ministry.

ZIEGEL
Bethel Township

The Lutheran congregation is first mentioned in the synod minutes of
1784. The congregation is Zoar, five miles northeast of Lebanon.

Sources:
Register, Translation, LTS, Gettysburg.

MORAVIAN

Bethel Moravian Church, Bethel Township, was organized by Count
Zinzendorf v.1743/4. Pastors were: Rev. Johannes Brandmueller,
Mr. Frederick Schlegel, 1756-1763. Egle published early tombstone
inscriptions (p. 176).

Hebron Moravian Church, South Lebanon Twp., was established in
1743. Until 1750 it was affiliated with Warwick Moravian in
Lancaster Co. Pastors were: Rev. Christian Rauch, 1750. Egle
published early tombstones (p. 159).

ROMAN CATHOLIC

St. Mary's Roman Catholic Church, Lebanon Borough, was one of the
oldest Catholic missions in Lebanon County, and was formed early
in the 18th Century (Egle, p. 143).

Priests included:
Fr. Louis DeBarth (later administrator of the Diocese of Philadelphia)
Fr. Fitzsimmons.

Robert W. Barnes

MAP OF LEBANON COUNTY

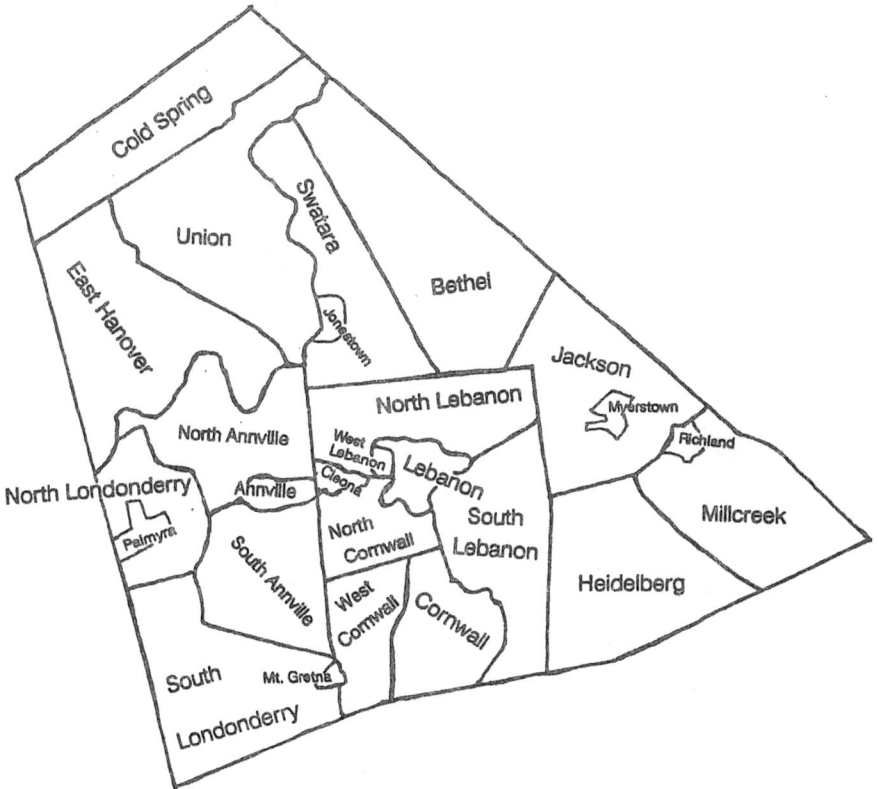

TABOR FIRST REFORMED CHURCH

BAPTISMS BY FREDERICK CASIMIR MUELLER, 1764-1766

Son of Jacob Graff and wife, bapt. Jul 30, 1765. Spon: Fridrich C.
Müller, (pastor) and wife.

Son of Nickolaus Lotz and wife, bapt. Sep 1, (1765). Spon: Henrich
Bauman and wife.

Son of Jacob Weibel and wife, bapt. Jul 30. Spon: Adam Weibel and
wife.

Dau. Melleh Rap and wife, bapt. Oct 12. Spon: Philip Grünewalt and
wife.

Dau. of Abraham (Rohland) and wife, bapt. Apr 26. Spon: Fridrich C.
Müller and wife.

Dau. of Abraham Rohland and wife, bapt. Sep 29. Spon: Abraham
Roland.

Susanna of Felix Müller and wife, bapt. Oct 15, 1759. Spon: Jacob
Bickel and Susanna Klein.

Carl of Felix Müller and wife, bapt. Oct 4, 1764. Spon: Carl Arnd and
wife.

Magdalena of Felix Müller and wife; b. Sep 26, 1767. Spon: Heinrich
Miller and wife.(This baptism by another hand.)

Son of Henrich Bauman and wife, bapt. Nov 25, 1765. Spon: Nicklas
Lotz and wife.

Dau. of Johannes Hambscher and wife, bapt. Nov 25, 1765. Spon:
Henrich Rewalt and Maria Schuhmacher.

Son of Peter Ritschart and wife, bapt. Nov 22, (1765). Spon:
Johannes Umberger and Catharine.

Son of --- Crumbein and wife, bapt. Jan 5, 1766. Spon: Jörg Gebhart
and wife.

Child of Johannes Fiessel and wife, bapt. Jan 2. Spon: Fridrich C.
Müller and wife.

Dau. of --- Bolman and wife, bapt. Mar 2, (1766). Spon: ---.

Son of Philip Dinges and wife, bapt. Mar 7. Spon: the father.

Son of Auren Jäckly and wife, bapt. Mar 30. Spon: Philip Gruenewald
and wife.

Son of Jacob Gundy and wife, bapt. Apr 5. Spon: Michel Keller.

(This is the last entry of Müeller.)

Maria Magdalena of Margaret Egstein, a widow, bapt. May 25, 1766. Spon: Heinrich Rewalt and wife.

Anna Catharine of Marty Zuber and wife, bapt. Jun 15, 1766. Spon: Georg Müller and wife.

David of John Rohrer and wife, bapt. Jul 27, 1766. Spon: David Deiss and wife.

Maria Elizabeth of Gottfried Keiser and wife, bapt. Jul 7, 1766. Spon: Michel Bush.

Johannes of Johannes Jäger and wife, bapt. Jul 30, 1767. Spon: Johan Brenner and wife.

Maria Elisabeth of Dewald Gerst and wife, bapt. May 29, 1768. Spon: Heinrich Schlosser and Maria Elisabetha Gerst.

(The next six baptisms entered by unknown hand.)

Barbara of Ludwig Istler and Appollonia, b. Feb 23, 1766; bapt ---. Spon: Conrad Menzinger and Barbara.

Barbara of Christian Meas and Charlotte, b. Sep 26, 1765. Spon: Caspar Diller and Barbara.

Catharine of Christian Meas and Charlotte, b. Oct 9, 1767. Spon: Joh. Rohrer and Barbara.

Georg of Georg McCunlde and Eva, b. Feb 24, 1770. Spon: John Rohrer and Barbara.

Maria Elisabeth of Heinrich Stephan and Louisa, b. Aug 19, 1770. Spon: Georg Wampler and Mary Elisabeth.

Johannes of Heinrich Stephan and Louisa, b. Jun 10, 1772. Spon: Michael Carmeny and Catharine.

Maria Catharine of Heinrich Stephan and Louisa, b. Sep 1, 1773. Spon: parents.

(These entries were made by Conrad Busher.[handwritten])

BAPTISMS BY REV. JOHN CONRAD BUCHER

Samuel of Georg Fée and Margaret, b. Jun 3, 1772. Spon: Samuel Myley and Catharine.

Michael of J. Nicklas Jaque and Maria Elizabetha, b. Nov 24, 1768. Spon: Adam Schally and Catharine.

Henrich of Rudolph Kelcker and Maria, b. Dec 5, 1768, bapt. Dec 18. Spon: Anthony Kelcker and Magdalene.

BAPTISMS ENTRIES BY REV. JOHN CONRAD BUCHER, 1769-1780

Joh. Christian and Heinrich Rehwald and Anna Maria, b. Jun 17, 1769; bapt. Nov 10, 1771. Spon: Christian Meas and Charlotte.

Catharine of Heinrich Rehwald and Anna Maria, b. Oct 25, 1771; bapt. Nov 10, 1771. Spon: Samuel Meyly and Catharine.

Anna Dorothea of Conrad Bucher and Maria Magdalena, b. Jul 17, 1769; bapt. Jul 19; d. Sep 3, 1770. Spon: J. Philip de Haas and Eleonora.

Johan David of Martin Meylin and Catharine, b. Jun 30, 1769. Spon: Joh. David Fortune and Catharina Merck.

Cath. Elizabeth of Jacob Weiser and Catharine, b. Aug 17, 1769. Spon: Peter Schlosser and wife.

Heinrich Peter of Matheys Rheinhart and Maria Catharina. bapt. Aug 17, 1769; bapt. Sep 10. Spon: Dan Bibell and Maria Margaret.

Johan Joseph of Heinrich Bouman and Barbara, Sep 19, 1769; bapt. Oct 1, 1769. Spon: Nicklaus Lutz and Rosina.

Johannes of Johannes Hemming and Elizabetha, b. Oct 8, 1769; bapt. Oct 29. Spon: Nicklaus Weiss and Barbara.

Georg of Jacob Folk and Maria, b. May 21, 1769; bapt. Dec 24. Spon: Jacob Schmidt and Catharine.

Johannes of Joh. Jacob Pfeiffer and Margaret, b. Nov 29, 1769; bapt. Dec 24. Spon: Joh. Adam Stein and Maria Magdalena.

Heinrich of Heinrich Jungst and Catharine, b. Nov 6, 1769; bapt. Jan 7, 1770. Spon: parents.

Susanna of Ludwig Istler and Apollonia, b. Dec 26, 1769; bapt. Jan 7, 1770. Spon: Georg Russlin and Susanna.

Johannes of Christian Meess and Charlotte, b. Dec 29, 1769; bapt. Jan 7, 1770. Spon: Johannes Schweyger and Eleonora.

Maria of John Thom and Anna Maria, b. Dec 30, 1769; bapt. Jan 7, 1770. Spon: Christopher Uhler and Barbara.

Maria Magdalena of Adam Heberlin and Martha, b. Nov 26, 1769; bapt. Jan 30, 1770. Spon: Mar. Magdalena Bucher.

Anna Margaretha of Caspar Jost and wife, b. ----; bapt. Mar 3, 1770. Spon: Anna Marg.

Maria Magdalena of Dewald Kerst and Maria Barbara, b. Feb 17, 1770; bapt. Mar 18. Spon: Heinrich Schlosser and Elizabeth Kerst.

Anna Christina of Jacob Ziegler and Juliana, b. Feb 18, 1770; bapt.

Mar 18. Spon: Martin Kirstetter and Elizabeth.

Margaretha of Bernhard Meyer and Anna Maria, b. Feb 11, 1770; bapt. Mar 22. Spon: mother.

Catharine of Georg Gruppensch and Elizabeth; bapt. Mar 14, 1770; bapt. Apr 1. Spon: Daniel Fitzberger and Catharine.

Maria of Samuel Hook and Hannah, b. Jun 11, 1765; bapt. Apr 14, 1770. Spon: mother.

Anna Maria of Baltaser Schally and Barbara, b. Apr 4, 1770; bapt. Apr 15. Spon: Heinrich Schlosser and Anna Maria Schallen.

Anna Barbara of Georg Atkinson and Barbara, b. May 19, 1770; bapt. May 27. Spon: Carl Arndt and Barbara.

Maria Elizabeth of Lucas Schally and Margaretha, b. May 4, 1770; bapt. Jun 24. Spon: Joh. Nicklaus Jaque and Mar. Elizabeth.

Eva Margaret of Felton Cornmann and Margaret, b. Jun 24, 1770; bapt. Jul 8. Spon: Johannes Lehn and Anna Eva.

Veronica of Peter Schally and Elizabeth, b. Sep 19, 1770; bapt. Sep 30. Spon: Carl Schally and Veronica Mattern.

Johann Jacob of Georg Adam Jaque and Maria Barbara, b. Nov 7, 1770; bapt. Nov 25. Spon: Jacob Zieger and Judith.

Anna Maria of Heinrich Miller and Elizabeth; bapt. Nov 17, 1770; bapt. Nov 25. Spon: Joh. Georg Stein and Maria Eva Heylman.

Johannes of Johannes Umberger and Elizabetha, b. Nov 9, 1770; bapt. Nov 25, 1770. Spon: Joh. Melchior Abmeyer and Anna Maria.

Elisabeth of Johannes Hemming and Elizabeth, b. Oct 4, 1770; bapt. Nov 25, 1770. Spon: Jacob Thomah and Ursula.

Catr. Elizabetha of Baltasar Steger and Elisabeth, b. Oct 14, 1770; bapt. Nov 25, 1770. Spon: Joh. Adam Stein and Cath. Eliz. Steger.

Johann Heinrich of Heinrich Gilpert and Susanna, b. Dec 22, 1770; bapt. Dec 25, 1770. Spon: Friedrich Steindorff and Anna Magdalena.

Abraham of Abraham Roland and Maria Eva, b. Jan 1, 1771; bapt. Jan 2, 1771. Spon: Catharine Finley.

Maria Margaret of Joseph County and Magdalena, b. Sep 2, 1770; bapt. Feb 17, 1771. Spon: Philip Grunewald and Margaret.

Johann Philip of Philip Greber and Cathrine, b. Jan 26, 1771; bapt. Feb 17, 1771. Spon: Philip Ebrecht and Elizabeth.

Susanna Barbara of Georg Dietrich and Dorothea, b. Mar 20, 1771; bapt. Mar 28, 1771. Spon: Friedrich Pollman and Susanna.

Eleonora Dorothea of Conrad Bucher and Maria Magdalena, b. Apr

22, 1771; bapt. May 12, 1771; d. Dec 18, 1772. Spon: Joh. Philip de Haas and Eleonora.

Johannes of Martin Imhoff and Maria Barbara, b. May 1, 1771; bapt. May 26, 1771. Spon: Wilhelm Denius and Anna Maria.

Daniel of Adam Schally and Catharina Elizabeth, b. May 22, 1771; bapt. Jun 9, 1771. Spon: Daniel Fizberger and Cattrine.

Cathr. Elizabeth of J. Nicklaus Jaque and Maria Elizabeth, b. May 16, 1771; bapt. Jun 23, 1771. Spon: Adam Schally and Cathr. Elizabeth.

Johannes of Johann Bouman and Elizabeth, b. Jun 20, 1771; bapt. Jul 21, 1771; d. Mar 4, 1773. Spon: Georg Stroh and Anna Angelica.

Barbara of Johannes Seyler and Maria, b. Jul 8, 1771; bapt. Jul 21, 1771. Spon: Nicklaus Weiss and Barbara.

Anna Maria of Jacob Pfeiffer and Margaretha, b. Jul 16, 1771; bapt. Aug 18, 1771. Spon: Baltasar Noll and Anna Maria.

Jacob of Heinrich Jüngst and Catharine, b. Sep 19, 1771; bapt. Sep 29, 1771. Spon: parents.

Barbara of David Theys and Elisabetha, b. Sep 24, 1771; bapt. Oct 13, 1771. Spon: Antony Doebler and Magdalena.

Elisabeth of Georg Gebhard and Elisabetha, b. Oct 19, 1771; bapt. Oct 21, 1771; d. Dec 31, 1771. Spon: Jacob Deney and Elisabeth Gebhard.

Johann Georg of Jacob Eichholtz and Anna Maria, b. Sep 21, 1771; bapt. Oct 28, 1771 Spon: Caspar Jost and Magdalena.

Johannes of Jacob Lämberlin and Hannah, b. Oct 8, 1771; bapt. Nov 10, 1771. Spon: J. Melchior Abmeyer and Maria.

Samuel of Heinrich Meyly and Catharine, b. Aug 27, 1771; bapt. Nov 22; d. Jul 27, 1774. Spon: Samuel Meyly and Catharine.

Anabella of James Britton and Mary, b. Jul 7, 1771; bapt. Dec 18, 1771. Spon: mother.

Maria Margretha of Heinrich Meyer and Maria Magdalena, b. Dec 20, 1771; bapt. Dec 25, 1771. Spon: Simon Boehler and Mar. Margretha.

Johannes of Jacob Weber and Margretha, Nov 27, 1771; bapt. Dec 25, 1771. Spon: Johann Rohrer and Barbara.

Johann Christoph of Johannes Rüger and Susanna, b. Nov 2, 1771; bapt. Jan 1, 1772. Spon: Christoph Meyer and Cathrina.

Cathrina of Caspar Jost and Magdalena, b. Dec 10, 1771; bapt. Feb 11, 1772; Oct 19, 1772. Spon: Jacob Fortune and Margaretha.

Johann Philip of Georg Grupensch and Elizabeth, b. Jan 22, 1722;

bapt. Feb 16, 1772. Spon: Joh. Philip Greber and Cathrina.

Joh. Philip of Joh. Umberger and Elizabetha, b. Jan 24, 1772; bapt.
Feb 21, 1772. Spon: Philip Grunewald and Margretha.

Joh. Heinrich of Heinrich Umberger and Margaretha, b. Jan 20, 1772;
bapt. Feb 21, 1772. Spon: Peter Jetter and Anna Maria.

Johannes of Georg Meess and Elizabeth, b. Jan 31, 1772; bapt. Mar
1, 1772. Spon: Martin Jensel and Cathrina Emptich.

Anna Barbara of Joh. Rohrer and Barbara, b. Feb 17, 1772; bapt.
Mar 15; d. Feb 26, 1773. Spon: Jacob Weber and Margaretha.

Joh. Georg of Michael Lauri and Jacobina, b. Mar 14, 1772; bapt. Mar
19, 1772. Spon: Joh. Georg Roesly and Susanna.

Joh. Jacob of Jacob Meyer and Barbara, b. Mar 23, 1772; bapt. Apr 3,
1772. Spon: Christoph Meyer and Cathrina.

Anna Maria of Jacob Ziegler and Juliana, b. Mar 22, 1772; bapt. Apr
16, 1772. Spon: Martin Kirchstetter and Elizabeth.

Cathrina of Felton Cornman and Margaretha, b. Apr 15, 1772; bapt.
Apr 26, 1772. Spon: Peter Lehn and Cathrina Cornman.

Cathrina of Michael Busch and Elisabeth; b. Apr 17, 1772; bapt. Apr
26, 1772. Spon: Joh. Brenner and Cathrina.

Eva Elisabetha of Jacob Dui and Cathrina, b. Mar 10, 1772; bapt. Apr
26, 1772. Spon: Eva Eliz. Ramler.

Susanna of Jacob Rudi and Susanna, b. Apr 2, 1772; bapt. Apr 26,
1772. Spon: Joh. Georg Roesly and Susanna.

Anna Margareth of Ludwig Schäffer and Anna Margaretha, b. May --,
1768; bapt. Apr 26, 1772. Spon: Heinrich Schäffer and Anna
Margreth.

Johannes of Ludwig Schäffer and Anna Margaretha, b. Dec 11, 1769;
bapt. Apr 26, 1772. Spon: parents.

Anna Elisabetha of Ludwig Schäffer and Anna Margaretha, b. Jan --,
1772; bapt. Apr 26, 1772. Joh. Georg Glassbrenner and Anna
Elizabeth.

Johannes of John Barr and Elizabetha, b. Apr 2, 1772; bapt. May 10,
1772. Spon: John Miller and Veronica.

Philip of Jacob Schaffner and Eva, b. Apr 14, 1772; bapt. May 10,
1772. Spon: Jacob Schmidt, Jr. and Elizabeth.

Joh. Jacob of Heinrich Bauman and Barbara, b. Apr 5, 1772; bapt.
May 15, 1772. Spon: Elizabeth Weiss.

Elizabeth of Georg Ellinger and Anna Maria, b. Apr 29, 1772; bapt.
May 19, 1772. Spon: Elisabeth Roland.

Talitha of Wm. Hunter and Mary, b. Mar 12, 1772; bapt. May 23.

Spon: *mater infantis.*

Jacob of Sebastian Rudy and Anna, b. Jul 8, 1741; bapt. Jun 3, 1772. Spon: ---.

Heinrich of Jacob Rudy and Susanna, b. Feb 20, 1769; bapt. Jun 3, 1772. Spon: ----.

Maria of Nicklaus Weiss and (Barbara), b. Jun 1, 1772; bapt. ---. Spon: Joh. Zollinger and Maria Imhoff.

Maria Elizabeth of Mattheys Reinhard and Maria Cathrina, b. Jun 14, 1772; bapt. Jul 5, 1772. Spon: Joh. Jacob Emptich and Maria Elis. Roland.

Anna Maria of Adam Bald and Christina, b. Jun 4, 1772; bapt. Jul 20, 1772. Spon: Bernhard Pfeiffer and Anna Sibilla.

Elizabeth of Georg. Michael Wolfensberger and Elizabeth, b. Aur 22, 1772; bapt. Sep 13, 1772. Spon: Georg Stein and Margaretha.

--- of John Thom and Anna Maria, b. ---; bapt. Sep 13, 1772. Spon: ----.

Jacob of Jacob Smith and Elizabeth, b. Sep 2, 1772; bapt. Sep 15, 1772. Spon: Jacob Swob and Elizabeth.

Joh. Matheys of Johannes Huber and A. Maria Magdalena, b. Jul --, 1770; bapt. Oct 9, 1772. Spon: Jost Werning and Ann Angelica.

William and Robert Laury and Mary, b. Aug 9, 1772; bapt. Oct 10, 1772. Spon: parents.

Cathrina of Wilhelm Denius and Anna Maria, b. Sep 21, 1772; bapt. Oct 11, 1772. Spon: Joh. Denius and Anna Dorothea.

Joh. Henrich of Geo. Michael Weiss and Elisabeth; b. Oct 2, 1772; bapt. Oct 13, 1772. Spon: Heinrich Baumann and Barbara.

Cathrina of Johannes Jeger and Anna Maria, b. Sep 23, 1772; bapt. Nov 8, 1772. Spon: Heinrich Rickes and Cathrina Ritter.

Joh. Georg of Ludwig Istler and Apollonia, b. Nov 19, 1772; bapt. Dec 6, 1772. Spon: Joh. Georg Roesly and Susanna.

Anna Margaretha of Christian Smith and Maria Elizabetha, b. Dec 6, 1771; bapt. Dec 20, 1772. Spon: Carl Philip Benner and Anna Marg. Steger.

Anna Margaretha of Georg Stein and Margaretha, b. Dec 6, 1772; bapt. Jan 1, 1773. Spon: Peter Wolfensberger and Anna Apollonia.

Maria Elisabetha of Philip Greber and Cathrina, b. Jan 27, 1773; bapt. Jan 31, 1773. Spon: Georg Michael Weiss and Elizabeth.

Johannes of Georg Atkinson and Anna Barbara, b. Jan 10, 1773; bapt. Jan 31, 1773. Spon: Joh. Umberger and Elizabeth.

Joseph of Joh. Stein and Barbara, b. Jan 9, 1773; bapt. Feb 4, 1773.

Spon: Christoph Kucher and Anna Maria.

Christina of Johannes Clever and Maria Magdalena, b. Jan 29, 1773; bapt. Feb 5, 1773. Spon: Heinrich Beckly and Anna Maria.

Jacob of Heinrich Schäffer and Anna Margaretha, b. Dec 16, 1772; bapt. Feb 14, 1773. Spon: Jacob Rudi.

Jacob of Jacob Fortune and Margaret, b. Mar 2, 1773; bapt. Apr 9, 1773. Spon: parents.

Cath. Elizabeth of Jacob German and Maria Cathrina, b. Apr 3, 1773; bapt. Apr 11, 1773. Spon: Jacob Schmidt, Sr. and Cathrina.

Maria Elisabetha of Conrad Bucher and Maria Magdalena, b. Apr 8, 1773; bapt. Apr 25, 1773. Spon: Joh. Philip de Haas and Eleonora.

Michael of Georg Ellinger and Maria Cathrina, b. Apr 18, 1773; bapt. May 6, 1773. Spon: Geo. Michael Weiss and Elisabetha.

Joh. Jacob of Jacob Ruger and Margaretha, b. Dec 25, 1772; bapt. Jun 20, 1773. Spon: Jacob Schmidt, Jr. and Elisabeth.

Johannes of Adam Stein and wife, b. ----; bapt. Jun 20, 1773. Spon: ---.

Joh. Georg of Jacob Shaque [Jaque] and Elisabeth, b. May 12, 1773; bapt. Jul 4, 1773. Spon: Joh. Georg Roeslin and Susanna.

Johann Heinrich of Rudolph Kelker and Anna Maria, b. Jul 10, 1773, b. Aug 1, 1773; d. Feb 13, 1774. Spon: Antony Doebler and Maria Magdalena.

Elisabeth of Georg McCundle and Eva, b. Jul 16, 1773; bapt. Aug 1, 1773. Spon: Johann Cornman and Elisabeth.

Maria Barbara of Adam Jaque and Barbara, b. Aug 5, 1773; bapt. Aug 15, 1773. Spon: Jacob Ziger and Judith.

Johannes of Johannes Denius and Dorothea, b. Aug 11, 1773; bapt. Aug 29, 1773. Spon: Wm. Denius and Anna Maria.

Anna Margaretha of Thomas Smith and Magdalena, b. Jul 13, 1773; bapt. Aug 29, 1773. Spon: Johannes Peter and Ann Christina.

Johannes of Heinrich Jungst and Cathrina b. Aug 17, 1773; bapt. Sep 12, 1773. Spon: parents.

Anna Elisabetha of Nicklaus Gebhard and Anna Apollonia, b. Sep 1, 1773; bapt. Sep 12, 1773. Spon: Peter Schindel and Margaretha.

Elisabetha of Ulrich Boeklin and Eva Margaretha, b. b. Aug 30, 1773; bapt. Sep 12, 1773. Spon: Maria Ursina Bocklin.

Maria Dorothea of Johannes Ruger and Susanna; bapt. Aug 30, 1773; bapt. Sep 12, 1773. Spon: Georg German and Dorothea.

Joh. Jacob of Jacob Schneider and Anna, b. Sep 19, 1773; bapt. Sep 26, 1773. Spon: Eva Schaffer.

Johann Philip of Abraham Roland and Maria Eva, b. Sep 10, 1773;
bapt. Sep 12, 1773. Spon: Philip Grunewald and Margaretha.

Joh. Heinrich of Nicklaus Denius and Regina; bapt. Aug 20, 1773;
bapt. Sep 26, 1773. Spon: Martin Imhoff and Barbara.

Joh. Heinrich of Johannes Bauman and Elizabeth, b. Jun 19, 1773;
bapt. Oct 15, 1773 Spon: Philip Grunewald and Margaret.

Johannes of Christian Gasser and Elisabeth, b. Sep 4, 1773; bapt. Oct
20, 1773. Spon: Jost Werning and Ann Angelica.

Regina of David Theys and Elizabetha, b. Oct 16, 1773; bapt. ---.
Spon: Johannes Theys and Regina.

Johann Martin of Martin Imhoff and Barbara, b. Nov. 15, 1773; bapt.
Dec. 19. Spon: Joh. Nicklaus Weis and Barbara.

Johannes of Johannes Cornman and Elisabeth, b. Dec. 15, 1773; bapt.
Dec 15, 1773. Spon: Peter Schindel and Margaretha.

Margaretha of Johannes Umberger and Elizabeth, b. Dec. 20, 1773;
bapt. Jan 28, 1774. Spon: Daniel Fezenberger and Cathrina.

Maria Barbara of Michael Busch and Elisabetha, b. Mar 2, 1774; bapt.
Mar 3, 1774. Spon: Abraham Breiner and Maria Barbara.

Elisabeth of Baltsar Schally and Barbara b. Mar 1, 1774; bapt. Mar
11, 1774. Spon: Adam Shally and Elisabeth.

Johannes of Adam Jacobi and Anna Margaretha, b. Feb 7, 1774; bapt.
Mar 13, 1774. Spon: Baltasar Lauber and Cathrina.

Joh. Philip of Felton Cornman and Margaretha, b. Feb 13, 1774; bapt.
Mar 13, 1774. Spon: Philip Mees and Cathrina.

Emmanuel of Martin Meilin and Eliz. Cathrina, b. Mar 26, 1774; bapt.
Apr 2, 1774. Spon: Peter --- and Rosina Fortune.

Maria Catharina of George Meilin and Rachel, b. Jan 31, 1774; bapt.
Apr 2, 1774. Spon: parents.

Johannes of Michael Krebs and Margaretha, b. Mar 29, 1774; bapt.
Apr 10, 1774; d. -- 11, 1775. Spon: Jacob Fortune and Margaretha.

Anna Magdalena of Jacob Ziegler and Juliana, b. Apr 8, 1774; bapt.
Apr 24, 1774. Spon: Friedrich Huber and Cathrina.

Maria Elisabetha of Adam Schally and Cathr. Elisabeth, b. Apr 13,
1774; bapt. May 8, 1774. Spon: Joh. Nicklaus Jaque and Maria
Elisabeth.

Johannes of Jacob Smith, Jr. and Elizabetha, b. May 26, 1774; bapt.
Jun 5, 1774. Spon: Jacob Schaffner and Eva.

Anna Barbara of Johannes Schneblin and Elizabtha, b. May 26, 1774,
bapt. Jun 5, 1774. Spon: Jacob Schaffner and Eva.

Joh. Jacob of Johannes Brenner and Cathrina, b. Jun 24, 1774; bapt.

Jul 5, 1774. Spon: parents.

Abraham of Heinrich Rehwald and Anna Maria, b. Jul --, 1774; bapt. Jul 31, 1774. Spon: Joh. Meyer and Anna Maria.

Cathrina of Johannes Meyer and Anna Maria, b. Jul --, 1774; bapt. Jul 31, 1774. Spon: Martin Lutz and Barbara.

Bernhard of Ludwig Ischler and Apollonia, b. Aug 1, 1774; bapt. Aug 1, 1774; d. Aug 3. Spon: Bernhard Pfeiffer and Anna Sybilla.

Joh. Heinrich of Heinrich Meyer and Magdalena, b. Aug 25, 1774; bapt. Aug 28, 1774; d. Mar 2, 1777. Spon: Heinrich Seyler and Eva Cathrina.

Susanna of Lambert Shielin and Cathrina, b. Feb 26, 1772; bapt. Sep 24, 1774. Spon: parents.

Christian of Peter Farney and Barbara, b. Jan 4, 1752; bapt. Sep 25, 1774. Spon:--- .

Margaretha of Christoph Loeb and Margaretha, b. Sep 18, 1774; bapt. Oct 9, 1774. Spon: Jacob Weber and Margaretha.

Maria Cathrina of Georg Gilbert and Eva, b. Nov 16, 1774; bapt. Dec 17, 1774. Spon: Jacob Laubscher and Juliana.

Cathrina of Christian Schmidt and Maria Elisabeth, b. Nov 13, 1774; bapt. Dec 22, 1774. Spon: Joh. Benner and Elisabetha.

Joh. Nicolaus of Nicklaus Weiss and Barbara, b. Dec 23, 1774; bapt. Jan 3, 1775. Spon: Martin Imhoff and Barbara.

Joh. Philip of Wm. Denius and Anna Maria, b. Dec 10, 1774; bapt. Jan 4, 1775. Spon: Philip Denius and Magdalena.

Barbara of Joh. Denius and Dorothea, b. Dec 11, 1774; bapt. Jan 4, 1775. Spon: Martin Imhoff and Barbara.

Joh. Philip of J. Philip Meess and Cathrina, b. Jan 3, 1775; bapt. Jan 28, 1775; d. Aug 7, 1776. Spon: parents.

Joh. Heinrich of Jost Blecher and Maria Elisabeth, b. Jan 8, 1775; bapt. Feb 7, 1775; d. May 25, 1775. Spon: Heinrich Mänchen and Maria Cathrina.

Anna Margaretha of David Theys and Elisabetha, b. Dec 29, 1774; bapt. Feb 7, 1775. Spon: Joh. Rohrer and Barbara.

Maria Magdalena of Bartholome Wicker and Mar. Dorothea Gunter, b. Jan 22, 1775; bapt. Feb 7, 1775. Spon: Heinrich Rewald and Anna Maria.

Catharina of Joh. Heinrich Münch and Mar. Cathrina, b. Mar 2, 1775; bapt. Mar 12, 1775. Spon: Jost Belcher and Mar. Elizabeth.

Heinrich of Heinrich Lang and Margaretha, b. Dec 9, 1774; bapt. Mar 12, 1775. Spon: Peter Brehm and Margaretha.

Barbara of Heinr. Bouman and Barbara, b. Feb 8, 1775; bapt. ---.
Spon: Jacob Hegy and Christina.

Johannes of Peter Spiker and Anna Maria; bapt. Feb 26, 1775; bapt.
---. Spon: Christoph Uhler and Barbara.

Geo. Michael of Matheys Dippel and wife, b. Mar 26, 1775; bapt. - --.
Spon: Geo. Michael Weiss and Elizabeth.

Jacob of Rudolph Kelker and Anna Maria, b. Mar 16, 1775; bapt. Apr
9, 1775. Spon: parents.

Christian of Joh. Jeger and Anna Maria, b. Mar 17, 1775; bapt. Apr
15, 1775, Spon: Christian Jeger.

Anna Elisabetha of Jacob Fortune and Margaretha, b. Apr 10, 1775;
bapt. May 21, 1775. Spon: parents.

George Matheys of Georg Meess and Maria Elisabeth, b. Dec 1, 1774;
bapt. Mary 30, 1775. Spon: Matheys Reinhard and Mar. Cathr.

Thomas of Georg Tee and Margaret, b. Apr 16, 1775; bapt. Jun 3,
1775. Spon: Jost Werning and Ann Angelica.

Anna Elizabetha of Christian Lup and Maria Elisabetha, b. May 16,
1775; bapt. Jun 4, 1775. Spon: Joh. Sassaman and A. Magd.
Steindorff.

Johann Conrad of Conrad Bucher and Maria Magdalena, b. Jun 18,
1775; bapt. Jul 16, 1775. Spon: Melchior Ram and Rebecca.

Eleonora of John Atkinson and Cathrina, b. May 27, 1775; bapt.Jul
26, 1775. Spon: Joh. Umberger and Elizabetha.

Robert of Robert Laury and Mary, b. Jul 23, 1775; bapt. Aug 25,
1775. Spon: parents.

Mar. Elisabetha of Georg Michael Weiss and Elisabeth, b. Aug 26,
1775; bapt. Sep 10, 1775. Spon: Ludwig Schott and Cathrina.

Philip Jacob of Philip Jacob Duboy and Elisabeth, b. Aug 2, 1775;
bapt. Sep 10, 17745. Spon: parents.

Philip of Johannes Meess and Elisabeth, b. Aug 14, 1774; bapt. Sep
14, 1775. Spon: Philip Faust and Margaretha.

Cathrina of Peter Bornn and Barbara, b. Feb --, 1757; bapt. Sep 30,
1775. Spon: ----.

Maria Cathrina of Peter Weyrich and Maria Cathrina, b. Aug 15,
1775; bapt. Oct 3, 1775. Spon: mother.

Anna of William Corroser and Mary, b. May 1, 1775; bapt. Oct 4,
1775. Spon: mother.

Joh. Jacob of Joh. Balsley and Margaretha, b. Sep 14, 1775; bapt. Oct
8, 1775. Spon: Jacob Meass and Cathrina.

Johannes of Jacob Hederich and Anna Maria, b. Sep 26, 1775; bapt.

Oct 22, 1775. Spon: Joh. Zolicker and Elizabeth Cor.

Elisabetha of Johann Umberger and Elisabeth, b. Sep 14, 1775; bapt.
Nov 5, 1775. Spon: Godfried Eichelberner and Juliana.

Cathr. Elisabeth of Adam Shaque and Barbara, b. Oct 17, 1775; bapt.
Nov 5, 1775. Spon: Joh. Zieger and Elis. Shaque.

Magdelena of J. Nicklaus Schaque and Maria Elisabetha, b. Sep 28,
1775; bapt. Nov 5, 1775. Spon: Adam Schally and Cathr. Elisab.

Margaretha of Johannes Stein and Barbara, b. Sep 23, 1775; bapt.
Nov 19, 1775. Spon: George Stein and Margaretha.

Joh. Godfried of Geo. Grupensch and Elisabeth, b. Oct 18, 1775; bapt.
Dec 3, 1775. Spon: Godfried Eichelberner and Juliana.

Maria Elisabeth of Adam Schally and Cathr. Elisabetha, b. Sep 27,
1775; bapt. Nov 5, 1775. Spon: J. Nicklaus Schaque and Maria
Elisab.

Maria Elisabeth of Jacob Weyrich and Margaretha, b. Dec 9, 1775;
bapt. Dec 26, 1775. Spon: Christoph Zebold and Barbara.

Elisabeth of Heinr. Schell and Margaretha, b. Dec 8, 1775; bapt. Jan
7, 1776. Spon: Elisabeth Fellenberger and Anna Maria
Fellenberger.

Abraham of Robert Patton and Elisabeth, b. Dec 23, 1775; bapt. Jan
15, 1776. Spon: parents.

Anna Maria of Abraham Duboy and Magdalena, b. Dec 21, 1775; bapt.
Jan 17, 1776. Spon: Jacob Tschopp and Anna.

Elisabetha of Christian Cramer and Maria, b. Dec 16, 1775; bapt. Jan
28, 1776. Spon: parents.

Johannes of Jacob Farney and wife; b. Jun 24, 1775; bapt. Jan 31,
1776. Spon: ---.

Christina Louisa of Ludwig Istler and Cathrina, b. Jan 20, 1776; bapt.
Feb 11, 1776. Spon: Friedrich Jensel and Louisa.

Susanna of Joh. Ruger and Susanna, b. Dec 26, 1775; bapt. Feb 11,
1776. Spon: David Wagoner and Anna Maria.

Cathr. Elisabeth of Georg Gilbert and Eva, b. Jan 12, 1776; bapt. Feb
25, 1776. Spon: Georg Simon and Elisabeth.

Jacob of Joh. Rohrer and Barbara, b. Jan 22, 1776; bapt. Feb 25,
1776. Spon: Jacob Schaffner and Eva.

Barbara of Mich. Krebs and Margaretha, b. Feb 19, 1776; bapt. Feb
26, 1776. Spon: Barbara Bush.

Johann Adams of Georg McCundle and Eva, b. Mar 16, 1776; bapt.
Mar 24, 1776. Spon: Felton Cornman and Cathrina.

Johannes of Joh. Zehring and Anna Eva Elisab., b. Mar 20, 1760;

bapt. Apr 2, 1776. Spon: ----.

Johannes of Martin Rudy and Anna Maria, b. Nov 24, 1775; bapt. Apr 2, 1776. Spon: Peter Bäry and Cathrina Swob.

Joh. Joseph of Jacob Ziegler and Juliana, b. Mar 6, 1776; bapt. Apr 7, 1776. Spon: Joseph Duboy and Christina.

Johann Georg of Philip Crum and Cathrina, b. Mar 23, 1776; bapt. May 4, 1776. Spon: J. Georg Schreiber and Christina.

Johannes of Jost Blecher and Maria Elisabeth, b. April 19, 1776; bapt. May 5, 1776. Spon: Joh. Blecher and Cathr. Weyrich.

Joh. Jacob of Peter Borgner and Cathrina, b. Feb 14, 1776; bapt. May 10, 1776. Spon: Jacob Keller and A. Cath. Dauber.

Maria Rebecca of Casper Kitzmiller and Juliana, b. Jan 26, 1776; bapt. May 10, 1776, Spon: Rebecca Miller.

Sarah of Wm. Tready and Nargareth, b. Jan 31, 1776; bapt. May 22, 1776, Spon: Cathr. Finley.

Anna Maria of Martin Imhoff and Maria Barbara, b. May 7, 1776; bapt. Jun 2, 1776. Spon: Michael Peyer and Anna Maria.

Joh. Heinrich of Friedrich Pollman and Susanna, b. May 11, 1776; bapt. Jun 2, 1776. Spon: Heinrich Seyler and Eva Cathrina.

Johannes of Leonhard Umberger and Maria, b. Mar 3, 1776; bapt. Jun 20, 1776. Spon: Adam Umberger and Maria.

Joh. Theobaldus of Baltasar Schally and Barbara, b. Jun 28, 1776; bapt. Jul 28, 1776. Spon: Peter Schlosser and Margaretha.

Margaretha of Felton Cornman and Margaretha, b. Aug 1, 1776; bapt. Aug 3, 1776. Spon: Geo. McGundle and Eva.

Anna Maria of Alexander Benjamin and Anna Elisabetha, b. Mar 15, 1776; bapt. Aug 5, 1776, Spon: Anna Maria Volmer.

Elisabeth of Jacob Kinzler and Elisabetha, b. Jul 18, 1776; bapt. Aug 11, 1776, Spon: Elis. Heckedorn.

Joh. Peter of Peter Hammah and Cathrina, b. Mar 3, 1776; bapt. Aug 11, 1776. Spon: Baltasar Stamgast and Mar. Elisabeth.

Heinrich of Joh. Cornman and Elisabeth, b. Sep 7, 1776; bapt. Sep 22, 1776. Spon: Heinrich Reinohl and Juliana.

Mar. Margaretha of Christoph Schlosser and Eva, b. Nov 1, 1776; bapt. Nov 3, 1776. Spon: Peter Schlosser and Mar. Margaretha.

Heinrich of Jost Schwartz and Susanna, b. Oct 11, 1776; bapt. Dec 15, 1776. Spon: Martin Kramer and Cathrina.

Anna Eva of J. Nicklaus Busch and Margretha, b. Nov 25, 1776; bapt. Dec 15, 1776, Spon: Anna Eva Sprecher.

Joh. Godlieb of Nicklas Gebhard and Anna Apollonia, b. Jan 4, 1777;

bapt. Jan 9, 1777. Spon: Godfried Eichelberner and Juliana.

Child of Jacob Weyrich and Margaretha, b. Jan 4, 1777; bapt. Jan 12, 1777. Spon: Georg Ellinger and Mar. Cathrina.

Child of Peter Spiker and Anna Maria, b. ---; bapt. Jan 12, 1777, Spon: Heinrich Boehler.

Mar. Elisabeth of John Schnebely and Anna Barbara, b. Jan 6, 1777; bapt. Jan 25, 1777. Spon: Peter Jetter and Anna Maria.

David of John Thom and Anna Maria, b. Mar 6, 1777; bapt. Mar 13, 1777. Spon: Christian Beistel.

Michael of Jacob Fortune and Margaretha, b. Feb 17, 1777; bapt. Mar 23, 1777. Spon: Michael Krebs and Margareth.

Susan Cathrina of Peter Swob and Cathrina, b. Feb 11, 1777; bapt. Mar 27, 1777, Spon: Cathr. Swab.

Anna Maria of Joh. Jerger and Anna Maria, b. Feb 16, 1777; bapt. Mar 31, 1777. Spon: Michael Peier and A. Maria.

Joh. Leonhard of Philip Grunewald and Margaretha, b. Mar 27, 1777; bapt. Apr 13, 1777. Spon: Leonhard Rupert and Christina.

Philip of Philip Mees and Cathrina, b. Apr 6, 1777; bapt. Apr 19, 1777. Spon: parents.

Joh. Martin of Christian Smith and Mar. Elisabeth, b. Mar 31, 1777; bapt. Apr 20, 1777. Spon: Joh. Martin Benner and Madg. Backenstoss.

Eva of Caspar Tschop and Barbara, b. Mar 20, 1777; bapt. Apr 20, 1777. Spon: Jacob Keller and Eva Tester.

Fridrich of Joh. Hefelfinger and Judith, b. ----; bapt. May 1, 1777. Spon: Joh. Brenner and Catharine.

Anna Margaret of Herman Spiess and Anna Margaret, b. Apr 15, 1777; bapt. May 1, 1777, Spon: Anna Margaret Mohr.

Christina of Henry Münche and Cathrina, b. Apr 4, 1777; bapt. May 4, 1777. Spon: Joh. Blecher and Cathr. Weyrich.

James of Jugan Bredon and Margaret, b. ---; bapt. May 9, 1777.

Anna Margretha of David Theys and Elisabeth, b. Apr 21, 1777; bapt. May 17, 1777. Spon: Antony Doebler and Magdalena.

Anna Maria of Joh. Umberger and Elisabeth, b. May 2, 1777; bapt. May 17, 1777. Spon: J. Melchior Abmeyer and A. Maria.

Maria Margaretha of Michael Krebs and Margaretha, b. Jul 18, 1777; bapt. Aug --, 1777. Spon: Philip Grünewald and Maria Margaretha.

Joh. Jacob of Johannes Mähs and Elisabetha, b. Jun 12, 1777; bapt. Jul 13, 1777. Spon: Philip Faust and Margreth.

Joh. Nicklaus of Michael Beyer and Anna Maria, b. Jul 10, 1777;

bapt. Jul 31, 1777. Spon: Nicklaus Weiss and Barbara.

Joh. Heinrich of Heinrich Rewald and Anna Maria, b. Aug 12, 1777; bapt. Aug 22, 1777. Spon: parents.

Barbara of Geo. Michael Weiss and Elisabetha, b. Aug 5, 1777; bapt. Aug 24, 1777. Spon: Jacob Stieb and Ottilia.

Elisabeth of Wilhelm Denius and Anna Maria, b. Aug 7, 1777; bapt. Sep 7, 1777. Spon: Joh. Denius and Dorothea.

Johannes of Johannes Meyer and Anna Maria, b. Sep 4, 1777; bapt. Sep 29, 1777; d. Oct 5, 1777. Spon: Henrich Rehwald and Anna Maria.

Magdalena of Christian Lup and Maria Elisabeth, b. Oct 5, 1777; bapt. Oct 9, 1777. Spon: Joh. Dittman and A. Elis. Strackbein.

Joh. Martin of Heinrich Meyly and Cathrina, b. Sep 8, 1777; bapt. Oct 14, 1777. Spon: Martin Meyly and Cathrina.

Wilhelm of Christian Kramer and Maria, b. Sep 5, 1777; bapt. Oct 19, 1777. Spon: parents.

Philip Bernhard of Jacob Pfeiffer and Margaretha, b. Oct 13, 1777; bapt. Nov 2, 1777. Spon: Bernhard Pfeiffer and Anna Sybilla.

Joh. Jacob of Heinrich Meyer and Mar. Magdalena, b. Aug 26, 1777; bapt. Nov 16, 1777, Spon: Elisabeth Sixin.

Regina of Heinrich Schell and Maria Margaretha, b. Dec 12, 1777; bapt. Feb 22, 1778. Spon: Nicklaus Denius and Regina.

Cathrina of Jacob Steger and Cathrina, b. Jan 16, 1777; bapt. Mar 6, 1777. Spon: parents.

Elisabetha of Joh. Steger and Elisabetha, b. Jan 31, 1778; bapt. Mar 6, 1778. Spon: parents.

Maria Magdalena of John Dubbs and Cathrina, b. Jan 19, 1778; bapt. Mar 8, 1778. Spon: Georg Stein and Margaretha.

Elisabeth of Joh. Stein and Barbara, b. Jan 22, 1778; bapt. Mar 8, 1778. Spon: David Schäffer and Elisabeth.

Joh. Conrad of Ludwig Istler and Cathrina, b. Jan 17, 1778; bapt. Mar 22, 1778. Spon: Conrad Menzinger and Barbara.

Joh. Jacob of Johannes Ruger and Susanna, b. Feb 4, 1778; bapt. Apr 5, 1778. Spon: Matheys Ruger and Hannah.

Anna Maria of Valentin Cornman and Elisabeth Margaret, b. Mar 14, 1778; bapt. Apr 5, 1778. Spon: Martin Weizel and A. Maria.

Joh. Georg of Jacob Hederich and Anna Maria, b. Apr 5, 1778, bapt. Apr 19, 1778. Spon: Joh. Backenstoss and Charlotta.

Mar. Cathrina of Laurenz Hauz and Anna Cathrina, b. Mar 28, 1778; bapt. Apr 19, 1778. Spon: Peter Borgner and Mar. Cathr.

Jacob of Alexander Benjamin and Anna Elisabeth, b. Jan 24, 1778; bapt. Apr 29, 1778. Spon: Matheys Bremer and Maria.

Robert of Joseph Quarrel and Susanna, b. Apr 26, 1778; bapt. May 2, 1778; d. next day. Spon: Joseph Cample (Campbell), and Mary Howart.

Johannes of Ludwig Kornman and Cathrina, b. Apr 9, 1778; bapt. May 3, 1778. Spon: Joh. Nunnenmacher and Susanna Maria.

Maria of Robert Laury and Mary, b. Mar. 2, 1778; bapt. May 16, 1778. Spon: John Rossly and Susanna.

Abraham of Philip Duboy and Elisabeth, b. Apr 1, 1778; bapt. May 17, 1778. Spon: Abraham Duboy and Magdalena.

Anna Maria of Christian Beck and Margaretha, b. Apr 25, 1778, bapt. May 20, 1778. Spon: Anna Maria Beck.

Joh. Georg of Christoph Schlosser and Eva, b. May 6, 1778; bapt. May 28, 1778. Spon: D. Georg Kop.

Susanna Mar. Magdalena of Friedrich Pollman and Susanna, b. May 5, 1778; bapt. May 28, 1778. Spon: A. Maria Denius, Dan. Oldenbrunch and Anna Maria, wife.

Elisabeth of Andreas Halter and Elisabeth, b. Jun 5, 1778, bapt. Jun 14, 1778. Spon: Christina Hauenstein.

Elisabeth of Georg Meyly and Rachel, b. Apr 28, 1778; bapt. Jun 18, 1778. Spon: Sam. Meyly and Cathrina.

Joh. Heinrich of Heinrich Bouman and Barbara, b. Jun 25, 1778, bapt. Jul 26, 1778. Spon: parents.

Salome of Ludwig Benter and Mar. Elisabeth, b. Aug --, 1755, bapt. Aug 7, 1778.

Anna of Georg Welsh and Maria Dorothea, b. Jul 10, 1778; bapt. Aug 7, 1778. Spon: Georg Gilbert and Eva.

Johannes of Jacob Hubler and M. Margretha, b. Aug 31, 1776, bapt. Aug 14, 1778. Spon: Peter Hederich and Philippina.

Mar. Cathrina of Adam Harper and Philippina, b. May 28, 1777, bapt. Aug 16, 1778. Spon: Kilian Merk and Cathr.

Maria of John McElreath and Nancy, b. Jan 8, 1778; bapt. Aug 24, 1778. Spon: parents.

Johan Bernhard of Nicklaus Gebhard and Anna Apollonia, b. Aug 19, 1778; bapt. Aug 29, 1778. Spon: Bernhard Pfeiffer and Sybilla.

Cathrina of Phil. Crum and Cathrina, b. Jul 17, 1778; bapt. Sep 20, 1778. Spon: Johannes Reuter and Amalia.

Joh. Peter of Peter Spiker and Anna Maria, b. Sep 7, 1778, bapt. Oct 4, 1778. Spon: Benj. Spiker and Cathr.

Elisabeth of Peter Swob and Cathrina, b. Sep 3, 1778; bapt. Oct 4, 1778. Spon: Jacob Swob and Elisabeth.

Joh. Heinrich of Johanna Meyer and Anna Maria, b. Sep 28, 1778; bapt. Oct 18, 1778. Spon: Heinrich Rehwald and Anna Maria.

Maria Elisabeth of Daniel Welshorn and Maria Magdalena, b. Oct 26, 1778; bapt. Dec 25, 1778. Spon: M. Elis. Smith.

Susanna of Georg Spaeth and Anna Maria, b. Oct 21, 1778; bapt. Jan 2, 1779. Spon: J. Adam Sharp and Susanna Ritter.

Joh. Jacob of Joh. Cornman and Elisabeth, b. Jan 5, 1779; bapt. Jan 17, 1779. Spon: Felton Cornman and Elis. Margr.

Mar. Margretha of Michl. Philippi and Elisabetha, b. Dec 15, 1778; bapt. Feb 15, 1779. Spon: Jacob Pfeiffer and Mar. Margretha.

Anna Cathrina of Jacob Hartman and Eva, b. Jan 28, 1779; bapt. Feb 21, 1779. Spon: Peter Andreas and Hannah Andreas.

Joh. Jacob of Jost Blecher and Anna Maria, b. Jan 9, 1779, bapt. Feb 21, 1779. Spon: Nicklaus Chaque and Mar. Elisabeth.

Jacob of Henrich Miller and Magdalena, b. Feb 23, 1779; bapt. Mar. 7, 1779. Spon: Jacob Sigs and Elisabeth.

Elisabeth of Johann Jager and Anna Maria, b. Feb 29, 1779, bapt. Mar. 7, 1779. Spon: Jacob Frey and Elisabeth.

Joh. Jacob of Martin Imhoff and Barbara, b. Mar. 10, 1779; bapt. Mar. 12, 1799. Spon: parents.

Johannes of Adam Heberlin and Martha, b. Feb 7, 1779; bapt. Mar. 31, 1779. Spon: Melchior Ram and Rebecca.

Daniel of Joh. Umberger and Elizabeth, b. Feb 28, 1779; bapt. Apr 18, 1779. Spon: Dan. Fezberger and Cathrina.

Joh. Christoph of Christoph Loeb and Margaretha, b. Apr 1, 1779; bapt. Apr 19, 1779. Spon: Christoph Emtick and Anna Maria.

Jacob of Jacob Weyrich and Margaretha, b. Apr 16, 1779; bapt. May 2, 1779. Spon: Mich. Ihly and A. Maria.

Anna Barbara of Joh. Richer and Susanna, b. Mar. 26, 1779; bapt. May 2, 1779. Spon: Mathys Richer and Anna.

Elisabeth of Christian Schmidt and Anna Elisabetha, b. May 18, 1779; bapt. May 22, 1779. Spon: Carl Brenner and Elisabeth.

Godfried of Alex. Benjamin and Elisabeth, b. May 8, 1779; bapt. Jun 13, 1779. Spon: Godfried Eichelberner and Juliana.

Cathrina of Christian Mertel and Susanna, b. Feb 6, 1779, bapt. Jun 19, 1799. Spon: Cathr. Jungst.

Cathrina of Abraham Becker and Sabina, b. Apr 14, 1779; bapt. Jun 25, 1779. Spon: mother.

Mary of Christian Fisher and Anna, b. Oct 13, 1763; bapt. Jul 7, 1779.

Johannes of J. Martin Weiss and Cathrina, b. Jun 26, 1779, bapt. Jul 18, 1779. Spon: Georg Meyli and Rahel.

Peter of Daniel Conrad and Anna Barbara, b. Jun 26, 1779; bapt. Aug 1, 1779. Spon: Martin Weiss and Cathr.

Cathrina of Heinrich Meyli and Cathrina, b. May 26, 1779; bapt. Aug 1, 1779. Spon: Samuel Meyli and Cathr.

Cathrina of Jacob Schmit and Elisabeth, b. Aug 26, 1779; bapt. Aug 29, 1779. Spon: Henrich Arnold and Cathrina.

Heinrich of John Rohrer and Barbara, b. Jul 19, 1779; bapt. Aug 29, 1779. Spon: Rudolph Kelker and Maria.

Joh. Heinrich of Heinr. Rehwald and Anna Maria, b. Aug 31, 1779; bapt. Sep 12, 1779. Spon: Ludwig Zehrung and Cathrina.

Anna Christina of Bartholome Wicker and Elis. Margaretha, b. Sep 5, 1779; bapt. Sep 12, 1779. Spon: Nicklaus Gebhard and Anna.

Cathrina of J. Conr. Naseman and Cathrina, b. Aug19, 1779, bapt. Sep 25, 1779. Spon: parents.

Joh. Georg of Joh. Fisher and Elisabetha, b. Aug 7, 1779; bapt. Oct 4, 1779. Spon: J. Nicklaus Shaque and M. Elis.

Joh. Jacob of Nicklaus Denius and Regina, b. Oct 3, 1779; bapt. Oct 24, 1779. Spon: Jacob Merk and Elis. Denius.

Cathrina of Benj. Spiker and Cathrina, b. Sep 23, 1779; bapt. Oct 24, 1779. Spon: Math. Reinhard and Cathr.

Eva Elisabeth of Abraham Bleystein and Christina, b. Sep 27, 1779; bapt. Oct 24, 1779. Spon: Adam Folmer and Barbara.

Anna Elisabeth of Felton Cornman and Elisabetha Margaret, b. Oct 20, 1799; bapt. Nov 7, 1799. Spon: Joh. Cornman and Elisabeth.

Anna Juliana of Johannes Reiter, (school master) and Amalia, b. Nov 14, 1779; bapt. Dec 5, 1799. Spon: Godfried Eichelberner and Juliana.

Mar. Barbara of David Theys and Elisabeth, b. Oct 31, 1779, bapt. Dec 9, 1779. Spon: Joh. German and Elizabeth.

Solomon of Georg Hamman and Juliana, b. Nov 16, 1779; bapt. Dec 9, 1779. Spon: Leonhard Koehler and Elisabeth.

Elisabeth Cathr. of Samuel Meyly and Cathrina, b. Nov 26, 1779, bapt. Dec 25, 1779. Spon: Elisabeth Schumacher.

Robert of Robert Patton and Elisabeth, b. Nov 3, 1779; bapt. Jan 1, 1780. Spon: parents.

Johannes of Peter Schindel and Anna Margreth, b. Dec 23, 1779, bapt. Jan 13, 1780. Spon: Nicklaus Gebhard and A. Apollonia.

Christian Ludwig of Peter Sprukman and Elizabeth, b. Dec 31, 1779; bapt. Jan 16, 1780. Spon: Christian Beck.

J. Michael of Georg Dietrich and Dorothea, b. Jan 24, 1780, bapt. Jan 25, 1780. Spon: Friedr. Pollman and Susanna.

Maria Catharina of Martin Weizel and A. Maria, b. Dec 13, 1779, bapt. Jan 26, 1780. Spon: Peter Cornman and Cathrina.

Elisabeth of Michael Krebs and Margaretha, b. Dec 13, 1779, bapt. Jan 30, 1780. Spon: Peter Miller and Margaretha.

Johannes of Caspar Loeb and Margaretha, b. Jan 10, 1780; bapt. Feb 2, 1780. Spon: Bernhard Reinhard and Magdal. Weiss.

Joh. Philip of Joh. Finkel and Nancy, b. Jun 2, 1779; bapt. Feb 6, 1780. Spon: parents.

Sarah of Georg Welsh and Dorothea, b. Jan 24, 1780; bapt. Feb 13, 1780. Spon: Thomas Morgan and Nancy.

Christoph of Martin Wagner and Charlotta, b. Jan 22, 1780, bapt. Feb 20, 1780. Spon: Christoph Seyler and Elisabeth.

J. Martin of Frantz Zerman and Eva, b. Dec 22, 1779; bapt. Feb 28, 1780. Spon: Martin Smith and M. A., wife.

Joh. Jacob of Georg Ellinger and Anna Maria, b. Jan 17, 1780, bapt. Feb 2, 1780. Spon: Joh. Graff and Elisabeth.

Mar. Cathr. of Philip Mees and Cathrina, b. Feb 18, 1780, bapt. Mar. 5, 1780. Spon: parents.

Johannes of Caspar Mees and Barbara, b. Nov 21, 1779; bapt. Mar. 6, 1780. Spon: Wilhelm Schumacher and Elisabeth, wife.

Mar. Cathrina of Johannes Dubs and Cathrina, b. Feb 26, 1780, bapt. Mar 19, 1780. Spon: Georg Stein and Margaretha.

Margareth of Heinr. Shaffner and Christina, b. Feb 26, 1780, bapt. Mar 26, 1780. Spon: Michael Krebs and Margareth.

Johannes of Joh. Steger and Elisabeth, b. Feb 2, 1780; bapt. Apr 9, 1780. Spon: Godfried Eichelberner and Juliana.

Salome of Thos. Gigins and Salome, b. Aug 5, 1775; bapt. Apr 9, 1780. Spon: Martin Weiss and M. Cathrina.

Cathrina Elisabeth of Joh. Peter and Salome, b. Nov 13, 1779, bapt. Apr 9, 1780. Spon: Martin Weiss and M. Cathrina.

Geo. Friedrich of Alex. McComeric and Cathr. Weyrich, b. Feb 25, 1780; bapt. Apr 23, 1780. Spon: Georg Stroh and M. Angelica.

Samuel of Christian Kramer and Maria, b. Mar. 20, 1780; bapt. Apr 23, 1780. Spon: parents.

Margaretha of John McBride and Elisabeth, b. Nov 2, 1779; bapt. Apr

24, 1780. Spon: parents.

Anna Margaretha of Nicklaus Gebhard and Anna Apollonia, b. Apr 21, 1780; bapt. May 4, 1780. Spon: Peter Schindel and Margaretha.

Georg of Georg Volmer and Juliana, b. Mar. 4, 1780; bapt. May 20, 1780. Spon: Joh. Bittner and Elisabeth.

Isaac of Friedr. Weyman and Cathrina, b. Mar 23, 1780; bapt. May 24, 1780. Spon: Geo. Volmer and Juliana.

Joh. Jacob of Peter Spiker and Anna Maria, b. Apr 25, 1780, bapt. May 21, 1780. Spon: Jacob Hartman and Eva.

Joh. Henrich of Jacob Hubler and M. Margaret, b. Dec 14, 1778, bapt. May 31, 1780. Spon: Franz Albert and M. Barbara.

Joh. Conrad of Jacob Peter and Cathrina, b. Jan 13, 1780; bapt. Jun 22, 1780. Spon: Conrad Bucher and Mar. Magd.

Anna Maria of Joh. Stein and Barbara, b. Apr 30, 1780; bapt. Jul 2, 1780. Spon: Christoph Kucher and Anna Maria. *(This is the last baptism of Bucher)*

Anna Juliana of Johannes Reuter and Amalia, b. Nov 12, 1779, bapt. Jul 19, 1779. Spon: Gottfried Eichelberner and Juliana. *(The last baptism was entered by the schoolmaster, John Reuter.)*

Joh. Friedrich of Anthony Kelker and Magdalena, b. Oct 29, 1780; bapt. Nov 26, 1780. Spon: Joh. Friedrich Bollman and Susanna.

Jacob of Jacob Scheuer and Magdalena, b. Oct 26, 1780; bapt. Nov 26, 1780. Spon: Dietrich Schultz and Anna.

Jacob of Jacob Eichelberner and Cathrina, b. Nov 6, 1780; bapt. Nov 26, 1780. Spon: Jacob Merck and Margaret Zimmerman.

(The last three baptisms were entered by rev. Joh. Wm. Runkel.)

Anna Maria of Johannes Finckel and Anna, b. Jun 25, 1780; bapt. Jan 1, 1781. Spon: Georg Stein and Margaretha.

Joh. Georg of Thomas Atkinson and wife, b. Jan 9, 1781; bapt. Jan 21, 1781. (by Rev. Hendel). Spon: Georg Stein and Margaretha.

Mar. Cathrina of David Scherck and Susanna, b. Jan 13, 1781; bapt. Jan 21, 1781 (by Rev. Hendel). Spon: Rudolph Kölker and Maria.

BAPTISMS BY THE REV. JOHN WM. RUNKEL, FEB 1781-NOV 1784

Georg David of Wilhelm Heidler and Magdalena, b. Jan 21, 1781, bapt. Feb 26, 1781. Spon: David Scherck and Susanna.

Henrich of Philip Duboy and Elisabetha, b. Dec 27, 1780; bapt. Jan 28, 1781. Spon: Henrich Rehwald and Maria.

Deborah of Bartholomew Barry and Bridget, b. Nov 6, 1780; bapt. Apr 6, 1781. Spon: parents.

Eleonora of Johannes Umberger and Elisabetha, b. Mar 20, 1781, bapt. Apr 17, 1781. Spon: Eleonora Rennels, widow.

Anna Maria of Henrich Schaffner and Christina, b. Sep 17, 1781; bapt. Sep 30, 1781. Spon: Jacob Sauder and Philippina.

Elisabetha of Benjamin Spicker and Catharina, b. Feb 7, 1782, bapt. Feb 23, 1782. Spon: Christoph Uller and Barbara.

Johannes of Johannes Reiter and Amalia, b. Feb 20, 1782; bapt. Mar 3, 1782. Spon: Michael Krebs and Margaretha.

Johannes of Joh. Christian Jäger and Margaretha, b. Oct 5, 1781; bapt. Mar 10, 1782. Spon: parents.

Henrich of Henrich Wild and Anna Elisabetha, b. Mar 25, 1782, bapt. Mar 30, 1782. Spon: Nicolaus Denius and Regina.

Adam of Henrich Wild and Anna Elisabetha, b. Mar 25, 1782; bapt. Mar 30, 1782. Spon: Adam Riess and Catharina.

Anna Maria of Henrich Meyer and Magdalena, b. Mar 22, 1782, bapt. Mar 31, 1782. Spon: Christoph Embich and Magdalena.

Salome of Valentin Kornman and Elis. Margaretha, b. Mar 3, 1782; bapt. Mar 31, 1782. Spon: Caspar Jungblut and Catharina.

Maria Barbara of Conrad Aubel and Barbara, b. Feb 8, 1782, bapt. Mar 10, 1782. Spon: Christoph Zibold and Barbara.

Johanna Regina of Peter Spicker (d. last Feb) and Anna Maria, b. Apr 21, 1782; bapt. May 9, 1782. Spon: Regina Spicker, widow.

Catharina of Nicolaus Denius and Regina, b. Apr 26, 1782; bapt. May 20, 1782. Spon: Casper Jungblut and Catharina.

Anna Maria of Johannes Kornman and Elisabetha, b. May 6, 1782, bapt. Jun 9, 1782. Spon: Anna Maria Jetter, widow.

David of Jacob Pfeiffer and Margaretha, b. May 24, 1782; bapt. Jun 25, 1782. Spon: parents.

Johannes of Christian Schmit and Maria, b. Jul 15, 1782; bapt. Aug 4, 1782. Spon: Martin Benner and Elisabeth.

Robert of Thomas McIRrath and Mary, b. Aug 12, 1782; bapt. Sep 6,

Robert of Thomas McIRrath and Mary, b. Aug 12, 1782; bapt. Sep 6, 1782. Spon: parents.

Anna Maria of Michael Krebs and Margaretha, b. Jul 26, 1782, bapt. Sep 17, 1782. Spon: parents.

Joh. Jacob of Jacob Weyrich and Margaretha, b. Aug 7, 1782, bapt. Sep 17, 1782. Spon: parents.

Michael of Johannes Stein and Barbara, b. Sep 16, 1782; bapt. Sep 27, 1782. Spon: Michael Zimmerman and Barbara.

Joh. Jacob of Jacob Eprecht and Elisabeth, b. Sep 18, 1782, bapt. Sep 29, 1782. Spon: Jacob Eprecht, Sen. and Catharina.

Joseph of Christian Krämer and Anna Maria, b. Aug 28, 1782, bapt. Sep 29, 1782. Spon: parents.

Catharina of Jacob Eichelberner and Catharina, b.---; bapt. Sep 29, 1782. Spon: Johannes Reiter and Amalia.

Johannes of Philip Miess and Catharina, b. Oct 18, 1782; bapt. Nov 11, 1782. Spon: Valentin Kornman and Elis. Margaretha.

Elisabetha of Edward Lang and Agnes, b. Oct 29, 1782; bapt. Nov 24, 1782. Spon: Georg Glassbrenner and Elisabetha.

David of David Deiss and Elisabetha, b. Oct 31, 1782; bapt. Nov 28, 1782. Spon: Nicolaus Killmer and Elisabetha.

Catharina of Christian Jäger and Catharina, b. Nov 8, 1782, bapt. Jan 1, 1783. Spon: parents.

Michael of Nicolaus Grünewald and Catharina, b. Jan 19, 1783, bapt. Feb 2, 1783. Spon: Michael Wagner and Anna Maria.

Johannes of Jacob Schop and Anna Maria, b. Dec 10, 1782; bapt. Feb 3, 1783. Spon: Peter Borger and Catharina.

Joh. Philip of Philip Huber and Susanna, b. Jan 19, 1783; bapt. Feb 28, 1783. Spon: parents.

Anna Rosina of Wilhelm Wart and Rosina, b. Jan 31, 1783; bapt. Mar 2, 1783. Spon: Jacob German and Anna.

Philip of Nicolaus Schütterle and Catharina, b. Mar 17, 1783, bapt. Apr 17, 1783. Spon: Michael Ensmenger and Anna Maria.

Elisabetha of Johannes Finckel and Anna, b. Aug 9, 1783; bapt. Apr 21, 1783. Spon: Geo. Kornman and Christina.

David of Georg McGundel and Regina, b. Apr 10, 1783; bapt. Apr 21, 1783. Spon: parents.

Joh. Jacob of Adam Kühner and Catharina, b. Mar 3, 1783; bapt. May 4, 1783. Spon: Clemens Scheuer and Margaretha.

Margaretha of Christoph Löb and Margaretha, b. May 26, 1783, bapt. May 27, 1783. Spon: Christoph Emich, Sr.

Jacob of Benedict Mellinger and Margaretha, b. Jul 22, 1756, bapt.
May 4, 1783. Spon: adult.

Rebecca of Joseph Gersch and Hannah, b. Feb 8, 1782; bapt. May 24,
1783. Spon: August Gersch and Elisabeth.

Elisabetha of Jesse Jones and Hannah, b. Jan 15, 1779; bapt. May 24,
1783. Spon: August Gersch and Elisabeth.

Anna Catharina of Philip Deboi (Duboy) and wife, b. Apr 13, 1783;
bapt. Jun 1, 1783. Spon: Jacob German and Anna.

Anna Margretha of David Schörck and Susanna, b. Feb 28, 1783,
bapt. Jun 1, 1783. Spon: Conradt Merck and Margaretha.

Susanna of Conradt Merck and Margretha, b. Apr 14, 1783; bapt. Jun
1, 1783. Spon: David Schörck and Susanna.

Catharina of Johannes Umberger and Elisabeth, b. May 10, 1783;
bapt. Jun 18, 1783. Spon: Daniel Vetzeberger and Cathr.

Johannes of Georg Gloninger and Maria, b. Apr 3, 1783; bapt. Jun 29,
1783. Spon: the father.

Maria Elisabeth of Casper Löb and Margaretha, b. Jul 6, 1783, bapt.
Jul 12, 1783. Spon: Elisabeth Weis, wife of G. M. Weis.

Anna Maria of Henrich Rehwald and Anna Maria, b. Jul 3, 1783,
bapt. Jul 14, 1783. Spon: Anna Maria Rehwald, widow.

Elisabetha of Casper Mies and Barbara, b. Jul 12, 1783; bapt. Aug 11,
1783. Spon: Elisabetha Meyer, widow.

Anna Elisabetha of Adam Sieber and Elisabetha, b. Oct 6, 1783, bapt.
Oct 21, 1783. Spon: parents.

Jacob of Georg Schambach and Catharina, b. Sep 26, 1783; bapt. Nov
23, 1783. Spon: Philip Schambaugh, single.

Barbara of Jacob Mellinger and Barbara, b. Nov 10, 1783; bapt. Nov
23, 1783. Spon: Simon Lauck and Catharina.

Philippina of Martin Imhoff and Barbara, b. Nov 8, 1783; bapt. Nov
28, 1783. Spon: Philippina Merck, single.

Margaretha of Johannes Itzenhäuser and Magdalena, b. Nov 3, 1783,
bapt. Dec 11, 1783. Spon: Peter Eichelberner and Margaretha.

Jacob of Henrich Jac. Wild and Anna Elisabetha, b. Dec 12, 1783;
bapt. Dec 26, 1783. Spon: parents.

Daniel of Christian Heckedorn and Veronica, b. Nov 22, 1783, bapt.
Feb 2, 1784. Spon: Susanna Heckedorn, widow.

Anna Catharina of Jacob Weyrich and Margaretha, b. Dec 30, 1783;
bapt. Feb 5, 1784. Spon: parents.

Anna Juliana of Henrich Mayer and Margaretha, b. Feb 9, 1784, bapt.
Feb 22, 1784. Spon: Gottfried Eichelberner and Juliana.

Catharina of Benjamin Spicker and Catharina, b. Jan 12, 1784, bapt.
Mar 16, 1784. Spon: Catharine Lobinger, single.

Veronica of Bernhardt Reinhard and Elisabetha, b. Mar 1, 1784, bapt.
Apr 11, 1784. Spon: Johannes Dubbs and Catharina.

Christina of Georg Kornman and Christina, b. Mar 22, 1784; bapt.
Apr 11, 1784. Spon: Philip Mies and Catharina.

Samuel of Samuel Graham and Elisabeth, b. Apr 2, 1784; bapt. Apr
24, 1784. Spon: parents.

Henrich of Henrich Schaffner and Christina, b. Apr 4, 1784; bapt.
Apr 25, 1784. Spon: Michael Krebs and Margaretha.

John of Thomas McElrath and Mary, b. Apr 12, 1784; bapt. Apr 26,
1784. Spon: parents.

Margaretha of Johannes Finckel and Anna, b. Apr 29, 1784; bapt.
May 30, 1784. Spon: Michael Funck and Marg.

Jacob of Carl Arndt and Margaretha, b. May 31, 1784; bapt. Jun 20,
1784. Spon: Gottfried Eichelberner and Juliana.

Michael of Michael Krebs and Margaretha, b. May 28, 1784; bapt. Jul
4, 1784. Spon: parents.

Joh. Henrich of Casper Loeb and Margaretha, b. Jun 7, 1784; bapt.
Jul 28, 1784. Spon: Maria Elis. Weis, wife of G. M. Weis.

Maria Magdalena of Johannes Blecher and Catharina, b. Jul 14, 1784;
bapt. Jul 28, 1784. Spon: Phil. Denius and Magdalena.

Christoph of Christoph Embich and Maria, b. Sep 4, 1784; bapt. Sep
5, 1784. Spon: parents.

Catharina of David Deiss and Elisabeth, b. Oct --, 1784; bapt. Nov 14,
1784. Spon: Cath. Kohr, wife of Christ. Kohr.

Peter of Peter Eichelberner and Margaretha, b. Oct 13, 1784; bapt.
Nov 14, 1784. Spon: Jacob Eichelberner and Cathr.

Elisabetha of Daniel Henning and Margaretha, b. Nov 1, 1784; bapt.
Nov 14, 1784. Spon: Joh. Dubs and Catharina.(This is the last
baptism of Rev. William Runkel.)

BAPTISMS BY REV. ANDREW LORETZ, FEB 1785-JAN 1786

Elisabetha of Jacob Eichelberner and Catharina Zimmermann, b. ---;
bapt. Feb 14, 1785. Spon: Peter Eichelberner and Elisabetha
Eichelberg.

Christina of Valentin Kornman and wife, bapt. Feb 14, 1785. Spon:
Jörg Kornman and Christina.

David of Christian Kramer and Anna Maria, b. ---; bapt. Feb 24, 1785.

Spon: parents.

Catharina of Johannes Kornman and Elisabeth, b. Apr 2, 1785; bapt. Apr 24, 1785. Spon: Cathrina Schindel.

Abraham of Philip Mihs and Catharina, b. Mar 23, 1785; bapt. Apr 24, 1785. Spon: Johannes Kornman and Elisabeth.

Thomas of Anthony McCreight and Abigail, b. Feb 19, 1783; bapt. Apr 25, 1785. Spon: parents.

Margaret of Conradt Merck and Margaretha, b. Apr 15, 1785; bapt. Apr 25, 1785. Spon: Michael Krebs and Margaretha.

(The last four baptisms were not entered by Rev. Andrew Loretz.)

Johann Philip of Johannes Stump(?) and Margaret Grünewald, b. ---; bapt. Aug 31, 1785. Spon: Johann Philip Grünewald and Margareth.

Johann Georg of Johannes Keller and Elisabeth Ort, b. ---; bapt. Aug 31, 1785. Spon: Antoni Töbler and Magdalena.

Johann Jacob of Peter Eichelberger and Margareth, b. Oct 12, 1785; bapt. Jan 1, 1785. Spon: Gottfried Eichelberger and Juliana.

Johannes of Johann Nicolaus Grünewald and Catharina, b. Dec 18, 1785; bapt. Jan 1, 1786. Spon: Georg Miggrundel [McGundel] and Regina.

Johann Georg of Georg Trany and Anna Barbara, b. Oct 4, 1785; bapt. Jan 1, 1786. Spon: Andreas Leu and Susanna Brun(?).

(This is the last baptism of Rev. Andrew Lorentz. The next three baptisms are by other hands.)

Cathrina of Michael Krebs and Margaretha, b. Jan 7, 1786; bapt. Feb 19, 1786. Spon: Henrich Schaffner and Christina.

Marilisabeth of Bernhardt Reinhardt and Elisabeth, b. Apr 10, 1786; bapt. Aug 27, 1786. Spon: parents.

Elisabetha of Jacob Steger and wife, b. Oct 28, 1784; bapt. Dec 19, 1784. Spon: Johannes Steger and wife.

BAPTISMS BY REV. LUDWIG LUPP, DEC 1786-JUN 1798.

---- of Johannes Steger and Elisabeth, b. Oct 11, 1786; bapt. Dec 6, 1786.

Maria Lisabetha of Georg Frantz and wife, b. Nov 2, 1786; bapt. Nov 19, 1786. Spon: Nicolaus Schaack and Elisabetha.

Maria Magdalena of Hannes Richer and wife, b. Oct 26, 1786; bapt. Dec 22, 1786. Spon: Anthon Kelcker and wife.

Jacob of Jacob Mellinger and wife, b. Dec 25, 1786; bapt. Jan 1, 1787.

Magdalena of Johannes Reuder and wife, b. Nov 28, 1786; bapt. Dec 24, 1786. Spon: Anthon Kelcker and wife.

Johannes of Johannes Müller, b. ---; bapt. Jan 19, 1787. Spon: mother.

Jacob of Johannes Müller, b. ---; bapt. Jan 19, 1787. Spon: mother.

Jacob of Johannes Keller and wife, b. Jan 5, 1787; bapt. Jan 21, 1787. Spon: Michael Krebs and wife.

Johann Georg of Cornelius Grün and wife, b. Jun 7, 1786; bapt. Feb 27, 1787. Spon: Johann Georg Dester and wife.

David of Andreas Huber and wife, b. Apr 4, 1785; bapt. Mar 4, 1787. Spon: parents.

Margaretha of Andreas Huber and wife, b. Jan 18, 1785; bapt. Mar 4, 1787. Spon: Margaretha Mohr.

Elisabetha of Peter Eigelberger and wife, b. Feb 30, 1787; bapt. Mar 25, 1787. Spon: Gottfried Eigelberger and wife.

Maria Elisabeth of Michael Boltz and wife, b. Jan 21, 1787; bapt. Mar 25, 1787. Spon: Margaretha Weyrich.

Philip of Henrich Schaffner and wife, b. Mar 17, 1787; bapt. Apr 9, 1787. Spon: Philip Grünewald and wife.

Sarah of Christoffel Löb and wife, b. Mar 22, 1787; bapt. Apr 9, 1787. Spon: Peter Fischer and wife.

Anna Barbara of Casper Miss and wife, b. Mar 5, 1787; bapt. Apr 25, 1787. Spon: Anna Barbara Mayer, widow.

Johann Philip of Friedrich Wolfersberger and wife, b. Feb 18, 1787; bapt. Apr 29, 1787. Spon: Daniel Henning and wife.

Johann Michael of Jacob Schaack and wife, b. Feb 21, 1787; bapt. Apr 29, 1787. Spon: Johann Nicolaus Schaack and wife.

Magdalena of Ludwig Dormann and wife, b. May 26, 1787; bapt. Jul 1, 1787. Spon: Maria Lis Schack.

Georg of Georg Kornman and wife, b. Jul 3, 1787; bapt. Jul 28, 1787. Spon: Georg Webert.

Johann Peter of Adam Steger and wife, b. Jul 4, 1787; bapt. Jul 29, 1787. Spon: parents.

Maria Sarah of Michael Gorwel and wife, b. Jan 29, 1787; bapt. Jul 29, 1787. Spon: Nicolaus Dunges and wife.

Anna Catharina of Carl Arnt and wife, b. Jul 26, 1787; bapt. Aug 12, 1787. Spon: Anna Arnd, widow.

Johannes of Henrich Steger and wife, b. Aug 24, 1787; bapt. Sep 23, 1787. Spon: Johannes Reuter and wife.

Anna Maria of Philip Peter and Catharina, b. Sep 11, 1787; bapt. Sep

23, 1787. Spon: Christian Dürcks.

Moses of Schims [James] Steer and wife, b. Jun 22, 1787; bapt. Jul 2, 1787. Spon: parents.

Barbara of Michael Krebs and wife, b. Oct 12, 1787; bapt. Nov 18, 1787. Spon: Hannes Keller and wife.

Jacob of Carl Miller and wife, b. Aug 30, 1787; bapt. Oct 15, 1787. Spon: parents.

Magdalena of Conrath Merck and wife, b. Nov 3, 1787; bapt. Dec 16, 1787. Spon: Magdalena Merck.

Anna Maria of Benjamin Schicker and wife, b. Aug 10, 1787; bapt. Jan 1, 1788. Spon: parents.

Elisabeth of Peter Jüngst and wife, b. Jun 10, 1787; bapt. Jul 1, 1788. Spon: Friedrich Steger and wife.

Johann Philip of Johannes Huber and wife, b. Mar 9, 1788; bapt. Apr 8, 1788. Spon: parents.

Philip of Johannes Gloninger and Catharina, b. Feb 17, 1788; bapt. Apr 24, 1788. Spon: ---. (This is the Rev. Philip Gloninger, 1788-1816.)

Hannah of Jörg Meile and wife, b. Jan 30, 1788; bapt. Apr 19, 1788. Spon: parents

Johann Jacob of David Deiss and wife, b. Mar 9, 1788; bapt. Apr 20, 1788. Spon: Johann Jacob Deiss and wife.

Anna Maria of Johannes Rohrer and wife, b. Nov 17, 1787; bapt. May 3, 1788. Spon: parents.

Johann Adam of Martin Bucher and wife, b. Apr 19, 1788; bapt. Jul 13, 1788. Spon: Johann Adam Bucher.

Johann Jacob of Frantz Alberthal and wife, b. Jun 20, 1788; bapt. Aug 11, 1788. Spon: Jacob Ferling and wife.

Christian of Christian Krämer and wife, b. Jul 12, 1788; bapt. Aug 24, 1788. Spon: parents.

Catharina of Johannes Keller and wife, b. Sep 22, 1788; b. Nov 7, 1788. Spon: parents.

Johann Philip of Johann Philip Grünewald and wife, b. Sep 29, 1788; bapt. Nov 2, 1788. Spon: parents.

Susanna of Juy Megeloch and wife, b. Oct 21, 1788; bapt. Nov 16, 1788. Spon: Johannes Ressler and wife.

Maria Margareth of Jacob Weyrich and wife, b. Oct 1, 1788; bapt. Dec 26, 1788. Spon: Maria Margaretha Weyrich.

Maria of Henrich Tubs and wife, b. Oct 12, 1788; bapt. Dec 26, 1788. Spon: Anthon Döbeler and wife.

Maria of Schims Steer and wife, b. Dec 15, 1788; bapt. Dec 26, 1788. Spon: parents.

Jacob of Johannes Vogel and wife, b. Sep 21, 1788; bapt. Dec 29, 1788. Spon: parents.

Hannah of Hannes Tünges and wife, b. Dec 15, 1788; bapt. Dec 30, 1788. Spon: Peter Andres and wife.

Elisabeth of Nicholaus Tünges and wife, b. Dec 18, 1788; bapt. Dec 30, 1788. Spon: Hannes Tünges and wife.

Johann Georg of Georg Clolinger and wife, b. Nov 16, 1788; bapt. Jan 4, 1789. Spon: parents.

William of Johann Gibsen and wife, b. Mar 4, 1788; bapt. Jan 24, 1789. Spon: Johannes Hemmerling and wife.

Cathrina of Johannes Mayer and wife, b. Aug 6, 1787; bapt. Nov --, 1789. Spon: Johannes Zimmerman and wife.

Elisabetha of Jacob Frölich and wife, b. Jun 4, 1788; bapt. Feb 7, 1789. Spon: Catharina Frölich, widow.

Johannes of Peter Buch and wife, b. May 19, 1788; bapt. Feb 8, 1789. Spon: Johannes Ressle and wife.

William of Carl Miller and wife, b. Dec 9, 1788; bapt. Feb 9, 1789. Spon: parents.

Susanna Cathrina of Bernhart Reinhart and wife, b. Oct 13, 1788; bapt. Feb 22, 1789. Spon: parents.

Johann Jacob of Henrich Kelcker and wife, b. Dec 17, 1788; bapt. Feb 22, 1789. Spon: Philip Grünewald and wife.

Johannes of Johannes Stöhr and wife, b. Feb 23, 1789; bapt. Mar 8, 1789. Spon: Johannes Schnee and wife.

Margaretha of Peter Eichelberger and wife, b. Dec 12, 1788; bapt. Mar 22, 1789. Spon: Michael Zimmermann and wife.

---- of Jacob Pfeiffer and wife, b. Jan 2, 1789; bapt. Mar 8, 1789. Spon: Peter Schicker and wife.

Johannes of Abraham Bleystein and wife, b. Jan 19, 1789; bapt. Feb 22, 1789. Spon: Leonhart Zimmermann.

Johannes of Johannes Schlotterbeck and wife, b. Dec 11, 1788; bapt. May 17, 1789. Spon: parents.

Susanna of Jacob Weyrich and wife, b. Mar 3, 1789; bapt. May 28, 1789. Spon: parents.

Juliana of Jacob Eichelberger and wife, b. Dec 10, 1788; bapt. Mar 22, 1789. Spon: Juliana Zimmermann.

Peter of Peter Weber and wife, b. May 22, 1789; bapt. Jun 2, 1789. Spon: parents.

Susanna of Ludwig Dormann and wife, b. May 9, 1789; bapt. Jun 14, 1789. Spon: Johannes Nicolaus Schack and wife.

Johann Peter of Hannes Steger and wife, b. May 24, 1789; bapt. Jun 19, 1789. Spon: Jacob Steger and wife.

Maria Magdalena of Johannes Miller and wife, b. Jun 11, 1789; bapt. Jul 26, 1789. Spon: Johannes Marther and wife.

Magdalena of Jacob Ely and wife, b. Jan 15, 1786; bapt. Aug 9, 1789. Spon: parents.

Jacob of Peter Ely and wife, b. May 30, 1789; bapt. Oct 18, 1789. Spon: parents.

Christian of Christian Jäger and Anna Maria, b. Aug 9, 1789; bapt. Oct 18, 1789. Spon: parents.

Susanna of Rudolf Müller and Susanna, b. Aug 31, 1789; bapt. Oct 19, 1789. Spon: Abraham Rigel and Elisabetha.

Susanna of Carl Korb and Susanna, b. Sep 11, 1789; bapt. Oct 19, 1789. Spon: Peter Jüngst and Catharina.

Johannes of Johannes Stroh and Anna Maria, b. Sep 7, 1789; bapt. Nov 2, 1789. Spon: Michael Mees.

Johannes of Johannes Gerst and Magdalena, b. Sep 13, 1789; bapt. Nov 15, 1789. Spon: parents.

Johann Georg of Lowis Gerstin, b. Aug 17, 1789; bapt. Dec 13, 1789. Spon: August Gerst and wife.

Johannes of Johannes Huber and wife, b. Nov 23, 1789; bapt. Jan 12, 1790. Spon: Carolus Kien and wife.

Johann Peter of Johannes Mayer and wife, b. Dec 5, 1789; bapt. Jan 12, 1790. Spon: Daniel Held.

Eva of Michael Krebs and wife, b. Sep 27, 1789; bapt. Jan 9, 1790. Spon: parents.

Anna Christina of Henrich Schaffner and wife, b. Nov 8, 1789; bapt. Dec 30, 1789. Spon: parents.

Elisabetha of Jacob Deiss and wife, b. Jan 9, 1790; bapt. Feb 27, 1790. Spon: Henrich Schaffner and wife.

Jacob of Johannes Megundel and wife, b. Jan 7, 1790; bapt. Feb 21, 1790. Spon: parents.

Anna Sibilla of Georg Kornman and wife, b. Jan 8, 1790; bapt. Feb 7, 1790. Spon: Philip Oberkirsch and wife.

Magdalena of Georg Wiland and wife, b. Feb 13, 1789; bapt. Mar 30, 1790. Spon: parents.

Anna Maria of Johann Grünewald and wife, b. Mar 2, 1790; bapt. May 2, 1790. Spon: Anna Maria Steer, widow.

Philip of August Braun and Juliana, b. Jan 1, 1790; bapt. May 3, 1790. Spon: parents.

Schems (James) of Robert Laury and wife, b. Nov 2, 1790 (1789); bapt. May 25, 1790. Spon: parents.

Catharina of Johannes Rohrer and wife, b. Feb 8, 1790; bapt. May 23, 1790. Spon: Samuel Meyle and wife.

David of Henrich Lang and wife, b. Jan 22, 1790; bapt. Jun 12, 1790. Spon: parents.

Elisa of Joseph Mecul and wife, b. Jul 3, 1790; bapt. Jul 11, 1790. Spon: parents.

Johann Jacob of Henrich Steger and Barbara, b. Jul 3, 1790; bapt. Aug 6, 1790. Spon: Jacob Steger and Catharina.

Johannes of Peter Eichelberger and wife, b. Jul 10, 1790; bapt. Aug 10, 1790. Spon: Abraham Bleystein and wife.

Henrich of Jacob Schaack and wife, b. Aug 31, 1790; bapt. Oct 3, 1790. Spon: Henrich Schantzen and wife.

Catharina of Michael Leuman and wife, b. Aug 25, 1790; bapt. Oct 3, 1790. Spon: Catharina Schaack.

Catharina Barbara of Jacob Goldmann and Mary Magdalena, b. Sep 24, 1789; bapt. Oct 18, 1790. Spon: Catharina Orth, widow.

Regina of Andreas Huber and wife, b. Jan 25, 1789; bapt. Oct 19, 1790. Spon: parents.

Matthäus of Philip Grünewald and wife, b. Sep 9, 1790; bapt. Oct 17, 1790. Spon: parents.

William of Juy Megoloch and wife, b. Oct 2, 1790; bapt. Oct 20, 1790. Spon: Peter Schindel and wife.

Daniel of Johannes Keller and wife, b. Sep 30, 1790; bapt. Oct 31, 1790. Spon: Johannes Klolinger and wife.

Johannes of Jacob Wutz and Catharina, b. Sep 20, 1790; bapt. Nov 13, 1790. Spon: Johannes Mayer and his sister, Eva.

Henrich of Henrich Kelcker and wife, b. Oct 10, 1790; bapt. Nov 14, 1790. Spon: parents.

Catharina of Peter Weyrich and wife, b. Nov 1, 1790; bapt. Nov 28, 1790. Spon: Georg Ellinger and Catharina.

Catharina Elisabeth of Johann Georg Drion and wife, b. Oct 28, 1790; bapt. Nov 30, 1790. Spon: Philip Grünewald and wife.

---- of Simon Meile and Anna Maria, bapt. Dec 3, 1790. Spon: Malle (Molly) Meister.

Johannes of Johannes Stehr and wife, b. Nov 27, 1790; bapt. Dec 26, 1790. Spon: Johannes Schnee and wife.

Johannes of Conrath Merck and wife, b. Dec 2, 1790; bapt. Dec 26, 1790. Spon: Georg Merck and wife.

Abraham of Abraham Belistein and wife; b. Dec 10, 1790; bapt. Jan 6, 1791. Spon: Peter Eichelberger and wife.

Johannes of Jacob Lehmann and wife, b. Mar 6, 1790; bapt. Jan 18, 1791. Spon: parents.

Johannes of Henrich Tubs and wife, b. Apr 5, 1790; bapt. Jan 23, 1791. Spon: parents.

Samuel of Carolus Müller and wife, b. Dec 26, 1790; bapt. Mar 6, 1791. Spon: parents.

Benjamin of Peter Weber and wife, b. Mar 26, 1791; bapt. Apr 1, 1791. Spon: Benjamin Zerbe and wife.

Elisa. Gretha of Christian Grünewald and wife, b. Feb 18, 1791; bapt. Apr 3, 1791. Spon: Philip Grünewald and wife.

Sarah of Henrich Schaffner and wife; b. Apr 3, 1791; bapt. Apr 5, 1791. Spon: Christina Schaffner.

Elisabeth of Adam Germann and wife, b. Feb 25, 1788; bapt. Apr 4, 1791. Spon: parents.

Johann Henrich of Adam Germann and wife, b. Mar 18, 1790; bapt. Apr 4, 1791. Spon: mother.

Johann Henrich of Jacob Pfeiffer and wife, b. Mar 31, 1791; bapt. May 15, 1791. Spon: parents.

Maria Catharina of Nicolaus Weyrich and wife, b. Apr 17, 1791; bapt. May 16, 1791. Spon: Georg Ellinger and wife.

Christian of Christian Farne and wife, b. Oct 12, 1790; bapt. May 28, 1791. Spon: parents.

Johann Peter of Dielmann Daub and wife, b. Apr 30, 1791; bapt. May 29, 1791. Spon: Johann Peter Daub.

Lisabetha Cathrina of Michael Dochtermann and wife, b. Feb 9, 1791; bapt. Jun 11, 1791. Spon: Elisabeth Weiss.

Johannes of Joseph Lewelle and Magdalena, b. May 28, 1791; bapt. Jun 11, 1791. Spon: Johannes Richer and wife.

Susanna of Jacob Ely and wife, b. Apr 19, 1791; bapt. Jun 12, 1791. Spon: parents.

Michael of Peter Ely and wife, b. Mar 22, 1791; bapt. Jun 12, 1791. Spon: parents.

Samuel of Casper Löw and wife, b. Jun 15, 1791; bapt. Jul 15, 1791. Spon: Johann Georg Drion and wife.

Joseph of Bernhart Reinhart and wife, b. Apr 21, 1791; bapt. Jul 26, 1791. Spon: parents.

Johann Georg of William Becker and Catharina, b. Jun 26, 1791; bapt. Jul 26, 1791. Spon: Johann Nicolaus Bressler.

Johann Conrath of Peter Burchener and wife, b. Apr 8, 1791; bapt. Jul 29, 1791. Spon: Johann Conrath Daub.

Dorothy of Michael Garrewel and wife, b. Dec 24, 1789; bapt. Aug 7, 1791. Spon: mother.

Johann Henrich of Michael Garrewel and wife, b. Dec 29, 1790; bapt. Aug 7, 1791. Spon: parents.

Johannes of Christian Jäger and wife, b. May 31, 1791; bapt. Aug 21, 1791. Spon: parents.

Johannes of Valentin Schultz and wife, b. Aug 9, 1791; bapt. Aug 21, 1791. Spon: Johannes Stehr and wife.

Magdalena of Johannes Megondel and wife, b. May 31, 1791; bapt. Sep 4, 1791. Spon: parents.

Magdalena of Henrich Mayer and wife, b. Aug 13, 1791; bapt. Sep 18, 1791. Spon: Jacob Groff and wife.

Philip of Georg Gloninger and wife, b. Jul 3, 1791; bapt. Oct 2, 1791. Spon: Ludwig Lupp and wife.

Elisabetha of Georg Gloninger and wife, b. Jul 3, 1791; bapt. Oct 2, 1791. Spon: parents.

Elisabeth of Henrich Kelcker and wife, b. Sep 8, 1791; bapt. Oct 2, 1791. Spon: parents.

Samuel of Benjamin Schicker and wife, b. Aug 18, 1791; bapt. Oct 2, 1791. Spon: parents.

Anna Maria of Georg Hammer and wife, b. Sep 9, 1791; bapt. Oct 16, 1791. Spon: Catharina Eichelberger.

David of Carolus Arnd and wife, b. Oct 19, 1791; bapt. Nov 12, 1791. Spon: Anna Arnd, widow.

Samuel of Johannes Finckel and wife, b. Aug 16, 1791; bapt. Nov 13, 1791. Spon: parents.

Magdalena of Jacob Weyrich and Magdalena, b. Nov 5, 1791; bapt. Dec 25, 1791. Spon: Elisabeth Gerst.

Johann Georg of Christoffel Braun and Maria, b. Aug 10, 1791; bapt. Dec 30, 1791. Spon: Johann Georg Dryon and wife.

Johann Georg of Peter Eichelberger and wife, b. Dec 10, 1791; bapt. Dec 25, 1791. Spon: Georg Megondel and Susanna.

Jacob of Jacob Merck and Catharina, b. Dec 15, 1791; bapt. Jan 1, 1792. Spon: Philip Tünges.

Anna Maria of Henrich Stecheer and Barbara, b. Nov 8, 1791; bapt. Jan 4, 1792. Spon: Gottfried Eichelberger and wife.

Jan 4, 1792. Spon: Gottfried Eichelberger and wife.

Jacob of Johannes Gerst and Molly [Malle], b. Oct 29, 1791; bapt. Jan 17, 1792. Spon: parents.

Johann Georg of Johann Leineweber and wife, b. Dec 9, 1791; bapt. Jan 22, 1792. Spon: Michael Meese and wife.

Hannah of Nicolaus Tünges and wife, b. Jan 15, 1792; bapt. Jan 25, 1792. Spon: Peter Entreas and wife.

Elias of Gottfried Xander (Alexander) and Elisabeth, b. Dec 23, 1791; bapt. Jan 27, 1792. Spon: parents.

Georg of Michael Krebs and wife, b. Nov 26, 1791; bapt. Feb 28, 1792. Spon: parents.

Barbara of Peter Weyrich and Jacobina, b. Feb 14, 1792; bapt. Mar 4, 1792. Spon: Philip Firntzler and wife.

Johann Jacob of Georg Schambach and wife, b. Sep 18, 1791; bapt. Mar 15, 1792. Spon: parents.

Elisabetha of Friedrich Thomas and wife, b. Feb 11, 1792; bapt. Mar 19, 1792. Spon: Elisabeth Schweitzer.

Johann Henrich of Henrich Tubs and Barbara, b. Dec 2, 1791; bapt. Mar 19, 1792. Spon: Anthony Deweler and wife.

Maria Magdalena of Jacob Körber and Susanna, b. Oct 2, 1791; bapt. Mar 31, 1792. Spon: Elisabetha Scharff.

Catharina of William Dewis and Susanna, b. Oct 16, 1791; bapt. Apr 4, 1792. Spon: Rosina Detweiler.

Cortius (Curtius) of Georg Meile and wife, b. ---; bapt. Apr 9, 1792. Spon: parents.

Johann Jacob of Michael Leymann and Elisabetha, b. Mar 22, 1792; bapt. Apr 29, 1792. Spon: Johann Jacob Schack.

Anna Maria of Jacob Deiss and Magdalena, b. Mar 9, 1792; bapt. Apr 29, 1792. Spon: David Deiss and wife.

Johannes of Jacob Schaack and wife, b. Apr 14, 1792; bapt. May 13, 1792. Spon: Peter Stecher and wife.

Elisabeth of Ludwig Dormann and wife, b. May 1, 1792; bapt. May 27, 1792. Spon: Gottfried Eichelberger and wife.

Christian of Jacob Schwab and Elisabeth, b. Jan 22, 1792; bapt. May 30, 1792. Spon: Johannes Schally and Barbara.

Johannes of Johannes Rohrer and wife, b. Nov 25, 1791; bapt. May 31, 1792. Spon: Samuel Meile and wife.

Elisabetha of Samuel Meile and wife, b. Mar 7, 1792; bapt. May 31, 1792. Spon: Johannes Rohrer and wife.

Joseph of Joseph Mecul and Catharina, b. Apr 3, 1792; bapt. Jul 16,

Andreas of Georg Kornman and Christina, b. Jul 1, 1792; bapt. Jul 22, 1792. Spon: Andreas Webert and wife.

Angnes (Agnes) of Thomas Elles and Eckes, b. Apr 30, 1792; bapt. May 27, 1792. Spon: Jacob Weyrich and Margaretha.

Catharina of Jacob Frölich and Catharina, b. Oct 20, 1791; bapt. Aug 17, 1792. Spon: parents.

Philip of Johannes Grünewald and wife, b. Jul 18, 1792; bapt. Aug 19, 1792. Spon: Philip Fawer and wife.

Johannes of Johannes Taunen and wife, b. Aug 29, 1791; bapt. Sep 30, 1792. Spon: Johannes Ressle and wife.

Johannes of Michael Huber and Regina, b. Sep 16, 1792; bapt. Oct 14, 1792. Spon: parents.

Rebecca of Adam German and wife, b. Sep 18, 1792; bapt. Oct 22, 1792. Spon: parents.

Elisabetha of Johannes Keller and wife, b. Aug 29, 1792; bapt. Aug 29, 1792. Spon: Henrich Schaffner and wife.

Regina of Valentin Kornman and wife, b. Jul 27, 1792; bapt. Nov 4, 1792. Spon: Regina Jungblut.

Jacob of Johannes Steger and Elisabeth, b. Nov 25, 1791; bapt. Dec 29, 1791. Spon: Conrath Hoffman and wife.

Maria Margaretha of Friedrich Schweitzer and wife, b. Oct 27, 1792; bapt. Nov 11, 1792. Spon: Maria Marg. Dussinger.

Elisabeth of Johannes Rewald and Susan, b. Nov 27, 1792; bapt. Dec 9, 1792. Spon: Henrich Schaffner and wife.

Georg Augustus and Elisabeth Augustin of Samuel Baumgertner and Elisabeth, b. Aug 1, 1792; bapt. Jan 2, 1793. Spon: parents.

Margaretha of Conrath Reinöhl and Eva Maria, b. Nov 30, 1792; bapt. Jan 4, 1793. Spon: parents.

Regina of Jacob Scheuer and wife, b. Nov 28, 1792; bapt. Jan 14, 1792 (1793?). Spon: Georg Scheuer and wife.

Anna Maria of Christoffel Schanck and wife, b. Jan 20, 1790; bapt. Jan 14, 1793. Spon: parents.

Sarah of Christoffel Schanck and wife, b. Aug 16, 1792; bapt. Jan 14, 1793. Spon: parents.

Anna of Michael Dochterman and wife, b. Nov 7, 1792; bapt. Jan 14, 1793. Spon: ----.

Marialis of Johannes Schettel and wife, b. Nov 12, 1792; bapt. Jan 14, 1793. Spon: parents.

Magdalena of Georg Scheuer and wife, b. Sep 16, 1792; bapt. Jan 14, 1793. Spon: Jacob Scheuer and wife.

Sella of Daniel Breuns and wife, b. Jun 15, 1791; bapt. Jan 14, 1793.
Spon: mother.

Casper Geiher of -----; bapt. Jan 14, 1793.

Scharlotte of Jacob Schumacher and wife, b. Aug 26, 1791; bapt. Jan
14, 1792. Spon: mother.

David of Philip Grünewald and wife, b. Nov 19, 1792; bapt. Jan 17,
1793. Spon: parents.

Elisabetha of Conrad Merck and wife, b. Jan 12, 1793; bapt. Jan 19,
1793. Spon: parents.

Johannes of Daniel Nunnenmacher and wife, b. Jan 18, 1793; bapt.
Jan 24, 1793. Spon: parents.

Anna Maria of Peter Steger and wife, b. Jan 1, 1793; bapt. Feb 3,
1793. Spon: Anna Maria Durst.

Johann Philip of Jacob Hornefius and wife, b. Oct 8, 1792; bapt. Feb
3, 1793. Spon: parents.

Alexander of Georg Megontel and Susanna, b. Jan 9, 1793; bapt. Feb
19, 1793. Spon: parents.

Anna Maria of Conrath Fassnacht and Catharina, b. Sep 18, 1793(2);
bapt. Feb 21, 1793. Spon: parents.

Johann Georg of Andreas Ley and Anna Maria; bapt. Mar 16, 1793;
bapt. Apr 12, 1793. Spon: Johannes Beyer and Anna Christina.

Hannah of Abraham Döbeler and wife, b. May 14, 1793; bapt. Jun 2,
1793. Spon: parents.

Barbara of Hannes Müller and wife, b. Mar 26, 1793; bapt. Jun 9,
1793. Spon: Barbara Ruland.

Henrich of Peter Fischer and wife, b. Mar 31, 1793; bapt. Jun 9,
1793. Spon: parents.

Margaretha of Georg Friedr. Nagel and Elisabetha, b. Jun 5, 1793;
bapt. Jun 11, 1793. Spon: parents.

William of William Griegbaum and wife, b. May 13, 1793; bapt. Jun
13, 1793. Spon: parents.

Elisabetha of Peter Wendling and Elisabetha, b. Apr 25, 1793; bapt.
Jun 15, 1793. Spon: parents.

David of Jacob Mellinger and Barbara, b. Jun 30, 1793; bapt. Jul 7,
1793. Spon: parents.

Anna Maria of Christoffel Embich and Anna Maria, b. May 2, 1793;
bapt. Jul 16, 1793. Spon: Johannes Bibel and Margaretha.

Conrath of Thielman Taub and Barbara, b. Jun 17, 1793; bapt. Jul
31, 1793. Spon: Conrath Taub.

Daniel of Peter Schrickman and Elisabeth, b. Jun 13, 1793; bapt. Jul

21, 1793. Spon: Anna Maria Beck.

Elisabetha of Johannes Schalle and Barbara, b. Mar 4, 1793; bapt. Aug 18, 1793. Spon: Elisabetha Schall.

Maria Catharina of Philip Firntzler and Barbara, b. Jul 12, 1793; bapt. Aug 18, 1793. Spon: Maria Catharina Ellinger.

Henrich of Georg Hammer and Anna Maria; bapt. Mar 30, 1793; bapt. Jul 21, 1793. Spon: Henrich Schaffner and wife.

Johannes of Johannes Schaack and Anna Maria, b. Jul 5, 1793; bapt. Aug 4, 1793. Spon: Jacob Schaack.

Jacob of Georg Hess and wife, b. Sep 1, 1793; bapt. Sep 7, 1793. Spon: Henrich Schaffner and wife.

Johannes of Peter Eigelberger and wife, b. May 1, 1793; bapt. Sep 15, 1793. Spon: parents.

Elisabetha of Thomas Klerck and Catharina, b. Sep 10, 1793; bapt. Sep 24, 1793. Spon: Rudolf Kelcker and wife.

---- of Rudolf Ressle and Catharina, b. Jul 27, 1793; bapt. Sep 29, 1793. Spon: Daniel Fetzeberger and Elisabeth.

David of Michael Steckbeck and wife, b. May 14, 1793; bapt. Oct 13, 1793. Spon: Martin Bucher and wife.

Elisabeth of Martin Bucher and wife, b. Apr 17, 1793; bapt. Oct 13, 1793. Spon: Michael Steckbeck and wife.

Anna Catharina of Andreas Fogel and Christina, b. Jun 7, 1793; bapt. Oct 13, 1793. Spon: Anna Catharina Bibel.

Elisabetha of Johann Philip Umberger and wife, b. Sep 13, 1793; bapt. Oct 13, 1793. Spon: Margaretha Schalle.

Johannes of Johann Philip Umberger and wife, b. Apr 19, 1792; bapt. Apr 14, 1792.? (These dates may be reversed.) Spon: Lucas Schalle and wife.

Joseph of Bernhart Embich and wife, b. Oct 8, 1793; bapt. Oct 13, 1793. Spon: parents.

Cathrina of Georg Tromb and wife, b. Aug 31, 1793; bapt. Oct 27, 1793. Spon: Andreas Ley.

Henrich of David Döbeler and Margaretha, b. Feb 14, 1792; bapt. Nov 10, 1793. Spon: parents.

Georg of Michael Fawer and wife, b. Sep 15, 1793; bapt. Nov 10, 1793. Spon: Georg Glassbrener and wife.

Valentin of Valentin Kob and wife, b. Oct 10, 1793, b. Nov 10, 1793. Spon: Georg Peter and wife.

Elisabetha of Johann Augustin Braun and wife, b. Sep 27, 1793; bapt. Nov 24, 1793. Spon: parents.

Nov 24, 1793. Spon: parents.

Johann Georg of Henrich Gilbert and wife, b. Nov 16, 1793; bapt. Nov 24, 1793. Spon: parents.

Elisabetha of Philip Tromb and wife, b. Jul 19, 1793; bapt. Feb 2, 1794. Spon: Georg Tromb and wife.

Samuel of Christoffel Uller and wife, b. Jan 22, 1794; bapt. Mar 1, 1794. Spon: parents.

Wilhelm of Michael Mees and Catharina, b. Dec 6, 1793; bapt. Mar 16, 1794. Spon: Philip Grünewald and wife.

Johannes of Conrath Mohr and Elisabeth, b. Jan 16, 1794; bapt. Mar 17, 1794. Spon: parents.

Joseph of Martin Jentzel and wife, b. Mar 19, 1794; bapt. Mar 20, 1794. Spon: parents.

Johann Michael of Johannes Schlotterbeck and wife, b. Jan 14, 1794; bapt. Apr 10, 1794. Spon: parents.

Eva Elisabetha of Jacob Deiss and Magdalena, b. Mar 2, 1794; bapt. Apr 13, 1794. Spon: Elisabetha Lauer.

Hannes of Hannes Leinweber and wife, b. Apr 1, 1794; bapt. Apr 14, 1794. Spon: parents.

Samuel of Johannes Beck and wife, b. Dec 3, 1793; bapt. Mar 23, 1794. Spon: parents.

Sarah of Benjamin Mohr and Magdalena, b. Feb 14, 1794; bapt. Apr 20, 1794. Spon: Anna Mohr.

Elisabetha of Peter Stecher and wife, b. Mar 23, 1794; bapt. Apr 25, 1794. Spon: parents.

Joseph of Henrich Imhoff and wife, b. Apr 10, 1794; bapt. Mar 2, 1794 (reversed dates?). Spon: parents.

Johannes of Schims Georg and Maria, b. Mar 5, 1794; bapt. May 3, 1794. Spon: parents.

Jacob of Peter Weyrich and Jacobina, b. Apr 13, 1794; bapt. May 4, 1794. Spon: Ludwig Lupp and wife.

Peter of Henrich Stecher and Barbara, b. Feb 21, 1794; bapt. May 9, 1794. Spon: Peter Stecher and Barbara.

Johannes of Frierich Schweitzer and Magdalena, b. Sep 10, 1794; bapt. May 12, 1794. Spon: Jacob Bicher and Catharina.

Susanna of Simon Lupp and Marialis, b. Aug 22, 1793; bapt. May 21, 1794. Spon: Susanna Lupp.

William of Matheis Grünewald and Barbara, b. May 23, 1794; bapt. May 30, 1794. Spon: parents.

Elisabeth of Friedrich Hubele and Anna Maria, b. Mar 21, 1794; bapt.

Jun 1, 1794. Spon: Elisabeth Grob and Maria Catharina Dering.

Susanna of Johannes Benner and Elisabetha, b. Mar 21, 1794; bapt. Jun 6, 1794. Spon: Susanna Lupp.

Samuel of Leonhart Reiss and wife, b. May 2, 1794; bapt. Jun 14, 1794. Spon: Anna Arnd.

Georg of Jacob Ellinger and wife, b. May 20, 1794; bapt. Jun 8, 1794. Spon: Catharina Ellinger, widow.

Catharina of Gottfried Zerbe and wife, b. Dec 15, 1790; bapt. Jun 29, 1794. Spon: parents.

Gottfried of Gottfried Zerbe and wife, b. Mar 26, 1794; bapt. Jun 29, 1794. Spon: parents.

Johann Henrich of Conrath Reinöhl and wife, b. Jun 24, 1794; bapt. Jul 11, 1794. Spon: parents.

Samuel of Philp Dünges and Christina, b. Jun 27, 1794; bapt. Aug 12, 1794. Spon: Nicolaus Dünges and wife.

Hannes of Hannes Umberger and Catharina, b. Aug 16, 1794; bapt. Aug 21, 1794. Spon: Elisabetha Umberger.

Elisabetha of Henrich Jüngst and Christina, b. Jul 28, 1794; bapt. Aug 22, 1794. Spon: Friedrich Stecher and Elisabeth.

Benjamin of Benjamin Schicker and wife, b. Jun 16, 1794; bapt. Jul 29, 1794. Spon: parents.

Elisabetha of Henrich Geib and wife, b. Oct 5, 1793; bapt. Sep 27, 1794. Spon: parents.

Johannes of Johannes Gloninger and Catharina, b. Aug 20, 1794; bapt. Oct 14, 1794. Spon: Georg Gloninger and wife.

Susanna of Johannes Megondel and Catharina, b. Sep 15, 1794; bapt. Oct 16, 1794. Spon: parents.

Johann Henrich of Casper Löw and wife, b. Sep 23, 1794; bapt. Oct 16, 1794. Spon: Anna Maria Löw.

Simon of Robert Meckling and wife, b. Dec 29, 1790; bapt. Oct 18, 1794. Spon: Anna Maria Kintzeler.

Johannes of Robert Meckling and wife, b. Oct 12, 1792; bapt. Oct 18, 1794. Spon: parents.

Catharina of Jue Gething and wife, b. Sep 7, 1793; bapt. Oct 18, 1794. Spon: parents.

Margaretha of Georg Conrath and wife, b. May 14, 1794; bapt. Oct 18, 1794. Spon: Catharina Gerli.

Anna Maria of Georg Conrath and wife, b. May 14, 1794; bapt. Oct 18, 1794. Spon: Catharina Kintzeler.

Samuel of Michael Huber and Regina, b. Sep 27, 1794; bapt. Oct 28, 1794. Spon: Christoffel Uhler and wife.

Maria Magdalena of Henrich Böshaar and wife, b. Sep 21, 1794; bapt. Nov 20, 1794. Spon: Juliana Laubscher.

Johannes of Johannes Scherer and wife, b. Nov 24, 1794; bapt. Jan 14, 1795. Spon: Henrich Schantzen and wife.

Anna Maria of Johannes Schack and wife, b. Nov 19, 1794; bapt. Feb 8, 1795. Spon: Jacob Empich and wife.

Sarah of Johann Georg Drion and Catharina, b. Jan 27, 1795; bapt. Feb 11, 1795. Spon: parents.

---- of Georg Embich and Catharina, b. Jan 12, 1794; bapt. Aug 4, 1794. Spon: ---.

Johann Georg of Conrath Merck and wife, b. Feb 6, 1795; bapt. Mar 8, 1795. Spon: Schims Justin and wife.

Margaretha of John Kelle and Maria, b. Mar 20, 1795; bapt. Mar 23, 1795. Spon: Catharina Bleistein, widow.

Sarah of John Kelle and Maria, b. Mar 20, 1795; bapt. Mar 23, 1795. Spon: Catharina Bleistein, widow.

Magdalena of Georg Kornman and Christina, b. Mar 31, 1795; bapt. Apr 19, 1795. Spon: Jacob Weiss and Margaretha.

Jacob of Dielmann Daub and Barbara, b. Feb 25, 1795; bapt. Apr 28, 1795. Spon: parents.

Johannes of Philip Grünewald and wife, b. Apr 17, 1795; bapt. May 29, 1795. Spon: Johannes Grünewald and wife.

Elisabetha of Philip Grünewald and wife, b. Apr 17, 1795; bapt. May 25, 1795. Spon: parents.

Georg of Conrath Gerhart and Cathr. b. Mar 13, 1795; bapt. Jun 7, 1795. Spon: Georg Schantzen and Maria Elisabeth.

Thomas of Joseph Meckmore and Elisabeth, b. Dec 21, 1783; bapt. May 14, 1795. Spon: parents.

Sarah of Joseph Meckmore and Elisabeth, b. Apr 28, 1789; bapt. May 14, 1795. Spon: parents.

Elisabetha of Joseph Meckmore and Elisabetha, b. Nov 6, 1791; bapt. May 14, 1795. Spon: parents.

Elisabetha of Nicolaus Weiss and Anna Maria, b. Jul 21, 1795; bapt. Aug 31, 1795. Spon: Dielmann Daub and Barbara.

Michael of Johannes Schlotterbeck and wife, b. Aug 14, 1795; bapt. Sep 11, 1795. Spon: parents.

Maria Magdalena of Johannes Dietz and Magdalena, b. Sep 6, 1795; bapt. Sep 15, 1795. Spon: Benjamin Mohr and Magdalena.

Anna Maria of Georg Gloninger and Maria, b. Jul 31, 1795; bapt. Oct 18, 1795. Spon: Johannes Gloninger and Cathrina.

Maria of Henrich Saltzberger and Juliana, b. Aug 23, 1795; bapt. Oct 18, 1795. Spon: Juliana Eigelberner, widow.

Johannes of Michael Krebs and Margareth, b. Aug 29, 1795; bapt. Oct 18, 1795. Spon: parents.

Margaretha of Johannes Schalle and wife, b. Sep 10, 1795; bapt. Nov 15, 1795. Spon: Margaretha Schalle.

Jacob of Henrich Sieg and Elisabeth, b. Oct 7, 1795; bapt. Nov 15, 1795. Spon: Ludwig Lupp.

William of Jacob Krebs and Catharina, b. Oct 30, 1795; bapt. Dec 18, 1795. Spon: Michael Krebs and Margaretha.

Samuel of Bernhart Reinhart and Elisabeth, b. Aug 6, 1795; bapt. Dec 31, 1795. Spon: Ludwig Lupp.

Samuel of Jacob Ebrecht and Elisabeth, b. Sep 25, 1795; bapt. Jan 1, 1796. Spon: Benjamin Mohr and Magdalena.

Catharina of Peter Eli and Cathr., b. ---; bapt. Jan 1, 1796. Spon: Valentin Schultz and Cathr.

Samuel of Jacob Mellinger and Barbara, b. Jan 17, 1796; bapt. Jan 25, 1796. Spon: parents.

Johannes of Philip Dünges and Christina, b. Feb 27, 1796; bapt. Mar 2, 1796. Spon: Christian Goldmann and wife.

Johann Philip of Mattheis Grünewald and Barbara, b. Mar 4, 1796; bapt. Mar 20, 1796. Spon: Philip Grünewald and Catharina.

Anna of Peter Fuhrman and Juliana, b. Jul 14, 1795; bapt. Apr 12, 1796. Spon: parents. *(Hand written entry.)*

William of Shimmy Gorry and Mary, b. Nov 2, 1795; bapt. Apr 13, 1796. Spon: parents.

Anna Maria of Johannes Huber and Elisabeth, b. Dec 29, 1795; bapt. Jun 27, 1796. Spon: Friedrich Hubele and Anna Maria.

David of Henrich William and Cathr., b. May 14, 1796; bapt. Jul 10, 1796. Spon: Michael Detweiler and Cathr.

Anna Maria of Henrich Schaffner and Christina, b. May 28, 1796; bapt. Jul 10, 1796. Spon: John Damm and Anna Maria.

Elisabeth of Johannes Alstadt and Elisabeth, b. May 29, 1796; bapt. Jul 10, 1796. Spon: parents.

Elisabetha of Henrich Berry and Maria Esther, b. Jul 3, 1796; bapt. Jul 12, 1796. Spon: --- Schertzer and wife.

Johannes of Johannes Fogel and Anna, b. Jun 23, 1795; bapt. Jul 12, 1796. Spon: Johannes Bard and wife.

Elisabetha of Georg Ischler and Susan, b. Jul 6, 1796; bapt. Jul 24, 1796. Spon: Barbara Müller.

Amos of Jacob Fuchs and Eva, b. May 29, 1796; bapt. Jul 24, 1796. Spon: David Sebold and Susanna.

Catharina of Jacob Ellinger and Elisabetha, b. Jun 2, 1796; bapt. Aug 9, 1796. Spon: Catharina Ellinger.

Johann Henrich of Johannes Müller and Salome, b. Jul 30, 1796; bapt. Sep 4, 1796. Spon: Henrich Richer and Margaretha.

Johannes of Lucas Schalle and Catharina, b. My 5, 1796; bapt. Sep 4, 1796. Spon: Johann Nicolaus Schack and Marilis.

Rebecca of Johannes Grünewald and Regina, b. Jul 18, 1796; bapt. Sep 4, 1796. Spon: Mattheis Grünewald and Barbara.

Johannes of Martin Rausch and Elisabeth, b. Nov 10, 1795; bapt. Sep 18, 1796. Spon: parents.

Georg of Michael Huber and Regina, b. Aug 20, 1796; bapt. Sep 18, 1796. Spon: Henrich Schantzin and Catharina.

Johannes of Henrich Imhoff and Christina, b. ----; bapt. Oct 4, 1796. Spon: parents.

Maria Cathrina of Johannes Stöhr and Margaretha, b. Jul 30, 1796; bapt. Nov 1, 1796. Spon: Johannes Zinn and Catharina.

Berthin of Daniel Meckmollen and Rebecca, b. Sep 22, 1795; bapt. Nov 21, 1796. Spon: parents.

Johannes of Peter Weyrich and Jacobina, b. Oct 30, 1796; bapt. Nov 26, 1796. Spon: Johannes Lautermilch and Christina.

Schimsrith of Liefa (Levi) Hallenswart and Sarah, b. Jul 13, 1796; bapt. Nov 28, 1796. Spon: parents.

Cathrina of Conrath Erhart and Catharina, b. Nov 25, 1796; bapt. Nov 30, 1796. Spon: parents.

Georg of Thomas Elles and wife, b. Jul 27, 1796; bapt. Dec 1, 1796. Spon: mother.

Henrich of Henrich Seng and Catharina, b. Sep 7, 1792; bapt. Jan 19, 1797. Spon: Johannes Schedel and Salome.

Catharina of Henrich Seng and Catharina, b. Oct 23, 1794; bapt. Jan 19, 1797. Spon: Johannes Schedel and Salome.

Daniel of Johannes Schedel and Salome, b. Nov 19, 1796; bapt. Jan 19, 1797. Spon: parents.

Margaretha of Jacob Richer and Margaretha, b. Oct 23, 1796; bapt. Jan 22, 1797. Spon: Philip Imboden and Elisabeth.

Johannes of Jacob Firntzler and Susanna, b. Oct 25, 1796; bapt. Feb 9, 1797. Spon: Johannes Neu and Catharina.

David of Henrich Peter and Christina, b. Jan 16, 1797; bapt. Feb 9, 1797. Spon: parents.

Salome of Johannes Rohrer and Elisabetha, b. Jul 15, 1796; bapt. Feb 18, 1797. Spon: parents.

Elisabetha of Conrath Merck and Margaretha, b. Jan 31, 1797; bapt. Feb 28, 1797. Spon: parents.

Samuel of Henrich Sieg and Elisabetha, b. Mar 5, 1797; bapt. Mar 6, 1797. Spon: parents.

Samuel of Samuel Kümmel and Elisabetha, b. Jan 1, 1797; bapt. Feb 23, 1797. Spon: Jacob Weyrich and Margaretha.

Margaretha of Henrich Saltzberry and Juliana, b. Mar 31, 1797; bapt. Apr 16, 1797. Spon: Johann Peter Ritschert and Margaretha.

Christophel of Jacob Hornefius and Elisabeth, b. Mar 6, 1797; bapt. Apr 19, 1797. Spon: parents.

Catharina of Henrich Kelcker and wife, b. Mar 23, 1797; bapt. Apr 30, 1797. Spon: parents.

Christina of Jacob Baumann and Anna, b. Feb 19, 1797; bapt. May 27, 1797. Spon: parents.

Jacob of Georg Baumann and Catharina, b. May 24, 1797; bapt. May 27, 1797. Spon: parents.

Johann Philip of Philip Schack and Magdalena, b. Apr 16, 1797; bapt. Jun 11, 1797. Spon: Jacob Schack.

Mattheis of Adam Brenner and Eva, b. Jun 12, 1797; bapt. Jun 17, 1797. Spon: Baltzer Gasser.

Magdalena of Martin Bucher and Catharina, b. May 17, 1797; bapt. Jul 23, 1797. Spon: Veronica Steckbeck.

Elisabetha of Henrich Steger and Barbara, b. Jun 5, 1797; bapt. Aug 6, 1797. Spon: parents.

Catharina of Georg Kornmann and Christina, b. Jun 18, 1797; bapt. Aug 6, 1797. Spon: Georg Vogt and Catharina.

Elisabetha of Daniel Meckmollen and Rebecca, b. Feb 19, 1797; bapt. Aug 28, 1797. Spon: parents.

Georg of Peter Eichelberner and Margaret, b. Dec 24, 1794; bapt. Aug 29, 1797. Spon: mother.

Friedrich of Henrich Williams and Catharina, b. Aug 21, 1797; bapt. Sep 29, 1797. Spon: Peter Killinger and Maria.

Jacob of Adam Stroh and Susan, b. Sep 24, 1796; bapt. Sep 29, 1797. Spon: Johannes Dutweiler and Maria.

Johann Carl of Philip Grünewald and wife, b. Aug 3, 1797; bapt. Oct 1, 1797. Spon: parents.

Wilhelm of Johannes Rewald and Susanna, b. Sep 25, 1797; bapt. Oct 2, 1797. Spon: Martin Schaffner and Veronica.

Johann Adam of Michael Errich and Catharina, b. Sep 20, 1797; bapt. Oct 2, 1797. Spon: Adam Heilmann and Cathr.

N. B. of Jacob Körber and Susanna, b. Jan 8, 1797; bapt. Nov 3, 1797. Spon: Melcher Walter and Barbara.

Maria Magdalena of Leonhart Dubs and Margaretha, b. May 4, 1794; bapt. Nov 9, 1797. Spon: Maria Magdalena Bucher.

Catharina of Leonhard Dubs and Margaretha, b. Mar 25, 1796; bapt. Nov 9, 1797. Spon: parents.

Johann Georg of Jacob Krebs and Catharina, b. Sep 16, 1797; bapt. Nov 21, 1797. Spon: Friederich Stöwer and Margaretha.

William of Georg Burcker and Christina, b. Aug 3, 1796; bapt. Nov 26, 1797. Spon: Jacob Zuber and Elisabetha.

Leah of Jacob Buschung and Elisabeth, b. Oct 28, 1797; bapt. Nov 29, 1797. Spon: parents.

Magdalena of Christian Weyrich and wife, b. Nov 29, 1788; bapt. Dec 7, 1797. Spon: Jacob Weyrich and Magdalena.

Elisabetha of Christian Weyrich and wife, b. May 8, 1791; bapt. Dec 7, 1797. Spon: Martin Jentzel and Elisabeth.

Christian of Christian Weyrich and wife, b. Oct 27, 1793; bapt. Dec 7, 1797. Spon: parents.

Margaretha of Christian Weyrich and wife, b. May 9, 1797; bapt. Dec 7, 1797. Spon: Margretha Weyrich.

Catharina of Johannes Weyrich and Elisabetha, b. Dec 15, 1797; bapt. Jan 21, 1798. Spon: Catharina Ley.

Henrich of Johannes Fogel and Hannah, b. Aug 16, 1797; bapt. Feb 1, 1798. Spon: Christian Howerder and Juli.

Rebecca of Philip Berry and Catharina, b. Jul 15, 1797; bapt. Feb 1, 1798. Spon: Jacob Bicher and Maria Catharina.

William of Johannes Alstadt and Elisabeth, b. Jan 10, 1798; bapt. Mar 23, 1798. Spon: Abraham Döbeler and Maria.

Anna Margaret of Christian Jäger and Anna Maria, b. Dec 30, 1797; bapt. Apr 1, 1798. Spon: parents.

Johannes of Philip Stecher and Regina, b. Jan 30, 1798; bapt. Mar 18, 1798. Spon: Henrich Stecher.

Johannes of Jacob Gontermann and Catharina, b. Mar 11, 1798; bapt. Apr 8, 1798. Spon: Michael Gontermann.

Johann Jacob of Johannes Scherer and Anna Maria, b. Mar 26, 1798; bapt. Apr 9, 1798. Spon: Johann Jacob Hornefius and Elisabeth.

Johann Jacob of Johannes Scherer and Anna Maria, b. Mar 26, 1798; bapt. Apr 9, 1798. Spon: Johann Jacob Hornefius and Elisabeth.

Johannes of Johannes Rohrer and wife, b. Feb 22, 1798; bapt. Apr 15, 1798. Spon: parents.

Susanna of Johannes Diel and Marilis, b. Aug 21, 1797; bapt. Apr 25, 1798. Spon: Johannes Scherer and Anna Maria.

Elisabetha of Henrich Müller and wife, b. Jan 6, 1798; bapt. Apr 27, 1798. Spon: Henrich Jegley and Barbara.

Johannes of David Marschall and Elisabetha, b. Feb 10, 1793; bapt. Apr 28, 1798. Spon: Christoggel Rickert and Maria.

Elisabeth of David Marschall and Elisabeth, b. Mar 3, 1798; bapt. Apr 28, 1798. Spon: Christoffel Rickert and Maria.

David of Jacob Weyrich and Magdalena, b. Mar 31, 1798; bapt. May 13, 1798. Spon: Christian Weyrich and Catharina.

Ludwig of Jacob Weyrich and Magdalena, b. Mar 31, 1798; bapt. May 13, 1798. Spon: Ludwig Lupp and Catharina.

Johannes of David Fortne and Anna Maria, b. Apr 27, 1798; bapt. May 27, 1798. Spon: Michael Krebs and Margaretha.

Magdalena of Lucas Schalle and Catharina, b. Jan 3, 1798; bapt. Jun 10, 1798. Spon: Magdalena Schallin.

(This is the last baptism entered by Mr. Lupp.)

Johannes Wilhelm of Johannes Reuther and Sarah, b. Dec 26, 1798; bapt. Jan 27, 1799 (by Rev. Wagner). Spon: parents.

Johannes of Wilhelm Hiester and Maria, b. Oct 21, 1797; bapt. Nov 13, 1797. Spon: parents.

Wilhelm of Wilhelm Hiester and Maria, b. Jan 1, 1800; bapt. Feb 2, 1800. Spon: parents.

BAPTISMS BY REV. WILLIAM HIESTER, SEP 1799-NOV 1827

Johann Georg of Joh. Peter Reuter and Sarah, b. Jul 11, 1799; bapt. Sep 22, 1799. Spon: Johannes Reuter and Sarah.

Johann Georg of Johannes Allstatt and Elisabeth, b. Dec 11, 1799; bapt. Jan 19, 1800. Spon: Georg Reinöhl and Catharina.

Israel of Bernhart Reinhart and Elisabeth, b. Dec 14, 1799; bapt. Apr 13, 1800. Spon: Henrich Sieg and Elisabeth.

Philippus of Jacob Buschong and Elisabeth, b. Apr 13, 1800; bapt. May 21, 1800. Spon: parents.

Phillippus of Johannes Baumann and Rebecca, b. Sep 8, 1796; bapt.

May 21, 1800. Spon: Jacob Stieb and Elisabeth.

Johannes of Peter Steger and Barbara, b. May 16, 1800; bapt. Jun 7, 1800. Spon: Johannes Steger and Elisabeth.

Sarah of William Sailsberry and Magdalena, b. Apr 19, 1800; bapt. Jul 6, 1800. Spon: Jacob Weiss and Margaretha.

Catharina of Philippus Umberger and Barbara, b. Feb 21, 1800; bapt. Jul 6, 1800. Spon: Christina Schally.

Anna Maria of Jacob Arndt and Susanna, b. Jul 5, 1800; bapt. Jul 15, 1800. Spon: Anna Arndt.

Johann Henrich of Andreas Lay and Anna Maria, b. May 21, 1800; bapt. Jul 20, 1800. Spon: Peter Borgener.

Johann Georg of Jacob Weyerich and Magdalena, b. Jun 19, 1800; bapt. Jul 26, 1800. Spon: Johannes Weyerich and Elisabeth.

Jacob of Johannes Schaag and Anna Maria, b. Oct 7, 1799; bapt. Aug 2, 1800. Spon: parents.

Maria Magdalena of Henrich Kelcker and Elisabeth, b. Jun 9, 1800; bapt. Aug 31, 1800. Spon: parents.

David of David Fortny and Anna Maria, b. Jul 9, 1800; bapt. Aug 31, 1800. Spon: Michael Steckbeck and Barbara.

Andreas Graf of Gustavus Stoy and Catharina, b. Jun 28, 1800; bapt. Sep 4, 1800. Spon: parents.

Sarah of Johannes Rewald and Susanna, b. Oct 5, 1800; bapt. Oct 24, 1800. Spon: Maria Rewald

Johann Georg of Johannes Meckgundel and Catharina, b. Mar 8, 1800; bapt. Oct 26, 1800. Spon: parents.

Henrich of Henrich Sieg and Elisabeth, b. Nov 14, 1800; bapt. Nov 21, 1800. Spon: parents.

Anna Catharina of Casper Löb and Margaretha, b. Nov 1, 1800; bapt. Nov 25, 1800. Spon: Martin Uler and Catharina.

Catharina of Henrich Bols and Anna Maria, b. Oct 1, 1800; bapt. Dec 4, 1800. Spon: parents.

Johannes of Philippus Greiss and Catharina, b. Dec 4, 1800; bapt. Feb 15, 1801. Spon: Johannes Brug.

Sarah of Georg Bauman and Catharina, b. Sep 24, 1800; bapt. Feb 23, 1801. Spon: mother.

David of Johannes Rohrer and Elisabeth, b. Apr 1, 1800; bapt. Mar 15, 1801. Spon: parents.

Salome of Jacob Bauman and Anna, b. Jul 30, 1800; bapt. Oct 20, 1801. Spon: mother.

Georg of Jacob Hornefius and Elisabeth, b. Mar 28, 1799; bapt. May 5, 1802. Spon: parents.

William of Johannes Schmidt and Maria, b. Sep 12, 1799; bapt. Mar 31, 1803. Spon: mother.

Wilhelm of Peter Gloninger and Elisabeth, b. Sep 7, 1800; bapt. Apr 28, 1803. Spon: parents.

Abraham of Jacob Pfeiffer and Esther, b. Feb 8, 1793; bapt. Apr 8, 1804. Spon: Peter Etschberger and Elisabeth.

Daniel of Georg Henning and Anna Maria, b. Jan 2, 1796; bapt. Aug 9, 1805. Spon: Friedrich Embig and Margaretha.

Sarah of Georg Aston and Elisabeth, b. Sep 29, 1799; bapt. Oct 18, 1807. Spon: parents.

Christina of Johannes Ott and Elisabeth, b. Apr 5, 1795; bapt. Mar 20, 1808. Spon: Elisabeth Hof.

Joseph of Johannes Ott and Elisabeth, b. May 5, 1797; bapt. Mar 20, 1808. Spon: ---.

William of Johannes Ott and Elisabeth, b. Sep 7, 1798; bapt. Mar 20, 1808. Spon: parents.

Andreas of John McCally and Maria, b. Apr 18, 1797; bapt. Oct 12, 1808. Spon: parents.

HEIDELBERG CONGREGATION CHURCH IN SCHAFFERSTOWN

John Peter of Jacob Sauter and wife, b. Oct 10, 1765; bapt. Jan 19, 1766. Spon: Jacob Sauter and Elizabeth Dome.

Abraham of Christian Bollinger and wife, b. Jun 28, 1762; bapt. Aug 16. Spon: Abraham Ruland and wife.

Maria Christine of Christian Bollinger and wife, b. Nov 3, 1763; bapt. Nov 12, 1763. Spon: Rudolph Bollinger and wife.

Anna Engel of Christian Bernhart and wife, b. Aug 31, 1766; bapt. Sep 14. Spon: Alexander Schäffer and wife.

Regina of John Tschopp and wife, b. Feb 2, 1770; bapt. Jun 4. Spon: Durst Thomen and Regina.

Alexander of Caspar Schweitzer and wife, b. Jan 8, 1766; bapt. Jan 19. Spon: Alexander Schaefer and wife.

John Henry of Johannes Schaefer and wife, b. Jan 12, 1766; bapt. Jan 19. Spon: George Schwengel and wife.

Maria Catharine of Christopher Meyer and wife, b. Feb 2, 1766; bapt. Feb 16. Spon: Alexander Schaefer and wife.

Catharine Margaret of Jacob Hamme and wife, b. Mar 13, 1766; bapt. Mar 30. Spon: Thomas Enders and wife.

Maria Catharine of Michael Haark and wife, b. Mar 13, 1766; bapt. Apr 6. Spon: Maria Catharine Schaefer.

Catharine Elizabeth of Adam Hoffman and wife, b. Mar 21, 1766; bapt. Apr 26. Spon: Henry Grim and wife.

Michael of Christian Kreyter and wife, b. Apr 25, 1766; bapt. May 16. Spon: Michael Winter and Catherine Kohlmann.

Anna Christine of John Schwertzel and wife, b. Jul 26, 1766; bapt. Aug 10. Spon: Frederick Faxius and wife.

Anna Christine of Abraham Stump and wife, b. Aug 13, 1766; bapt. Aug 24. Spon: Lorentz Keller and wife.

John George of Martin Götz and wife, b. Sep 7, 1766; bapt. Sep 14. Spon: George Kop and wife.

John Philip of Henry Meisser and wife, b. Oct 15, 1766; bapt. Nov 6. Spon: John Philip Mauerer and wife.

John Frederick of Martin Heffelfinger and wife, b. Nov 4, 1766; bapt. Nov 30. Spon: Frederick Wolfesberger and Catharine Wolfesberger.

Elizabeth of John Taub and wife, b. Oct 18, 1766; bapt. Nov 30. Spon: Jacob Heyser and wife.

John Philip of Paul Gemberling and wife, b. Nov 17, 1766; bapt. Nov

23, 1766. Spon: Justice Mr. De Haas and wife.

Christian of Christian Bollinger and wife, b. Dec 3, 1765; bapt. Dec 8. Spon: Rudolph Bollinger and wife.

Anna Catharine of Jacob Birger (Berger) and wife, b. Jul 8, 1765; bapt. Aug 8. Spon: Anna Margaret Wevers (Weber).

Anna Maria of George Trautman and wife, b. Dec 1, 1765; bapt. Dec 29. Spon: Hieronymus Trautman and wife.

John Jacob of Jacob Thume and wife, b. Jan 2, 1767; bapt. Feb 1. Spon: John Jacob Sauter and Anna Barbara Graef.

Philip of Christine Philippi, b. Mar 30, 1767; bapt. Apr 19. Spon: Philip Klein and wife.

John of Philip Wolfesberger and wife, b. Apr 12, 1767; bapt. Apr 19. Spon: John Wolfesberger and wife.

John Jacob of Hans Tschopp and Magdalene Stoler, b. Dec 5, 1767; bapt. Mar 28, 1768. Spon: Jacob Tomme and wife, Ursula Graef.

Margaret of Jacob Schaub and wife, b. Feb 28, 1758; bapt. Mar 11. Spon: Valentine Schneider and wife.

(The following baptisms were copied into the record from the earlier record book which is still preserved with the later book.)

John of Jacob Schaub and wife, b. Dec 31, 1759; bapt. Jan 13, 1760. Spon: John Schaefer and Anna Maria Nef.

Alexander of Jacob Schaub and wife, b. Jun 28, 1761; bapt. Jul 19. Spon: Alexander Schaefer and wife.

Michael of Jacob Wittmer and wife, b. Mar 29, 1761; bapt. Apr 12. Spon: Abraham Stumb and wife.

Henry of John Brecht and wife, b. Nov 24, 1760; bapt. ---. Spon: Alexander Schaefer and wife.

Michael of John Brecht and wife, b. Sep 10, 1762; bapt. ---. Spon: Michael Hark and wife.

Anna Barbara of Caspar Schweitzer and wife, b. Feb 7, 1763; bapt. ---. Spon: John Schaefer and wife.

Catharine of Christian Bernhard and wife, b. Nov 1, 1764; bapt. Nov. 7. Spon: Ludwig Michel and wife.

John of Jacob Due and wife, b. Jun 27, 1764; bapt. Jul 22. Spon: John Wolfesberger and wife.

John Adam of Jacob Wittmer and wife, b. Jul 10, 1764; bapt. Jul 29. Spon: Lorentz Arnold and wife.

Gottfried of Conrad Eichelberg and wife, b. Aug 18, 1764; bapt. Sep 2. Spon: Gottfried Eichelberg and wife.

John of John Schaefer and wife, b. May 9, 1764; bapt. May 27. Spon:

Alexander Schaefer and wife.

Catharine and Jacob Schaub and wife, b. Mar 3, 1764; bapt. Mar 18. Spon: John Meyer and Catharine Schaefer.

Maria Catharine of John Rosweiler and wife, b. ---; bapt. Mar 18, 1764. Spon: Jacob Due and wife.

Anna Barbara of Jacob Dumme and wife, b. Mar 3, 1764; bapt. Apr 4. Spon: Elizabeth Dumme.

Matthias of Mathias Jacobi and wife, b. ---; bapt. Apr 15, 1764. Spon: Lorentz Hergelrath and wife.

Michael of Michael Hark and wife, b. Apr 29, 1764; bapt. May 27. Spon: Jacob Wittmer and wife.

John Michael of Ludwig Maus and wife, b. May 1, 1764; bapt. Oct 14. Spon: John Michael Dumme and Elizabeth.

Dau of Melchior Lautermilch and wife, b. Oct 1, 1764; bapt. Oct 28. Spon: Henry Meyer and wife.

Jacob of Christian Kreiter and wife, b. Oct 25, 1764; bapt. Dec 9. Spon: Jacob Kreyter and wife.

Conrad of John Daub and wife, b. Oct 17, 1764; bapt. Dec 9. Spon: Conrad Orendorf and wife.

John of John Brecht and wife, b. Nov 11, 1764; bapt. Dec 9. Spon: John Meier and Catharine Schaefer.

Peter of Martin Heffelfinger and wife, b. Oct 19, 1764; bapt. Dec 9. Spon: Peter Wolfersberger and wife.

Valentine of Lorentz Keller and wife, b. Nov 16, 1764; bapt. Dec 9. Spon: Valentine Dienes and wife.

Abraham of Abraham Stumpf and wife, b. Dec 3, 1764; bapt. Dec 25. Spon: Abraham Rein and wife.

Andrew of Bastian Burkert and wife, b. ---; bapt. Dec 25, 1764. Spon: ---.

Andrew of Jost Schwertzler and wife, b. Feb 25, 1765; bapt. Mar 17. Spon: Andrew Ley and wife.

Michael of Adam Bohlender and wife, b. Aug 14, 1765; bapt. Sep 1. Spon: Michael Meyer and Anna Maria Neff.

John of Jacob Pfeiffer and wife, b. Aug 12, 1765; bapt. Oct 6. Spon: John Daub and wife.

Maria Catharine of Peter Schuy and Magdalene, b. Dec 1, 1768; bapt. Dec 29, 1768. Spon: Jacob Sältzer and Maria Catharine.

Maria Elizabeth of Michael Borgert and Anna Eva, b. Dec 20, 1768; bapt. Dec 29. Spon: Jacob Ised and Maria Elizabeth.

John of Jacob Spengler and Maria Elizabeth, b. Dec 4, 1768; bapt.

Jan 11, 1769. Spon: John Roth and Maria Barbara.

Magdalene Dorothea of Samuel Gaehy and Maria Dorothea, b. Jan 8, 1769; bapt. Jan 19. Spon: Philip Erb and Anna Dorothea.

Juliana of William Cafferoth and Mary Magdalene, b. Feb 16, 1769; bapt. Mar 5. Spon: Jacob Brücker and Margaret Walter.

Susanna Sophia of Caspar Viehman and Eva Christine, b. Feb 20, 1769; bapt. Mar 5. Spon: Valentine Viehman and Susanna Margaret.

Catharine of Caspar Schweitzer and Anna Maria, b. Apr 1, 1769; bapt. Apr 9. Spon: Henry Pfeffer and Catharine.

Catharine of Adam Weynant and Barbara, b. Mar 16, 1769; bapt. Apr 23. Spon: David Weynant and Catharine Gelbert.

John Adam of John Fale and Anna Maria, b. Apr 12, 1769; bapt. May 14. Spon: Adam Balmer and Barbara.

John George of George Kriesing and Catharine, b. May 3, 1769; bapt. Jun 9. Spon: George Maurer and Anna Maria Hoffmann, both single.

Philip of Christian Kreuter and Catharina, b. Jun 5, 1769; bapt. Jun 11. Spon: Philip Erb and Magdalene.

John George of John Nicholas Bechten and Eva Margaret, b. Apr 23, 1769; bapt. Jul 20. Spon: John George Raab and Anna Maria.

Catharine of John Geyer and Anna Maria, b. Jun 17, 1769; bapt. Jul 23. Spon: Martin Weiss and Catharine.

Elizabeth of Matthew Jacobi and Elizabeth, b. Aug 2, 1769; bapt. Sep 3. Spon: Frederick Wolfersberger and Eva Baur.

Son of John Nicholas Maes and Susanna, b. Aug 5, 1769; bapt. Sep 12. Spon: ---.

Anna Elizabeth of Paul Gemberling and Elizabeth, b. Aug 18, 1769; bapt. Sep 12. Spon: Jacob Gemberling and Catharine.

John Leonard and George Baurmann and Elizabeth, b. May 23, 1769; bapt. Sep 11. Spon: Leonard Kurtz and Ursula.

J. Jacob of Martin Höffelfinger and Anna Maria, b. Aug 24, 1769; bapt. Oct 1. Spon: Jacob Spengler and Maria Elizabeth.

Fredericka Magdalene of Adam Hoffmann and Barbara, b. Sep 24, 1769; bapt. Oct 27. Spon: Gerhard Cafferoth and Eva Fredericka.

John Philip of Philip Wolfersberger and Margaret, b. Sep 28, 1769; bapt. Oct 29. Spon: Peter Wolfersberger and Apollonia.

Conrad of Conrad Raam and Catharine, b. Oct 5, 1796; bapt. Oct 29. Spon: John Unger and Eva.

(This is the last baptism by Dom. Zufall, The next eight baptisms

were entered by Rev. William Hendel.)
Jacob of Jacob Zauter and Elizabeth, b. Apr 5, 1779; bapt. Apr 18.
Spon: Leonard Krumbein and Anna Maria.
John of Abraham Schwanger and Anna Elizabeth, b. May 5, 1779;
bapt. May 16. Spon: Magnus Conrad and Margaret.
Jacob of John Thome and Anna, b. Jun 16, 1779; bapt. Aug 6. Spon:
Jacob Zollinger and Barbara.
Catharine of Frederick Wolfersberger and Elizabeth, b. Jun 11, 1779;
bapt. Aug 6. Spon: Catharine Mock.
Catharine of Henry Herchelroth and Christine, b. Jul 15, 1779; bapt.
Aug 27. Spon: Catharine Mock.
Elizabeth of Nicholas Bahnert and Margaret; bapt. May 2, 1779; bapt.
Jul 17. Spon: Elizabeth Stäger.
Catharine of John Stager and Elizabeth, b. May 7, 1779; bapt. Jul 17.
Spon: Jacob Stager and Catharine.
Elizabeth of Ludwig Hauser and Elizabeth, b. Sep 9, 1779; bapt. Sep
25. Spon: Elizabeth Trautmann.
The next baptism of the children of Henry Shäfer were entered by the
Rev. Wm. Runkel.
Catharine of Henry Schäfer and Anna Eva, b. Nov 27, 1774; bapt. ---.
Spon: Alexander Schäfer and Catharine.
Susanna of Henry Schäfer and Anna Eva, b. Oct 29, 1776. Spon:
Henry Schweitzer and Elizabeth.
Anna Maria of Henry Schäfer and Anna Eva, b. Jul 9, 1779. Spon:
Christopher Meyer and Anna Marg.
John of Henry Schäfer and Anna Eva, b. Jun 15, 1782. Spon:
Alexander Schaefer and Catharine.
(The following nine baptisms were entered by different hands.)
John George of John Krum and Anna Maria, b. Mar 9, 1780. Spon:
George Stautt and Margaret.
Eva Catharine of John Krum and Anna Maria, b. Sep 29, 1781. Spon:
Eva Catharine Wolff, single.
John Henry of John Krum and Anna Maria, b. Sep 5, 1786. Spon:
Henry Krum and Anna Maria.
Catharine of John Krum and Anna Maria, b. May 25, 1796. Spon:
Frederick Mieller and Catharine.
Leonard of Henry Krum and Anna Maria, b. Sep 13, 1785. Spon:
Leonard Schwartz and Elizabeth.
John of Henry Krum and Anna Maria, b. Mar 13, 1787. Spon: John
Krum and Anna Maria.

John Henry of Henry Krum and Anna Maria, b. Apr 24, 1789. Spon: Valentine Miller and Magdalene.

Philip of Henry Krum and Anna Maria, b. Nov 22, 1790. Spon: John Krum and Anna Maria.

John Henry of Henry Meier and Elizabeth, b. May 14, 1794; bapt. May 18, 1794. Spon: Henry Krum and Anna Maria.

BAPTISMS BY REV. WILLIAM RUNKEL, JAN 1783-SEP 1784

John Henry of Casper Schweitzer and Anna Maria, b. Jan 4, 1783; bapt. Jan 5. Spon: John Krum and Anna Maria.

Sophia of Peter Jäger and Margaret, b. Dec 6, 1782; bapt. Mar 9. Spon: Sophia Brunner, single.

Elizabeth of George Maes and Elizabeth, b. Feb 12, 1783; bapt. Mar 9. Spon: George Holstein and Elizabeth.

Jacob of Adam Viehman and Susanna, b. Jan 11, 1783; bapt. Mar 9. Spon: Parents.

Elizabeth of Philip Gruse and Catharine, b. Feb 3, 1783; bapt. Apr 18. Spon: Elizabeth Christ.

John of John Paul Schumacher and Catharine, b. Mar 29, 1783; bapt. Apr 18. Spon: Adam Jacoby and Anna Maria.

Maria Elizabeth of Jacob Garte and Maria Elizabeth, b. Feb 25, 1783; bapt. Apr 18. Spon: John Paul Schumacher and Catharine.

Anna Maria of John Krum and Anna Maria, b. Jun 4, 1783; bapt. Jun 29. Spon: Eva Catharine Wolff, single.

Elizabeth of Peter Spengler and Catharine, b. Sep 23, 1783; bapt. Oct 12. Spon: Henry Kring and Elizabeth.

Child of Michael Stump and Catharine, b. ---; bapt. Oct 12, 1783. Spon: Michael Miller and Margaret.

Maria Margaret of Henry Hübschmann and Catharine, b. Oct 8, 1783; bapt. Nov 10. Spon: Henry Strack and Anna Rosina.

John of George Trautman and Maria Christine, b. Dec 15, 1783; bapt. Dec 21. Spon: John Krum and Anna Maria.

John George of John Mayer and Catharine, b. Sep 7, 1783; bapt. Jan 18, 1784. Spon: John Mayer, Sr. and Anna Barbara.

Maria Margaret of Casper Schweitzer and Maria, b. Feb 12, 1784; bapt. Feb 15. Spon: Frederick Speyer and Anna Margaret.

Margaret of John Thoma and Anna, b. Nov 3, 1783; bapt. Mar 9, 1784. Spon: Philip Wolfersberger and Margaret.

Benjamin of Nicholas Maess and Susanna, b. Jan 31, 1784; bapt. Mar

14. Spon: Henry Hergelroth and Christine.

Margaret of Valentine Miller and Mary Magdalene, b. Feb 11, 1784; bapt. Mar 14. Spon: Michael Miller and Margaret.

John Henry of Henry Mayer and Angelica, b. Jan 4, 1784; bapt. Mar 14. Spon: Henry Schaefer and Eva.

Michael of John Balsle and Margaret, b. Mar 13, 1784; bapt. Apr 9. Spon: Michael Mees and Catharine.

Anna Maria of Philip Eckert and Lydia, b. Mar 15, 1784; bapt. Apr 9. Spon: John Krum and Anna Maria.

Anna Eva of John Ditman and Anna Margaret, b. Jun 11, 1784; bapt. Jun 18. Spon: Henry Schaefer and Anna Eva.

Mary Magdalene of Jacob Gemberling and Catharine, b. Jun 14, 1784; bapt. Sep 5. Spon: Henry Bercki and Mary Magdalene.

Mary Catharine of John Paul Schumacher and Maria Catharine, b. Aug 2, 1784; bapt. Sep 5, 1784. Spon: Adam Jacobi and Margaret.

(This is the last entry of Hunkel, the next two were made by Rev. John Henry Helffrich.)

John of Peter Gally and Catharine, b. ---; bapt. Dec 6, 1784. Spon: John Balsly and Margaret.

BAPTISMS BY REV. ANDREW LORTEZ, FEB-NOV 1785

John Jacob of Jacob Maes and Catharine, b. ---; bapt. Dec 6, 1784. Spon: George Maes and Elizabeth.

John of Frederick Tobler(?) and Catharine Schell b. Jan 25, 1785; bapt. Feb 13, 1785. Spon: John Dietmann and Anna Margaretha Dietmann.

Mary Magdalene of Michael Müller and Margaret Stump, b. Jan 26, 1785; bapt. Feb 13. Spon: Valentin Müller Bagistoff.

John of Jacob Hoft and Catharine, b. Jan 16, 1785; bapt. Feb 13. Spon: Adam Schweitzer and Eva Maria Schmaltzer.

John Philip of George Trautmann and Christine Eggert, b. ---; bapt. Mar 6, 1785. Spon: Jacob Philippi and Christine Philippi.

Catharine of Michael Weiss and Catharine Bayer, b. Feb 21, 1785; bapt. Mar 6, 1785. Spon: George Bayer and Anna Maria Bayer.

Catharine of Peter Hauser and Barbara Brecht, b. Mar 22, 1785; bapt. Mar 28. Spon: Catharine Mogg.

Eva Christine of Henry Herchelroth and Christine Momma, b. Mar 11, 1785; bapt. Apr 3. Spon: Henry Mogg and Eva Mogg.

Michael of George Becker and Juliana Huber, b. ---; bapt. May 1.

Spon: Michael Meyer and Elizabeth.

John of Henry Hubschmann and Catharine Leissi, b. Mar 1, 1785; bapt. May 1. Spon: Peter Spengler and Catharine Spengler.

Catharine Susan of Philip Eggert and Lydia Beck, b. Nov 15, 1785; bapt. Dec 18. Spon: Valentine Seiler and Margaret.

Susanna of Henry Schäfer and Eva Schweitzer, b. Oct 2, 1785; bapt. Nov 13. Spon: Sabina Hägi, nee Schäfer.

Sophia Barbara of Michael Mees and Catharine, b. May 28, 1786; bapt. Jul 9. Spon: Martin Albrecht and Sophia.

(The following baptisms between 1786 and 1794 were entered by different hands.)

Philip of Jacob Guth and Hannah Christine, b. Sep 21, 1784; bapt. Nov 1. Spon: Parents.

Daniel of Jacob Guth and Hannah Christine, b. Dec 11, 1786; bapt. Dec 25. Spon: Parents. *(This is the ancestor of Dr. J. I. Good, who arrived in Pa. on Sep 9, 1765. The entires, in beautiful script, were evidently mde by Jacob Guth himself, who was a schoolmaster.)*

John George of Adam Schreiber and Sarah, b. May 10, 1787; bapt. May 20. Spon: Adam Fried and Catharine.

Child of Philip Eckert and wife, b. May 28, 1788; bapt. Jul 13. Spon: John Krumm and Anna Maria.

John of William Duin and Margaret, b. Apr 17, 1788; bapt. Jul 13. Spon: John Juin and Anna Maria.

George of George Mes and Elizabeth, b. Jul 12, 1788; bapt. Aug 3. Spon: Francis Seibert and wife.

Child of Henry Schäfer and Eva, b. Oct 5, 1788; bapt. Nov 2. Spon: John Mayer and wife.

Elizabeth of John Krum and Anna Maria, b. Aug 2, 1788; bapt. Aug 21. Spon: George Von Nieda and Catharine.

Anna Maria of Peter Spengler and Catharine, b. Oct 13, 1788; bapt. Jan 4, 1789. Spon: John Krum and Anna Maria.

John of John Jost Schramm and Eva Maria, b. Mar 30, (1788); bapt. Jun 1. Spon: Henry Weber and Anna Maria.

Anna Eva of Henry Schäfer and Anna Eva, b. Oct 5, 1788; bapt. ---. Spon: John Meyer and Catharine.

Sarah of George Hofman and Juliana, b. Dec 10, 1789; bapt. ---. Spon: John Krum and Anna Maria.

Peter of Philip Eckert and Lydia, b. May 4, 1790; bapt. Jun 13. Spon: Peter Spycker and Catharine.

Daniel of Adam Fieman and wife, b. Feb 19, 1791; bapt. Apr 3. Spon:

Parents.
Catharine of Adam Schreiber and Sarah, b. Mar 22, 1791; bapt. Apr 17. Spon: John Dickman and Margaret.
Eva Maria of Jost Schramm and Eva Maria, b. Jan 12, 1791; bapt. Apr 17. Spon: Anna Maria Lautermilch.
Margaret and Catharine of Matthias Armischong and Gertrude, b. Aug 5, 1791; bapt. Aug 21, 1791. Spon: Barbara Geyer and Catharine Geyer.
Magdalene of Jacob Mieller and Margaret, b. Nov 21, 1790; bapt. ---. Spon: Henry Krig and Susanna.
Catharine of George Pleistein and Anna Maria, b. Mar 19, 1791; bapt. ---. Spon: Jacob Schack and wife.
John Peter of Peter Wewer (Weber) and Barbara, b. Oct 4, 1792; bapt. Sep 20, 1795. Spon: John Krum and Anna Maria.
Veronica of Peter Wewer (Weber) and Barbara, b. Dec 4, 1794; bapt. Sep 20, 1795. Spon: Catharine Wever, widow.
Anna Maria of John Wanderlich and Catharine, b. Sep 4, 1792; bapt. ---. Spon: John Krum and Anna Maria.
Wilhelm of John Wanderlich and Catharine, b. Nov 24, 1794; bapt. ---. Spon: John Dittman and Margaret.

BAPTISMS BY THE REV. LUDWIG LUPP

Christian of Henry Strack and Rosina, b. Nov 3, 1793; bapt. Apr 20, 1794. Spon: Parents.
William of Henry Schraer and Rosina, b. Feb 17, 1794; bapt. May 31, 1795. Spon: John Braun and Juliana.
John of George Wolfersberger and Eva, b. Apr 23, 1795; bapt. May 31, 1795. Spon: Jacob Müller and Christine.
Rebecca of John Barry and Christine, b. Nov 11, 1795; bapt. Jun 13, 1796. Spon: Parents.
Elizabeth of Peter Leydich and Magdalene, b. Jan 31, 1796; bapt. Feb 7, 1796. Spon: Martin Leydich and Elizabeth.
Catharine of Jim Magolloch and Susanna, b. Jan 18, 1796; bapt. May 1, 1796. Spon: Susanna Scherck.
Jacob of George Battorf and Dorothea, b. Jan 13, 1796; bapt. May 15, 1796. Spon: Jacob Sauter and wife.
Catharine of Valentine Müller and Magdalene, b. Dec 25, 1796; bapt. Jan 12, 1797. Spon: Frederick Müller and Catharine.

Catharine of Frederick Dobler and Elizabeth, b. Mar 16, 1797; bapt. Apr 3, 1797. Spon: Catharine Dobler.

Sarah of Mathias Armaschon and Barbara, b. May 4, 1797; bapt. Jun 5, 1797. Spon: Parents.

Maria Catharine of Peter Reidel and Barbara, b. Jan 19, 1797; bapt. Jun 5, 1797. Spon: John Reidel and Christine.

William of Francis Seubert and Susanna, b. Aug 21, 1797; bapt. Sep 17, 1797. Spon: John Seubert.

Charlotte of Augustinus Steiner and Sarah, b. Nov 23, 1796; bapt. Oct 8, 1797. Spon: Sarah Schreiber.

(The next six baptisms are entered by an untrained hand.)

Catharine of Jacob Klein and Elizabeth, b. Nov 23, 1797; bapt. Jan 7, 1798. Spon: Parents.

William of Charles Münch and Margaret, b. Feb 10, 1799; bapt. Feb 24. Spon: Elizabeth Ditmann.

John of Jacob Krobb and Elizabeth, b. Dec 5, 1799; bapt. Dec 24. Spon: Henry Iba and Barbara.

Elizabeth of David Baier and Elizabeth, b. Jul 19, 1796; bapt. Mar 28, 1799. Spon: Elizabeth Diettmann.

Anna of Jacob Sontag and Anna Maria, b. Jan 23, 1799; bapt. May 19. Spon: Anna Thomas.

Anna Margaret of Andrew Baier and Elizabeth, b. Jan 28, 1798; bapt. Jul 2, 1799. Spon: John Krumm and Anna Maria.

Elizabeth of Jacob Grob and Elizabeth, b. Oct 26, 1800; bapt. Dec 14, 1800. Spon: the mother.

Peter of George Wolfersberger and Eva, b. Sep 27, 1800; bapt. Jan 10, 1801. Spon: Peter Wolfersberger.

Jacob of Jacob Klein and Elizabeth, b. Nov 24, 1800; bapt. Jan 11, 1801. Spon: Valentine Miller and Magdalene.

Margaret of John Reidel and Christine, b. Dec 17, 1800; bapt. Feb 8, 1801. Spon: Jacob Gehrhart and Catharine.

Hannah of Henry Kumler and Susanna, b. Oct 12, 1798; bapt. Apr 5, 1801. Spon: Parents.

Joseph of Elias Krieg and Anna Maria, b. Oct 30, 1797; bapt. May 2, 1801. Spon: the mother.

John of Elias Krieg and Anna Maria, b. Jan 29, 1799; bapt. May 2, 1801. Spon: John Schmidt and Margaret.

John George of Elias Krieg and Anna Maria, b. Sep 14, 1800; bapt. May 2, 1801. Spon: Jacob Freyberger.

Catharine of Henry Krieg and Elizabeth Trautman, b. May 22; bapt.

May 29, 1785. Spon: Henry Krug and Elizabeth Krug.
Barbara of John Thoma and Anna Wolfersberger, b. Jul 20; bapt. Oct
16, 1785. Spon: Daniel Henning and Margaret.

MARRIAGES BY REV. JOHN JACOB ZUFALL

Jan 5, 1769   William Jüngst m. Catharine Schwanger.
Feb 20, 1769   John George Noll m. Anna Maria Zoller.
Feb 14, 1769   Jacob Benny m. Anna Maria Diel.
Mar 20, 1769   I, John Jacob Zufall, pro tem minister at Heidelberg
and Mühlbach, m. Veronica Brunner, dau. of Henry Brunner, by
the Rev. Bucher, in my house.
Mar 28, 1769   John Meisser, widower, m. Christine Lang, widow.
Apr 11, 1769   Isaac Brand m. Maria Margaret Zollicker.
Apr 25, 1769   William Gilbertry m. Susanna Thomas, widow.
May 2, 1769   Nicholas Dönges m. Regina Merck.
May 15, 1769   Christian Thiel m. Susanna Reyer, a Dunker.
Jun 27, 1769   Noy Giesi m. Elizabeth Merckle.
Aug 1, 1769   John Giesi m. Catharine Merckle.
Oct 3, 1769   Daniel Möller m. Susanna Margaret Schleucher.
Oct 12, 1769   Michael Hahn m. Anna Maria Mee.

BURIALS, 1769

Jan 22, 1769, Frederick Möller, son of Dewald Möller, bur. age 1 yr,
less 1 mo, 5 das.
Feb 1, 1769, Michael Dumme, son of Jacob Dumme, bur. age 3 yrs
less 10 das.
Feb 5, 1769, John Trautmann, son of George Trautmann, bur. age 9
mos.
Feb 13, 1769, John Michael, son of John Meiser, bur. age 2 yrs, 1 mo.
Feb 15, 1769, John Jacob, son of Adam Bollender, bur. age 3 mos,
less two das.
Feb 20, 1769, Andrew, son of George Magnus Conrad, bur. age 2 yrs,
7 mos.
Mar 3, 1769, Maria Elizabeth, dau. of Michael Winter, bur. age 3 wks.
Mar 7, 1769, John Michael, son of Jacob Hauser, bur. age 9 yrs, less 5
wks.

Mar 11, 1769, Maria Barbara, dau. of George Hetzler, bur. age 6 yrs, 4 mos, 8 das.

Mar 19, 1769, Henry, son of Nicholas Ensminger, bur. age 6 yrs, 6 mos, 3 das.

Mar 19, 1769, Catharine, dau. of Peter Wolfersberger, bur. age 9 mos.

Apr 4, 1769, Catharine and Jacob, children of Henry Wolff, bur. the first, age 2 yrs, 7 mos; the son age 9 1/2 mos.

Apr 9, 1769, John Henry, son of William Cafferoth, bur. age 4 yrs, 7 mos.

Apr 10, 1769, John, son of Michael Leidig, bur. age 1 yr, 2 mos.

Apr 14, 1769, Andrew, son of Philip Dönges, bur. age 3 yrs, 1 mo, 9 das.

Apr 26, 1769, Catharine, dau. of Peter Merckle, bur. age 6 mos, 7 das, at Wendel Horniss Church.

Apr 28, 1769, Margaret, dau. of George Weymann, bur. age 11 yrs, 8 mos, at Horniss church.

Jun 28, 1769, Susanna, dau. of John Ochsenmann, bur. age 1 yr, 4 wks.

Jun 15, 1769, John, son of Andrew Heffer, bur. age 11 weeks, 3 days.

Sep 31, 1769, Melchior Lautermilch, bur. age about 60 yrs.

Mar 25, 1785, Jacob, a son of Jacob Bager, bur.

Apr 3, 1785, A child, Elizabeth, bur. age 1 year 8 mos.

ST PAUL'S (OR KLOPP'S) - BETHEL TOWNSHIP

BAPTISMS BY REV. HENRY WILLIAM STOY, 1755-1756

Anna Barbara of Gottfried Stembel and Anna Margaret, b. Feb,
1755. Spon: John Heffler and Anna Barbara.

Francis of Peter Dietrich and Maria Catharina, b. Apr 1755. Spon:
Jacob Wolfing and Catharine Wolfing, single.

Catharine of Nicholas Jungblut and Anna Maria, b. Feb 1755. Spon:
John Schuy and wife Catharine.

Balthasar of Michael Gunkel and Maria, b. Jan 6, 1756. Spon:
Balthasar Noll.

Anna Catharine of Isaiah Cuschwa and Anna Christina, b. Feb 8,
1756. Spon: Tobias Bickel and wife.

John of Peter Klein and Anna Margaret, b. Feb 2, 1756. Spon: John
Christman and wife.

BAPTISMS BY JOHN WILLIAM HENDEL, 1770-1784

John Daniel of Georg Dany and Elisabeth, b. May 6; bapt. May, 1770.
Spon: Daniel Kabel and Maria Barbara.

Philip Henry of Henry Hautz and Maria Barbara, b, Jul 5; bapt, Jul,
1770. Spon: Philip Lorentz Hautz and Anna Maria.

Peter of ---; bapt. Jul 23, 1770. Spon: ---.

Catharine of Christian Hautz and Barbara, b. Aug 24; bapt. Sep 30,
1770. Spon: John Kunkel and Catharine.

John Jacob of Peter Schmeltzer, b. Sep 16; bapt. Oct 14, 1770. Spon:
Jacob Becker and Anna Maria.

Christopher of Samuel Reyer and Maria Elisabeth, b. Oct 25; bapt.
Dec 16, 1770. Spon: Christoph Reyer and Catharine.

Maria Catharine of John Gunkel and Catharine, b. Feb 22, 1770;
bapt. Jan 13, 1771. Spon: George Schafer and Maria Catharine.

Daniel of Daniel Kabel and Barbara, b. Dec 12, 1770; bapt. Feb 24,
1771. Spon: Caspar Kabel and Anna Maria.

Maria Catharine of Nicholas Noll and Catharine, b. Jan 26; bapt.
Mar 17, 1771. Spon: Peter Leitner and Anna Maria.

Anna Maria of John Schaeffer and Catharine, b. Mar 2; bapt. May 5,
1771. Spon: Anna Maria Beyer.

Balthasar of Balthasar Noll and Anna Maria, b. ---- 20; bapt. May 5,
1771. Spon: (torn).

Laurence of Isaac Wolf and Catharine, b. Feb 1; bapt. Apr 7, 1771.
Spon: ---- and Maria Catharine (torn).

Christian of George Tany and Elisabeth, b. Sep 11; bapt. Sep, 1771.
Spon: Christian Hautz and Barbara.

John of Henry Hautz and Barbara, b. Aug 24; bapt. Sep, 1771. Spon:
John --- (torn).

Christina of Stephan Biry and Margaret, b.---; bapt. Dec 22, 1772.
Spon: Michael Wolf and Maria Margaret.

Maria Christina of Wendel Wolf and Maria Christina, b. Dec 13;
bapt. Jan 19, 1772. Spon: Maria Magd. Bender, widow.

Martin of Martin Battorf and Maria Barbara, b. --- 29; bapt. Mar 15,
1772. Spon: Leonard Schwartz and Elisabeth.

Benjamin of George Leonard Emmert and Catharine, b. Feb 29; bapt.
Apr, 1772. Spon: Christian Hautz and Barbara.

Christian of Christian Miller and Veronica, b. Oct 1; bapt. Nov 8,
1772. Spon: Lawrence Hautz and Anna Maria.

Anna Catharine of Peter Schmid and Eva, b. Oct 25; bapt. Jan, 1773.
Spon: Anna Catharine Guschwa.

Anna Maria of Jacob Wolf and Catharine, b. Oct 15; bapt. Feb, 1773.
Spon: Balthasar Noll and Anna Maria.

John of Samuel Reyer and Maria Elisabeth, b. Mar 4; bapt. Apr 4,
1773. Spon: Caspar Thome and Anna Barbara.

Leonard of Nicholas Noll and Maria Catharine, b. Mar 3; bapt. 1773.
Spon: Leonard Noll.

Anna Margaret of Leonard Noll and Anna Maria, b.---; bapt. Mar 13,
1774. Spon: Peter Mayer and Margaret.

Susanna Catharine of George Lentz and Rosina, b.---; bapt. Mar 13,
1774. Spon: Henry Zehring and Susanna.

Maria Barbara of George Adam Stumb and M. Apollonia, b. Feb 8;
bapt. Mar 13, 1774. Spon: Christopher Peter and Barbara.

Christian of Henry Stumb and Elisabeth, b. Feb 22; bapt. Apr 4,
1774. Spon: (Christian) Hautz and Barbara.

Elisabeth of Daniel Wolf and Elisabeth, b. Nov 12, 1773; bapt. Apr 4,
1774. Spon: Apollonia Wolf.

Eva Elisabeth of Martin Battorf and Maria Barbara, b. Apr 26; bapt.
May 8, 1774. Spon: Lawrence Hautz and Eva.

Jacob of Caspar Dschob and Barbara, b. Jun 18; bapt. Jul 14, 1774.
Spon: Jacob Dschob and Anna.

Catharine of George Battorf and Maria Dorothea, b. Aug 1; bapt.
Aug 14, 1774. Spon: Henry Holtzman and Anna Maria.

Daniel of George Stattler and Eva Catharine, b. Jul 31; bapt. Aug 28,
   1774. Spon: Daniel Hoffman and Eva.
Eva Christina of Melchior Ditzler and Eva, b. May 10; bapt. Jan 19,
   (?). Spon: Christina Schafer.[This is probably Jun rather than
   Jan.]
Magdalena and Dorothea of Peter Mayer and Margaret, b. May 9, ---;
   bapt. Aug 14, 1774. Spon: George Battorf and Magdalena Schug.
Hen of John Daub and Catharine, b. Sep 20; bapt. Oct 9, 1774. Spon:
   (Christian) Hautz and Barbara.
Catharina of John Schaffer and Catharine, b. Feb 4, 1774; bapt, 1774.
   Spon: Christina Schaefer.
Maria Magdalena of Thomas Hedman and wife, b. Nov 2; bapt. 1774.
   Spon: Peter Leitner and Anna Maria.
Catharine of Henry Hautz and Barbara, b. May 15; bapt. Jun, 1774.
   Spon: Susanna Dups.
Maria Eva of Philip Lawrence Hautz and Anna Maria, b. Jun 6; Jun,
   1774. Spon: George Emmert and Maria Eva.
Maria Barbara of Balthasar Lesch and Christina, b. May 31; bapt.
   Jun, 1774. Spon: Christian Hautz and Barbara.
Catharine of John Keblinger and Catharine, b. Aug 18; bapt. Aug 29,
   1774. Spon: Anna Cath. Mayer.
Anna Elisabeth of Henry Werner and Anna Maria, b. Jul 10; bapt.
   Aug 29, 1774. Spon: Samuel Reyer and M. Elisabeth.
Margaret of Conrad Lind and Anna Maria, b. Jun 8; bapt. Aug 29,
   1774. Spon: Sebastian Wolf and Margaret.
John of Conrad Lind and Anna Maria, b. Feb 21, 1771; bapt. ---.
   Spon: Jost Schreckengast and wife.
Maria Barbara of Nicholas Gillmer and Elisabeth, b. Aug 11; bapt.
   Sep 26, 1774. Spon: Peter Mayer and Margaret.
David of Peter Schmid and Eva, b. Sep 28; bapt. Oct 2, 1774. Spon:
   David Schmid.
Catharine of Jacob Liebengut and --- Decker, b. Dec 25, 1770; bapt.
   Oct 2, 1774. Spon: Christoph Peter and Barbara, foster parents.
Anna Margaret of John Knis(?) and Elisabeth, b. Oct 30; bapt. Nov
   20, 1774. Spon: Anna Marg. Wolf.
Benjamin of Nicholas Noll and Maria Catharine, b. Oct 16; bapt. Nov
   20, 1774. Spon: John Georg Noll.
John of John Schaefer and Catharine, b. Dec 26, 1774; bapt. Jan 8,
   1775. Spon: Peter Ditzler.
Jacob of Jonas Rudy and Barbara, b. Dec 17, 1774; bapt. Jan 29,

1775. Spon: Jacob Keller.

John Martin of Martin Schuy and Catharine, b. Feb 1, 1775; bapt. Feb 19, 1775. Spon: Martin Schy and Elisabeth.

Anna Margaret of Frederick Wolf and Barbara, b. Aug 26, 1774; bapt. Feb 27, 1775. Spon: Nicholas Ponzius and Anna Margaret.

Salome of Adam Schmid and Maria Elisabeth, b. Jan 29; bapt. Mar 12, 1775. Spon: Salome Kassel.

Philip Lawrence of Adam Werner and Catharine, b. Dec 31; bapt. Mar 12, 1775. Spon: Lawrence Hautz and Eva.

Juliana of Daniel Angst and Maria Elisabetha, b. Feb 3; bapt. Mar 12, 1775. Spon: Balthasar Schmid and Juliana.

Christian of Henry Hautz and Barbara, b. Mar 19; bapt. Apr 16, 1775. Spon: (Christian) Hautz and Barbara.

Anna Catharine of Balthasar Lesch and Christina, b. Apr 10; bapt 1775. Spon: John Gunckel and Anna Catharine.

George Philip of Martin Gundrum and Maria Catharine, b. Apr 21; bapt. 1775. Spon: Philip Gundrum and Elisabeth.

Juliana of Georg Lentz and Rosina, b. May 19; bapt. Jul 6, 1775. Spon: Henry Mayer and Juliana.

Regina of Jacob Michel and Maria, b. Aug 19; bapt. Sep 10, 1775. Spon: Jacob Tany and Regina.

The next three baptisms were entered by a different hand.

Christian of Peter Schmitt and Eva, b. Oct 25; Nov, 1775. Spon: Martin Schuy and Cath. Elisabeth.

William of William Runkel and Catharine, b. Nov 12; bapt. Nov 30, 1775. Spon: Parents.

Maria Magdalene of Nicholas Killmer and Elisabeth, b. Oct 9; bapt. Nov 30, 1775. Spon: Andrew Eder and Anna Margaret.

The handwriting is that of Runkel.

Magdalene of Balthasar Noll and Anna Maria, b. Dec 14; bapt. Dec 26, 1775. Spon: Melchior Ditzler and Eva.

Elisabeth of Christian Hautz and Barbara, b. Jul 10; bapt. Jul, 1775. Spon: Balthasar Lesch and Christina.

Eva Elisabeth and Simon Schürman and Anna Maria, b. Dec 17, 1775; bapt. Jan 25, 1776. Spon: Eva Elisabeth Schürman.

John of John Knis and Elisabeth, b. Jan 22; bapt. Feb 17, 1776. Spon: Paul Wolf and Magdalena.

John of Martin Schuy, Jr. and Cath. Elisabeth, b. Feb 6; bapt. Feb 28, 1776. Spon: John Schuy.

Anna Maria of Jacob Leitner and Margaret, b. Feb 27; bapt. Mar 10,

1776. Spon: Balthasar Noll and Anna Maria.

Peter of Peter Schmeltzer and Catharine, b. Feb 15; bapt. Mar 10, 1776. Spon: Paul Tany, Jr. and Margaret.

Anna Maria of George Nicholas Wentzel and Christina, b. Feb 20; bapt. Mar 10, 1776. Spon: Rosina Schaefer.

Maria Salome of Conrad Wolf and Catharine Elisabeth, b. Apr 26; bapt. May 26, 1776. Spon: Anna Catharine Guschwa.

William of George Stättler and Eva, b. Mar 22; Jun 16, 1776. Spon: William Kirschbaum and Gertrude.

Rosina of John Schäefer and Catharine, b. Aug 6; bapt. Aug 11, 1776. Spon: Rosina Schäfer.

John of Jacob Gunckel and Margaret, b. Jun 21; bapt. Sep 22, 1776. Spon: parents.

Catharine Elisabeth of Christopher Stumb and Maria, b. May; bapt. Sep 22, 1776. Spon: Maria Catharina Stumb.

Eva of George Bresler and Catharine, b. Sep 5; Oct 27, 1776. Spon: Jacob Gebhard and Eva Maria.

John George, of John George Battorf and Dorthea, b. Oct 17; bapt. Oct. 27, 1776. Spon: Leonard Schwartz and Elisabeth.

John Adam of Henry Stumb and Elisabeth, b. Sep 3; bapt. Oct 27, 1776. Spon: John Adam ---? and Elisabeth.

Christina of Daniel Wolf and Elisabeth b. Apr 13; bapt. May 18, 1777. Spon: Philip Gebhard and Christine.

Anna Maria of Henry Hautz and Barbara, b. Apr 9; bapt. May 18, 1777. Spon: John Dubs and Barbara.

John Jacob of John Christian Willems and Johanna Catharine, b. Jul 30; bapt. Aug 10, 1777. Spon: Jacob Albert and Maria Margaret.

John David of John Guschwa and Cath. Elisabeth, b. Aug 10; bapt. Aug 24, 1777. Spon: Philip Gebhard and Anna Christina.

Maria Elisabetha of Daniel Angst and Maria Elisabeth, b. Nov 11, 1775; bapt. Sep, 1777. Spon: Melchior Ditzler and Maria Eva.

Maria Eva of Melchior Ditzler and Maria Eva, b. Sep 12; bapt. Sep 21, 1777. Spon: Maria Barbara Noll wife of Matthew Noll.

John Leonard of Leonard Noll and Anna Margaret, b. Sep 5; Sep 21, 1777. Spon: Andrew Eder and Anna Margaret.

Maria Magdalena of Jacob Knebel and Maria Salome, b. Feb 8; bapt. Mar 8, 1778. Spon: Herman Knebel and Margaret.

Catharina Elisabeth of Georg Scherer and Magdalena, b. Feb 2; bapt. Mar 8, 1778. Spon: Martin Schuy and Elisabeth.

John Jonas of Jonas Rudy and Barbara, b. Jan 4; bapt. Mar 8, 1778.

Spon: Hieronymus Rudy and Catharine.

Maria Magdalena of John Schafer and Catharine, b. Nov 3; bapt. Nov 25, 1778. Spon: Christian Battorf and Rosina.

Maria Catharine of Martin Burkhard and Catharine, b. Sep 10; bapt. Nov 25, 1778. Spon: Anna Maria Schmid.

Catharine Elisabeth of Jacob Michel and Eva Maria, b. Oct 22; bapt. Nov 25, 1778. Spon: Catharine Burkhard.

John George of Henry Stumb and Elisabeth, b. Nov 9; bapt. Jan 17, 1779. Spon: George Graff and Barbara.

John Philip of Philip Zehring and Catharine, b. Nov 12; bapt. Jan 17, 1779. Spon: Francis Zeller and Elisabeth.

Anna Margaret of Simon Schürman and (Anna Maria), b. Jan 3; bapt. Feb 3, 1779. Spon: --- Wolff and Anna Margaret.

John of Henry Hautz and Barbara, b. ---; bapt. Feb 14, 1779. Spon: George Hautz and Elisabeth.

Catharine Margaret of Conrad Wolff and Elisabeth, b. Jan 20; bapt. Mar 3, 1779. Spon: John Guschwa and Cath. Elisabeth.

John of Andrew Eder and A. Margaret, b. Feb 28; bapt. Apr 5, 1779. Spon: Peter Leitner and Anna Maria.

John Michael of Nicholas Noll and Maria Catharine, b. Apr 23; bapt. Jun 6, 1779. Spon: Michael Nusshack and Anna Maria.

Elisabeth of Jonas Rudy and Barbara, b. Jul 24; bapt. Oct 10, 1779. Spon: Elisabeth Strohm, single.

---- of Jacob Leitner and Margaret, b. ----; bapt. Feb 12, 1779. Spon: Peter Leitner.

Maria Magdalena of John Georg Battorf and Maria Dorothea, b. Jan 24; bapt. Feb 8, 1779. Spon: Henry Holtzman and Maria Magdalena.

John Peter of George Weil and Catharine, b. Dec 10, 1778; bapt. Mar 5, 1779. Spon: Peter Mayer and Anna Maria.

John Nicholas of Nicholas Gillmer and Elisabeth, b. Feb 15; bapt. Mar 5, 1779. Spon: Nicholas Kiseler and Margaret.

Anna Elisabeth of Peter Schmid and Anna, b. Mar 22; bapt. Apr 20, 1779. Spon: John Guschwa and Elisabeth.

Caspar of Peter Borgner and Maria Catharina, b. May 27; bapt. Jun, 1779. Spon: Caspar Tschob and Anna Barbara.

Daniel of John Eder and Christina, b. Sep 4, 1777; bapt. 1779. Spon: parents.

Maria Magdalena of Christian Battorf and Rosina, b. Jun 21; bapt. Jul, 1779. Spon: Lawrence Hautz and Eva.

John Henry of John Henry Schreckengast and Maria Catharina, b. Jun 10; bapt. Jul 19, 1779. Spon: Samuel Reyer and Maria Elisabeth.

Simon of Peter Schmeltzer and Catharine, b. Aug 19; bapt. Oct 28, 1779. Spon: Simon Schürman and Anna Maria.

John Adam of Nicholas Wentzel and Christina, b. Oct 26; bapt. Nov 7, 1779. Spon: John Guschwa and Elisabeth.

Maria Regina of Jacob Leitner and Anna Maria, b. Jan 24, 1780; bapt. Feb 27, 1780. Spon: Regina Ditzler.

Jacob of Abraham Diehl and Catharine, b. May 28, 1780; bapt. Jul 2, 1780. Spon: Jacob Rohrer and Anna.

Elisabeth of Leonard Noll and Anna Margaret, b. Aug 11, 1780; bapt. Aug 27, 1780. Spon: Elisabeth Mayer, single.

John of George Scherer and Magdalena, b. Jul 16, 1780; bapt. Aug 27, 1780. Spon: John Schuy, single.

Magdalena of Peter Schmeltzer and Catharine, b. Aug 6, 1780; bapt. Sep 24, 1780. Spon: Jacob Diefenbach and Sabina.

Veronica of John Schäfer and Catharine, b. Dec 22, 1780, Jan, 1781. Spon: Regina Ditzler.

Christian of Jacob Michel and Margaret, b. Dec 30, 1780; bapt. Feb 4, 1781. Spon: Christian Battorf and Rosina.

Eva of Henry Stumb and Elisabeth, b. Dec 11, 1780; bapt. Feb 4, 1781. Spon: Eva Battorf.

Margaret of Andrew Eder and Margaret, b. May 10, 1781; bapt. Jul 29, 1781. Spon: Jacob Leitner and Margaret.

Wendel of Samuel Reyer and Elisabeth, b. Jun 14, 1781; bapt. Aug 26, 1781. Spon: Wendel Hautz.

Anna Eva of Balthasar Hautz and Elisabeth, b. Jul 6, 1781; bapt. Aug 26, 1781. Spon: Lawrence Hautz and Anna Eva.

Anna of Henry Hautz and Barbara, b. Aug 23, 1781; bapt. Sep 23, 1781. Spon: Jacob Gasser and Anna.

Magdalena of Jacob Leitner and Anna Margaret, b. Oct 19, 1981; bapt. Nov 18, 1781. Spon: Magdalena Eder.

Maria Catharine of Martin Gundrum and M. Catharina, b. Oct 22, 1781; bapt. Nov 18, 1781. Spon: George May and Catharina.

Anna Maria of Nicholas Noll and Maria Catharina, b. Oct 22, 1781; bapt. Mar 17, 1782. Spon: Anna Maria Noll, single.

Anna Maria of Peter Schmid and Eva, b. Oct 30, 1781; bapt. Mar 17, 1782. Spon: Simon Schürman and Anna Maria.

Martin of Martin Mayer and Anna Maria, b. Jun 9, 1782; bapt. Aug

25, 1782. Spon: John George Winter and Magdalena.

George of George Hautz and Elisabeth, b. Jul 21, 1782; bapt. Aug 25, 1782. Spon: John Ditzler and Margaret.

Christina of Geo. Nicholas Wentzel and Christina, b. Aug 30, 1782; bapt. Sep 22, 1782. Spon: Melchior Ditzler and Eva.

Eva Christina of John Caechog (Rehoe?) and Catharina, b. Oct 9, 1782; bapt. Nov 5, 1782. Spon: Herman Ruebel and Eva Maria.

Catharine of Conrad Schürman and Catharine, b. Oct 17, 1782; bapt. Nov 28, 1782. Spon: Catharine Schürman.

Catharina of Peter Fieser and M. Regina, b. May 9, 1782; bapt. Jun 24, 1782. Spon: Catharina Ditzler.

John Philip of Matthew Neidig and Catharina, b. Oct 13, 1782; bapt. Oct 29, 1782. Spon: Philip Lucas.

Eva Catharine of Peter Schmid and Maria Eva, b. Nov 26, 178??; bapt. Oct 29, 1782. Spon: Catharine Seibert.

Peter of Philip Mayer and Catharine, b. Oct 7, 1782, Oct 29, 1782. Spon: Martin Mayer and Anna Maria.

(The last three baptisms were entered by Hendel, probably while on a visit. He was pastor at Lancaster, since Sep 1782.)

The next entry was made by John Wm. Runckel.

Michael of Nicholas Berry and Eva, b. Feb 26, 1783; bapt. Mar 3, 1883. Spon: Michael Wolf and Margaret.

(The baptisms from Jun 1784 to Jun 1785 were entered by an unknown hand.)

Magdalena of Henry Hautz and Barbara, b. May 20, 1783; bapt. Jun 20, 1784. Spon: Peter Fischer and Regina.

Maria Magdalena of Peter Fischer and Maria Regina, b. Nov 3, 1784; bapt. Dec 5, 1784. Spon: Christian Schuy and wife.

John Jacob of Melchior Ditzler and Maria Eva, b. Nov 21, 1784; bapt. Dec 5, 1784. Spon: Jacob Leitner and wife.

John of Philip Gunckel and Catharine, b. Mar 6; bapt. Apr 24, 1785. Spon: George Schaefer, Jr and wife.

Margaret of Jacob Kons (Kuntz) and Eva Catharine, b. Mar 25; bapt. Apr 24, 1785. Spon: Wendel Hautz and wife.

Tobias of Henry Pickel (Bickel) and Magdalena, b. Feb 19; bapt. May 8, 1785. Spon: Henry Schnaterly and Elisabeth Eisenhauer.

Catharine Elisabeth of Alexander Benjamin and Margaret Eicheler, b. Nov 14, 1784; bapt. Jun 5, 1785. Spon: Elisabeth Eisenhauer.

Elisabeth of Jacob Michael and Maria, b. Apr 20; bapt. Jun 5, 1785. Spon: Caspar Tanie (?) and wife.

f Conrad Schürman and Catharine, b. Mar 11; bapt. Jun 5,
Spon: Isaiah Guschwa and wife.
ob of Simon Schürman and Anna Maria, b. May 13; bapt.
, 1785. Spon: John Jacob Cohren and wife, Anna.
f Samuel Reyer and wife, b. Sep 3; bapt. Mar 25, 1785.
Jacob Geyer and Maria Margaret.

APTISMS ENTERED BY REV. WILLIAM HENDEL

John Häberling and Margaret, b. May 11; bapt. Sep 15,
Spon: Peter Schmid.
f Henry Hautz and Barbara, b. Sep 8; bapt. Sep 15, [1785?].
Martin Schuy, Jr. and Margaret Elisabeth.
t baptism was entered by same hand as above.)
orge of Jacob Kohns and Eva Catharine, b. Dec 3, 1786; bapt.
, 1787. Spon: George Neidig and Salome.
t baptisms were entered by unknown hand.)
ria of George Battorf and Maria Dorothea, b. Jan 7, 1787;
Apr 17, 1787. Spon: John Schuy and Catharine.
John George Heyd and Magdalena, b. May 6, 1787; bapt.
19, 1787. Spon: Jacob Kuntz and Catharine.
ia of Jacob Bordner and Anna Maria, b. Nov 2, 1787; bapt.
25, 1787. Spon: Daniel Bordner and Eva Maria.
John Bordner and Susanna, b. Oct 25, 1787; bapt. Nov 25,
Spon: Christian Walborn and Elisabeth.
of Philip Kunkel and Catharine, b. Nov 13, 1787; bapt. Nov
787. Spon: Michael Schaefer.
ia of Christian Battorf and Rosina, b. May 16; bapt. Jun 8,
Spon: Spon: Samuel Reyer and Elisabeth.
etrich Walch and Margaret, b. May 22; bapt. Jul 6, 1788.
George Schaefer and Catharine.
  of Jacob Leitner and Margaret, b. Aug 14; bapt. Aug 24,
pon: John Schuy and Catharine.

PTISMS ENTERED FROM SEP 1788-DEC 1789.

  ander Greck(?) and Anna Maria, b. Sep 12, 1788; bapt.
788. Spon: Melchior Ditzler and Maria Eva.
  George Noll and Anna Maria, b. Oct 26; bapt. Nov 23,
  John Noll.

Maria Catharine of Christian Litsch and Susanna, b. Jan 13; bap
  Dec 21, 1788. Spon: John Spengeler and Maria Salome.
John William of George Heyd and Magdalena, b. Jan 16; bapt. M
  15, 1789. Spon: William Wetzen (?) and Anna Barbara.
John Philip of Jacob Kuntz and Eva Catharine, b. Mar 1; bapt. A
  12, 1789. Spon: Georg Lentz and Rosina.
Anna Margaret of Balthasar Loesch and Salome, b. Mar 9; bapt.
  12, 1789. Spon: Valentin Seyler and Anna Maria.
Christian of Andrew Jungling and Veronica, b. Apr 24, 1788; bap
  Apr 12, 1789. Spon: Christian Battorf and Rosina.
Susanna of Henry Hautz and Barbara, b. Aug 7; bapt. Sep 6, 178
  Spon: Anna Maria Dubs.
John of John Heberling and Anna Margaret, b. Oct 17; bapt. Nov
  1789. Spon: George Lentz and Rosina.
Catharine Schefer b. Apr 5, 1795. Spon: Elisabeth Choren.
Maria Schmid, b. Sep 1, 1794. Spon: Wendel Hautz and Maria
  Magdalena. Note: Harry W. Leing states: In our research, we
  always known of that person as the 15th child of Revolutiona
  Soldier, Johann Adam Schmidt, Sr. of "the Tulpehocken" and
  9th child of his 2nd wife, Elisabeth Barbara Miller. The child'
  name was, actually, Maria Magdalena: and here in Perry Co.,
  married Samuel Weary. They spent their entire married life, i
  Ohio, where they reared a large family.
Anna Maria of Georg Mueller and Elisabeth, b. Sep 13; bapt. Sep
  1794. Spon: Georg Meyer and Elisabeth.
Anna Maria of Gottfried Thomas and Anna Maria, b. Aug 26; bap
  Sep 27, 1794. Spon: Maria Thomas.
Martin of Martin Gundrum and Maria Catharine, b. Nov 24; bapt
  Nov 24, 1794. Spon: Jacob Bortner and Eva.
Margaret of John Artzt and Anna Maria, b. Mar 16; bapt. Apr 3,
  1795. Spon: Jacob Leitner and Anna Margaret.
Anna Maria of Nicholas Albert and Anna Maria, b. Apr 9; bapt.
  26, [1795]. Spon: Nicholas Moser and Anna Maria.
Maria Catharine of Christian Schuy and Magdalena, b. Jun 20;
  Aug 3, [1795]. Spon: Catharine Noll.
Sarah of Henry Hautz and Barbara, b. Sep 15; bapt. Oct 26, 1
  Spon: John Syrer and Susanna.
Christina of Peter Fieser and Regina, b. Aug 22; bapt. Oct 26,
  Spon: Christina Ditzler.
John Peter of John Noll and Elisabeth, b. Jun 25; bapt. Jun

Spon: Peter Fieser and Regina.

Martin of Philip Mayer and Catharine Elisabeth, b. Feb 25; bapt. Feb 26, [1794]. Spon: Jacob Diefenbach and Sabina.

Anna Maria of Balthasar Noll and Maria, b. Sep 14; bapt. Oct 25, 1795. Spon: Regina Leitner.

Peter of George Krebb and Salome, b. May 28, 1787; bapt. Jan 16, 1796. Spon: George Reyer and Elisabeth.

Daniel of Henry Dornmeyer and Catharine, b. Jan 15; bapt. Feb 8, 1796. Spon: Jacob Reyer and Maria Magdalena.

(The baptisms from Mar 1796-Jan 1813, are in a beautiful script, perhaps that of the schoolmaster.)

Anna Maria of Christian Thomas and Maria Elisabeth, b. Jan 2; Mar 13, 1796. Spon: Gottfied Thomas and Anna Maria.

Martin of Peter Fieser and Regina, b. Jan 6; bapt. Mar 13, 1796. Spon: Martin Schuy and Margaret Elisabeth.

David of Isaiah Guschwa and Margaret; bapt. Mar 1; bapt. Mar 27, 1796. Spon: Christian Schuy and Magdalena.

John of John Reyer and Susanna, b. Feb 27; bapt. Mar 27, 1796. Spon: John Fölcker and Elisabeth.

Peter of Frederick Camper and Elisabeth, b. Apr 15; bapt. May 22, 1796. Spon: Peter Ries and Susanna.

John Jacob of Paul Ziebach and Eva, b. May 1; bapt. Jun 26, 1796. Spon: John Jacob Reyer.

George Peter of Christian Battorf and Rosina, b. Jul 26; bapt. Sep 18, 1796. Spon: John Lehman and Elisabeth.

Anna Maria of John Edman and Catharine, b. Nov 18; bapt. Dec 4, 1796. Spon: Barbara Kilmer.

John of Christian Schuy and Magdalena, b. Nov 27; bapt. Dec 26, 1796. Spon: Andrew Eder, single.

Maria Magdalena of Henry Daub and Catharine, b. Feb 9; Mar 27, 1797. Spon: Peter Daub and Magdalena.

John of George Loesch and Veronica, b. Jan 4; bapt. Mar 12, 1797. Spon: Peter Loesch and Catharine.

John of Peter Ries and Susanna, b. Feb 11; bapt. Apr 14, 1797. Spon: Wendel Schmidt and Barbara.

John George of Frederick Camper and Elisabeth, b. Sep 11; bapt. Oct 22, 1797. Spon: John George Stätler and Christina.

Catharina of John Noll and Elisabeth, b. Mar 10; bapt. Dec 10, 1797. Spon: Elisabeth Noll.

John George of John George Miller and Elisabeth, b. Nov 16; bapt.

Dec 10, 1797. Spon: Adam Stump and Anna Maria.

John of Peter Daub and Magdalena, b. Aug 6, 1797; bapt. Sep 5, (?).
Spon: Michael Noll, single.

Anna Maria of John Saltzer and Catharine, b. Dec 17, 1797; bapt. Jan
1, 1798. Spon: Anna Maria Saltzer, single.

Catharine of Leonard Eder and Magdalena, b. Mar 1; bapt. Apr 9,
1798. Spon: Balthasar Noll and Maria Elisabeth.

Michael of Henry Schucker and Catharine, b. Dec 11, 1797; bapt. Jun
17, 1798. Spon: Frederick Deck and Catharine.

Elisabeth of Henry Schucker and Catharine, b. Dec 11, 1797; bapt.
Jun 17, 1798. Spon: Valentin Seiler and Maria Margaret.

Catharine of Balthasar Noll and Maria Elisabeth, b. Mar 1; bapt. Apr
9, 1799. Spon: Anna Margaret Eder, single.

Catharine of Paul Ziebach and Eva, b. Jan 2; bapt. Jan 13, [1799].
Spon: Catharine Ziebach, single.

Michael of Philip Meyer and Catharine, b. Jul 17, 1798; bapt. Mar 9,
[1799]. Spon: John Noll, single.

Elisabeth of Henry Hautz and Christina, b. Feb 20; bapt. Mar 9,
[1799]. Spon: Elisabeth Breitenbach, single.

Susanna of John Gerhart and Christina, b. Oct 16, 1798; bapt. Mar
10, [1799]. Spon: Frederick Gerhard and Susanna.

Catharine of John Hautz and Catharine, b. Jan 25; ba. May 5, 1799.
Spon: Elisabeth Finckel.

Elisabeth of John George Mimmian and Elisabeth, b. Dec 4, 1798;
bapt. Jan 1, 1799. Spon: Emmanuel Zerbe and Barbara.

Maria Magdalena of John Edman and Catharine, b. Dec 22, 1798;
bapt. Jan 1, 1799. Spon: Magdalena Fehler.

Philip of Jacob Wenner and Magdalena, b. Sep 6, [1799]; bapt. Nov
17, 1801. Spon: Philip Weber and Maria.

Catharine of Christian Stump and Catharine, b. Dec 11, 1800; bapt.
Feb 8, 1801. Spon: Eva Stump.

Catharine of Henry Spittler and Catharine, b. Dec 31; bapt.
Feb 8, 1801. Spon: Christina Schuy.

John Henry of Andrew Eder and Catharine, b. Jan 30; bapt. Mar 8, --
-. Spon: Andrew Eder and Margaret.

Anna Maria of Leonard Noll and Barbara, b. Mar 14; bapt. Apr 3, ---.
Spon: John Schuy and Catharine.

Anna Maria of John Artzt and Anna Maria, b. Sep 3; bapt. Oct 3, ---.
Spon: Adam Stein and Regina.

John Jacob of Henry Schucker and Catharine, b. Apr 19; bapt.

Oct 3, ---. Spon: Christian Schuy and Magdalena.

Eva of Leonard Viehman and Elisabeth; bapt. Aug 22; bapt. Oct 3, ---. Spon: Eva Viehman.

John of John Jung and Barbara, b. Aug 4; bapt. Oct 3, ---. Spon: John Schmitt and Anna Maria.

ST. JACOB'S KIMMERLING'S REFORMED CHURCH

BAPTISMS NOT ENTERED BY REV. CONRAD TEMPLEMANN

Elizabeth of John George Miller and Anna, b. Dec 14, 1753; bapt. Dec 27. Spon: John Nicholas Beyer and Barbara Meiry.

Michael of John George Miller and Anna; bapt. Nov 20, 1758. Spon: Michael Theiss and wife.

Daughter of John George Miller and Anna, b. Oct 6, (1760); bapt. Oct 14. Spon: Michael Theiss and Wife.

Anna Catharine of Carl Philip Bonner and Elizabeth, b. Jun 23; bapt. Jun 29. Spon: John George Mueller and wife.

John Christian of Carl Philip Benner and Elizabeth, b. Jan 4, (1780); bapt. Feb 3, 1780. Spon: George Mueller and Mary Magdalene Backenstoss.

BAPTISMS BY CONRAD TEMPELMAN, SEP 1754 - SEP 1755.

John Michael of Christopher Miller and Barbara, b. Nov 4, 1754. Spon: Thomas Mattern and Veronica.

Simon of Jacob Kunterman and Catharine, b. Sep 26, 1754. Spon: Simon Bassler and Elizabeth Kimmerling.

Anna Maria of Martin Imhoff and Ursula, b. Dec 6, 1754. Spon: John Seiller and Anna Maria Flubach.

Elizabeth of Jacob Schwob and Elizabeth, b. Oct 28, 1754. Spon: Frederick Ruth and wife.

George of John George Miller and Anna, b. May 20, 1755. Spon: George Meir, single and Verena Meier.

Jonas of Frederick Ruy and Elizabeth, b. Jan 8, 1751. Spon: Jonas Wolff and Catharine.

Elizabeth of Frederick Ruy and Elizabeth, b. Apr 1, 1755. Spon: Jacob Schwob and Elizabeth.

John George of John Seiller and Maria, b. Jun 3, 1755. Spon: John George Faetter and Marcia Meier, single.

John Peter of Christian Burger (decd.) and Barbara, b. Jun 12, 1749; bapt. Pentecost 1755.

John of Christian Burger (decd.) and Barbara, b. Apr 16, 1751; bapt. Pentecost, 1755.

Anna Barbara of Christian Burger, (decd.) and Barbara, b. Jul 17,

1753; bapt. Pentecost, 1755.
Henry of Nicholas Schanty and Elizabeth, b. Mar 26, 1754. Spon:
Henry Weschenbauh, and wife.
John Frederick of John Adam Gramlich and Anna Maria, b. Jun 8,
1755. Spon: John Frederick Schlosser and Elizabeth Kimmerling,
single.
Magdalene Barbara of Herman Eckel and Anna Maria, b. Sep 12,
1755. Spon: Ludwig Michel, single, and Barbara Schlosser.

BAPTISMS BY HENRY WILLIAM STOY, JAN-APR 1756

Anna Maria of Christian Gortner and Maria Elizabeth, b. Jan 10;
bapt. Jan 28, 1755(/56). Spon: Nicholas Weis and Anna Maria
Weschenbach.
Barbara of Simon Ebbert and Barbara, b. Feb 10, 1756; bapt. Feb 18.
Spon: John Mees and Barbara Schlosser.
Eva Elizabeth of Peter Dester and Barbara, b. Mar 14, 1756; bapt.
Apr 4. Spon: Anthony Keleker and Elizabeth Kimmerling.
Michael of Ludwig Weidner and Mar. Engel, b. Mar 19, (1756); bapt.
Apr 4, 1756. Spon: Michael Theiss and Elizabeth.

BAPTISMS BY JOHN HENRY DECKER, JUN, 1757-1763

Anna Barbara of John Adam Gramlich and Anna Maria, b. Mar.19,
1757; bapt. Jun 6. Spon: Jacob Zolicker and wife.
Daughter of Jacob Zolicker and Anna Barbara, b. Jul 19, 1756;
bapt.---. Spon: John Spickert and Regina.
John George of John Mess and Elizabeth, b. Dec 17, 1757; bapt. Jan
25, 1758. Spon: John George Miller and wife.
Maria Christine of David Biegelt and Maria Catharine, b. Dec 24,
1757; bapt. ----. Spon: parents.
Anna Maria of John Miller and Maria, b. May, 1758. Spon: Jacob
Schwab and wife, Elizabeth.
Catharine of Jacob Schwob and Elizabeth, b. May, 1758.
John of John Seeler and Maria, b. Jun 10, 1758. Spon: John Graf and
wife.
Catharine of Ludwig Weidner and Engel, b. Aug 16, 1757. Spon:
Dewalt Gerst and wife.
John of John Meess and Elizabeth, b. Jan 31, 1759; bapt. Feb 25,
1759. Spon: John Backestoss and Maria Weschenbauch, single.

Anna Barbara of John Meess and Eva Elizabeth, b. May 23, 1760; bapt. Jul 13, 1760.

Jacob of Peter Dester and wife, b. Nov 1, (1759); bapt. Apr 5, 1760. Spon: Jacob Conrad and Elizabeth Conrad.

Son of Christopher Miller and wife, b.---; bapt. Feb 1, 1762. Spon: George Mueller and wife.

John Jacob of John Adam Reifwein and wife, b. Feb 11, 1762; bapt. Mar 1, 1762. Spon: Jacob German and wife.

Anna Christine of Frederick Schlosser and Anna Collica, b. Sep 8, 1762; bapt. Sep 23. Spon: John Lucas Schalle and Anna Christrine Schlosser.

Catharine Elizabeth of John Meess and Eva Elizabeth, b. Apr 29, 1762; bapt. Sep 26. Spon: John Adam Wagner and Catharine Elizabeth.

Jacob of John Misch and Anna Margaret, b. Jun 22, 1757; bapt. ---. Spon: Nicholas Weiss.

Elizabeth of John Misch and Anna Margaret, b. Feb 20, 1759. Spon: Elizabeth Rath.

Anna Maria of John Misch and Anna Margaret, b. Feb 2, 1761. Spon: Jacob Schwab and wife.

Maria Barbara of John Misch and Anna Margaret, b. Feb 14, 1763. Spon: Maria Barbara Schwob and Martin Roth.

Peter of Jacob Schwab and wife, b. Dec 15, 1751. Spon: Peter Schlosser and wife.

Elizabeth of Jacob Schwab and wife, b. Sep 18, 1754. Spon: Frederick Rute and wife.

Anna Maria of Jacob Schwab and wife, b. May 1, 1759. Spon: John Miller and wife.

Anna Barbara of Jacob Schwab and wife, b. Mar 1, 1761. Spon: John Miesch and wife.

Susanna of Jacob Schwab and wife, b. Jun 4, 1763. Spon: Conrad Reinmeye.(?).

(Next three baptisms were entered by Pastor at Lancaster.)

Maria Catharine of John Mess and Elisabeth, b. Oct 20, 1764; bapt. Dec 23. Spon: Jacob Kämmerling and Maria Catharine.

Anna Maria of John Mess and Elizabeth, b. Apr 18, 1766; bapt. Jun 8, 1766. Spon: George Mess and Anna Maria.

Maria Susanna of John Mess and Elisabeth, b. Apr 9, 1768; bapt. May 24, 1768. Spon: Nicholas Mess and Maria Susanna.

The next baptism was entered by the father, Henry Miller.
Henry, (first son) of Henry Miller and Anna Maria, nee Kimmerling,
b.----; bapt. Sep 5, 1767. Spon: Henry Hautz and Catharine
Reifwein.

BAPTISMS BY JOHN JACOB ZUFALL, FEB 1766-SEP 1769

Maria Barbara of Dawelt Gerst and Maria Barbara, b. Jan 28, 1767;
bapt.Feb 15, 767. Spon: Catharine Schlosser, single.
Eva Margaret of Jacob Weibell and Catharine, b. Jan 27, 1767; bapt.
Mar 8, 1767. Spon: Valentine Korman and Margaret Lenin.
Anna Maria of John Bernard Eisenhut and wife, b. ---; bapt. Nov 5,
1769. Spon: Andrew Baddorf and Anna Maria Thomas.
John Michael of John Mess and Elizabeth, b. Jan 1, 1770; bapt. Feb
1, 1770. Spon: John Michael Theiss and wife.
John of Jacob Conterman and wife, b.---; bapt. Feb 1, 1770. Spon:
John Uhry and wife.
Peter of Henry Miller and wife, b. Mar 6, 1770; bapt. Mar 22. Spon:
Peter Tester and wife.
Margaret of Conrad Helm and wife, b. ---; bapt. Feb 3, 1771. Spon:
Peter Schlosser and wife.

BAPTISMS BY REV. WILLIAM HENDEL, FROM OCT 1771

John Peter of Theobald Gerst and Maria Barbara, b. Oct 14, 1771;
bapt. Oct 20, 1772. Spon: Peter Schlosser and Maria Margaret.
Christian of Casper Tschop (Job) and Barbara, b. Dec 25, 1771; bapt.
Jan 13, 1772. Spon: Christian Borgner.
John of Christian Weyhrich and Margaret, b. Jan 19, 1772; bapt. Feb
23. Spon: William Rauch and Barbara.
Christopher Frederick of Henry Muller and Anna Maria, b. Feb 27,
1772; bapt. Mar 15. Spon: Christopher Wegman and Eva.
John of John Backenstos and Charlotte, b. Jan, 1772; bapt. Mar 15.
Spon: John Zollinger.
Jacob of Isaac Brand and Margaret, b. Mar [6?], 1772; bapt. Apr 20.
Spon: Jacob Zollinger and Anna Barbara.
George of John Miesch and Margaret, b. Mar 13, 1772; bapt. May 5.
Spon: Hieronimus Rudy and Eva Maria.

Margaret of Balthasar Schalle and Barbara, b. Apr 29, 1772; bapt.
    May 5. Spon: Peter Schlosser and Maria Margaret.
Jacob of Martin Rudy and Maria, b. Apr 24, 1772; bapt. Jun 8. Spon:
    Jonas Rudy.
Maria Christine of John Daub and Maria Catharine, b. Aug 29, 1772;
    bapt, Oct 4. Spon: Maria Christine Kaemmerling.
Peter of Christian Borgner and Anna Maria, b. Feb 14, 1773; bapt.
    Mar 14. Spon: Peter Dester and Anna Barbara.
Regina of John Backenstos and Charlotte, b. Mar 5, 1773; bapt. Apr
    18. Spon: Regina Zollinger.
Philip of Michael Theiss and Elizabeth, b. May 3, 1773; bapt. Jun 13.
    Spon: Michael Leg and Magdalene.
John of Philip Mutterbauch and Anna Margaret, b. Jun 5, 1773; bapt.
    Jul 11. Spon: Christian Borgner and Anna Maria.

BAPTISMS BY JOHN CONRAD BUCHER, NOV 1774-MAY 1780

Anna Maria of Martin Rudi and Anna Maria, b. Oct 14, 1774; bapt.
    Nov 29. Spon: Conrad Reiniger and Susanna Margaret.
John of Henry Miller and wife, b. Aug. 13, 1774; bapt. ---, in the brick
    church. Spon: Melchior Abmeier and Anna Maria.
Barbara of Henry Miller and wife, b. Jun 14, 1777; bapt. Jun 26.
    Spon: Barbara Meier and John Kuhn.
(Last two baptisms entered by the father, Henry Miller)
John George of Michael Spengler and Magdalene, b. Jan 6, 1779;
    bapt. Feb 7, 1779. Spon: George Spengler.
John Peter of Casper Tschop and Barbara, b. Nov 22, 1778; bapt. Dec
    20, 1778. Spon: Peter Teschler and Barbara.
Mary Magdalene of Balthasar --- and Barbara, b. Jan 8, 1779; bapt.
    Feb 9, 1779. Spon: John Schlosser and Magdalene Schally.
John of John Benter and Elisabeth, b. Mar 7, 1778; bapt. Mar 14.
    Spon: Carl Philip Benter and Anna Elizabeth.
John Leonard of Jacob Gunderman and Elizabeth, b. Mar 11, 1779;
    bapt. Mar 14. Spon: John Leonard Biegler and Elizabeth.
John Jacob of John Jacob Keller and Eva Elizabeth, b. Feb 20, 1779;
    bapt. Mar 14. Spon: Casper Schop and Barbara.
Mary Magdalene of Isaac Brand and Margaret, b. Feb 9, 1779; bapt.
    Mar 14. Spon: Mary Magdalene Backenstoss.
John of Michael Lentz and Elizabeth, b. Mar 18, 1779; bapt. Apr 1.
    Spon: John Kuster and Catharine.

John Leonard of Nicholas Fehler and Barbara, b. May 30, 1779; bapt. Jun 13. Spon: John Jacob Georg and Anna Maria Koch.
Maria Margaret of Peter Baeri and Margaret, b. Jul 29, 1779; bapt. Aug 8. Spon: Conrad Hoster and Margaret.
John William of John Maess and Elizabeth, b. Aug 21, 1779; bapt. Aug 29. Spon: John Zehrung.

BAPTISMS ENTERED BY SCHOOLMASTER, JOHN WEBER, MAR 1780-JUN 1781

Maria Margaret of Jacob Hatrich and Anna Maria, b. Mar 8, 1780; bapt. Mar 19, 1780. Spon: Adam Menges and Margaret.
Catharine Barbara of John Casper Tschopp and Anna Barbara, b. Feb 8, 1780; bapt. Mar 19. Spon: Peter Borgner and Catharine.
Anna Catharine of Philip Lorentz Hautz and Anna Catharine, b. Mar 8, 1780; bapt. Mar 19. Spon: Jacob German and Catharine.
Margaret of Matthew Faederhafe and Maria Elizabeth, b. Feb 2, 1780; bapt. Mar 19, 1780. Spon: Margaret Faederhafe.
Daniel of Daniel Mueller and Anna, b. Mar 28, 1780; bapt. Apr 16. Spon: David Mueller and Catharine Elizabeth.
John George of Jacob Wolff and Catharine, b. Feb 27, 1780; bapt. Apr 16. Spon: Martin Baender and Elizabeth.
Peter of Jacob Baery and Christine, b. Mar 28, 1780; bapt. Apr 16. Spon: Peter Baery and Anna Margaret.
John Christian of Michael Korr and Anna Barbara, b. Mar 23, 1780; bapt. May 7. Spon: William Rauch and Anna Barbara.
(Last baptism is in the handwriting of J. C. Bucher.)
Anna Maria of Martin Ruth and Anna Maria, b. Jun 15, 1780; bapt. Jul 9. Spon: Susanna Schwaebin (Schwab).
Anna Barbara of Adam Schwarm and Anna Christine, b. Jun 24, 1780; bapt. Jul 9. Spon: Anna Barbara, wife, of Christopher Koppenhefer.
John Michael of John Michael Mueller and Eva, b. Jul 28, 1780; bapt. ---. Spon: John Nicholas Schnee and Anna Barbara.
Elizabeth of John Benner and Elizabeth, b. May 13, 1781; bapt. ---. Spon: Martin Benner and Elizabeth Benner.
John Henry of John Weber, (schoolmaster here), and Anna Christine, b. Jun 6, 1781; bapt. ---. Spon: John Henry Sarter, also a schoolmaster.

BAPTISMS BY JOHN WILLIAM RUNKEL, OCT 1781-AUG 1784

Anna Christine of John Maes and Elizabeth, b. Oct 6, 1781; bapt. Oct 15. Spon: John Daub and Anna.

Henry of Henry Schop and Magdalene, b. Feb 23, 1782; bapt. Mar 10, 1782. Spon: John Schally, single.

Anna Barbara of Michael Lentz and Elizabeth, b. Feb 23, 1782; bapt. Mar 10, 1782. Spon: Christian Schmit and Maria Elizabeth.

John George of Carl Benner and Elizabeth, b. Aug. 1, 1782; bapt. Aug. 4. Spon: George Miller and Anna.

Anna Christine of Jacob Tschop and Anna Maria, b. Jan 13, 1781; bapt. Sep 5, 1782. Spon: Eva Kaemmerling, single.

Catharine of Jacob Berry and Christine, b. Sep 12, 1782; bapt. Sep 17. Spon: Peter Berry and Margaret.

John Jacob of Adam German and Rebecca, b. Aug. 22, 1782; bapt. Sep 29. Spon: Jacob German and Maria Catharine.

Catharine Elizabeth of John Matthew Steingruber and Anna Catharine, b. Oct 22, 1782; bapt. Oct 27. Spon: John Mees and Elizabeth.

John Frederick of Jerome Rudy and Marg. Elizabeth, b. Oct 7, 1782; bapt. Nov 14. Spon: John Kuhn and Barbara.

Anna Barbara of Daniel Miller and Anna, b. Nov 17, 1782; bapt. Dec 22, 1782. Spon: Barbara Schwab, single.

John Adam of John Maes and Elizabeth, b. Mar 4, 1783; bapt. Mar 18. Spon: parents.

John Philip of Jacob Hetterich and Anna Maria, b. Mar 8, 1783; bapt. Mar 20. Spon: Michael Kohr and Barbara.

John of Jacob Kuhns and Catharine, b. Mar 1, 1783; bapt. Mar 30. Spon: John German and Elizabeth.

Matthew of John Benner and Elizabeth, b. Apr 30, 1783; bapt. May 31. Spon: Christian Jaeger, Sr.

John of Adam Schwarm and Anna Christine, b. Jun 1, 1783; bapt. Jun 25. Spon: John Uhrich, single.

Eva Catharine of Peter Berry and Margaret, b. May 19, 1783; bapt. Jul 3. Spon: Frederick Noecker and Eva Catharine.

Gottlieb of Daniel Miller and Eliza Catharine, b. Sep 12, 1783; bapt. Oct 2. Spon: Daniel Miller and Ana.

Barbara of Jacob Keller and Eva, b. Dec 28, 1783; bapt. Feb 3, 1784. Spon: Peter Dester and Barbara.

Susanna of Michael Kohr and Barbara, b. Feb 19, 1784; bapt. Mar 11.

Spon: Nicholas Weiss and Barbara.

Anna Elizabeth of Peter Borger and Catharine, b. Feb 4, 1784; bapt. Mar 21. Spon: Elizabeth Daub, single.

Anna Maria of Conrad Aubel and Barbara, b. Apr 24, 1784; bapt. May 9. Spon: Anna Maria Bayer.

Anna Christine of Philip Lorentz Hautz and Anna, b. Jul 31, 1784; bapt. Aug. 15. Spon: John Daub and Anna.

(This the last entry of John William Runkel, the next by unknown hand)

Elizabeth of John Mess and Elizabeth, b. Feb 17, 1785; bapt. Mar 14, 1785. Spon: George Mess and Elizabeth.

ENTRIES BY LUDWIG LUPP, MAY 1786-MAY 1798
Note: not all entries were made by Lupp, those made by him personally are marked by an asterisk.

Anna Elizabeth of Daniel Miller and Anna, b. Apr 25, 1786; bapt. May 14. Spon: Anna Elizabeth Reifwein.*

Anna Elizabeth of Peter Borgner and Catharine, b. Mar 6, 1788; bapt. Apr 6. Spon: Anna Elizabeth ---.

Magdalene of Daniel Miller and Anna, b. May 8, 1789; bapt. Jun 14. Spon: Jacob Keller and wife.

George Michael of Michael Riegel and wife, b. Feb 4, 1788; bapt. May 7, 1788. Spon: George Mueller and wife.*

John Jacob of John Zehrung and wife, b. Mar 13, 1788; bapt. May 7, 1788. Spon: Michael Meess.*

John Adam of Adam Schwarm and wife, b. Dec 19, 1788; bapt. Feb 8, 1789. Spon: Jacob Decker and wife.*

John Jacob of Christian Kantzer and wife, b. Jul 4, 1789; bapt. Aug 16. Spon: Christian Miller and wife.

John of Michael Maier and wife, b. Jul 5, 1789; bapt. Aug 16. Spon: parents.

Susanna of Michael Rigel and wife, b. Aug 28, 1790; bapt. Jan 10, 1791. Spon: Benjamin Zerbe and wife.

Maria Elizabeth of Carl Brenner and Elizabeth, b. Aug 26, 1791; bapt. Sep 15. Spon: Nicholas Bohr and wife.

Anna Catharine of Jacob Rittel and wife, b. Aug. 6, 1791; bapt. Sep 15. Spon: John George Lentz and wife.

John of John George Mueller and wife, b. Oct 8, 1793; bapt. Oct 27. Spon: John Noll and wife.*

Barbara of Andrew Webert and wife, b. Oct 22, 1793; bapt. Nov 29, 1793. Spon: John Glueck and wife.*

John of Daniel Miller and wife, b. Oct 9, 1794; bapt.---. Spon: parents.

John Adam of John Gunterman and wife, b. May 20, 1795; bapt. Jun 7, 1795. Spon: John Adam Gunterman.

John of Joseph Eckley and wife. b. May 10, 1795; bapt. Jun 7, 1795. Spon: Lucas Schally and wife.

John Jacob of William Baecker and wife, b. Feb 2, 1796; bapt. Feb 14, 1796. Spon: parents.

Elizabeth of Philip Eckert and wife, b. Dec 28, 1796; bapt. Mar 13, 1796. Spon: John Steger and wife.

John of Conrad Aubel and wife, b. Feb 8, 1796; bapt. Mar 13, 1796. Spon: Carl Benner and wife.

John George of Jacob Loos and wife, b. Jun 29, 1796; bapt. Aug 28, 1796. Spon: Jacob Keller and wife.

Henry of Jacob Schwab and Elizabeth, b. Dec 21, 1796; bapt. Mar 12, 1797. Spon: Daniel Mueller and Anna.*

John Philip of Carolus Benner and Elizabeth, b. Jan 16, 1797; bapt. Feb 12, 1797. Spon: Conrad Aubel and Anna.*

Jacob of Jacob Schwab and Elizabeth, b. May 4, 1794; bapt. Jun 19, 1794. Spon: parents.

John Michael of William Backer and Catharine, b. Dec 28, 1797; bapt. Feb 11, 1798. Spon: parents.

John Henry of Jacob Bloss and wife, b. Apr 8, 1798; bapt. May 6, 1798. Spon: Henry Ruetel and wife, Barbara.

BAPTISMS BY REV. WILLIAM HIESTER, MAY 1801-JUN 1820

Anna Maria of Jacob Loss and Catharine, b. Oct 6, 1800; bapt. soon afterwards. Spon: Anna Elizabeth Miller.

TRINITY TULPEHOCKEN CHURCH

BAPTISMS BY REV. DOMINICUS BARTHOLOMAEUS, 1748-1751

Elizabeth of --- Basler and wife, bapt. Nov 6, (1748). Spon: (Elizabeth) Lein.

John Adam of Nicholas Gelbert and wife, bapt. Feb 27, 1752. Spon: John Adam Diefebach and wife, Maria Sibylla. (Entered by a different hand.)

Eva Margaret of Dominicus Batholomae, (pastor), bapt. Oct 21, 1748; Spon: Mrs. Weiser, Mr. and Mrs. Reiss.

John George of Jonas Lerue, bapt. Jan --, 1749. Spon: J. G. Zoeller.

Eva Christine of A. Bullman and wife, bapt. Jan 29, 1749. Spon: N. Bullman and Mr. E. Moor.

Eva Christine of W. Hoster and wife, bapt. Mar 12, 1749. Spon: Mrs. Burksthaler.

Anna Susanna of P. Kloss and wife, bapt. Apr 30, 1749. Spon: Mrs. Seubert and bro. of Hoster.

Anna Catharine of John Kunckel and wife, bapt. May 15, 1749. Spon: Mrs. Stein and Noll.

John Peter of Hartman Zoeller and wife, bapt. May 15, 1749. Spon: -- - Zoeller.

Anna Margaret of Nicholas Noll and wife, bapt. May 15, 1749. Spon: Mrs. Noll.

John Frederick of Peter Summi and wife, bapt. May 28, 1749. Spon: Mr. Stein.

John Thomas of George Huber and wife, bapt. Jun 11, 1749. Spon: --- Kopenheber.

Magdalene of Michael Summi and wife, bapt. Jun 11, 1749. Spon: Mrs. Summi, grandmother.

John Peter of Michael Spengler and wife, bapt. Jul 23, 1749. Spon: Mr. Schell and wife.

Maria Catharine of Nicholas Gelbert and wife, bapt. Oct 8, 1749. Spon: Mr. and Mrs. Schilling.

Elizabeth of John Zollner and wife, bapt. Dec 10, 1749. Spon: Mrs. Dollinger and Mr. Zollner.

Maria of Jacob Itzberger and wife, bapt. Dec 10, 1749. Spon: Mr. and Mrs. Dollinger.

Eva Elizabeth of Jacob Hamme and wife, bapt. Dec 24, 1749. Spon: Mr. and Mrs. Loch.

Catharine Barbara of Nicholas Mueller and wife, bapt. Feb 9, 1750. Spon: Jacob Mueller and Mrs. Jansser.

Regina Anna of Peter Becker and wife, bapt. Feb 23, 1750. Spon: Mr. and Mrs. Bathdorf.

Abraham of P. Tiehle and wife, bapt. Feb 11, 1750. Spon: Mr. and Mrs. Libo.

Anna Elizabeth of Peter Loch and wife, bapt. Mar 11, 1750. Spon: Mrs. Herchelroth and Mr. Fortine.

Anna Margaret of John Ederich and wife, bapt. Apr 8, 1750. Spon: Peter Summi and wife.

Dorothy of John Lein and wife, bapt. Jun 3, 1750. Spon: Mr. Lein.

Michael of Jacob Dinges and wife, bapt. Sep --, 1750. Spon: Mr. Spengler.

George Michael of --- Maus and wife, bapt. Oct 21, 1750. Spon: --- Stumpf.

John George ---, bapt. Oct 23, 1750. Spon: --- Dickert and Huber.

John Adam of John Adam Stein and wife, bapt. Nov 4, 1750. Spon: (John) Stein.

Anna Margaret of John Stein and wife, bapt. Nov 4, 1750. Spon: John Adam Stein and wife.

Hannah of Jacob Dinges and wife, bapt. Dec 2, 1750. Spon: --- Hoster.

Anna Margaret of Christian Orndorff and wife, bapt. Dec 16, 1750. Spon: Herman Orndorff and wife.

Anna Elizabeth of Jacob Simon and wife, bapt. Dec --, 1750. Spon: Thomas Koppenheber.

Maria Catharine of --- Poepli and wife, bapt. Dec --, 1750. Spon: Holb Buschelmacher's son.

John of John Kunckel and wife, bapt. Apr 8, 1751. Spon: Michael ----.

BAPTISMS BY H. W. STOY OCT 1752-NOV 1755

Christopher of Christian Ohrendorf, bapt. Oct 15, 1752. Spon: Christopher Noecker and wife, Catharine.

Anna Margaret of Michael Gunckel of Little Swartara, bapt. Oct 8, 1752 by Rev. Mr. Kurtz. Spon: John Henry Noll and Anna Marg. Weyand.

John Jacob of Jacob Keller, bapt. Mar 25, 1753. Spon: Jacob Lehman and Anna Marg. Kitzmueller.

John Jacob of Adam Stein, bapt. Mar 25, 1753. Spon: John Jacob Mueller and wife.

John George of Peter Summois, bapt. Mar 26, 1753. Spon: George Dollinger and wife.

Anna Catharine of John Zoeller, bapt. Apr 23, 1753. Spon: Christian Lauer and wife.

John Conrad of John William Hoster, bapt. Aug 5, 1753. Spon: Conrad Goldman and Joanna Hoster, single.

John Adam of Abraham Lebbo, bapt. Aug 12, 1753. Spon: John Adam Stein and wife.

Barbara Elizabeth of Frederick Summois and Anna Mar., b. 5 yrs old; bapt. Jun 14, 1753. Spon: William Leitner and wife.

John Michael of Frederick Summois and wife, b. 3 yrs old; bapt. Jun 14, 1753. Spon: Michael Summois and wife.

Anna Margaret of Frederick Summois and wife, b. 1 yr old; bapt. Jun 14, 1753. Spon: John Cuswa and wife, Anna Marg.

Maria Elizabeth of Peter Mueller and Maria Catharine, b. ---; bapt. Jun 14, 1753. Spon: George Schaefer and Maria Eliz. Leitner, now married.

Gertrude of John Adam Forne and Elizabeth, bapt. Jun 14, 1753. Spon: Veitt Capp and wife, Gertrude.

Henry of Peter Spycker, bapt. Sep 3, 1753. Spon: John Henry Marsteller of Skippack.

John of Jacob Etschberger and Esther, b. Jul 27, 1753; bapt. Sep 30, 1753. Spon: John Ferrer of Lancaster twp.

John Martin of Michael Spengler and Elizabeth Margaret, b. Nov 22, 1753; bapt. Jan 3, 1754. Spon: Jacob Ramler and wife, Eva Margaret.

Maria Barbara of John Kniss and Catharine Elizabeth, b. Dec 30, 1753; bapt. Jan 20, 1754. Spon: Christopher Mueller and wife, Maria Barbara.

Maria Dorothy of John Gunckel and Margaret, b. Jan 11, 1754; bapt. Feb 19, 1754. Spon: John Etherich and wife.

John Adam of William Leitner and Maria Elizabeth, b. Feb 13, 1754; bapt. Feb 19, 1754. Spon: John Adam Stein and wife.

Catharine of John George Stahlschmidt and Anna Margaret, b. Feb 16, 1754; bapt. Feb 22, 1754. Spon: Daniel Mauenshagen and wife, Catharine.

John Michael and Nicholas Simon and Maria Margaret, b. Jan 14, 1754; bapt. Mar 3, 1754. Spon: Michael Spengler and wife.

Johanna Elizabeth of Michael Kor and Mary Magdalene of Quitobehilla, b. Feb 4, 1754; bapt. Mar 3, 1754. Spon: Christian

Ohrendorf and wife, Joanna Elizabeth.

John of John Lein and Dorothy, b. Dec 11, 1753; bapt. Apr 15, 1754. Spon: John Weidler, Leacock twp, Conestoga.

Anna Maria of Michael Gunckel and Anna Mar., b. Apr 11, 1754; bapt. Apr 21, 1754. Spon: Balthasar Noll and Anna Maria Stein, single and now married.

John of John Wohlleber, (Luth.) and Anna Margaret, b. Apr 14, 1754; bapt. Apr 23, 1754. Spon: John Gunckel and wife.

Maria Catharine of Peter Mayer and Anna Margaret, b. Mar 30, 1754; bapt. Apr 23, 1754. Spon: John Cuswa and wife, Anna Margaret.

Elizabeth of Jonas le Rouche and Anna Bar. Elizabeth, b. Feb 19, 1754; bapt. Jun 2, 1754. Spon: Andrew Salzgeber and Elizabeth Ferrer, single.

John Jacob of Jacob Rossel and Maria Margaret, b. Jun 2, 1754; bapt. Jun 9, 1754. Spon: Jacob Gasser and Maria Elizabeth Lesch, both single.

John Henry of Jonas Fortune and wife, b. ---; bapt. Jun 10, 1754. Spon: John Henry Herchelroth and Catharine Meyer, wife of Isaac Meyer of Conestoga.

Anna Maria of George Zoeller and Barbara, b. Jun 14, 1754; bapt. Jun 26, 154. Spon: Henry Zoeller and wife.

John George of Elizabeth Stein at George Rommel's, b. ---; bapt. Jun 26, 1754. Spon: George Zoeller and wife, Barbara.

John Adam of Jacob Mueller and wife, bapt. Jul 7, 1754. Spon: John Adam Stein and wife.

John William of Jacob Seifert and wife, b. Jul 2, 1754; bapt. Jul 7, 1754. Spon: John Wm. Hoster and wife.

Son (John?) of John Diehm and Christine, b. Dec 4, 1754; bapt. Dec 15, 1754. Spon: Marcus Breunig and wife, Maria Catharine.

Margaret of John Zoeller and Catharine, b. Jan 13, 1755; bapt. Feb 3, 1755. Spon: Henry Linn and Elizabeth Ferrer.

Catharine Elizabeth of Christian Ohrendorf and Elizabeth, b. ---; bapt. Feb 3, 1755. Spon: Henry Koppenhoefer and Elizabeth Debeler, both single.

Henry Ludwig (Lewis) of Conrad Hartman and Elizabeth, both dead, b. 6 yrs old; bapt. Feb 10, 1755. Spon: Henry Ludwig Schwarz and wife.

Mary Magdalene of Philip Koester and Maria Margaret, b. Jan 10, 1755; bapt. Feb 10, 1755. Spon: Jacob Lutz and Mary Magdalene.

Catharine Elizabeth of John Adam Kassel and Elizabeth, b. Oct 5, 1754; bapt. Mar 24, 1755. Spon: Peter Kuntz and wife, Eliz. Catharine.

Elizabeth of Daniel Mauenshagen and Catharine, b. ---; bapt. Mar 31, 1755. Spon: Elizabeth Wolf.

Anna Margaret of Balthasar Noll and Anna Maria, b. Mar 28, 1755; bapt. Apr 27, 1755. Spon: John George Noll and wife, Anna Margaret.

John Peter of John Adam Stein and Maria Catharine, b. Apr 10, 1755; bapt. Apr 27, 1755. Spon: Peter Poppel and wife, Magdalene.

Elizabeth of Isaac Meyer and Catharine, b. ---; bapt. Jul 4, 1755. Spon: Valentine Herchelroth and wife, Barbara.

John Michael of Jacob Keller and Barbara, b. Jul 7, 1755; bapt. Jul 27, 1755. Spon: Jacob Schnellbacher and wife, Catharine.

John Peter of John Adam Diefenbach and Sibylla, b. Jul 15, 1755; bapt. Aug 2, 1755. Spon: John Peter Anspach and wife, Mary Magdalene.

Maria Elizabeth of Adam Forne and Elizabeth, b. Jul 14, 1755; bapt. Aug 3, 1755. Spon: John Nicholas Weigand and Maria Elizabeth Dredenbach.

Anna Catharine of John Adam Hartman and Anna Maria, b. Aug 22, 1755; bapt. Aug 31, 1755. Spon: --- Michael and wife, Anna Maria.

Andrew of George Zoeller and Barbara, b. Jul 18, 1755; bapt. Sep --, 1755. Spon: Andrew Saltzgeber and wife, Anna Maria.

John of John Adam Stein and Anna Margaret, b. Aug 7, 1755; bapt. Sep 7, 1755. Spon: John Etherich and wife, Dorothy.

Susanna Elizabeth of John William Hoster and Anna Elizabeth, b. ---; bapt. Nov 2, 1755. Spon: Jacob Seifert and wife, Susanna.

BAPTISMS BY REV. JOHN WALDSCHMIDT, DEC 1756-SEP 1757

Esther of Nicholas Wiant and Maria Elizabeth, b. Dec 17, 1756; bapt. Dec 25, 1756. Spon: Francis Wenrich and Esther.

Anna Maria of John Herckert and Elizabeth, b. Jan 6, 1757; bapt. Apr 9, 1757. Spon: Anna Maria Steiner, wife of John Steiner.

Maria Elizabeth of Jacob Mueller and Margaret, bapt. Jun 22, 1756; bapt. Jul 11, 1756. Spon: John Schwartz and wife, Maria Elizabeth.

John Henry of Peter Winckelblech and Margaret, b. Sep 25, 1756; bapt. Oct 17, 1756. Spon: John Henry Wurst and Catharine Schuler, both single.

John Nicholas of John Diehm and Anna Christine, b. Nov 21, 1756;
bapt. Nov 28, 1756. Spon: Nicholas Zimmerman and wife, Anna
Catharine.

Catharine of Jacob Seibert and Susanna, b. Feb 25, 1757; bapt. Mar
20, 1757. Spon: Peter Klopp and wife, Werrine.

John Jacob of Abraham Lebbo and Anna Margaret, b. Feb 16; bapt.
Mar 20, 1757. Spon: Jacob Loewenguth and wife, Catharine.

Ludwig (Lewis) of Daniel Mauenshagen and Catharine, b. Apr 14,
1757; bapt. May --, 1757. Spon: Ludwig Michael and Cath. Noll,
single.

John of Balser Noll and Anna Maria, b. Apr 14, 1757; bapt. May --,
1757. Spon: John Noll and Maria Elizabeth.

Elizabeth of George Zeller and Maria Barbara, b. May 31, 1757; bapt.
Jun --, 1757. Spon: John Schwartz and wife, Elizabeth.

Mary Magdalene of Jacob Kroeninger and Dorothy, b. Feb 3, 1757;
bapt. Feb --, 1757. Spon: Adam Diefebach and Sibylla.

John Henry of Joseph Bubikofer and Anna Maria, b. Jan 22, 1757;
bapt. Feb, ---. Spon: John Henry Mayer and Eva Sorber.

Conrad of Conrad Goldman and Hannah, b. Aug 20, 1757; bapt. Sep -
--. Spon: William Hoster and Anna Elizabeth.

Anna Maria of Henry Schmitt and Maria Barbara, b. Aug 27, 1757;
bapt. Sep, --. Spon: John Laferre and Anna Maria.

*BAPTISMS BY REV. J. WILLIAM OTTERBEIN, NOV 1758-JUL
1760 Not entered by him, but by schoolmaster Bäcker.*

Barbara of Philip Ziegler and Reg(ina), b. Oct 29, 1758; bapt. Nov 19,
1758. Spon: John Schnaebele and Barbara.

John of Conrad Goldman and Hannah, b. Oct 27, 1758; bapt. Nov 19,
1758. Spon: John Rammel and Barbara.

Margaret Elizabeth of George Zeller and Maria Barbara, b. Jun 19,
1758; bapt. Jul 15, 1759. Spon: Margaret Eliza. Haas, single.

Son of Valentine Schuler and Apollonia, b.---; bapt. Jul 22, 1759.
Spon: John Sc(hwartz?) and wife, Elizabeth.

Anna Barbara of Christian Ohrendorff and Elizabeth, b. Aug 21,
1759; bapt. Sep 2, 1759. Spon: Caster Chor and Anna Barbara.

Anna Elizabeth of John Michael Baecker and wife, Elizabeth,
schoolmaster at present, b. Sep 23, 1759; bapt. Sep 30, 1759. Spon:
Michael Saenger and Anna Gertrude.

Jacob of Jacob Walter and wife, b. ---; bapt. Oct 28, 1759. Spon: Jacob

Gassert and wife.

Michael of Jacob Tinius and Maria Ursula, b. ---; bapt. Nov 11, 1759. Spon: Michael Im(hoff), single.

John Peter of John Michael Diefenbach and Anna Margaret, b. Dec 16, 1759; bapt. Dec 23, 1759. Spon: Peter Anspach and Mary Magdalene.

John of Leonard Schwartz and Elizabeth, b. --; bapt. Dec 23, 1759. Spon: John Zeller and wife, Catharine.

Catharine Elizabeth of George Deiss and Anna Margaret, b. Apr 11, 1760; bapt. May 4, 1760. Spon: Maria Eliz. Deiss, single.

John Peter of Jacob Etschberger and Esther, b. --; bapt. May 18, 1760. Spon: John Peter Anspach and Mary Magdalene.

John Michael of John Adam Stein and Margaret, b. Apr 12, 1760; bapt. May 18, 1760. Spon: John Michael Nussheuer and wife.

Leonard of John Schwartz and Elizabeth, b. May 11, 1760; bapt. May 25, 1760. Spon: Leonard Schwartz and Anna Elizabeth.

Elizabeth Margaret of Peter Spengler and Margaret, b. Dec 10, 1759; bapt. May 25, 1760. Spon: Michael Spengeler and Elizabeth.

John of Jacob Gassert and wife, b. ---; bapt. Jun 29, 1760. Spon: Jacob Rossel and wife.

Dau of John Dutweiler and wife, b. --; bapt. Jul 29, 1760. Spon: ---.

BAPTISMS BY REV. H. W. STOY, OCT 1760-1762

John Peter of Martin Schell and Catharine, b. Sep 6, 1760; bapt. Oct 5, 1760. Spon: Christian Cassenitz, single.

Eva of Conrad Goldman and Hannah, b. Dec 1, 1760; bapt. Dec 23, 1760. Spon: William Hoster and Anna Elizabeth.

Henry Ludwig of Leonard Schwartz and Elizabeth, b. Apr 17, 1761; bapt. Jun 7, 1761. Spon: Henry Ludwig Schwartz and Maria Elizabeth.

Maria Salome of Jacob Rossel and Margaret, b. May 29, 1761; bapt. Jun 7, 1761. Spon: Francis Brossman and Maria Salome.

Maria Elizabeth of William Hoster and Anna Elizabeth, b. Aug 4, 1761; bapt. Aug 19, 1761. Spon: Magdalene Goldman, single.

Jacob of Jacob Mueller and wife, b. Aug 30, 1761; bapt. Sep 16, 1761. Spon: Jacob Etschberger and wife.

Eva Elizabeth of George Stahlschmidt and Anna Margaret, b. ---; bapt. Sep 27, 1761. Spon: John Adam Christ and wife.

John of John Adam Stein and Maria Catharine, b. Sep 9, 1761; bapt.

Oct 4, 1761. Spon: John Schwartz and Elizabeth.

Catharine of John Schwartz and Elizabeth, b. Dec 24, 1761; bapt. Jan 24, 1762. Spon: John Adam Stein and Catharine.

John Michael of John Michael Baecker, (schoolmaster here), and wife, Elizabeth, b. May 8, 1762; bapt. Jun 20, 1762. Spon: John Eberth Michel and Anna Catharine.

Anna Maria of Balser (Balthasar) Noll and Anna Maria, b. ---; bapt. Jul 11, 1762. Spon: ---.

Maria Barbara of Jacob Etschberger and Esther, b. ---, ba. Dec 28, 1762. Spon: John Maercke and Barbara.

(This is the last entry of schoolmaster Baecker)

(The next two entries were made by perhaps the new schoolmaster.)

John William of Jacob Mueller and Margaret, b. Dec 3, 1764; bapt. Apr 16, 1765. Spon: William Hoster and Anna Elizabeth.

Maria Catharine of John Adam Stein and Anna Margaret, b. Dec 4, 1764; bapt. Apr 16, 1765. Spon: Adam Stein and Magdalene.

George of Balthasar Noll and Anna Maria, b. Feb 17, 1764; bapt. Mar 15, 1764. Spon: George Noll and Barbara Groo, single. (Baptism entered by Rev. Zufall.)

BAPTISMS BY REV. JOHN JACOB ZUFALL, SEP 1764-SEP 1767.

Anna Margaret of Michael Schwartz and Susanna Barbara, b. Sep 17, 1765; bapt. Oct 28, 1765. Spon: John Lora and Anna Margaret.

Child of Laurence Wolff and wife, b. ---; bapt. Dec 15, 1765. Spon: George Zoeller.

Catharine of Nicholas Moser and Catharine, b. Jun 30, 1766; bapt. Jan 31, 1766. Spon: John Rammeler and Barbara.

Henrietta Elizabeth of John Leicht, (schoolmaster pro tem), and Anna Catharine, b. Jan 27, 1766; bapt. Feb 2, 1766. Spon: John Henry Schmidt and Elizabeth Woeller.

Anna Margaret of John Hoeffelfinger and Judith, b. Jan 1, 1766; bapt. Feb 26, 1766. Spon: Adam Hartmann and Anna Margaret.

Maria Catharine of Jacob Spengler and Maria Elizabeth, b. Feb 2, 1766; bapt. Mar 8, 1766. Spon: Peter Menges and Maria Catharine.

Anna Maria of Balthasar Noll and Anna Maria, b. Apr 7, 1766; bapt. Apr 11, 1766. Spon: George Wolff and Susanna.

George of John Gelber and Catharine, b. Feb 13, 1766; bapt. Apr 13, 1766. Spon: George Gall and Elizabeth.

Anna Maria of Leonard Schwartz and Elizabeth, b. Oct 28, 1766;

bapt. Dec 14, 1766. Spon: Andrew Saltzgeber and Anna Maria.

Christian of Henry Moser and Maria Cath. Elizabeth, b. Jan 26, 1767; bapt. Jan 30, 1767. Spon: Christian Urich and Elizabeth.

Maria Elizabeth of John Roth and Barbara, b. Jan 16, 1767; bapt. Feb 8, 1767. Spon: Jacob Spengler and Maria Elizabeth.

Andrew of Valentine Schuler and Apollonia, b. Mar 22, 1767; bapt. Mar 31, 1767. Spon: Andrew Neves and wife.

Dorothy of Henry Buch and Dorothy, b. Aug 25, 1767; bapt. Aug 25, 1767. Spon: the mother.

Catharine Elizabeth of Martin Schell and Anna Catharine, b. May 8, 1767; bapt. Jun 14, 1767. Spon: Nicholas Hussecker and Catharine Elizabeth.

Barbara of Jacob Kitzmoller and Maria, b. Jul 2, 1767; bapt. Jul --, 1767. Spon: John Kitzmoller and wife.

Eva Barbara of Christian Seibert and Catharaine, b. Apr 3, 1767; bapt. Apr 27, 1767. Spon: Peter Schuetz and Eva Barbara.

Susanna of George Zoeller and Maria Barbara, b. May 24, 1767; bapt. Jun 15, 1767. Spon: Leonard Schwartz and Anna Elizabeth.

John Nicholas of Jacob Moller and Anna Margaret, b. Jun 27, 1767; bapt. Jun 28, 1767. Spon: Nicholas Moeller and Anna Maria, of Muehlbach.

Anna Maria of Michael Moeller and Margaret Elizabeth, b. Jul 8, 1767; bapt. Jul 20, 1767. Spon: Diederich Marcky and Anna Maria.

John Jacob of John Adam Stein and Maria Catharine, b. Sep 2, 1767; bapt. Sep 7, 1767. Spon: John Jacob Cattermann and Anna Margaret.

Jacob Michael of Henry Kiblinger and Sibylla, b. Aug 16, 1767; bapt. Nov 2, 1767. Spon: Michael Schwartz and Susanna.

Catharine of Isaac Meuer and Maria Catharine, b. Nov 18, 1767; bapt. Nov 18, 1767. Spon: the mother.

Maria Catharine of John Jacob Schmidt and Elizabeth, b. Dec 7, 1767; bapt. Dec 8, 1767. Spon: Maria Catharine Meuer.

Maria Elizabeth of Mathias Noll and Maria Barbara, b. Apr 22, 1767; bapt. May 6, 1767. Spon: John Weber and Eva.

Dau. of Jacob Gasser and wife, b. May 16, 1767; bapt. May 26, 1767. Spon: Henry Brey(?) and Mrs. Spengler.

Maria Catharine of Adam Stein and Maria Catharine, b. Aug 18, 1767; bapt. Sep 13, 1767. Spon: George Battorf and Maria Catharine, single. (Last entry of Mr. Zufall.)

John Peter of Peter Schell and Susanna Margaret, b. Nov 2, 1767;

bapt. Jan 16, 1768. Spon: Peter Wallmer and wife, Anna Margaret. (Entered by unknown hand.)

BAPTISMS BY REV. WILLIAM HENDEL, OCT 1769-NOV 1782

Elizabeth of Henry Moser and Elizabeth, b. Aug 22, 1769; bapt. Oct 29, 1769. Spon: Elizabeth Schutz.

Peter of William Leitner and Maria Elizabeth, b. Dec 14, 1769; bapt. Dec 25, 1769. Spon: Peter Leitner and Anna Maria.

John Jacob of Michael Hack and Sabina, b. Nov --, 1769; bapt. Dec 25, 1769. Spon: Jacob Hack and Anna Maria Kreutzer.

Child of Peter Schell and Susanna Margaret, b. --; bapt. Dec 31, 1769. Spon: Adam Schutz and ---.

Barbara of Conrad Mayer and Elizabeth, b. Jan 11, 1770; bapt. Jan 24, 1770. Spon: Barbara Ried.

Jacob of George Zeller and Maria Barbara, b. Jan 5, 1770; bapt. Jan 25, 1770. Spon: Jacob Etschberger and Esther.

George Valentine of Michael Schwartz and Susanna, b. Jan 6, 1770; bapt. Jan 25, 1770. Spon: George Lora.

Margaret Elizabeth of John Schwartz and Elizabeth, b. Jan 19, 1770; bapt. Jan 25, 1770. Spon: Christian Karstnitz and Catharine.

Jacob of Christopher Zimmerman and Elizabeth, b. Feb 14, 1770; bapt. Mar 7, 1770. Spon: Jacob Gasser and Mary Magdalene.

John George of Jacob Fehler and Eva, b. Jul 4, 1770; bapt. Jul 15, 1770. Spon: George Weiss and Barbara.

John Adam of Nicholas Seibert and Catharine, b. Jul 12, 1770; bapt. Jul 15, 1770. Spon: George Wolff.

John Michael of Christopher Reichard and wife, b. Nov 16, 1767; bapt. Aug 5, 1770. Spon: John Michael Faust.

Marian Elizabeth of William Hendel (pastor) and Elizabeth, b. Sep 2, 1770; bapt. Sep 16, 1770. Spon: Anna Maria Le Roy, (sister of Mrs. Hendel).

Anna Maria of Daniel Muller and Susanna, b. Sep 3, 1770; bapt. Sep 16, 1770. Spon: Philip Pfeffer and Anna Maria.

Michael of John Roth and Barbara, b. Oct 15, 1770; bapt. Oct 21, 1770. Spon: Michael Haack and Sabina.

John of Christian Seibert and Catharine, b. Nov 3, 1770; bapt. Dec 2, 1770. Spon: John Mercke and Barbara.

Henry of Henry Muller and Elizabeth, b. Oct 28, 1770; bapt. Dec 2, 1770. Spon: John Kiblinger and Catharine.

George of George Weiss and Barbara, b. Dec 28, 1770; bapt. Dec 29, 1770. Spon: Martin Battorf.

Peter of George Wendel Wolf and Anna Elizabeth, b. Jan 9, 1771; bapt. Feb --, 1771. Spon: Peter Schuetz and Barbara.

Catharine of Henry Leineweber and Juliana, b. Mar 30, 1771; bapt. May 5, 1771. Spon: Martin Schell and Catharine.

Jacob of Jacob Bene and Anna Maria, b. May 5, 1771; bapt. May 26, 1771. Spon: Jacob Stahlschmidt.

Anna Maria of Michael Haack and Sabina, b. Jun 9, 1771; bapt. Jul 7, 1771. Spon: Alexander Schaeffer and Angelica.

Maria Margaret of Jacob Spengler and Elizabeth, b. Jun 30, 1771; bapt. Jul 21, 1771. Spon: Jacob Gasser and Maria Margaret.

Eva Margaret of Nicholas Killmer and Elizabeth, b. Aug 17, 1771; bapt. Oct 13, 1771. Spon: Margaret Theiss.

Peter of George Zeller and Maria Barbara, b. Dec 2, 1771; bapt. Dec 25, 1771. Spon: Peter Battorf and Margaret.

Maria Barbara of Philip Nied and Hannah, b. Feb 6, 1772; bapt. Mar 1, 1772. Spon: John Mercke and Barbara.

Christine of Henry Kiblinger and Sibylla, b. Mar 20, 1772; bapt. Apr 12, 1772. Spon: Peter Berry and Margaret.

---- of John Christmann and Rosina, b. --- 10, 1772; bapt. Aug 2, 1772. Spon: Nicholas Seibert and Catharine.

George Henry of Henry Rost and Anna Maria, b. Apr 19, 1772; bapt. Aug 2, 1772. Spon: Henry Lebbo and Catharine.

Maria Barbara of John Lora and Anna Maria, b. Aug 27, 1772; bapt. Sep 13, 1772. Spon: Georg Zeller and Maria Barbara.

Jacob of William Hendel (Pastor) and Elizabeth, b. Sep 21, 1772; bapt. Sep 30, 1772. Spon: (Rev) Christopher Gobretch and wife.

Maria Catharine of Nicholas Seibert and Catharine, b. Nov 25, 1772; bapt. Dec 6, 1772. Spon: Michael Diefebach and Margaret.

Barbara of Georg Gensemer and Margaret, b. Dec 13, 1772; bapt. Dec 18, 1772. Spon: Peter Kuster and Dorothy.

Henry of Michael Haack and Sabina, b. Nov 29, 1772; bapt. Jan 1, 1773. Spon: Henry Schaffer.

John of Wendel Weber and Elizabeth, b. Dec 21, 1772; bapt. Jan 17, 1773. Spon: John Balsle.

Magdalene of Michael Diefebach and Margaret, b. Feb 14, 1773; bapt. Feb 21, 1773. Spon: John Mercke and Barbara.

Catharine of John Neumann and Elizabeth, b. Jan 17, 1773; bapt. Feb 28, 1773. Spon: Christian Noecker and Catharine.

Georg of William Neumann and Catharine, b. Jan 8, 1773; bapt. Feb 28, 1773. Spon: Georg Schiffler and Catharine.

Jonathan of Georg Wolff and Elizabeth, b. Jan 14, 1773; bapt. Mar 21, 1773. Spon: Christian Seibert and Catharine.

Maria Catharine of Jacob Diefebach and Sabina, b. Mar 8, 1773; bapt. Mar 21, 1773. Spon: Catharine Heffner.

Mary Magdalene of John Roth and Barbara, b. Apr 19, 1773; bapt. Apr --, 1773. Spon: Mary Magdalene Kreutzer.

Maria Barbara of John Albert and Barbara, b. Mar 8, 1773; bapt. May 22(?), 1773. Spon: parents.

John Adam of Jacob Gasser and Maria Margaret, b. May 12, 1773; bapt. May 30, 1773. Spon: Adam Spengler and Eva.

Christian of Christian Seibert and Catharine, b. Jun 22, 1773; bapt. Jul 18, 1773. Spon: Nicholas Seibert and Catharine.

Jacob of Jacob Schmid and Elizabeth, b. Aug 8, 1773; bapt. Aug 16, 1773. Spon: Jacob Rammler and Eva.

Catharine of Rudolph Kunsle and Catharine, b. Oct 3, 1773; bapt. Nov 7, 1773. Spon: Michael Haack and Sabina.

John Peter of ----, b. Feb 12, 1774; bapt. Mar 7, 1774. Spon: ---.

John of John Neumann and Elizabeth, b. Feb 11, 1774; bapt. Mar 27, 1774. Spon: John Roth.

John of John Roth and Barbara; bapt. Apr 4, 1774; bapt. Apr 14, 1774. Spon: John Kuster and Catharine.

Christine of Nicholas Moser and Catharine, b. Dec 17, 1773; bapt. Jan 7, 1774. Spon: Martin Wallborn and Maria.

Andrew of John Lora and Anna Maria, b. Mar 2, 1774; bapt. Apr 4, 1774. Spon: Andrew Zeller.

Magdalene of Jacob Spengler and Elizabeth, b. Jun 8, 1774; bapt. Jul 12, 1774. Spon: Adam Hoffman and Maria Barbara.

Elizabeth of Georg Wolff and Elizabeth, b. Aug 16, 1774; bapt. Aug 21, 1774. Spon: Anna Maria Thornmayer.

Abraham of William Hendel (pastor) and Elizabeth, b. Aug 18, 1774; bapt. Aug 28, 1774. Spon: Jacob Etschberger and Esther.

Christine of Henry Leineweber and Juliana, b. Jan 31, 1774; bapt. Aug 28, 1774. Spon: Henry Koppenhofer and Christine.

Catharine of Georg Nied and Catharine, b. Sep 30, 1774; bapt. Oct 23, 1774. Spon: Eva Catharine Wolff.

Eva Elizabeth of Christopher Leis and Elizabeth, b. Oct 16, 1774; bapt. Nov 6, 1774. Spon: Eva Trautmann, widow.

Peter of Nicholas Seibert and Catharine, b. Nov 26, 1774; bapt. Dec

4, 1774. Spon: Adam Schuetz and Catharine.

Maria Eva of Georg Simon and Elizabeth, b. Nov 1, 1774; bapt. Dec 4, 1774. Spon: Henry Hautz and Maria Barbara.

Christine of Georg Preis and Barbara, b. Dec 21, 1774; bapt. Dec 25, 1774. Spon: Martin Stub and Christine.

Catharine of Wendel Weber and Anna Elizabeth, b. Feb 4, 1775; bapt. Feb 26, 1775. Spon: Catharine Kobel, wife of John Kobel.

Anna Maria of Jacob Bene and Anna Maria, b. Mar 11, 1775; bapt. Apr 9, 1775. Spon: Engel Dunges and Elizabeth.

Elizabeth of John Neumann and Elizabeth, b. Apr 18, 1775; bapt. May 21, 1775. Spon: Elizabeth Koppenhoefer.

Elizabeth of Georg Ebinger and Elizabeth, b. Jul 7, 1775; bapt. Sep 10, 1775. Spon: Elizabeth Stammgast.

Maria Barbara of Martin Hoefelfinger and Anna Maria, b. Jan 10, 1776; bapt. Jan 25, 1776. Spon: Maria Barbara Rammler, dau of Jacob Rammler.

John of George Wolff and Maria Elizabeth, b. Mar 15, 1776; bapt. Apr 21, 1776. Spon: John Katermann, single.

John Henry of John Neumann and Elizabeth, b. Jun 4, 1776; bapt. Jun 30, 1776. Spon: Henry Koppenhoefer and Christine.

Christine of Wendel Weber and Elizabeth, b. Jun 15, 1776; bapt. Jul 28, 1776. Spon: Susanna Kobel.

George of William Hendel and Elisabeth, b. Jul 21, 1776; bapt. Aug 6, 1776. Spon: Christopher Gobrecht in the name of William Otterbein.

Eva of Christian Seibert and Catharine, b. Sep 10, 1776; bapt. Oct 6, 1776. Spon: Francis Seibert and Eva.

Gottlieb of Rudolph Kintzle and Catharine, b. Sep 13, 1776; bapt. Oct 25, 1776. Spon: Nicholas Moser and Catharine.

Maria Catharine of Jonas Fortne and Regina, b. Sep 6, 1776; bapt. Dec 1, 1776. Spon: Elizabeth Schmid.

William of Nicholas Seibert and Catharine, b. Feb 14, 1776; bapt. Dec 26, 1776. Spon: William Seibert.

Jacob of Jacob Spengler and Maria Elizabeth, b. Nov 28, 1776; bapt. Jan 1, 1777. Spon: Peter Spengler.

Anna Maria of William Neumann and Catharine, b. Dec 24, 1776; bapt. Feb 12, 1777. Spon: Elizabeth Neumann, wife of John Neumann.

John of John Riegel and Elizabeth, b. Jan 30, 1777; bapt. Feb 23, 1777. Spon: John Lora and Anna Maria.

David of Michael Diefebach and Margaret, b. Mar 18, 1777; bapt. Mar 23, 1777. Spon: Peter Diefebach.

Anna Maria of Georg Simon and Elizabeth, b. Feb 10, 1777; bapt. Mar 23, 1777. Spon: Anna Maria Hautz.

Elizabeth of Georg von Nied and Catharine, b. Apr 16, 1777; bapt. May 18, 1777. Spon: Maria Wolf.

Christine Elizabeth of John Schwartz and Elizabeth, b. Jun 28, 1777; bapt. Jun 29, 1777. Spon: William Hoster and Elizabeth.

Catharine of Christian Leis and Maria Elizabeth, b. Jun 13, 1777; bapt. Jul 13, 1777. Spon: John Adam Christ and Catharine.

John Georg of Georg Wolff and Elizabeth, b. Oct 10, 1777; bapt. Nov 28, 1777. Spon: Georg von Nied and Catharine.

John of Georg Wendel Wollf and Anna Elizabeth, b. Jul 17, 1777; bapt. Aug 10, 1777. Spon: Frederick Ried and Maria Angelica.

John Henry of Henry Battorf and Sophia, b. Sep 6, 1777; bapt. Sep 12, 1777. Spon: Leonard Schwartz and Elizabeth.

Michael of Thomas Schmid and Christine, b. Sep 7, 1777; bapt. Oct 5, 1777. Spon: Michael Schmid and Susanna.

Maria Barbara of Martin von Nied and Maria Barbara, b. Oct 7, 1777; bapt. Oct 19, 1777. Spon: Elizabeth Decker, single.

Isaac Mayer of John Reily and Elizabeth, b. ---; bapt. ---, 1777. Spon: Catharine Mayer.

John Henry of Thomas Basler and Elizabeth, b. Oct ---, 1777; bapt. Dec 11, 1777. Spon: Henry Brill and Anna Maria.

John of Henry Brill and Anna Maria, b. Sep 25, 1777; bapt. Dec 11, 1777. Spon: Thomas Basler and Elizabeth.

John of John Lein and Catharine, b. Nov 24, 1777; bapt. Dec 14, 1777. Spon: John Adam Schutz and Catharine.

Elizabeth of Adam Spengler and Eva, b. Oct 20, 1777; bapt. Feb 22, 1778. Spon: Jacob Gasser and Maria Margaret.

Barbara of Jacob Bene and Anna Maria, b. Jan 14, 1778; bapt. Mar 22, 1778. Spon: Barbara Weber.

Anna Barbara of Henry Kiblinger and Sibylla, b. Mar 15, 1778; bapt. Apr 5, 1778. Spon: Martin von Nied and Maria Barbara.

Barbara of Michael Schwartz and Susanna, b. Apr 21, 1778; bapt. May 24, 1778. Spon: Nicholas Gillmer and Elizabeth.

John of John Aurand and Maria Elizabeth, b. Jul 5, 1778; bapt. Aug 2, 1778. Spon: Georg Lochner and M. Elizabeth.

Elizabeth of Nicholas Moser and Catharine, b. Jul 20, 1778, b. Aug 14, 1778. Spon: Elizabeth Urich, widow.

Maria Sibylla of William Hendel and Elizabeth, b. Sep 25, 1778; bapt. Sep 27, 1778. Spon: Anna Maria Le Roy.

Margaret of Adam Schleich and wife, b. Oct 11, 1778; bapt. Oct 25, 1778. Spon: Michael Diefebach and Margaret.

Child of Henry Battorf and Sophia, b. ---; bapt. Oct 25, 1778. Spon: Ludwig Schwartz.

John of Leonard Noll and Margaret, b. Sep 29, 1778; bapt. Nov 8, 1778. Spon: John Noll and Maria Elizabeth.

Conrad of Conrad Hoster and Maria Elizabeth Schwartz, b. Feb 12, 1779; bapt. Feb 25, 1779. Spon: John Schwartz and wife.

Child of Adam Spengler and wife, b. ---; bapt. Mar 5, 1779. Spon: Henry Brill and Anna Maria.

Child of Jacob Bene and Anna Maria, b. Feb 8, 1779; bapt. Mar 14, 1779. Spon: Elizabeth Schmid, single.

John of John Lora and A. Maria, b. Jan 31, 1779; bapt. Mar 17, 1779. Spon: John Katermann and Marg. Elizabeth.

Henry of Georg Simon and Elizabeth, b. Feb 23, 1779; bapt. Apr 5, 1779. Spon: Henry Brill and Anna Maria.

John Jacob of Rudolph Kuntzle and Catharine, b. Feb 25, 1779; bapt. Apr 5, 1779. Spon: Daniel Koenig and Anna.

Christian of Georg Wendel Wolf and A. Elizabeth, b. Apr 1, 1779; bapt. Apr 25, 1779. Spon: Michael Ried and Catharine.

John Adam of Jacob Diefebach and Sabina, b. ---; bapt. Apr 25, 1779. Spon: John Adam Schuetz and Catharine.

Maria Barbara of Georg Zeller and Maria Barbara, b. Apr 7, 1779; bapt. May 9, 1779. Spon: Jacob Katermann and Anna Catharine.

Elizabeth of John Lein and Catharine, b. May 24, 1779; bapt. Jul 4, 1779. Spon: Christopher Leis and M. Elizabeth.

Georg of Francis Stahlschmid and Barbara, b. Jun 9, 1779; bapt. Jul 18, 1779. Spon: Georg Simon and Elizabeth.

Anna Catharine of Francis Zeller and Elizabeth, b. Aug 22, 1779; bapt. Sep 26, 1779. Spon: John Zeller and Catharine.

Margaret of Georg von Nied and Catharine, b. Feb 15, 1779; bapt. Oct 10, 1779. Spon: Margaret Lechner, single.

Catharine of Andrew Zeller and Maria Catharine, b. Nov 23, 1779; bapt. Dec 26, 1779. Spon: Georg Forrer and Catharine.

Eva Barbara of Wendel Weber and Elizabeth, b. Nov 6, 1779; bapt. Dec 26, 1779. Spon: Barbara Rammler, wife of John Rammler.

Child of Henry Brill and Anna Maria, b. Nov 11, 1779; bapt. Dec 30, 1779. Spon: Valentine Mueller and wife.

Child of --- German and wife, b. ---; bapt. Feb 13, 1780. Spon: Jacob Gasser and wife.

Catharine Christine of Jacob Spengler and Elizabeth, b. Jan 8, 1780; bapt. Feb 28, 1780. Spon: John Noecker and Catharine.

Elizabeth of Georg Weyl and Catharine, b. Feb 18, 1780; bapt. Apr 23, 1780. Spon: Nicholas Gillmer and Elizabeth.

Joseph of Jack Gibbs and Bruh, both slaves of A. Schutz, b. Apr 3, 1780; bapt. May 9, 1780. Spon: William Juengst and Catharine.

Elizabeth of Christopher Leis and Elizabeth, b. May 11, 1780; bapt. Jul 3, 1780. Spon: Catharine Leis.

Elizabeth of Jacob Aurand and Anna Maria, b. Jun 2, 1780; bapt. Aug 13, 1780. Spon: Leonard Schwartz and Elizabeth.

Maria Catharine of Nicholas Haack and Catharine, b. Aug 22, 1780; bapt. Sep 13, 1780. Spon: Catharine Ruth, wife of Michael Ruth.

Anna Elizabeth of Nicholas Gillmer and Elizabeth, b. Sep 5, 1780; bapt. Oct 31, 1780. Spon: Anna Eliz. Lauer, widow.

Child of Daniel Graff and Margaret, b. ---; bapt. ---, 1780. Spon: Michael Ruth and Catharine.

Maria Salome of William Hendel and Elizabeth, b. Jan 6, 1781; bapt. Jan 11, 1781. Spon: Leonard Schwartz and Elizabeth.

M. Magdalene of Adam Schleich and Magdalene, b. Mar 12, 1781; bapt. Mar 25, 1781. Spon: Michael Diefenbach and Margaret.

Susanna of Martin von Nied and Maria Barbara, b. Aug 28, 1780; bapt. Apr 5, 1781. Spon: Albert Heu and Susanna.

Elizabeth of Henry Fortine and Margaret, b. Feb 25, 1781; bapt. Jul 28, 1781. Spon: Elizabeth Schmid, single.

John of Andrew Zeller and Catharine, b. Jul 14, 1781; bapt. Jul 29, 1781. Spon: John Katermann and Margr. Elizabeth.

John Jacob of John Jacob Decker and Eva Barbara, b. Aug 23, 1781; bapt. Sep 22, 1781. Spon: Carl Decker, single.

John George of John Noll, Jr. and Catharine, b. Sep 1, 1781; bapt. Sep 22, 1781. Spon: John George Neff and Elizabeth.

John George of George Simon and Elizabeth, b. Jun 1, 1781; bapt. Jul ---, 1781. Spon: Nicholas Moser and wife.

Henry of Wendel Weber and Elizabeth, b. May 29, 1781; bapt. Jun ---, 1781. Spon: Martin Heffelginger and A. Maria.

Anna Catharine of Christian Heckendorn and Veronica, b. Mar 23, 1782; bapt. Apr 21, 1782. Spon: Rudolph Kunsle and Catharine.

Benjamin of Francis Zeller and Elizabeth, b. Aug 1, 1782; bapt. Aug 25, 1782. Spon: Christian Lauer, Jr. and Christine.

John of Jacob Aurand and Anna Maria, b. Oct 15, 1782; bapt. Oct 20, 1782. Spon: Philip Mayer and Catharine.

Christian of Rudolph Kunsele and Catharine, b. Aug 23, 1782; bapt. Oct 20, 1782. Spon: Christian Heckendorn and Veronica.

Christian of Wendel Weber and Elizabeth, b. Sep 17, 1782; bapt. Nov 3, 1782. Spon: John Kayser and Susanna.

(Entries by unknown hand.)

Christine of Christopher Leiss and Maria Elizabeth, b. Apr 6, 1783; bapt. Apr 27, 1783. Spon: Henry Koppenhoefer and Christine.

Eva Maria of Francis Stahlschmid and Barbara, b. Apr 6, 1783; bapt. Apr 27, 1783. Spon: Eva Stahlschmid.

Maria Sarah of Philip Staut and Margaret, b. Oct 5, 1783; bapt. Nov 9, 1783. Spon: Martin Walborn and Maria.

BAPTISMS BY REV. ANDREW LORETZ, JAN 1785-FEB 1786

Andrew of Henry Brill and Anna Maria Bickel, b. ---; bapt. Jan 18, 1785. Spon: Andrew Loretz, Jr. born at Chur.

Elizabeth of Thomas Basler and Elizabeth Schmal; bapt. Feb 10, 1785. Spon: Elizabeth Basler.

Margaret of Peter Bene and Anna Maria Thiel, b. Feb 7, 1785; bapt. Mar 26, 1785. Spon: Francis Ruthi and Elizabeth.

Andrew of Henry Brill and Anna Maria Bickel, b. Feb 7, 1785; bapt. Feb 18, 1785. Spon: Andrew Loretz from Chur in Buenden.

John Michael of Arnold Hebelmann and Eva Susanna, b. Mar 9, 1785; bapt. Apr 23, 1785. Spon: Michael Haag and Sabina Schaefer.

Elizabeth of Francis Stahlschmid and Barbara Weber, b. Feb 21, 1785; bapt. Apr 24, 1785. Spon: ---.

Elizabeth of Benjamin Tiefenbach and wife, b. Apr 18, 1785; bapt. May 15, 1785. Spon: Michael Tiefenbach and Maria Margaret.

Maria Catharine of Martin Spengler and Christine Riegel, b. ---; bapt. May 15, 1785. Spon: Georg Spengler and Barbara Spengler.

Elizabeth of Christian Seibert and Catharine Hollstein, b. Apr 22, 1785; bapt. May 15, 1785. Spon: Georg Wendel Wald and wife.

John Philip of John Noll and Catharine Noll; bapt. Oct 9, 1785. Spon: Philip Noll and Magdalene Noll.

Margaret of John Weyer and Catharine Haen, bapt. Nov 10, 1785. Spon: ---.

Barbara of Nicholas Haag and Catharine Rudi, bapt. Nov 20, 1785. Spon: Barbara Rudi.

Child of Michael Haag and wife, bapt. Nov 21, 1785. Spon: ---.

Margaret of Peter Behne and Anna Maria Thiel, b. Feb 7, 1785; bapt. Mar 26, 1785. Spon: Hieronymus Ruthi and Elizabeth.

Peter of Peter Weyrich and Maria Weyrich, b. Mar 8, 1785; bapt. Sep 11, 1785. Spon: ---.

John Jacob of Henry Strack and Anna Rosina, b. Nov 15, 1785; bapt. Feb 12, 1786. Spon: Henry Huebschman and Catharine Huebschman.

Henry of John Nicholas Banner and Maria Margaret, b. Oct 28, 1785; bapt. Feb 12, 1786. Spon: Frederick Staeger and Elizabeth.

Salome of Elizabeth Foessler, b. Jan 18, 1786; bapt. Feb 14, 1786. Spon: Salome Radmann.

John of John Zehring and Maria Barbara, b. Oct 30, 1785; bapt. Feb 16, 1786. Spon: Christopher Moench and Maria Sarah Moench.

John of Andrew Zeller and Catharine, b. Nov 14, 1785; bapt. Dec 13, 1785. Spon: John Georg Zeller and Barbara. (This is the last entry of Mr. Loretz.)

BAPTISMS BY REV. DANIEL WAGNER, JAN 1787-SEP 1793

Ann Maria of Henry Fortne and Margaret, b. Jul 11, 1786; bapt. Jan 27, 1787. Spon: Ann Maria Schmitt.

Maria Catharine of Henry Achy and Margaret, b. Dec 22, 1786; bapt. Jan 28, 1787. Spon: Maria Catharine Spengler.

Maria Elizabeth of Christian Lutz and Eva, b. Jan 11, 1787; bapt. Jan 28, 1787. Spon: Elizabeth Stahlschmid.

John Peter of John Peter Diefenbach and Magdalene, b. Jan 30, 1787; bapt. Feb 11, 1787. Spon: Nicholas Seibert and Catharine.

Anna Susanna of John Reily and Elizabeth, b. Dec 17, 1786; bapt. Jan 22, 1787. Spon: Frederick Bolman and Susanna.

Christopher of Peter Behn and Anna Maria, b. Jan 29, 1787; bapt. Feb 11, 1787. Spon: Christopher Loser.

John of Michael Spengler and Mary Magdalene, b. Dec 21, 1786; bapt. Feb 11, 1787. Spon: John Gasser and Maria Margaret.

John of John Gasser and Margaret, b. --- 27, 1787; bapt. 4 weeks later. Spon: Christian Leyn.

Elizabeth of Christian Hoster and Catharine, b. --- 27, 1787; bapt. Apr 9, 1787. Spon: Elizabeth Hoster.

Child of James Basford and Susanna, b. --- 6, --; bapt. Apr ---, 1787. Spon: Peter Radenbach and Catharine.

Elizabeth of Georg Schmitt and Elizabeth, b. Jan 16, 1787; bapt. Apr 22, 1787. Spon: Catharine Schmitt.

Eva Elizabeth of Peter Forn and Catharine, b. Apr 5, 1787; bapt. May 4, 1787. Spon: Christian Lutz and Eva Elizabeth.

Catharine of Adam Fuehman and Susanna, b. Apr 17, 1787; bapt. May 27, 1787. Spon: parents.

Jonathan of Michael Schmitt and Susanna, b. Apr 30, 1787; bapt. May 27, 1787. Spon: Thomas Schmitt and Christine.

Francis Stahlschmit and Barbara, b. May 1, 1787; bapt. Jun 10, 1787. Spon: Adam Schuetz and Catharine.

John Jacob of Georg Roth and Anna Maria, b. Jun 21, 1787; bapt. Jul 15, 1787. Spon: John Jacob Gasser.

Elizabeth of Martin Spengler and Christine, b. Aug 22, 1787; bapt. Oct 7, 1787. Spon: Elizabeth Ried.

John of Peter Etschberger and Elizabeth, b. Sep 27, 1787; bapt. Nov 4, 1787. Spon: Jacob Etschberger and Esther.

Catharine of Micahel Haack and Magdalene, b. Feb 27, 1788; bapt. Mar 8, 1788. Spon: Catharine Rammler.

John of Christian Hoster and Catharine, b. May 24, 1788; bapt. Jul 15, 1788. Spon: William Hoster.

Maria of Francis Zeller and Elizabeth, b. Jun 8, 1788; bapt. Jul 13, 1788. Spon: Margaret Lechner.

Elizabeth of John Adam Schuetz and Susanna, b. Jun 27, 1788; bapt. Jul 13, 1788. Spon: Elizabeth Fischbach.

Catharine Barbara of John Grill and Barbara, b. May 22, 1788; bapt. Jul 27, 1788. Spon: Catharine Rammler.

Peter of John Schwalm and Margaret, b. Jul 10, 1788; bapt. (Aug) 10, 1788. Spon: Peter Battorf and Maria.

Elizabeth of Conrad Spillman and Dorothy, b. Jul 29, 1788; bapt. Sep 21, 1788. Spon: Elizabeth Thrumbach (?).

Maria Elizabeth of John Gasser and Maria Margaret, b. Sep 2, 1788; bapt. Oct 5, 1788. Spon: Elizabeth Spengler.

Maria Elizabeth of Georg Roth and Maria Barbara, b. Sep 7, 1788; bapt. Oct 5, 1788. Spon: Elizabeth Bollman.

Ann Catharine of John Mohr and Elizabeth, b. Jul 7, 1788; bapt. Aug 17, 1788. Spon: John Bollman and Catharine.

Maria of Peter Diefenbach and Catharine, b. Sep 7, 1788; bapt. Oct 19, 1788. Spon: John Bateman and Catharine.

Eva Elizabeth of Christian Lutz and Eva Elizabeth, b. Sep 20, 1788; bapt. Oct 18, 1788. Spon: Francis Stahlschmid and Barbara.

Peter of Jacob Decker and Barbara, b. Oct 2, 1788; bapt. Oct 19, 1788. Spon: Valentine Urich and Susanna.

Susanna of Dietrich Griess and Magdalene, b. Sep 22, 1788; bapt. Oct 23, 1788. Spon: parents.

Michael of Andrew Zeller and Catharine, b. Aug 27, 1788; bapt. Oct 9, 1788. Spon: Michael Forney and Catharine.

Maria Margaret of Nicholas Moser and Margaret, b. Oct 12, 1788; bapt. Jan 15, 1789. Spon: Valentine Urich and Susanna.

John Michael of John Noll and Catharine, b. Jan 18, 1789; bapt. Feb 8, 1789. Spon: John Bollman and Anna Maria.

John of Peter Derst and Elizabeth, b. Mar 1, 1789; bapt. Apr 9, 1789. Spon: Catharine Grusius.

John Jacob of Conrad Widders and Susanna, b. Mar 14, 1789; bapt. Apr 13, 1789. Spon: Jacob Kuellinger.

Barbara of George Weyrich and Margaret, b. May 3, 1789; bapt. May --, 1789. Spon: Barbara Kilmer.

John of Peter Spengler and Maria, b. Apr 28, 1789; bapt. Jun 14, 1789. Spon: Erhard Thurmwaechter and Catharine.

Susanna of Georg Schmitt and Elizabeth, b. Jun 21, 1789; bapt. Sep 6, 1789. Spon: Eliz. Thurmwaechter.

Elizabeth of Christian Riehm and Catharine, b. Dec 24, 1788; bapt. Sep 6, 1789. Spon: Elizabeth Spengler.

John of Martin Spengler and Christine, b. Sep 29, 1789; bapt. Nov 15, 1789. Spon: Daniel Ried.

Elizabeth of Philip Noll and Magdalene, b. Oct 27; bapt. Nov 15, 1789. Spon: M. Elizabeth Noll.

Anna Maria of Georg Riehm and Catharine, b. Oct 7, 1789; bapt. Nov 15, 1789. Spon: Anna Maria Lutzinger.

John Michael of Adam Boeshahr and Margaret, b. Nov 19, 1789; bapt. Dec 26, 1789. Spon: John Michael Nusshaack and Anna Maria.

John Jacob of Adam Schuetz and Susanna, b. Sep 8, 1789; bapt. Oct 4, 1789. Spon: John Jacob Scheutz.

Catharine of Jacob Decker and Barbara, b. Mar 16, 1790; bapt. Apr 3, 1790. Spon: Catharine Zehring.

Michael of Jacob Decker and Barbara, b. Aug 23, 1786; bapt. soon afterwards. Spon: John Urich and Elizabeth.

John of David Theiss and Barbara, b. Apr 9, 1790; bapt. May 23, 1790. Spon: Thomas Kopenhefer and Catharine.

Maria of Peter Etschberger and Elizabeth, b. Aug 17, 1790; bapt. Sep 5, 1790. Spon: Jacob --- and Maria.

John Peter of Peter Spengler and Maria, b. Oct 5, 1790; bapt. Oct 21, 1790. Spon: Nicholas Seibert and Catharine.

Anna Maria of Christian Lutz and Eva, b. Sep 5, 1790; bapt. Oct 31, 1790. Spon: John Adam Leiss and Magdalene.

John Adam of John Zeller and Elizabeth, b. Nov 17, 1789; bapt. Mar 7, 1790. Spon: Georg Zeller and Elizabeth.

Maria Eva of Valentine Miller and Christine, b. Dec 11, 1789; bapt. Jan 20, 1790. Spon: Maria Eva Miller.

Elizabeth of Daniel Wagner (pastor) and Maria, b. Mar 4, 1790; bapt. Apr 4. Spon: William Leimeister and Elizabeth.

Georg Michael of Michael Noll and Magdalene, b. Feb 13, 1791; bapt. Mar 7, 1791. Spon: Georg Noll.

John of Christian Riehm and Catharine, b. Dec 24, 1790; bapt. Feb 6, 1791. Spon: Frederick Steiner and Elizabeth.

Michael of Nicholas Haack and Catharine, b. Mar 9, 1791; bapt. Apr 17, 1791. Spon: Michael Dieffenbach and Margaret.

Maria Salome of Daniel Mayer and Christine, b. Dec 11, 1790; bapt. May 1, 1791. Spon: Jacob Schoenfelder and Catharine.

Maria of Jacob Steiner and Catharine, b. Feb --, 1791; bapt. May 1, 1791. Spon: Eva Kapp.

Catharine (?) of William Arnold and Anna Maria, b. May 1, 1791; bapt. Jun 13, 1791. Spon: Catharine Christman.

John of Dieter Griess and Mary Magdalene, b. Feb 27, 1791; bapt. soon afterwards. Spon: parents.

Jacob of John Scharf and Anna Maria, b. Jul 8, 1790; bapt. Sep 4, 1791. Spon: Thomas Fister.

Christian of Christian Hoster and Catharine, b. Aug 28, 1791; bapt. Sep 18, 1791. Spon: Christian Seiler and Elizabeth.

John Daniel of John Schwalm and Ottilia, b. Aug 24, 1791; bapt. Oct 2, 1791. Spon: Daniel Boby and Salome.

Maria Catharine of Peter Lein and Catharine, b. Sep 4, 1791; bapt. Oct 30, 1791. Spon: Maria Cath. Seibert.

Margaret Elizabeth of Christian Seibert and Catharine, b. Sep 29, 1791; bapt. Oct 30, 1791. Spon: Francis Seibert and Eva.

Maria Elizabeth of William Hoster and Catharine, b. Dec 1, 1791; bapt. Dec 10, 1791. Spon: Philip Braun and Maria Elizabeth.

Anna Maria of Adam Leiss and Magdalene, b. Oct 21, 1791; bapt. Nov 27, 1791. Spon: Michael Kei(ser?) and Ca(tharine).

John of Jacob Blecher and Margaret, b. Oct 29, 1791; bapt. Dec 5, 1791. Spon: Christian Noe(cker) and wife.

John of John Adam Schuetz and Susanna, b. Jan 17, 1792; bapt. Feb 18, 1792. Spon: John Lein and Catharine.

Maria Barbara of John Zeller and Elizabeth, b. Jan 9, 1792; bapt. Feb 12, 1792. Spon: Georg Zeller and Barbara.

Lydia of Martin Spengler and Christine, b. Jan 28, 1792; bapt. Mar 9, 1792. Spon: Leonard Rammler and Anna Maria.

Catharine of John Mayer and Catharine, b. Feb 17, 1792; bapt. Mar 23, 1792. Spon: James Woods and Catharine.

Susanna Maria of Jacob Decker and Barbara, b. Apr 17, 1792; bapt. May 13, 1792. Spon: Henry Zehring and Susanna.

Maria Catharine of Peter Zeller and Catharine, b. May 7, 1792; bapt. Jun 19, 1792. Spon: Catharine Noll.

Daniel of Francis Zeller and Elizabeth, b. May 27, 1792; bapt. Jun 29, 1792. Spon: Daniel Wagner (pastor) and Anna Maria.

John of John Heffelfaenger and Christine, b. Jun 14, 1792; bapt. Jul 22, 1792. Spon: Martin Heffelfaenger.

John of Jacob Christman and Catharine, b. Jun 17, 1792; bapt. Jul 28, 1792. Spon: John Matthias Gast and Margaret.

Sarah of James McDarmet and Elizabeth, b. --- 11, 1792; bapt. Jul 28, 1792. Spon: Jacob Christman and Catharine.

Child of Peter Spengler and Anna Maria, b. Feb 2, 1792; bapt. Aug 1, 1792. Spon: Georg Spengler and Barbara.

Child of Daniel Mayer and Christine, b. ---; bapt. Oct 28, 1792. Spon: Eva Mayer.

Maria of Henry Achy and Elizabeth, b. Aug 14, 1792; bapt. Sep 21, 1792. Spon: Philip Philbert and Ann Maria.

John of Peter Heffelfaenger and Margaret, b. Oct 13, 1792; bapt. Dec 19, 1792. Spon: Martin Heffelfaenger.

Eva Catharine of William Hoster and Mary Catharine, b. Feb 2, 1793; bapt. Feb 19, 1793. Spon: Maria Eva Mauntz.

Magdalene of John Lein and Catharine, b. Feb 9, 1793; bapt. Mar 13, 1793. Spon: Peter Schlessman and Elizabeth.

John Jacob of Valentine Mayer and Catharine, b. Jan 4, 1793; bapt. Mar 29, 1793. Spon: John Jacob Mayer.

Sarah (?) of John Gasser and Mary Margaret, b. ---; bapt. Mar 20, 1793. Spon: Georg --- and Elizabeth.

Ann Margaret of Christian Riehm and Catharine, b. Mar 3, 1793; bapt. May 20, 1793. Spon: John Adam Pracht and Margaret.

Susanna of Michael Schmitt and Susan, b. Mar 15, 1793; bapt. May 21, 1793. Spon: William Hoster and Catharine.

John of Jacob Steiner and Catharine, b. Apr 4, 1793; bapt. Jun 23, 1793. Spon: John Berckner and Magdalene.

Maria Elizabeth of Michael Noll and Magdalene, b. May 27, 1793; bapt. Jun 23, 1793. Spon: Maria Elizabeth Noll.

Esther of Peter Diefenbach and Catharine, b. Jun 20, 1793; bapt. Aug 4, 1793. Spon: Peter Etschberger and Elizabeth.

William of Nicholas Haack and Catharine, b. Jun 21, 1793; bapt. Sep 28, 1793. Spon: Michael Moser and Margaret.

BAPTISMS BY REV. WILLIAM HENDEL, JR., NOV 1793-DEC 1794

William of John Mayer and Catharine, b. Oct 30, 1793; bapt. Nov 21, 1793. Spon: William Hiester and Maria.

Child of Georg Schwartz and Eva Rosina, b. Oct 25, 1793; bapt. Nov 24, 1793. Spon: Margaret Schwartz.

Joseph of Daniel Greff and Margaret, b. Oct 31, 1793; bapt. Dec 17, 1793. Spon: parents.

Michael of Georg Weyrich and Anna Margaret, b. Oct 15, 1793; bapt. Dec 22, 1793. Spon: Michael Moser and Margaret.

Maria Christine of John Christman and Catharine, b. Sep 14, 1793; bapt. Dec 25, 1793. Spon: John Georg Roth and Maria.

Catharine of Georg Riehm and Catharine, b. Nov 3, 1793; bapt. Dec 25, 1793. Spon: Christian Riehm and Catharine.

Georg Jacob of William Arnoldt and Magdalene, b. Dec 15, 1793; bapt. Dec 29, 1793. Spon: Georg Robolt and Magdalene.

Eva Rosina of Adam Leiss and Magdalene, b. Dec 26, 1793; bapt. Feb 6, 1794. Spon: Georg Schwartz and Eva Rosina.

Christian of Jacob Decker and Eva Barbara, b. Jan 30, 1794; bapt. Feb 8, 1794. Spon: Henry Zehring and Susan Maria.

Elizabeth of Michael Moser and Margaret, b. Feb 1, 1794; bapt. Mar 7, 1794. Spon: David Theis and Barbara.

John Georg of Georg Ferly and Susan, b. Apr 11, 1794; bapt. May 11, 1794. Spon: Henry Schaeffer and Margaret.

Maria Elizabeth of Peter Spengler and Maria, b. Mar 28, 1794; bapt. May 11, 1794. Spon: Elizabeth Spengler.

David of David Kilmer and Barbara, b. May 12, 1794; bapt. Jun 22, 1794. Spon: Jonathan Kilmer.

Elizabeth of Peter Lein and Catharine, b. Mar 18, 1794; bapt. Jul 6, 1794. Spon: Matthew Gast and Margaret.

Maria Elizabeth of Georg Zeller and Maria Elizabeth, b. Jul 5, 1794; bapt. Aug 3, 1794. Spon: Abraham Bayer and Barbara.

Elizabeth of Valentine Mayer and Catharine, b. Jun 14, 1794; bapt. Aug 30, 1794. Spon: Elizabeth Mayer.

Valentine of Francis Zeller and Elizabeth, b. Aug 1, 1794; bapt. Sep 14, 1794. Spon: Valentine Seiler and Margaret.

Luther of John Reyley and Elizabeth, b. ---; bapt. Oct 3, 1794. Spon: Doctor Luther and Eva.

William of Christian Seibert and Catharine, b. Sep 14, 1794; bapt. Oct 5, 1794. Spon: Francis Seibert and Eva.

Ludwig of Benjamin Diefenbach and Charlotte, b. Sep 3, 1794; bapt. Oct 9, 1794. Spon: John Mercky and Elizabeth.

John of Simon Bassler and Catharine, b. Sep 16, 1794; bapt. Oct 16, 1794. Spon: John Bassler.

Anna Maria of John Jacob Zeller and Christine, b. Sep 27, 1794; bapt. Nov 6, 1794. Spon: Ann Maria Bucher.

Elizabeth of John Georg Wengert and Catharine, b. Jul 15, 1794; bapt. Nov 9, 1794. Spon: Jacob Weiser and Maria Elizabeth.

Sarah of Thomas Butler and Isabel, b. Nov 10, 1794; bapt. Nov 19, 1794. Spon: parents.

John Peter of Peter Etschberger and Elizabeth, b. Nov 4, 1794; bapt. Nov 23, 1794. Spon: Peter Spycker and Catharine.

Benjamin of John Zeller and Elizabeth, b. Nov 7, 1794; bapt. Dec 15, 1794. Spon: John Jacob Zeller and Christine.

John Jacob of Peter Derscht and Elizabeth, b. Jul 12, 1794; bapt. Dec 14, 1794. Spon: parents.

John Georg of Georg Heyd and Magdalene, b. Oct 1, 1794; bapt. Dec 25, 1794. Spon: John Georg Rullman and Magdalene.

Christian of Christian Riehm and Catharine, b. Oct 20, 1794; bapt. Dec 25, 1794. Spon: John Spengler and Magdalene.

Salome of Daniel Mayer and Christine, b. Feb 10, 1795; bapt. Feb 16, 1795. Spon: Magdalene Mayer.

Sarah of Georg Schwartz and Eva Rosina, b. Dec 5, 1794; bapt. Jan 18, 1795. Spon: Adam Leiss and Magdalene.

Eva Barbara of Jacob Decker and Catharine, b. Jan 21, 1795; bapt. Feb 1, 1795. Spon: Margaret Zehring.

Maria Catharine of J. Adam Schuetz, Jr. and Susanna, b. Jan 8, 1795; bapt. Feb 12, 1795. Spon: John Adam Schuetz, Sr. and A. Mar. Catharine.

Mary Anne of William Carr and Rachel, b. Jan 27, 1795; bapt. ---.

Spon: parents.

Samuel of John Saltzer and Catharine, b. Jun 14, 1795; bapt. Jul 26, 1795. Spon: Valentine Seiler and Catharine.

Anna Margaret of Andrew Zeller and Catharine, b. Feb 14, 1795; bapt. Mar 1, 1795. Spon: Jacob Kienser and Barbara.

Anna Maria of John Eckart and Catharine, b. Feb 20, 1795; bapt. Mar 22, 1795. Spon: Elizabeth Eckart.

David of Peter Eckert and Susanna, b. Mar 18, 1795; bapt. Apr 5, 1795. Spon: Georg Eckert.

Henry of George Stettler and Christine, b. Dec 12, 1794; bapt. Apr 11, 1795. Spon: Henry Stettler.

George of John van der Schleuss and Catharine, b. Nov 11, 1794; bapt. May 10, 1795. Spon: parents.

David of John Meuhut and Sarah, b. Feb 29, 1795; bapt. May 10, 1795. Spon: parents.

Catharine of Martin Batteiger and Catharine, b. May 10, 1795; bapt. May 18, 1795. Spon: Eva Bickel.

Catharine of Doctor J. Luther and Eva, b. May 16, 1795; bapt. May 24, 1795. Spon: Catharine Mayer.

Eva of John Scherff and Anna Maria, b. Jul 16, 1794; bapt. May 24, 1795. Spon: Elizabeth Hendel.

John of Georg Loescher and Catharine, b. Jun 18, 1795; bapt. Jun 19, 1795. Spon: John Philip Loescher and Elizabeth.

Sarah of John --- and Florey, b. May 20, 1795; bapt. Jun 21, 1795. Spon: Sibylla ---.

Anna Maria of Jonathan Mueller and Catharine, b. Jul 24, 1795; bapt. Aug 16, 1795. Spon: Magdalene Flick and He.

Maria Elizabeth of Adam Dock and Catharine, b. Aug 18, 1795; bapt. Sep 13, 1795. Spon: Philip Weber and Maria Elizabeth.

Maria Elizabeth of Frederick Mueller and Catharine, b. Aug 18, 1795; bapt. Sep 20, 1795. Spon: --- Kunckel and Catharine.

William of Francis Riddle and Phoebe, b. Sep 20, 1795; bapt. Sep 26, 1795. Spon: parents.

Jonas of Valentine Mueller, Jr. and Christine, b. Aug 16, 1795; bapt. Oct 9, 1795. Spon: Valentine Mueller, Sr. and Eva.

Henry of Conrad Christ and Elizabeth, b. Sep 30, 1795; bapt. Oct 7, 1795. Spon: Henry Rieth and Elizabeth.

Jonathan of Jonathan Zerbe and Margaret, b. May 31, 1795; bapt. Oct 11, 1795. Spon: Benjamin Weiser.

Christine of John Adam Leiss and Magdalene, b. Sep 6, 1795; bapt.

Oct 25, 1795. Spon: Henry Koppenheber and Christine.

Maria of Thomas Kirkpatrick and Maria, b. Sep 19, 1795; bapt. Oct 28, 1795. Spon: parents.

George Henry of Michael Noll and Magdalene, b. Sep 27, 1795; bapt. Nov 8, 1795. Spon: Wendel Wolff and Anna Elizabeth.

Philip of John Mayer and Catharine, b. Oct 31, 1795; bapt. Nov 7, 1795. Spon: Philip Han and Margaret.

Anna Catharine of John Whagner and Margaret, b. Oct 28, 1795; bapt. Nov 11, 1795. Spon: Catharine Wagner.

Michael of David Theis and Barbara, b. Nov 12, 1795; bapt. Dec 17, 1795. Spon: Michael Theis and Elizabeth.

Susanna of Adam Gasser and Catharine, b. Apr 27, 1795; bapt. ---. Spon: Frederick Bollman and Susanna.

Catharine of Adam Dinius and Catharine, b. Oct 17, 1795; bapt. Nov 24, 1795. Spon: John Schiffler and Catharine.

John Henry of Georg Schwartz and Eva Rosina, b. Dec 28, 1795; bapt. Feb 13, 1796. Spon: Henry Knox and Catharine.

John Jacob of Jacob Blecher and Maria Margaret, b. Dec 13, 1795; bapt. Feb 26, 1796. Spon: Jacob Fischer.

Catharine of Peter Wolff and Maria Elizabeth, b. Feb 3, 1796; bapt. Mar 27, 1796. Spon: Georg Wendel Wolff and Anna Elizabeth.

Peter of Peter Lein and Catharine, b. Mar 7, 1796; bapt. Apr 4, 1796. Spon: Gottlieb Kienser.

John of David Killmer and Barbara, b. Mar 11, 1796; bapt. Apr 10, 1796. Spon: Frederick Seibert and Eva.

Susanna of John Krill and Barbara, b. Mar 16, 1796; bapt. Jun 5, 1796. Spon: Martin Meyer and Hannah Elizabeth.

Eva Elizabeth of Henry Theiss and Magdalene, b. Apr 29, 1796; bapt. Jun 5, 1796. Spon: Eva Elizabeth Lauer.

John William of Christian Seibert and Susanna, b. Jun 17, 1796; bapt. Jun 29, 1796. Spon: Andrew Graff, Jr.

John Adam of Jacob Decker and Catharine, b. Jun 17, 1796; bapt. Aug 28, 1796. Spon: Peter Diefenbach and Catharine.

Anna Margaret of Francis Zeller and Elizabeth, b. Jul 13, 1796; bapt. Aug 21, 1796. Spon: John Peter Aurandt and Anna Catharine.

David of John George Heyd and Magdalene, b. Aug 4, 1796; bapt. Sep 25, 1796. Spon: David Killmer and Maria Barbara.

John of Martin Spengler and Anna Maria, b. Sep 6, 1796; bapt. Sep 26, 1796. Spon: John Litzinger.

William of Michael Moser and Anna Maria, b. Sep 2, 1796; bapt. Oct

4, 1796. Spon: Nicholas Moser and Anna Maria.

Anna Maria of John Jacob Schuetz and Magdalene, b. Jun 28, 1796; bapt. Jul 31, 1796. Spon: Maria Cath. Schuetz.

John of Jacob Ebling and Maria, b. Jan 2, 1795; bapt. Oct 31, 1796. Spon: parents.

Elizabeth of Jacob Ebling and Maria, b. Jul 16, 1796; bapt. Oct 31, 1796. Spon: parents.

Maria Catharine of Peter Schuetz and Elizabeth, b. Oct 10, 1796; bapt. Nov 12, 1796. Spon: Maria Cath. Schuetz.

Henry of Georg Noll and Anna Maria, b. Nov 18, 1796; bapt. Dec 1, 1796. Spon: Jacob Leitner and Margaret.

Elizabeth of Nicholas Haack and Catharine, b. Oct 10, 1796; bapt. Jan 1, 1797. Spon: Jonas Eckert and Maria Catharine.

Maria Catharine of Simon Bassler and Catharine, b.Apr 5, 1796; bapt. May 9, 1796. Spon: Catharine Bassler.

Maria Magdalene of Valentine Bender and Eva, b. Dec 31, 1796; bapt. Jan 17, 1797. Spon: Nicholas Killmer and Elizabeth.

Christine of Gottfried Mueller and Elizabeth, b. Jan 9, 1797; bapt. Feb 5, 1797. Spon: Frederick Rieth and Christine.

Maria Margaret of John Georg Weirich and Maria Margaret, b. Dec 4, 1796; bapt. Feb 12, 1797. Spon: Michael Zerbe and Anna Maria.

Maria of Peter Spengler and Maria, b. Nov 7, 1796; bapt. Feb 26, 1797. Spon: Christine Spengler.

Susan Barbara of Peter Schell and Barbara, b. Feb 2, 1797; bapt. Feb 27, 1797. Spon: Jacob Kunckel and Susanna.

Daniel Hendel of John Meyer and Catharine, b. Mar 8, 1797; bapt. Mar 27, 1797. Spon: William Hendel (pastor) and Margaret.

Salome of Benjamin Diefenbach and Charlotte, b. Mar 7, 1797; bapt. Apr 19, 1797. Spon: Michael Diefenbach and Maria Margaret.

Henry of Christian Lutz and Eva, b. May 1, 1797; bapt. Jun 4, 1797. Spon: Nicholas Killmer and Elizabeth.

John Georg of Georg Schwartz and Eva Rosina, b. Apr 30, 1797; bapt. Jun 4, 1797. Spon: Jacob Kunckel and Susanna.

Charlotte of Adam Braun and Catharine, b. Jul 6, 1797; bapt. Aug 27, 1797. Spon: Benjamin Diefenbach and Charlotte.

William of Thomas Zerbe and Catharine, b. Jul 2, 1797; bapt. Aug 29, 1797. Spon: John Mueller.

Elizabeth of John Adam Bassler and Maria, b. Jun 1, 1797; bapt. Aug 29, 1797. Spon: Elizabeth ---.

Eva of Peter Welter and Magdalene, b. Oct 2, 1797; bapt. Dec 25,

1797. Spon: Elizabeth Welter.

Henry of Christian Seibert and Susanna, b. Sep 22, 1797; bapt. ---. Spon: Henry Kahlbach and Maria.

Henry of Simon Bassler and Catharine, b. Dec 11, 1797; bapt. Feb 11, 1798. Spon: Henry Hautz and Christine.

Susan Anna Maria of Jacob Deckert and Catharine, b. Feb 8, 1798; bapt. Feb 27, 1798. Spon: John Georg Rayer and Elizabeth.

Maria Christine of Andrew Zoeller and Catharine, b. Dec 29, 1797; bapt. Feb 9, 1798. Spon: Jacob Zoeller and Christine.

John of John Zoeller and Elizabeth, b. Oct 22, 1797; bapt. Feb 9, 1798. Spon: Andrew Zoeller and Catharine.

John of Michael Mayer and Catharine, b. Sep 5, 1795; bapt. Sep 9, 1798. Spon: Peter Weyl.

Elizabeth of Michael Mayer and Catharine, b. Apr 18, 1797; bapt. Feb 9, 1798. Spon: Elizabeth Weyl.

Barbara of John Jacob Schuetz and Magdalene, b. Feb 4, 1798; bapt. Mar 25, 1798. Spon: John Walborn and Elizabeth.

Elizabeth of John Bernet and Catharine, b. Jul 30, 1797; bapt. Apr 22, 1798. Spon: Georg Stettler and Christine.

Mary Magdalene of Peter Seibert and Elizabeth, b. Mar 27, 1798; bapt. Apr 22, 1798. Spon: John Jacob Schuetz and Mary Magdalene.

Anna Maria of John Adam Schuetz and Susanna, b. Apr 14, 1798; bapt. May 9, 1798. Spon: Maria Weiser.

John Georg of Peter Schuetz and Elizabeth, b. Mar 24, 1798; bapt. May 9, 1798. Spon: John Lein and Catharine.

Peter of John Scherff and Anna Maria, b. Oct 20, 1796; bapt. Jun 2, 1798. Spon: William Hendel and Margaret.

John Jacob of Nicholas Meyer and Elizabeth, b. Jan 26, 1798; bapt. Apr 2, 1798. Spon: John Jacob Kienser and Catharine.

Catharine of Peter Etschberger and Elizabeth, b. Jun 9, 1798; bapt. Jul 29, 1798. Spon: John Weiser and Elizabeth.

Elizabeth of Leonard Schertel and Elizabeth, b. May 19, 1798; bapt. Jun 17, 1798. Spon: Georg Zeller and Elizabeth.

Susanna of Peter Lein and Catharine, b. Jun 19, 1798; bapt. Jul 30, 1798. Spon: Frederick Bollman and Susanna.

John Georg of Jacob Mueller and Christine, b. Jul 15, 1798; bapt. Aug 4, 1798. Spon: John Georg Mueller.

Henry of John Glantz and Catharine, b. Feb 6, 1798; bapt. Sep 26, 1798. Spon: Henry Schneider and Barbara.

Barbara of Valentine Bender and Eva, b. Jul 20, 1798; bapt. Sep 21, 1798. Spon: David Killmer and Maria Barbara.

Thomas of Adam Bassler and Magdalene, b. Aug 26, 1798; bapt. Sep 25, 1798. Spon: Henry Huebschman.

Elizabeth of John Scholl and Maria, b. Jan 21, 1798; bapt. Sep 25, 1798. Spon: Magdalene Bassler.

Valentine of Valentine Mueller and Barbara Christine, b. Jul 26, 1798; bapt. Oct 5, 1798. Spon: Leonard Stump and Eva.

John Michael of Philip Fischbach and Anna Maria, b. Aug 2, 1798; bapt. Oct 7, 1798. Spon: Michael Haack, Sr. and Sabina.

Benjamin of Philip Weil and Eva, b. Sep 17, 1798; bapt. Sep 26, 1798. Spon: Charles Bamberger.

Catharine of Martin Spengler and Anna Maria, b. Sep 17, 1798; bapt. Oct 11, 1798. Spon: Adam Gasser and Catharine.

William of Jacob Blecher and Margaret, b. Sep 9, 1798; bapt. Nov 18, 1798. Spon: Georg Blecher.

Salome of Ludwig Schwartz and Anna Maria, b. Oct 11, 1798; bapt. Nov 18, 1798. Spon: Margaret Eliz. ---.

Elizabeth of Henry Haack and Elizabeth, b. Nov 13, 1798; bapt. Dec 25, 1798. Spon: Elizabeth Haack.

Magdalene of David Killmer and Barbara, b. Oct 26, 1798; bapt. Dec 26, 1798. Spon: Henry Koppenheber and Mary Magd. Killmer.

David of Peter Bene and Anna Maria, b. Nov 30, 1797; bapt. Dec 26, 1798. Spon: David Killmer and Barbara.

John Henry of John Eckert and Catharine, b. Nov 13, 1798; bapt. Dec 27, 1798. Spon: Henry Heubschman and Catharine.

William of John Krill and Eva, b. Dec 27, 1798; bapt. Dec 27, 1798. Spon: parents.

Henry of Peter Schell and Barbara, b. Sep 14, 1798; bapt. Dec 29, 1798. Spon: Henry Schell.

Anna Margaret of Peter Hettinger and Maria Catharine, b. Jan 3, 1799; bapt. Feb 10, 1799. Spon: Peter Wohleben and Margaret Elizabeth.

John Jacob of Georg Blecher and Elizabeth, b. Dec 13, 1798; bapt. Feb 26, 1799. Spon: John Jacob Blecher and Maria Margaret.

William of John Garden and Mary Magdalene, b. Jan 26, 1799; bapt. Mar 10, 1799. Spon: Jacob Frantz.

Elizabeth Catharine of William Seibert and Catharine, b. Feb 1, 1799; bapt. Mar 10, 1799. Spon: Peter Seibert and Elizabeth.

John of Michael Moser and Anna Margaret, b. Feb 22, 1799; bapt.

Mar 16, 1799. Spon: Christian Walborn and Anna Margaret.

Christine of Peter Spengler and Maria, b. Sep 23, 1798; bapt. Mar 26, 1799. Spon: Christian Spengler.

Jonathan of Gottlieb Kinsley and Barbara, b. Feb 18, 1799; bapt. Apr 7, 1799. Spon: Rudolph Kiensley and Anna Catharine.

Daniel of John Berlot and Catharine, b. Nov 22, 1798; bapt. Apr 28, 1799. Spon: Daniel Stettler.

Mary Magdalene of Christian Geim (Keim) and Mary Magdalene, b. Dec 28, 1798; bapt. May 12, 1799. Spon: Jacob Goldman and Mary Magdalene.

Salome of John Jacob Schutz and Magdalene, b. Jun 9, 1799; bapt. Jul 28, 1799. Spon: Catharine Lebbo.

Christian of Nicholas Haack and Catharine, b. Jun 23, 1799; bapt. Aug 11, 1799. Spon: Christian Walborn and Catharine.

Catharine of Daniel Mayer and Christine, b. Sep 3, 1799; bapt. Sep 10, 1799. Spon: ---- Schoenfelder and Catharine.

Magdalene of Georg Weyrich and Anna Margaret, b. Aug 31, 1799; bapt. Nov 3, 1799. Spon: John Battorf and Elizabeth.

John of William Stettler and Catharine, b. Aug 21, 1799; bapt. Oct 20, 1799. Spon: John Berlott and Catharine.

Simon of Simon Bassler and Catharine, b. Aug 25, 1799; bapt. Nov 8, 1799. Spon: Simon Bassler.

Jonathan of Francis Zeller and Elizabeth, b. Oct 22, 1799; bapt. Dec 25, 1799. Spon: John Merckly and Elizabeth.

Daniel of Benjamin Diefenbach and Charlotte, b. Sep 15, 1799; bapt. Nov 27, 1799. Spon: John Diefenbach.

John of John Georg Blecher and Catharine, b. Nov 15, 1799; bapt. Jan 28, 1800. Spon: John Wenrich and Catharine.

Maria Catharine of Robert Mordig and Catharine, b. Dec 5, 1799; bapt. Feb 13, 1800. Spon: Maria Barbara Blechman.

John of Philip Werhiem and Elizabeth, b. Jun 5, 1797; bapt. Feb 11, 1800. Spon: parents.

Isaac of Philip Werhiem and Elizabeth, b. Feb 24, 1799; bapt. Feb 11, 1800. Spon: parents.

John of Peter Schuetz and Elizabeth, b. Jan 19, 1800; bapt. Feb 17, 1800. Spon: John Haehn and Anna Margaret.

Elizabeth of Christian Riehm and Catharine, b. Jan 6, 1800; bapt. Feb 25, 1800. Spon: Henry Ache and Elizabeth.

Henry of Samuel Ache and Elizabeth, b. Jan 7, 1800; bapt. Feb 25, 1800. Spon: Henry Heubschman and Catharine.

Samuel of Valentine Trautman and Margaret, b. Jan 13, 1800; bapt. Mar 26, 1800. Spon: John Georg Preiss and Elizabeth.

John Frederick of John Adam Gasser and Catharine, b. Oct 23, 1799; bapt. Jan 12, 1800. Spon: Georg Spengler and Barbara.

John of Martin Heffelfenger and Anna Maria, b, Sep 8, 1799; bapt. Apr 6, 1800. Spon: Jacob Goldman and Magdalene.

John Georg of Peter Schuetz and Elizabeth, b. Mar 13, 1800; bapt. Apr 10, 1800. Spon: Matthew Gast and Margaret.

Eliza of Henry Belcher and Anna, b. Feb 17, 1800; bapt. Apr 22, 1800. Spon: Henry Bunner and Christine.

Mary Magdalene of Bernard Schaertel and Elizabeth, b. Feb 23, 1800; bapt. Jun 1, 1800. Spon: Mary Magdalene Bens.

John of Peter Schmidt and Susanna, b. Mar 24, 1800; bapt. Jun 1, 1800. Spon: John Georg Weirich and Margaret.

Margaret of John Schreiner and Catharine, b. Dec 14, 1799; bapt. Jun 5, 1800. Spon: John Adam Gasser and Catharine.

Barbara of Henry Haack and Elizabeth, b. May 23, 1800; bapt. Jul 13, 1800. Spon: Frederick Steiner and Anna Margaret.

Joel of Georg Gibs and Sybilla, b. Jan 10, 1800; bapt. Aug 24, 1800. Spon: Peter Schutz and Elizabeth.

John of Peter Seibert and Elizabeth, b. Oct 2, 1800; bapt. Nov 2, 1800. Spon: John Walborn and Elizabeth.

Henry of Martin Spengler and Anna Maria, b. Oct 10, 1800; bapt. Nov 16, 1800. Spon: John Adam Spengler.

Elizabeth of Gottlieb Kiensley and Barbara, b. Sep 13, 1800; bapt. Nov 16, 1800. Spon: Michael Haack and wife.

Isaac of John Nicholas Killmer and Catharine, b. Sep 11, 1800; bapt. Oct 18, 1800. Spon: Nicholas Killmer and Elizabeth.

Henry of Michael Peiffer and Anna Maria, b. Nov 30, 1800; bapt. Dec 25, 1800. Spon: Henry Peiffer.

Maria of Peter Lein and Magdalene, b. Dec 17, 1800; bapt. Feb 1, 1801. Spon: Eva ---.

Georg of John Adam Schuetz and Susanna, b. Dec 24, 1800; bapt. Feb 12, 1801. Spon: Ludwig Fischer and Elizabeth.

Peter of Peter Schell and Barbara, b. Jan 27, 1799; bapt. Sep 17, 1800. Spon: parents.

Frederick of Adam Dinius and Catharine, b. Dec 23, 1799; bapt. Mar 8, 1801. Spon: Matthew Gast and Margaret.

Elizabeth of John Kapp and Magdalene, b. Mar 20, 1799; bapt. May 31, 1799. Spon: William Hendel and Margaret.

Margaret of John Scherff and Maria, b. Jul 9, 1800; bapt. Mar 13, 1802. Spon: parents.

Henry of Peter Bene and Anna Maria, b. Oct 25, 1798; bapt. May 30, 1802. Spon: Christian Lutz and Eva.

MARRIAGES OF THE REV. WM. HENDEL, NOV 1769-AUG 1779

Nov 5, 1769   David Le Febre and Maria Zeller, both single.

Apr 5, 1770   Thomas Bassler and Elizabeth Schmel, both single.

Apr 30, 1770   Barnabas Parsons and Catharine Geyer, single.

Jun 30, 1770   Christian Lauer and Elizabeth Haffner, both widowed.

Aug 7, 1770   Thomas Schmid and Christine Hoster, both single.

Oct 16, 1770   Adam Mell and Maria Barbara Felleban, both single.

Oct 22, 1770   Bernard Dachs and Susanna Magdalene Brucker, both single.

Dec 31, 1770   Martin Battorf and Maria Barbara Hautz, both single.

Dec 18, 1770   Henry Schuy and Barbar Theiss, both single.

Dec 20, 1770   Jacob Walther and Susanna Groh, both single.

Jan 15, 1771   Michael Trautman and Susanna Hoffmann, both single.

Jan 22, 1771   Adam Heilman and Catharine Schmid, both single.

Jan 29, 1771   Christopher Heckman and Anna Marg. Kessler, both single.

-- --, 1771   Casper Dschob and Barbara Borgner, both single.

Apr 1, 1771   George Leonard Emmert and Anna Catharine Gunckel, both single.

Apr 14, 1771   Francis Seibert and Eva Hollstein.

Apr 15, 1771   Abraham Fellman and --- Siffrich.

Jun 10, 1771   John Krebs and Elizabeth Schneider.

Jun 16, 1771   Krafft Hachenbach and Catharine Hippenstiel.

Jun 16, 1771   John Peter Ziegler and Maria Eichelberger, widow.

Jun 19, 1771   Christian Muller and Veronica Brucker.

Jul -, 1771   Jacob Neff and Anna Maria Etschberger, single.

Feb 23, 1772   --- Weis and -- Wengert, single.

Apr 20, 1772   George Wolf and Elizabeth Thormayer, single.

Apr 28, 1772   Hieronymus Rudy and Eva Maria Kucher, single.

Apr 28, 1772   Peter Spicker and Anna Maria Buhler, single.

May 10, 1772   Jacob Anspach and Maria Elizabeth Ried, single.

May 19, 1772   William Stein and Catharine Steeger, single.

May 26, 1772   Isaac Heller and Anna Catharine Wallborn.

Jan 19, 1773 Frederick Jung and Margaret Diel, single.
Jan 19, 1773 Jacob Mess and Catharine Dunges.
Feb 2, 1773 Henry Brunner and Susanna Bollinger.
Feb 2, 1773 John Mohr and Elizabeth Mayer.
Mar 9, 1773 Henry Schaeffer and Eva Schweitzer.
Jan 16, 1775 Leonard Gunckel and Rosina Meylin.
Jan 16, 1775 Andrew Zeller and Catharine Forrer.
Feb 16, 1779 Jacob Bayer and Barbara Numann, single.
Feb 24, 1779 Adam Viehmann (widower) and Susanna Catharine Guest.
Mar 30, 1779 Jacob Hoff and Maria Catharine Schmeltzer.
Apr 20, 1779 Jacob Loos and Catharine Reichard.
Apr 20, 1779 Carl Reichard and Elizabeth Stauch.
Apr 26, 1779 Nicholas Theissinger and Eva Catharine Sicher.
May 7, 1779 Henry Velde and Catharine Huber.
Jun 7, 1779 John Brecht and Anna Maria Leiss.
Jun 9, 1779 Jacob Berry and Christine Germann.
Jun 29, 1779 John Michael Miller and Margaret Stumb.
Jul --, 1779 Peter Schuck and Barbara Riesser.
Aug 15, 1779 Martin Schuy and Marg. Eliz. Conrad.

MARRIAGE BY THE REV. ANDREW LORETZ, APR 1785

Apr 18, 1785   Wendel Hautz and Catharine Tiezler.

MARRIAGES BY REV. WILLIAM HENDEL, OCT 1793-APR 1823

Oct 29, 1793   Jacob Kaucher and Anna Maria Leiss.
Nov 5, 1793   John Jacob Zoeller and Christine Bucher.
Nov 7, 1793   Simon Kantner and Juliana Unckschen.
Nov 19, 1793   John Gros and Catharine Reyer.
Dec 10, 1793   Peter Weber and Catharine Peiffer.
Apr 15, 1794   John Artzt and Anna Maria Leitner.
May 12, 1794   Jacob Decker and Catharine Zehring.
Jun 10, 1794   Jacob Hubler and Anna Margaret Braun.
Jul 29, 1794   Reigert Schreiner and Maria Conrath.
Jul 29, 1794   John Seltzer and Catharine Schiffler.
Sep 18, 1794   James McCleary and Elizabeth Anderson.
Oct 30, 1794   Jacob Klar and Christian Ulrich.

Nov 25, 1794	Adam Gasser and Catharine Bollman.
Dec 14, 1794	Peter Kinckelman and Catharine Bellemann.
Jan 11, 1795	John Schultz and Barbara Etschberger.
Mar 31, 1795	Frederick Kraffert and Catharine Schuger.
Mar 15, 1795	Michael Mayer and Catharine Kiblinger.
Apr 2, 1795	James Young and Rebecca Steel.
Apr 6, 1795	William McFarling and Anna Stuart.
Apr 7, 1795	George Grundruh and Cath. Elizabeth Weiss.
Apr 10, 1795	Michael Schaeffer and Anna Maria Diezler.
Apr 21, 1795	Conrad Loos and Christine Brendel.
May 12, 1795	Martin Scheib and Anna Maria Braun.
May 17, 1795	Henry Stettler and Anna Margaret Gundruh.
May 17, 1795	John Reber and Salome Steiner.
May --, 1795	John Hey and Anna Maria Berger.
Jul --, 1795	John George Schneider and Barbara Kochendoerfer.
Sep 20, 1795	-- Braun and -- Kern.
Sep 29, 1795	John Ross and Juliana Moth.
Oct 11, 1795	George Hepfer and Elizabeth Fischer.
Nov 29, 1795	Casper Laux and Barbara Lora.
Jan 21, 1796	Samuel Roland and Elizabeth McCabe.
Feb 2, 1796	John Nicholas Schneider and Maria Elizabeth Kern.
Mar 6, 1796	John Jacob Wolff and Catharine Boeshor.
Mar 20, 1796	George Huber and Anna Maria Roth.
Mar 22, 1796	Frederick Brendel and Magdalene Loos.
Mar 22, 1796	Martin Spengler and Anna Maria Litzinger.
Apr 17, 1796	Philip Theiss and Eva Moser.
Apr 17, 1796	John Gerhart and Christine Dietzler.
May 1, 1796	George Blecher and Elizabeth Formwalt.
May 29, 1796	Francis Seibert and Susanna Zwelle.
Oct 9, 1796	Henry Lebo and Regina Theiss.
Oct 15, 1796	Martin Benner and Maria Muller.
Nov 12, 1796	Peter Schell and Barbara Schwerth.
Dec 20, 1796	William Seybert and Catharine Moser.
Dec 17, 1796	Benjami Rutter and Catharine Meiser.
Feb 2, 1797	Jacob Spang and Magdalene Beyer.
Feb 7, 1797	Thomas Zerbe and Catharine Bassler.
Feb 21, 1797	John Adam Stump and Anna Maria Eissauer.
Mar 7, 1797	Adam Bassler and Maria Hibschmann.
Mar 14, 1797	Peter Thomas and Regina Ziegler.
Apr 16, 1797	Bernard Schaerdel and Elizabeth Bens.

Apr 21, 1797   John Berlot and Catharine Stettler.
Apr 23, 1797   Jacob Gerhardt and Barbara Leiss.
May 2, 1797   John Scholl and Anna Maria Bassler.
May 21, 1797   John Braun and Salome Wegelin.
Aug 15, 1797   Christopher Liweringshaus and Catharine
Dollendorffer.
Nov 21, 1797   John Frederick Muth and Elizabeth Zerwe.
Nov 25, 1797   Samuel Clarck and Catharine Ries.
Nov 28, 1797   Abraham Reber and Catharine Christ.
Feb 20, 1798   Peter Schmidt and Susanna Himmelberger.
Feb 27, 1798   Henry Haack and Elizabeth Stein.
Mar 6, 1798   Nicholas Aulenbach and Catharine Bohn.
Apr 1, 1798   John Rietzel and Anna Maria Riess.
Apr 22, 1798   John Kreim and Catharine Rieth.
Jun 3, 1798   Jacob Achenbach and Anna Maria Meutz.
May 27, 1798   John Kapp and Magdalene Dieffenbach.
Jul 31, 1798   John Bamberger and Catharine Schaeffer.
Aug 12, 1798   Gottlieb Kiensley and Barbara Haack.
Aug 14, 1798   Frederick Becker and Catharine Bergman.
Sep 16, 1798   Peter Wendel and Veronica Eischauer.
-- 1, 1798   Henry Hix and Elizabeth Lauer.
Dec 23, 1798   Christian Dibbon and Rebecca Wore.
Dec 31, 1798   Philip Schaertel and Barbara Klar.
Jan 15, 1799   George Kahlbach and Magdalene Ruth.
Jan 20, 1799   John Freyberger and Elizabeth Guth.
Feb 12, 1799   Robert Mordig and Catharine Blecher.
Mar 24, 1799   Abraham Luckenbill and Eva Staller.
Apr 2, 1799   John George Hey and Barbara Rieth.
Apr 7, 1799   John Philbert and Anna Marai Leiss.
Apr 7, 1799   Jacob Wenrich and Susanna Formwalt.
Apr 7, 1799   George Muller and Susanna Stein.
Apr 7, 1799   Ludwig Schuy and Anna Margaret Athern.
Apr 23, 1799   Henry Blecher and Nancy Garden.
Apr 28, 1799   Simon Gutmann and Barbara Forrey.
Apr 30, 1799   Henry Spittler and Catharine Schuy.
Jun 16, 1799   Peter Schmidt and Margaret Wenrich.
Jul 31, 1799   Henry Spengler and Nancy Bittner.
Aug 7, 1799   John Jacobi and Anna Maria Mess.
Nov 3, 1799   William Gutmann and Regina Mohr.
Nov 26, 1799   Daniel Mayer and Elizabeth Lora.

Dec 10, 1799   Christian Baertsch and Regina Michel.
Dec 17, 1799   Joseph Klein and Catharine Wittemeyer.
Dec 17, 1799   John Schuy and Elizabeth Breitebach.
Dec 17, 1799   Michael Meyer and Magdalene Klar.
Dec 24, 1799   Christopher Lebo and Catharine Bortner.
Jan 11, 1800   George Egge and Maria Margaret Vonnöth.
Jan 2, 1800   Michael Mohr and Barbara Backer.
Feb 9, 1800   Daniel Haehn and Maria Haehn.
Mar 16, 1800   John Nicholas Killmer and Catharine Leiss.
Mar 18, 1800   Peter Mayer and Catharine Gundruh(m).
Apr 23, 1800   Arthur Russel and Margaret Conrad.
Apr 14, 1800   Michael Reber and Anna Maria Machemer.
Apr 27, 1800   Peter Klopp and Eva Ulrich.
Apr 27, 1800   John George Pontius and Catharine Mayer.
May 6, 1800   Samuel Fetter and Catharine Katermann.
Jun 24, 1800   Joshua Kelger and Anna Maria Mayer.
Jun 12, 1800   Daniel Wummeldorf and Eva Mayer.
Aug 12, 1800   Jost Hey and Margaret Reber.
Sep 21, 1800   John Gundrum and Margaret Elizabeth Bender.
Sep 21, 1800   John Jacob Battorf and Catharine Reber.
Sep 23, 1800   Henry Schumacher and Anna Maria Schaeffer.
Nov 23, 1800   Henry Von Nieth and Anna Maria Reber.
Dec 18, 1800   John Stein and Eva Hetzel.
Dec 30, 1800   Jacob Formwald and Maria Staudt.

SWATARA REFORMED CONGREGATION, JONESTOWN

BAPTISMS BY CONRAD TEMPLE-MANN, but not entered by him.

John Henry of Martin Capler and Margaret, bapt. Oct 1, 1740. Spon: Henry Dubs and wife.

Philip Lorentz of Philip Hautz and Anna Margaret, bapt. Dec 16, 1740. Spon: Philip Lorentz and wife Eva.

John Henry of Ottmar Schnaeble and Anna Margaret, bapt. Oct 14, 1740. Spon: Philip Hautz and wife.

Anna Maria of Ludwig Born and Anna Maria, bapt. Jan 28, 1740/41. Spon: Henry Dubs and wife Anna Maria.

Anna Christine of John Heyl and Maria, bapt. Jun 16, 1740. Spon: Isaiah Guschweyd and wife Anna Christine.

Anna Margaret of Thomas Matern and Anna Margaret, bapt. Jun 18, 1741. Spon: Daniel Schuy and wife Anna Maria.

John Christian of Philip Lorentz Hautz and Eva, bapt. Aug 16, 1741. Spon: Christian Walborn and wife Cath. Elizabeth.

Anna Maria of William Fischer and Christine, bapt. Apr 4, 1741. Spon: Ludwig Born and wife Anna Maria.

Barbara of Daniel Schuy and Anna Maria, bapt. Jun 25, 1741. Spon: George Meyer and Barbara.

John Herman of Herman Muller and Catherine, bapt. Mar 8, 1742. Spon: John Sigmund Haehnle and wife Anna Maria.

Daniel of Nicholas Jungbluth and Anna Maria, bapt. Sep 17, 1742. Spon: Daniel Born, single and Maria Gottlin.

Anna Maria of Nicholas Lang and Recilla (Regula), bapt. Aug 16, 1742. Spon: Ludwig Born and wife Anna Maria.

John of Jacob Gurle and Susanna, bapt. Oct 29, 1742. Spon: John Bindnagel and wife Regula.

Catharine of Martin Capler and Margaret, bapt. Apr 20, 1742. Spon: Henry Dups and wife Anna Maria.

Anna Maria of John Heyl and Maria, bapt. Aug 10, 1742. Spon: Ludwig Born and wife Anna Maria.

Catharine of Frederick Cremer and Maria Barbara, bapt. Dec 4, 1742. Spon: Herman Muller and wife Catharine.

John George of Nicholas Nol (Noll) and Margaret, bapt. Feb 15, 1742. Spon: John George Nol and wife Margaret.

Christian of John Winckelblech and Anna Elizabeth, bapt. Mar 15, 1745. Spon: Martin Capler and wife Margaret.

John Henry of Casper Schnaeble and Barbara, bapt. Aug 29, 1747.
Spon: Henry Sauder and Anna Margaret Schuy, single.

Elizabeth of Ottmar Schnaebele and Barbara, bapt. Sep 9, 1747.
Spon: Philip Hautz and wife Anna Margaret.

John Martin of Henry Dubs and Anna Maria, bapt. Dec 10, 1747.
Spon: Martin Cramer, single and Hanna Maria Muller, single.

John Henry of Peter Bucher and Anna Maria, bapt. Dec 28, 1747.
Spon: John Dubs and wife.

Anna Maria of Adam Schmal and Cacaterde, bapt. Oct 10, 1747.
Spon: Margaret Zimmerman, single.

Catharine Elizabeth of Daniel Schuy and Maria Martha, bapt. Jun 8,
1747. Spon: Peter Schell and wife Maria Catharine.

Philip of Felix Lang and Regina, bapt. Aug 2, 1747, Spon: Thomas
Matern and Veronica.

John Martin of Peter Winckelblech and Anna Margaret, bapt. Aug 10,
1747. Spon: Martin Capler and wife Anna Margaret.

Anna Catharine of Henry Bachmann and Christine, bapt. Jul 13,
1747. Spon: Peter Hetrich and wife Anna Delila.

Anna Maria of John Bruner and Anna Margaret, bapt. Jun 5, 1747.
Spon: Casper Jost and wife Anna Elizabeth.

Anna Maria of Jacob Rieger and Anäs (?), bapt. Jun 27, 1747. Spon:
Henry Klein and wife Anna Maria.

Elizabeth of Henry Wagner and Barbara, bapt. May 18, 1748. Spon:
Peter Tittel, single and mother Elizabeth Tittel.

John Casper of Jacob Dojy and Anna, bapt. Jun 15, 1748. Spon:
Casper Crob and Hannah Millen, single.

John Henry of Ludwig Henry Schuy and Maria Elizabeth, bapt. Mar
9, 1748. Spon: Henry Sauder and Anna Marg. Schuy, single.

Thomas of Nicholas Jungblut and Anna Maria, bapt. Jan 30, 1748.
Spon: Thomas Krick and wife Margaret.

Maria Barbara of John Dubs and Barbara, bapt. Jan 30, 1748. Spon:
Henry Dubs and wife Anna Maria.

John Peter of John Bruner and wife, bapt. --- --, 1749. Spon: Peter
Getel and wife Maria Eva.

John Leonard of Peter Winckelblech and wife, bapt. May 9, 1749.
Spon: Leonard Capler and Maria Winckelblech, single.

Barbara of Bernard Raug and Anna Elizabeth, bapt. Feb 1, 1749.
Spon: Moritz Dubel and wife Anna Barbara.

Rudolph of Henry Sauter and Sabina, bapt. Oct 30, 1749. Spon:
Philip Kolb and wife Dorothy.

Anna Maria of Philip Kolb and Anna Dorothy, bapt. Feb 13, 1748.
Spon: Christopher Kolb and wife Anna Maria.
John Bernard of Martin Kapler and Christine, bapt. Jan 2, 1750.
Spon: John Bernard ---- and wife Dorothy.
John Henry of Ottmar Schnaebler and wife, bapt. Feb 3, 1750. Spon:
Jacob Schnaeble, single.
Anna Maria of Philip Kolb and Anna Dorothy, bapt. Mar 1, 1750.
Spon: Christopher Kolb and wife Anna Maria.
Anna Elizabeth of Paul Schaefer and Anna Elizabeth, bapt. Mar 15,
1750. Spon: Adam Bulman and wife Anna Elizabeth.
John Jacob of Nicholas Ullant and Juliana, bapt. Dec 25, 1749. Spon:
Jacob Schober and wife Dorothy.
John Martin of Ludwig Schuy and Elizabeth, bapt. Jun 15, 1750.
Spon: John Martin Schuy, single.
Anna Maria of Philip Lorentz Hautz and Eva, bapt. eight before
Pentecost. Spon: Casper Schnaeble and wife Barbara.
Magdalena of Peter Kiny and Catharine, bapt. Feb 3, 1751. Spon:
Samuel Diessler and Dorothy.
John of John Nicholas Weyrig and Anna Barbara, bapt. Feb 2, 1751.
Spon: John Brenneisen and wife Christine.
Moses ---, bapt. Dec 10, 1751. Spon: Jacob Wagener and wife
Magdalene.
Maria Barbara of Nicholas Jungblut and Anna Maria, bapt. May 7,
1751. Spon: Casper Schnaeble and wife.
Christian of Dewalt Annias and Catharine, bapt. Dec 23, 1750. Spon:
Christian Lang and Anna Maria of Peter Hedrich.
John Henry of Nicholas Noll and Anna Margaret, bapt. Aug 8, 1751.
Spon: Henry Noll and Elizabeth Stein, both single.
Margaret of Peter Gettel and Maria Eva, bapt. Apr 18, 1752. Spon:
John Brunner and wife Margaret.
Sabina of John Fock and Eva, bapt. Apr 3, 1752. Spon: Sabina
Schnaettler and Valentine Gerhard.
Melchior of Melchior Leitert and Salome, bapt. Jul 5, 1752. Spon:
Henry Dubs and wife Anna Maria
Magdalene Catharine of Christine Lentz and Anna Barbara, bapt. Jun
7, 1752. Spon: Dewald Gerst and Magdalene Catharine.
Anna Maria of Henry Wagener and Barbara, bapt. Jun 1, 1752. Spon:
Dewalt Nawiner.
Barbara of Ulrich Schwinch and Ursula, bapt. Nov 27, 1752. Spon:
Jacob Hengschig and Barbara Spittler(?).

BAPTISMS ENTERED BY REV. CONRAD TEMPLEMAN
JAN 1753-MAY 1756.

Anna Maria of Peter Kiny and Catharine, b. Jan 7, 1753, bapt. ____.
Spon: Jacob Krieger and wife Annäs.

Elizabeth of Peter Diterich and Maria Catharine, b. Dec 27, 1752;
bapt. -----. Spon: Nicholas Wolf and wife Elizabeth.

Catharine Elizabeth of William Salsmann and Maria Catharine, b. Dec
7, 1753(?). Spon: Wendel Roemer and Catharine Elizabeth.

Mary Engel of Nicholas Schaeffer and Magdalene, b. Dec 8, 1752.
Spon: Engel Gerst and Jacob Labster.

John of Ludwig Schuy and Elizabeth, b. Dec 7, 1752. Spon: John
Schuy and wife Catharine.

Elizabeth of John Dubs and Barbara, b. Jan 26, 1752. Spon: Rudolph
Hauck and wife Elizabeth.

Susanna of John Dubs and Barbara, b. Sep 8, 1750. Spon: Henry
Schnaeble and Susanna Buchman.

Henry of John Dubs and Barbara, b. Mar 2, 1745. Spon: Henry Dubs
and wife Anna Maria.

John of John Dubs and Barbara, b. Nov 28, 1746. Spon: Henry Dubs
and Anna Mila (Maria).

John Christopher of Philip Hautz and Anna Margaret, b. Jan 29,
1753. Spon: Christopher Reier and wife Catharine.

Anna of Casper Schnaeble and Barbara, b. Jan 28, 1753. Spon:
Ottmar Schnaeble and wife Barbara.

John and Daniel of Martin Schneider and Eva, b. Dec 18, 1752. Spon:
Anthony Kelcker, Catharine Mattern, Jonas Focht and Eva.

Anna Barbara of Peter Schmidt and Anna Barbara, b. May 8, 1753.
Spon: Jacob Lebengut and wife Anna Catharine.

Bernhart of Bernhart Rauch and Anna Elizabeth, b. Jul 27, 1753.
Spon: Elizabeth Meier, single.

John of Jacob Tschofft and Hannah, b. Jul 14, 1753. Spon: John
Schweitzer and Anna Hamm.

Susanna Catharine of George Michael Wildfang and Susanna
Catharine, b. Aug 28, 1753. Spon: Abraham Hubler and wife
Salome.

Christine Margaret of John Gottfried Stempfel and Margaret, b. Aug
16, 1753. Spon: Conrad Raumer and Christine Margaret Stempfel.

Anna Catharine of John William Notz and Elizabeth, b. Oct 19, 1753.
Spon: Nicholas Weininger and wife Anna Catharine.

Maria Catharine of Philip Kolb and Dorothy, b. Aug 21, 1753. Spon: Casper Henn and Maria Catharine.

John Frederick of Peter Winckelblech and Maria, b. Nov 1, 1753. Spon: John Frederick Kramer and wife Maria Barbara.

Daughter of John Schnaeble, (decd.) and wife, age 16 years, bapt. Jan 25, 1754. Spon: ---.

Anna Maria of Frederick Kramer and Maria Barbara, b. Jun --, 1753. Spon: George Winckelblech and Anna Maria Dubs, single.

Henry of Melchior Leydert and Salome, b. Feb 24, 1754. Spon: Henry Dubs and wife Magdalene.

Sabina of Peter Bucher and Barbara, b. Jan 14, 1754. Spon: Henry Sauter and wife Sabina.

John Henry of Henry Wagner and Barbara, b. Feb 21, 1754. Spon: Henry Dubs and wife Anna Maria.

Michael of Jonas Focht and Eva, b. Jan 30, 1754. Spon: Michael Hergeheimer and Barbara Schnaeble, both single.

John Jacob of Henry Miller and Anna nee Meili, b. Jun 22, 1751; bapt. Jan 28, 1854. Spon: Adam Lerch and wife Maria Margaret.

Henry of Henry Miller and Anna nee Meili, b. Jan 23, 1753; bapt. Jan 28, 1754. Spon: John Rontel and wife Elizabeth.

Catharine Barbara of Christian Lentz and Barbara, b. Jan 7, 1754. Spon: Dewald Gerst and wife Catharine Magd.

Elizabeth of Jacob Libs and Elizabeth, b. Mar 3, 1754. Spon: Felix Winsch and wife Ursula.

John Martin of Martin Kramer and Anna, b. Mar 17, 1754. Spon: Frederick Kramer and wife Maria Barbara.

Maria Magdalene of Jacob Ulm and Mary Magdalene, b. Apr 28, 1754. Spon: George Scheffer and Anna Maria.

Catharine of Valentine Gerhard and Catharine, b. Jun 6, 1754. Spon: John George Obenmeier and Magdalene.

Maria Elizabeth of Jacob Laman and Maria Catharine, b. Jun 15, 1754. Spon: John Adam Loch and Maria Eva Detter.

Maria Elizabeth of Peter Winckelblech and Maria Margaret, b. Nov 30, 1754. Spon: Michael Gleber and wife.

Margaret of Nicholas Weyrich and Barbara, b. Nov 17, 1754. Spon: William Weyrich and Margaret Gerst.

John of Henry Mueller and Anna, b. Jan 3, 1755. Spon: John Dickert and wife Catharine.

Anna Maria of Bernard Boessohr and Caroline, b. Feb 10, 1755; bapt. Mar 2, 1755. Spon: Dewald Nawinger and wife, Anna Maria.

Catharine of Philip Kobb and Dorothy, b. Feb 15, 1755; bapt. Mar 31, 1755. Spon: Barbara Weber and Anthony Kelcker.

Henry of Henry Schneble and Anna, b. Apr 5, 1755; bapt. Apr 17, 1755. Spon: John Dubs and wife.

Daniel of John Bossohr and Anna Maria, b. E(a)ster 1755; bapt. May 24, 1755. Spon: Daniel Bossohr and Christine Renninger.

John of Daniel North and Maria, b. Jul 16, 1755; bapt. Jul 20, 1755. Spon: John Dickert.

Jacob of John Dubs and Barbara, b. Aug 29, 1755; bapt. Oct 12, 1755. Spon: Henry Schneble.

Frederick of Frederick Kramer and Barbara, b. Jan 26, 1756; bapt. Feb 15, 1756. Spon: Martin Krohmer and wife.

Anna Maria of Bernard Rauch and Elizabeth, b. Feb 2, 1756; bapt. Feb 15, 1756. Spon: Henry Dubs and wife.

Gertrude of John Titteler and Anna Catharine, b. May 12, 1756; bapt. May 30, 1756. Spon: Michel Horchesheimer and Gertrude Staehner.

Jacob of Jacob Schnebele and Anna Maria, b. Apr 1, 1756; bapt. May 30, 1756. Spon: Conrad Schneble and Susan Schneble.

(The preceding is the last baptism of Templeman, the next two are by an unknown hand.)

John Adam of Valentine Gerhart and Catharine, b. Jun 1, 1756. Spon: Adam Moser and Magdalene Dubs, single.

John George of John Boeshar and Anna Maria, b. Nov --, 1756. Spon: George Harges and Wilhelmina Lang, single.

BAPTISMS BY HENRY DECKER, 1757-1760

Anna Maria of Adam Schneider and Anna Maria, b. Nov 6, 1751. Spon: Martin Kieffer and wife.

Anna of Adam Schneider and wife, b. Sep 3, 1754. Spon: Henry Miller and wife.

Elizabeth of Adam Schneider and wife, b. Nov 21, 1757. Spon: John Adam Wegner and wife.

Anna Barbara of Adam Schneider and wife, b. Sep 18, 1759. Spon: Ottmar Schnebele.

Anna of John Dubs and Anna Barbara, b. Aug 21, 1757. Spon: Henry Schnebele and wife.

Veronica of John Dubs and wife, b. Jan 14, 1760. Spon: Henry Lowhmiller and wife.

BAPTISMS BY FREDERICK C. MEULLER, APR 1762-JUL 1769

Son of Valentine Gerhart and wife, b. Apr 25, 1762. Spon: William
Rauch and Regina Gerhart.

Anna Maria of John Braun and wife, b. Mar 25, 1762. Spon: Henry
Dubs and wife.

Anna Maria of Adam Sattelzan(?) and wife, b. Mar 25, 1762. Spon:
Leonard Fischer and wife.

Catharine of John Dubs and wife, b. Oct 20, 1761. Spon: John
Titler(?) and wife.

John of George Geistweit and wife, b. --- --, 1761. Spon: John Dubs
and Margaret Rauch.

John George of George Geistweit and wife, b. --- --, 1762. Spon: John
George Hatz and wife.

Anna Maria of Henry Christ and wife, b. Mar 11, 1762. Spon: Adam
Sattelzan(?) and wife.

Elizabeth of Martin Schuy and wife, b. Aug 1, 1762. Spon: Ludwig
Schuy and wife Elizabeth.

Susanna of Henry Wagener and wife, b. Aug 1, 1762. Spon: John
Braun and wife.

*(The next three baptisms were not entered by Mueller but were
performed by him.)*

Catharine of John Braun and wife, b. May 22, 1763; bapt. by Rev.
Frederick Mueller. Spon: John Dubs and wife Catharine.

Henry of John Braun and wife, b. Apr 20, 1765; bapt. by Rev.
Frederick Mueller. Spon: John Wolfersberger and wife Hannah.

John Braun of John Braun and wife, b. Dec 26, 1766; bapt. by Rev.
Frederick Mueller. Spon: John Bruner and Barbara Dubs.

(The next two baptisms were in the handwriting of Mueller.)

Son of John Brechbil and wife; bapt. Jun 19, 1768. Spon: John Leydig
and wife.

Anna Maria of Kilian Lang and wife; bapt. Jul 3, (1768). Spon: John
Boeshor and wife.

BAPTISMS OF REV. JOHN JACOB ZUFALL, JUL-DEC 1769

Anna Catharine of Jacob Brunner and Maria Margaret, b. Jun 18,
1769; bapt. Jul 2, 1769. Spon: John Adam Kleeman and wife Anna
Catharine.

Eva Elizabeth of Philip Heu and Barbara, b. Jul 24, 1769; bapt. Aug

22, 1769. Spon: Carl Heu and wife Eva.
Son of John Moller and Elizabeth, b. Sep 6, 1769; bapt. Oct 22, 1769.
Spon: Daniel Angst and Maria Margaret Fuchs.
Barbara of George Kuntz and Elizabeth, b. Oct 15, 1769; bapt. Nov 5,
1769. Spon: John Scherp and Barbara Rauch.
Maria Barbara of Frederick Guntrum and Anna, b. Oct 2, 1769; bapt.
Nov 5, 1769. Spon: Daniel Schuy and Anna Barbara.
John of John Braun and Maria, b. Oct 21, 1769; bapt. Nov 5, 1769.
Spon: John Teben and wife Catharine.
Adam of Wendel Bartholomae and Maria Elizabeth, b. Nov 10, 1769;
bapt. Dec 17, 1769. Spon: Adam Philipps and wife Magdalene.

BAPTISMS OF REV. JOHN CONRAD BUCHER, APR 1770-JUN 1779

John Henry of Henry Huber and Elizabeth, b. Nov 27, 1769; bapt.
Dec 17, 1769. Spon: Michael Wild and Amelia Tibi.
John of Christian Weyrich and Margaret, b. Feb 17, 1770; bapt. Apr
12, 1770. Spon: John Bickel and Maria Elizabeth Gerst.
Catharine Margaret of Adam Baldt and Christine, b. May 9, 1770;
bapt. May 24, 1770. Spon: Peter Winkelblech and wife Margaret.
Maria Eva of John Boesshaar and Anna Maria, b. Apr 10, 1770; bapt.
May 24, 1770. Spon: Matthias Boesshaar and wife Maria
Apollonia.
John Frederick of John Schuy and Catharine, b. Dec 11, 1769; bapt.
May 24, 1770. Spon: Daniel Schuy and wife Barbara.
John Henry of John Baumgaertner and Catharine, b. Apr 15, 1770;
bapt. May 24, 1770. Spon: Henry Baumgaertner and wife Rosina.
John Michael of John Dubbs and Catharine, b. May 13, 1770; bapt.
May 24, 1770. John Michael Naeff and wife.
Maria Margaret of Peter Wallmer and Maria Barbara, b. Jun 3, 1770;
bapt. Jun 21, 1770. Spon: Peter Wallmer, Sr. and wife Maria
Margaret.
Anna Margaret of Christopher Hennich and Maria Catharine, b. Jul
3, 1770; bapt. Aug 5, 1770. Spon: Simon Duy and wife Anna
Catharine.
Catharine Elizabeth of Michael Burckert and Elizabeth, b. Jun 13,
1770; bapt. Aug 5, 1770. Spon: John Kniss and wife Catharine.
*(The next two baptisms were entered by the father of the children,
Henry Umholtz.)*

Henry of Henry Umholtz and wife, b. Jun 16, 1764. Spon: William Rauch and Barbara Rauch.

Jacob of Henry Umholtz and wife, b. Nov 19, 1766. Spon: Jacob Rauch and Anna Maria Jeckel.

John of Henry Umholtz and Margaret, b. -----; bapt. Aug 30, 1770. Spon: Jacob Fischer and wife Sabina.

John George of David Dueben and Elizabeth, b. Aug --, 1770; bapt. Aug 30, 1770. Spon: Frederick Boeshaar and wife Barbara.

John George of John Adam Stein and Maria Catharine, b. Sep 23, 1770; bapt. Oct 11, 1770. Spon: John George Stein and Amelia Tuebin.

Bernard of William Rauch and Barbara, b. Sep 19, 1770; bapt. Oct 30, 1770. Spon: Bernard Rauch and wife Anna Elizabeth.

Abraham of Killian Merck and Anna Maria, b. Nov 21, 1770; bapt. Nov 22, 1770. Spon: Conrad Merck and Philippina, wife of Henry Merck.

Maria Catharine of William Weyrich and Elizabeth Margaret, b. Aug 23, 1770; bapt. Dec 22, 1770. Spon: Peter Brechtbihl and Maria Catharine Simon.

John Christopher of Rudolph Baer and Catharine, b. Oct 11, 1770; bapt. Dec 23, 1770. Spon: John Dietz and wife Elizabeth.

John Henry of John Henry Dubbs and Anna Maria, b. Dec 4, 1770; bapt. Jan 16, 1771. Spon: John Dubbs and wife Catharine.

Maria Barbara of Jacob Brunner and Maria Margaret, b. Feb 6, 1771; bapt. Feb 13, 1771. Spon: Philip Kunselmann and wife Maria Barbara.

John Henry of Daniel Moser and Anna Maria, b. Feb 24, 1771; bapt. Apr 28, 1771. Spon: John Adam Guthman and wife Regina.

Abraham of Killian Lang and Magdalene, b. Dec 20, 1770; bapt. Apr 28, 1771. Spon: Martin Kueffer and wife Elizabeth.

John Jacob of John Braun and Anna Maria, b. -----; bapt. Jun 10, 1771. Spon: Jacob Henning and Amelia Tuben.

Conrad of Conrad Gerhard and Anna Maria, b. Jul 10, 1771; bapt. Aug 4, 1771. Spon: John Ulrich Jegly and wife Elizabeth.

John Henry of Daniel Stober and Anna Maria, b. Jul 16, 1771; bapt. Aug 4, 1771. Spon: Conrad Felton and Barbara Jegley.

John Henry of Peter Hederich and Philippina, b. Sep 11, 1771; bapt. Sep 29, 1771. Spon: Henry Schuy and wife.

John Wendel of John Wendel Fortune and Elizabeth, b. Aug 31, 1771; bapt. Sep 29, 1771. Spon: John Wendel Hautz and wife

Catharine.

John Henry of Jacob Rauch and Anna Margaret, b. Oct 4, 1771; bapt. Oct 27, 1771. Spon: Henry Umholtz and wife Anna Margaret.

Anna Maria of Adam Herper and Catharine, b. -----; bapt. Dec 23, 1771. Spon: Nicholas Albert and Anna Maria Duebin.

Eva Margaret of George Wallmer and Eva, b. -----; bapt. Dec 23, 1771. Spon: Adam Guthman and wife Regina.

Christine of Jacob Dubbs and Susanna, b. Nov 22, 1771; bapt. Dec 23, 1771. Spon: John Merck and Susanna Dubbs.

Anna Catharine of Henry Miller and Regina, b. -----; bapt. Mar 2, 1772. Spon: Rudolph Jaegly and Anna Catharine Merck.

Mary Magdalene of John Spittler and Catharine, b. Jan 22, 1772; bapt. Mar 30, 1772. Spon: Jacob Blank and wife Magdalene.

John Phillip of Jacob Roth and Elizabeth, b. Jan 21, 1772; bapt. Apr 26, 1772. Spon: Wendel Stoltz and wife Catharine.

John of Jacob Weber and Susanna, b. Apr 4, 1772; bapt. Apr 26, 1772. Spon: John Weber and wife Barbara.

Maria Margaret of John Wallmer and Christine, b. Mar 18, 1772; bapt. Apr 26, 1772. Spon: Jacob Moser and Margaret Hooch(?).

Anna Maria of Henry Lohmiller and Veronica, b. Apr 15, 1772; bapt. May 24, 1772. Spon: Frederick Gundrum and wife Anna.

John Peter of John Boeshaar and Anna Maria, b. Apr 15, 1772; bapt. May 24, 1772. Spon: Matthias Boeshaar and wife Apollonia.

Anna Maria of John Brechtbihl and Elizabeth, b. Apr 11, 1772; bapt. May 24, 1772. Spon: Anna Maria Brechtbihl.

John of John Jacob Tueben and Catharine, b. May 22, 1772; bapt. Jun 9, 1772. Spon: John Gasser and Anna Amelia Tueben.

John Henry of John George Kuntz and Elizabeth, b. Jun 21, 1772; bapt. Jul 19, 1772. Spon: Michael Cor (Kohr) and wife Barbara.

Maria Catharine of George Hederich and Catharine, b. Jun 20, 1772; bapt. Jul 19, 1772. Spon: Michael Philippi and Catharine Becker.

Catharine of Henry Zehrung and Susanna, b. Jul 24, 1772; bapt. Aug 16, 1772. Spon: Ludwig Zehrung and Catharine.

Maria Barbara of Peter Wallmer, Junior and Maria Barbara, b. Jul 16, 1772; bapt. Aug 16, 1772. Spon: John Wallmer and Christine.

Anna Margaret of Francis Albert and Maria Barbara, b. Aug 2, 1772; bapt. Sep 13, 1772. Spon: Jacob Hubler and Margaret Harper.

Bernard of Henry Umholtz and Anna Margaret, b. Sep 22, 1772; bapt. Nov 9, 1772. Spon: Bernard Rauch and Anna Maria.

John Jacob of Adam Gudtmann and Regina, b. Jan 2, 1773; bapt. Feb

1, 1773. Spon: John Jacob Moser and Catharine.
John Henry of William Rauch and Barbara, b. Jan 22, 1773; bapt. Mar 1, 1773. Spon: Leonard Neff and Anna Maria Kinny.
Barbara of Matthias Henning and Barbara, b. Jan 15, 1773; bapt. Mar 1, 1773. Spon: Barbara Scherblin.
John of Wendel Fortune and Elizabeth, b. Mar 25, 1773; bapt. Apr 12, 1773. Spon: Killian Merck and Catharine.
Elizabeth of George Geistweit and Maria, b. Apr 25, 1773; bapt. May 23, 1773. Spon: Philip Baumgartner and Margaret Taud.
John Jacob of Conrad Meyer and Elizabeth, b. May 30, 1773; bapt. Jun 20, 1773. Spon: John Jacob Moser and Eva Margaret Meyer.
John Jacob of Jacob Brunner and Anna Maria, b. Jun 18, 1773; bapt. Jun 20, 1773. Spon: George Kuntz and Anna Elizabeth.
John of Abraham Bleystein and Louisa, b. Mar 1, 1773; bapt. Aug 15, 1773. Spon: John Neff and Salome Vollhaefen.
Anna Catharine of John Bickel, Jr. and Sabina, b. Jul 28, 1773; bapt. Aug 15, 1773. Spon: Conrad Steinman and Anna.
John Henry of John Brechtbihl and Elizabeth, b. Jun 22, 1773; bapt. Aug 15, 1773. Spon: John Henry Dubbs and Anna Maria.
John Adam of John Adam Stein and Maria Catharine, b. Aug 2, 1773; bapt. Sep 12, 1773. Spon: Adam Harper and Catharine.
John Jacob of William Lang and Magdalene, b. Aug 4, 1773; bapt. Sep 12, 1773. Spon: Henry Zehring and Susanna Maria.
John of Balthasar Baumgartner and Magdalene, b. -----; bapt. Sep 12, 1773. Spon: Philip Kister and Margaret.
Anna Catharine of John Baer and Catharine, b. Sep 13, 1773; bapt. Oct 10, 1773. Spon: George Dollinger and Catharine.
Maria Elizabeth of Michael Wolff and Maria Elizabeth, b. Oct 12, 1773; bapt. Nov 8, 1773. Spon: Peter Wallmer and Barbara.
Daniel of John Schuy and Catharine, b. Aug 26, 1773; bapt. Nov 8, 1773. Spon: Daniel Schuy and Maria.
Elizabeth Barbara of Peter Reuber and Maria Barbara, b. Oct 11, 1773; bapt. Nov 8, 1773. Spon: John Adam Schmidt and Maria Elizabeth.
Jacob of Nicholas Hebling and Dorothy, b. Oct 11, 1773; bapt. Nov 8, 1773. Spon: Jacob Henning and Magdalene.
John Wendel of John Wendel Bartlime and Maria Elizabeth, b. Oct 4, 1773; bapt. Dec 6, 1773. Spon: Simon Duy and Catharine.
John Henry of Henry Miller and Regina, b. Oct 16, 1773; bapt. Dec 6, 1773. Spon: Henry Jegly and Anna Maria Rauch.

John of Jacob Rauch and Anna Margaret, b. Jan 7, 1774; bapt. Jan 28, 1774. Spon: Martin Kueffer and Elizabeth.

Anna Maria Elizabeth of Jacob Tuebin and Catharine, b. Feb 14, 1774; bapt. Feb 28, 1774. Spon: John Spittler and Catharine.

Maria Elizabeth of Jacob Weber and Susanna, b. Feb 8, 1774; bapt. Feb 28, 1774. Spon: Jacob Seltzer and Anna Maria.

John of Adam Harper and Philippina, b. Feb 28, 1774; bapt. Mar 31, 1774. Spon: John Simon and Anna Catharine Herper.

Anna Margaret of Henry Brunner and Catharine, b. Mar 26, 1774; bapt. Mar 31, 1774. Spon: John Brunner and Anna Margaret.

Christine of Jacob Boeshaar and Christine, b. Apr 5, 1774; bapt. Apr 25, 1774. Spon: George Schnatterlin and Anna Margaret.

John Peter of John Peter Wallmer and Barbara, b. Apr 13, 1774; bapt. Apr 25, 1774. Spon: George Wallmer and Eva.

John of Daniel Buerki and Catharine, b. Feb 1, 1774; bapt. Apr 25, 1774. Spon: Henry Lampert and Magdalene.

Anna Maria of Jacob Henning and Magdalene, b. Apr 5, 1774; bapt. Apr 25, 1774. Spon: Jacob Gasser and Margaret.

John William of Wendel Fortune and Elizabeth, b. -----; bapt. May 23, 1774. Spon: Michael Stroh and Eva.

John Adam of John Miller and Elizabeth, b. May 26, 1774; bapt. Jun 19, 1774. Spon: John Adam Stein and Maria Catharine.

Mary Magdalene of Michael Philippi and Maria Elizabeth, b. May 30, 1774; bapt. Jun 19, 1774. Spon: Adam Philippi and Anna Magdalene.

Christine of Simon Duy and Catharine, b. May 22, 1774; bapt. Jun 26, 1774. Spon: Frederick Schuetz and Catharine.

Rudolph of Erasmus Rosenberg and Regina, b. Jan 17, 1774; bapt. Jul 17, 1774. Spon: Rudolph Jeglin and Philippina Merck.

Christine of John Wallmer and Christine, b. Jun 13, 1774; bapt. Jun 29, 1774. Spon: Peter Wallmer and Maria Barbara.

Susanna Maria of Henry Zehrung and Susanna, b. Jul 13, 1774; bapt. Aug 17, 1774. Spon: Matthias Zehrung and Susanna Dubbs.

George Jacob of John Gerberich and Elizabeth, b. -----; bapt. Aug 17, 1774. Spon: George Dollinger and Catharine.

John Adam of George Hederich and Catharine, b. -----; bapt. Aug 17, 1774. Spon: Nicholas Simon and Maria Margaret.

John of Christian Seltzer and Maria, b. Aug 9, 1774; bapt. Aug 17, 1774. Spon: John Tueben and Anna Catharine.

John Peter of Peter Brunner and Anna Maria, b. Aug 5, 1774; bapt.

Aug 17, 1774. Spon: John Brunner and Margaret.

Maria Barbara of Balthasar Baumgartner and Mary Magdalene, b. Jul 21, 1774; bapt. Aug 17, 1774. Spon: Andrew Gerberich and Barbara.

John Jacob of Jacob Dubbs and Susanna, b. Jul 28, 1774; bapt. Aug 17, 1774. Spon: Henry Lohmiller and Veronica.

John of John Spittler and Catharine, b. Jul 26, 1774; bapt. Aug 17, 1774. Spon: Jacob Duben and Catharine.

John Jacob of Jacob Henning and Anna Barbara, b. Aug 4, 1774; bapt. Sep 11, 1774. Spon: Jacob Gasser and Margaret.

Maria Catharine of Christian Stucky and Anna Maria, b. Jun 24, 1774; bapt. Aug 17, 1774. Spon: Michael Velten and Maria Margaret Buhr.

Anna Maria Margaret of John Boeshaar and Anna Maria, b. Aug 30, 1774; bapt. Oct 9, 1774. Spon: Matthias Boeshaar and Maria Apollonia.

Catharine Margaret of George Wallmer and Eva Barbara, b. Oct 13, 1774; bapt. Nov 5, 1774. Spon: Adam Stober and Catharine Margaret Munich.

Maria Catharine of John Neff and Salome, b. Oct 24, 1774; bapt. Nov 5, 1774. Spon: John Dubbs and Catharine Vollhaver.

Maria Elizabeth of Jacob Mosser and Eva Margaret, b. Sep 26, 1774; bapt. Nov 5, 1774. Spon: Conrad Meyer and Maria Elizabeth.

Anna Maria of Michael Kohr and Barbara, b. Nov 3, 1774; bapt. Dec 5, 1774. Spon: Henry Schnetterlin and Barbara.

Frederick Adam of Frederick Adam Huber and Catharine, b. Nov 5, 1774; bapt. Dec 5, 1774. Spon: parents.

John Adam of Francis Albert and Maria Barbara, b. Jan 14, 1775; bapt. Jan 30, 1775. Spon: John Adam Dittler and Maria Catharine Hubler.

Anna Maria of Conrad Gerhardt and Anna Maria, b. Dec 27, 1774; bapt. Jan 30, 1774. Spon: Philip Gasser and Anna Maria Kiny.

John Adam of John Brechtbihl and Elizabeth, b. Dec 19, 1774; bapt. Feb 27, 1775. Spon: John Adam Baumgartner and Elizabeth.

Susanna Catharine of James Laller (Lawler) and Anna Maria, b. Feb 4, 1775; bapt. Feb 27, 1775. Spon: Henry Zehrung and Susanna.

John of Henry Dubbs and Anna Maria, b. Jan 2, 1775; bapt. Feb 27, 1775. Spon: John Gasser and Christine Maurer.

Catharine Barbara of Henry Bickel and Magdalene, b. Feb 8, 1775; bapt. Feb 27, 1775. Spon: Michael Hoffman and Barbara Bickel.

John Henry of John Henry Lampert and Magdalene, b. Feb 25, 1775; bapt. Mar 27, 1775. Spon: John Henry Fretzler and Juliana.

Maria Catharine of Wendel Bartholomeh and Maria Elizabeth, b. Feb 24, 1775; bapt. Apr 14, 1775. Spon: Catharine Duy.

Magdalene of Daniel Moser and Anna Maria, b. Mar 3, 1775; bapt. May 22, 1775. Spon: Daniel Brunner and Ottilia.

Catharine of John Story and Dorothy Elizabeth Geist, b. Sep --, 1774; bapt. May 22, 1775. Spon: Catharine Grumm.

George of Thomas Friedrich and Margaret, b. Jul 2, 1775; bapt. Jul 6, 1775. Spon: George Boeshaar and Anna Maria Tueben.

John of William Rauch and Barbara, b. Jul 12, 1775; bapt. Aug 12, 1775. Spon: Michael Cohr and Barbara.

John of John Bickel and Sabina, b. Jul 16, 1775; bapt. Aug 13, 1775. Spon: John Dubbs and Barbara.

John of William Hedrich and Maria Margaret, b. Jul 20, 1775; bapt. Aug 13, 1775. Spon: Peter Fay and Apollonia.

Maria Catharine of Adam Baumgartner and Elizabeth, b. Aug 23, 1775; bapt. Sep 10, 1775. Spon: Adam Dittler and Catharine Boeshaar.

Nicholas of Nicholas Hebling and Dorothy, b. Jan 10, 1776; bapt. Jan 28, 1776. Spon: Carl Schmidt and Esther.

Magdalene of John Faber and Margaret, b. Nov 26, 1775; bapt. Jan 28, 1776. Spon: Killian Lang and Magdalene.

John of John Tueben and Dorothy, b. Jan 24, 1776; bapt. Feb 26, 1776. Spon: John Gasser and Anna Maria.

Mary Magdalene of Henry Miller and Regina, b. Jan 30, 1776; bapt. Feb 26, 1776. Spon: George Beydelmeyer and Magdalene.

Anna Barbara, daughter of Peter Hederich and Philippina, b. Mar 2, 1776; bapt. Mar 25, 1776. Spon: Andrew Gerberich and Anna Barbara.

John George of Peter Wallmer and Maria Barbara, b. Feb 29, 1776; bapt. Mar 25, 1776. Spon: Peter Reuber and Barbara.

John Henry of Jacob Weber and Susanna, b. Feb 21, 1776; bapt. Mar 25, 1776. Spon: Henry Schnatterly and Barbara.

Anna Margaret of Henry Zehrung and Susanna Maria, b. Mar 8, 1776; bapt. Mar 25, 1776. Spon: Philip Zehrung and Catharine.

Henry of Henry Dubs and Catharine, b. Feb 3, 1776; bapt. Mar 25, 1776. Spon: John Adam Gassel and Elizabeth.

Anna Barbara of Bernard Rauch and Margaret, b. May 10, 1776; bapt. Jun 16, 1776. Spon: William Rauch and Barbara.

Mary Magdalene of Adam Stein and Maria, b. -----; bapt. Jun 16, 1776. Spon: John Tueben and Catharine.

Maria Barbara of Michael Korr and Barbara, b. Aug 4, 1776; bapt. Sep 8, 1776. Spon: George Michael Weiss and Elizabeth.

Elizabeth of John Boeshaar and Anna Maria, b. Jul 12, 1776; bapt. Sep 26, 1776. Spon: Killian Lang and Magdalene.

John of John Wallmer and Christine, b. Aug 29, 1776; bapt. Oct 6, 1776. Spon: George Wallmer and Eva.

Margaret of Philip Gasser and Anna Maria, b. Jun 19, 1776; bapt. Oct 6, 1776. Spon: Jacob Gasser and Margaret.

Catharine of Thomas Friedrich and Margaret, b. Oct 6, 1776; bapt. Oct 27, 1776. Spon: John Tueben and Catharine.

Maria Catharine of Matthias Henning and Anna Barbara, b. Jul 19, 1776; bapt. Oct 26, 1776. Spon: Jacob Neff and Margaret.

Elizabeth of Andrew Scherck and Anna Maria, b. Oct 5, 1776; bapt. Oct 27, 1776. Spon: Anthony Krumm and Catharine.

Adam of Adam Baumgartner and Elizabeth, b. Feb 3, 1777; bapt. Mar 24, 1777. Spon: Jacob Boeshaar and Ottilia.

Frederick of Simon Duy and Catharine, b. Jan 23, 1777; bapt. Mar 24, 1777. Spon: John Brunner and Anna Margaret.

John of Balthasar Baumgartner and Magdalene, b. Mar 18, 1777; bapt. Apr 21, 1777. Spon: John Gerberich and Catharine Hess.

John of John Faber and Margaret, b. Mar 30, 1777; bapt. Apr 21, 1777. Spon: John Spittler and Catharine.

William of William Hederich and Margaret, b. Mar 17, 1777; bapt. May 19, 1777. Spon: Jacob Gluck (?) and Elizabeth.

Mary Magdalene of Wendel Fortune and Elizabeth, b. -----; bapt. Jul 13, 1777. Spon: J. Adam Stein and Maria Catharine.

John Henry of Christian Zehrung and Christine, b. May 26, 1777; bapt. Jul 13, 1777. Spon: Henry Zehrung and Susanna.

Anna Regina of Conrad Gerhardt and Anna Maria, b. Sep 25, 1777; bapt. Oct 2, 1777. Spon: Henry Miller and Regina.

Anna Elizabeth of Conrad Gerhardt and Anna Maria, b. Sep 25, 1777; bapt. Oct 2, 1777. Spon: Rudolph Jegly and Juliana Veltin.

George of John Dricki(?) and Dorothy, b. -----; bapt. Oct 2, 1777. Spon: John Seyler and Barbara Bickel.

Catharine Barbara of Frederick Boeshaar and Barbara, b. -----; bapt. Oct 2, 1777. Spon: George Boeshaar and Catharine.

Rosina of Casper Brentzenkofer and Susanna, b. Oct 28, 1777; bapt. Dec 1, 1777. Spon: Rosina Schauffler.

Christian of Daniel Heckedorn and Elizabeth, b. Dec 5, 1777; bapt.
Dec 26, 1777. Spon: Anthony Krumm and Anna Catharine.

Abraham of Peter Hederich and Philippina, b. Jan 5, 1778; bapt. Jan
26, 1778. Spon: Nicholas Albert.

John William of William Rauch and Barbara, b. Nov 29, 1777; bapt.
Jan 26, 1778. Spon: Philip Gasser and Anna Maria.

John Jacob of Jacob Scherblin and Brisilla (Priscilla), b. Feb 21, 1778;
bapt. Mar 22, 1778. Spon: Henry Zehrung and Susanna Maria.

Anna Elizabeth of Bernard Rauch, Jr. and Margaret, b. Jan 19, 1778;
bapt. Mar 22, 1778. Spon: Bernard Rauch, Sr. and Anna
Elizabeth.

Maria Barbara of Nicholas Albert and Catharine, b. Feb 8, 1778; bapt.
Mar 22, 1778. Spon: Francis Albert and Maria Barbara.

Henry of John Dubbs and Christine, b. Dec 22, 1778; bapt. Mar 22,
1778. Spon: Nicholas Schneider and Maria.

John Michael of Jacob Rauch and Anna Margaret, b. May 24, 1778;
bapt. Jun 14, 1778. Spon: Michael Henly and Anna Maria.

John of Philip Gasser and Anna Maria, b. Jun 22, 1778; bapt. Jul 12,
1778. Spon: William Rauch and Barbara.

Benjamin of John Booshaar and Anna Maria, b. Oct 16, 1778; bapt.
Dec 29, 1778. Spon: Matthias Booshaar and Maria Apollonia.

Abraham of Thomas Belz and wife, b. Jan 5, 1782; bapt. -----. Spon:
Abraham Duboi and Magdalene. *(This baptism entered by a
different hand.)*

Maria Salome of John Neff and Maria Salome, b. Jan 29, 1779; bapt.
Apr 5, 1779. Spon: John Jacob Lohman and Catharine Vollhaver.

Catharine Elizabeth of John Wallmer and Christine, b. Feb 23, 1779;
bapt. Apr 25, 1779. Spon: Henry Brunner and Catharine.

Maria Catharine of Adam Dittler and Catharine, b. May 14, 1779;
bapt. Jun 27, 1779. Spon: Jacob Moser and Sabina Tueben.

John Adam of Balthasar Baumgartner and Magdalene, b. May 7,
1779; bapt. Jun 27, 1779. Spon: Adam Merck and Catharine
Vollhafer.

Maria Elizabeth of Francis Albert and Maria Barbara, b. Jul 21, 1779;
bapt. Aug 4, 1779. Spon: Jacob Rauch and Anna Margaret.

Jacob of William Rauch and Barbara, b. Feb 19, 1780; bapt. Mar 23,
1780. Spon: Jacob Eberecht and Catharine.

Elizabeth of Abraham Duboy and Magdalene, b. Feb 13, 1780; bapt.
Mar 23, 1780. Spon: Abraham Latscher and Catharine.

BAPTISMS BY WM. HENDEL

John Jacob of John Seyler and Maria, b. May 22, (1780); bapt. Jun
    25, (1780). Spon: John Bickel and Margaret.
Susanna of Philip Zehring and Catharine, b. Sep 12, 1780; bapt. Oct
    30, 1780. Spon: Henry Zehring and Susanna.
John of John Dups and Elizabeth, b. Apr 30, 1779; bapt. May 16,
    1779. Spon: John Dups and Barbara.
Jacob of Henry Mueller and Regina, b. Aug 22, 1781; bapt. Sep 30,
    1781. Spon: Jacob Bickel and Maria Gerhardt.

BAPTISMS BY REV. JOHN WM RUNDEL, OCT 1781-MAY 1784

John Jacob of Henry Lohmiller and Veronica, b. Sep 8, 1781; bapt.
    Oct 15, 1781. Spon: John Schneble and Sabina.
John of Michael Brecht and wife, b. Dec 24, 1781; bapt. Mar 4, 1782.
    Spon: John Winter and Margaret.
David of John Brecht and Margaret, b. Jan 22, 1782; bapt. May 19,
    1782. Spon: parents.
Anna Barbara of John Gundrum and Susanna, b. Nov 16, 1781; bapt.
    May 19, 1782. Spon: Michael Selser and Barbara.
Maria Catharine of Christian Hirschberger and Catharine, b. May 24,
    1782; bapt. Jul 14, 1782. Spon: Magdalena Merck, single.
George of George Lohs and Maria Elizabeth, b. Jul 5, 1782; bapt. Aug
    11, 1782. Spon: Anthony Fuchs and Elizabeth.
Mary Magdalene of Abraham Duboy and Magdalene, b. Jul 30, 1782;
    bapt. Aug 11, 1782. Spon: Christian Selzer and Mary Magdalene.
Daniel of Philip Ranck and Magdalene, b. Nov 11, 1777; bapt. Aug 12,
    1782. Spon: Casper Viehman and Catharine.
Abraham of Philip Ranck and Magdalene, b. Oct 11, 1780; bapt. Aug
    12, 1782. Spon: Abraham Stein and Anna Maria.
Magdalene of Bernard Eisenhuth and Elizabeth, b. Apr 10, 1782;
    bapt. Sep 8, 1782. Spon: Abraham Duboy and Mary Magdalene.
John Henry of Henry Dubs and Catharine, b. Nov 6, 1782; bapt. Dec
    3, 1782. Spon: John Dubs and Catharine.
John of Thomas Friederich and Margaret, b. Oct 11, 1782; bapt. Dec
    3, 1782. Spon: parents.
Catharine Susanna of Joseph von Gundy and Magdalene, b. Jun 26,
    1782; bapt. Dec 3, 1782. Spon: Henry Dubs and Catharine.
Henry of John Bickel and Sabina, b. Nov 18, 1782; bapt. Jan 19,

1783. Spon: Henry Bickel and Magdalene.

Jacob of John Baer and Catharine, b. Dec 6, 1782; bapt. Jan 19, 1783. Spon: Jacob Blanck and Magdalene.

Philip of Balthasar Baumgartner and Magdalene, b. Jan 7, 1783; bapt. Feb 8, 1783. Spon: Philip Baumgartner and Magdalene.

Philip of William Rauch and Barbara, b. Jan 1, 1783; bapt. Feb 16, 1783. Spon: Philip Gassert and Anna Maria.

Elizabeth of John Dubs, Jr. and Elizabeth, b. Jan 27, 1783; bapt. Feb 16, 1783. Spon: Henry Hautz and Barbara.

Benjamin of Philip Zehring and Catharine, b. Jan 22, 1783; bapt. Feb 27, 1783. Spon: Henry Dubs and Catharine.

Jacob of Michael Brecht and Barbara, b. Jun 5, 1783; bapt. Jun 29, 1783. Spon: John Dubs and Elizabeth.

Maria Margaret of John Jacob Judt and Eva Catharine, b. Jul 7, 1783; bapt. Aug 2, 1783. Spon: the father

Barbara Stehli, adult, dau. of ----- Stehli, b. -----; bapt. Aug 3, 1783. Spon: -----.

Adam of John Spitler and Catharine, b. Aug 5, 1783; bapt. Oct 5, 1783. Spon: Henry Dubs and Catharine.

Elizabeth of Jacob Gassert and Anna, b. Sep 1, 1783; bapt. Oct 5, 1783. Spon: John Dubs, Sr. and wife.

Jacob of Jacob Weyerich and Magdalene, b. Jun 24, 1783; bapt. Jul 18, 1783. Spon: Michael Streher and Susanna.

John of Jacob Loos and Maria Catharine, b. Aug 20, 1783; bapt. Oct 5, 1783. Spon: John Schwartz and Catharine.

John Henry of Henry Zehring and Elizabeth, b. Sep 26, 1783; bapt. Nov 2, 1783. Spon: Henry Zehring, Sr. and Susanna Maria.

Catharine of Philip Gassert and Anna Maria, b. Sep 5, 1783; bapt. Nov 29, 1783. Spon: Michael Seltzer and Barbara.

John of Ludwig Zehring and Julianna, b. Sep 21, 1783; bapt. Nov 30, 1783. Spon: John Besshor and Anna Maria.

Ludwig of Ludwig Zehring and Julianna, b. Sep 21, 1783; bapt. Nov 30, 1783. Spon: Henry Zehring and Elizabeth.

Michael of John Neef and Salome, b. Oct 31, 1783; bapt. Nov 30, 1783. Spon: John Becker and Elizabeth.

Jacob of Thomas Friederich and Margaret, b. Sep 19, 1783; bapt. Dec 26, 1783. Spon: parents.

John George of Jacob Dueven and Catharine, b. Nov 15, 1783; bapt. Dec 27, 1783. Spon: parents.

John George of Daniel Weidel and Sarah, b. Feb 1, 1784; bapt. Feb

29, 1784. Spon: George Schaller and Barbara.

Sarah of Jacob Goettel and Magdalene, b. Dec 31, 1783; bapt. Feb 29, 1784. Spon: Abraham Stein and Maria.

John of Nicholas Schneider and Maria, b. Feb 4, 1784; bapt. Feb 29, 1784. Spon: Jacob Bortner and Susanna.

William of Michael Ehler and Anna Maria, b. Dec 10, 1783; bapt. Feb 29, 1784. Spon: Daniel Weidel and Sarah.

Jacob of Peter Bross and Magdalene, b. Dec 17, 1783; bapt. Feb 29, 1784. Spon: Jacob Schneider, single.

John George of Anthony Fuchs and Elizabeth, b. Nov 20, 1783; bapt. Mar 28, 1784. Spon: George Loos and Maria Elizabeth.

John of Michael Selsser and Barbara, b. Dec 3, 1783; bapt. Mar 28, 1784. Spon: Philip Gasser and Anna Maria.

Maria Catharine of Nicholas Alberthal and Maria, b. Dec 30, 1783; bapt. May 13, 1784. Spon: Daniel Miller and Maria Catharine.

BAPTISMS BY REV. LUDWIG LUPP, JAN 1785-APR 1798

Regina of Henry Mueller and Anna Regina, b. Dec 24, 1784; bapt. ---. Spon: ---.

Catharine of Henry Hammer and Julianna, b. Jan 22, 1785; bapt. ---. Spon: ---.

Anna Barbara of Jacob Bickel and Mary, b. Jan 22, 1785; bapt. ---. Spon: ---.

John of Jacob Bickel and Mary, b. Mar 25, 1783; bapt. ---. Spon: ---.

Christian of Jacob Weyrich and wife, b. Dec 8, 1784; bapt. Jan 9, 1785. Spon: Anthony Fuchs and wife.

Jonas of Henry Zehrung and wife, b. May 8, 1785; bapt. Jun 12, 1785. Spon: Jonas Rub (Rupp) and wife.

Philip of Philip Baumgartner and wife, b. Mar 16, 1785; bapt. Apr 16, 1785. Spon: Anthony Fuchs and wife.

Catharine of John Schwartz and wife, b. Apr 16, 1785; bapt. May 12, 1785. Spon: John Loos and wife.

David of Christian Hirschberger and wife, b. -----; bapt. -----. Spon: Anthony Fuchs and wife.

John Henry of John Petri and wife, b. Sep 22, 1785; bapt. Nov 13, 1785. Spon: John Henry Lohmueller and wife.

John Jacob of John Boesshaar and wife, b. Oct 4, 1785; bapt. Nov 13, 1785. Spon: Jacob Blanck and wife.

Abraham of Abraham Debo (Duboy) and wife, b. Oct 11, 1785; bapt.

Nov 13, 1785. Spon: Michael Stroh and wife.

John George of John Seiler and wife, b. Nov 4, 1785; bapt. Nov 13, 1785. Spon: Jacob Baltz and wife.

John Henry of Adam Wendling and wife, b. Apr 8, 1786; bapt. May 14, 1786. Spon: John Brecht and wife.

Barbara of John Faber and wife, b. Apr 2, 1786; bapt. May 14, 1786. Spon: George Roland and wife.

Magdalene of Adam Merck and wife, b. Mar 25, 1786; bapt. May 14, 1786. Spon: Philip Baumgertner and wife.

Catharine of Hannes Scholtz and wife, b. Mar 25, 1786; bapt. Apr 17, 1786. Spon: Anthony Fuchs and wife.

John of Ezechiel Rembo and wife, b. Mar 12, 1786; bapt. May 14, 1786. Spon: Nicholas Alberta(l) and wife.

John of John Winder and wife, b. Apr 17, 1786; bapt. May 14, 1786. Spon: Valentine Schauffler and wife.

Barbara of William Rauch and wife, b. Apr 15, 1786; bapt. Jun 3, 1786. Spon: Jacob Rauch and wife.

John Jacob of Philip Gasser and wife, b. Sep 15, 1786; bapt. Nov 25, 1786. Spon: Jacob Brecht and wife.

Catharine of Peter Herrauf and wife, b. Sep 9, 1786; bapt. Mar 10, 1787. Spon: Christian Herschberger and wife.

Maria Sarah of Jacob Dubs and wife, b. Nov 7, 1786; bapt. Nov 26, [1786]. Spon: Jacob Wild and wife.

Anna Maria of Frederick Haman and wife, b. Nov 5, 1786; bapt. Nov 26, [1786]. Spon: Abraham Stein and wife.

Susanna of Frederick Haman and wife, b. Dec 25, 1786; bapt. -----. Spon: John Bickel and wife.

Ludwig of Henry Zehrung and wife, b. Jan 15, 1787; bapt. Jan 17, 1787. Spon: Ludwig Zehrung and wife.

John of George Ruhland (Roland) and wife, b. Jan 5, 1787; bapt. Jan 28, 1787. Spon: John Waver (Weber) and wife.

Elizabeth of Nicholas Alberthal and wife, b. Feb 6, 1787; bapt. Mar 18, 1787. Spon: Elizabeth Herber.

John George of John George Huber and wife, b. Mar 29, 1787; bapt. Apr 8, 1787. Spon: Philip Stein and wife.

John Adam of John Boeshaar and wife, b. Feb 19, 1787; bapt. Apr 8, 1787. Spon: John Adam Boeshaar and wife.

Catharine of Martin Bucher and wife, b. Jan 10, 1787; bapt. -----. Spon: George Unger and wife.

Abraham of John Loos and wife, b. Nov 12, 1786; bapt. Dec 15, 1786.

Spon: Abraham Loos and wife.
John Jacob of Jacob Bickel and wife, b. Mar 25, [1787]; bapt. May 6,
[1787]. Spon: Jacob Boltz and wife.
Jacob of Jacob Goettel and wife, b. Nov 18, [1787]; bapt. Mar 16,
[1788]. Spon: Henry Stein and wife.
Anna Maria of Henry Miller and wife, b. Dec 30, 1787; bapt. Mar 15,
1788. Spon: Rudolf Jegli and wife.
Catharine of Jacob Dubs and wife, b. Mar 21, 1788; bapt. Mar 26,
1788. Spon: John Dubs and wife.
Elizabeth of John Petry and wife, b. Jan 5, 1788; bapt. Apr 16, 1788.
Spon: Michael Ehler and wife.
Barbara of John Seyler and wife, b. Jul 15, 1788; bapt. Aug 17, 1788.
Spon: John Heyl and wife.
Anna Margaret of John Seyler and wife, b. Jul 15, 1788; bapt. Aug
17, 1788. Spon: John Bickel and wife.
George Frederick of Christian Krautler and wife, b. Dec 26, 1788;
bapt. Jan 14, 1789. Spon: Philip Gassert and wife.
Catharine of Jacob Bickel and Maria, b. Oct 11, 1789; bapt. -----.
Spon: Rudolf Joeckli and Catharine.
Mary Magdalene of Jacob Dups and Barbara, b. Nov 7, 1789; bapt.
Nov 14, 1789. Spon: George Hening and Anna Maria.
George of George Roland and Maria, b. Oct 15, 1789; bapt. Nov 26,
1789. Spon: George Huber and Anna Maria.
Elizabeth of Peter Zimmermann and Magdalene, b. Oct 4, 1789; bapt.
Nov 26, 1789. Spon: Philip Gasser and Anna Maria.
Anna Maria of Jacob Dieben and Catharine, b. Jan 1, 1790; bapt. Mar
27, 1790. Spon: Jacob Dieben and wife.
Elizabeth of Killian Lang and Barbara, b. Jun 10, 1790; bapt. Jun 20,
1790. Spon: Christian Leitner and Eva.
Christian of John Spittler and Catharine, b. Aug 20, 1790; bapt. Oct
17, 1790. Spon: Ludwig Zehrung and wife.
Anna Maria of John Schwartz and Catharine, b. Sep 15, 1790; bapt.
Oct 17, 1790. Spon: Henry Schwartz and Catharine.
Jacob of John Schultz and Catharine, b. Apr 22, 1790; bapt. May 23,
1790. Spon: Frederick Fetterh of and Susanna.
Sarah of John Rudolf Jegle and Eva Catharine, b. Sep 8, 1790; bapt.
Dec 1, 1790. Spon: Peter Seyler and Elizabeth.
Peter of Peter Boeshaar and Magdalene, b. Nov 1, 1790; bapt. Dec 1,
1790. Spon: Jacob Roehrer and Anna Maria.
John of John Kaempf and Margaret, b. Dec 3, 1790; bapt. Dec 25,

1790. Spon: Michael Stroh and wife.

Jacob of Jacob Moser and Rosina, b. Dec 14, 1790; bapt. Dec 25, 1790. Spon: Jacob Blanck and wife.

Mary Magdalene of Adam Wendling and Elizabeth, b. Aug 29, 1790; bapt. Dec 15, 1790. Spon: Anna Maria Wendling.

John of Henry Miller and Regina, b. May 22, 1790; bapt. Aug 15, 1790. Spon: Henry Joeckli and Anna Barbara.

Philip of Frederick Federh of and Susanna, b. Sep 2, 1788; bapt. Nov 20, 1788. Spon: Philip Heckert and Maria.

John of Frederick Federh of and Susanna, b. Oct 12, 1790; bapt. Apr 3, 1791. Spon: John Schultz and Catharine.

John of Isaac Lang and Magdalene, b. Feb 3, 1791; bapt. Apr 23, 1791. Spon: Killian Lang and Magdalene.

Catharine of Frederick Stroh and Susanna, b. Apr 17, 1791; bapt. May 15, 1791. Spon: John Brecht and Margaret.

Catharine of Benjamin Klarck and Margaret, b. Jun 20, 1791; bapt. Aug 15, 1791. Spon: Nelly -----.

Susanna of Jacob Bickel and Anna Maria, b. Sep 13, 1791; bapt. Oct 30, 1791. Spon: Henry Jegly and Anna Barbara.

Elizabeth of Jacob Dubs and wife, b. Oct 24, 1791; bapt. Nov 27, 1791. Spon: Christian Seltzer and wife.

Jacob of John Kaempf and Margaret, b. Dec 26, 1791; bapt. Jan 22, 1792. Spon: Henry Stein and Elizabeth.

Catharine of George Hubert and Anna Maria, b. Jan 23, 1792; bapt. Feb 19, 1792. Spon: Henry Weigand and Elizabeth.

Sarah of Henry Lang and wife, b. Jan 29, 1792; bapt. May 10, 1792. Spon: Jacob Kab and wife.

Barbara of Rudolf Jegly and wife, b. -----; bapt. Nov 25, 1792. Spon: Henry Voelcker and wife.

John Adam of Ludwig Zehrung and wife, b. Nov 2, 1792; bapt. Nov 25, 1792. Spon: Henry Zehrung and wife.

Peter of Ludwig Zehrung and wife, b. Nov 2, 1792; bapt. Nov 25, 1792. Spon: John Boeshaar and wife.

John of Henry Zehrung and wife, b. Oct 4, 1792; bapt. Nov 25, 1792. Spon: Henry Zehrung and wife.

Jacob of Jacob Merck and wife, b. Sep 16, 1792; bapt. Oct 28, 1792. Spon: David Merck and wife.

John Henry of John Winter and Margaret, b. Jan 13, 1793; bapt. Feb 9, 1793. Spon: Henry Henckel and Anna Maria.

John Henry of John Boeshar and Anna Maria, b. Jan 28, 1793; bapt.

Mar 17, 1793. Spon: John Boeshar and Anna Maria.

Elizabeth of Christopher Miller and Rosina,b. Jun 30, 1793; bapt. Aug 4, 1793. Spon: George Merk and Anna.

Catharine of George Miller and Margaret Elizabeth, b. Aug 23, 1793; bapt. Sep 7, 1793. Spon: Jacob Kraemer and Catharine.

Christine Elizabeth of John Kaempf and Margaret, b. Dec 25, 1793; bapt. Feb 25, 1794. Spon: Martin Meili and Christine.

Elizabeth of Jacob Sattelzaum and Magdalene, b. Feb 15, 1794; bapt. Apr 13, 1794. Spon: Martin Walb. and Elizabeth.

Abraham of Henry Lang and Mary Magdalene, b. Jan 8, 1794; bapt. Apr 18, 1794. Spon: John Boeshar and Anna Maria.

Anna Maria of Nicholas Albert and Catharine, b. Mar 12, 1794; bapt. Apr 21, 1794. Spon: Henry Henkel and Anna Maria.

John Frederick of Adam Stoever and Veronica, b. Mar 10, 1794; bapt. May 11, 1794. Spon: John Frederick Stoever.

George Henry of George Henry Mees and Dorothy, b. Mar 13, 1794; bapt. May 11, 1794. Spon: George Henry Merk.

Catharine of George Gassert and Christine, b. Nov 29, 1792; bapt. Dec 28, 1792. Spon: Peter Spicker and Catharine.

John of George Gassert and Christine, b. Mar 6, 1794; bapt. Jun 15, 1794. Spon: John Bickel and Sabina.

Sophia Catharine of George Schwartz and wife, b. Jul 28, 1794; bapt. Aug 31, 1794. Spon: John Bickel and Sabina.

Elizabeth of Werner Olwein and Catharine, b. Jun 22, 1794; bapt. Aug 31, 1794. Spon: John Bickel and Sabina.

John Rudolf of Rudolf Jegly and Eva Catharine, b. Oct 2, 1794; bapt. Jan 18, 1795. Spon: Christopher Loerch and Anna Maria.

Catharine of John Lohmiller and Susanna, b. Mar 11, 1795; bapt. Apr 12, 1795. Spon: Veronica Lohmiller.

Elizabeth of John Rang (Ranck) and Elizabeth, b. Feb 12, 1795; bapt. Apr 6, 1795. Spon: Henry Stein.

Margaret of Frederick Boeshaar and Elizabeth, b. -----; bapt. Apr 6, 1795. Spon: Margaret Boeshaar.

John of Benjamin Klarck and Margaret, b. Mar 21, 1795; bapt. Jun 7, 1795. Spon: Peter Spicker and Catharine.

Maria Catharine of Jacob Gassert and Elizabeth, b. Jun 7, 1795; bapt. Sep 18, 1795. Spon: parents.

Anna Maria of John Fischer and Hannah, b. -----; bapt. Jul 5, 1795. Spon: Daniel Lehme and Anna Maria.

Catharine of Peter Zimmermann and Magdalene, b. Nov 9, 1794;

bapt. Aug 30, 1795. Spon: Michael Zimmermann and Elizabeth.

Jacob of Christian Gengrich and Eva, b. Jun 23, 1795; bapt. -----.
Spon: Jacob Wendling and Anna Maria.

Elizabeth of John Ache and Elizabeth, b. Sep 11, 1795; bapt. Oct 25,
1795. Spon: Catharine Huber, widow.

Susanna of Jacob Dubs and Barbara, b. Sep 10, 1795; bapt. Oct 22,
1795. Spon: Philip Stein and Susanna.

Elizabeth of Henry Jegly and Anna Barbara, b. Mar 5, 1789; bapt.
Apr 26, 1789. Spon: Ulrich Felty and Elizabeth.

John of Henry Jegly and Anna Barbara, b. Nov 2, 1793; bapt. Apr 13,
1794. Spon: Sebastian Felty and Elizabeth.

Maria Margaret of Christopher Miller and Rosina, b. Oct 15, 1795;
bapt. Dec 25, 1795. Spon: John Zimmerman and Margaret.

Elizabeth of Henry Hammer and Anna Maria, b. Sep 16, 1795; bapt.
Jan 17, 1796. Spon: Martin Meili and Christine.

Maria of William Rieser and Catharine, b. -----; bapt. Jan 17, 1796.
Spon: Martin Meili and Christine.

John of John Diwin (Tueben) and Elizabeth, b. Jan 10, 1796; bapt.
Feb 14, 1796. Spon: John Boeshaar and Elizabeth.

Mary Magdalene of William Feycker and Magdalene, b. Feb 4, 1796;
bapt. Apr 10, 1796. Spon: Henry Dittel and Maria.

Susanna of Jacob Sattezahn and Magdalene, b. Feb 19, 1796; bapt.
Apr 10, 1796. Spon: Catharine Faber.

Elizabeth of George Mueller and Anna Margaret, b. Apr 10, 1796;
bapt. Dec 23, 1796. Spon: George Hen and Catharine.

George of George Hiller and Barbara, b. Feb 11, 1796; bapt. Apr 10,
1796. Spon: George Merck and wife.

Christian of Jacob Gassert and Catharine, b. Feb 19, 1796; bapt. Apr
10, 1796. Spon: Christian Seltzer and wife.

John of Andrew Beck and Elizabeth, b. Mar 31, 1796; bapt. Jun 5,
1793. Spon: parents.

George of John Runckel and Catharine, b. Jun 30, 1796; bapt. Jul 31,
1796. Spon: George Merck and Anna.

Peter of Michael Zimmermann and Elizabeth, b. Jul, 22, 1796; bapt.
Aug 28, 1796. Spon: George Merck and Anna.

Peter of Peter Zimmerman and Magdalene, b. Jan 2, 1796; bapt. Aug
28, 1796. Spon: George Bross and Elizabeth.

Catharine of Jacobus Wutz and Catharine, b. Sep 3, 1796; bapt. Oct
23, 1796. Spon: parents.

Magdalene of John Schwartz and Catharine, b. Sep 13, 1796; bapt.

Oct 23, 1796. Spon: John Runckel and Catharine.

Catharine of John Rang and Elizabeth, b. Oct 12, 1796; bapt. Nov 20, 1796. Spon: Catharine Franck.

Daniel of Henry Spittler and Margaret, b. Sep 14, 1796; bapt. Nov 20, 1796. Spon: Daniel Spittler.

Elizabeth of John Boeshaar and Elizabeth, b. Nov 19, 1796; bapt. Feb 12, 1797. Spon: Peter Boeshaar and Magdalene.

Catharine of John Lerch and Catharine, b. Feb 4, 1797; bapt. Mar 12, 1797. Spon: Peter Spicker and Catharine.

David of David Merck and Gertrude, b. Feb 3, 1797; bapt. Apr 17, 1797. Spon: John Schwartz and Catharine.

Susan of John Lohmueller and Susan, b. Oct 11, 1796; bapt. Apr 17, 1797. Spon: Adam Ulrich and Maria.

Elizabeth of Christian Kembel and Sarah, b. Aug 26, 1796; bapt. Apr 17, 1797. Spon: Elizabeth Mayer.

Susan of Christian Huber and Johanna Salome, b. Sep 16, 1796; bapt. Apr 17, 1797. Spon: parents.

Rudolph of Jacob Boltz and Margaret, b. Mar 16, 1797; bapt. Apr 17, 1797. Spon: parents.

Christopher and John William of Christopher Loerch and Anna Maria, b. Mar 25, 1797; bapt. Apr 17, 1797. Spon: parents.

Samuel of John Diwin (Tueben) and Elizabeth, b. Mar 5, 1797; bapt. May 7, 1797. Spon: Valentine Schauffler and Magdalene.

Elizabeth of Henry Schuy and Barbara, b. Apr 18, 1797; bapt. Jul 2, 1797. Spon: Henry Schuy and Barbara.

Margaret of Benjamin Klerck and Margaret, b. Feb 3, 1797; bapt. Jul 2, 1797. Spon: Adam Stein and Regina.

Elizabeth of Christian Volck and Margaret, b. May 17, 1797; bapt. Jul 2, 1797. Spon: John Boeshaar and Rosina.

Elizabeth of Michael Stroh and Apollonia, b. Apr 16, 1797; bapt. Jul 30, 1797. Spon: John Ache and Elizabeth.

Susanna of Daniel Weidel and Sarah, b. May 12, 1797; bapt. Jul 29, 1797. Spon: parents.

Henry of John Gerberich and Catharine, b. Jun 7, 1797; bapt. Aug 27, 1797. Spon: Henry Schuy and Barbara.

John of John Adam Mueller and Catharine, b. Jul 16, 1797; bapt. Aug 27, 1797. Spon: George Mueller and Margaret Elizabeth.

William of Alexander Robens and Maria, b. Jul 28, 1797; bapt. Aug 27, 1797. Spon: Jacob Wendling and Anna Maria.

John Jacob of Jacob Gasser and Elizabeth, b. Dec 18, 1796; bapt. Sep

24, 1797. Spon: parents.

John Jacob of Jacob Dubs and Barbara, b. Aug 5, 1797; bapt. Aug 30, 1797. Spon: John Walmer and Christine.

John Jacob of Andrew Beck and Elizabeth, b. Jul 6, 1797; bapt. Sep 24, 1797. Spon: Conrad Helm and Barbara.

Christine of Adam Merck and Margaret, b. Aug 23, 1797; bapt. Oct 21, 1797. Spon: parents.

Elizabeth of John Bickel and Sabina, b. Sep 7, 1797; bapt. Oct 22, 1797. Spon: parents.

Maria of Thomas Kobeheber (Kopenhaver) and Catharine, b. Oct 5, 1797; bapt. Dec 17, 1797. Spon: Henry Schuy and Barbara.

Anna Magdalene of Peter Seiler and Elizabeth, b. Sep 30, 1797; bapt. Dec 17, 1797. Spon: Magdalene Mueller.

Henry of Henry Rauch and Catharine, b. Nov 16, 1797; bapt. Dec 17, 1797. Spon: John Rauch and Margaret.

John of Jacob Backestoss and Barbara, b. Oct 23, 1797; bapt. Dec 17, 1797. Spon: John Herber and Barbara.

Samuel of Peter Ranck and Eva, b. Nov 22, 1797; bapt. Dec 23, 1797. Spon: parents.

Peter of John Jacob Zehrung and Catharine, b. Nov 16, 1797; bapt. Dec 26, 1797. Spon: John Nicholas Goetz and Barbara.

John Jacob of John Schnebely and Catharine, b. Nov 18, 1797; bapt. Dec 26, 1797. Spon: Rudolf Bickel and Catharine.

Catharine of John Henry Lang and Magdalene, b. Nov 20, 1797; bapt. Jan 14, 1798. Spon: Rachel Lang.

Maria Catharine of Christopher Mueller and Rosina, b. Dec 2, 1797; bapt. Jan 14, 1798. Spon: Adam Merck and Margaret.

Christine of Philip Gerberich and Anna Maria, b. Nov 22, 1797; bapt. Jan 14, 1798. Spon: Christine Schuy.

George of Ulrich Feldy and Elizabeth, b. Oct 16, 1797; bapt. Dec 26, 1797. Spon: Henry Jeckily and Barbara.

Margaret of John George Schwartz and Margaret, b. Nov 23, 1797; bapt. Apr 8, 1798. Spon: Adam Merck and Margaret.

(this is the last entry of Rev. Lupp. The next two were made by an unknown hand.)

Samuel of Abraham Herschberger and Veronica, b. Mar 3, 1798; bapt. May 28, 1798. Spon: Samuel Herschberger and Elizabeth.

John of John Lauck and Elizabeth, b. Aug 15, 1798; bapt. Sep 3, 1798. Spon: John Bickel and Sabina.

Eva of Henry Schuy, Jr. and Barbara, b. Sep 1, 1799; bapt. Oct 27,

1799. Spon: Eva Schuy.
Barbara of Henry Schuy, Jr. and Barbara, b. Jul 12, 1798; bapt. Sep
3, [1798]. Spon: Andrew Gerberich and Barbara.

ST. JOHN'S UNION CHURCH, FREDERICKSBURG

Elisabeth of Michael Wolf and Margaret, b. Mar 13, 1774; bapt. Apr 20, 1774. Spon: John Knies and wife Elisabeth.

Anna Margaret of Adam Sattezaum and A. Maria, b. Nov 19, 1773; bapt. Apr 20, 1774. Spon: Anna Margaret Winkelblech.

J. Jacob of J. Adam Gramlich and A. Maria, b. Apr 8, 1774; bapt. May 15, 1774. Spon: Jacob German and wife Maria Catherine.

Christina of John Henry Bucher and Barbara, b. Feb 28, 1774; bapt. May 15, 1774. Spon: Albert Kleinfelder and wife Christina.

Andreas of Sebastian Wolf and Margaret, b. ---; bapt. May 15, 1774. Spon: Andreas Wolf and wife Margaret.

Margaret of Jacob Hauer and Margaret, b. Jun 16, 1774; bapt. 17, 1774. Spon: Peter Deisinger and Margaret.

Susanna of Jacob Dany (Denny) and Margaret, b. Jul 18, 1774; bapt. 17, 1774. Spon: Geo. Walteberger and Susanna.

John of Gottlieb Roth and Elisabeth, b. Jul 26, 1774; bapt. Sep 7, 1774. Spon: John Kleinfelder and Catharine.

Michel of Daniel Boshaar and A. Maria (Boeshore), b. Jul 27, 1774; bapt. Sep 7, 1774. Spon: Michel Wolf and Margaret.

Margaret of J. George Meyer and A. Eva, b. Sep 12, 1774; bapt. Oct 5, 1774. Spon: Sebastian Wolf and Margaret.

J. Michel of J. Michel Eisenhauer and Catharine, b. Aug 28, 1774; bapt. Oct 5, 1774. Spon: Peter Schauer and Ester.

Jacob of Friedrich Kamper and Elisabeth, b. Oct 18, 1774; bapt. Nov 2, 1774. Spon: Cath. Meilyn.

Henry of Christian Meyer and A. Margaret, b. Apr 23, 1773; bapt. Nov 2, 1774. Spon: Peter Schauer and Ester.

Christian of Christian Mäyer (Moyer), b. Jun 21, 1774; bapt. Nov 2, 1774. Spon: George Schaefer and Catharine.

Susanna Maria of Peter Deisinger and Margaret, b. Dec(?) 26, 1773; bapt. Feb(?) 9, 1774. Spon: Jacob Geib and A. Maria.

Andreas of George Walborn and Catharine, b. Jan 1 (?), 1775; bapt. Jan 6 (?), 1775. Spon: Andreas Klunk and Magdalene.

J. Peter of Wendel Fischer and Eva, b. Nov 15, 1774; bapt. Jan 6, 1775. Spon: Peter Schauer and Ester.

John of Thomas Schmidt and Christina, b. Jan 25, 1775; bapt. Feb 1 (?), 1775. Spon: Christian Hoster, single.

Margaret of George Schaefer and Catharine, b. Feb 10, 1775; bapt. Mar 1, 1775. Spon: Sebastian Wolf and Margaret.

Christina Regina of Charles Klinger and Veronica, b. Mar 15, 1775; bapt. Mar 29, 1775. Spon: Jacob Schaefer and Regina.

Christoph David of Peter Schauer and Ester, b. Mar 31, 1775; bapt. Apr 23, 1775. Spon: Chris. David Schauer and Eva Margaret.

Marie Catharine of Anthon Hauer and Maria Barbara, b. Apr 17, 1775; bapt. Apr 23, 1775. Spon: Jacob Geib and A. Maria.

George Valentin of Adam Bender and Christina, b. May 11, 1775; bapt. May 25, 1775. Spon: Valentine Bender and Barbara Benye (Behney).

Cath. Margaret of George Walteberger and Susanna, b. Apr 21, 1775; bapt. May 25, 1775. Spon: Jacob Hauer and Margaret.

Eva Catharine of Henry Titel and Magdalena, b. Apr 29, 1775; bapt. May 25, 1775. Spon: Jacob Eckler and Margaret.

Peter of Peter Diel (Diehl?) and A. Maria, b. Apr 4, 1775; bapt. Jun 7, 1775. Spon: Peter Foltz and Cath. Meilun (Meily).

A. Rosine of Henry Mayer (Moyer) and Juliana, b. Jun 19, 1775; bapt. Jul 19, 1775. Spon: George Lentz and Rosine.

Elisabeth of Michel Burkert and Elisabeth, b. May 2, 1775; bapt. Sep 13, 1775. Spon: Peter Maurer and Elisabeth.

Carl of Sebastian Wolf and Margaret, b. Oct 17, 1775; bapt. Nov 5, 1775. Spon: Carl Rorig (Rehrig) and Margaret.

J. Michel of Christian Kohr and Marie Catherine, b. Oct 3, 1775; bapt. Dec 6 (?), 1775. Spon: Casper Kohr and A. Marie.

Cath. Elisabeth of Friedrich Kamper and Elisabeth (Gamber), b. Sep 26, 1775; bapt. Oct 9 (?), 1775. Spon: Cath. Meiun.

Marie Barbara of Peter Bucher and A. Marie, b. Apr 14, 1775; bapt. Nov 5, 1775. Spon: Marie Barb. Knies.

J. Friedrich of Carl Klinger and Frany (Veronica), b. Nov 4, 1775; bapt. Dec 13, 1775. Spon: Friedr. Kamper and Elisabeth.

Cath. Elisabeth of Carl Rorig and Anna Margaret, b. Dec 24, 1775; bapt. Jan 6, 1776. Spon: Sebastian Wolf and Margaret.

J. Peter of Peter Deisinger and Margaret, b. Dec 23, 1775; bapt. Jan 6, 1776. Spon: Peter Fols (Foltz).

J. Henry of J. Henry Bucher and A. Barbara, b. Dec 2, 1775; bapt. Jan 6, 1776. Spon: Albert Kleinfelder and Christina.

Barbara of Jacob Rauch and A. Margaret, b. Dec 6, 1775; bapt. Jan 6, 1776. Spon: Michel Kohr and Barbara.

J. Adam of Adam Schauer and Elisabeth, b. Jan 21, 1776. baptized Feb 7, 1776. Spon: Adam Bender and Christine.

J. Philip of Philip Desch and Margaret, b. Jan 28, 1776; bapt. Feb 7,

1776. Spon: Philip Zehring and Catherine.

Marie Catherine of Jacob Hauer and Margaret, b. Mar 13, 1776; bapt. Mar 19, 1776. Spon: Caspar Diel (Diehl) and Catherine.

Peter of Lenert (Leonard) Yerrier and Eva (Yerger), b. Feb 4, 1776; bapt. Mar 31, 1776. Spon: Peter Schauer and Ester.

Eva of Michel Wolf and Margaret, b. Feb 19, 1776; bapt. Mar 31, 1776. Spon: Eva Gottel (Gettle).

Marie Barbara of Johannes Wolf and Margaret, b. Jan --, 1774; bapt. Mar 31, 1776. Spon: Marie Barbara Schnebele (Snavely).

Catherine of Andreas Fricker and Marie Magdalena, b. May 8, 1776; bapt. Jun 19, 1776. Spon: parents.

Marie Elisabeth of Bernd. (Bernhardt) Hauer and Catherina, b. May 13, 1776; bapt. Jun 19, 1776. Spon: Henry Stump and wife.

Cath. Elisabeth of Adam Bender and Christina, b. Jul 24, 1776; bapt. Sep 11, 1776. Spon: Adam Schauer and Elisabeth.

Cath. Margaret of Lenert Winkelblech and Cath. Elisabeth, b. 11, 1776; bapt. Sep 11, 1776. Spon: Cath. Elisabeth Winkelblech.

Elisb. Margaret of Paul Wolf and Magdalene, b. Aug 8, 1776; bapt. Sep 11, 1776. Spon: Margaret Wolf.

Christina of Johannes Wolf and Magdalena (Margaret?), b. Aug 8, 1776; bapt. Sep 11, 1776. Spon: Christoph. Petry and Maria Barbara.

Margaret of Wendel Fischer and Eva, b. Dec 14, 1776; bapt. Jan 29, 1777. Spon: Andreas Walborn and Margaret Hofman.

J. George of Jacob Dany (Denny) and Margaret, b. Dec 11, 1776. baptized Jan 29, 1777. Spon: Peter Schmeitzer and Catherine.

J. Heinrich of Henrich Titel and Magdalena, b. Jan 15, 1777; bapt. Jan 29, 1777. Spon: Henrich Buckel (Bickel) and Magdalena.

Marie Elisabeth of Michel Eisenhauer and Catherine, b. Sep 1, 1776; bapt. Dec(?) 29, 1776 (?). Spon: Elis. Eisenhauer.

Marie Barbara of Jacob Weidman and Marg. Elisabeth, b. Feb 10, 1777; bapt. Feb 26, 1777. Spon: Niclas (Nicholas) Schwengel and Marie Barbara.

Johannes of Johan Emrich and Elisabeth (Emerich), b. Feb 5, 1777; bapt. Feb 26, 1777. Spon: Carl Rorig and A. Margaret.

J. Jacob of Peter Deisinger and Margaret, b. Mar 2, 1777; bapt. Mar 4, 1777. Spon: Jacob Hauer and Margaret.

Cath. Dorothea of Gottlieb Roth and A. Elisabeth, b. Nov 14, 1776; bapt. Apr 1, 1777. Spon: Martin Bardo (Berto) and Dorothea (Barto).

J. Jacob of George Schaefer and Catharine, b. Apr 1, 1777; bapt. May 11, 1777. Spon: Michel Wolf and Margaret.

Cath. Margaret of George Walteberger and Susanna, b. Apr 10, 1777; bapt. May 11, 1777. Spon: Jacob Dany and Margaret.

--- of Philip Desch and Margaret, b. ---; bapt. May 11, 1777. Spon: George Emmert and wife.

Marie Barbara of Henrich Bucher and Barbara; bapt. Jul 16, 1777; bapt. 6, 1777. Spon: Henrich Dubs (Dubbs) and wife.

Marie Elisabeth of Henrich Bucher and Barbara; bapt. Jul 16, 1777; bapt. 6, 1777. Spon: Philip Schmitt and Eva Kleinfelder.

A. Marie of Peter Bucher and A. Marie, b. Jan 14, 1777; bapt. 6, 1777. Spon: A. Marie Schmitt.

Eva Catherine of Peter Schauer and Ester, b. Jul 14, 1777; bapt. 6, 1777. Spon: Wendel Fischer and Eva Catherine.

Juliana of Henrich Mayer and Juliana, b. 3, 1777; bapt. Sep 3, 1777. Spon: Margaret Emrich (Emerich).

Niclaus (Nicholas) of Sebastian Wolf and Margaret, b. Oct 4, 1777; bapt. Nov 2, 1777. Spon: Niclas Wolf and Elisabeth.

J. Christian of Christian Kohr and M. Catherine, b. Nov 21, 1777; bapt. Dec 4, 1777. Spon: Michel Nehf (Neff?) and A. Marie.

A. Marie of Jacob Hauer and A. Margaret, b. Nov 10, 1777; bapt. Dec 28, 1777. Spon: Caspar Diel and Catharine.

Caspar of Daniel Boshaar and Elisabeth (Boeshore), b. Nov 16, 1777; bapt. Dec 28, 1777. Spon: Adam Schauer and Elisabeth.

Christina of Carl Rohrig and Margaret, b. Dec 12, 1777; bapt. Dec 28, 1777. Spon: Christina Roth.

Elisabeth of Peter Kapp and Christina, b. Dec 10, 1777; bapt. Dec 28, 1777. Spon: Elisabeth Nef.

J. Jacob of Frantz (Francis) Braun and Marie (Brown), b. Nov 26, 1777; bapt. Feb 25, 1778. Spon: Jacob Gashert (Goshert) and Barbara Steckbeck.

J. Adam of Lenert Winkelblech and Elisabeth, b. Feb 2, 1778; bapt. Feb 25, 1778. Spon: Adam Schauer and Cath. Elisabeth.

A. Barbara of Anthon Hauer and A. Barbara, b. Mar 29, 1778; bapt. May 3 (?), 1778. Spon: A. Barbara Braun (Brown).

Jacob of Wendel Fischer and Eva, b. May 3 (?), 1778; bapt. May 9 (?), 1778. Spon: Jacob Adam Sattetzaum and A. Marie.

Martinus of George Walborn and Catharine, b. 13, 1778; bapt. Aug 26, 1778. Spon: Martinus Walborn and Eva Kleinfelder.

Michel of MichelWolf and Margaret, b. Sep 17, 1778; bapt. Oct 21,

1778. Spon: Michel Stroh and Eva.

Johannes of Peter Eisenhauer and A. Marie, b. ---, 1778; bapt. Oct 21, 1778. Spon: Carl Rohrig.

J. Heinrich of Carl Klinger and Frenie, b. Nov 22, 1778; bapt. Nov 28, 1778. Spon: Henrich Siegfried.

Cath. Margaret of John Emrich and Elisabeth, b. Oct 16, 1778; bapt. Nov 28, 1778. Spon: Michel Horner and Margaret.

J. Jacob of Michel Eisenhauer and Catharine, b. Sep 21, 1778; bapt. Nov 28, 1778. Spon: Peter Eisenhauer and Anna.

Samuel of Eva Schuick (Shick), "Hure" (bastard), b. Nov 20, 1778; bapt. Nov 28, 1778. Spon: George Schaefer and Catharine.

Cath. Dorothea of Peter Deisinger and Margaret, b. Dec 14, 1778; bapt. Jan 6, 1779. Spon: Martin Berdaw (Barto) and Cath. Dorothea.

Bernd. (Bernhardt) of Bernd. Hauer and Catharine, b. Dec 17, 1778; bapt. Jan 6, 1779. Spon: Jacob Geib and A. Marie.

Magdalena of Paul Wolf and Magdalena, b. Dec 18, 1778; bapt. Jan 6, 1779. Spon: John Kempel and Magdalena Beny.

Heinrich of Peter Bucher and A. Marie, b. Nov 8, 1778; bapt. Jan 6, 1779. Spon: Henrich Dubs and A. Marie.

J. Philip of Andreas Fricker and Marie Magdalena, b. Feb 12, 1779; bapt. Mar 3, 1779. Spon: Johan Emrich and Elisabeth.

Adam of Johannes Eisenhauer and Barbara, b. Jan 4, 1779; bapt. Mar 3, 1779. Spon: Peter Schauer and Ester.

J. Jacob of Peter Brunner and Barbara, b. Mar 13, 1779; bapt. Apr 11, 1779. Spon: Jacob Gottel and Catharine Brunner.

Johannes of Friederich Kamper and Elisabeth, b. Mar 30, 1779; bapt. Apr 29, 1779. Spon: Jacob Gottel and Catharine Meily.

Marie Magdalena of Henrich Mayer and Juliana (Moyer), b. Mar 15, 1779; bapt. Apr 29, 1779. Spon: Paul Wolf and Marie Magdalena.

Christina of Jacob Dany and Margaret, b. Apr 6, 1779; bapt. May 16, 1779. Spon: Albert Kleinfelder and Christina.

A. Marie of Henrich Bucher and Barbara, b. Apr 10, 1779; bapt. May 16, 1779. Spon: Philip Schmidt and A. Marie Kunkelin.

A. Marie of Peter Schauer and Ester, b. Jun 4, 1779; bapt. Jul 16, 1779. Spon: Sigmund Schauer and A. Marie.

Friederich of Lenert Winkelblech and Elisabeth, b. Jun 10, 1779; bapt. Jul 21, 1779. Spon: Johannes Schaefer and Margaret Rausch.

Magdalena of Jacob Fosler and Eva, b. 25, 1779; bapt. Sep 8, 1779.

Spon: John Kempel and Magdalena.

Johannes of Henrich Titel and Madlene (Magdalena), b. Aug 15, 1779; bapt. Sep 8, 1779. Spon: Johan Rauch and Catharine Brunner.

George Michel of Henrich Herman and Madlene, b. Jul 27, 1779; bapt. Sep 8, 1779. Spon: George Wild and wife.

A. Marie of Sebastian Wolf and Margaret, b. Sep 26, 1779; bapt. Oct 13, 1779. Spon: Marie Boshaar (Boeshore).

Anna Eva of Johannes Wolf and Margaret, b. Aug 9, 1779; bapt. Oct 13, 1779. Spon: Michel Stroh and wife.

Cath. Elisabeth of Jacob Rauch and Margaret, b. Oct 22, 1779; bapt. - --. Spon: Elis. Eisenhauer.

Johannes of Carl Rorig and Margaret, b. Nov 25, 1779; bapt. Dec 15, 1779. Spon: Johannes Emrich and Elisabeth.

J. Henrich of George Schaefer and Catharine, b. Jan 22, 1780; bapt. Mar 8, 1780. Spon: Albert Kleinfelder and Christina.

J. Jacob of Peter Deisinger and Margaret, b. Mar 23, 1780; bapt. Apr 2, 1780. Spon: Jacob Geib and A. Marie.

Joseph of Joseph Gundy and Magdalena, b. Oct --, 1779; bapt. Apr 2, 1780. Spon: Friederich Kamper and Elisabeth (Gamber).

Jacob of Gottlieg Roth and Hanna(h), b. Dec 9, 1779; bapt. Apr 2, 1780. Spon: Adam Schauer and Elisabeth.

A. Marie of Nichlas Conrad and Margaret, b. Apr 3, 1780; bapt. May 3, 1780. Spon: Wilhelm German and A. Marie Bönyn.

Peter of Melchoir Beni and Barbara, b. Aapr 18, 1780; bapt. May 3, 1780. Spon: Paul Wolf and M. Magdalena.

Marie Eva of Anton Bauer and M. Barbara (?), b. Apr 1, 1780; bapt. Jun 7, 1780. Spon: Vincent Braun and A. Marie.

Johannes of Johannes Schmidt and Barbara (Smith), b. Mar 27, 1780; bapt. Jun 7, 1780. Spon: Velte Schmidt and Elisabeth Fürer.

Catharine of Daniel Clarke and A. Marie, b. May 16, 1780; bapt. Jun 7, 1780. Spon: Henrich Schnatterle and Elisabeth Brunner.

George Michel of Wendel Fischer and Eva, b. May 23, 1780; bapt. Jul 5, 1780. Spon: George Walborn and Catharine.

J. Henrich of George Lentz and Rosine, b. Jun 22, 1780; bapt. Jul 30, 1780. Spon: Henrich Zehring and Susanna Schaefer.

Johannes of Adam Schauer and Elisabeth, b. Aug 4, 1780; bapt. Aug 30, 1780. Spon: Johan Wohlleber and Madlena.

Magdalena of Jacob Hauer and Margaret, b. Sep 13, 1780; bapt. Sep 27, 1780. Spon: Andreas Walborn and Madalena.

Johannes of Daniel Kössler and Elisabeth, b. Sep 13, 1780; bapt. Sep

27, 1780. Spon: Johannes Böshaar and Marie.

Andreas of Johan Emrich and Elisabeth, b. Sep 22, 1780; bapt. Oct 1, 1780. Spon: Andreas Emrich and Margaret.

Cath. Elisabeth of Johan Gempel and M. Magdalena, b. Nov 1, 1780; bapt. Nov 29, 1780. Spon: Adam Schauer and Cath. Elisabeth.

Marie Cath. of Christian Kohr and M. Catharine, b. Nov 23, 1780; bapt. Jan 6, 1781. Spon: Jacob Hederich and A. Marie.

Marie Cath. of George Heilman and Marie, b. Jan 29, 1781; bapt. Mar 11, 1781. Spon: Jacob Wild and Catharine.

Jacob of Carl Klinger and Frane, b. Dec 4, 1780; bapt. Mar 11, 1781. Spon: Jacob Dany and Margaret.

Johannes of Peter Bucher and Marie, b. Feb 7, 1781; bapt. Mar 11, 1781. Spon: Peter Brunner and Barbara.

Gertraud of Henrich Mayer and Juliana, b. Mar 17, 1781; bapt. Apr 8, 1781. Spon: George Schaefer and Catharine.

Elisabeth of Philip Eisenhauer and Eva, b. Mar 12, 1781; bapt. Apr 8, 1781. Spon: Johannes Emrich and Elisabeth.

J. Jacob of Jacob Hederich and A. Marie, b. Jan 5, 1781; bapt. Apr 29, 1781. Spon: Jacob Geib and A. Marie.

Elisabeth of Barbara Eisenhauer (single), b. Mar 18, 1781; bapt. May 24, 1781. Spon: Baltzer Vetterhafe and Marie (Fetterhoff).

J. George of Nicklas Sauter and A. Marie (Souders), b. May 2, 1782; bapt. May 24, 1781. Spon: George Schaefer and wife.

George Peter of George Walborn and Catharine, b. Jun 12, 1781; bapt. Jul 8, 1781. Spon: Wendel Fischer and Eva.

Benjamin of Henrich Bucher and Barbara, b. Nov 22, 1780; bapt. Jul 8, 1781. Spon: Peter Klein and Margaret.

Adam of Jacob Dany and "Gret." (Margaret), b. Jul 25, 1781; bapt. Aug 1, 1781. Spon: Adam Schmidt and Catharine.

Marie Susanna of Andres Walborn and Helena (Magdalena)(?), b. Jul 15, 1781; bapt. 1, 1781. Spon: Susanna Kramer (Kremer).

Johannes of Bernd (Hauer) and Catharine, b. 9, 1781; bapt. Sep 2, 1781. Spon: Philip Eisenhauer and Eva.

Johannes of Johannes Ditzler and Marie Margaret, b. Sep 10, 1781; bapt. Oct 3, 1781. Spon: George Hautz and Elisabeth.

--- of Lenert Winkelblech and Elisabeth, b. Sep 16, 1781; bapt. Oct 3, 1781. Spon: Johannes Wohlleb(er) and "Gret."

M. Barbara of Peter Brunner and Barbara, b. 15, 1781; bapt. Oct 3, 1781. Spon: Peter Bucher and A. Marie.

J. Friederich of Friederich Walter Marte, and Susanna, b. Aug 15,

1781; bapt. Oct 3, 1781. Spon: Bernd. Hauer and Catharine.

M. Christina of Catharine Marte (Martin), "Hure" (bastard), b. Sep 10, 1781; bapt. Oct 3, 1781. Spon: Eva Koch.

Barbara of Paul Wolf and Madlena, b. Sep 24 1781; bapt. Nov 4, 1781. Spon: J. George Schaefer and Elisabeth Wolf.

Margaret of Michel Wolf and "Gret.", b. Sep 13, 1781; bapt. Nov 4, 1781. Spon: Sebastian Wolf and Margaret.

Elisabeth of Gottlieb Roth and A. M., b. Oct 18, 1781; bapt. Dec 23, 1781. Spon: Adam Schauer and Elisabeth.

Johannes of Johannes Huber and "Lies. Gret." (Elisab. Marg.?), b. Nov 15, 1781; bapt. Dec 23, 1781. Spon: Jacob Wolf.

M. Madlena of Henrich Titel and Magdalena, b. Dec 11, 1781; bapt. Dec 23, 1781. Spon: Margaret Eckler.

Anna Marie of Jacob Fohler and Eva, b. Oct 24, 1781; bapt. Mar 14, 1782. Spon: Adam Sattezaum and A. M.

Barbara of Niclas Schaefer and Barbara, b. Jan 13, 1782; bapt. Mar 14, 1782. Spon: Martin Kreitter and Barbara.

Christina of Wendel Fischer and Eva, b. Dec 25, 1781; bapt. Mar 14, 1782. Spon: Johannes Desch and Margaret Walborn.

Sabina of Johannes Kitzmiller and A. M., b. Dec 17, 1781; bapt. Mar 14, 1782. Spon: Johannes Emrich and Elisabeth.

Johannes of Peter Sattezaum and Barbara, b. Feb 4, 1782; bapt. May 9, 1782. Spon: Peter Volz.

Marie Magd. of Adam Bender and M. Christina, b. Oct 28, 1777; bapt. Jun 8, 1782. Spon: Marie Magd. Bender.

M. Christina of Adam Bender and M. Christina, b. Nov 7, 1779; bapt. Jun 8, 1782. Spon: Albert Kleinfelder and wife Christina.

Johannes of Adam Bender and M. Christine, b. Sep 12, 1781; bapt. Jun 8, 1782. Spon: Peter Winkelblech and "Gret."

Eva of Christoph Knabel and A. M. (Kneb), b. May 18, 1782; bapt. Jun 29, 1782. Spon: Wendel Hautz and Elisabeth Knobel.

J. Daniel of Adam Schmidt and Barbara, b. Feb 19, 1782; bapt. Jun 29, 1782. Spon: George Lentz and Rosina.

Johannes of Henrich Bickel and Magdalena, b. Jun 9, 1782; bapt. Aug 11, 1782. Spon: Johannes Bickel and Sabina.

Johannes of Johannes German and Elisabeth, b. Jun 10, 1782; bapt. Aug 11, 1782. Spon: Johannes Schallie and Barbara Schwab.

Marie Margaret of Johannes Winkelblech and Christina, b. Jul 16, 1782; bapt. Aug 11, 1782. Spon: Peter Winkelblech and M. "Gret."

M. Gertraud of George Schaefer and Catharine, b. Jul 23, 1782; bapt.

Aug 11, 1782. Spon: Henrich Mayer and Juliana.

Christina of Carl Rorig and "Gret.", b. Apr 28, 1782; bapt. Oct 9, 1782. Spon: Elisabeth Wagner.

J. Philip of George Philip Eisenhauer and Eva, b. Sep 2, 1782; bapt. Oct 9, 1782. Spon: Philip Peter Hautz and Catharine.

Johannes of Niclas Sauter and A. Marie, b. Oct 28, 1782; bapt. Nov 10, 1782. Spon: J. Emrich and wife.

Christina Barbara of Jonas Rudy and Barbara, b. 10, 1782; bapt. Dec 22, 1782. Spon: Albert Kleinfelder and Christina.

A. Margaret of Andres Walborn and Magdalene, b. Dec 20, 1782; bapt. Jan 16, 1783. Spon: Margaret Desch, widow.

Eva Barbara of Carl Klinger and Frany, b. Dec 20, 1782; bapt. Apr 10, 1783. Spon: Wendel Fischer and Eva.

M. Sabina of Ann Marie Clark, "Hure" (bastard), b. Mar 30, 1783; bapt. Apr 2, 1783. Spon: Rosina Ekler.

Christian of Lenert Winkelblech and Elisabeth, b. Jan 4, 1783; bapt. Apr 28, 1783. Spon: Peter Winkelblech and M. Margaret.

Carl of Adam Schmidt and Barbara, b. Mar 12, 1783; bapt. Apr 23, 1783. Spon: Carl Schmidt.

Jacob of Peter Bernhard and Magdalena, b. Mar 24, 1783; bapt. May 18, 1783. Spon: Jacob Ebrecht and wife.

A. Barbara of Daniel Boshaar and Elisabeth, b. Apr 19, 1783; bapt. May 18, 1783. Spon: Peter Schauer and Ester.

M. Magdalena of Peter Bucher and A. Marie, b. Apr 16, 1783; bapt. May 16, 1783. Spon: John Kampel and Magdalena.

M. Catharine of Peter Ditzler and M. Margaret, b. Jun 6, 1783; bapt. Jun 15, 1783. Spon: M. Catharine Ditzler.

Daniel of Henrich Huber and Catharine, b. May 19, 1783; bapt. Jun 13, 1783. Spon: Daniel North and Margaret.

J. Jacob of Johannes Emrich and Elisabeth, b. May 17, 1783; bapt. Jun 15, 1783. Spon: Johannes Desch and Margaret Kleinfelder.

Henrich of Philp Kunzelman and Barbara, b. May 17, 1783; bapt. Jun 15, 1783. Spon: Henrich Bickel and Magdalena.

Johannes of Johannes Stein and Elisabeth, b. Apr 12, 1783; bapt. Jun 15, 1783. Spon: Valentine Scheuffler and Eva.

Catharine of Johannes Schonaur (Schoener, Shaner), b. Jun 2, 1783; bapt. Jun 15, 1783. Spon: Jacob Ebrecht and Catharine.

M. Catharine of Johann Kempel and Magdalena, b. Jun 25, 1783; bapt. Jul 13, 1783. Spon: Henrich Kempel and M. Catharine.

Magdalena of Adam Schauer and Elisabeth, b. Jul 13, 1783; bapt. Jul

27, 1783. Spon: Henrich Bickel and Magdalena.

J. Adam of Adam Bender and Christina b. Jul 19, 1783; bapt. Aug 17, 1783. Spon: Adam Sattezaum and A. Marie.

Marg. Elisabeth of Johann Stetler ("Mennonite") and Margaret, b. Jul 13, 1783; bapt. Sep 7, 1783. Spon: Elisa. (daughter of Sebastian Wolf).

Johannes of Wilhelm Wetzel and A. Barbara, b. Sep 24, 1783; bapt. Oct 5, 1783. Spon: Henrich Berry and Elisabeth Wel(l)s.

Johannes of George Schaefer and Catharine, b. Sep 28, 1783; bapt. Oct 5, 1783. Spon: Caspar Stover and Barbara.

Christina Marg. of Fried. "Woltemade" and Susanna (Martin), b. Aug 28, 1783. bapt. Oct 5, 1783. Spon: Peter Deisinger and Margaret.

Elisabeth of Friederich Kamper and Elisabeth, b. Sep 12, 1783; bapt. Nov 3, 1783. Spon: Johann Emrich and Elisabeth.

J. Philip of Johannes Storzer (Stertzer, Stetzer), b. Sep 17, 1783; bapt. Dec 26, 1783. Spon: Peter Deisinger and Margaret.

M. Catharina of Johannes Ditzler and Marie Margaret, b. Jan 23, 1784; bapt. Mar 28, 1784. Spon: Christian S(c)huey and M. Cath. Ditzler.

Elisabeth of Jacob Hauer and Margaret, b. Feb 26, 1784; bapt. Apr 11, 1784. Spon: Johann Emrich and Elisabeth.

Jacob of Johann Kitzmiller and A. Marie, b. Dec 9, 1783; bapt. Apr 11, 1784. Spon: Jacob Hauer and Margaret.

Elisabeth of Michel Keller and Elisabeth, age 8 weeks; bapt. May 9, 1784. Spon: Johann Kempel and Madlene.

Elisabeth of Johannes Faber and Margaret, b. Apr 10, 1784; bapt. May 23, 1784. Spon: Peter Schauer and Ester.

--- of Gottlieb Roth and Hanna(h), b. Oct 27, 1783; bapt. May 23, 1784. Spon: Jacob Ebrecht and Catharine.

Friederich of Michel Wolf and Margaret, b. May 29, 1784; bapt. Jun 20, 1784. Spon: Friederich Seibert.

J. Henrich of Henrich Bickel and Margaret, b. May 20, 1784; bapt. Jun 20, 1784. Spon: Philp Kunzelman and Barbara.

Catharine of Henrich Schräder and Rosina, b. May 28, 1784; bapt. Jun 20, 1784. Spon: Andres Emrich and Margaret.

Catharine of Peter Sattezaum and Barbara, b. May 10, 1784; bapt. Jun 20, 1784. Spon: Andres Emrich and Margaret.

Barbara of Johann Winkelblech and Christine, b. Mar 21, 1784; bapt. Jun 20, 1784. Spon: Adam Sattezaum and A. Marie.

M. Catharine of George Walborn, b. Aug 1, 1784; bapt. 24, 1784.

Spon: Gottlieb Kayser and Catharine.

M. Magdalena of Jonas Rudy and Barbara, b. May 14, 1784; bapt.
Nov 11, 1784. Spon: Baltzer Ober Kirsch and M. Magdalena
(Kirst?).

Johannes of Peter Deisinger and Margaret, b. Nov 5, 1784; bapt. Dec
25, 1784. Spon: J. Emrich and mother Margaret (D).

Christina of Philip Eisenhauer and Eva, b. Feb 18, 1784; bapt. Jan 16,
1785. Spon: Albert Kleinfelder.

M. Margaret of Wilhelm Wetzel and Barbara, b. Jan 5, 1785; bapt.
Jan 16, 1785. Spon: Michel Wolf and "Gret."

E. Barbara of Jacob Goldman and M. Magdalena, b. Jan 27, 1785;
bapt. Mar 16, 1785. Spon: Henrich Herman and M. Magdl.
Goldman.

Michel of Johannes Eisenhauer and Barbara, b. ---; bapt. Mar 27,
1785. Spon: Michel Wolf and "Gret."

Peter of Johann Emrich and Elisabeth, b. Apr 15, 1785; bapt. Apr 24,
1785. Spon: Peter Schauer and Ester.

Johannes of Wendel Fischer and Eva, b. Apr 26, 1785; bapt. May 29,
1785. Spon: Albert Kleinfelder and wife.

Elisabeth of Carl Klinger and Frany, b. Mar 8, 1785; bapt. May 29,
1785. Spon: the mother.

Peter. son of George Schaeffer and Catharine, b. May 21, 1785; bapt.
Jun 26, 1785. Spon: George Lentz and Rosina.

Catharine of Peter Bernhard(t), b. ---; bapt. Jun 26, 1785. Spon:
Caspar Vic(h)man and wife.

J. George of Matthias Vetterhafe and M. Elisabeth, b. Jun 12, 1785;
bapt. Jul 24, 1785. Spon: George Fetterhafe and Catharine.

Johannes of Philp Eisenhauer and Eva, b. Mar 26, 1785; bapt. Aug 7,
1785. Spon: Wendel Fischer and Eva.

Susanna and Louisa (twins) of Matthias Köler and Catharine, b. Jan
20, 1785; bapt. Aug 7, 1785. Spon: the wife, their widowed
mother.

Catharine of Peter Brunner and Barbara, b. May 20, 1785; bapt. Sep
23, 1785. Spon: Catharine Hauer.

J. George of George Schaefer, Jr. and Catharine, b. Oct 24, 1785;
bapt. Nov 20, 1785. Spon: George Schaefer, Sr. and Catharine.

Johannes of Henrich Kempel and Catharine, b. Oct 19, 1785; bapt.
Nov 20, 1785. Spon: Johannes Desch.

A. Magdalena of Daniel Beshaar and Elisabeth, b. Nov 17, 1785; bapt.
Dec 18, 1785. Spon: Magdalena Beshaar.

Barbara of Baltzer Fetterhafe and M. Barbara, b. Feb 1, 1786; bapt.
Apr 16 (?), 1786. Spon: Johannes Eisenhauer and Barbara.
Catharine of Jacob Gundy and Madlena, b. Feb 4, 1786; bapt. ---.
Spon: Catharine Meily.
Johannes of Adam Grosbart and Sibylla, b. Nov 23, 1785; bapt. Jan
15, 1786. Spon: the parents.
Barbara of Melchior Beny and Barbara, b. Dec 1, 1775; bapt. Jan 24,
1786. Spon: The Father himself answered.
Martin of Melchior Beny and Barbara, b. May 15, 1778; bapt. Jan 24,
1786. Spon: The Father himself answered.
--- of Melchior Beny and Barbara, b. Feb 6, 1782; bapt. Jan 24, 1786.
Spon: Barbara Patz.
Catharine of Melchior Beny and Barbara, b. Jan 6, 1784; bapt. Jan
24, 1786. Spon: Peter Sattezaum and Catharine.
M. Margaret of Melchior Beny and Barbara, b. Oct 18, 1785; bapt.
Jan 24, 1786. Spon: Peter Winkelblech and M. "Gret."
Magdalena of Andres Walborn, b. Feb 23, 1786; bapt. Mar 26, 1786.
Spon: Magdalena Walborn.
J. Nicolaus of Johannes Seeger and Anna, b. Feb 15, 1786; bapt. Mar
26, 1786. Spon: Niclas Sauter and A. Marie.
Daniel of Jacob Bolander and Magdalena, b. Mar 4, 1786; bapt. Mar
26, 1786. Spon: Daniel Boshaar.
Dietrich of Dieter Walk and Margaret (Walker?), b. Mar 24, 1786;
bapt. May 14, 1786. Spon: Christian Schmitt and Catharine (?).
Magdalena of Peter Bucher and A. M. (Anna Marie?), b. Feb 9, 1786;
bapt. Jul 30, 1786. Spon: Philip Smith (lit.)
Marie of Christian Schmith and A. Marie (?), b. Jul 19, 1786; bapt.
Jul 30, 1786. Spon: Dieter Walk and Margaret.
Peter of Michel Wolf and Margaret, b. Jan 14, 1786; bapt. Jul 30,
1786. Spon: Friederich Seibert and Ann Eva.
Henrich of Friederich Kamper and Elizabeth, b. Jul 17, 1786; bapt.
Aug 27, 1786. Spon: Johann Kempel and Madlena.
Friederich of Wendel Fischer and Eva, b. Sep 15, 1786; bapt. Sep 21,
1786. Spon: Albert Kleinfelder, Jr. and Magdalena.
J. Friederich of Wilhelm Wetzel and Barbara, b. Nov 25, 1786; bapt.
Jan 14, 1787. Spon: Friederich Kamper and wife.
M. Magdalena of Johann Kempel and Magdalena, b. Dec 14, 1786;
bapt. Jan 14, 1787. Spon: Jacob Wenner and M. Magdalena.
George Henrich of Henrich Schrader and Rosina, b. Dec 23, 1786;
bapt. Feb 18, 1787. Spon: Friederich Waltemarte and Susanna.

Michel of Johannes Eisenhauer and Barbara, b. Mar 23, 1787; bapt. Apr 8, 1787. Spon: Michel Wolf and "Gret."

Catharine of Paul Wolf and Magdalena, b. Feb 3, 1787; bapt. Apr 8, 1787. Spon: Johann Fuchs and Catharine.

Jacob of Johannes Eisenhauer and Charlat, b. Jan 13, 1787; bapt. Apr 8, 1787. Spon: Jacob Becker and A. Marie.

J. Adam of Christoph(er) Schneider and "Gret.", "will be 5 weeks old in Apr"; bapt. Apr 8, 1787. Spon: J. Adam Moser and Barbara.

Marie "Lisb" of Jacob Heberling and Magdalena, 114 weeks old; bapt. Apr 8, 1787. Spon: J. Eisenhauer, Sr. and wife.

Ann Elisabeth of Johannes Klienfelder and Magdalena (?), b. Feb 6, 1787(?); bapt. Apr 8, 1787. Spon: Johannes Dösh and Ann "Lisb."

Johannes of Albert Kleinfelder and Magdalena, b. Mar 19, 1787; bapt. May 13, 1787. Spon: Jacob Walborn.

A. Catharine of Niclas Sauter and A. Marie, b. Mar 27, 1787; bapt. May 13, 1787. Spon: George Schaefer, Jr. and Catharine.

Peter of George Schaefer, Jr. and Catarine, b. May 12, 1787; bapt. May 28, 1787. Spon: George Lentz and Frany.

George Henry of Henrich Huber and Catharine, b. May 5, 1787; bapt. May 28, 1787. Spon: George Motz and Ester.

Michael of Johann Emrich and "Lib.", b. Jun 3, 1787; bapt. Jun 24, 1787. Spon: Johannes Schaefer and Magdalena Desch.

M. Magdalena of Jacob Wenner and Magdalena, b. May 16, 1787; bapt. Jun 24, 1787. Spon: Johannes Kempel and Magdalena.

Johannes of Jacob Hauer and "Gret.", b. Jun 16, 1787; bapt. Jul 22, 1787. Spon: Johannes Seeger and M. Barbara.

Barbara of Philip Eisenhauer and Eva, b. Jul 15, 1787; bapt. Aug 19, 1787. Spon: Johannes Eisenhauer and Barbara.

Henrich of Conrad Wagner and A. M., b. Jun 16, 1787; bapt. Aug 19, 1787. Spon: Henrich Schnatterly and A. Marie.

Magdalena of Carl Klinger and Rosina, b. Mar 31, 1787; bapt. Aug 19, 1787. Spon: Andres Walborn and Madlen.

Henrich of Henrich Kampel and Catharine, b. Feb 16, 1788; bapt. Mar 16, 1788. Spon: Henrich Dubbs and Catharine.

Marg. Elisabeth of Johann Seeger and Barbara, b. Feb 13, 1788; bapt. Mar 16, 1788. Spon: Jacob Hauer and Margaret.

--- of Henrich Emrich and Catharine, b. Apr 2, 1788; bapt. May 11, 1788. Spon: ---.

A. Catharine of Jacob Wenner and Magdalena, b. Jan 6, 1788; bapt. Jul 6, 1788. Spon: Johannes Desch and Elisabeth.

Ann Barbara of Johannes Eisenhauer and Charlott(e), b. Apr 8, 1788;
bapt. Jul 6, 1788. Spon: Johannes Eisenhauer, Sr. and Cath.

Cath. Elisabeth of Wendel Fischer and Eva, b. Jun 13, 1788; bapt. 4,
1788. Spon: Gottlieb Kayser and wife.

Marie Catharine of Bernd. Hauer and Catharine, b. Aug 17, 1788;
bapt. Sep 14, 1788. Spon: Philip Gunkel and Catharine.

Samuel of Jacob Gundy and Magdalena, b. ---; bapt. Dec 6, 1788.
Spon: Henrich Kempel and Catharine.

M. Catharine of Jacob Walborn and Juliana, b. Nov 16, 1788; bapt.
Dec 21, 1788. Spon: Gottlieb Kayser and M. Catharine.

Marie Catharine of Caspar Derker and Sara(h), b. Nov 15, 1788;
bapt. Jan 18, 1789. Spon: George Schaefer and Catharine.

J. Jacob of George Walborn and Catharine, b. Dec 29, 1788; bapt. Jan
18, 1789. Spon: Jacob Albert and M. Margaret.

Joseph of Daniel Böshaar (Baschore), b. Dec 9, 1788; bapt. Jan 21,
1789. Spon: Peter Bucher.

Johannes of Friederich Böshaar, b. Nov 15, 1788; bapt. Jan 21, 1789.
Spon: Jacob Kaster.

J. Adam of Andres Walborn and Magd. Elisabeth, b. Jan 18, 1789;
bapt. Feb 15, 1789. Spon: Adam Sattezaum and A. Marie.

Magdalena (?) (Moth name) (Son Christian Rec.), child of Albert
Kleinfelder and Magdalena (blank), b. May 20, 1788; bapt. Feb
2(?), 1789. Spon: Christian Walborn.

Catharine of Jacob Walborn and Juliana, b. Nov 16, 1788; bapt. ---.
Spon: Gottlieb Kayser and Catharine.

Jacob of Melcher Beny and Barbara, b. Feb 12, 1788; bapt. Apr 26,
1789. Spon: Jacob Fohler and Eva.

Lenert of Jacob Fohler and Eva, b. 4, 1788; bapt. Apr 26, 1789.
Spon: Caspar Greiser.

Isaac of Philip Eisenhauer and Eva, b. Dec 5, 1788; bapt. Apr 26,
1789. Spon: Johann (Albert?) Kleinfelder and Magd.

A. Margaret of Henrich Schrader and Catharine, b. Feb 23, 1789;
bapt. Apr 12, 1789. Spon: Samuel Bär and Margaret Hauer.

Catharine of Wilhelm Wetzel, b. May 8, 1789; bapt. May 16, 1789.
Spon: Catharine Berde.

J. Adam (duplicate?) of Michel Wolf and "Gret.", b. Mar 12, 1789;
bapt. May 21, 789. Spon: J. Adam Cassel.

A. Marie of Niclas Sauter and A. Marie, b. Mar 21, 1789; bapt. May
21, 1789. Spon: Bernd Hauer and Catharine.

J.Adam (duplicate?) of Paul Wolf and Margaret, b. Mar 12, 1789;

bapt. May 21, 1789. Spon: J. Adam Cassel.

A. Catharine of Philip Gunkel, b. May 16, 1789; bapt. Jun 1, 1789. Spon: Eva Gunkel.

Catharine of Michel Hunter, b. Apr 15, 1789; bapt. Jun 1, 1789. Spon: Johann Batz.

Catharine of Johannes Desch and Elisabeth, b. Apr 7, 1789; bapt. May 21, 1789. Spon: Henrich Kempel and Catharine.

David of Henrich Bickel and Magdalena, b. 20, 1789; bapt. Sep 20, 1789. Spon: Philip Gunckel and Catharine.

Johannes of Samuel Bähr and Margaret, b. Nov 13, 1789; bapt. Nov 28, 1789. Spon: Catharine Hauer.

Barbara of Jacob Benner and M. Magdalena, b. Oct 31, 1789; bapt. Dec 13, 1789. Spon: Rudy Merck and Barbara Walteberger.

M. Catharine of Christian Walborn and Magdalena, b. Nov 13, 1789; bapt. Dec 13, 1789. Spon: Catharine Fischer.

Catharine of Henrich Schnabele, b. Dec 4, 1789; bapt. Jan 1, 1790. Spon: Henrich Dubs and Catharine.

Jacob of Philip Eisenhauer and Eva, b. Dec 5, 1789; bapt. May 2, 1790. Spon: Jacob Gottel and Marie.

M. Elisabeth of Jacob Walborn and Juliana, b. Feb 13, 1790; bapt. May 2, 1790. Spon: Wendel Fischer and Eva.

A. Marie of Carl Klinger and Frany, b. Apr 2, 1790; bapt. Jun 20, 1790. Spon: Henrich Sigfrüh and A. M.

J. Andres of Johannes Seeger and Barbara, b. Jun 8, 1790; bapt. Aug 1, 1790. Spon: Andres.

--- of Martin Walborn, b. Jun 29, 1790; bapt. Sep 12, 1790. Spon: Johannes Walborn.

A. Marie of Friederich Kamper and Elizabeth, b. Sep --, 1790; bapt. Oct 10, 1790. Spon: Peter Schauer and Marie.

J. Jacob of Henrich Okam and Elizabeth, b. Jul 2, 1790; bapt. Nov 21, 1790. Spon: Jacob Gottel and Marie.

Elisabeth of Johannes Desch and A. Elisabeth, b. Sep 17, 1790; bapt. Nov 21, 1790. Spon: Elizabeth Desch.

Johannes of Andres Walborn, b. Oct 16, 1790; bapt. Nov 21, 1790. Spon: Wendel Fischer and Eva.

Cath. Barbara of Henrich Schnatterle and Ann Marie, b. Oct 20, 1790; bapt. Nov 21, 1790. Spon: David Böshaar and Barbara.

Johannes of Jacob Cassel and Magdalena, b. Nov 18, 1790; bapt. Dec 19, 1790. Spon: Johannes Desch.

Marie Margaret of Johann Eisenhauer and Charlott(e), b. Apr 30,

1791; bapt. Jul 1, 1791. Spon: Jacob Dany and "Gret."

J. Henrich of Henrich Okam and Elizabeth, b. Jan 13, 1791(?); bapt. - --. Spon: Henrich Schnabele(?) (doubtful) and A. M. (Probably H. and A. M. Schnatterly).

J. Jacob of Christian Walborn and Magdalena, b. Jul 26, 1791; bapt. 28, 1791. Spon: Jacob Walborn and Juliana.

Magdalena of Samuel Bahr and Margaret, age 7 weeks old; bapt. Aug 28, 1791. Spon: Jacob Gottel and Marie.

M. Elisabeth of Henrich Schnabele and Catharine, b. Oct 8, 1791; bapt. Dec 11, 1971. Spon: Henrich Stein and M. Elizabeth.

--- of Philip Schrack and Catharine, b. Oct 28, 1791; bapt. Dec 11, 1791. Spon: parents.

Susanna of Paul Wolf and Susanna, b. Oct 29, 1791; bapt. Dec 25, 1791. Spon: Widow Ph. Zerbe.

Margaret of Johannes (Albert?) Kleinfelder and Marie (?)(Magdalena), b. Dec 1, 1791; bapt. Apr 6, 1792. Spon: Margaret Boshaar.

George of Johann Caspar Weber and Veronica, b. Jan 11, 1792; bapt. May 20, 1792. Spon: Gottlieb Kayser.

Joseph of Carl Klinger and Veronica, b. Mar 8, 1792; bapt. May 20, 1792. Spon: Johann Wingert and Barbara.

Christina of Johannes Desch and A. Margaret (?)(A. Elizabeth), b. Apr 5, 1792; bapt. May 20, 1792. Spon: Albert Kleinfelder and Christina.

Cath. Elisabeth of Henrich Okam and Elizabeth, b. Aug 2, 1792; bapt. Nov 18, 1792. Spon: Catharine Meily.

Jacob of Jacob Cassel and Magdalena, b. Aug 23, 1792; bapt. Sep 29, 1792. Spon: Jacob Wenner and Magdalena.

J. George of Conrad Ernst and Elizabeth, b. Sep 5, 1792; bapt. Oct 7, 1792. Spon: George Schaefer and Catharine.

Elizabeth of Johannes Kettner and Eva, age 15 weeks; bapt. Oct 21, 1792. Spon: Michel Wolf and Margaret.

Michel of Christian Walborn, b. Feb 3, 1793; bapt. Apr 6, 1793. Spon: Wendel Fischer and Eva.

Magdalena of Peter Batz and Elizabeth, b. Dec 16, 1793; bapt. Jul 14, 1793. Spon: Magdalena Schmith, widow.

Magdalena of Johannes Desch and Margaret (?)(A. Elis.), b. Jun 11, 1793; bapt. Sep 22, 1793. Spon: Jacob Kassel and Magdalena.

J. Jacob of Conrad Wagner and A. M., b. Mar 26, 1793; bapt. Oct 20, 1793. Spon: Peter Bohr and Catharine.

A. Barbara of Henrich Schnabele and Catharine, b. 24, 1793; bapt.
Oct 20, 1793. Spon: Barbara Koppeheber, widow.
J. Jacob of Albert Kleinfelder and Magdalena, b. Sep 17, 1793; bapt.
Oct 20, 1793. Spon: Jacob Walborn.
M. Catharine of Henrich Uhrich and Catharine, b. Jun 26, 1793; bapt.
Jul 28 (?), 1793. Spon: Johannes Jones.
--- of Israel Lang, b. Dec 15, 17--; bapt. ---. Spon: ---.
Sara(h) of Samuel Gilbert and Catharine, age 7 weeks old; bapt. Feb
9, 1794. Spon: Johannes Fuche.
Johannes of Conrad Ernst and Elizabeth, b. Mar 6, 1794, Apr 6, 1794.
Spon: Johannes Wagner and Hanna(h).
Johann Nichlas of George Walborn and wife, b. Dec 10, 1794(93);
bapt. Dec 26, 1794(?)(93). Spon: Johann Niclas Albert and wife.

(All of the following entries for 1794 are doubtful.)

--- (Ann Rosina?) of Johannes Kleinfelder (J. Albert Klien), b. Feb
(26?), 1794 (?95); bapt. Apr 20, 1794 (?95). Spon: ---.
--- of Johannes Weber, b. ---; bapt. Apr 20, 1794(5?). Spon: ---.
--- of Henrich Kempel, b. Apr 7, 1794(5?); bapt. Jun 9, 1794(5?).
Spon: J. Kampel and wife.
Elizabeth of Johannes Desch, b. May 26, 1794(5?); bapt. Jun 29,
1794(5?). Spon: Adam Bucher and Elizabeth.
Eva Magdalena of Peter Feg and Appolonia, b. Feb 7, 1794(5?); bapt.
24, 1794(5?). Spon: Eva Chafin.
M. Magdalena of Caspar Pfatteicher and M. Sabina, b. May 27,
1794(5?); bapt. Jul 27, 1794(5?). Spon: Peter Schauer and Ester.
Elizabeth of Friederich Camper and Elizabeth, b. Apr 6, 1794(5?);
bapt. 24, 1794(5?). Spon: Joseph Wengert and Barbara.
Johannes of Henrich Schnebele and Catharine, b. Aug 31, 1794(5?);
bapt. Oct 5, 1794(5?). Spon: Johannes Spittler and Catharine.
Marg. Elisabeth of Christian Walborn and Magdalena, b. Sep 5,
1794(5?); bapt. Nov 16, 1794(5?). Spon: Elizabeth Kayser.
J. Martin of Peter Batz and Catharine, b. Oct 29, 1794(5?); bapt. Dec
10, 1794(5?). Spon: Martin Kleinfelder and Marie Rebok.
Johannes of Margaret Junker and ("Jacob Wenner"), b. Oct 31,
1794(5?); bapt. Dec 14, 1794(5?). Spon: Johann Campbell and
Magdalena.
J. Jacob of Johannes Seeger and M. Barbara, b. Oct 27, 1795; bapt.
Jan 11, 1796. Spon: Johann Viel and Eva.

--- of George Walborn and Catharine, b. Dec 10, 1795; bapt. Jan 11, 1796. Spon: J. Niclas Albert and A. Marie.

Elizabeth of George Bader and Catharine, b. Jan 5, 1796; bapt. Feb 15, 1796. Spon: Henrich Urich and Catharine.

Elizabeth of Henrich Urich and Catharine, b. Jan 17, 1796; bapt. Feb 15, 1796. Spon: Johann Urich and Elizabeth.

Jacob of Henrich Huber and Elizabeth, b. Feb 8, 1796; bapt. Mar 22, 1796. Spon: Henrich Kempel and wife.

A. Marie of Christian Walborn, b. Apr 13, 1796; bapt. May 25, 1796. Spon: George Walborn.

A. Catharine of J. Albert Kleinfelder and Magdalena, b. Jan 25, 1796; bapt. May 25, 1796. Spon: Johann Herman and wife.

Cath. Elizabeth of Johann Wingert, b. Oct 12, 1796; bapt. Nov 1, 1796. Spon: Catharine Pfatteiger.

Elizabeeth of Michel Wagner and Magdalena, b. Oct 29, 1796; bapt. Nov 1, 1796. Spon: Catharine Spengler.

J. Conrad of Conrad Miller and Frany, b. Sep 29, 1796; bapt. Dec 13, 1796. Spon: Andres Sarg and A. Catharine.

A. Catharine of Jacob Egler and Barbara, b. Nov 8, 1796; bapt. Mar 6, 1797. Spon: Magdalena Viel.

Martin of Martin Walborn and Elizabeth, b. Apr 10, 1797; bapt. Jun 26, 1797. Spon: Adam Sattelzaum and Elizabeth.

David of George Weber and Peggy (Rebecca), b. Mar 30, 1797; bapt. Jul 10, 1797. Spon: Conrad Wordt.

Elizabeth of Johann Mayer and Christina, b. Jul 24, 1797; bapt. 21, 1797. Spon: J. Kempel and M. Magdalena.

George Adam of Jacob Walborn and Juliana, b. Oct 2, 1797; bapt. Nov 13, 1797. Spon: Andres Walborn and Rosina Keiser.

J. Jocobus of Johann Luk and "Sally," b. Aug 21 (?), 1796; bapt. Nov 13, 1797. Spon: Dr. J. Eckel.

Sara(h) of Georg(e) Bader and Catharine, age 6 weeks; bapt. Jan 22, 1798. Spon: John Herman and Sara(h).

--- of Jonathan Grunzweig and Elizabeth, b. Dec 24, 1797; bapt. Mar 5, 1798. Spon: ---.

Christian of Henrich Urich and Catharine, b. Mar 10, 1798; bapt. Apr 14, 1798. Spon: Christian Urich.

Henrich of Henrich Schnabele and Catharine, b. Mar 30, 1798; bapt. May 28, 1798. Spon: Henrich Dubbs and wife.

Israel of Israel Lang and Rachel, b. Sep 19, 1798; bapt. Nov 26, 1798. Spon: Christian Lang.

Maria of Samuel Gilbert and Catharine, b. Oct --, 1798; bapt. Nov 26, 1798. Spon: Johann Fuchs and M. Catharine.

Elizabeth of J. George Schneider, b. Oct 26, 1798; bapt. Dec 1, 1798. Spon: Michel Schwenck and Catharine.

Marie Margaret of Melchior Beny, b. Nov 20, 1798; bapt. Jan 14, 1799. Spon: Margaret Fischer.

Children of Joseph Worril (Worrall, Worrell); "baptized 9 children on Feb 25, 1799. Spon: ---.

Hanna(h) of Johannes Kettner and Eva, 1 month old in Sep; bapt. Mar 27, 1799. Spon: Johannes Fuchs and Catharine.

Daniel of Caspar Pfatteicher and Sabina, b. Apr 2, 1798; bapt. Jun 17, 1799. Spon: parents.

Margaret of Johannes Desch and Elizabeth, b. Mar 14, 1798; bapt. Jul 1, 1799, Spon: Margaret Desch, widow.

Michel of Paul Wolf and Sophia, b. Jan 1, 1799; bapt. Jul 1, 1799. Spon: Michel Wolf and "Gret."

A. Marie of Johann Field and Eva, b. Jun 2, 1799; bapt. Jul 1, 1799. Spon: A. Marie Hauer.

Wilhelm of Henrich Stetzer (brickmaker) and Maria, 7 weeks old; bapt. Aug 26, 1799. Spon: the father.

Christian of Christian Walborn and Magdalena, b. Jul 27, 1798; bapt. Sep 9, 1799. Spon: Albert Kleinfelder, Jr.

M. Catharine of Michael Schwenck and wife, b. Sep 28, 1799; bapt. Oct 7, 1799. Spon: Margaret Bohr.

Johannes of Jacob Walborn and wife, b. Sep 2, 1799 (1800?); bapt. Oct 7, 1799 (1800?). Spon: Philip Keiser.

David of Jacob Walborn ?(transposed) and wife, Jul 6, 1799 (1802?); bapt. Sep 16, 1799 (1802?). Spon: Albert Kleinfelder, Jr. (?) and Magdalena (?).

Catarina of Paul Wolf and wife, b. Oct 12, 1799; bapt. ---, 1799. Spon: Jacob Willt and wife.

Johann Jacob of Henrich Schnebly and Catharine, b. Mar 27, 1799; bapt. ---, 1799. Spon: Johannes Wagner and wife Hanna(h).

George of Melchior Beny, b. Dec 6, 1799; bapt. Jan 30, 1800. Spon: Jacob Walborn's wife.

Johann Martinus of Andres Walborn and wife, b. Jan 15, 1800; bapt. Feb 27, 1800. Spon: Martinus Walborn.

Madlena of Jacob Rudy and wife, b. Feb 6, 1800; bapt. Mar --, 1800. Spon: Madlena Wendel.

Johannes of Philip Desch and wife, b. Feb 5, 1800; bapt. Mar --, 1800.

Spon: Johannes Herman and wife.

Johann Henrich of Conrad Miller and wife, b. Feb 6, 1800; bapt. Mar --, 1800. Spon: Friederich Waltemardy (Fred. W. Martin).

Christina of Johann Kettner and wife, b. Sep 8, 1799; bapt. Mar --, 1800. Spon: George Raier.

Elizabeth of Peter Peifer and wife, b. Dec 10, 1799; bapt. May --, 1800. Spon: Peter Bieber and Elizabeth Gilbert.

Elizabeth of Abraham Strohm and wife, b. Mar 10, 1800; bapt. May --, 1800. Spon: Henr(y) Windbiegler and wife.

Catharine of Johannes Luck and Sarah, b. Jan 8, 1800?; bapt. May 18, 1800. Spon: Catharine Stang.

Margaret of Jacob Gettel and Maria, b. ---; bapt. May 13, 1800. Spon: Michael Wolf, Sr. and wife.

Johannes of Conrad Wagner and Anna Maria, b. Jan. 3, ---; bapt. May 18, 1800. Spon: Sebastian Wagner and wife.

Wilhelm of Christian Mayer and wife Christina, b. May 30, 1800; bapt. Jul 20, 1800. Spon: Jacob Gilbert and Catharine Gilbert.

Johann Jacob of Philip Weber and Anna Maria, b. Jun 22, 1800; bapt. Jul 20, 1800. Spon: Jacob Weber.

Johannes of Henrich Urich and wife, b. Jun 4, 1800; bapt. (Jul 20, 1800?). Spon: Johann Urich.

George Peter of Caspar Ludwig and wife, b. Jun 26, 1800; bapt. Jul (20?), 1800. Spon: Peter Walborn and wife.

Johann Conrad of Caspar Ludwig and wife, b. Jun 26, 1800; bapt. Jul (20?), 1800?. Spon: Conrad Wirth and wife.

Jacob of Johannes Bohny and wife, b. Jun 10, 1800; bapt. Oct 10, 1800. Spon: Jacob Fisher, single.

Johannes of Jacob Walborn and wife, b. Sep 1, 1800; bapt. Nov 10, 1800. Spon: Philip Keiser.

Johan Conrad of Caspar Ludwig and wife, b. Jun 26 (Nov.?); bapt. Apr 6, 1801. Spon: Conrad Worth and wife.

Paul of Michael Wagner and wife, b. Jun 24, 1800; bapt. --- (1801). Spon: Paul Wolf and wife.

Barbara of Johann Nicholas Gebhardt and wife, b. Apr 23, 1800 (?); bapt. --- (1801?). Spon: Wilheln Wetzel and wife.

Johann Adam of Henrich Emrich and wife, b. Nov 27, 1800; bapt. --- (1801?). Spon: Johannes Mayer and wife.

Johann Adam of Henrich Emrich and wife, b. Apr 17, 1798; bapt. --- (1801?). Spon: Johann Adam Stump and wife.

MILLBACH REFORMED CONGREGATION
MILLBACH TOWNSHIP

BAPTISMS BY TEMPLE-MANN, 1747-1751

(These baptisms although performed by Temple-mann, were not entered by him.)

George Michael of Peter Wolfsperger and Apollonia, bapt. Mar 15, 1747. Spon: George Michael Brunner and Anna Catharine Wolfberger.

Anna Maria of Henry Zöller and wife, bapt. Mar 15, 1747. Spon: Anna Mila Zöller.

Susanna Margaret of John Noll and Elizabeth, bapt. Mar 15, 1747. Spon: John George Noll and Anna Margaret.

John of Peter Numann and Magdalene, bapt. Aug 6, 1747. Spon: John Noll and wife.

John Michael of John George Meuser and Anna, bapt. Sep 7, 1747. Spon: Michael Näff and Anna Mila.

John Jost of Henry Hofmann and wife, bapt. Nov 4, 1747. Spon: John Jost Hof(man) and wife.

John Jacob of Paulus Schäfer and Anna Eliza, bapt. Dec 8, 1747. Spon: George Schäfer an Anna Maria.

John Adam of Gottfried Lautermilch and Anna Margaret, bapt. Mar 5, 1748. Spon: John Adam Stumpff and Anna Margaret.

John George of Jost Hofmann and Maria Catharine, bapt. Mar 8, 1748. Spon: George Schwengel and Anna Margaret.

John Henry of William Abell and Anna Maria, bapt. Apr 6, 1748. Spon: Andrew Saltzgeber and Anna Maria.

Elizabeth of George Schäfer and wife, bapt. May 22, 1748. Spon: John Adam Bollmann and Elizabeth.

Anna Elizabeth of William Blecher and Dorothy, bapt. Jul 18, 1748. Spon: Henry Hofmann and Anna Elizabeth.

John of Peter Eckert and Anna Barbara, bapt. Oct 2, 1748. Spon: John Schick and Anna Maria Witter.

George of John George Meuser and Anna, bapt. Jan 25, 1749. Spon: George Müller and Maria Catharine.

Peter of Peter Bersch and Anna Elizabeth, bapt. Aug 6, 1749. Spon: Francis Neukommer and Regina.

Maria Elizabeth of John Trautmann and Eva Elizabeth, bapt. Aug 6,

1749. Spon: Hieronimus Trautmann and Anna Maria.
John Nicholas of Jacob Zimmermann and Anna Margaret, bapt. Aug
30, 1749. Spon: Nicholas Schnes, single Anna Elizabeth
Herchelroth, single.
John George of John Haack and Dorothy (Diffenbach, dau. of Conrad
and Barbara Diffenbach), bapt. Sep 2, 1749. Spon: George Müller
and Maria Catharine.
Maria Margaret of William Apffel and wife, bapt. Dec 4, 1749. Spon:
Daniel Eichelbener and Margaret.
Anna Barbara of Peter Eckert and wife, bapt. Dec 23, 1749. Spon:
John Meyer and Barbara.
Catharine Elizabeth of Jost Hoffmann and Maria Catharine, bapt.
Dec 2, 1749. Spon: Henry Hoffmann and Elizabeth.
Anna Elizabeth of Peter Numann and Magdalene, bapt. Jan 20, 1750.
Spon: Henry Stahl and wife.
John Jost of Peter Hulpe and Maria, bapt. Jan 17, 1750. Spon: Jost
Blecher and Magdalene.
Anna Maria of Jacob Rickardt and wife, bapt. Jan 18, 1750. Spon:
Jacob Wittmer and Anna Maria.
John of David Zöller and wife, bapt. Jan 22, 1750. Spon: John George
Alberdt and Margaret, wife of Henry Zöller.
John Peter of Francis Neukommer and wife, bapt. Mar 12, 1750.
Spon: John Peter Bersch and Anna Elizabeth.
John of Henry Hofmann and Elizabeth, bapt. Apr 8, 1750. Spon: John
Mohr and Susanna.
Anna Engel of Casper Leb and Anna Margaret, bapt. Apr 8, 1750.
Spon: Sander Schäfer and Anna Engel.
John of Andrew Ketterley and wife, bapt. Jun 8, 1750. Spon: John
Mohr and Susanna.
Maria Catharine of Seydt (Feydt) Numann and Anna Margaret, bapt.
Jul 20, 1750. Spon: George Daniel Gentzemar and M. Catharine.
John Peter of Peter Numann and Magdalene, bapt. Sep 9, 1750.
Spon: Peter Werner and wife.
Jost William of William Blecher and Dorothy, bapt. Oct 18, 1750.
Spon: Jost Blecher and Magdalene.
John Daniel of Daniel Nort and Elizabeth, bapt. Nov 15, 1750. Spon:
John Jacob Meyer and Anna Maria Messer (Miesserid).
John Andrew of John William Pesch (Busch) and Anna Maria, bapt.
Dec 29, 1750. Spon: John Andrew Peischlein and Elsa Rosina.
John Henry of Peter Schmidt and Elizabeth, bapt. Jan 3, 1751. Spon:

Henry Hoffmann and Elizabeth.

Maria Catharine of Jost Blecher and Magdalene, bapt. Jan 18, 1751. Spon: Catharine Müller, single.

Anna Catharine of John Spittler and Catharine, bapt. Jan 15, 1751. Spon: John Jacob Braun and Ursula.

Peter of Peter Ecker and Barbara, bapt. Feb 20, 1751. Spon: John Schupp and his sister, Mrs. Meyer.

Anna Margaret of George Adam Gura and Elizabeth, bapt. Feb 28, 1751. Spon: John Fischer, single and Anna Margaret N., single.

Maria Margaret of Jacob Zöller (Zolker) and Anna Barbara, bapt. Apr 14, 1751. Spon: Jacob Wittmer, single and Maria Margaret Strickler, single.

Maria Catharine of Adam Bulman and Elizabeth, bapt. May 6, 1751. Spon: Abraham Bullmann and Maria Catharine Müller, single.

John Henry of John Mayer and Barbara, bapt. May 19, 1751. Spon: Henry Mayer and Anna Mayer.

John of Martin Bayer and Barbara, bapt. May 19, 1751. Spon: John Thoma of Martin Thoma, and Anna Maria Stahl, (single).

John George of Henry Hoffman and Elizabeth, bapt. Jul 6, 1751. Spon: John George Meisser and Anna.

John of George Meisser and Anna, bapt. Aug 30, 1751. Spon: John Fack and Anna Barbara.

Maria Barbara of Jacob Meyer and Susanna, bapt. Jun 30, 1751. Spon: John Meyer and Barbara.

Maria Catharine of John Nicholas Siemon and Maria Catharine, bapt. Sep 2, 1751. Spon: Elizabeth Müller, single.

Anna Margaret of Seitly (Veitly) Numann and Anna Margaret, bapt. Sep 23, 1751. Spon: Peter Numann and Magdalene.

Maria Susanna of Philip Adam Schiermann and Catharine, bapt. Oct 6, 1751. Spon: John Mohr and Maria Susanna.

John of Jacob Rickert and Maria Sybilla, bapt. Oct 14, 1751. Spon: John Blubacher and wife.

(The baptisms in 1753 and 1754 were performed by H. W. Stoy, but were not entered by him. Those of 1753 were entered by the same hand that entered the earlier baptisms.)

John Henry of David Zöller and wife, bapt. Aug 26, 1753. Spon: John Henry Zöller and Anna Margaret.

Mary Elizabeth of Andrew Strickler and wife, bapt. Aug 28, 1753. Spon: Gerhart Reyck (Meyer) and wife.

Magdalene of John Adam Pollmann (Bollman) and Elizabeth, bapt.

Oct 21, 1753. Spon: John Pollmann (Bollman), single and
Magdalene Lautermilch, (single).

Maria Magdalene of Peter Röcker and wife, bapt. Oct 21, 1753. Spon:
Maria Magdalene Gräff, single.

John Philip of Philip Carl Schenck and Maria Elizabeth, bapt. Oct 21,
1753. Spon: John Philip Bieg and wife.

John Peter of Seitel Numann and Margaret, bapt. Nov 18, 1753.
Spon: Peter Werner and wife.

John of John Mohr and Maria Susanna, bapt. Dec 12, 1753. Spon:
John Mey(er) and Anna Barbara.

John of Michael Riger and Catharine, bapt. Mar 31, 1754. Spon:
John Meyer and Barbara.

John of Andrew Ricker and Elizabeth, bapt. Mar 31, 1754. Spon:
John Maier and Elizabeth.

Martin of John Stele and Elizabeth, bapt. Mar 31, 1754. Spon: Martin
Thuma and (and his wife) Barbara.

John George of Michael Müller and Maria Elizabeth, bapt. Apr 25,
1756. Spon: John George Meusser and Anna.

Anna Margaret of Peter Zöller and wife, bapt. Sep 16, 1754. Spon:
Henry Bassler and wife.

Andrew of John Nagel and Eva, bapt. Oct 19, 1756. Spon: Andrew
Ricker and Elizabeth.

Maria Magdalene of Andrew Ricker and Elizabeth, bapt. Apr 8, 1757.
Spon: Andrew Kraus and Magdalene.

John Henry of John George Meisser and Anna, bapt. Apr 8, 1757.
Spon: Henry Zöller and wife.

Anna Maria of Jacob Hamme and Maria Catharine, bapt. Apr 17,
1757. Spon: John Nicholas Müller and Anna Maria.

Dau. of Jost Hoffman and Maria Catharine, bapt. Jun 17, 1757. Spon:
Michel Müller and Elizabeth.

John Adam of Lorentz Arnold and Anna Maria, bapt. Oct 9, 1757.
Spon: John Adam Bollinger and Elizabeth.

Anna Maria of Ludwig Maus and Anna Margaret, bapt. Oct 9, 1757.
Spon: Anna Maria Stump.

John of John George Beler and Catharine, bapt. Oct 9, 1757. Spon:
John Mohr and Susanna.

Barbara of John Fischer and Sabina, bapt. Jan 5, 1758. Spon: John
Meyer and Barbara.

Anna Barbara of Adam Bulmann and Catharine Elizabeth, bapt. Mar
27, 1758. Spon: John George Meyser and Anna Barbara.

John George of Jacob Meyer and Susanna, bapt. Mar 27, 1758. Spon: Sebastian Zimmerman and Mary.

Benjamin of Michael Müller and Maria Elizabeth, bapt. Mar 27, 1758. Spon: Benedict Hoff and Magdalene.

George Michael of John Meiser and Catharine, bapt. Mar 27, 1758. Spon: John George Meiser and Anna.

John Adam of Peter Leiss and Catharine Elizabeth, bapt. Oct 15, 1758. Spon: John Adam Hiltenbeitel and Maria Ursula.

Maria Barbara of Leonard Miller and Gertrude, bapt. Nov 4, 1757. Spon: Maria Barbara Miller, (single).

John of Jacob Schaub and Catharine, bapt. Jan 28, 1759. Spon: John Schäffer and Maria Neff, single.

(This and the following baptisms is entered in a script which resembles very much that of Frederick C. Miller.)

Eva Maria of Bernard Weber and Rosina, bapt. Feb 25, 1759. Spon: George Drautman and Eva Maria Illick.

Maria Catharine of George Numann and Barbara, bapt. Feb 25, 1759. Spon: Henry Saltzgeber and Maria Catharine Illick.

John Peter of Leonard Miller and Gertrude, bapt. Mar 25, 1759. Spon: John Peter Anspach and Magdalene.

Maria Margaret of Jacob Keiser and wife, bapt. Mar 25, 1759. Spon: Henry Zöller and wife.

Maria Elizabeth of Jacob Eichelbrener and wife, bapt. Sep 20, 1759. Spon: Elizabeth Numann, single.

Anna Barbara of Christian Willi and Anna, bapt. Oct 6, 1759. Spon: George Stoler and Anna.

John of Jacob Wittmer and Elizabeth, bapt. May 24, 1759. Spon: Jacob Greininger and wife.

John Henry of Henry Gring and Elizabeth, bapt. May 24, 1759. Spon: John Henry Strack (and) youngest daughter of Jacob Kreiter.

George Leonard of Christopher Stump and Gretrude (Gerta), bapt. May 24, 1759. Spon: Leonard Miller and Gertrude.

Maria Elizabeth of Adam Hiltenbeitel and Ursula, bapt. Jun 11, 1759. Spon: Maria Elizabeth Miller.

Elizabeth of Andrew Klein and wife, bapt. Oct 5, [1759]. Spon: John Adam Bohlender and wife.

Eva of Conrad Wohlfahrt and Margaret, bapt. Sep 4, 1757. Spon: David Zöller and Christine.

Catharine Elizabeth of Peter Zöller and Hannah, b. Sep 18, 1757; bapt. Dec 18, [1757]. Spon: David Zöller and wife.

John Adam of John Meuser and Catharine, bapt. Apr 2, 1760. Spon: John Adam Meuser (single), Mary Catharine Hoff (Hass, single), John Peter Leiss and Catharine Eliza.

John Jacob of Jacob Thoma and Maria Margaret, bapt. Apr 20, 1760. Spon: Jacob Meyer and Susanna.

Anna Maria of Conrad Wohlfahrt and Maria Margaret, bapt. Apr 22, 1760. Spon: Henry Heill and Anna Maria from Elizabeth township.

John Frederick of John Adam Bohlender and Elizabeth, bapt. Jun 1, 1760. Spon: John Frederick Sentzel and Wilhelmina.

Susanna of Andrew Schaub and Susanna, bapt. Jun 1, 1760. Spon: Valentine Viehmann and Susanna.

Anna Christine of Peter Numann and Magdalene, bapt. Jul 21, 1760. Spon: Jacob Kinser and wife.

John of Martin Noecker and Mary Magdalene, bapt. Jul 3, 1760. Spon: John George Wehrheim and Mary Magdalene Noecker.

Mary Elizabeth of Michael Driann (Tryon) and wife, bapt. Aug 25, 1760. Spon: Michael Krau and Elizabeth.

Andrew of Philip Wagstein and wife, bapt. Aug 17, 1760. Spon: Andrew Ricker and wife.

(John) Daniel of Conrad Eichelberner (Eügenberner) and wife, bapt. Dec 14, 1760. Spon: Daniel Stroh and Miss Ensmenger.

John of George Adam Stumpf and wife, bapt. Feb 15, 1761. Spon: John Meiser and Catharine.

John Conrad of Seyler Numann and Margaret, b. Feb 2, 1761; bapt. Mar 15, 1761. Spon: Conrad Wohlfahrt and Mary Margaret.

John Jost of Henry Schram and wife, bapt. Mar 15, 1761. Spon: Jost Hoffman and wife.

Anna Barbara of John Mayer and Anna Barbara, bapt. Mar 15, 1761. Spon: Peter Wolfersberger and Apollonia.

Mary Catharine of Michael Miller and Anna Elizabeth, bapt. Apr 9, 1761. Spon: Barbara Miller, single.

John Peter of Jacob Kinser and wife, bapt. Apr 9, 1761. Spon: Peter Numann and Magdalene.

John Martin of David Zöller and Mary Christine, bapt. Apr 9, 1761. Spon: Martin Kast, Conrad Wohlfahrt and Mary Margaret.

Daughter of Ludwig Maus and wife, bapt. Apr 9, 1761. Spon: -----

Mary Christine of Adam Bollmann (Pollmann) and Elizabeth, bapt. May 24, 1761. Spon: John Meyer and Barbara.

Eva Margaret of Peter Schuy and wife, bapt. May 24, 1761. Spon: Carl Baumberger and wife.

Alexander of Jacob Schaub and wife, bapt. Jul 19, 1761. Spon: Alexander Schäfer and Engel.

Mary Elizabeth of John Mäuser and Catharine, bapt. Jul 19, 1761. Spon: Adam Bollmann (Pollmann) and Mary Elizabeth.

John Jacob of Adam Hiltenbeitel and Ursula, bapt. Aug 16, 1761. Spon: John Jacob Eicholtz and Mary Barbara Miller.

John Jacob of Andrew Numann and wife, bapt. Sep 20, 1761. Spon: Jacob Kinser and Margaret.

Christopher of Henry Mayer and Catharine, bapt. Sep 20, 1761. Spon: Christopher Mayer, single.

Anna Catharine of Adam Mäuser and Anna Catharine, bapt. Sep 20, 1761. Spon: (Johann) George Mäuser and Anna.

John Michael of Michael Meiser and Anna Barbara, bapt. Oct 18, 1761. Spon: Michael Drian and Elizabeth.

John Jacob of John Numann and wife, bapt. Oct 18, 1761. Spon: Jacob Kinser and wife.

Walter of John Numann and wife, bapt. Oct 18, 1761. Spon: Walter Numann and Elizabeth.

Margaret of Christopher Stumpf and Anna Margaret, bapt. Oct 18, 1761. Spon: George Leonard Schmidt and Margaret.

Tobias of Henry Zöller and Maria Margaret, bapt. Nov 15, 1761. Spon: David Zöller and Mary Christine.

John of Jacob Becker and wife, bapt. Jan 31, 1762. Spon: John Mayer and wife.

Anna Maria of Georg Becker (?) and wife, bapt. Jan 31, 1762. Spon: Maria Neff, single.

Anna Catharine of John Noll and Mary Elizabeth, bapt. Apr 4, 1762. Spon: Ludwig Michael and Catharine.

John Jacob of Jost Hoffmann and Mary Catharine, bapt. Apr 4, 1762. Spon: Jacob Wagner and wife.

Valentine of Valentine Miller and wife, bapt. Apr 4, 1762. Spon: Nicholas Miller and wife.

Leonard of (George) Adam Stumpff and wife, bapt. Jun 27, 1762. Spon: Leonard Köller and Magdalene Stumpff.

Son of Peter Numann and wife, bapt. Jun 27, 1762. Spon: Henry Numann and Magdalene Mäuser.

George of George Schmitt and Dorothy, bapt. Jul 25, 1762. Spon: Mary Margaret ----, the sister-in-law.

John Conrad of Andrew Strückler and Anna Margaret, bapt. Aug 29, 1762. Spon: Conrad Wohlfahrt and Mary Margaret.

Eva Maria of Peter Zöller and Hannah, bapt. Aug 29, 1762. Spon: Simon Bassler and Eva Maria.

John George of John Mäuser and Catharine, bapt. Oct 17, 1762. Spon: John Mohr and Susanna.

Catharine Elizabeth of Peter Leiss and wife, bapt. Oct 17, 1762. Spon: Christian Sehler and wife.

Son of Nicholas Miller and wife, bapt. Sep 14, 1762. Spon: -----.

John of Adam Bollender and wife, bapt. Sep 14, 1762. Spon: John Schaffer and Barbara (Miller).

Frederick of Nicholas Miller and Anna Maria, bapt. Sep 14, 1762. Spon: Frederick Sintzel and wife.

John George of Säudler Numann and wife, bapt. Feb 6, 1763. Spon: Walter Numann and wife.

Mary Eliza of Abraham Bollmann and Elizabeth, bapt. Feb 6, 1763. Spon: Adam Bollmann and wife.

John Adam of Mathew Schroff and wife, bapt. Mar 6, 1763. Spon: Peter Schuy and wife.

John Michael of Michael Miller and Mary Elizabeth, bapt. May 3, 1763. Spon: George Schwingel and wife.

Dau. of John Weber and wife, bapt. May 3, 1763. Spon: -----.

Child of Rudolph Bollinger and wife, bapt. Jan 3, 1764. Spon: -----.

John Frederick of Michael Miller and Mary Elisabeth, bapt. Feb 17, 1764. Spon: Philip Erpff.

Abraham of Abraham Bollmann and Elizabeth, bapt. Feb 17, 1764. Spon: Adam Schermann and wife.

David of David Zöller and wife, bapt. Mar 25, 1764. Spon: Peter Zöller and Hannah.

Mary Susanna of George Adam Stumpff and wife, bapt. Mar 25, 1764. Spon: Jacob Schwanger and wife.

Son of Henry Zöller and wife, bapt. Apr 23, 1764. Spon: Peter Zöller and wife.

John Michael of Henry Meiser and Anna Mary, bapt. Jul 5, 1764. Spon: Michael Schwingel and Elizabeth Zöller, single.

Anna Maria of Jost Hoffmann and Catharine, bapt. Aug 5, 1764. Spon: Michael Neff and Anna Maria.

John Jacob of Andrew Rücker and wife, bapt. Aug 5, 1764. Spon: Jacob Schwanger and Susanna.

John Michael of John Noll and Mary Elizabeth, bapt. Aug 4, 1765. Spon: Michael Kroh and Elizabeth.

Anna Catharine of Nicholas Bressler and Catharine, bapt. Aug 4,

1765. Spon: John Geo. Lautermilch and Anna Catharine.

Maria Dorothea of John Fischer and (Eva) Elizabeth, b. Sep 9, 1765;
bapt. Nov 17, 1765. Spon: Leonard Illick and Maria Dorothea.

(This last entry was made apparently by John Waldschmidt.)

(On Oct 20, 1765 the first child was baptized by the Rev. Zufall.)

Mary Susanna of Conrad Wohlfahrt and Mary Margaret, bapt. Oct
27, 1765. Spon: John Mohr and Mary Susanna.

*(This is the last entry in the hand that began making entires in 1759.
It was probably one of the elders.)*

Catharine of Henry Mayer and Catharine, b. Mar 1, 1759. Spon:
Peter Ruth.

Christopher of Henry Mayer and Catharine, b. Sep 5, 1761. Spon:
Christopher Mayer and Catharine Becker.

John George of Henry Mayer and Catharine, b. Nov 16, 1765. Spon:
John George Lautermilch and Catharine.

Michael of Henry Mayer and Catharine, b. Nov 25, 1768. Spon:
Michael Mayer and Elizabeth.

(These baptisms were entered by Henry Mayer himself ...)

Jonathan of Michael Miller and Mary Elizabeth, bapt. Sep 16, 1769.
Spon: Philip Marsteller and Magdalene, from Lebanon.

BAPTISMS BY THE REV. WILLIAM HENDEL, DEC 1769-1780

John Henry of John Schultz and Anna Maria, b. Dec 10, 1769; bapt.
Dec 24, 1769. Spon: John Henry Eisenmenger and Susanna
Catharine.

John George of Henry Saltzgeber and Eva, b. Dec 29, 1769; bapt. Jan
1, 1770. Spon: George Meiser and Anna.

Catharine of Adam Knauer and Margaret, b. Dec 15, 1769; bapt. Jan
28, 1770. Spon: Daniel Stein and Catharine (Seid).

Anna Catharine of Benedict Lang and Anna Maria, b. Feb 14, 1770;
bapt. Feb 18, 1770. Spon: George Meiser and Anna.

John George of William Blecher and Barbara, b. Jan 6, 1770; bapt.
Feb 18, 1770. Spon: George Hederich and Maria Elizabeth.

John George of Jacob Wagner and Catharine, b. Jan 5, 1770; bapt.
Mar 10, 1770. Spon: George Hoffmann.

Eva Christine of Jost Hoffmann and Maria Catharine, b. Mar 29,
1770; bapt. Apr 29, 1770. Spon: Caspar Viehmann and Eva
Christine.

Maria Elizabeth of Melchior Lautermilch and Catharine, b. Apr 21,

1770; bapt. May 13, 1770. Spon: Henry Gring and Elizabeth.

Eva Margaret of Michael Schwengel and Elizabeth, b. Jan 15, 1770; bapt. Jun 4, 1770. Spon: Margaret Elisabeth Hass.

Maria Christine of William Brenckel and Maria, b. Jun 19, 1770; bapt. Jul 8, 1770. Spon: Maria Christine Würtz.

Barbara of Matthew Reich and Barbara, b. Jun 21, 1770; bapt. Jul 22, 1770. Spon: Barbara Fehg.

Christine of George Gensemer and Margaret, b. Jun 5, 1770; bapt. Aug 12, 1770. Spon: John Blum and Christine.

George of Peter Schutz and wife, b. Aug 13, 1770; bapt. Aug 26, 1770. Spon: George Hollstein and Elizabeth.

John Henry of Abraham Schaffer and Catharine, b. Sep 4, 1770; bapt. Oct 7, 1770. Spon: Peter Numann and Magdalene.

Catharine of Christian Wolf and Catharine, b. Sep 12, 1770; bapt. Oct 21, 1770. Spon: Melchior Lautermilch and Catharine.

Henry of Henry Strack and (Anna) Elizabeth, b. Aug --, 1770; bapt. Oct 28, 1770. Spon: Adam Hoffmann and Barbara.

George of Peter Zöller and Anna Maria, b. Nov 29, 1770; bapt. Dec 30, 1770. Spon: Henry Zeller and Maria Margaret.

Maria Elizabeth of Henry Munich and Catharine, b. Dec 14, 1770; bapt. Jan 20, 1771. Spon: Maria Elizabeth Müller.

George of Caspar Viehmann and Christine, b. Jan 18, 1771; bapt. Feb 10, 1771. Spon: George Albrecht.

Philip of John Weber and Elizabeth, b. Feb 9, 1771; bapt. Mar 24, 1771. Spon: Philip Lorentz Hautz and Catharine.

Henry of John Schultz and Barbara, b. Feb 8, 1771; bapt. Mar 24, 1771. Spon: John Henry Eisenmenger and Susanna.

Barbara of Jacob Schwanger and Susanna, b. Mar 18, 1771; bapt. Mar 24, 1771. Spon: Nicholas Zollinger and Barbara.

Julianna of John Fischer and wife, b. Apr 5, 1771; bapt. Apr 14, 1771. Spon: Julianna Becker.

Michael of David Numann and Magdalene, b. Feb 22, 1771; bapt. Apr 28, 1771. Spon: Michael Wenrich and Elizabeth.

John of William Blecher and Barbara, b. Mar 28, 1771; bapt. May 12, 1771. Spon: John Roth and Barbara.

John Jacob of George Becker and Juliana, b. Jun 5, 1771; bapt. Jul 14, 1771. Spon: Michael Tryon and Elizabeth.

George of Leonard Strickler and Catharine, b. Aug 12, 1771; bapt. Aug 25, 1771. Spon: George Strickler and Barbara.

Jacob of John Schmid and Elizabeth, b. Sep 11, 1771; bapt. Oct 6,

1771. Spon: Jacob Wagner and Catharine.

George of Michael Munich and Christine, b. Sep 27, 1771; bapt. Nov 10, 1771. Spon: Michael Mayer and Elizabeth.

Margaret of Benedict Lang and Anna Maria, b. Nov 13, 1771; bapt. Dec 15, 1771. Spon: Margaret Kiesecker.

Michael of Michael Müller and Maria Elizabeth, b. Feb 15, 1772; bapt. Mar 8, 1772. Spon: Michael Mayer and Elizabeth.

John of Henry Saltzgeber and Eva, b. May 21, 1772; bapt. May 31, 1772. Spon: John Saltzgeber and Catharine.

John George of Henry Meiser and Anna Maria, b. Dec 26, 1771; bapt. Jun 7, 1772. Spon: George Meiser, (Jr.) and Catharine.

Maria Elizabeth of Jacob Paulus and Margaret, b. Jun 10, 1772; bapt. Jul 12, 1772. Spon: Michael Tryon and Eliza.

Frederick of John George Becker and Juliana, b. Nov 4, 1772; bapt. Dec 13, 1772. Spon: John Mohr and Susanna.

Philip of Henry Münch and Catharine, b. Nov 11, 1772; bapt. Dec 13, 1772. Spon: Philip Dunjes and Magdalene.

Maria Margaret of Abraham Schaffer and Catharine, b. Mar 22, 1773; bapt. Apr 18, 1773. Spon: Carl Schenckel and Maria Elizabeth.

Sophia Elizabeth of Mauritius Duppel and Anna Maria, b. Jun 5, 1773; bapt. Jun 13, 1773. Spon: Anna Maria Lang.

Philip of Michael Miller and Elizabeth, b. -----; bapt. Jun 27, 1773. Spon: Philip Erb and Magdalene.

George of Christopher Stumb and Margaret, b. -----; bapt. Jun 27, 1773. Spon: George Schmid and Dorothy.

John of John Mohr, Jr. and Elizabeth, b. Oct 14, 1773; bapt. Nov 21, 1773. Spon: John Mayer, Jr. and Catharine.

Catharine of Andrew Strickler and Catharine, b. Nov 14, 1773; bapt. Nov 21, 1773. Spon: George Meiser, Jr. and Catharine.

Abraham of Benedict Lang and Anna Maria, b. Dec 22, 1773; bapt. Jan 16, 1774. Spon: Jacob Schwanger and Susanna.

Christian of Jacob Hähn and Magdalene, b. Nov 20, 1773; bapt. Feb 6, 1774. Spon: Christian Fremdling.

Christine of Henry Brunner and Susanna, b. Mar 17, 1774; bapt. Apr 17, 1774. Spon: Conrad Reuler and Catharine.

Michael of Andrew Numann and (Eva), b. Mar 23, 1774; bapt. May 23, 1774. Spon: Michael Tryon and wife.

Elizabeth of David Numann and Magdalene, b. Mar 6, 1774; bapt. May 23, 1774. Spon: Elizabeth Stub.

Elizabeth of George Becker and Juliana, b. Apr 26, 1774; bapt. May

29, 1774. Spon: Michael Mayer and Elizabeth.

George of Nicholas Müller and Anna Maria, b. May 6, 1774; bapt. Jun 12, 1774. Spon: Melchior Lautermilch and Catharine.

Henry of Christopher Bayer and Catharine, b. Mar 13, 1774; bapt. Jun 12, 1774. Spon: Peter Lebo and wife.

Michael of Michael Zöller and Catharine, b. May 13, 1774; bapt. May 16, 1774. Spon: Michael Trion and wife.

Henry of William Blecher and Barbara, b. Jul 23, 1774; bapt. Aug 21, 1774. Spon: Henry Strack and Anna Elizabeth.

Catharine Margaret of Moritz Duppel and Anna Maria, b. Oct 8, 1774; bapt. Oct 16, 1774. Spon: Jacob Mohr and Catharine.

John George of George Meiser, Jr. and Catharine, b. Oct 13, 1774; bapt. Oct 30, 1774. Spon: Andrew Strickler and Catharine.

John George of George Hoffmann and Julianna, b. Oct 23, 1774; bapt. Nov 27, 1774. Spon: George Schmid and Dorothy.

Maria Catharine of John Meiser and Catharine, b. Dec 24, 1774; bapt. Jan 22, 1775. Spon: Jacob Britzius and Magdalene.

Catharine of George Schmid and Dorothy, b. Sep 7, 1767; bapt. --- --, 1767. Spon: Margaret Schmid.

Henry of George Schmid and Dorothy, b. Feb 7, 1771; bapt. Feb --, 1771. Spon: Henry Mayer and Catharine.

John of George Schmid and Dorothy, b. Dec 18, 1774; bapt. Feb 12, 1775. Spon: John Mohr, Jr. and Elizabeth.

Leonard of Leonard Strickler and Elizabeth, b. May 20, 1775; bapt. Jun 25, 1775. Spon: Andrew Strickler and Catharine.

Martinus of John Schmid and Anna Elizabeth, b. Nov 7, 1774; bapt. Dec 17, 1775. Spon: Martin Weiser and Catharine.

Maria Elizabeth of Michael Miller and Mary Elizabeth, b. -----; bapt. Mar 12, (1775). Spon: Maria Catharine Müller.

John of Moritz Duppel and Maria, b. Jan 14, 1776; bapt. Feb 14, 1776. Spon: John Saltzgeber and Catharine.

John Michael of John Mohr, Jr. and Elizabeth, b. Feb 3, 1776; bapt. Feb 14, 1776. Spon: John Mayer and Anna Barbara.

Barbara of Henry Mayer and Angelina, b. Feb 10, 1776; bapt. Mar 3, 1776. Spon: John Mayer and Anna Barbara.

Henry of Henry Brunner and Susanna, b. Jan 27, 1776; bapt. Mar 3, 1776. Spon: Ludwig Höfer and Catharine.

John William of William Blecher and Barbara, b. Mar 19, 1776; bapt. Mar 31, 1776. Spon: Jacob Spengler and Maria Elizabeth.

Elizabeth of Jacob Hähn and Magdalene, b. Apr 7, 1776; bapt. Apr

28, 1776. Spon: Valentine Kaufman and Agnes.

Child of Jacob Wagner and Catharine, b. -----; bapt. May 6, 1776. Spon: Theobald Mayer and wife.

John George of Michael Zeller and Catharine, b. Apr 26, 1776; bapt. May 12, 1776. Spon: George Meiser and Catharine.

John of John Meiser and Catharine, b. Jul 26, 1776; bapt. Aug 4, 1776. Spon: Henry Eisenmenger and Catharine.

Juliana of John George Becker and Juliana, b. Sep 13, 1776; bapt. Oct 13, 1776. Spon: George Hofmann and Juliana.

Benjamin of Michael Münich and Christine, b. Sep 17, 1776; bapt. Oct 13, 1776. Spon: Benjamin Müller.

George Peter of Christopher Bayer and Catharine, b. Dec 20, 1775; bapt. Dec 1, 1776. Spon: Peter Lebo and Margaret.

Christopher of Leonard Strickler (?) and Maria Catharine, b. Dec 9, 1776; bapt. Dec 25, 1776. Spon: Margaret Stump.

Catharine of George Reitenauer and Catharine, b. Dec 5, 1776; bapt. Dec 25, 1775. Spon: Andrew Strickler and Catharine.

Benjamin of John Numann and Christiana, b. Jan 18, 1777; bapt. Feb 16, 1777. Spon: Margaret Brosius.

Joseph of John Bayer and Esther, b. Aug 10, 1776; bapt. Feb 16, 1777. Spon: Jacob Brosius (?).

Maria Catharine of George Meiser, Jr. and Anna Catharine, b. Feb 25, 1777; bapt. Mar 16, 1777. Spon: John Meiser and Maria Catharine.

Michael of William Jüngst and Catharine, b. Apr 9, 1777; bapt. Apr 13, 1777. Spon: Michael Trion and wife.

John of Michael Zeller and Catharine, b. Nov 16, 1777; bapt. Dec 7, 1777. Spon: John Saltzgeber and Catharine.

Michael of Henry Mayer, Jr. and Anna Angelica, b. Jul 5, 1777; bapt. Aug --, 1777. Spon: Michael Mayer and Elizabeth.

John of Henry Brunner and Susanna, b. Jan 20, 1778; bapt. Mar 1, 1778. Spon: Adam Popele and Catharine.

Elizabeth of John Mohr, Jr. and Elizabeth, b. Jul 1, 1778; bapt. Jul 7, 1778. Spon: John Mohr and Susanna.

John of Henry Mayer, Jr. and Angelica, b. Oct 21, 1778; bapt. Nov 30, 1778. Spon: John Mohr, Jr. and Elizabeth.

Jonathan of Michael Munch and Christine, b. Apr 9, 1778; bapt. Jul 12, 1778. Spon: George Zimmermann and Maria Salome.

Anna Catharine of John Weber and Anna Christine, b. Mar 10, 1779; bapt. Mar 21, 1779. Spon: Anna Catharine Schmeltzer.

Christian of Christian Theiss and Maria Elizabeth Bollinger, b. -----;
bapt. Mar 21, 1779. Spon: Ehrhard Thürwächter.

John of Ludwig Miller and Barbara, b. Jul 17, 1779; bapt. Aug 8,
1779. Spon: John Mayer and Barbara.

John of Adam Scherman and Anna Maria, who died 4 weeks after
birth, b. May 29, 1778; bapt. Aug 8, 1779. Spon: the Father and
Susanna, stepmother.

Maria Christine of John George Becker and Juliana, b. Jan 20, 1780;
bapt. Feb 20, 1780. Spon: Michael Münch and Christine.

Child of Andrew Strickler and wife, b. -----; bapt. Mar 6, 1780. Spon:
Andrew Graff and Catharine.

Maria Catharine of Henry Mayer and Christine, b. Feb 26, 1780;
bapt. Mar 10, 1780. Spon: Michael Zeller and Catharine.

Benjamin and Maria Catharine of Samuel Hartmann and Elizabeth, b.
-----; bapt. May 15, 1780. Spon: Benjamin Müller and Catharine
Müller.

George of John Mohr, Jr. and Elizabeth, b. Sep 3, 1780; bapt. Oct 1,
1780. Spon: John George Miller.

John of Henry Heckroth and Elizabeth, b. Nov 4, 1780; bapt. Nov 26,
1780. Spon: Michael Leonhard and Elizabeth.

John of Christian Heckendorn and Veronica, b. Nov 21, 1780; bapt.
Nov 26, 1780. Spon: William Bergenhoff and Rosina.

Mary Magdalene of John Miller and Veronica, b. Nov 1, 1780; bapt.
Nov 26, 1780. Spon: Frederick Imhoff and Mary Magdalene.

Catharine of Michael Heber (Zeber) and Catharine, b. Nov 26, 1780;
bapt. Dec 7, 1780. Spon: John Meiser and Catharine.

(This is the last baptism entered by Rev. Wm. Hendel.)

John George of John Neuman and Christine, b. Feb 9, 1793; bapt.
Jun 2, 1793. Spon: George Person.

Anna Maria of Philip Noll and Magdalene, b. Sep 18, 1793; bapt. Oct
13, 1793. Spon: John Noll and Catharine.

Jacob of Henry Müller and Catharine, b. Jun 5, 1793; bapt. Oct 13,
1793. Spon: Martin Müller and Anna Maria.

John of Henry Numan and Eva, b. Jul 31, 1793; bapt. Oct 13, 1793.
Spon: John Adam Schmidt and Susanna.

John George of John Frederick Dryon and Barbara, b. Sep 26, 1793;
bapt. Dec 1, 1793. Spon: George Mayser.

(This is the first child baptised by Rev. Hendel, (Jr.) at the
Mühlbach.)

Anna Catharine of John Bollman and Anna Maria, b. Nov 11, 1793;

bapt. Dec 29, 1793. Spon: Adam Moor and Barbara.

Eva of Michael Müller and Margaret, b. Jan 23, 1794; bapt. Feb 18, 1794. Spon: Eva Stichel.

Catharine of Christopher Liveringshaus and Sarah, b. Feb 12, 1794; bapt. Feb 19, 1794. Spon: Catharine Weick.

Samuel of Sebastian Kohle and Anna Maria, b. Sep 29, 1793; bapt. Nov 14, 1795. Spon: Jost Hoffman and Catharine.

Anna Maria of Sebastian Kohle and Anna Maria, b. Aug 14, 1794; bapt. Nov 14, 1795. Spon: Anna Maria Lautermilch.

Eva Margaret of Michael Haack and Magdalene, b. Aug 18, 1795; bapt. Nov 10, 1795. Spon: Barbara Ramler.

George Leonard of Leonard Stump and Eva, b. Sep 25, 1795; bapt. Nov 18, 1795. Spon: Parents

Maria Elizabeth of Tobias Zeller and Catharine, b. Nov 12, 1795; bapt. Dec 13, 1795. Spon: Peter Zeller and Catharine.

Jacob of Balser Wittmer and Catharine, b. Nov 13, 1795; bapt. Feb 23, 1796. Spon: parents.

Philip of John Mohr and Elizabeth, b. Feb 18, 1796; bapt. Mar 28, 1796. Spon: Philip Noll and Magdalene.

John of John Bollman and Anna Maria, b. Dec 12, 1796; bapt. Jan 8, 1797. Spon: John Moor and Elizabeth.

John of Michael Müller and wife, b. Feb 1, 1797; bapt. Apr 2, 1797. Spon: Leonard Strickler.

Catharine of Frederick Müller and Catharine, b. Jan 6, 1797; bapt. Apr 2, 1797. Spon: Henry Schultz and Maria Elizabeth.

Sarah of John Müller and Catharine, b. Apr 7, 1797; bapt. May 25, 1797. Spon: parents.

John of Jacob Weiss and Maria, b. Dec 20, 1797; bapt. Feb 4, 1798. Spon: John Brossman and Barbara.

George Peter of J. George Strickler and Eva, b. Nov 22, 1797; bapt. Feb 4, 1798. Spon: John Geo. Wagner and Catharine.

John of John Binckly and Elizabeth, b. Mar 7, 1797; bapt. Apr --, 1797. Spon: John Ruth and Elizabeth.

Jacob of John George Mayer and Catharine, b. Mar 28, 1798; bapt. May 20, 1798. Spon: Jacob Harnisch and Magdalene.

Anna Maria of Jacob Steiner and Catharine, b. Feb 9, 1798; bapt. -----. Spon: parents.

Mary Magdalene of Samuel Becker and Juliana, b. Jan 27, 1798; bapt. Mar 4, 1798. Spon: Juliana Becker.

Maria Catharine of Conrad Erits and Elizabeth, b. Jul 9, 1797; bapt.

Jul 29, 1798. Spon: Benjamin Miller and Catharine.

Catharine of Christopher Ziegler and Catharine, b. Sep --, 1792; bapt. Sep 22, 1798. Spon: Catharine Müller.

Eva of John Bollman and Anna Maria, b. Aug 25, 1798; bapt. Oct 12, 1798. Spon: Eva Philipi.

Anna Maria of John George Schmidt and Elizabeth, b. Jul 2, 1798; bapt. Jan 22, 1799. Spon: Erhardt Thürwächter and Catharine.

John of Michael Haack and Salome, b. Dec 25, 1798; bapt. Jan 28, 1799. Spon: John Stower and Maria Salome.

Daniel of Michael Kunckel and Catharine, b. Dec 8, 1798; bapt. Feb 3, 1799. Spon: Henry Schultz and Maria Elizabeth.

Daniel of Christian Seibert and Susanna, b. Dec 20, 1798; bapt. Feb 13, 1799. Spon: Barbara Seibert.

Susanna of Henry Strack and Susanna, b. Jan 4, 1799; bapt. Mar 28, 1799. Spon: Rosina Strack.

George of Peter Zeller and Catharine, b. Mar 15, 1799; bapt. May 12, 1799. Spon: George Person and Catharine.

Sarah of George Müller and Anna Maria, b. Jan 7, 1799; bapt. May 12, 1799. Spon: Catharine Strickler.

Maria Catharine of George Wagner and Catharine, b. Dec 21, 1799; bapt. May 12, 1799. Spon: Leonard Strickler and Catharine.

Anna Maria of Peter Zeller and Catharine, b. Mar 24, 1797; bapt. May 25, 1799. Spon: Maria Marg. Zeller.

Sarah of Leonard Stump and Eva, b. Apr 7, 1799; bapt. Aug 24, 1799. Spon: Leonard Strickler and Catharine.

Magdalene of John George Müller and Catharine, b. Nov 23, 1799; bapt. Jan 5, 1800. Spon: John George Mayer and Catharine.

Margaret of Michael Müller and Eva, b. Jun 19, 1800; bapt. Aug 10, 1800. Spon: Samuel Becker and Juliana.

Henry of Henry Strack and Susanna, b. May 21, 1800; bapt. Aug 10, 1800. Spon: George Kochendorf and Maria Elizabeth.

Henry of Henry Spengler and Anna, b. May 28, 1800; bapt. Aug 10, 1800. Spon: Henry Strack and Anna.

Samuel of Christian Seibert and Susanna, b. Sep 21, 1800; bapt. Nov 1, 1800. Spon: John Jacob Rieth and Eva.

Elizabeth of Christopher Liweringshaus and wife, b. Jun 6, 1798; bapt. -----. Spon: Michael Müller and wife.

Sarah of Christopher Liweringshaus and wife, b. Sep 15, 1800. Spon: George Haack and wife.

Frederick of Christopher Liweringshaus and wife, b. Dec 19, 1788;

bapt. --- 1801. Spon: Frederick Kob and wife.

MARRIAGES

John George Zöller, son of Henry Zöller, Sr. of Tulpehocken m. Anna
Barbara Hast, dau of Ludwig Hast (Haas) of Muehlbach Feb 6, 1753.
John Michael Mäuser, son of the late Michael Mäuser m. Mary
Barbara --- Nov 2, 1760.
John Adam Meusser, youngest son of Michael Meusser m. Anna
Catharina Haas, dau of George Ludwig Hass, all of Muehlbach Dec 8,
1760.
Nicholas Bollman, son of Abraham Bolman m. Elizabeth, dau of the
late George Mehr, all of Muehlbach Aug 14, 1761.
John Henry Strack, the younger son of John Jost Strack, from
Germany, County of Wittgenstein m. Anna Elizabeth, dau of Henry
Hoffman, in Heidelberg twp Aug 6, 1762.

THE QUITOPAHILLA (HILL) CHURCH (LUTHERAN)

"Church Record of (for) The Evangelical Lutheran Congregation at the Quitapohila ..." From *Egle's Notes*, vol. 1898 (published in 1899).

Susanna Elizabeth of Daniel Angst, b. Jan 27, 1749; bapt. Feb 19, 1749. Spon: Philip Beyer and Elizabeth Stroeher.

John Daniel of Daniel Angst, b. Dec --, 1750; bapt. Jan 2, 1751. Spon: Matthias Stroeher and Elizabeth Stroeher.

John Nicholas, b. Nov --, 1754; bapt. Dec 2, 1754. Spon: John Nicholas Stroeher and Mary Elizabeth Stroeher.

John Michael of Daniel Angst, b. Mar --, 1762; bapt. Apr 8, 1762. Spon: Michael Neu (Nye) and Anna Catharine Stroeher.

John Philip of John Achenbach and wife Anna Mary, b. Nov 7, 1761; bapt. Nov 22, 1761. Spon: Philip Firnsler and Christina Stotter.

Anna Catharine of John Achenbach and wife Anna Mary, b. Jun 28, 1765; bapt. Jun 30, 1765. Spon: Peter Jetter (Yetter) and Elizabeth Heylman.

Christian, child of John Nic. Busch and wife Margaret, b. Apr 14, 1782; bapt. Apr 17, 1783. Spon: Kraft Kolz and wife Eva.

Anna Sabina of John Bindnagel and wife Regina, b. Sep 11, 1733; bapt. Sep 17, 1733. Spon: Martin Meyly and wife.

John of John Bindnagel and wife Regina, b. Feb 7, 1735; bapt. Mar 23, 1735. Spon: Melchoir Heuter.

John Martin of John Bindnagel and wife Regina, b. Sep 7, 1736; bapt. Oct 3, 1736. Spon: Joh. Martin Meyly.

Anna Dorothea of Michael Boltz, b. Feb 18, 1738; bapt. Mar 30, 1738. Spon: Balthaser Ort and wife Barbara; also Anastasius Uhler and wife Dorothea.

Elizabeth of Michael Boltz, b. May 10, 1741; bapt. Oct 4, 1741. Spon: George Buerger and wife.

Catharine Barbara of Michael Boltz, b. Jun 23, 1745, baptized Aug 24, 1745. Spon: George Buerg(er) and wife.

Anna Sabina of Michael Boltz, b. Sep 6, 1750; bapt. Oct 9, 1750. Spon: Joh. Wolff Kissner and his betrothed wife Anna Sabina Bindnagel, on the day of marriage.

Anna Mary Elizabeth of Michael Borst, b. Mar 9, 1735; bapt. Aug 29, 1735. Spon: Martin Kirstaetter and wife.

Susanna of Michael Borst, b. Dec 8, 1736; bapt. Sep 11, 1737. Spon: Dorothea Kirstaetter.

Anna Dorothea of Michael Borst, b. Dec 25, 1738; bapt. Jan 29, 1739.
Spon: Anastasius Uhler and Dorothea.

Elizabeth of Jacob Birckel, b. Dec 24, 1741; bapt. Mar 18, 1744. Spon:
Peter Kucher and his wife Barbara; also Sarah Jones.

John of John Brown, b. Apr 15, 1744; bapt. May 13, 1744. Spon: John
Bindnagel and wife.

Joh. Valentine of John Brown, b. Apr 7, 1748; bapt. Apr 17, 1748.
Spon: John Bindnagel and wife.

Eva Mary of John Brown, b. Jan 30, 1751; bapt. Feb 22, 1751. Spon:
Vincens Kueffer and wife.

John of Peter Baumgaertner, b. May 13, 1740; bapt. May 26, 1740.
Spon: John Brechbiel and wife.

Joh. Dorst of Peter Baumgaertner, b. May 9, 1742; bapt. Jul 18,
1742. Spon: Dorst Brechbiel and Anna Barbara Brechbiel, wife of
John Brechbiel.

Catharine of Philip Bayer and wife Susanna, b. Jul 15, 1744; bapt.
Aug 12, 1744. Spon: Adam Ulrich and Catharine Buerger.

Eva of Philip Bayer and wife Susanna, b. Jul 18, 1746; bapt. Jul 20,
1746. Spon: Jacob Dietz and Eva Kuenig.

Susanna Mary of Philip Bayer and wife Susanna, b. Sep 8, 1747;
bapt. Oct 11, 1747. Spon: George Buerger and wife Catharine.

Elizabeth Catharine of Philip Bayer and wife Susanna, b. Oct 18,
1748; bapt. Oct 30, 1748. Spon: Michael Berches and Elizabeth
Catharine Stroeher.

Joh. Adam of Philip Bayer and wife Susanna, b. Oct 12, 1750; bapt.
Oct 28, 1750. Spon: Joh. Adam Neu and wife Elizabeth; and
Nicholas Goebel.

Juliana of Philip Bayer and wife Susanna, b. Sep 21, 1752; bapt. Oct
8, 1752. Spon: Nicholas Neu and Barbara Firnssler.

Joh. Philip of Philip Bayer and wife Susanna, b. May 21, 1754; bapt.
May 23, 1754. Spon: Nicholas Wederts and wife Elizabeth.

Joh. Michael of Philip Bayer and wife Susanna, b. Mar 16, 1756; bapt.
Apr 15, 1756. Spon: Michael Bohr and Barbara Firnssler.

Mary Barbara of Philip Bayer and wife Susanna, b. Oct 26, 1757;
bapt. Nov 27, 1757. Spon: Michael Holderbaum and Mary
Barbara Firnssler.

Joh. Frederic of Philip Bayer and wife Susanna, b. Jan 20, 1760; bapt.
Feb 17, 1760. Spon: Christopher Frederic Wegman and wife
Anna Mary.

Christina of Philip Bayer and wife Susanna, b. Apr 8, 1762; bapt. Apr

24, 1762. Spon: John Weber and wife Susanna.

Joh. Peter of Philip Bayer and wife Susanna, b. Oct 29, 1763; bapt. Nov 30, 1763. Spon: Peter Brechbiel and wife Catharine.

John of Philip Bayer and wife Susanna, b. Oct --, 1765; bapt. Nov 10, 1765. Spon: Michael Firnssler and wife Catharine.

(This appears to be a corrected record. Another on page 15 contains the first eleven names as here given. The twelfth differs, being John Christoph instead of John Frederic. There are, however, four additional names, which we give as there recorded.)

Joh. Michael of Philip Bayer and wife Susanna, b. Aug 17, 1746; bapt. Sep 14, 1746. Spon: Adam Ulrich and wife Juliana.

Mary Magdalene of Philip Bayer and wife Susanna, b. b. ----, 1748; bapt. Feb 25, 1748. Spon: Abraham Heydt and wife.

Mary Barbara of Philip Bayer and wife Susanna, b. ----, 1749; bapt. Oct 17, 1749. Spon: Michael Ackerman and wife.

John of Philip Bayer and wife Susanna, b. ----, 1751; bapt. Jul 28, 1751. Spon: John Schaeffer and wife (mistake somewhere).

Joh. Michael of Jacob Brenn Eissen (Brenneisen) and wife Veronica, b. Oct 6, 1747; bapt. Nov 8, 1747. Spon: Joh. Michael Warmpstler and ----.

Joh. Jacob of Jacob Brenn Eissen (Brenneisen) and wife Veronica, b. Sep 28, 1749; bapt. Nov 1, 1749. Spon: Joh. Peter Warmpstler and wife Mary Barbara.

Anna Elizabeth of Jacob Brenn Eissen (Brenneisen) and wife Veronica, b. ----, 1750; bapt. Apr 28, 1750. Spon: Michael Warmpstler and wife. (The above three entries (Breneisern) "Renounced the Et. Lutheran church and became Tunkers.)

Catharine of Michael Braun and wife Anna, b. Dec 31, 1747; bapt. Jul 8, 1750. Spon: Christopher Meyer and wife.

Christopher of Michael Braun and wife Anna, b. Jun 7, 1750; bapt. Jul 8, 1750. Spon: Christopher Meyer and wife.

Joh. Michael of Michael Braun and wife Anna, b. Oct 22, 1751; bapt. Oct 27, 1751. Spon: Christopher Meyer and wife.

Andrew of Michael Braun and wife Anna, b. May 19, 1753; bapt. May 20, 1753. Spon: Andrew Kissinger and wife Susanna.

Anna Margaret of Michael Braun and wife Anna, b. Jun 7, 1755; bapt. Jun 19, 1755. Spon: Martin Oberbeck and Catharine Seltzer.

Eva Margaret of Michael Braun and wife Anna, b. Sep 9, 1759; bapt. Sep 30, 1759. Spon: George Sprecher and wife.

Anna Mary of Michael Braun and wife Anna, b. March 28, 1762; bapt.

Apr 29, 1762. Spon: George Sprecher and wife Anna Elizabeth.

Anna Elizabeth of Michael Braun and wife Anna, b. Apr 7, 1764; bapt. Apr 13, 1764. Spon: Philip Bayer and wife.

Dorothea of Michael Braun and wife Anna, b. May 13, 1767; bapt. May 17, 1767. Spon: Frederic Bickel and wife Dorothea.

Mary Magdalene of Michael Braun and wife Anna, b. Nov 19, 1757; bapt. --, ----. Spon: George Dillman and wife Margaret.

Anna Mary of Michael Bohr, b. Nov 25, 1750; bapt. Jan 25, 1751. Spon: Abraham Heydt and wife Anna Mary.

Joh. William of Michael Bohr, b. Jan 19, 1753; bapt. Feb 25, 1753. Spon: William Litz and ----.

Anna Margaret of Michael Bohr, b. Apr 20, 1756; bapt. May 16, 1756. Spon: John Oppenhauser and wife.

Joh. Michael of Michael Bohr, b. Sep 10, 1757; bapt. Oct 2, 1757. Spon: Michael Holderaum and Mary Elizabeth Bohr.

Margaret Barbara of Jacob Brandtstaetter (of Swatara), b. Jul 15, 1751; bapt. Aug 25, 1751. Spon: George Steyer and wife Anna Margaret.

Joh. Jacob of Gottfried Baumgaertner, b. Nov 22, 1751; bapt. Dec 2, 1751. Spon: Wendel Heyl and wife Anna.

Christina of Philip Adam Balmer, b. Nov 30, 1751; bapt. Dec 26, 1751. Spon: Henry Motz and wife Barbara.

John Michael of Adam Bach and wife Barbara, b. May 21, 1753; bapt. Jun 11, 1753. Spon: Joh. Michael Braun and wife Anna.

Anna Elizabeth of Adam Bach and wife Barbara, b. Jul 14, 1760; bapt. Aug 10, 1760. Spon: George Dietz and wife.

Anna Mary of Moritz (Maurice) Bauer, b. Aug 17, 1753; bapt. Sep 3, 1753. Spon: Jacob Meyer and sister Anna Mary Meyer.

John Jacob of Moritz (Maurice) Bauer, b. Oct 12, 1754; bapt. Nov 3, 1754. Spon: Jacob Meyer and sister Anna Mary Meyer.

John Matthias of John Becker and wife Catharine, b. Nov --, 1753; bapt. Dec 2, 1753. Spon: Joh. Matthias Bohr and wife.

John of John Becker and wife Catharine, b. Apr --, 1756; bapt. May 16, 1756. Spon: Michael Umberger and wife.

Mary Elizabeth of John Becker and wife Catharine, b. March --, 1766; bapt. March 28, 1766. Spon: Jacob Thuy (Duy or Dewey) and wife.

Justina of Adam Barth, b. Feb 20, 1754; bapt. Apr 21, 1754. Spon: Valentine Keller and wife Justina.

Mary Elizabeth of Adam Barth, b. Apr --, 1757; bapt. ----, ----. Spon:

Joh. Nichol Stroeher and Mary Elizabeth Stroeher.

Joh. Adam of Adam Barth, b. Apr 9, 1761; bapt. Apr 30, 1761. Spon: Michael Holderbaum and Anna Christina Stroeher.

Anna Barbara of Adam Barth, b. Jun --, 1765; bapt. Jun 30, 1765. Spon: John Nichol. Neu and Anna Barbara Heylman.

Anna Catharine of ----, 1767; bapt. March 17, 1767. Spon: Valentine Keller and wife Justina Mary.

Philip Adam of Antonius (Anthony) Blessing, b. Jan 7, 1755; bapt. ----, ----. Spon: Philip Adam Balmer and Regina Siechele.

Joh. Valentine of Matthias Boger, b. March 10, 1756; bapt. March 26, 1756. Spon: Valentine Keller and wife.

Anna Magdalene of Matthias Boger, b. Nov --, 1762; bapt. Dec 5, 1762. Spon: George Wampstler and wife.

Mary Catharine of Jacob Boltz and wife Catharine, b. Aug --, 1757; bapt. Sep 4, 1757. Spon: John Daniel Madern and Mary Catharine Uhler.

Joh. Michael of Jacob Boltz and wife Catharine, b. Oct 22, 1759; bapt. Oct 28, 1759. Spon: Joh. Michael Holderbaum and Barbara Uhler.

Joh. Jacob of Jacob Boltz and wife Catharine, b. Sep 24, 1761; bapt. Oct 25, 1761. Spon: Michael Wagner and wife Elizabeth.

Anna Mary of Jacob Boltz and wife Catharine, b. Sep --, 1767; bapt. Sep 20, 1767. Spon: Henry ---- and wife.

Joh. George of Henry Bauman and wife, b. Sep 11, 1758; bapt. Oct 22, 1758. Spon: George Meyer and Margaret Bauman.

Anna Christina of Nocholas Brechtbiel and wife Juliana, b. May 17, 1760; bapt. May 26, 1760. Spon: Caspar Diller and Anna Christina Stoever.

Anna Juliana of Nocholas Brechtbiel and wife Juliana, b. Jan --, 1762; bapt. Feb 2, 1762. Spon: Caspar Diller and Anna Christina Stoever.

Anna Margaret of Nocholas Brechtbiel and wife Juliana, b. Jan 29, 1764; bapt. Feb 12, 1764. Spon: Michael Kaineth and wife Anna Margaret.

Anna Mary of Nocholas Brechtbiel and wife Juliana, b. Jan --, 1766; bapt. Jan 26, 1766. Spon: John Stroh and wife.

Rebecca of Nocholas Brechtbiel and wife Juliana, b. Jan --, 1772; bapt. Feb 22, 1772. Spon: Caspar Diller, Jr. and wife.

Catharine of Martin Busch and wife Anna Mary, b. May end, 1761; bapt. Jun 7, 1761. Spon: Jacob Ludwig and wife Catharine.

Juliana of Martin Busch and wife Anna Mary; bapt. Apr --, 1763;
bapt. May 8, 1763. Spon: Adam Ulrich and wife Juliana.

Mary Barbara and Catharine Sophia, twins of Michael Boltz, Jr. and
wife Veronica, of Swatara, to Bindnagle's Cong., b. Oct 28, 1761;
bapt. Nov 22, 1761. Spon: (none given).

George of Michael Boltz, Jr. and wife Veronica, of Swatara, to
Bindnagle's Cong., b. Nov --, 1765; bapt. Dec 8, 1765. Spon:
George Firnssler and Sabina Boltz.

John of Martin Bindnagel and wife Mary Elizabeth, b. May 7, 1762;
bapt. May 23, 1762. Spon: Jacob Ruecker and wife Christina.

Christina Elizabeth of Martin Bindnagel and wife Mary Elizabeth, b. -
---, 1763; bapt. Nov 6, 1763. Spon: Jacob Ruecker and wife
Christina; and Elizabeth Wessner.

Elizabeth of Matthias Bohr and wife Mary Elizabeth, b. Feb 23, 1764;
bapt. March 11, 1764. Spon: John Dietz and wife Elizabeth.

Eve Catharine of Peter Brechbiel and wife Catharine, b. Apr 24,
1764; bapt. May 1, 1764. Spon: Henry Weiss and Eve Catharine
Fuchs.

Joh. Henry of Peter Brechbiel and wife Catharine, b. Sep --, 1766;
bapt. Oct 12, 1766. Spon: Joh. Henry Peter and Anna Mary
Schall(y).

John of Peter Brechbiel and wife Catharine, b. Apr 4, 1770; bapt. Apr
8, 1770. Spon: John Mueller and wife.

Eva Elizabeth of George Michael Balmer and wife, b. Jan 31, 1765;
bapt. Feb 24, 1765. Spon: Peter Hetzel and wife Eva Elizabeth.

Joh. Adam of Joh. Adam Balmer and wife Barbara, b. March 3, 1767;
bapt. March 8, 1767. Spon: Geo. Mich. Balmer and wife Anna
Elizabeth.

Mary Barbara of Matthias Boger, Jr. and wife Barbara, b. Jul 12,
1780; bapt. Aug --, 1780. Spon: Luke Schally and wife Mary
Elizabeth.

Joseph of Matthias Boger, Jr. and wife Barbara, b. Sep 19, 1781;
bapt. Oct 14, 1781. Spon: Matthias Boger, Sr., and wife
Magdalene.

Benjamin of Matthias Boger, Jr. and wife Barbara, b. ----, ----; bapt.
Nov 20, 1784. Spon: father and mother.

Catharine Barbara of John Boeshar and wife Cathar. Barbara, b.
March 31, 1784; bapt. May 19, 1784. Spon: John Sauter and wife
Catharine.

Arthur of Charles Cannoway, b. Nov 3, 1745; bapt. Feb 11, 1746.

Spon: Abraham Heydt and wife.

Catharine of Charles Cannoway, b. Feb 19, 1747; bapt. Apr 4, 1747.
Spon: Jacob Shilling and Barbara.

James of Charles Cannoway, b. Aug 27, 1748; bapt. Sep 12, 1749.
Godships used: Michael Ackerman and wife Mary Barbara.

Eleonore of James Carrighen and wife Isabella, b. Dec 5, 1760; bapt.
Dec 8, 1760. Spon: John Atkinson and wife Eleonore, Thomas
Atkinson, and Elizabeth Williams.

Sarah of Henry Childs, b. March 4, 1761; bapt. March 23, 1761. Spon:
James Carrighen and wife Isabella, and Richard Trotter.

Joh. George of John Diebl, b. Nov 6, 1734; bapt. Jul 29, 1735. Spon:
George Steitz.

Mary Catharine of John Diebl, b. Sep --, 1737; bapt. Feb 6, 1738.
Spon: Mary Catharine and Joanna Cath. Blum.

Joh. Henry of David Dreher, b. March 29, 1743; bapt. May 23, 1743.
Spon: Henry Merck and wife.

Adam of David Dreher, b. Sep 18, 1749; bapt. Oct 17, 1749. Spon:
Adam Faber and wife.

John of Jacob Dietz, b. ----, 1749; bapt. ----, 1749. Spon: John
Bindnagel and wife.

Anna Magdalena of Jacob Dietz, b. Aug 4, 1751; bapt. Sep 1, 1751.
Spon: Martin Kirstaetter and wife.

George Hanss of George Hanss Dietrich and wife Dorothea, b. March
25, 1758; bapt. March 26, 1758. Spon: Joh. Geo. Ulrich and Cath.
Barbara Ulrich.

Joh. Philip of George Hanss Dietrich and wife Dorothea, b. Nov 10,
1759; bapt. Nov 25, 1759. Spon: Philip Firnsler and Catharine
Barbara Boltz.

Anna Margaret of George Hanss Dietrich and wife Dorothea, b.
March 3, 1761; bapt. March 20, 1761. Spon: Michael Kaineth and
wife Anna Margaret.

Adam of George Hanss Dietrich and wife Dorothea, b. Oct --, 1764;
bapt. Oct 21, 1764. Spon: Adam Ulrich and wife Juliana.

Christopher Frederick of George Hanss Dietrich and wife Dorothea,
b. March --, 1767; bapt. Jun 7, 1767. Spon: Christopher Frederic
Wegman and wife Eva Mary.

John of John Deitz and Elizabeth, b. Aug 17, 1762; bapt. Sep 5, 1762.
Spon: Michael Kirstaetter and wife Dorothea.

Abraham of Antonius (Anthony) Doebler and wife Magdalena, b.
March 10, 1765; bapt. March 24, 1765. Spon: Abraham Weidman

and wife.

Anna Barbara of Antonius (Anthony) Doebler and wife Magdalena, b. Dec 16, 1766; bapt. Dec 25, 1766. Spon: Jacob Rohrer and wife Barbara.

John of Henry Doerges and wife Dorothea, b. Jan 5, 1760; bapt. Jan 19, 1760. Spon: Peter Eisenhauer and wife Elizabeth.

Valentine of Philip Dietz and wife Catharine, b. Jan 1, 1784; bapt. May 19, ----. Spon: John Imboden and wife Catharine.

Lydia of Samuel Etder (Etter) and wife Anna Mary Metdern (Madern), b. Feb 2, 1788; bapt. March 16, 1788. Spon: Henry Reinoehl.

Catharine of John George Ergebrecht, b. March 26, 1733; bapt. Sep 17, 1733. Spon: Anna Catharine Mast (Mrs.).

Anna Elizabeth of John George Ergebrecht, b. Feb 25, 1735; bapt. Apr 27, 1735. Spon: Joh. Jacob Mast and wife.

Anna Barbara of Caspar Eberhardt, (Swatara), b. Apr 15, 1753; bapt. Jun 11, 1753. Spon: Wendel Stoltz and wife Barbara.

John Adam of Martin Ergebrecht, b. Oct 30, 1753; bapt. Dec 26, 1753. Spon: Adam Bach and wife.

Juliana of Matthias Eck, of Conewago, b. Jan 2, 1754; bapt. Aug 11, 1754. Spon: Adam Ulrich and wife Juliana.

Mary Elizabeth of Henry Eller (or Etter), of Lebanon, b. Sep 7, 1752; bapt. Nov 7, 1752. Spon: Elizabeth Ackerman.

Joh. Michael of Michael Fischer (died before birth of child), b. Dec 29, 1757; bapt. Feb 2, 1758. Spon: Nicholas Eissenhauer and wife.

Lawrence (Lorentz) of David Fischer, b. Sep 24, 1733; bapt. Nov 11, 1733. Spon: Lawrence Herchelrodt and wife Elizabeth.

Mary Barbara of David Fischer, b. Dec 12, 1736; bapt. Feb 19, 1737. Spon: Peter Gaentzler and wife Mary Barbara.

Anna Barbara of David Fischer, b. Nov 13, 1739; bapt. Dec 2, 1739. Spon: George Unruh and wife Anna Barbara.

Joh. George of David Fischer, b. Nov 28, 1743; bapt. Dec 18, 1743. Spon: Joh. George Graff, Jr.and wife Mary Magdalene.

Joh. Jacob of David Fischer, b. Apr 3, 1748; bapt. Apr 17, 1748. Spon: Joh. Jacob Weynandt and (Mrs.) Margaret Sober.

Anna Catharine of Jacob Froelich, b. Oct --, 1741; bapt. Apr 15, 1742. Spon: Geroge Burger and wife Catharine.

Dorothea of Philip Firnsler and wife Barbara, b. Aug 14, 1747; bapt. Oct 11, 1747. Spon: Anastasius Uhler and wife Dorothea.

Juliana of Philip Firnsler and wife Barbara, b. May 28, 1749; bapt. Jul

9, 1749. Spon: Anastasius Uhler and wife Dorothea.

John of Frantz Fuchs (Francis Fox), b. May 9, 1749; bapt. ----, ----.
Spon: John Bindnagel and wife Regina.

Catharine Margaret, of Joh. Peter Felten (Felty) and wife Mary
Catharine, b. b. Jul 4, 1752; bapt. Jul 13, 1752. Spon: Nicholas
Goebel, Catharine Stroeher and Margaret Neu.

John Michael of Joh. Peter Felten (Felty) and wife Mary Catharine,
b. Jan 1, 1754; bapt. Jan 27, 1754. Spon: Joh. Michael Malvir,
Joh. Nich. Stroeher, and Mary Elizabeth Bohr.

Joh. Peter of Joh. Peter Felten (Felty) and wife Mary Catharine, b.
March 8, 1756; bapt. March 21, 1756. Spon: Peter Holderbaum,
Joh. Adam Neu and Catharine Stroeher.

Mary Christina of Joh. Peter Felten (Felty) and wife Mary Catharine,
b. Sep 18, 1772; bapt. Sep 20, 1772. Spon: Michael Neu and
Mary Elizabeth Neu.

Mary Catharine of Michael Firnssler and wife Mary Catharine, b. Jul
20, 1761; bapt. Aug 2, 1761. Spon: Joh. Daniel Stroh and wife
Catharine.

Joh. Frederick of Michael Firnssler and wife Mary Catharine, b. Apr -
-, 1768; bapt. Apr 17, 1768. Spon: Frederick Firnssler.

Mary Catharine of Philip Firnssler (Jr.) and wife Anna Christina, of
Lebanon, b. Aug 27, 1763; bapt. Aug 31, 1763. Spon: Mary
Catharine Stoever.

Joh. Frederic of Philip Firnssler (Jr.) and wife Anna Christina, of
Lebanon, b. Feb 9, 1765; bapt. Feb 10, 1765. Spon: Frederic
Firnssler and Anna Mary Stoever.

Joh. Philip of Philip Firnssler (Jr.) and wife Anna Christina, of
Lebanon, b. Apr 21, 1768; bapt. Apr 22, 1768. Spon: Philip
Gruenewaldt and wife Margaret.

Joh. Philip of Philip Firnssler (Jr.) and wife Anna Christina, of
Lebanon, b. Apr 12, 1770; bapt. Apr 16, 1770. Spon: Joh. Caspar
Stoever and wife Anna Mary Barbara.

Joh. Jacob of Jacob Firnssler and wife Magdalene, b. Jan 9, 1765;
bapt. Jan 25, 1765. Spon: Joh. Ulrich Huber, Jr. and wife
Elizabeth.

Anna Margaret of Jacob Firnssler and wife Magdalene, b. Dec --,
1767; bapt. Dec 6, 1767. Spon: Henry Peter, Sr. and wife
Margaret.

Joh. Frederic of Joh. Henry Frey and wife Anna Mary, of Lebanon, b.
March 21, 1770; bapt. Apr 8, 1770. Spon: Joh. Frederic Boger

and Anna Mary Bieder.

Joh. Jacob of George Goeckel, b. Oct 8, 1764; bapt. Oct 9, 1764. Spon: Jacob Bender and Catharine Weiss.

Joh. George of George Goeckel, b. March 31, 1766; bapt. Apr 8, 1766. Spon: John Stroh and wife Elizabeth.

Anna Mary of George Goeckel, b. Apr --, 1768; bapt. Apr 17, 1768. Spon: John Stroh and wife Anna Mary.

Anna Catharine of John German and wife Anna Mary, b. May 13, 1783; bapt. May 24, 1783. Spon: John Adam Bardt and wife Catharine.

Rosina of Joh. George Haedderich, b. Jan 16, 1743; bapt. March 27, 1743. Spon: Christopher Meyer and wife Rosina.

Mary Barbara of Joh. George Haedderich, b. March 31, 1744; bapt. May 13, 1744. Spon: Joh. Peter Kucher and wife.

Joh. George of Peter Haedderich, b. Sep 12, 1743; bapt. Oct 23, 1743. Spon: Joh. George Huber and wife.

Anna Oteliana of George Huber and wife, b. Nov 19, 1745; bapt. Dec 12, 1745. Spon: Peter Hetterich and wife.

Mary Elizabeth of William Huber, b. Oct 13, 1743; bapt. Dec 18, 1743. Spon: Mary Elizabeth Rathfang.

Catharine of Adam Heylman and wife, b. Apr 7, 1740; bapt. May 26, 1740. Spon: Anastasius Uhler and wife Dorothea.

Anna Elizabeth of Adam Heylman and wife, b. March 2, 1742; bapt. Apr 15, 1742. Spon: Anastasius Uhler and wife.

Anna Mary of Anthony (Antonius) Hemperle and wife, b. Dec 15, 1744; bapt. Jan 6, 1745. Spon: John Bindtnagel and wife.

Martin of Anthony (Antonius) Hemperle and wife, b. ----, 1747; bapt. Jun 21, 1747. Spon: John Bindtnagel and wife.

Eva Mary of Anthony (Antonius) Hemperle and wife, b. March 24, 1750; bapt. Apr 15, 1750. Spon: John Keller and wife Anna Mary.

Elizabeth of George Hatz and wife Elizabeth, b. Jul 2, 1745; bapt. Aug 18, 1745. Spon: Joh. Adam Hambrecht and wife.

Eva Catharine of George Hatz and wife Elizabeth, b. Feb 18, 1748; bapt. Feb 25, 1748. Spon: Catharine Buerger.

Abraham of Peter Heydt, b. March 15, 1747; bapt. Apr 4, 1747. Spon: Abraham Heydt and wife Magdalene, Caspar Lowe and wife

Margaret.

Catharine Elizabeth, of Jacob Hornberger, b. Nov 15, 1750; bapt. Feb 22, 1751. Spon: Christopher Suess and wife.

Catharine of Jacob Huppman, b. Sep 17, 1751; bapt. Sep 27, 1751. Spon: Christopher Meyer and wife Catharine.

Joh. Valentine of Frederick Hummel, of (Swatara), b. Feb 17, 1753; bapt. Feb 24, 1753. Spon: Joh. Valentine Kittring and Julia Grasser.

Mary Catharine of Peter Holderbaum, of (Swatara), b. Oct 2, 1753; bapt. Oct 8, 1735 (1753). Spon: Peter Feltin, Michael Bohr and Mary Catharine Sprecher.

Joh. Michael of Michael Holderbaum and wife Juliana, b. Jul 19, 1762; bapt. Aug 16, 1762. Spon: Michael Bohr and wife.

Martin of Michael Holderbaum and wife Juliana, b. Dec --, 1764; bapt. Jan 13, 1765. Spon: Martin Busch and wife Anna Mary.

Anna Mary of Michael Holderbaum and wife Juliana, b. Jul 17, 1767; bapt. Jul 19, 1767. Spon: Martin Busch and wife.

Peter of Michael Holderbaum and wife Juliana, b. Aug 20, 1780; bapt. Sep 3, 1780. Spon: Henry Weigandt and wife Catharine.

Anna Catharine of Michael Holderbaum and wife Juliana, b. Nov 10, 1783; bapt. Feb 12, 1784. Spon: Joh. Nic. Morrel and Anna Mary Busch, both single.

John of David Herbster, b. Aug 18, 1765; bapt. Aug 23, 1765. Spon: John Hamster and wife.

Agnes Mary, of David Herbster, b. Apr --, 1768; bapt. Apr 22, 1768. Spon: Jacob Haecker and wife Agnes.

Juliana Dorothea of Ulrich Huber and wife Elizabeth, b. Aug --, 1766; bapt. Aug 17, 1766. Spon: Henry Firnssler and wife Juliana.

Frederic of Anastasius Heylmann and wife Rosina Barbara, b. Dec 5, 1766; bapt. Dec 25, 1766. Spon: Joh. Nicholas Maurer and Elizabeth Heylmann.

Anna Catharine of Anastasius Heylmann and wife Rosina Barbara, b. Dec 3, 1768; bapt. Dec 3, 1768. Spon: Peter Heylman, Sr. and wife Salome.

John Adam of Anastasius Heylmann and wife Rosina Barbara, b. Sep 29, 1771; bapt. Oct 12, 1771. Spon: Anthony (Anton) Stoever and wife.

Mary Christina of Anastasius Heylmann and wife Rosina Barbara, b. Sep 14, 1773; bapt. Oct 21, 1773. Spon: John Heylmann and wife.

Rosina Barbara of Anastasius Heylmann and wife Rosina Barbara, b.
Apr 4, 1776; bapt. Apr 18, 1776. Spon: John Heylmann and wife.
John of Anastasius Heylmann and wife Rosina Barbara, b. Oct 17,
1778; bapt. Oct 20, 1778. Spon: John Heylmann and wife.
John George of Anastasius Heylmann and wife Rosina Barbara, b.
Jun 16, 1780; bapt. Sep 3, 1780. Spon: John George Heylmann
and wife Anna Mary.
Simon John of Peter Heylman, Jr. and wife Barbara, nee Heymann
(evidently meant for Heylmann), b. Feb 3, 1767; bapt. March 1,
1767. Spon: John Heylmann and Anna Mary Heylmann.
Anna Catharine of Peter Heylman, Jr. and wife Barbara, nee
Heymann (evidently meant for Heylmann), b. Sep 2, 1768; bapt.
Sep 11, 1768. Spon: Adam Heylman and Catharine Heylman.
John Frederic of Peter Heylman, Jr. and wife Barbara, nee Heymann
(evidently meant for Heylmann), b. March 30, 1771; bapt. Apr
17, 1771. Spon: Peter Eiderholt and wife Elizabeth.
John Adam of Peter Heylman, Jr. and wife Barbara, nee Heymann
(evidently meant for Heylmann), b. Nov 27, 1774; bapt. Dec 12,
1774. Spon: Adam Heylman and wife Catharine.
Peter of Peter Heylman, Jr. and wife Barbara, nee Heymann
(evidently meant for Heylmann), b. Jul 22, 1777; bapt. Aug 10,
1777. Spon: George Heylman and Barbara Umberger.
Jacob of George Holtz and wife Elizabeth, b. Nov 16, 1759; bapt. Dec
15, 1759. Spon: Sebastian ----.
Anna Mary of John Heylman and wife Anna Mary, b. Sep 24, 1779;
bapt. Oct 17, 1779. Spon: John George Heylman and Anna
Magdalena Keller, both single.
Henry of John Henry Heylman and wife Christina, b. Oct 14, 1779;
bapt. Oct 17, 1779. Spon: Peter Heylman and wife Barbara.
Mary Christina of John Henry Heylman and wife Christina, b. Apr
22, 1781; bapt. Apr 28, 1781. Spon: Anastasius Heylman and
wife Rosina Barbara.
Anna Christina of John (Jacob in index) Hix and wife Elizabeth, b.
Dec 24, 1780; bapt. Dec 26, 1780. Spon: Michael Holderbaum
and wife Juliana.
John Henry of John Happel and wife Margaret, b. Jul 28, 1782; bapt.
Sep 9, 1782. Spon: father and mother.
Mary Barbara of Philip Holinger and wife (Olinger in index), b. Nov
2, 1744; bapt. Nov 3, 1744. Spon: Leonard Umberger and Philip
Olinger and wife Juliana.

Elizabeth of Philip Holinger and wife (Olinger in index), b. Aug 11, 1746; bapt. Aug 14, 1746. Spon: Peter Kucher and wife.

Mary Magdalene of Jost Jotter and wife Eve, b. March 18, 1757; bapt. Apr 16, 1757. Spon: Christian Kauffman and wife.

John of Jost Jotter and wife Eve, b. Sep 27, 1759; bapt. Sep 3, 1759. Spon: John Kuemmerling and wife.

Anna Christina of John Schweickhard Imboden and wife Eleonora, b. Aug 27, 1759; bapt. Sep 2, 1759. Spon: Michael Holderbaum and Anna Christina Stoever, both single.

John of John Schweickhard Imboden and wife Eleonora, b. Sep 20, 1761; bapt. Oct 25, 1761. Spon: Caspar Diller, Jr. and Juliana Ulrich.

John Adam of John Schweickhard Imboden and wife Eleonora, b. Oct --, 1765; bapt. Nov 10, 1765. Spon: Joh. Adam Weiss and Eva Meyer.

Joh. George of John Schweickhard Imboden and wife Eleonora, b. Jan 25, 1772; bapt. Feb 22, 1772. Spon: John Mueller and wife Susanna.

Joh. Philip of John Schweickhard Imboden and wife Eleonora, b. March 26, 1774; bapt. Apr 17, 1774. Spon: John Philip Firnsler and wife Anna Christina.

Solomon and Eleonara, twins of John Schweickhard Imboden and wife Eleonora, b. ----, ----; bapt. Aug 22, 1781. Spon: Anastasius Heylman and wife Rosina, Anton Carmini and wife Anna Christina.

Jacob of John Schweickhard Imboden and wife Eleonora, b. Dec 25, 1783; bapt. Jul 8, 1784. Spon: John Wunderlig and wife Mary Elizabeth.

John of John Imboden and wife Christina, b. Apr 10, 1784; bapt. Apr 21, 1784. Spon: Henry Peter and wife Mary Christina.

Juliana of Daniel Jungblut and wife Anna Mary Elizabeth, b. Dec --, 1767; bapt. Dec 21, 1767. Spon: Martin Ulrich and Juliana Heinrich.

Eva Mary of Peter Jetter and wife Anna Mary, b. March 10, 1768; bapt. Apr 1, 1768. Spon: George Sprecher and wife Eva Margaret.

Mary Catharine of Peter Jetter and wife Anna Mary, b. Dec 16, 1769; bapt. Jan 17, 1770. Spon: Mary Catharine Stoever.

Anna Mary of Peter Jetter and wife Anna Mary, b. Jul 10, 1772; bapt. Aug 2, 1772. Spon: Tobias Stoever and wife Hannah.

Catharine of Peter Johnsen and wife Anna Mary, b. Dec 30, 1783; bapt. May 30, 1784. Spon: John Sauter and wife Catharine.

Joh. Frederic of Michael Jensel, b. Jul 12, 1760; bapt. Aug 3, 1760. Spon: Joh. George Jensel and Salome Huber.

John Francis of Peter Kucher, b. Jul 13, 1736; bapt. Aug 1, 1736. Spon: John Frantz Fuchs and wife Margaret.

Anna Catharine of Peter Kucher, b. Jan 12, 1738; bapt. Feb 7, 1738. Spon: Joh. George Graff, Jr. and (Mrs.) Catharine Koppenhoeffer.

Joh. Christopher of Peter Kucher, b. March 15, 1739; bapt. Apr 22, 1739. Spon: Christopher Meyer and wife Rosina.

Rosina of Peter Kucher, b. March 20, 1741; bapt. May 25, 1741. Spon: Christopher Meyer and wife.

Joh. Peter of Peter Kucher, b. Feb 12, 1743; bapt. March 27, 1743. Spon: Albrecht Siechele and wife.

Eva Barbara of Peter Kucher, b. Jan 19, 1745; bapt. Feb 3, 1745. Spon: Albrecht Siechele and wife.

George Mich. of Peter Kucher, b. Feb 10, 1747; bapt. March 3, 1747. Spon: Joh. George Hettericht and wife.

Anna Elizabeth of Joh. Dietrich Kober, b. May 12, 1734; bapt. Jul 21, 1734. Spon: Joh. Adam Heyl and wife.

Joh. Egidius of Joh. Dietrich Kober, b. Dec 18, 1738; bapt. Dec 24, 1738. Spon: Joh. Egidius Hoffman.

Joh. George of Joh. Dietrich Kober, b. Jan 27, 1741; bapt. Feb 22, 1741. Spon: Joh. Egidius Hoffman and wife.

Anna Margaret of Joh. Dietrich Kober, b. May 13, 1743; bapt. May 23, 1743. Spon: Thomas Kreuel and wife Margaret.

George Michael of John Adam Kittring, b. Dec 11, 1741; bapt. Jan 3, 1742. Spon: Michael Boltz and wife Mary Barbara.

Mary Margaret of John Adam Kittring, b. Aug 4, 1743; bapt. Nov 15, 1743. Spon: Michael Boltz and wife Mary Barbara.

Sarah of William Kally, b. Apr 6, 1742; bapt. Apr 15, 1742. Spon: Andrew Weltz and wife.

Mary Margaret of Joh. Adam Kreuel, b. Oct 17, 1743; bapt. Nov 20, 1743. Spon: Thomas Kreuel and wife Mary Margaret.

Valentine of Vincens Kueffer and wife Margaret, b. March 5, 1745; bapt. March 31, 1745. Spon: Valentine Kueffer and wife Barbara.

Joh. George of Vincens Kueffer and wife Margaret, b. Oct 13, 1748; bapt. Nov 27, 1748. Spon: George Buerger and wife.

Anna Margaret of Valentine Kueffer and wife Barbara, b. Oct 27,

1744; bapt. Nov 10, 1744. Spon: Vincens Kueffer and wife.
Elizabeth daughter of Valentine Kueffer and wife Barbara, b. March
17, 1747; bapt. March 29, 1747. Spon: George Velty and wife.
Mary Barbara of Valentine Kueffer and wife Barbara, b. Feb 18,
1749; bapt. March 3, 1749. Spon: Peter Heylman and wife.
Valentine of Valentine Kueffer and wife Barbara, b. Apr 23, 1751;
bapt. May 12, 1751. Spon: Peter Wampstler and wife.
John of Valentine Kueffer and wife Barbara, b. May 9, 1753; bapt.
May 20, 1753. Spon: Joh. George Friedrich and wife; also
Anthony Nagel and wife Margaret.
Mary Regina of John Wolff Kissner and wife Sabina, b. Jul 5, 1751;
bapt. Jul 7, 1751. Spon: Joh. Jacob Kantz and Mary Regina
Siechle; her parents, Albrecht Siechle and his wife representing
her in minority.
Mary Eve of John Wolff Kissner and wife Sabina, b. Jan 23, 1754;
bapt. Jan 25, 1754. Spon: Joh. Jacob Kautz.
Joh. Michael of John Wolff Kissner and wife Sabina, b. Apr --, 1755;
bapt. Apr 20, 1755. Spon: Joh. Michael Pfrang and wife; Joh.
Jacob Kantz.
John of John Wolff Kissner and wife Sabina, b. March 13, 1757; bapt.
March 20, 1757. Spon: Jacob Ruecker and Eva Pfrang.
Mary Barbara of John Wolff Kissner and wife Sabina, b. Jul 8, 1759;
bapt. Jul 10, 1759. Spon: Martin Bindtnagel and Mary Barbara
Siechle.
Daniel of John Wolff Kissner and wife Sabina, b. Oct 30, 1762; bapt.
Nov 7, 1762. Spon: Daniel Wunderlich and Mary Barbara
Siechle.
Joh. Jacob of John Adam Kleeman, b. Jul 9, 1751; bapt. ----, ----.
Spon: Joh. Nicholas Frank, Joh. Jacob Herber and Anna
Elizabeth, wife of Philip Herber.
Joh. Valentine of Valentine Keller, b. Feb 28, 1752; bapt. Apr 12,
1752. Spon: Charles Schally and wife Esther.
Mary Elizabeth of Valentine Keller, b. Sep 15, 1753; bapt. Oct 7,
1753. Spon: Joh. Nich. Stroeher and Elizabeth Schall (or
Schally).
Joh. Adam of Valentine Keller, b. Aug 8, 1756; bapt. Aug 24, 1756.
Spon: Adam Barth and wife Elizabeth.
Anna Magdalene of Valentine Keller, b. Oct --, 1757; bapt. Oct 30,
1757. Spon: Matthias Boger and wife.
Joh. George of Valentine Keller, b. March --, 1759; bapt. Apr 12,

1759. Spon: Joh. George Kob and Anna Mary Schall (or Schally).

Joh. Jacob of Valentine Keller, b. Jan 19, 1762; bapt. Feb 2, 1762. Spon: Jacob Ludwig and wife.

Vernonica of Sebastian Kirstaetter and wife Magdalena, b. Apr 9, 1752; bapt. Apr 12, 1752. Spon: Thomas Madern and wife Veronica.

Joh. Martin of Sebastian Kirstaetter and wife Magdalena, b. March 7, 1754; bapt. March 24, 1754. Spon: Martin Kirstaetter, Jr.

Joh. Leonard of Sebastian Kirstaetter and wife Magdalena, b. Apr 12, 1756; bapt. Apr 15, 1756. Spon: Joh. Leonard Kirstaetter and Sarah Elizabeth.

Anna Catharine of Sebastian Kirstaetter and wife Magdalena, b. Jun 1, 1758; bapt. Jun 4, 1758. Spon: Joh. Leonard Kirstaetter and Anna Catharine Uhler.

Mary Elizabeth of Michael Kirstaetter, b. March 23, 1754; bapt. March 24, 1754. Spon: John Dietz and wife Mary Elizabeth.

Joh. Martin of Michael Kirstaetter, b. May 30, 1756; bapt. Jun 4, 1756. Spon: Joh. Martin Kirstaetter and Anna Mary Heylman.

John of Michael Kirstaetter, b. Oct 31, 1761; bapt. Nov 22, 1762. Spon: John Schally and Mary Elizabeth Bohr.

John of Michael Kirstaetter, b. ----, 1769; bapt. Apr 21, 1770. Spon: Joh. Nicol. New and wife Anna Margaret.

Joh. Adam of Martin Kirstaetter and wife Elizabeth, b. Aug 28, 1757; bapt. Sep 3, 1757. Spon: Adam Stoehr and wife Eve Catharine.

Anna Margaret of Martin Kirstaetter and wife Elizabeth, b. Jul --, 1766; bapt. Aug 17, 1766. Spon: Frantz Fuchs and wife Anna Margaret. (A line is drawn through this last.)

George Michael of Michael Kaineth and wife Anna Margaret (changed to read Kaemeth), b. Oct 15, 1758; bapt. Oct 23, 1758. Spon: George Hanss Dietrich and wife Dorothea.

Anna Elizabeth of Michael Kaineth and wife Anna Margaret (changed to read Kaemeth), b. Oct 21, 1760; bapt. Nov 23, 1760. Spon: Joh.Wm. Stoehr and wife Anna Elizabeth.

Anna Mary of Michael Kaineth and wife Anna Margaret (changed to read Kaemeth), b. Sep 1, 1762; bapt. Sep 21, 1762. Spon: Thomas Kinsel and wife Anna Mary.

John Caspar of Michael Kaineth and wife Anna Margaret (changed to read Kaemeth), b. Sep 29, 1764; bapt. Sep 30, 1764. Spon: George Henry Peter and Eva Meyer.

Catharine of Michael Kaineth and wife Anna Margaret (changed to read Kaemeth), b. ----, 1766; bapt. Aug 17, 1766. Spon: Nicholas Brechtbiel and wife Juliana.

Joh. Adam of Joh. George Kupper and wife Elizabeth, b. Jul 1, 1759; bapt. Aug 5, 1759. Spon: Joh. George Ulrich and sister Anna.

Jacob of Joh. George Kupper and wife Elizabeth, b. Aug 1, 1761; bapt. Sep 1, 1764. Spon: Jacob Derry and wife Mary Ulrich.

Joh. Frederic of Martin Kueffer and wife Elizabeth, b. Oct 18, 1759; bapt. Nov 25, 1759. Spon: Joh. Frederic Kueffer and Elizabeth Feltin.

Joh. Peter of Martin Kueffer and wife Elizabeth, b. Mar 20, 1761; bapt. Apr 12, 1761. Spon: Peter Kueffer and Anna Waibel.

Anna Margaret of John Krueger, b. Jan 5, 1758; bapt. Feb 2, 1758. Spon: Abraham Heydt, Jr., Anna Mary Heydt, and Anna Margaret Jetter.

Joh. George of John Krueger and wife Anna Margaret (apparently same as above), b. Nov 8, 1759; bapt. Nov 25, 1759. Spon: Michael Killinger and wife.

Elizabeth of George Kob and wife Elizabeth, b. Jul --, 1760; bapt. Aug 17, 1760. Spon: Adam Barth and wife Elizabeth.

Anna Catharine of George Kob and wife Elizabeth, b. Mar 2, 1762; bapt. Mar 22, 1762. Spon: Peter Kober and Mary Catharine Beyer.

Joh. Valentine of George Kob and wife Elizabeth, b. Feb 10, 1764; bapt. Mar 11, 1764. Spon: Joh. Valentine Keller and wife.

Mary Elizabeth of Michael Kirber and wife Anna Mary, b. Nov 2, 1761; bapt. Nov 30, 1761. Spon: Martin Heinrich and wife Mary Elizabeth.

Anna Elizabeth of Peter Kober and wife Margaret, b. Jul --, 1765; bapt. Aug 17, 1765. Spon: Michael Warmpstler and wife Elizabeth.

Joh. Nicholas of Peter Kober and wife Margaret, b. Nov 20, 1766; bapt. Dec 17, 1766. Spon: Joh. Nichol. New, Jr. and Anna Catharine Stroeher, both single.

Anna Christina of Martin Kolmar and wife Anna Magdalene, b. Oct 11, 1768, (or 1767); bapt. Oct 20, 1767 (or 1768). Spon: Antonius Karmeni and wife Anna Christina.

Susanna of Martin Koch and wife Elizabeth, b. Dec --, 1767; bapt. Dec 6, 1767. Spon: Andrew Karg and wife Susanna.

Joh. David of Christopher Kucher and wife ("Belongs to congregation at Lebanon at present."), b. Jan 19, 1769; bapt. Feb 6, 1769.

Spon: David Schaeffer and wife. In their absence Peter Kucher, Sr. and wife Barbara were their representatives.

Joh. Philip of Christopher Kucher and wife ("Belongs to congregation at Lebanon at present."), b. Nov --, 1770; bapt. Feb --, 1771. Spon: Philip De Haas and wife Eleonora.

Joh. Philip of Antonius Karmenie and wife Christina, b. Dec 2, 1758; bapt. Dec 18, 1758. Spon: Philip Fishborn and wife Catharine Elizabeth.

John of Antonius Karmenie and wife Christina, b. Jun 15, 1760; bapt. on the day of birth. Spon: John Karmenie.

Antonius of Antonius Karmenie and wife Christina, b. Nov 14, 1764; bapt. Nov 19, 1764. Spon: Antonius Blessle and wife Mary Salome.

John Martin of Antonius Karmenie and wife Christina, b. Sep 12, 1766; bapt. Oct 19, 1766. Spon: Joh. Martin Kolmar and wife Anna Magdalene.

Catharine Elizabeth of John Karmenie and wife Juliana, b. Oct 10, 1763; bapt. Nov 6, 1763. Spon: Henry Dietz and wife Catharine Elizabeth.

Rebecca of John Karmenie and wife Juliana, b. Apr 14, 1765; bapt. May 16, 1765. Spon: Michael Karmenie and Rebecca Guenther, both single.

Mary Barbara of John Karmenie and wife Juliana, b. Jul 22, 1766; bapt. at next opportunity. Spon: Antonius Blessle and wife Mary Salome.

John of John Karmenie and wife Juliana, b. Oct 19, 1767; bapt. Nov 1, 1767. Spon: Antonius Karmenie and wife Anna Christina.

Anna Christina of John Karmenie and wife Juliana, b. Aug 18, 1769; bapt. "at first opportunity." Spon: Antonius Karmenie and wife Anna Christina.

Antonius of John Karmenie and wife Juliana, b. Jun 13, 1771; bapt. "at next opportunity." Spon: Antonius Karmenie (evidently Blessle) and wife Mary Salome.

John George of John Karmenie and wife Juliana, b. Apr 2, 1775; bapt. Apr 13, 1775. Spon: John Schweighard Imboden and wife Eleonora.

George Adam of John Karmenie and wife Juliana, b. Mar 31, 1777; bapt. May 10, 1777. Spon: John Schweighard and wife Eleonora.

John Philip of John Karmenie and wife Juliana, b. Jul 14, 1779; bapt. Jul 27, 1779. Spon: John Philip Karmenie and Anna Matter, both single.

John David of John Karmenie and wife Juliana, b. Jan 2, 1782; bapt.
Jan 12, 1782. Spon: John David Wagner and wife Anna Mary,
after the father's death.

Joh. George of Michael Karmenie and wife Catharine, b. Sep 29,
1775; bapt. Oct 15, 1775. Spon: George Wampster and wife
Elizabeth.

Anna Mary of Philip Karmini and wife Anna, b. Jan 10, 1782; bapt.
Jan 22, 1782. Spon: John Carmini and Anna Mary Matter, both
single.

John of Philip Karmini and wife Anna, b. Dec 25, 1783; bapt. Jan 11,
1784. Spon: John Matter and Barbara Carmini, both single.

John of John Klein and wife Barbara, b. Dec 20, 1782; bapt. Dec 26,
1781. Spon: John Stroh and Anna Mary Nase, boh single.

Anna Mary of Michael Kleber and wife Catharine, b. Oct 14, 1776;
bapt. Oct 27, 1776. Spon: Jacob Matter and wife.

John Michael of Michael Kleber and wife Mary Catharine, b. Jan 17,
1784; bapt. Apr 4, 1784. Spon: John Matter and Juliana
Imboden, both single.

Catharine of George Kimmerling and wife Veronica, b. Apr 1, 1784;
bapt. May 2, 1784. Spon: Jacob Bolz and Elizabeth Wagner, both
single.

Anna of Philip Karmini and wife Anna, b. Jun 16, 1788; bapt. Jun 22,
1788. Spon: Jacob Marder (Matter) and wife.

Walther of Jacob Kintzer and wife, b. Sep 21, 1746; bapt. Nov 9,
1746. Spon: Sadeler Neuman and Sabina Bindtnagel.

Joh. Frederic of Joh. Frederic Kueffer and wife Sabina, b. Dec 9,
1761; bapt. Dec 20, 1761. Spon: Ulrich Joeckel and wife.

John of Michael Lauer, b. Apr 28, 1744; bapt. May 13, 1744. Spon:
Henry Merck and wife Philippina.

Anna Regina of Joh. Leonard Lang, of (Swatara), b. Sep --, 1750;
bapt. Oct 9, 1750. Spon: John Bindtnagel and wife Regina.

Leonard of John Leonard Lang, of (Swatara), b. March 29, 1752;
bapt. Apr 13, 1752. Spon: George Buerger and wife.

Antonius of Joh. Leonard Lang, of (Swatara), b. Nov 9, 1753; bapt.
Feb 24, 1754. Spon: George Buerger and wife Catharine.

Margaret of John William Litz and wife Catharine, b. Sep 12, 1758;
bapt. Oct 2, 1758. Spon: Dietrich Morrel and wife Margaret.

Joh. William of Joh. William Litz and wife Catharine, b. Oct 16, 1759;
bapt. Dec 26, 1759. Spon: Albrecht Mueller and Catharine Beyer.

Christina of William Lang (Long) and wife Elizabeth, b. Jul 3, 1782; bapt. Jul 28, 1782. Spon: Mary Elizabeth Kop.

Juliana of Henry Martin, b. Mar --, 1753; bapt. Mar 9, 1753. Spon: Matthias ---- and Catharine Schnock.

Mary Elizabeth of Peter Marcker and wife, b. Apr 21, 1743; bapt. May 23, 1743. Spon: Christopher Zimmer and wife.

Juliana of Peter Marcker and wife, b. Feb 3, 1746; bapt. March 3, 1746. Spon: Adam Ulrich and wife Juliana.

Catharine of Peter Marcker and wife, b. Feb 4, 1751. baptized March 17, 1751. Spon: George Mueller.

Isaac of James McNees, b. Jul --, 1737; bapt. Feb 7, 1738. Spon: Peter Kucher and wife Anna Barbara.

James of James McNees, b. Sep 4, 1741; bapt. Jul 18, 1742. Spon: Anastasius Uhler and wife Dorothea.

Elizabeth of Joh. Martin Meyle and wife Sabina, b. Nov 7, 1733; bapt. Apr 28, 1734. Spon: Michael Baeltel and wife Elizabeth.

John of Joh. Martin Meyle and wife Sabina, b. Jan 25, 1735; bapt. May 25, 1735. Spon: John Bindtnagel and wife.

Joh. Martin of Joh. Martin Meyle and wife Sabina, b. Jul 25, 1737; bapt. Dec 25, 1737. Spon: Michael Baeltel and wife.

Henry of Joh. Martin Meyle and wife Sabina, b. Jan 16, 1742; bapt. Apr 15, 1742. Spon: Henry Klein and wife.

George of Joh. Martin Meyle and wife Sabina, b. Oct 2, 1743; bapt. Dec 18, 1743. Spon: Henry Klein and wife.

Anna Catharine of George Meyer, b. Jul 2, 1740; bapt. Aug 10, 1740. Spon: Peter Ruth and wife Barbara.

Joh. Henry of George Meyer, b. Dec 19, 1741; bapt. Apr 26, 1742. Spon: Henry Beyer and wife.

Michael of George Meyer, b. Feb 28, 1743; bapt. May 23, 1743. Spon: Michael Meyer and wife.

George Peter of George Meyer, b. Oct 19, 1744; bapt. Apr 28, 1745. Spon: Peter Marcker, Ulrich Peter and (Mrs.) Elizabeth Hatz.

Joh. Jacob of George Meyer, b. Aug 28, 1746; bapt. Nov 9, 1746. Spon: Jacob Schlauch and wife Ursula Elizabeth.

Christopher Jonathan of George Meyer, b. Sep 3, 1748; bapt. Oct 2, 1748. Spon: Christopher Zimmer and wife Sarah Barbara.

George of Christopher Meyer (the Miller), b. Dec 4, 1735; bapt. Apr 18, 1736. Spon: Joh. George Klein and wife Anna.

Mary Barbara of Christopher Meyer (the Miller), b. Aug 12, 1738; bapt. Aug 21, 1738. Spon: Joh. Peter Kucher and wife Mary

Barbara.

Anna Mary of Christopher Meyer (the Miller), b. Jun 18, 1742; bapt. Jul 18, 1742. Spon: Thomas Koppenhoeffer and wife Anna Mary.

Christopher of Michael Meyer, b. Oct 20, 1736; bapt. Nov 7, 1736. Spon: Christopher Meyer and wife.

George of Michael Meyer, b. Oct 2, 1743; bapt. Dec 2, 1743. Spon: George Meyer and wife Barbara.

Joh. Charles of John Meyer, b. March 7, 1749; bapt. March 19, 1749. Spon: Joh. Charles Schally and Veronica Brennkissen.

Conrad of Christopher Meyer and wife Catharine (in index the Blacksmith), b. Jul 26, 1749; bapt. Aug 6, 1749. Spon: Jacob Faber, and Michael Braun and wife Anna.

Mary Catharine of Christopher Meyer and wife Catharine (in index The Blacksmith), b. Dec 25, 1750; bapt. Jan 2, 1751. Spon: Michael Braun and wife Anna.

John Michael of Christopher Meyer and wife Catharine (in index The Blacksmith), b. Feb 26, 1752; bapt. March 15, 1752. Spon: Michael Braun and wife.

Christopher of Christopher Meyer and wife Catharine (in index The Blacksmith), b. Feb 12, 1754; bapt. Feb 24, 1754. Spon: Conrad Braun and wife Catharine.

Eva Margaret of Christopher Meyer and wife Catharine (in index The Blacksmith), b. May 12, 1755; bapt. Jun 15, 1775. Spon: George Sprecher and wife Eva Margaret.

Anna Mary of Christopher Meyer and wife Catharine (in index The Blacksmith), b. Sep 3, 1758; bapt. Sep 24, 1758. Spon: Christopher Wegman and wife.

Anna Mary Elizabeth of Christopher Meyer and wife Catharine (in index The Blacksmith), b. March 3, 1760; bapt. March 23, 1760. Spon: Christopher Wegman and wife.

Christopher Frederic of Christopher Meyer and wife Catharine (in index The Blacksmith), b. Jan --, 1763; bapt. Jan 25, 1763. Spon: Christopher Frederic Wegman and Catharine Ludwig.

Anna Christina of Christopher Meyer and wife Catharine (in index The Blacksmith), b. Feb --, 1764; bapt. Feb 24, 1764. Spon: John Stroh and wife.

John of Christopher Meyer and wife Catharine (in index The Blacksmith), b. Feb 27, 1765; bapt. Oct 12, 1765. Spon: John Stroh and wife Elizabeth.

Christopher Frederic of Christopher Meyer and wife Catharine (in

index The Blacksmith), b. Feb 17, 1770; bapt. Feb 25, 1775.
Spon: Christopher Frederic Wegman and wife Mary Eve.

Mary Regina of George Adam Mueller, of (Swatara), b. Oct 4, 1751;
bapt. Oct 7, 1751. Spon: John Bindtnagel and wife Mary Regina.

Christina Dorothea of George Adam Mueller, of (Swatara), b. Feb 3,
1753; bapt. Feb 24, 1753. Spon: Martin Bindtnagel and Dorothea
Boltz.

John of George Adam Mueller, of (Swatara), b. Nov 9, 1755; bapt.
Dec 1, 1755. Spon: Joh. Kissnes and wife Sabina, and Dorothea
Boltz.

Joh. Adam of George Michael Mueller, b. Apr 9, 1754; bapt. Apr 11,
1754. Spon: Joh. Adam Herbert and wife.

John of Rudolph Mueller, b. May 17, 1760; bapt. Jun 8, 1760. Spon:
John Schnock, Jr. and Catharine Elizabeth Schall, or Schalle.

Mary Margaret of George Mueller, b. Dec 5, 1760; bapt. Dec 8, 1760.
Spon: ---- Schweinfurt and wife Mary Margaret.

Elizabeth Catharine of Joh. George Maeintzer and wife, b. Apr 13,
1741; bapt. May 16, 1741. Spon: Jacob Spanseiler.

Anna Catharine of Joh. George Maeintzer and wife, b. May 23, 1742;
bapt. Jul 18, 1742. Spon: George Buerger and wife.

Mary Elizabeth of Joh. George Maeintzer and wife, b. Oct 1, 1743;
bapt. Dec 21, 1743. Spon: Mary Elizabeth Klettleri.

George Christopher of Joh. George Maeintzer and wife, b. May 21,
1748; bapt. May 30, 1748. Spon: George Hatz and wife
Elizabeth.

Rosina Barbara of Nicholas Maurer and wife Mary Catharine, b. Nov
22, 1769; bapt. Dec 2, 1769. Spon: Anastasius Heylman and wife
Rosina Barbara.

Frederic Theodore Melsheimer, b. Sep 29, 1749 near Holminden,
Principality of Brunswick, m. Jan 3, 1779.

Mary Agnes Mau, of Bethlehem, b. Nov 16, 1759, m. Jan 3, 1779.

Charles Theodore of Frederic Theodore Melsheimer and wife Mary
Agnes Mau, b. Apr 16, 1780; bapt. May 14, 1780. Spon:
Valentine Keller and wife Justina.

Frederic Ernst of Frederic Theodore Melsheimer and wife Mary
Agnes Mau, b. Apr 20, 1782; bapt. May 17, 1782. Spon: Adam
Bardt and wife.

John Frederic of Frederic Theodore Melsheimer and wife Mary Agnes
Mau, b. Jul 12, 1784; bapt. Aug 1, 1784. Spon: Anthony Karmini
and wife Christina.

William of Thomas Morgan and wife Anna, b. Jul 20, 1780; bapt. Sep 1, 1780. Spon: Siegmund Schauer and wife Anna Mary.

Thomas of Thomas Morgan and wife Anna, b. Nov 4, 1782; bapt. Dec 26, 1782. Spon: father and mother.

John Adam of John Samuel Mau and wife Eva Esther, b. Nov 29, 1782; bapt. Dec 16, 1782. Spon: John Adam Bart and Catharine Achenbach, both single.

Anna Magdalene of Jacob Matter and wife Elizabeth, b. Apr 14, 1784; bapt. May 2, 1784. Spon: Philip Karmini and wife Anna.

John Jacob of John Matter and wife Magdalene, b. Oct 26, 1787; bapt. Nov 12, 1787. Spon: Jacob Matter and wife.

Joh. Philip of Joh. Nicholas Neu (Nye and Ney), b. Oct 3, 1750; bapt. Oct 28, 1750. Spon: Joh. Philip Bayer and Joh. Nicholas Weder and wife.

Joh. Peter of Joh. Nicholas Neu (Nye and Ney), b. Jul --, 1753; bapt. Aug 12, 1753. Spon: Peter Feltin and wife.

Mary Elizabeth of John Adam Neu and wife Eve Elizabeth, b. Apr 30, 1751; bapt. May 16, 1751. Spon: Nicholas Wederts and wife Mary Elizabeth, also Elizabeth Catharine Stroeher.

Fredric of John Adam Neu and wife Eve Elizabeth, b. Feb 9, 1753; bapt. ----, ----. Sponsors were to have been Matthias Bohr and his wife, but on account of high water Christopher Wegman and Margaret Neu acted in their stead.

Mary Christina of John Adam Neu and wife Eve Elizabeth, b. Oct 27, 1759; bapt. Oct 28, 1759. Spon: Matthias Bohr and wife.

Anna Margaret of John Adam Neu and wife Eve Elizabeth, b. Apr 11, 1761; bapt. Apr 12, 1761. Spon: Michael Malfir (Maulfair) and wife.

Joh. Peter of John Adam Neu and wife Eve Elizabeth, b. Sep 29, 1762; bapt. Oct 10, 1762. Spon: Joh. Peter Feltin and wife Mary Catharine.

Joh. Michael of John Adam Neu and wife Eve Elizabeth, b. ----, 1764; bapt. Nov 11, 1764. Spon: (none given.)

Joh. Henry of John Adam Neu and wife Eve Elizabeth, b. Jul --, 1766; bapt. Jul 2, 1766. Spon: Henry Firnsler and wife Juliana.

Michael Neu (oldest son of John Nicholas Neu), b. Oct 4, 1744, Elennich, Magistracy of Traebach, at the Moselle, Germany; bapt. Oct 7, 1744. Spon: Peter Lahm, Michael Lahm and Anna Margaret Neu. Married Justina Bardt in Feb 1773. The following children were the fruit of this marriage:

Anna Christina of Michael Neu and wife Justine, b. Aug 26, 1774; bapt. Sep 3, 1774. Spon: John Peter Neu and Elizabeth Bardt.

Anna Catharine of Michael Neu and wife Justine, b. Feb 21, 1776; bapt. March 3, 1776. Spon: John Neu and Anna Mary Bardt.

John Michael of Michael Neu and wife Justine, b. Nov 4, 1777; bapt. Nov 23, 1777, died Aug 4, 1778. Spon: Adam Stoever and wife Mary Catharine.

Elizabeth of Michael Neu and wife Justine, b. March 14, 1779; bapt. March 30, 1779. Spon: John Adam Bardt and Elizabeth Kopp.

John Peter of Peter Neu and wife Juliana, b. March 19, 1780; bapt. March 28, 1780. Spon: John Nicholas Neu and wife Mary Margaret.

Catharine of Peter Neu and wife Juliana, b. Apr 9, 1781; bapt. Apr 19, 1781. Spon: John Peter Neu and Catharine Karmini, both single.

John George of Michael Naef and wife Anna Christina Barbara, b. Sep 28, 1779; bapt. Oct 17, 1779. Spon: George Guntrum and wife Susanna.

Anna Elizabeth of John Oppenhauser and wife Anna Elizabeth, b. Aug 17, 1747; bapt. Sep 13, 1747. Spon: John Anspach and wife.

Mary Catharine of John Oppenhauser and wife Anna Elizabeth, b. Dec --, 1748; bapt. Feb 26, 1749. Spon: John Schwab and Cath. Elizabeth Schall, or Schally, and Mary Elizabeth Schall, or Schally.

Catharine Barbara of John Oppenhauser and wife Anna Elizabeth, b. Nov 1, 1750; bapt. Nov 25, 1750. Spon: Catharine Doner and Elizabeth Labengeiger.

Anna Margaret of John Oppenhauser and wife Anna Elizabeth, b. Nov 19, 1753; bapt. Dec 2, 1753. Spon: Michael Bohr and wife.

John of John Oppenhauser and wife Anna Elizabeth, b. March 1, 1755; bapt. Apr 8, 1755. Spon: John Schally and ---- Heydt.

John of John Oehrle (Early) and wife Regina of (Swatara), b. Aug 1, 1757; bapt. Aug 7, 1757. Spon: Albrecht Siechle and wife. Belongs to Bindnagle congregation now.

Catharine of George Henry Peter, b. Jun (close), 1741; bapt. Oct 4, 1741. Spon: George Buerger and wife.

Juliana of Matthias Pflantz and wife Elizabeth, b. Feb --, 1750; bapt. March 18, 1750. Spon: John Grasser and Catharine Kueffer.

Rosina of Matthias Pflantz and wife Elizabeth, b. March 21, 1751; bapt. March 25, 1751. Spon: William Stober and wife, also

Christopher Suess and wife.

Catharine and Anna Mary, twins of Matthias Pflantz and wife
Elizabeth, b. Apr 11, 1753; bapt. Apr 17, 1753. Spon: George
Buerger and wife Catharine, and Michael Gassel and wife Anna
Mary.

Joh. George of Peter Pannekuchen and wife Catharine, b. March 30,
1756; bapt. Apr 15, 1756. Spon: Joh. George Hatz and Catharine
Uhler.

Joh. Valentine of Peter Pannekuchen and wife Catharine, b. Jan 21,
1758; bapt. Jan 22, 1758. Spon: Joh. Valentine Keller and wife.

Joh. Peter of Peter Pannekuchen and wife Catharine, b. Jan 27,
1760; bapt. Feb 17, 1760. Spon: Joh. Peter Fetter and Anna
Margaret Stoever.

Mary Catharine of Peter Pannekuchen and wife Catharine, b. May --,
1762; bapt. Jun 20, 1762. Spon: Valentine Keller and wife.

Mary Barbara of William Ernst Persohn and wife, b. Aug --, 1766;
bapt. Aug 17, 1766. Spon: George Obermeyer and wife Barbara.

Catharine Regina of George Peter and wife Catharine, b. Jan 30,
1771; bapt. Feb 10, 1771. Spon: John Oehrle (Early) and wife
Regina.

Mary Elizabeth of John Penter and wife, b. ----, ----; bapt. Oct 17,
1779. Spon: (none given).

John of John Penter and wife, b. Sep 6, 1782; bapt. Dec 26, 1782.
Spon: Jacob Becker and Catharine Schauer, both single.

Magdalene of Jacob Penter and wife Magdalene, b. Sep 20, 1784;
bapt. Nov 20, 1784. Spon: Martin Ulrich and wife Dorothea.

Joh. Jacob of Jacob Rueger, b. Aug 19, 1743; bapt. Oct 23, 1743.
Spon: Henry Klein and wife.

Anna Catharine of Peter Ruth, b. Jan 29, 1735; bapt. Jun 20, 1735.
Spon: (Mrs.) Susanna Barbara Teuss.

Mary Catharine of Peter Ruth, b. Oct 27, 1741; bapt. Jan 3, 1742.
Spon: Michael Meyer and wife.

Mary Barbara of Peter Ruth, b. Nov 25, 1742; bapt. Dec 20, 1742.
Spon: John Immel and wife Barbara.

George of Francis Reynolds, b. Feb 23, 1732; bapt. May 20, 1732.
Spon: John Barbara, John Reynolds, Jr. and Anna Van Bebe.

Joh. Martin of George Caspar Rauch, b. Sep 24, 1743; bapt. Dec 18,
1743. Spon: Joh. Martin Meyle and wife.

Elizabeth of George Caspar Rauch, b. Jan 29, 1745; bapt. May 1,
1745. Spon: Salome Ort.

Anna Magdalene of George Caspar Rauch, b. Jan 4, 1747; bapt.
March 29, 1747. Spon: Anna Mary Ergebrecht.

Sophia of George Caspar Rauch, b. May 21, 1748; bapt. Aug 5, 1748.
Spon: Christopher Widder and wife Rosina.

Joh. Jacob of George Caspar Rauch, b. Jul 22, 1751; bapt. Sep 1,
1751. Spon: Abraham Heydt and wife Magdalene.

Joh. George of George Caspar Rauch, b. Aug 2, 1753; bapt. Sep 2,
1753. Spon: George Happes and wife.

John Leonard of Frederic Rathforn and wife, b. Jan 5, 1746; bapt.
Feb 11, 1746. Spon: John C. Bender.

Susanna Catharine of Philip Rudiesiel, b. Jul 29, 1749; bapt. Aug 6,
1749. Spon: Susanna Rudiesiel and Anna Mary Mueller.

Mary Elizabeth of Philip Rudiesiel, b. Nov --, 1751; bapt. Nov 30,
1751. Spon: Nicholas Wederts and wife.

Philip Adam of Philip Rudiesiel, b. Jan --, 1754; bapt. Jan 25, 1754.
Spon: Adam New and wife.

Eve Catharine of Philip Rudiesiel, b. ----, 1756; bapt. Feb 22, 1756.
Spon: Adam New and wife.

Joh. Charles of Valentine Rein, b. Jan 23, 1754; bapt. Jan 27, 1754.
Spon: Charles Rally and wife, and Valentine Keller and wife.

Joh. Christian of Valentine Rein, b. Apr 13, 1755; bapt. Apr 20, 1755.
Spon: John Schalley and Dorothea Borst.

Joh. Michael of Valentine Rein, b. May --, 1757; bapt. May 30, 1757.
Spon: Joh. Michael Wagner and wife.

Hannah Justina of Valentine Rein, b. Nov 10, 1758; bapt. Nov 15,
1758. Spon: Valentine Keller and wife.

Anna Barbara of Valentine Rein, b. Apr --, 1761; bapt. May 17, 1761.
Spon: George Meyer and wife.

Joh. George of Valentine Rein, b. Jul 23, 1763; bapt. Jul 26, 1763.
Spon: George Meyer and wife.

Joh. Martin of Valentine Rein, b. Jan 18, 1766; bapt. Feb 9, 1766.
Spon: Joh. Martin Uhler and Juliana Umberger.

Catharine of George Reynolds, b. Oct 2, 1756; bapt. Dec 9, 1756.
Spon: George Steitz, John Reynolds and wife, and Margaret Nas
(Naes).

Anna Barbara of Erasmus Rosenberger and wife Anna Catharine, b.
Jan 1, 1758; bapt. Jan 22, 1758. Spon: Joh. Ulrich Joeckel and
wife.

John Frederic of Erasmus Rosenberger and wife Anna Catharine, b.
Jul 15, 1760; bapt. Aug 3, 1760. Spon: Frederic Kueffer and

Anna Margaret Stoever.

John of Erasmus Rosenberger and wife Anna Catharine, b. Oct --, 1761; bapt. Oct 25, 1761. Spon: John Kissner and wife Sabina.

Joh. Christopher of Lawrence (Lorentz) Reuter, b. Feb 21, 1762; bapt. Feb 28, 1762. Spon: Christopher Labengeiger and Elizabeth Heylmann.

John of Lawrence (Lorentz) Reuter, b. Dec 17, 1768; bapt. Jan 2, 1769. Spon: John Heylmann and Justina Bardt.

John of John Reyer (Reiher in index) and wife Elizabeth, b. May 26, 1769; bapt. Jun 4, 1769. Spon: Joh. Nicholas New, Jr. and Catharine Schaeffer.

Christian, child of John Reyer (Reiher in index) and wife Elizabeth, b. Feb 23, 1782; bapt. Apr 1, 1782. Spon: Andrew Gerberich and wife.

George of Christian Ramberger and wife Elizabeth, b. Apr 8, 1760; bapt. May 6, 1760. Spon: George Berger (Buerger) and wife Catharine.

Anna Mary of Henry Reinoehl and wife Ima (?) Juliana, b. Aug 24, 1771; bapt. Sep 22, 1771. Spon: George Pawter (Pawter?) and wife Anna Mary.

Anna Catharine of Henry Reinoehl and wife Ima (?) Juliana, b. Oct 4, 1773; bapt. Oct 17, 1773. Spon: George Henry Reinoehl and wife Eva Catharine.

Mary Elizabeth of Henry Reinoehl and wife Ima (?) Juliana, b. March 15, 1778; bapt. March 20, 1778. Spon: Mary Elizabeth Schomacher, single.

Anna Christiana of Henry Reinoehl and wife Ima (?) Juliana, b. Oct 26, 1780; bapt. Nov 12, 1780. Spon: George Reinoehl and wife Anna Christina.

Juliana of Henry Reinoehl and wife Ima (?) Juliana, b. Jan 2, 1783; bapt. Jan 12, 1783. Spon: Jacocb Matter, Sr. and wife.

Dorothea of John Henry Reichart and wife Barbara, b. Aug 20, 1781; bapt. Sep 16, 1781. Spon: father and mother.

Henry of John Henry Reichart and wife Barbara, b. Feb 8, 1783; bapt. Apr 6, 1783. Spon: father and mother.

Catharine of Charles Reichard and wife Elizabeth, b. Oct 16, 1783; bapt. Mar 24, 1784. Spon: Catharine Schumacher.

Anna Catharine of Christian Schnug and wife Catharine, b. Feb 1, 1765; bapt. Feb 3, 1765. Spon: Jacob Wolff and Susanna Bayer.

Mary Elizabeth of Christian Schnug and wife Catharine, b. May 11,

1766; bapt. May 17, 1766. Spon: Frederic Fuchs (Fox) and
Elizabeth Bayer.

Mary of James Stuart, b. Oct 1, 1736; bapt. Feb 19, 1737.

Joh. Peter of Charles Schalley or Schally, b. Sep 29, 1741; bapt. Jan
3, 1742. Spon: Joh. PeterKucher and wife Barbara.

Joh. Valentine of Charles Schalley or Schally, b. Dec 6, 1743; bapt.
Dec 21, 1743. Spon: Joh. Valentine Kittring.

Mary Elizabeth of John Albrecht Siechele, b. ----, ----; bapt. Feb 7,
1738. Spon: *(Whether the line was left blank for the insertion of
Mary Regina, who subsequently became the wife of John Early,
Sen., or whether a vacant space was left because of uncertainty
about the whole matter, can, of course, not be said. But
apparently Stoever made this record of the first daughter of J.
Albrecht Sichele from memory, and it must always remain a
question whether he mistakenly put Mary Elizabeth for Mary
Regina, or whether there were six children besides her. But the
writer entertains a very strong suspicion that the baptism of
Christina Regina of J. Albrecht Schell in the published "Record"
of Stoever's Baptisms, was intended for J. Albrecht Sichele, as
there apparently was no Schell family residing in the vicinity
during the 18th century. The name Schell occurs much later and
even then there is no John Albrecht Schell.)*

Joh. Peter of John Albrecht Siechele, b. Mar 7, 1741; bapt. Apr 15,
1742. Spon: Peter Kucher and wife.

Eva Barbara of John Albrecht Siechele, b. Oct 2, 1744; bapt. Oct 28,
1744. Spon: Peter Kucher and wife.

Anna Catharine of John Albrecht Siechele, b. Mar 1, 1747; bapt. Mar
29, 1747. Spon: Anna Catharine Baseler and Mary Catharine
Stoever.

Anna Margaret of John Albrecht Siechele, b. Jul 20, 1749; bapt. Aug
6, 1749. Spon: Mary Catharine Stoever and Sabina Bindtnagel.

Joh. Jacob of John Albrecht Siechele, b. Nov 22, 1755; bapt. Dec 17,
1755. Spon: Joh. Kissner and wife Sabina, and Joh. Jacob Cantz.

Mary Barbara of Peter Schlosser, b. Jan 14, 1745; bapt. Feb 3, 1745.
Spon: Peter Kucher and wife.

George Ernst of Peter Schlosser, b. Aug 8, 1746; bapt. Sep 4, 1746.
Spon: George Steitz and Margaret Morr (Mohr).

Catharine Margaret, daughter of Peter Schlosser, b. Jan 10, 1748;
bapt. Feb 8, 1748. Spon: George Steitz and wife Barbara, and
Margaret Mor (Mohr).

John of Peter Schlosser, b. Sep 10, 1754; bapt. Dec 3, 1754. Spon:
John and Catharine Uhler.

John Peter of Adam and Dorothea Schmaal, b. Feb 22, 1746; bapt.
Mar 31, 1747. Spon: Peter Kucher and wife.

Joh. Matthias of Matthias Stroeher, b. Jul 27, 1749; bapt. Aug 6,
1749. Spon: Philip Beyer, Sr., Daniel Angst, and Anna Margaret
Ziegeler.

Mary Catharine of Matthias Stroeher, b. Dec 11, 1750; bapt. Dec 21,
1750. Spon: Peter Velty, Margaret New and Catharine Neu.

Catharine Elizabeth of Matthias Stroeher, b. Mar 25, 1752; bapt. Apr
12, 1752. Spon: John Adam Neu and wife, and Anna Catharine
Stroeher.

Joh. Michael of Matthias Stroeher, b. Dec 10, 1759; bapt. Dec 23,
1759. Spon: Michael Bohr and wife.

William of Willam and Margaret Stober, b. Sep 25, 1749; bapt. Oct 1,
1749. Spon: Valentine Stober and wife Eve Elizabeth.

Mary Barbara of Jacob and Anna Catharine Stober, b. Dec 6, 1749;
bapt. Dec 15, 1749. Spon: Henry Motzel and wife Mary Barbara
(in their absence represented by William Stober and wife
Margaret).

Adam of Jacob and Anna Catharine Stober, b. Dec 22, 1751; bapt.
Dec 26, 1751. Spon: Philip Adam Balmer and Barbara Pflantz.

John of Jacob and Anna Catharine Stober, b. Feb 7, 1754; bapt. Feb
24, 1754. Spon: Michael Firnsler and Barbara Pflantz.

Mary Elizabeth of Jacob and Anna Catharine Stober, b. Aug 11, 1756;
bapt. Sep 5, 1756. Spon: Michael Firnsler and Mary Elizabeth
Oberlin.

Mary Elizabeth of Jacob and Anna Catharine Stober, b. Jun 17, 1761;
bapt. Jul 5, 1761. Spon: Christopher Frederick Wegman and wife
Anna Mary.

John of John Schnock, b. Apr 30, 1750; bapt. May 30, 1750. Spon:
John Schally, Michael Boltz, Jr. and Ursula Peter.

Anna Barbara of John and Eva Margaret Schwab, b. Jan 18, 1751;
bapt. Feb 11, 1751. Spon: John Ramler and Barbara Schwab.

Elizabeth of John and Eva Margaret Schwab, b. Oct 2, 1752; bapt.
Oct 18, 1752. Spon: Anastasius Uhler and wife Dorothea.

Mary Dorthea of John and Eva Margaret Schwab, b. Oct 12, 1754;
bapt. Nov 3, 1754. Spon: Anastasius Uhler and wife Dorothea.

Margaret Catharine of Christopher Suess, b. Nov 14, 1748; bapt. Nov
27, 1748. Spon: Joh. Adam Oberlin and wife.

Mary Barbara of Christopher and Catharine Elizabeth Suess
(apparently same as above), b. Apr 9, 1751; bapt. Apr 25, 1751.
Spon: Adam Oberlin and wife Catharine Agatha.

Joh. Balthaser of Christopher and Catharine Elizabeth Suess
(apparently same as above), b. Jan 19, 1754; bapt. Jan 25, 1754.
Spon: Frederic William Hager and Margaret Stober.

Anna Catharine of Peter Stroeher, b. Nov 22, 1751; bapt. Dec 21,
1751. Spon: Matthias Stroeher and Anna Catharine Stroeher.

Catharine Elizabeth of Matthias Stroeher, Sr., b. Feb 18, 1753; bapt.
Feb 25, 1753. Spon: Peter Feltin and wife Mary Catharine, and
Anna Elizabeth Holderbaum.

Mary Magdalene of Matthias Stroeher, Sr., b. ----, 1755; bapt. Apr 25,
1755. Spon: Matthias Boger and wife.

Anna Mary of Matthias Stroeher, Sr., b. Oct 26, 1756; bapt. Nov 28,
1756. Spon: John Schweickert and Anna Mary Schall, or Schally.

Joh. Jacob of Jacob Strebich, b. Apr 15, 1754; bapt. Apr 17, 1754.
Spon: Herman Bickel and wife.

Anna Elizabeth and Christina Regina, twins of Matthias Schmidt, b.
Jun 23, 1754; bapt. Jul 14, 1754. Spon: Christopher Wegman and
wife Anna Mary, Michael Boltz and Regina Sichele.

Mary Catharine of George and Eve Margaret Sprecher, b. Aug 24,
1756; bapt. Aug 27, 1756. Spon: Mary Catharine Stoever.

Anna Margaret of George and Eve Margaret Sprecher, b. Jul 16,
1758; bapt. Jul 30, 1758. Spon: Michael Braun and wife Anna
Juliana.

Anna Eve of George and Eve Margaret Sprecher, b. Mar 26, 1760;
bapt. Apr 4, 1760. Spon: Michael Braun and wife.

Catharine Rosina of George and Eve Margaret Sprecher, b. Dec 10,
1761; bapt. Dec 20, 1761. Spon: Peter Jetter and Catharine
Braun, both single.

Anna Rosina of George and Eve Margaret Sprecher, b. Nov 13, 1763;
bapt. Nov 21, 1763. Spon: Elizabeth Barbara Wessner.

Anna Justina of George and Eve Margaret Sprecher, b. Dec 13, 1765;
bapt. Dec 29, 1765. Spon: Valentine Keller and wife Anna
Justina.

John. George of George and Eve Margaret Sprecher, b. Feb 20, 1769;
bapt. Feb 28, 1769. Spon: Valentine Keller and wife Justina.

Elizabeth of George and Eve Margaret Sprecher, b. Aug 26, 1776;
bapt. Sep 1, 1776. Spon: George Rheinoehl and wife Catharine.

Mary Elizabeth of George and Eve Margaret Sprecher, b. ----, ----;

bapt. Jul 23, 1780. Spon: Martin Bindnagel and wife Mary
Elizabeth.
Mary Barbara of Frederic Stroh, b. Oct 17, 1757; bapt. Oct 19, 1757.
Spon: Adam Bach and wife.
George Andrew of Michael Singhaas, b. Nov 28, 1759; bapt. Dec 20,
1759. Spon: George Reynold and Andrew Klein.
John Daniel of Daniel and Catharine Stroh, b. May 11, 1762; bapt.
May 16, 1762. Spon: Anastasius Uhler and wife Dorothea.
Joh. Michael of Daniel and Catharine Stroh, b. Apr --, 1763; bapt.
May 8, 1763. Spon: Joh. Michael Firnssler and wife Catharine.
Anna Elizabeth of Daniel and Catharine Stroh, b. Dec 26, 1765; bapt.
Dec 29, 1765. Spon: Christopher Uhler and Anna Elizabeth
Stroh, both single.
Christiana Dorothea of Daniel and Catharine Stroh, b. Jan 15, 1768;
bapt. Jan 17, 1768. Spon: Philip Firnsler and wife Anna
Christina.
Christopher Frederic of Daniel and Catharine Stroh, b. Jan 15, 1769;
bapt. Jan 17, 1769. Spon: Christopher Uhler and wife Margaret
Catharine.
Eva Mary of Daniel and Catharine Stroh, b. Mar 10, 1772; bapt. Mar
22, 1772. Spon: Christopher Frederic Wegman and wife Eva
Mary.
John Adam of John and Elizabeth Stroh (see below), b. Sep 12, 1766;
bapt. Sep 13, 1766. Spon: Christopher Meyer and wife
Catharine.
Daniel of John and Elizabeth Stroh (see below), b. Aug 27, 1771;
bapt. Sep 8, 1771. Spon: Abraham Heydt and wife Elizabeth.
John Stroh, b. in Germany on Feb 4, 1736; bapt. Feb 9, 1736. Spon:
Matthias Dietinger and Anna Christina Mueller. And his wife,
Anna Mary Fischer, b. Apr 3, 1740; bapt. ----, ----. Spon: Ludwig B.
and wife Anna. Were m. May 23, 1758 and had the following
children:
Mary Catharine of John Stroh and wife Anna Mary Fischer, b. May 9,
1760; bapt. ----, ----. Spon: Christopher Meyer and wife
Catharine.
John of John Stroh and wife Anna Mary Fischer, b. May 11, 1762;
bapt. ----, ----. Spon: Martin Herman and wife Dorothea.
Joh. Adam of John Stroh and wife Anna Mary Fischer, b. Sep 12,
1766; bapt. ----, ----. Spon: Christopher Meyer and wife.
Daniel of John Stroh and wife Anna Mary Fischer, b. Aug 27, 1771;

bapt. Sep 8, 1771. Spon: Abraham Heyd and wife.

Joh. Philip of George Stroh and wife Anna Engel (belongs to Lebanon), b. Dec 22, 1768; bapt. ----, ----. Spon: Joh. Philip Marsteller and wife Magdalene.

George of Jacob Sprecher and wife Dorothea, b. Jan 6, 1760; bapt. Jan 13, 1760. Spon: Joh. Nicholas Schaack and wife.

Adam of John Adam Stoever and wife Esther Elizabeth, b. Aug 4, 1770; bapt. Aug 31, 1770. Spon: Philip Firnsler and wife Christina.

Catharine of John Adam Stoever and wife Esther Elizabeth, b. Nov 30, 1772; bapt. Dec 7, 1772. Spon: Philip Firnsler and wife Christina.

Philip of John Adam Stoever and wife Esther Elizabeth, b. Jun 23, 1773; bapt. Aug 3, 1773. Spon: Philip Firnsler and wife Christina.

John of John Adam Stoever and wife Esther Elizabeth, b. Feb 1, 1775; bapt. Feb 10, 1775. Spon: John Stoever and wife Anna Engel.

Anna Mary of John Adam Stoever and wife Esther Elizabeth, b. Jun 15, 1777; bapt. Jun 22, 1777. Spon: Peter Yetter and wife Anna Mary.

Christina of John Adam Stoever and wife Esther Elizabeth, b. Jun 9, 1779; bapt. Jun 27, 1779. Spon: Philip Firnsler and wife Christina.

Tobias of John Adam Stoever and wife Esther Elizabeth, b. Feb 16, 1781; bapt. March 15, 1781. Spon: Tobias Stoever and wife Hannah.

Anna Magdalene of John Adam Stoever and wife Esther Elizabeth, b. Dec 20, 1783; bapt. Feb 6, 1784. Spon: Anna Mary Yetter.

Eve Catharine of Tobias Stoever and wife Hannah, b. Jan 2, 1778; bapt. ----, ----. Spon: Frederic Stoever and Anna Catharine Zimmerman.

Anna Mary of Tobias Stoever and wife Hannah, b. Dec 2, 1779; bapt. Dec 19, 1779. Spon: Peter Yetter and wife Anna Mary.

Christina of Tobias Stoever and wife Hannah, b. Oct 20, 1781; bapt. Oct 28, 1781. Spon: Adam Stoever and wife Catharine Elizabeth.

Elizabeth of Tobias Stoever and wife Hannah, b. Oct 24, 1783; bapt. ----, ----. Spon: John Stoever and wife.

Magdalene of Tobias Stoever and wife Hannah, b. Nov 19, 1785; bapt. ----, ----. Spon: John Stoever and wife.

John of Tobias Stoever and wife Hannah, b. Jan 19, 1788; bapt. ----, --

--. Spon: John Lautermilch and wife.

Anna Margaret of Tobias Stoever and wife Hannah, b. March 4, 1791; bapt. ----, ----. Spon: Henry Miller and wife.

Anna Christina of John Stoever and wife Anna Engel, b. Dec 3, 1780; bapt. Dec 14, 1780. Spon: Caspar Stoever and wife Anna Mary Barbara.

Joh. Michael of George Schlotterbeck and wife, b. March --, 1766; bapt. March 30, 1766. Spon: Joh. Michael Hahn.

Anna Elizabeth of Peter Schindel and wife Margaret; b. March 17, 1772; bapt. March 18, 1772. Spon: Nicholas Gebhardt and wife Anna Appolonia.

Joh. George of George Tittel, b. Oct --, 1761; bapt. Nov 22, 1761. Spon: ----.

Catharine Barbara of Anastasius Uhler and wife Dorothea, b. Oct 29, 1738; bapt. Jan 29, 1739. Spon: Michael Boltz and wife Catharine, Balthaser Ort and wife Barbara.

Christopher of Anastasius Uhler and wife Dorothea, b. Feb 2, 1741; bapt. March 25, 1741. Spon: Balthaser Ort and wife Barbara.

Anna Barbara of Anastasius Uhler and wife Dorothea, b. March 20, 1743; bapt. March 27, 1743. Spon: Balthaser Ort and wife.

Joh. Martin of Anastasius Uhler and wife Dorothea, b. Sep 24, 1744; bapt. Oct 28, 1744. Spon: Martin Kirstaetter and wife.

Michael of Anastasius Uhler and wife Dorothea, b. Apr 22, 1746; bapt. May 25, 1746. Spon: Michael Wagener and Margaret Roth.

John of Leonard Umberger, b. Feb 7, 1743; bapt. March 27, 1743. Spon: John Umberger and wife Elizabeth.

Joh. Leonard of Michael Umberger, b. Aug 8, 1743; bapt. May 23, 1743. Spon: Leonard Rammler and wife.

Joh. Michael of Michael Umberger, b. Feb 15, 1757; bapt. Feb 24, 1757. Spon: Adam Herbert and wife.

John of Michael Umberger, b. May 4, 1759; bapt. May 12, 1759. Spon: John Ramler and wife Barbara.

Christopher of Adam Ulrich and wife Juliana, b. Aug 23, 1746; bapt. Sep 14, 1746. Spon: Christopher Widder and wife.

Martin of Adam Ulrich and wife Juliana, b. Aug 7, 1749; bapt. Sep 3, 1749. Spon: Anastasius Uhler and wife.

Catharine of Adam Ulrich and wife Juliana, b. Sep 1752; bapt. Oct 8, 1752. Spon: Jacob Cantz and Catharine Firnsler.

Adam of George Ulrich and wife Elizabeth, b. Sep 20, 1761; bapt. Sep 27, 1761. Spon: Adam Ulirch and wife Juliana.

Anna Mary of George Ulrich and wife Elizabeth, b. Apr 7, 1763; bapt. Apr 10, 1763. Spon: Martin Busch and wife.

Christopher Frederic of George Ulrich and wife Elizabeth, b. Aug --, 1764; bapt. Sep 2, 1764. Spon: Christopher Frederic Wegman and wife Mary Eve.

Anna Mary of Christopher and Juliana Ulrich, b. Dec 31, 1767; bapt. Jan 1768. Spon: Martin Busch and wife Anna Mary.

Adam of Christopher and Juliana Ulrich, b. March 1, 1772; bapt. March 8, 1772. Spon: Adam Ulrich and wife Juliana.

Joh. Jacob of Christopher and Juliana Ulrich, b. Jan 31, 1780; bapt. Feb 4, 1780. Spon: Henry Voigt and wife Juliana.

Joh. Nicholas of Martin and Eva Dorothea Ulrich, b. Jul 25, 1777; bapt. Aug 3, 1777. Spon: Christopher Ulrich and wife Juliana.

Margaret of Martin and Eva Dorothea Ulrich, b. Aug 17, 1782; bapt. ----, ----. Spon: Martin Ulrich and wife.

Elizabeth of Jacob Von Der Weide, b. Sep 30, 1756; bapt. Nov 5, 1756. Spon: Adam Barth and wife Elizabeth.

Anna Mary of Jacob Von Der Weide, b. Sep 30, 1756; bapt. Nov 5, 1756. Spon: Anna Mary Holderbaum.

Anna Catharine of Michael and Elizabeth Wagner, b. Jan 1, 1750; bapt. Jan 22, 1750. Spon: Christopher Zimmerman and wife.

Joh. Martin of Michael and Elizabeth Wagner, b. Jul 16, 1751; bapt. Aug 3, 1751. Spon: Joh. Martin Kirstaetter and wife.

Joh. Christopher of Michael and Elizabeth Wagner, b. Jan 8, 1753; bapt. Jan 28, 1753. Spon: Joh. Christopher Zimmerman and wife Anna Catharine.

Joh. Michael of Michael and Elizabeth Wagner, b. Feb 4, 1755; bapt. Feb 22, 1755, Spon: Michael Killinger and Catharine Madern.

Joh. Daniel of Michael and Elizabeth Wagner, b. Dec 4, 1756; bapt. Jan 5, 1757. Spon: Joh. Daniel Madern and Catharine Uhler.

Joh. Jacob of Michael and Elizabeth Wagner, b. Apr 5, 1761; bapt. Apr 12, 1761. Spon: Jacob Boltz and wife Catharine.

Anna Elizabeth of Michael and Elizabeth Wagner, b. Feb 14, 1763; bapt. March 14, 1763. Spon: Jacob Boltz and wife Catharine.

Mary Magdalene of Michael and Elizabeth Wagner, b. Dec 9, 1764; bapt. Dec 25, 1764. Spon: Jacob Boltz and wife Catharine.

Henry of Michael and Elizabeth Wagner, b. Sep 15, 1766; bapt. Oct 10, 1766. Spon: Henry Wegner and wife.

Joh. Casper of Michael and Elizabeth Wagner, b. March 26, 1769; bapt. Apr 22, 1769. Spon: Jacob Boltz and wife Catharine.

Joh. Jacob of Jonas Wolff, b. Jan 4, 1742; bapt. Apr 15, 1742. Spon:
Joh. Jacob Kuemmerling and wife.
Joh. Herman of Jonas Wolff, b. Aug 5, 1743; bapt. Aug 28, 1743.
Spon: Herman Trott and wife.
Anna Mary of Jonas Wolff, b. Jan 7, 1745; bapt. Jan 15, 1745. Spon:
Herman Trott and wife.
Simon of Jonas Wolff, b. Oct 28, 1746; bapt. Dec 7, 1746. Spon:
George Wagner and wife Anna Elizabeth.
Anna Elizabeth of Jonas Wolff, b. March 4, 1748; bapt. March 20,
1748. Spon: Joh. Jacob Kuemmerling and wife.
Anna Cather. of Joh. George and Anna Elizabeth Wagner, b. Feb 27,
1746; bapt. Apr 3, 1746. Spon: John Wolff and wife Anna Cath.
John of Peter and Hannah Wolff, b. Feb 2, 1747; bapt. Mar 31, 1747.
Spon: Peter Kucher and wife.
Joh. George of Henry Weber and wife, b. Dec 6, 1747; bapt. Jan 25,
1748. Spon: George Buerger and wife Catharine Mary.
Eve Catharine of Henry Weber and wife, b. Aug 23, 1751; bapt. Sep
22, 1751. Spon: Michael Zimmerman and wife.
Joh. Henry of Henry Weber and wife, b. Apr 30, 1757; bapt. May 15,
1757. Spon: George Buerger and wife Catharine.
Mary Barbara of Jacob Wolff, b. Dec 20, 1747; bapt. Mar 20, 1748.
Spon: Michael Boltz and wife.
John of Jacob Wolff, b. Jan 13, 1750; bapt. Mar 18, 1750. Spon: Joh.
Jacob Oberkirsch and wife.
Mary Eve of Adam Wegner and wife, b. Aug 13, 1749; bapt. Oct 17,
1749. Spon: John Immel and wife.
(After a space on the same page, the following entry is made:
Catharine of ---- and ----, b. Dec 17, 1780; bapt. Feb 4, 1782. Spon:
Jacob Kitzmiller and wife Catharine.
N. B. — neither the name of the father nor that of the mother was
known, both being dead.)
Joh. Jacob of Jacob Wagner, b. Aug 1, 1751; bapt. Aug 4, 1751. Spon:
Valentine Gerhardt and Sabina Schnatterle.
Magdalene of Jacob Wagner, b. ----, 1753; bapt. Mar 9, 1753. Spon:
(none given).
John of Caspar and Margaret Wagner, b. Nov 19, 1754; bapt. Dec 4,
1754. Spon: John Kissner and wife Sabina.
Joh. Martin of Caspar and Margaret Wagner, b. Apr 1, 1757; bapt.
Apr 16, 1757. Spon: Martin Kirstaetter and wife.
Joh. Michael of Caspar and Margaret Wagner, b. Jun 28, 1759; bapt.

Jul 9, 1759. Spon: Michael Kirstaetter and wife Dorothea.

Mary Elizabeth of Caspar and Margaret Wagner, b. Feb --, 1763; bapt. Mar 6, 1763. Spon: Sebastian Kirstaetter and wife Magdalene.

Christina Catharine of John Martin Wolff, b. Jul 27, 1751; bapt. Aug 25, 1751. Spon: George Adam Mueller and wife (maiden name Christina Catharine).

John Jacob of Joh. Jacob and Anna Margaret Wolff, b. Aug --, 1766; bapt. Aug 17, 1766. Spon: Christian Schnug and wife Catharine.

Mary Catharine of Henry and Eva Catharine Weiss, b. Nov --, 1766; bapt. Nov 9, 1766. Spon: Peter Brechbiel and wife Mary Catharine.

Mary Catharine of Adam and Mary Eva Weiss, b. Feb --, 1767; bapt. March 1, 1767. Spon: Andrew Keuffer and Mary Catharine Meyer.

Elizabeth of Adam and Mary Eva Weiss, b. March --, 1768; bapt. March 27, 1768. Spon: Conrad Meyer and Elizabeth Meyer.

Gotthilff John Philip of Christopher Frederic Wegman and wife Mary (to Philadelphia), b. Aug 5, 1769; bapt. Aug 13, 1796. Spon: John Casper Stoever, Sr., Philip Marsteller, and Anna Mary Thome, John Thome's wife.

John Frederic of Christopher Frederic Wegman and wife Mary (to Philadelphia), b. Jan 19, 1773; bapt. Jan 28, 1773. Spon: John Casper Stover, Sr. and wife Mary Catharine.

Jacob of Daniel Wunderlig and Eva Barbara, b. Jun 7, 1782; bapt. Jul 28, 1782. Spon: Jacob Sichele and wife Susanna.

Simeon (Simeun) of Daniel Wunderlig and Eva Barbara, b. Apr 26, 1785; bapt. ----, ----. Spon: John Oehrle and wife Margaret.

Mary of John Wilhelm and wife Elizabeth, b. ----, ----; bapt. May 30, 1784. Spon: Catharine Schauer (single person).

Mary Eliz. of Henry Weschenbach and wife Elizabeth, b. Jan 27, 1746; bapt. May 14, 1746. Spon: Jacob Kemmerlin and wife M. Eliz.

Mary Barbara of John Nicholas Weynrich and Anna Barbara, b. Apr 3, 1746; bapt. Apr 5, 1747. Spon: Ernst Leonard George and Mary Susanna.

Joh. Thomas of Andrew Ziegler, b. Dec 15, 1745; bapt. Feb 2, 1746. Spon: Thomas Madern and wife.

Joh. Christopher of Christopher Zimmerman and wife, b. Aug 10, 1747; bapt. Nov 9, 1747. Spon: Christopher Zimmer and wife

Anna Catharine.

John of Joseph Zieffle, b. Apr 14, 1750; bapt. May 13, 1750. Spon:
John Schwab and wife Eve.

Mary Eve of Joseph Zieffle, b. Jan 4, 1753; bapt. Jan 11, 1753. Spon:
Andrew Weltz and wife.

Joh. George of Michael Zimmerman and wife Eve, b. Apr 20, 1751;
bapt. Apr 25, 1751. Spon: George Buerger, Catharine
Zimmerman, and Henry Weber and wife.

Hannah of Michael Zimmerman and wife Eve, b. Jun --, 1752; bapt.
Jul 5, 1752. Spon: William Stober and wife Margaret.

Joh. Michael of Michael Zimmerman and wife Eve, b. Apr 13, 1754;
bapt. 15, 1754. Spon: Joachim Nagel and wife.

John of Michael Zimmerman and wife Eve, b. Apr 11, 1756; bapt. Apr
19, 1756. Spon: John Oehrle and wife Regina.

Joh. Adam of Michael Zimmerman and wife Eve, b. Dec 26, 1757;
bapt. Dec 26, 1757. Spon: John Oehrle and wife Regina.

Gotfried of Michael Zimmerman and wife Eve, b. Dec --, 1763; bapt.
Dec 31, 1763. Spon: John Oehrle and wife Regina.

Elizabeth of Christian Zimmerman and wife Catharine, b. Apr 8,
1782; bapt. Aug 18, 1782. Spon: father and mother.

Catharine of Christian Zimmerman and wife Catharine, b. Apr 15,
1784; bapt. Jul 31, 1784. Spon: father and mother.

Anna Barbara of Jacob Ziegler and wife, b. Dec 3, 1744; bapt. March
3, 1745. Spon: Jacob Schober and Ann Barbara Uhler.

*(Here follow a few baptisms separately recorded by [John Casper]
Hoerner:)*

Francis (Frantz) of John Schock and wife Anna Mary Stein, b. March
14, 1788; bapt. Apr 15, 1788. Spon: (none given).

Thomas of Thomas Luden and wife Rebecca, b. March 24, 1788; bapt.
Apr 23, 1788. Spon: (none given).

Elizabeth of John German and wife Mary, b. May 1, 1788; bapt. Jun
8, 1788. Spon: Elizabeth Achenbach (Achabach).

John of Christian Gingrich (Gyngrich) and wife Eve, b. Dec 2, 1788;
bapt. Apr 12, 1789. Spon: John Dietz (Diesz) and wife Elizabeth.

(Baptisms by Rev. George Lochman.)

Elizabeth of George and Elizabeth Ache, b. Dec 21, 1794; bapt. Feb 8,
1795. Spon: Jacob Hoffman and wife Magdalene.

Joh. Jacob of John Achenbach and wife, b. Sep 26, 1795; bapt. Nov 2,
1795. Spon: Jacob Rueger and wife.

Margaret of John Arndt Achenbach and wife Anna Mary, b. Feb 2,

1796; bapt. May 26, 1797. Spon: Anna Mary Busch.

Anna Mary of (John) Arndt Achenbach and wife, b. Jul 21, 1798; bapt. Aug --, ----. Spon: Joh. Carmini and wife.

--- Allen of James Allen and wife, b. ---, bapt. ----. Spon: (none given)

Sarah of Adam Alt and wife Mary, b. Oct 6, 1791; bapt. Mar 5, 1796. Spon: Joh. Carmini.

Mary of Adam Alt and wife Mary, b. Feb 22, 1793; bapt. Mar 5, 1796. Spon: Joh. Carmini.

John of Adam Alt and wife Mary, b. Feb --, 1795; bapt. Mar 5, 1796. Spon: Joh. Carmin.

Elizabeth of Adam Alt and wife, b. Apr 28, 1797; bapt. Jul 2, 1797. Spon: Elias Weitzel and wife.

Anna Mary of John Bardt and wife Eve, b. Mar 1, 1796; bapt. Mar 12, 1796. Spon: Christopher Riechert and wife.

John of John Barth and wife, b. Feb 11, 1798; bapt. Mar --, 1798. Spon: John Scherzer and wife.

Mar. Magdalene of John Barth and wife, b. Apr 13, 1800; bapt. Jun 15, 1800. Spon: Joh. Dietrich Bieber and wife.

John of Joh. Adam Baumgartner and wife, b. Oct 10, 1797; bapt. Nov 21, 1797. Spon: Francis Boehler and wife.

John George of Adam Baumgartner and wife, b. May 10, 1800; bapt. Mar 29, 1801. Spon: George Buehler and wife.

Philip of Philip Bayer and wife, b. May 9, 1795; bapt. Aug 16, 1795. Spon: John Maulfuer.

Barbara of Frederic Bayer and wife, b. Dec 27, 1795; bapt. Jan 31, 1796. Spon: Barbara Jalle.

David of Frederic Bayer and wife, b. Mar 10, 1798; bapt. Apr 8, 1798. Spon: William Lang and wife.

Joh. George of Peter Bayer and wife, b. Oct 4, 1798; bapt. Oct 15, 1798. Spon: Philip Fernsler, Jr.and wife.

Christina of Frederic Bayer and wife, b. Sep 27, 1800; bapt. Nov 30, 1800. Spon: Michael Killinger and wife.

Mary of ---- Bergman, b. Mar 20, 1780; bapt. Mar 5, 179. Spon: (none given).

Margaret of Conrad Berry and wife, b. Jan 22, 1798; bapt. Jul 3, 1799. Spon: Christian Cassel.

Paul of Jacob Boger and Catharine, b. Aug 5, 1792; bapt. Jun 23, 1795. Spon: mother.

Anna Mary of Jacob Boger and Catharine, b. Dec 21, 1794; bapt. Jun 23, 1795. Spon: Christpher Rickert and wife.

Christina of Valentine Boger and wife, b. March 25, 1796; bapt. May 5, 1796. Spon: Henry Peter and wife Christina.

Catharine of Christian Boger and wife, b. Aug 15, 1796; bapt. Oct 20, 1799. Spon: Valentine Boger and wife.

Mar. Christina of Joh. Nich. Bohr (Bor), b. Oct 12, 1795; bapt. Nov 28, 1795. Spon: Petter Bohr and wife.

Anna Mary of Joh. Nich. Bohr, b. Jan 2, 1797; bapt. May 12, 1797. Spon: Michael Clfer and wife.

Mary Magdalene of Joh. Nich. Bohr, b. Jul 15, 1798; bapt. ----, 1798. Spon: Charles Benner and wife.

John of Joh. Nich. Bohr, b. Dec 27, 1799; bapt. March --, 1800. Spon: Peter Neu and wife.

Elizabeth of George Boltz and wife, b. Jun 6, 1798; bapt. Aug 12, 1798. Spon: Christian Boger and wife.

Susanna of Jacob Boltz and wife, b. Aug 25, 1798; bapt. Sep --, 1798. Spon: John Umberger and wife.

Adam of Jacob Boltz and wife, b. Feb 20, 1800; bapt. March --, 1800. Spon: parents.

Margaret of Jacob Braun and wife, b. Aug 11, 1797; bapt. Sep 24, 1797. Spon: William Long and wife.

John Peter of Jacob Braun and wife, b. March 30, 1800; bapt. Jun 15, 1800. Spon: Valentine Boger.

John of John Brubatcher and wife, b. Nov 4, 1799; bapt. Apr 11, 1800. Spon: Joh. Dietrich Bieber and wife.

Mary of John Buchter and wife, b. Aug 4, 1798; bapt. Nov --, 1799. Spon: Anthony Barto and wife.

Elizabeth of George Buehler and wife, b. Feb 13, 1800; bapt. Apr 11, 1800. Spon: Elizabeth Schaeffer, widow.

Anna Catharine of Martin Busch and wife, b. Nov 1, 1795; bapt. Nov 2, 1795. Spon: Martin Ulrich.

John of Martin Busch and wife, b. Sep 22, 1798; bapt. Jan 1, 1799. Spon: Jacob Kitzmiller and wife.

John Philip of Philip Carmini and wife Anna, b. March 1, 1794; bapt. Apr 20, 1794. Spon: John Carmene and wife Barbara.

Elizabeth of Gorge Carmini and wife, b. Nov 5, 1795; bapt. Nov --, 1795. Spon: Christopher Riekert and wife.

Henry of Martin Carmini and wife Catharine, b. Sep 20, 1796; bapt. Nov 9, 1796. Spon: Solomon Siegchrist and Christina.

Elizabeth of Philip Carmini and wife Anna, b. Oct 20, 1796; bapt. Nov 20, 1796. Spon: Anthony Carmini and Anna Mary.

Elizabeth of Martin Carmini and wife, b. Sep 16, 1799; bapt. Nov 17, 1799. Spon: Gottfried Zimmerman and wife.

Anna Mary of George Carmini and wife, b. Feb 4, 1800; bapt. ----, 1800. Spon: John Achenbach and wife.

----, child of ---- Cassel and wife, b. ----; bapt. May 6, 1798. Spon: Adam Riechert.

----, child of Leonard Cassel and wife, b. ----; bapt. Jul 20, 1799. Spon: Christina Ulrich.

Philip Jacob of Philip Dietrich and Salome, b. Dec 30, 1797; bapt. Jan 18, 1798. Spon: Henry Reinoel and wife.

Jane Dolan, a married woman; bapt. Jan 14, 1798

Daniel of Daniel Dolan (Dohlen) and wife Jane, 8 yrs. of age; bapt. Jan 20, 1788. Spon: mother.

Elizabeth of Jacob Ebersoll and wife, b. March 15, 1800; bapt. May 4, 1800. Spon: Lucas Schally and wife.

Jacob of John Emrich and wife, b. Jul 16, 1800; bapt. Sep --, 1800. Spon: William Lang and wife.

Elizabeth of Jonathan Ensminger and wife, b. May 28, 1797; bapt. Jul 16, 1797. Spon: Daniel Ensminger.

Margaret Barbara of Philip Faernsler and Margaret Barbara, b. Feb 12, 1795; bapt. March 26, 1795. Spon: Peter Weirich and Jacobina.

John William of Frederic and Catharine Fernsler, b. Jan 9, 1797; bapt. Feb 26, 1797. Spon: Philip Fernsler and wife.

John Jacob of Philip Fernsler and wife, b. Sep 7, 1797; bapt. Oct 28, 1797. Spon: Peter Bayer and wife.

Molly of Frederic Fernsler and wife, b. Jun 7, 1798; bapt. Jul 14, 1798. Spon: Michael Bamberger and wife.

John of Philip Fernsler and wife, b. Nov 13, 1799; bapt. ----, 1800. Spon: John Neu and wife.

John of John and Elizabeth Fegen, b. Feb 11, 1797; bapt. Apr 9, 1797. Spon: Jacob Rinehart and wife.

Elizabeth of Jacob Fiddri and wife, b. Feb 16, 1800; bapt. March --,. 1800. Spon: Christian Clever.

Catharine of Paul and Christina Frank, b. March 6, 1795; bapt. May 25, 1795. Spon: Catharine Ischler.

Jacob of Jacob Fuetterer and wife, b. March 12, 1798; bapt. Aug --, 1798. Spon: Philip Carminie and wife.

John of Benjamin Geiger and wife, b. Jul 17, 1798; bapt. Aug 12, 1798. Spon: George Schneider and wife.

Michael of Christian Gingrich and wife, b. Dec --, 1797; bapt. Apr 22,
1798. Spon: Michael Celser and wife.

Jacob of Adam Graemer (Kraemer) and wife, b. Sep 22, 1798; bapt.
Nov --, 1799. Spon: Jacob Michael.

Elizabeth of Christian Gruber and wife, b. Apr 5, 1797; bapt. Jul 2,
1797. Spon: John Schw. Imboden and wife.

Susanna of Christian Gruber and wife, b. Aug 21, 1799; bapt. Jan --,
1800. Spon: Schweikart Imboden.

John of Andrew Haerter and wife Salome, b. Aug 15, 1794; bapt. Aug
24, 1794. Spon: John Haerter and wife Elizabeth.

Catharine of John Heylman and wife, b. Jan 30, 1798; bapt. Feb --
1799. Spon: Adam Heylman and wife.

John of George Hicks and wife, b. Aug 8, 1799; bapt. Oct 20, 1799.
Spon: John Romich and wife.

John of Abraham Hirschberger and wife, b. Nov 16, 1799; bapt. Jun --
, 1800. Spon: John Hirschberger and wife.

Elizabeth of Christian and Juliana Howerter, b. Jan 12, 1795; bapt.
Jul 17, 1796. Spon: Christian Cassel and wife Barbara.

Jacob of Christian Howerter and wife, b. Dec 1, 1797; bapt. Dec 31,
1797. Spon: Jacob Hoffman and wife.

George of Christian Howerter and wife, b. Feb 18, 1799; bapt. ----,
1800. Spon: Philip Carmini.

Samuel of Christian Howerter and wife, b. Nov 15, 1800; bapt. Dec
27, 1800. Spon: Tobial Ulrich and wife.

Elizabeth of Adam Imboden and wife Mary, b. Sep 25, 1795; bapt.
Oct 12, 1794. Spon: John Schweickard Imboden and wife
Leonora.

Christina of Adam Imboden and wife Mary, b. Feb 18, 1796; bapt.
March 12, 1796. Spon: Henry Peter and wife Christina.

Henry of Adam and Catharine Imboden, b. Jan 6, 1796; bapt. Apr 10,
1796. Spon: Henry and Christina Peter.

Anna Mary of George Imboden and wife Elizabeth, b. May 3, 1795;
bapt. Jul 17, 1796. Spon: Jacob Hoffman.

Magdalene of Adam Imboden and wife, b. March 17, 1797; bapt. Apr
23, 1797. Spon: Magdalene Siegchrist.

Elenora of Philip Imboden and wife, b. Apr 1, 1797; bapt. Apr 7,
1797. Spon: Joh. Schweick Imboden and wife.

Margaret of Adam Imboden and wife, b. Oct 3, 1798; bapt. Nov 16,
1798. Spon: parents.

Philip of Philip Imboden and wife, b. Jul --, 1799; bapt. ----, 1799.

Spon: Jacob Riechert and wife.

Eleonora of Adam Imboden and wife, b. Dec 29, 1799; bapt. ----, 1800. Spon: Solomon Siegchrist and wife.

Margaret of ---- Jenny (illegit.), b. Oct --, 1795; bapt. Dec 20, 1801. Spon: Joh. Schw. Imboden.

Samuel of ---- Juengst (Yingst) and wife, b. ----; bapt. Mar3, 1795. Spon: Christopher Rieker and Anna Mar. Ulrich.

John of John Juengst (Yingst) and wife, b. Oct 12, 1795; bapt. Nov 2, 1795. Spon: Christopher Ulrich.

Anna Mary of John Juengst (Yingst) and wife, b. Jun 7, 1797; bapt. Sep 24, 1797. Spon: Christopher Rhinehart and wife.

John of Abraham Juengst (Yingst) and wife, b. Oct 9, 1797; bapt. May 6, 1798. Spon: Joh. Carmini.

Rebecca of John Juengst (Yingst) and wife, b. Aug 21, 1799; bapt. Oct 6, 1799. Spon: Widow of Ulrich.

Elizabeth of Abraham Juengst (Yingst) and wife, b. Oct 22, 1798; bapt. ----, 1801. Spon: John Schmidt and wife.

Barbara of George Keller and wife Eve, b. Oct 3, 1794; bapt. Dec 31, 1794. Spon: parents.

Elizabeth of Jacob Keller and wife, b. Oct 10, 1795; bapt. Jan 31, 1796. Spon: Magdalene Keller.

Catharine of George Keller and wife Eve, b. Jul 8, 1796; bapt. Jul 30, 1796. Spon: Miss Magdalene Keller.

Joh. Jacob of Jacob Keller and wife, b. Feb 20, 1798; bapt. Feb 27, 1798. Spon: parents.

Benjamin of Jacob Keller and wife, b. Feb 20, 1798. Spon: Feb 27, 1798. Spon: parents.

Catharine of Jacob Keller and wife, b. Jan 11, 1800; bapt. Feb --, 1800. Spon: John Scherzer and wife.

John of George Keller and wife, b. Dec 6, 1800; bapt. Dec --, 1800. Spon: Jacob Keller and wife.

Susan of Peter Killinger and wife, b. Jul 2, 1798; bapt. Sep --, 1798. Spon: John Killinger and wife.

Christina of Jacob Kitzmiller and wife, b. Apr 20, 1800; bapt. Jun 15, 1800. Spon: Martin Busch and wife.

Anna Dorothea of John Klever and Margaret Dietrich (ill.), b. Sep 25, 1799; bapt. Nov --, 1799. Spon: Christian Hepting and wife.

Anna Mary of John Knochen and wife Anna Margaret, b. Jul 24, 1794; bapt. Sep 7, 1794. Spon: Lucas and Mary Elizabeth Schalle.

Barbara of John Knochen and wife, b. Jun 9, 1797; bapt. Nov 19, 1797. Spon: Miss Barbara Schalle.

Sarah Hoch, Adult daughter of John Muenzger and wife, b. --- 1763; bapt. Mar 2, 1795.

Mary of Henry Koch and wife Sarah, b. Mar 23, 1785; bapt. Mar 2, 1795. Spon: Mrs. Siegchrist.

Catharine of Henry Koch and wife Sarah, b. Nov 11, 1787; bapt. Mar 2, 1795. Spon: Mrs. Siegchrist.

John of Henry Koch and wife, Sarah, b. Jul 18, 1789; bapt. Mar 2, 1795. Spon: Mrs. Siegchrist.

Anna of Henry Koch and wife Sarah, b. Jan 10, 1793; bapt. Mar 2, 1795. Spon: Mrs. Siegchrist.

----, child of Henry Koch and wife Sarah, b. ----, 1797; bapt. Oct 22, 1797. Spon: Christopher Rinehart and wife.

Jacob of Henry Koch and wife Sarah, b. Mar 12, 1798; bapt. Mar 14, 1800. Spon: Jacob Hoffman and wife.

Elenora of Henry Koch and wife Sarah, b. Sep 20, 1800; bapt. Mar 14, 1800. Spon: Joh. Schw. Imboden.

John of Joh. Nichls Kopp and wife Veronica, b. Jan 17, 1797; bapt. May 26, 1797. Spon: Geo. Schreckengast and wife Elizabeth.

Jacob of George Kunz and wife, b. Feb --, 1799; bapt. Apr --, 1799. Spon: Philip Selzer.

Anna Mary of Philip Kunz and wife, b. Feb 2, 1800; bapt. Dec --, 1800. Spon: Abraham Hirschberger.

John of William and Elizabeth Lang, b. ----, 1794; bapt. Oct 26, 1794. Spon: Frederick Faernsler.

Mary of John and Elizabeth Lehr, b. Apr 17, 1795; bapt. Jul 28, 1796. Spon: Dorothea Hepting.

Elizabeth of John and Elizabeth Lehr, b. Apr 17, 1795; bapt. Jul 28, 1796. Spon: Miss Mary Schmidt.

Sophia of Christopher Marzal, b. Oct 28, 1800; bapt. ----, 1801. Spon: parents.

George of George Matter and wife, b. March 31, 1799; bapt. Jun --, 1799. Spon: Philip Carmini and wife.

Jacob of George Matter and wife, b. May 8, 1800; bapt. Jun 15, 1800. Spon: Philip Carmini and wife.

Rosini of John McGill and wife An. Mar., b. Dec 18, 1796; bapt. Jan 19, 1797. Spon: Wm. Bergenhof and wife.

John of John McGill and wife, b. Jul 20, 1799; bapt. ----, 1799. Spon: John Achenbach and wife.

John of Charles McLaughlin and wife, b. March 9, 1798; bapt. Apr 29, 1798. Spon: Elias Weizel and wife.

Mary of Charles McLaughlin and wife, b. Feb 13 1800; bapt. Mar --, 1800. Spon: Christian Schmidt.

John Williams of Jacob Merck and wife, b. March 26, 1795; bapt. Aug 16, 1795. Spon: Willam Lang and wife.

Samuel son of Jacob Merck and wife, b. Sep 16, 1799; bapt. Jan --, 1800. Spon: George Merck and wife.

William of Robert Morrison and wife, b. Dec 18, 1798; bapt. Jan 2, 1799. Spon: William Bergenhoff and wife.

Catharine of Conrad Muenzinger and wife Barbara, b. May 6, 1795; bapt. May 25, 1795. Spon: George Ischler and wife Susanna.

Jacob of Michael Neu (Ney) and wife, b. Nov 22, 1797; bapt. Dec 17, 1797. Spon: Jacob Hoffman and wife.

Anna Catharine of Peter Neu (Ney) and wife, b. Jul 25, 1799; bapt. Aug --, 1799. Spon: Adam Riechert and wife.

Samuel of Michael Neu (Ney), b. Oct 8, 1799; bapt. Dec 1, 1799. Spon: John Scherzer.

John George of Henry Peter (Peters) and wife, b. Jun 14, 1798; bapt. Jul --, 1798. Spon: parents.

Elizabeth of ---- Ramberger and wife, b. ----, 1798; bapt. ----, 1798. Spon: parents.

Daniel of Adam Ramberger and wife, b. Jun 23, 1800; bapt. Aug --, 1800. Spon: Daniel Wagner.

Eve of John Rau (Rowe) and wife, b. Dec 23, 1797; bapt. Apr 22, 1798. Spon: parents.

George of John Rauch and wife, b. Jun --, 1799; bapt. Jul 20, 1799. Spon: George Ramberger and Anna Mar. Heylman.

Abraham of Abraham Regel and wife, b. Jan 30 or beginning Feb, 1796; bapt. Feb 28, 1796. Spon: David Thom and Elizabeth Miller.

Sarah of Abraham Regel and wife, b. Aug 31, 1798; bapt. Sep --, 1798. Spon: David Daily.

Elizabeth of Peter Reist, decd., and wife Catharine, b. March 12, 1793; bapt. ----, 1805. Spon: Abraham Reguel and wife.

Susanna of Peter Reist, decd., and wife Catharine, b. March 12, 1793; bapt. ----, 1805. Spon: Anthony Carmini and wife.

Catharine of Peter Reist, decd., and wife Catharine, b. Feb 27, 1798; bapt. ----, 1805. Spon: Martin Carmini and wife.

Christina of Peter Reist, decd., and wife Catharine, b. Oct 6, 1799;

bapt. ----, 1805. Spon: John Barth and wife.

Elizabeth of ---- and Elizabeth Rettig (ill.), b. Dec 14, 1796; bapt. Apr 3, 1797. Spon: Anna Mary Stroh.

John of Jacob Riechert and wife, b. Feb 16, 1799; bapt. Apr 1, 1799. Spon: Matthias Riechert.

Samuel of Philip Schauer and wife Regina, b. Dec 9, 1796; bapt. Jan 13, 1797. Spon: David Schauer and Anna Peter.

Catharine of Philip Schauer and wife, b. Jan 13, 1799; bapt. March 24, 1799. Spon: John Carmini and wife.

Joseph of John Schmidt and wife Christina, b. Sep 1, 1795; bapt. March 5, 1796. Spon: parents.

Anna of John Schmidt and wife Christina, b. March 28, 1798; bapt. Apr 29, 1798. Spon: parents.

Magdalene of John Scherer and wife, b. Oct 26, 1797; bapt. March --, 1798. Spon: Anna Mary Bayer, wife of Peter Bayer.

Catharine of Joh. Scherzer and wife Barbara, b. Aug 6, 1796; bapt. Sep 11, 1796. Spon: Henry Berry and wife.

John of Joh. Scherzer and wife, b. Apr 1, 1799; bapt. Jul 3, 179. Spon: parents.

Elizabeth of George Schroekengeist and wife, b. Feb 20, 1796; bapt. Apr 24, 1796. Spon: Adam Reichert and wife.

Anna Mary of David Sebold and wife, b. Dec 2, 1795; bapt. Apr 3, 1797. Spon: Daniel Stroh and wife.

Jacob of David Sebold and wife, b. Jun 8, 1798; bapt. Oct 7, 1798. Spon: Jacob Fuchs (Fox).

John of Joseph Sergeant and wife, b. May 27, 1797; bapt. Jul 2, 1797. Spon: Andrew Karstschnitz and wife.

Jacob of Joseph Sergeant and wife, b. Sep 11, 1799; bapt. ----, 1799. Spon: Henry Martin and wife.

Magdalene of Solomon Siegchrist and wife, b. Jul 29, 1795; bapt. Sep 28, 1795. Spon: Magdalene Siegchrist.

Catharine of Lorenz and Magdalene Siegchrist, b. Feb 12, 1796; bapt. March 27, 1796. Spon: Martin Carmini and wife.

Catharine of Solomon Siegchrist and wife, b. Jan 22, 1797; bapt. Feb 26, 1797. Spon: Adam Imboden and wife.

John of Solomon Siegchrist and wife, b. Sep 10, 1798; bapt. Nov 18, 1798. Spon: John Stoever and wife.

Henry of Solomon Siegchrist and wife, b. ----, 1800; bapt. May 3, 1800. Spon: John Scherzer and wife.

Josiah of Michael Singer and wife Hannah, b. March 23, 1790; bapt.

Sep 1, 1799. Spon: Jacob Hoffman and wife.

David of Michael Singer and wife Hannah, b. Oct 8, 1791; bapt. Sep 1, 1799. Spon: Tobias Ulrich.

Benedict of Michael Singer and wife Hannah, b. Aug 24, 1793; bapt. Sep 1, 1799. Spon: Christian Howerter and wife.

Elizabeth of Michael Singer and wife Hannah, b. Jul 23, 1796; bapt. Sep 1, 1799. Spon: Abraham Regel and wife.

Elizabeth of John and Margaret Stauffer, b. Jan 30, 1796; bapt. Oct 30, 1803. Spon: John Barth and wife.

Margaret of John and Margaret Stauffer, b. Sep 3, 1799; bapt. Oct 30, 1803. Spon: George Maurer and wife.

Tobias of Tobias Stoever and wife Anna, b. Nov 19, 1794; bapt. Nov 26, 1734 (?). Spon: father.

Elizabeth of John Stoever and wife, b. Feb 26, 1798; bapt. Apr 8, 1798. Spon: Christina Uhler.

John of John Strehr and wife, b. May 9, 1797; bapt. Jul 2, 1797. Spon: John Guntrum and wife.

Elizabeth of John Strehr and wife Anna Mary, b. Oct 28, 1799; bapt. Dec 2, 1799. Spon: William Bohr and wife.

John of Daniel Stroh and wife Eve, b. May 7, 1795; bapt. Jun 23, 1795. Spon: John Bardt and wife.

Anna Mary of John Stroh and Anna Mary, b. Oct 6, 1795; bapt. Feb 8, 1796. Spon: George and Elizabeth Carmini.

Anna Mary of Daniel Stroh and wife, b. Feb 26, 1797; bapt. Apr 3, 1797. Spon: Jacob Hoffman.

Sarah of John Stroh and wife, b. Aug 8, 1800; bapt. Sep --, 1800. Spon: Miss Sarah Kopenhafer.

Elizabeth of Daniel Stroh and wife, b. Dec 25, 1800; bapt. Dec 27, 1800. Spon: Mrs. Stroh, the grandmother.

Daniel of Adam Stroh and wife, b. Apr 26, 1798; bapt. Jun --, 1807. Spon: Daniel Kroh and wife.

John of John Troxel and wife, b. Dec 11, 1800; bapt. March 3, 1801. Spon: Peter Wendling and wife.

Susan of Adam Ulrich and wife Anna Mary, b. Feb 3, 1796; bapt. Apr 10, 1796. Spon: Christopher Riechert and wife.

Adam of Christopher Ulrich and wife, b. March 10, 1797; bapt. Apr 23, 1797. Spon: Adam Ulrich and wife.

Tobias of Adam Ulrich and wife, b. Aug 19, 1797; bapt. Sep 24, 1797. Spon: Tobias Ulrich, single.

Anna Mary of Joh. Nichl. Ulrich, b. Feb 26, 1798; bapt. Apr 8, 1798.

Spon: Jacob Hoffman and wife.

Mary of Adam Ulrich and wife, b. May 3, 1799; bapt. Jul 14, 1799. Spon: John Lohmiller and wife.

Elizabeth of Tobias Ulrich and wife, b. Sep 12, 1799; bapt. Nov --, 1797 [sic]. Spon: Christopher Riechert and wife.

Sanuel of Christopher Ulrich and wife, b. March 8, 1800; bapt. March --, 1800. Spon: Christopher Riechert and wife.

Jacob of Philip Umberger and wife, b. Apr 22, 1798; bapt. Aug 12, 1798. Spon: John Umberger and wife.

Barbara of Daniel Wagner and wife, b. ----, 1796; bapt. Apr 24, 1806. Spon: William Lang.

John of George Wagner and wife, b. Dec 27, 1800; bapt. Mar 16, 1801. Spon: parents.

Jacob of Patrick Ward (Wharte) and wife, b. Nov 8, 1795; bapt. Jan 3, 1796. Spon: John Oehrly and wife.

Samuel of Patrick Ward (Wharte) and wife, b. Nov 11, 1797; bapt. Dec 31, 1797. Spon: Philip Carmini and wife.

Margaret of Patrick Ward (Wharte) and wife, b. Jul 26, 1799; bapt. ---, 1799. Spon: Philip Carmini.

Jacob of Henry Williams and wife, b. Jan 26, 1799; bapt. Feb --, 1799. Spon: Frederic Williams.

Elizabeth of Ludwig Wirth and wife Elizabeth, b. Nov 9, 1794; bapt. Feb 7, 1795. Spon: Christian and Anna Barbara Wirth.

John of Christian and Barbara Wirth, b. Jan 17, 1795; bapt. Feb 7, 1795. Spon: Ludwig Wirth and wife Elizabeth.

Joh. George of Christian Wirth and wife Barbara, b. Feb 15, 1797; bapt. May 26, 1797. Spon: Joh. Runkel and wife Mar. Cath.

Anna Catharine of Christian Wirth and wife Barbara, b. Oct 10, 1799; bapt. Nov 17, 1799. Spon: Henry Peter and wife.

Elizabeth of Christian Wolf and wife, b. Oct 9, 1800; bapt. Mar 29, 1801. Spon: parents.

BURIALS

Adam of G. Maurer and wife Elizabeth, b. Nov 1, 1793. Spon: Adam Barth. Buried Aug 3, 1794. Swelling of the throat, sick 9 days, aged 9 mos. 1 day.

Henry Maurer, of George Maurer and wife Elizabeth, b. Dec 9, 1789. Spon: John Schnock and wife Margaret. Buried Aug 5, 1794. Sore throat, sick 9 days, aged 4 yr.s 8 mos. less 4 days.

Anna Mary Schauer, b. in Germany, 3 children, 6 grandchildren.
Buried Sep 28, 1794. Daysentery for six wks, aged 70 yr.s.

Anna Mary of John Stroh and wife Anna Mary, b. Jan 4, 1787. Spon:
grandparents, J. Stroh and Anna Mary. Buried Oct 11, 1794.
Fever for 13 days, aged 7 yr.s 4 mos. 5 days.

Jacob of J. Stroh and A. M., b. Nov 21, 1793. Spon: Jacob Seman and
wife Susan. Buried Oct 19, 1794. Whooping cough and
daysentery, aged 10 mos. 28 days.

Anna Neu, b. Feb 28, 1776 of Daniel Stauffer and wife Eve; bapt.
Reformed. Married 1793 for 1 year 2 mos. 3 wks. Had 1 child, it
died. Anna Neu buried Oct 21, 1794. Daysentery for 16 days,
aged 18 yrs. 7 mos. 3 wks 1 day.

Catharine of Jacob Bolz and wife Anna Marg. Spon: Jacob Bolz, Sr.
and Catharine. Buried March 7, 1795. Cough, spasms and
swollen throat, aged 4 yrs. 5 mos. 20 days.

Anna Mar. Holderbaum, b. Mar 23, 1736, in Oberklanich, of Joh.
Peter Holderbaum and Anna Elizabeth; bapt. and confirmed;
came to this county in 1751. In 1761 joined in marriage to
Thomas Kniesly, surviving. No children. Buried Jul 23, 1795.
Asthma, aged 59 yrs. 4 mos.

Elizabeth of John Scherzer and wife Barbara, b. Feb 20, 1795. Spon:
Henry Baerry and wife Esther. Buried Sep 22, 1795 (died on the
20th). Whooping cough, age 7 mos.

Elizabeth of Adam Stover and wife Elizabeth Catharine, b. Nov ---,
1785. Spon: parents. Buried Sep 25, 1795. Typhoid fever for 3
days, aged 9 yrs. 10 mos. several days.

Mary Catharine Stoever of Christian Merkling and Mary Catharine,
b. May 14, 1715, at Lampsheim, Chur-Pfaltz. Spon: Catharine
Scheudling. Catechised and confirmed. Apr 8, 1733 united in
marriage to Rev. John Caspar Stoever, Ev. Lutheran minister.
Lived therein 46 yrs. 1 mo. 5 days. They had 11 children: 6 yet
living, 5 sons and 1 daugher. Sickness was fever. Buried Oct 7,
1795, aged 80 yrs. 4 mos. 3 wks (actually 80 yrs. 4 mos. 23 days).
"Remarkable that she lived to see 75 grandchildren and 52 great-
grandchildren".

Lydia of John Schmidt and wife Christina; bapt. Apr 21, 1791. Spon:
parents. Buried Oct 8, 1795. Sickness was a burning fever and
spasms, aged 4 yrs. 5 mos. 2 wks.

Elizabeth of Frederick Fernsler and wife Magd., b. Apr 18, 1795.
Spon: Christina Bamberger. Buried Nov 23, 1795. Cough and

Asthma, aged 7 mos. 3 days.

Frederic of Adam Reichert and wife Elizabeth, b. Aug 24, 1793. Spon: John Diez and Barbara Beck. Buried Jan 7, 1796. Fever and spasms, sick 1½ days, aged 2 yrs. 4 mos. 12 days.

Henry Kurz, b. in the Palatinate in 1709; bapt. and confirmed as Reformed, came to this country in 1739, married Catharine Adelberger. They had 7 children, only 4 survive, 22 grandchildren. Buried Apr 7, 1796, aged 87 yrs. Walmer's church.

An insane woman, widow of the schoolmaster at Millerstown. No burial date.

Elizabeth of Philip Carminy and wife Anna, b. Oct 20, 1796. Spon: Anthony Carminy, Jr. and wife Anna Mary. Buried Jan 25, 1797. Spasms, continuing from Sunday until Monday night at 11 o'clock, aged 3 mos. 3 days.

John Adam of Jacob Braun and wife Elizabeth, b. Mar 17, 1794; bapt. Buried Sep 26, 1797. Daysentery, aged 3 yrs. 6 mos. 13 days.

John of Daniel Wagner and wife Anna Mary, b. Jul 15, 1793; bapt. Buried Sep 28, 1797. Daysentery, aged 4 yrs. 2 mos. 12 days.

Anna Christina of Christian Wirth and wife, b. Nov 9, 1790. Spon: Henry Peter and wife. Buried Nov 21, 1797. Malarial fever, aged 7 yrs. 10 days.

Magdalene Matter, wife of John Matter, nee Siech (Sieg), b. Dec 9, 1764; bapt. and confirmed in Luth. church. Married to John Matter A. D. 1786. Mother of 5 children, 2 living sons, buried Nov 24, 1797. Presumably paralysis, sickly for 5 yrs. Aged 32 yrs. 11 mos. 2 wks.

Hannah Stoever, b. Jun 15, 1752 of Michael Zimmerman and wife Eve. Spon: William Stober and wife. Confirmed in Ev. Lutheran faith. Apr 21, 1772 united in marriage with Tobias Stover, the surviving widower. They had 12 children, only 8 survive: 6 daughters and 2 sons. No burial date. Dropsical for 3 yrs., confined to bed for 13 days, vomiting and an internal tumor, aged 54 yrs. 6 mos. less 6 days.

Christian Studel, b. about 1729 in Germany; bapt. and confirmed as a member of the Lutheran church. When about in his 13th year he came to this country, married Catharine ----; 2 children died young. He was a captain in the late war, afterwards a school teacher. Buried Jan 28, 1798. Pleurisy, on previous Sunday his wife was buried and 8 days later himself. Aged about 62 yrs.

Infant daughter of Adam Reichert. Buried Feb 10, 1798.

(Rev. Dr. Lochman's Burials.)

Justina Catharine Keller of John Trapp and Catharine, b. 1721 at Danenfels, at the Donnersberg; bapt. and confirmed. Came to this country in 1743. Married to Valentine Keller. Had 9 children: 2 sons and 3 daughters survive. Buried Feb 27, 1798. Cough and pleurisy, aged 77 yrs.

Joh. George of Peter Berger and wife, b. Jan 31, 1797. Spon: Philip Fernsler and wife. No burial date. Smallpox, aged 1 year 1 mo. 4 days.

Elizabeth of John Scherer and wife, b. Jan 23, 1795. Spon: Frederic Guntramm and wife. Buried March 30, 1798. Smallpox, aged 3 yrs. 2 mos. 5 days.

Joh. George of Christian Wirth and wife Anna Barbara, b. Feb 15, 1796. Spon: John Runkel and wife. Buried Apr 2, 1798. Smallpox, aged 1 year 1 mo. 15 days.

John of John Rau and wife, b. Jul 22, 1795. Spon: parents. Buried Apr --, 1798. Smallpox, aged 2 yrs. 8 mos. 3 wks.

Eve of John Rau and wife, b. Dec 23, 1797. Spon: parents. Buried May --, 1798. Smallpox, aged 5 mos. less 5 days (i.e. 4 mos. and 25 days).

Christina Elizabeth of Henry Lang and wife Margaret, b. Jun 1, 1774. Spon: Anthony Carmini and wife Christina. Confirmed. Buried Aug --, 1798. A raging fever and a swollen leg, aged 24 yrs. 2 mos. some days.

Samuel of Patrick Ward and wife Mary, b. Oct 11, 1797. Spon: Philip Carmini and wife. Buried Oct --, 1798. Vomiting and spasms, aged 10 mos. 3 wks.

Catharine of Conrad Baerry and wife Elizabeth, b. Nov 11, 1797. Spon: Tobias Ulrich and wife. Buried Dec 1, 1798. Sore throat and asthma, aged 3 yrs. 8 mos.

Anna of Joseph Sanderson and wife Anna, b. Jan 4, 1791. Spon: Catharine Kleber. Buried Feb 1799. Swollen throat, sick 4 days, aged 8 yrs. less 4 days.

Frederic Guntram, b. Feb 1743 in Germany. Baptized and confirmed in Reformed church. Married 1st: Anna nee Schnebele, they had 5 children of whom 4 survive, she died in 1792; married 2nd Mrs. Elizabeth ---- nee Brechbiel, issue 1 child. Buried Apr 4, 1799. Pleurisy and pains in the head, suffered 8 days, aged 56 yrs. and 1 mo..

Rosina Barbara, of Michael Maurer and wife, and wife of Anastasius
Heylman, b. Jan 29, 1746 bapt. and confirmed Lutheran. Apr 8,
1766 married Anastasius Heylman, lived together 33 yrs. and
had 8 chldren, of whom 7 survive. Buried Apr 11, 1799.
Consumption for 17 yrs., aged 52 yrs. 2 mos. 9 days.
Soloman of Joh. Schweickert Imboden and wife Eleonora, b. Jun 29,
1781. Spon: Anastasius Heylman and wife. Confirmed last year.
Buried May 16, 1799. Consumption, suffered 7 wks, aged 17 yrs.
10 mos. 2 wks.
Joh. Adam Killinger of Michael Killinger and wife Catharine, b. Jul 7,
1772. Spon: John Dutweiler and wife. Confirmed as a member of
the Reformed church. Buried Aug 3, 1799. Consumption, aged 27
yrs. 3 wks.
Jacob Conrad Maenzinger, b. in Eppingen, in the Palatinate, Sep 17,
1715. Confirmed as Reformed. Nov 17, 1739 was united in
marriage to Barbara Eyerman; no children. Came to this country
in 1753. 1783 married Barbara Ischler, has 2 children. Buried
Jan --, 1800. Sickness caused by a broken leg, aged 84 yrs. 4
mos.
Catharine of Christian Boger and wife Elizabeth, b. Aug 15, 1799.
Spon: Valentine Boger and wife Juliana. Buried March 26, 1800.
Cough and croup, aged 7 mos. 11 days.
Christian Schally, b. in 1726 in Palatinate, Germany. Baptized,
catechised and confirmed as Reformed. Came to this country in
youth. In his 30th year he married Rebecca Wartman, had 2
children. Buried Apr 24, 1800, aged 74 yrs.
John of Solomon Siegchrist and wife Christina, b. Sep 10, 1798. Spon:
John Stoever and wife ---- Engel. Buried May 22, 1800. Supposed
worms with spasms, aged 1 year 8 mos. 10 days.
Susan of Christian Gruber and wife Catharine. Spon: Joh. Schw.
Imboden and wife. Buried Jun 3, 1800. Whooping cough, aged 9
mos. 1 day.
Mrs. Barbara Peter of Philip Fernsler and wife; b. 1742 in Lebanon
township; bapt. and confirmed Lutheran. In her 25th year
married to John Peter, had 7 children, of whom 3 are living. No
burial date. Probably comsumption for 15 yrs., aged 58 yrs.
Samuel of Philip Schauer and wife Regina, b. Dec 9, 1796. Spon:
David Schauer and Anna Peter. Buried Sep 2, 1800. "Gichtfluss,"
aged 3 yrs. 8 mos. 3 wks 2 days.
Benjamin of Jacob Keller and wife Catharine, b. Feb 20, 1788. Spon:

Adam Stoever, Jr. and wife. Buried Sep 13, 1800.
Hydrocephalous since 5 wks old, aged 2 yrs. 6 mos. 3 wks 2 days.

Mary of Charles McLaughlin and wife Margra., b. Feb 13, 1800. Spon:
Christian Schmidt. No burial date. Smallpox, aged 7 wks 2 days.

Bartholomew Ramberger, b. May 4, 1716 in "Fraukenland;" bapt. and
confirmed a Catholic. In his married state he begot 5 children, of
whom 4 are living. A widower for 24 yrs. No date of burial, aged
84 yrs. 4 mos. 3 wks.

Joh. George of George Keller and wife Eve, b. Feb 4, 1799. Spon:
parents. Buried Oct --, 1800. Swollen throat, aged 1 year 8 mos.
2 wks 3 days.

Michael Fernsler, b. Aug 26, 1772 of Jacob Fernsler and wife
Magdalene. Spon: Michael Fernsler and wife. Confirmed,
Lutheran. No burial date. Probably consumption, aged a little
over 28 yrs.

Catharine of Jacob Keller and wife Catharine, b. Jan 11. Spon: John
Scherzer and wife. Buried Nov --, 1800. Croup, aged 2 days less
than 10 mos.

Elizabeth of George Buehler and wife, b. Feb 13, 1800. Spon:
Elizabeth Schaeffer. No burial date. Smallpox, aged 3 days less
than 9 mos.

John of John Fernsler and wife Susan, b. Oct 25, 1796. Spon: John
Neu and wife Catharine. Buried in 1801. Vomiting and spasms,
aged 4 yrs. and 5 days less than 3 mos.

Thomas Kniesel, b. May 29, 1830 [1730?] in Schoeckingen,
Wurtemburg; bapt. in infancy. After instruction admitted to
Lord's Supper. Came to this country in 1751. Married Anna
Mary Holderbaum in 1761, no children. Buried in 1801.
Constipation, aged 70 yrs. 7 mos. 10 days.

Mrs. Keller. Buried in 1801.

John Simeon Boehler, b. 1720, earldom of Duerkheim; bapt. and
confirmed Jul 13, 1745. Married Anna Margaret Behr. Came
over in 1766, had 4 sons and 2 daughters, 1 son and 2 daughters
living. Buried in 1801. Aged 81 yrs.

Elizabeth of Tobias Ulrich, b. Oct 12, 1799. Spon: Christopher
Riechert and wife. Buried Easter Monday in 1801. Vomiting and
spasms, aged 1 year 8 mos. 10 days.

John of George Keller and wife Mary Eve, b. Dec 6, 1800. Spon:
Jacob Keller and wife. Buried in 1801. Croup, aged 6 days less
than 5 mos.

Anna Mary of George Carmini and wife Elizabeth, b. Feb 4, 1800.
Spon: John Achenbach and wife. Buried Nov 8, 1801. Whooping
cough and spasms, aged 1 year and 3 days less than 9 mos.

William of Robert Morrison and wife Eve, b. Dec 18, 1798. Spon:
William Bergenhoff and wife Rosina. Buried Nov 27, 1801.
Whooping cough and spasms, aged 2 yrs. 11 mos. 9 days.

Elizabeth of Adam Barth and wife Catharine, b. Oct 17, 1792. Spon:
Henry Henkel and wife Anna Mary. Buried Dec 26, 1801. Fever
and spasms, aged 9 yrs. 2 mos. 7 days.

Tobias Stoever of Adam Stoever and wife Cath. Elizabeth, b. Feb 26,
1780. Spon: Tobias Stoever and wife. Confirmed. Buried Dec 29,
1801. Fever, aged 21 yrs. 10 mos. 7 days.

Susan Catharine Fuchs (Fox) of Martin Batteicher and wife and wife
of Jacob Fuchs, b. Jul 25, 1764 . Spon: Jacob Ernst and wife.
Confirmed. Married to Jacob Fuchs in 1791 and had 3 children.
Buried Jan 1, 1802. Consumption, aged 37 yrs. 5 mos. 3 days.

Mary of Arendt Achenbach and wife, b. Apr 21, 1799. Spon: John
Carmini and wife Barbara. Buried ca 1802. Measles, aged 2 yrs.
5 mos. 4 days.

Jacob Seiler, b. Aug 22, 1757 in the Earldom Leiningen in the Central
Palatinate. Spon: Jacob Herman. Confirmed a Lutheran. Came
to this country in 1772. ---- 23, 1775 married Mrs. ----, nee Koch;
16 children, 10 surviving. Teaching school. No burial date. Gravel
or gall stones, aged 64 yrs. 5 mos. 11 days.

Elizabeth of Christian Lang and wife, b. Sep 22, 1800. Spon:
Elizabeth Neip. Buried ca 1802. Asthma or pneumonia, aged 1
year 5 mos. 27 days.

Anna Barbara Stoever of John Emerich and wife Anna Gertrude, b.
Dec 10, 1759; bapt. and confirmed Lutheran. Married Nov 10,
1778 to Christian Wirth; 8 children, 1 son and 5 daughters
survive. Husband died on May 24, 1798, 3 yrs. a widow. Married
Tobias Stoever on Aug 11, 1801; 1 child. Buried Apr --, 1803.
Slow cancer, aged 43 yrs. and 2 days less than 4 mos.

Peggy Wilson of Alexander and Mary Wilson, b. in Philadelphia in
1787. In fifth year left an orphan, then her uncle, Charles
Downey, took her in care; bapt. in infancy. Buried Apr 28, 1803.
Sick about 8 days, aged between 16 and 17 yrs.

Elizabeth Dietz of Christopher Labegeyer and wife, b. Feb 1, 1733 in
Warwick township; bapt. and confirmed in Lutheran church.
Married to John Dietz on Aug 17, 1751; had 2 children, both

died, married 52 yrs. Buried Jul --, 1803. Aged 70 yrs. 5 mos. 15 days.

Magdalene Angst, b. Sep 20, 1737; bapt. and confirmed a Lutheran. Married to Daniel Angst on Nov 11, 1766; had 5 children, who survive. Buried Aug --, 183(?)[1803]. Weakness and fainting spells, aged 18 days less than 66 yrs.

John Stroh of John Stroh and wife Anna Mary, b. May 11, 1762; bapt., confirmed a Lutheran. Arrived at manhood he married Elizabeth Trump; had one child, it and the mother died. Married secondly Anna Mary Muese in 1784; had 9 children of whom 1 son and 6 daughters are living. Buried Feb --, 1804. Consumption, aged 41 yrs. 9 mos. 9 days.

Anna Mary Stroh of Wm. Fischer and wife Christina, b. Apr 3, 1740 "in der Hohl;" bapt. and confirmed a Lutheran. Married May 23,1758 to the survivor John Stroh, had 5 children, 2 sons and 1 daughter living, 26 grandchildren, married 46 yrs. Buried Apr 4, 1804. Gripes and vomiting for 6 days, aged 1 day less than 64 yrs.

Elias of Adam Stoever and wife Cath., b. Jul 15, 1789. Spon: parents. Buried Aug --, 1804. Fever, in bed for 3 days. Aged 15 yrs. and 3 days less than 1 mo.

Catharine of John Stroh and Anna Mary, b. Aug 1, 1791. Spon: Elizabeth Nes (Nace). Buried Oct --, 1804. Fever and finally pleurisy. Aged 13 yrs. 1 mo. 20 days.

Eve Elizabeth Stauffer of George Peter and wife Catharine, b. Oct 23, 1780. Spon: Jacob Sichely and wife. Married to Christian Stauffer on March 15, 1803, on child. Buried Nov --, 1804. Fever, aged 24 yrs. 10 days.

Catharine Reuter of William Reuter and wife Cath., b. May --, 1775; bapt. and confirmed Reformed. Buried ca 1804. Fever, aged 28 yrs. 5 mos.

----, child of Valentine Boger, b. March 26, 1796. Spon: Henry Peters and wife Christina. Buried Feb 28, 1805. Croup and spasms: Monday at school and died Tuesday at 4 p.m. Aged 9 yrs. 11 mos. 1 day.

John Leman, a Saxon, b. about 1769; bapt. and confirmed in the Evangelical doctrine. Came to this country in his 27th year, a tailor. Buried Aug --, 1805. Hurt by a wagon, aged 36 yrs.

Mary Busch of Adam Ulrich and wife Juliana, b. 1732; bapt. and confirmed. Married to Martin Busch, with whom she lived 10 yrs.

and had 5 children, a widow for 36 yrs. Buried Dec 7, 1805. Aged 63 yrs.

Andrew Karschnitz, b. Oct --, 1719 in Germany. Married twice and had 10 children, 5 surviving. Buried in 1806. Aged 83 yrs. 3 mos.

John Hettrich of Peter Hettrich, b. Jul 14, 1793; bapt. Served with Philip Imboden. Buried in 1806. Fell from loft and died 2 hours after. Aged 12 yrs. 7 mos. 14 days.

Mar. Eliz. Sprecher of Henry Reinoel and wife, b. March 10, 1778; bapt. and confirmed. Married Aug --, 1802, 2 children yet living. Buried Jan --, 1806. Dropsy, aged 27 yrs. 2 days less than 10 mos.

Christian Heveling, b. 1718 in Germany; bapt. and confirmed. Married in 27th year and came to this country, wife died in 1790, childless. In 1791 married Dorothea Dietrich. Buried May --, 1806. Pleurisy, aged 88 yrs.

Susan Fuetterer of Christopher Wagner and wife, b. Feb 10, 1783; bapt. and confirmed. Married Sep 14, 1802; 4 children, 2 survive. Buried ----, 1806. Fever and confinement, aged 23 yrs. 6 mos. 15 days.

John Stroh, b. Feb 4, 1736 in Germany; bapt. and in 10th year came to this country, confirmed a Lutheran. On Apr 3, 1758 married Anna Mary Fischer, had 5 children, 3 surviving. Buried ----, 1806. Fever, aged 70 yrs. 8 mos. 3 days.

Anna Catharine Peter, nee Sichely, b. March 3, 1747; bapt. and confirmed. In 1768 married George Peter; 5 children, 3 survive. Buried Oct 11, 1806. Fever, aged 59 yrs. 7 mos. 6 days.

Anthony Carmini of Anthony Carmini, Sr., b. Nov 14, 1764; bapt. and confirmed Lutheran. On Apr 4, 1786 m. Anna Mary of Casper Stoever; had 8 children, 7 surviving. Buried ----, 1806. Fever and spasms, aged 42 yrs. less 25 days.

Elizabeth Berry (nee Hartman), b. in Macungy; confirmed in the Evang. faith. Married to Conrad Berry on May 4, 1784; 10 children, 8 surviving. Buried Oct --, 1806. Fever, aged 42 yrs.

John of Chas. and Mary McLaughlin, b. March 9, 1798; bapt., was blind. Buried ----, 1806. Fever, aged 8 yrs. 7 mos. 19 days.

Jacob Kitzmiller of Jacob Kitzmiller and wife Anna Mary, b. Jul 25, 1732; bapt. and confirmed a Lutheran. Married twice; no children with first wife; with second wife, Widow Vogt, had 4 children, yet living. Buried ----, 1807. Consumption, aged 74 yrs. 5 mos. 8 days.

Elizabeth of George Carmini and wife Elizabeth, b. Nov 5, 1795. Buried ----, 1807. Chills and spasms, sick for 3 days. Aged 11 yrs. 2 mos. 25 days.

Magdalene Siegchrist of George Noll and wife, b. Jan 31, 1751; bapt. Married to Lawrence Siegchrist on Sep 29, 1767; had 13 children, 9 yet living. Buried ----, 1808. Pleurisy and Fever, aged 55 yrs. 6 mos. 13 days.

Elizabeth of Jacob Fuetterer and wife, b. Feb 6, 1800. Buried ----, 1808. Fever, aged 6 yrs. 6 mos. 19 days.

Joh. Adam Heilman of Anastasius Heilman, b. Sep 29, 1771; bapt. and confirmed. On Jan 31, 1808 married Eleonora Imboden. Buried Feb --, 1809. Killed suddenly by falling under a wagon, aged 37 yrs. 4 mos. 24 days.

Elizabeth Barth, b. 1733, confirmed in Ev. Luth. church. Was married to Adam Barth in 1752; hasd 12 children, 2 sons and 5 daughters survive. Buried Aug --, 1809. Diseased spleen, aged 76 yrs.

Mary Matter, nee Wendling, b. March 24, 1720 in Alsace, village of Buchsweiler. Came over in her 25th year. Married to Jacob Matter; had 8 children, 3 sons and 4 daughters survive; 53 grandchildren, 22 great grandchildren. A widow for 19 yrs. Buried Sep 1, 1809. Vomiting and diarrhoea, aged 83 yrs. 5 mos. 6 days.

Henry Peters' wife, nee Imboden. Buried ----, 1810. Aged 50 yrs. 5 mos. 19 days.

Susan Fernsler of Joh. Franz and wife Cath., b. Jan 11, 1770. Married to Jacob Fernsler; had 6 children, 4 survive. Buried Apr --, 1810. Consumption, aged 40 yrs. 2 mos. 22 days.

Frederic Fernsler (omited several yrs. ago) of Philip and Barbara Fernsler, b. Apr --, 1730; bapt. and confirmed. In 1789 married Magdalene Bamberger; had 6 children. Buried ca 1810-1. Consumption, aged 68 yrs. 6 mos.

Fredr. Haupt, b. Sep 29, 1744; bapt. and confirmed in Germany. Buried ----. Aged 58 yrs. 9 mos. 27 days.

Elizabeth of Jacob Fernsler and wife Susan, b. Jan 9, 1793; bapt. and confirmed. Buried Nov --, 1812. Consumption, aged 19 yrs. 10 mos. 2 days.

John Dietz, b. Apr 24, 1725 at Gauersheim. In 1741 he came to America. Married Elizabeth Labegeyer; had 2 children, both died. Buried Mar --, 1813. Died suddenly, aged 88 yrs. and several wks. Bequethed £20 to Hill Church, £20 to Lebanon, £20 to Bindnagel's and £20 to Jonestown — £80.

Eleonora Imboden, nee Diller, b. Jun 29, 1741; bapt. and confirmed. On Nov 16, 1758 married Joh. Schw. Imboden; had 13 children, 8 survive, 77 grandchildren, a number of great grandchildren. Buried Jul --, 1813. Sick a long time; dropsy. age 72 yrs. 17 days.

John Rupp, b. Oct 1, 1762 in Cocalico; bapt. and confirmed. On Apr 18, 1786 married Cath. Heilman; 14 children. Buried ca 1813-15. Consumption, aged 52 yrs. 2 mos. 19 days.

Anastasius Heilman, b. Mar 30, 1742; bapt. and confirmed. On Apr 8, 1766 married Ros. Barbara Maurer; 8 children. Buried ----, 1815. A wound at little finger. Aged 73 yrs. 12 days.

Joh. Mich. Bohr, b. Aug 12, 1752; bapt. and confirmed. When in 4th day he already took fits (epileptic?). Buried Aug --, 1815. Aged 6 days less than 63 yrs.

Alexander Benson, b. in 1770; bapt. Buried Jan 11, 1816. Died suddenly from internal injuries, aged 46 yrs.

Joh. Adam Bardt of Joh. Nichl. and wife Mary, b. in Germany in 1773; bapt. and confirmed. Married; 12 children. Died Jul 30, 1860 [1816], buried Aug 1, 1816. Feebleness of age, aged 83 yrs.

Mrs. Salome Heilman, wife of Philip H. of Adam and Elizabeth Bardt, b. Jun 5, 1786; bapt. and confirmed. Died Nov 12, 1816, buried Nov 14, 1816. Aged 30 yrs. 5 mos. 7 days.

John Schnebele, b. ----; bapt. and confirmed, married. Buried Nov 22, 1817. Aged 29 yrs.

John Laber. Buried Mar 1, 1818. Aged 20 yrs. 6 mos. 6 days.

Mrs. Magdalene Fernsler, b. Jan --, 1769; bapt., confirmed, married twice. Buried Mar 13, 1819. Fever, aged 49 yrs. 9 mos. 5 days.

John Schweigert Imboden of Diel Imboden and wife Elizabeth, b. Oct 23, 1733 at Hanau, Germany; bapt. and confirmed. In his 16th year he came to America. Married Eleonora of Casper Diller; had 13 children, 8 sons 5 daughters. Resided here a long time, useful member of this congregation. Died Jul 29, 1819, buried Jul 31, 1819. Aged 85 yrs. 9 mos. 6 days.

Joh. Jac. Keller of Valentine and Justina K., b. Jan 19, 1762; bapt. and confirmed. Married Catharine Stoever, had 13 children. Died Mar 29, 1820, buried Mar 31, 1820. Consumption, aged 58 yrs. 2 mos. 10 days.

Philip Fernsler, b. Apr 12, 1770; bapt. and confirmed. Married, had 9 children. Died Oct 9, 1821, buried Oct 11, 1821. Fever, aged 51 yrs. 6 mos. 3 days.

Mrs. Rachel Kleimer of John Kohlman and wife, b. Aug 11, 1738 in
Oley, Berks County; bapt. and confirmed. Married to Abraham
Kleimer, had 9 children. Died Nov 6, 1822, buried Nov 7, 1822.
Aged 84 yrs. 3 mos.

Adam Heilman of John and Anna M. H., b. Feb 10, 1771; bapt. and
confirmed. Married Cath. Maury, had 2 children. Died Mar 11,
1823, buried Mar 13, 1823. Aged 52 yrs. 1 mo. 1 day.

Mrs. Barbara Meinzinger, nee Ischler, b. Feb 23, 1766; bapt. and
confirmed. Married to Conrad Meinzinger, had 2 children. Died
Mar 28, 1823, buried Mar 30, 1823. Aged 56 yrs. 1 mo. 5 days.

Mrs. Anna Mary Blauch, nee Haupt, b. Jan 15, 1789; bapt. and
confirmed. Married to John Blauch, had 5 children. Died Aug 25,
[1823] , buried Aug 27, 1823. Fever, aged 34 yrs. 7 mos. 10 days.

Mrs. Cath. Elizabeth Stoever, nee Heilman, wife of Joh. Ad. Stoever,
b. Nov 29, 1750; bapt. and confirmed. Had 12 children. Died Apr
7, 1824, buried Apr 9, 1824. Aged 73 yrs. 4 mos. 13 days.

John Haupt, b. Mar 29, 1774; bapt. and confirmed. Married Christina
Behm, had 6 children. Died May 9, 1824, buried May 10, 1824.
Aged 50 yrs. 1 mo. 9 days.

Henry Reinoehl of Henry and Cath. Reinoehl, b. Dec 18, 1741 in
Germany; bapt., came to America in 8th year, confirmed.
Married Juliana Gephart, had 4 children. Married (2nd) Cath.
Matter, had 6 children. Died Feb 14, 1824(?), buried Feb 16,
1825. Aged 83 yrs. 2 mos.

Mrs. Elizabeth Steher, b. May 1, 1789; bapt. and confirmed. Married
to George Streher, had 9 children. Died Aug 28, 1825, buried
Aug 9, 1825. Consumption, aged 36 yrs. 3 mos. 7 days.

Valentine Boger of Matthias and Anna Magdalene, b. Oct 16, 1758;
bapt. and confirmed. Married Juliana Imboden, had 4 children.
Died Jul (?) 24, 1826, buried Jun 26, 1826. Aged 67 yrs. 9 mos. 3
days.

Mrs. Barbara Streher, b. May 16, 1750; bapt. and confirmed. Married
to John Streher, had 6 children. Buried May 23, 1827. Aged 77
yrs. 6 days.

John Strecher, b. Aug 25, 1743 in Europe; bapt. and confirmed.
Married. Buried Sep 25, 1827. Aged 84 yrs. 1 mo..

Mrs. Rachel Heilman, nee Lang, b. Dec 14, 1774; bapt. and confirmed.
Married to John Heilman, had 7 children. Died Feb 24, 1828,
buried Feb 26, 1828. Aged 53 yrs. 2 mos. 10 days.

John Adam Stoever of Rev. J. C. Stoever and wife Cath., b. Jun 18,

1748; bapt. and confirmed a Lutheran. Married Cath. Elizabeth
Heilman, had 12 children; 7 sons and 5 daughters. Useful
member for many yrs. Married 54 yrs., many descendants.
Buried Sep 7, 1828. Fever, aged 80 yrs. and 3 days less than 3
mos.

Joseph Blecher, and old soldier. Died Jan 11, 1829, buried Jan 13,
1829.

John Fredr. Haupt, b. March 1, 1772; bapt. and confirmed, Lutheran.
Married Hannah Mayer. Died of fever on Sep 12, 1829, buried
Sep 14, 1829. Aged 57 yrs. 13 days.

Joh. Nicholas Bohr of Matthias and Mary Bohr, b. Oct 11, 1758; bapt.
and confirmed a Lutheran. Married Cath., nee Schnock, had 10
children. Long a member. Buried Dec 9, 1829. Aged 71 yrs. 26
days.

Mrs. Cath. Keller, nee Stoever, b. Nov 30, 1772; bapt. and confirmed
a Lutheran. Married to Jacob Keller, had 13 children. Buried Jan
3, 1830. Aged 57 yrs. 1 mo. 2 days.

Mrs. Cath. Stoever, nee Misch, b. Feb 3, 1793; bapt. and confirmed
Reformed. Married to Fredr. Stoever, had 9 children. Buried Jan
9, 1830. Aged 36 yrs. 11 mos. 5 days.

John Stoever of John Adam and Cath. St[oever], b. Feb 1, 1775;
bapt. and confirmed. Married Catharine Uhler, had 9 children.
Buried Feb 8, 1830. Aged 55 yrs. 3 days.

Jacob Imboden of Joh. Schw. Imboden, b. Dec 25, 1783; bapt. and
confirmed. Married Christina Carmeme, had 10 children. Buried
Dec 21, 1831. Aged 48 yrs. 8 days.

Anna Mary Blecher, nee Rupp, b. Jan 6, 1751; bapt. and confirmed.
Married to Joseph Blecher, had 10 children. Died Jan 28, 1832,
buried Jan 30, 1832. Aged 81 yrs. 22 days.

Mrs. Mary Magdln. Juengst, b. Oct 31, 1783; bapt. and confirmed.
Married to Henry Juengst, had 9 children. Buried March 1832.
Aged 46 yrs. and 3 days less than 5 mos.

Adam Bardt of Jacob and Elizabeth B., b. Apr 9, 1761; bapt. and
confirmed. Married Anna Achenbach, had 6 children. Sick a long
time. Buried Aug 6, 1832. Aged 71 yrs. 3 mos. 27 days.

Mrs. Susan Schnebele, nee Haupt, b. Oct 18, 1781; bapt. and
confirmed. Married to John Schnebele, had 4 children. Married
secondly to Jacob Schnebele, had 4 children. Buried Jan 21,
1834. Aged 52 yrs. 3 mos. 2 days.

Mrs. Anna Cath. Rupp, nee Heilman, b. Sep 3, 1768; bapt. and

confirmed. Married to John Rupp, had 14 children. Died May 10, 1835, buried May 13, 1835. Aged 66 yrs. 6 mos. 7 days.
Joh. George Keller of Valentine and Justin K., b. March 6, 1759; bapt. and confirmed. Married Mary Eve Laubscher, had 10 children. Long a member. Buried March 3, 1836. Aged 77 yrs. and 3 days less.
David Schad, b. ----, 1777; bapt. and confirmed. Married Magdalene Hauer, had 10 children. Buried Nov 11, 1836. Aged 59 yrs.

MARRIAGES

Francis Reynolds m. Catharine Steitz on Feb 25, 1731.
Christopher Meyer m. Anna Rosina Koppenhoeffer on Dec 18, 1734.
John Peter Kucher m. Anna Barbara Koppenhoeffer on Oct 6, 1735.
Anastasius Uhler m. Dorothea Jerg (Jorg, apparently for Georg) on May 3, 1737.
John Welsh m. Elizabeth Whitside on Feb 6, 1738.
John George Glassbrenner m. Elizabeth Fischer on Feb 7, 1738.
Matthias Schmeisser m. Elizabeth Koppenhoeffer on Aug 2, 1738.
Francis Reynolds m. Eleonore Thistle on Dec 12, 1738.
Peter Heylman m. Salome Frey on Jan 29, 1739.
James Russell m. Jane Russell on Jun 12, 1739.
Matthew Clark m. Elizabeth Ingerham on Nov 6, 1739.
Nicholas Kintzer m. Anna Catharine Hoester, or Hoeffer on Jan 3, 1742. *(J. C. Stoever almost invariably forms "ff" exactly like "st" in German. It is therefore impossible to decide whether he meant to write Hoeffer or Hoester, but as the name Hoeffer elsewhere occurs we incline to the opinion that the name is Hoeffer. The same remark applies to Hoffer and Hoster.)*
Leonard Umberger m. Barbara Borst on Apr 15, 1742.
John Welsh m. Anna Sharp on Jun 9, 1742.
Peter Wolff m. Hannah Wolff on Aug 8, 1742.
Michael Umberger m. Anna Mary Rammler on Oct 18, 1742.
Caspar Loewe m. Margaret Ess Kuch on Oct 25, 1742.
John Peter Schmidt m. Mary Margaret Huber (A line is drawn through.) on Nov 28, 1742.
Joh. George Huber m. Catharine Hoster, or Hoffer, on Feb 20, 1742.
John Herman Ickel m. Anna Margaret Ohrendurff on Oct 23, 1743.
Joh Tomson m. Susan Hammon on Jan 31, 1744.
Vincens Kueffer m. Anna Margaret Vollmer on Feb 24, 1744.

Joh. Philip Holinger m. Juliana Umberger on Feb 24, 1744.
Daniel Gray m. Mary Patton on March 3, 1744.
Joh. Martin Kirstaetter m. Magdalene Kuckenberger on Jul 19, 1744.
James Carr m. Mary Hyde on Sep 19, 1744.
Joh. Conrad Tempelman m. Mary Elizabeth Buch on Sep 24, 1744.
Matthias Boger m. Anna Magdalene Wampstler on Jan 7, 1746.
Michael Ackerman m. Anna Barbara Albert on Feb 11, 1746.
James Clarck m. Margaret Tratter, or Trotter, on May 15, 1746.
Dennis Druggan m. Joanna Conner on Dec 3, 1746.
Jacob Breneissen m. Anna Veronica Wampstler on Jan 13, 1747.
William Preese (hardly Freese) m. Mary Griffith on Jun 3, 1747.
Jacob Rees m. Rachel Dyx on Oct 12, 1747.
James Barnet m. Martha Rogers on Oct 13, 1747.
Joseph McCorry m. Roas (apparently for Rose) Feere on Nov 14,
    1747.
William Grace m. Mary McNealy on Dec 14, 1747.
Valentine Herchelrodt m. Elizabeth Meusser on Dec 29, 1747.
Jacob Schober m. Mary Dorothea Zimmerman on Dec 29, 1747.
Thomas Mackey m. Mary Meben on March 21, 1748.
Moses Moor m. Jane Gillighin on May 10, 1748.
Abraham Richardson m. Mary Margaret Mintz on Jun 15, 1748.
Adam Slhneider m. Anna Mary Bor on Jun 21, 1748.
George Michael Bronner m. Barbara Tempelmann on Jun 21, 1748.
Joh. Michael Wagner m. Elizabeth Madern on Oct 25, 1748.
Joh. Jacob Dietz m. Catharine Holtzwart on Dec 21, 1748.
George Velty m. Anna Mary Meyer on Oct 24, 1749.
Vincens Keuffer m.Eva Mary Hubeler on Nov 14, 1749.
Adam Buerger m. Mary Barbara Meyer on Apr 26, 1750.
Michael Zimmerman m. Eva Kuenig on May 15, 1750.
Gottfried Baumgaertner m. Anna Catharine Dueffer on May 28, 1750.
John Matthias Bohr m. Mary Elizabeth Neu on Aug 14, 1750.
Jacob Wagner m. Magdalena Gerhardt on Oct 9, 1750.
John Wolff Kissner m. Anna Sabina Bindtnagel on Oct 9, 1750.
John Becker m. Catharine Umberger on Jan 10, 1751.
John Peter Felten m. Mary Catharine Neu on Feb 5, 1751.
Joseph Ziefle m. Mary Catharine Guenther on May 16, 1751.
Sebastian Kirstaetter m. Magdalena Diebler on Jun 11, 1751.
Melchoir Winckelman m. Barbara Siegchrist on Jun 18, 1751.
Frantz Caspar Wagner m. Margaret Kirstaetter on Oct 8, 1751.
Peter Kraemer m. Magdalena Leydy, or Leyde (in feminine) on Jan 2,

1752.

Leonard Mueller m. Anna Mary Raetelsperger on March 31, 1752.

Philip Weigandt m. Magdalene Baur on Nov 14, 1752.

James McNeese and Margaret Allen on Dec 20, 1752.

Joh. Adam Barth m. Elizabeth Waeissen-Kind on Jan 30, 1753.

John Huber m. Mary Elizabeth Ritscher on May 6, 1753.

Joh. Michael Kirstaetter m. Mary Dorothea Dietz on Jun 5, 173.

Henry Hertle m. Catharine Firnsler on Aug 12, 1753.

Christopher Frederic Wegman m. Anna Mary Keller on Nov 27, 1753.

Casper Hssler m. Rosina Schnellbecher on Jun 25, 1754.

Simon Burckhardt m. Catharine Brandt on Aug 27, 1754.

Ludwig Weidner m. Mary Engel Gerst on Nov 3, 1754.

George Sprecher m. Eva Margaret Schwab on May 28, 1755.

John Adam Bohr m. Anna Barbara Labengeiger on Jul 21, 1755.

John Peter Pannekuchen m. Catharine Dietz on Jul 21, 1755.

Lawrence (Lorentz) Kurtz m. Mary Elizabeth Saur on Oct 5, 1755.

John Adam Stoehr m. Eva Catharine Jetter (Yetter) on Nov 18, 1755.

George Rein m. Anna Mary Meyer on Feb 10, 1756.

Abraham Clark m. Jane Clark on March 23, 1756.

Michael Malfir m. Anna Eve Schnug on March 25, 1756.

Jost Jotter m. Eva Catharine Hubler on March 30, 1756.

Joh. Martin Kirstaetter m. Elizabeth Bickel on Jun 1, 1756.

George Hanss Dietrich m. Anna Dorothea Boltz on Jun 15, 1756.

Erasmus Rosenberger m. Anna Catharine Baumgaertner on Jul 27, 1756.

Joseph Scot m. Anna Kalliah on Aug 26, 1756.

John Peter Ritscher m. Anna Margaret Kirber on Feb 15, 1757.

Matthias Schmutz m. Regina Zwerentzer on March 2, 1757.

John Lerkin m. Margaret Thompson on March 14, 1757.

Wendell Keller m. Catharine Dorothea Haberland on March 14, 1757.

Joh. Jacob Boltz m. Catharine Madern on March 22, 1757.

John Krueger m. Anna Margaret Heydt on March 29, 1757.

Jacob Zimpffer m. Anna Margaret Lorentz on Apr 12, 1757.

Joh. Caspar Stoever m. Anna Mary Barbara Nagel on Apr 26, 1757.

John Kuemmerling m. Anna Mary Pfrang on May 31, 1757.

George Hatz m. Anna Margaret Dieb on May 31, 1757.

Martin Schmidt m. Catharine Fischer on Aug 7, 1757.

Hanss Ulrich Huber m. Elizabeth Firnsler on Sep 4, 1757.

Peter Kraemer m. Anna Margaret Ernst on Oct 18, 1757.

Joh. Henry Hertle m. Catharine Kuehn on Nov 22, 1757.

Joh. Nicholas Brechbiel m. Juliana Diller on Nov 22, 1757.

Adam Stephan m. Mary Agnes Pfrang on Dec 20, 1757.

George Fisher m. Elizabeth Knopf on Jan 3, 1758.

Matthias Weimar m. Barbara Vollmar on Jan 5, 1758.

John Jacob Bickel m. Eva Margaret Jetter on Feb 14, 1758.

Anthony Karmenie m. Anna Christina Hetzler on Feb 27, 1758.

Andrew Bartruff m. Christina Sophia Klein on March 29, 1758.

Joh. Martin Kuemmerling m. Elizabeth Kirstaetter on Apr 4, 1758.

Abraham Heydt m. Elizabeth Sieg on Apr 24, 1758.

John Stroh m. Anna Mary Fischer on May 23, 1758.

Robert Rogers m. Anna Christina Ramberg on Jun 15, 1758.

Peter Fischer m. Catharine Boeckl or Boeckle (plainly not Bockle) on Jul 2, 1758.

John Schweickhardt Imboden m. Eleonora Diller on Nov 14, 1758.

John Stholer (apparently for Stohler) m. Anna Mary Glassbrenner on Jan 29, 1759.

Jacob Sprecher m. Dorothea Blecher on March 5, 1759.

Peter Brechbiel m. Mary Catharine Franck on Aug 21, 1759.

Martin Herman m. Anna Dorothea Borst on Sep 18, 1759.

Philip Baass m. Anna Weimer on Oct 28, 1759.

Joh. Ernst Curt m. Margaret Riedt on Oct 28, 1759.

Jacob Ziegeler m. Juliana Kirstaetter on Jan 21, 1760.

Abraham Schaeffer m. Mary Barbara Sirer on Jan 21, 1760.

Adam Dumme m. Catharine Hydt on Jan 22, 1760.

David Herbster m. Anna Mary Barbara Haecker on Feb 19, 1760.

Frantz Caspar Wagner m. Elizabeth Wirtz on Feb 26, 1760.

Michael Kirber m. Anna Mary Schlatter on Jun 26, 1760.

Adam Bayer m. Mary Sarah Ritscher on Jul 6, 1760.

Abraham Kroh m. Mary Schaeffer on Aug 30, 1760.

Joh. Christopher Friedrich m. Anna Mary Wagner on Sep 2, 1760.

Christian Mueller m. Elizabeth Ried on Sep 16, 1760.

Peter Benedict m. Mary Elizabeth Lauckster on Oct 14, 1760.

Joh. Michael Firnssler m. Mary Catharine Hedderich on Oct 23, 1760.

Matthias Staub m. Sophia Fischer on Oct 28, 1760.

George Ulrich m. Elizabeth Naess on Nov 18, 1760.

James Atkinson m. Anna Camill (probably for Campbell) on Nov 18, 1760.

Matthias Schwertzel m. Catharine Barbara Laey on Dec 2, 1760.

Joh. Christian Demmen m. Margaret Magdalena Mueller on Dec 30, 1760.

John George Heldt m. Mary Magdalene Wolff on Feb 3, 1761.

Thomas Kintzel m. Anna Mary Holderbaum on Feb 17, 1761.

John Lewis (Ludwig) Kleber m. Anna Magdalene Ellinger on Apr 7, 1761.

Owen Davies m. Anna Mary Weber (not in Stoever's Record) on Apr 17, 1761.

Joh. Frederick Kuehbauch m. Anna Catharine Felt (for Felten or Felty) on Apr 30, 1761.

Joh. George Meyer m. Anna Barbara Felt (for Felten or Felty) on Apr 30, 1761.

Joh. Christian Goellnitz m. Mary Elizabeth Steg on May 11, 1761.

John Peter Kueffer m. Anna Waeibel on May 19, 1761.

Joh. Daniel Stroh m. Catharine Barbara Uhler on Jun 16, 1761.

Henry Schnatterle m. Anna Barbara Uhler on Jun 16, 1761.

Joh. Philip Firnssler m. Anna Christina Stoever on Apr 18, 1762.

Frantz Caspar Wagner m. Elizabeth Haehnle on Apr 20, 1762.

John Frederic Danninger m. Anna Mary Balmus on Apr 20, 1762.

George Fischer m. Elizabeth Cunradt on Aug 24, 1762.

Jacob Scherertz m. Elizabeth Rausch on Oct 23, 1763.

Nicholas Kilimer m. Elizabeth Teiss on Dec 13, 1763.

Jacob Firnssler m. Magdalene Peter on March 6, 1764.

Philip Lorentz Hautz m. Anna Mary Mueller on March 7, 1764.

George Balmer m. Barbara Olinger on March 20, 1764.

Christian Schnuck m. Catharine Bayer on Apr 10, 1764.

John Peter m. Barbara Firnssler on Apr 10, 1764.

Christopher Frederic Wegman m. Mary Eva Pfrang on Jul 23, 1764.

John Atkinson, Jr. m. Catharine Dieb or Diebi on Aug 7, 1764. *(In the original it is Diebin the general feminine ending. As there were people named Deibi in this vicinity and we know of none of the name Dieb, it is probably the former.)*

Joh. Henry Firnssler m. Juliana Simon on Oct 9, 1764.

Henry Weiss m. Eva Catharine Fuchs on Oct 9, 1764.

Peter Kober m. Margaret Stroeher on Oct 9, 1764.

George Federhoff m. Anna Elizabeth Schnaebele on Oct 28, 1764.

Joh. Adam Maennig m. Anna Margaret Holtz on March 5, 1765.

Andrew Kastnitz m. Elizabeth Geckel on Mar 19, 1765.

George Ellinger m. Mary Catharine Weyrich on Apr 5, 1765.

Henry Boeckle m. Anna Mary Ellinger on Apr 23, 1765.

Christian Fremdling m. Hannah Wolff on Sep 29, 1765.

Joh. Jacob Wolff m. Anna Margaret Schnug on Oct 8, 1765.

Jacob Frederic Danninger m. Anna Mary Fauler on Feb 3, 1766.
John Stein m. Eva Barbara Kucher on Feb 6, 1766.
Joh. Nicholas Bohr m. Mary Margaret Kolmar on March 4, 1766.
Joh. Martin Kolmar m. Anna Magdalena Hertzler on March 4, 1766.
Joh. Jacob Bickel m. Mary Catharine Braun (not in Stoever's Record) on March 4, 1766.
Joh. Martin Kuemmerling m. Anna Margaret Edelmann on Apr 8, 1766.
Anastasius Heylman m. Rosina Barbara Maurer on Apr 8, 1766.
George Maurer m. Magdalene Heylman on Apr 8, 1766.
Caspar Elias Diller m. Eva Magdalene Meyer on Apr 14, 1766.
Joh. Adam Balmer m. Barbara Schauffler on May 27, 1766.
John Schnug, widower, m. Catharine Dulibam on Jun 4, 1766.
John Hicks m. Elizabeth Holderbaum on Jul 29, 1766.
Joh. Adam Weiss m. Mary Eve Meyer on Aug 4, 1766.
Martin Koch m. Elizabeth Schanst (very plainly but probably for Schanz) on Oct 28, 1766.
Daniel Angst m. Magdalene Fischer on Nov 10, 1766.
Andrew Karg m. Susan Mary Heinrich (Henry) on Nov 18, 1766.
Daniel Jungblut m. Anna Mary Elizabeth Heinrich on Nov 18, 1766.
Christopher Ulrich m. Juliana Umberger on March 10, 1767.
George Meyer m. Mary Elizabeth Stoehr on Apr 21, 1767.
John Thome m. Anna Mary Reiss on May 1, 1767.
John Reyer m. Mary Elizabeth Neu on Oct 20, 1767.
Andrew Kueffer m. Elizabeth Bickel on Oct 27, 1767.
Lucas Schally m. Mary Elizabeth Boger on Jan 5, 1768.
Christopher Meyer m. Anna Margaret Ili (Ely) on Jan 19, 1768.
Joh. Martin Uhler m. Anna Elizabeth Stroh on March 15, 1768.
Rudolph Koellicker m. Anna Mary Weidman on March 22, 1768.
George Volck m. Catharine Germann on Jun 21, 1768.
John Hermann m. Catharine Hermann on Jul 5, 1768.
Leonard Albrecht m. Catharine Stroeher on Aug 16, 1768.
Andrew Endress m. Anna Mary Gingrich on Dec 12, 1768.
Joh. Peter Fischer m. Anna Elizabeth Heylman on Jan 2, 1769.
Balthasser Laber m. Rosina Wentz on Feb 7, 1769.
Anastasius Ellinger m. Catharine Olinger on Feb 2, 1769.
Michael Bosch m. Elizabeth Koch on Mar 16, 1769.
Conrad Braun m. Agnes Weiss (not Schneider) on Apr 10, 1769.
Joh. William Neu m. Juliana Firnssler on Apr 18, 1769.
Daniel Scherertz m. Mary Catharine Meyer on Apr 25, 1769.

Joh. Melchoir Abmeyer m. Anna Mary Kuemmerling on May 2, 1769.
Joh. Henry Frey m. Anna Mary Boger on May 23, 1769.
Joh. Henry Rheinoehl m. Juliana Gebhardt on Jun 20, 1769.
Jacob Schenck m. Dorothea Speck on Aug 15, 1769.
Caspar Jungblut m. Anna Catharine Felleberger on Aug 22, 1769.
Philip Mattheis m. Catharine Kinzel on Nov 2, 1769.
Michel Kleber m. Catharine Holderbaum on Dec 12, 1769.
John Nicholas Neu m. Anna Margaret Schaeffer on Dec 28, 1769.
John Ulrich Ohlinger m. Catharine Roessle on Mar 27, 1770.
John Adam Stoever m. Catharine Elizabeth Heylman on Apr 24, 1770.
Thomas Atkinson m. Magdalene Kintzel on May 8, 1770.
Christopher Fuchs m. Susanna Mary Bayer on Jul 3, 1770.
Andrew Lay m. Hannah Dinniss on Aug 21, 1770.
John Heckendorn m. Mary Catharine Hammann on Aug 21, 1770.
Christopher Frederic Seiler m. Mary Elizabeth Kintzel on Nov 20, 1770.
Martin Ulrich m. Regina Felt (Felty or Felten) on Feb 19, 1771.
Joh. Nicholas Neu m. Eva Catharine Rudisiehl on Mar 26, 1771.
George Sprecher m. Margaret Boger on May 2, 1771.
Andrew Beistel m. Christina Pflantz on May 28, 1771.
Jacob Sauter m. Philippina Beistel on May 28, 1771.
Jacob Kleeman m. Elizabeth Catharine Bayer on Jun 18, 1771.
Martin Lang m. Elizabeth Huber on Oct 1, 1771.
Peter Etter m. Elizabeth Daut on Dec 31, 1771.
Tobias Stoever m. Hannah Zimmerman on Apr 21, 1772.
John Schnug m. Anna Christina Heylmann on May 19, 1772.
Stephen Huck m. Christina Decker on May 31, 1772.
John Schmidt m. Christina Nennemacher on Jun 16, 1772.
Michael Karmenie m. Catharine Meyer on Jun 21, 1772.
Albrecht Siechle m. Mary Preiss (plainly so) on Sep 22, 1772.
Peter Koch m. Juliana Heinrich (Henry) on Dec 15, 1772.
Joh. Michel Neu m. Justina Bart on Feb 9, 1773.
John Frantz Boehler m. Catharine Breit on Apr 18, 1773.
Joh. Michael Uhler m. Anna Mary Elizabeth Stroh on Apr 29, 1773.
Joh. Martin Wagner m. Charlotte Kintzel on Jun 29, 1773.
John Adam Fischer m. Mary Elizabeth Becker on Feb 22, 1774.
John Stoever m. Anna Engel Kissecker on May 24, 1774.
John Philip New m. Elizabeth Preiss on Jul 17, 1774.
John Christopher Frank m. Anna Margaret Maurer on Aug 30, 1774.

John Nicholas Bopp m. Catharine Margaret Felt on Dec 20, 1774.

Matthias Stroeher m. Anna Barbara Brechbiel on Mar 21, 1775.

George Adam Eckhardt m. Mary Margaret Kraemer on Sep 5, 1775.

Andrew Braun m. Magdalene Malfir on Dec 19, 1775.

Henry Peter m. Anna Christina Imboden on Mar 26, 1776.

John Conrad Kachel m. Margaret Schwab on Oct 13, 1776.

John Schnug, (widower), m. Anna Margaret Bohr, from Lebanon and Hanover, on Oct 30, 1776.

John Jacob Bickel m. Christina Schindel, from Lebanon, on Nov 28, 1776.

Jacob Epprecht m. Elizabeth Weitzel on Feb 18, 1777.

Jacob Siechle m. Susanna Muench on Feb 18, 1777.

John George Glasbrenner m. Catharine Rudy on Mar 30, 1777.

John Peter Neu m. Mary Regina Rausch (very plainly) on Apr 8, 1777.

Jacob Wolandie m. Catharine Bickel on Jun 17, 1777.

Matthias Boger, Jr. m. Barbara Foerster on Dec 23, 1777.

John Peter m. Salome Bender on Aug 22, 1778.

John Beltz m. Mary Heyr (plainly so written) on Oct 27, 1778.

Jacob Palm m. Mary Dorothea Bischoff on Feb 16, 1779.

Joh. Peter Neu m. Juliana Karmeni on Feb 16, 1779.

Nicholas Heinrich m. Catharine Elizabeth Becker on Feb 23, 1779.

John Wilhelm Bohr m. Anna Magdal. Boger on Apr 19, 1779.

(This ends entries made by Stoever. Those following until 1784 are apparently almost certainly [Frederick] Melsheimer's hand.)

John George Reinoehl, (widower), m. Catharine Matter on Jul 23, 1779.

Anton Lange m. Esther Wilhelm on Aug 17, 1779.

George Kimmerling m. Veronica (Freni) Wagner on Sep 7, 1779.

John Walter m. Anna Boehn (daugther of a Mennonite) on Oct 11, 1779.

John Frederic Stoever m. Anna Margaret Daenschaertz (Schaefferstadt crossed out and Lebanon added) on Nov 8, 1779.

Michael Stucki m. Elizabeth Huber on Feb 21, 1780.

John George Heylman m. Anna Mary Wild on May 2, 1780.

Jacob Brechbiehl m. Rachel Henry on Sep 5, 1780.

George Kornmann m. Christina Webber on Oct 24, 1780.

John William Lang m. Elizabeth Kog, or Kag (possibly intended for Koch) on Nov 14, 1780.

Jacob Matter m. Elizabeth Wolf on Nov 14, 1780.

John Philip Karmini m. Anna Matter on Apr 17, 1781.

John German m. Anna Mary Achenbach on March 19, 1782.

John Philip Achenbach m. Anna Mary Herter on Aug 13, 1782.

John Adam Bardt m. Catharine Achenbach on Dec 4, 1782.

Jacob Becker m. Magdalene Hunsridter on March 9, 1783.

John Hener m. Mary Elizabeth Becker on Apr 6, 1783.

John Imboden m. Catharine Fernsler on Jun 3, 1783.

John Stroh m. Elizabeth Trumpf on Nov 11, 1783.

John Bock m. Elizabeth Herter on Apr 14, 1784.

Valentine Boger m. Juliana Imboden on May 25, 1784.

John Ahrendt (Arndt) Achenbach m. Anna Mary Busch on Aug 10, 1784.

Peter Walborn m. Catharine Kehler, single persons, on Aug 24, 1794. Witnesses: Parents and friends.

Paul Frank m. Christian Isler, single, on Oct 27, 1794. Witnesses: Jacob Kupp and John Kupp.

George Karmini m. Elizabeth Benter, single, on Oct 28, 1794. Witnesses: John Benter and wife Barbara.

Anthony Karmini m. Christina Biel, single, on Dec 16, 1794. Witness: Mrs. Beck, widow.

Christian Howerter m. Julia (July) Carmini, on Apr 21, 1795. Witnesses: George Carmini and John Neu.

Adam Ulrich m. Anna Mary Lomiller, single, on Apr 21, 1795. Witnesses: Martin Ulrich and a number of friends.

Adam Ensminger m. Christina Fahrny, single, on Jun 23, 1795. Witnesses: Jonathan Ensminger and Christian Fahrny. Two pairs —— names forgotten.

George Imboden m. Elizabeth Foltz on May 23, 1795. Witnesses: Philip Imboden, Frederic Wolfelsberger and some others.

Jacob Walther m. Magdalene Zug on Apr 13, 1795. Witnesses: Peter Walther and John Walther.

Michael Neu m. Susan Romich on Apr 19, 1795. Witnesses: the parents of the bride.

Joseph Sergeant m. Catharine Karstschnitz, single, on Aug 2, 1795. Witnesses: the parents of the bride and many others.

Jonathan Ensminger m. Veronica Fern on Jan 3, 1797. Witnesses: many friends on both sides.

Leonard Cassel, Paxton, Dauphin county, m. Christina Barth, Lebanon, both single, on Feb 21, 1797. Witnesses: Adam Barth, Frederick Cassel and various others.

Philip Baerry m. Margaret Esterrllein on March 14, 1797. Witnesses: Adam Alt, Henry Schauer and various others.

Philip Dietrich m. Salome Xander (Sanders) on ----, 1797. Witnesses: Emanuel Xander, Margaret Dietrich, &c. &c. "Several omitted."

George Matter m. Christina Kennedy on Apr 29, 1797. Witnesses: Joh. Carmini, &c. &c.

Christian Boger m. Elizabeth Boltz, both single, on May 29, 1797. Witnesses: Valentine Boger and wife, Henry Bolz and wife.

THE QUITOPAHILLA (HILL) CHURCH (REFORMED)

Barbara of Jörg Schambach and wife, b. Feb 13, 1761. Spon: Jörg Ullerich and wife.

Joerg of Jörg Schambach and wife, b. Nov 21, 1763. Spon: Jorg Ullerich.

Margaretha of Jörg Schambach, b. May 31, 1751. Spon: --- Lieber.

Jacob of Jörg Schambach and wife, b. Nov 1, 1754. Spon: Jacob Lutwig and wife.

Jacob of Peter --- (?), b. 1761. Spon: Jacob Lutwig and wife.

Johann Philip Schambach, b. Mar 31, 1761. Spon: Philip Grinewalt and wife.

(These entries made by Fred. Casimir Mueller.)

Magdalena of Heinrich Seitz and wife, b.---, 1761. Spon: Johannes Mueller and wife.

Elisabetha of Abraham Heid and wife, b.---, 1761 spon: Jacob Sieg and Magdalena Sieg.

Dau of Wendel Hatz and wife, bapt. July 28, 1765. Spon: Simon Riegel and wife.

Anna Maria of Heinrich Koellicker, bapt. Nov 12, 1745. Spon: Johann Conrad Gerhart and wife.

Anna Liesbet of Heinrich Koellicker and wife, bapt. Dec 12, 1746. Spon: Hans Ulrich Jägel and wife.

(These entered by Heinrich Koellicker.)

Rudolf of Heinrich Koellicker and wife, bapt. Dec 6, 1747. Spon: Rudolf Haab and Maria Tempelmann.

Regina of Hans Ulrich Jaegeli and Lisbet, bapt. Oct 19, 1746. Spon: Heinrich Kollicker and wife.

Maria of Hans Ulrich Jaegeli and Liesbet, bapt. Apr 20, 1748. Spon: Johann Conrad Gerhart and wife.

(The following baptisms were entered by Tempelmann)

Barbara of Henrich Altdörfer and Ursula, b. Nov 22, 1741. Spon: Jacob Huetmann and Barbara.

Eva of Henrich Weber and Anna Margareta, b. Oct 4, 1749. Spon: Eva Kinigin.

Anna Sabina of Jacob Kintzer and Anna, b. Feb 5, 1750. Spon: Johannes Küstner and Anna Sabina Bindnagel.

Johann Thomas of Felix Lang and Regina, b. Mar 5, 1750. Spon: Thomas Mackern.

Lenhart of Henrich Stall and Anna, b. Mar 2, 1750. Spon: Lenhart

Schnäbele and Anna Maria.

Johann Peter of Hans Brechbill and wife, b.---, 1750. Spon: Peter Brechbill and Eva Künigin.

Johann Peter of Jacob Jugerle and Susanna, b. Jun 18, 1750. Spon: Johannes Bintnagel and Regina.

Maria Barbara of Lenhart Umberger and Maria Barbara, b. Aug 28, 1750. Spon: Carl Schally and Esther.

Carl of David Bigler and wife, b. Jun 12, 1751. Spon: Carl Schally and Esther.

Johann Valentin of Jörg Meier and Barbara, b. Feb 14, 1751. Spon: Christoffel Zimmer and Catrina.

Anna Maria of Friedr. Stroh and Anna Elisabetha, b. Mar 8, 1751. Spon: Johannes Tempelmann, single; Catrina Elis. Grün; Lenhart Miller and wife, Anna Maria nee Templemann.

(The next two baptisms entered by unknown hands.)

Anna Christina of Johannes Achebach and Anna Maria, b. Nov 9, 1766. Spon: Federades(?) Holt and Anna Elisabeth.

Johann Henrich of Martin Imhoff and wife, b. Nov 4, 1766. Spon: Rudi Kölcker and Regina Martin.

(The next two baptisms were entered by Heinr. Kelcker.)

Anna Maria of Jacob Hutmann and wife, bapt. Sep 14, 1746. Spon: Jorg Peter and wife.

Maria Barbara of Jacob Hutmann and wife, bapt. Sep 4, 1746. Spon: Rudolf Peter and Maria Barbara.

Barbara of Johannes Achenbach and Anna Maria, bapt. Mar 27, 1768. Spon: Peter Heilman and wife.

Michel of Johannes Trauertman (Trautman), bapt. Mar 22, 1747. Spon: Michel Tempelmann and sister Barbara.

Johann Heinrich of Christoffel Meyer and wife, bapt. Apr 19, 1747. Spon: Heinr. Bumann and wife.

Johann Heinrich of Jörg Heinr. Peter and wife, bapt. Apr 19, 1747. Spon: Jörg Peter and wife.

Johann Jacob of Jorg Heinrich Peter and wife, bapt. Jul 2, 1749. Spon: Jacob Fröli and wife.

Johann Conrad of Johann Conradt Gerhart and wife, bapt. Jun 14, 1747. Spon: Henrich Köllicker and wife.

Anna Catrina of Michael Umberger and wife, bapt. Jun 14, 1747. Spon: Heinrich Umberger and dau. Catrina.

Barbara of Casper Lieb and wife, bapt. Aug 9, 1747. Spon: Michel Meyer and wife.

Johannes of Johann Adam Wagener and wife, bapt. Jun 30, 1747.
Spon: Johannes Tiell and wife.
Johann Martin of Jacob Gugerli and wife, bapt. Sep 20, 1747. Spon:
Johannes Biegel and wife.
Anna Maria of Adam Heilmann and wife, bapt. Aug 26, 1747. Spon:
Johannes Umberger and Catrina Umberger.
(The next four entries, exc. first, entered by Kelcker)
Son of Adam Schally and wife, bapt.-----26, 1768. Spon: Peter Schmidt
and wife.
Juliana of Lenhart Umberger and wife, bapt. Dec 13, 1747. Spon:
Johannes Umberger and Catrina Umberger.
Regina of Heinrich Merck and wife, bapt. Dec 13, 1747, spon: Heinr.
Köllicker and wife.
Elisabetha of Johannes Flender and wife, bapt. Jan 15, 1748. Spon:
Rudolf Peter and Elisabeth Peter.
(The next two baptisims made by unknown hand.)
Abraham of Johannes Eriger and wife, bapt. Mar 11, 1765. Spon:
Abraham Heid, Jr. and wife.
Anna Maria of Peter Aderholt and wife, bapt. Feb 28, 1766. Spon:
Johannes Achenbach and wife.
(The next four baptisms enterd by H. Kelcker.)
Johannes Heinrich of Jacob Fröli and wife, bapt. Feb 13, 1748. Spon:
Jörg Heinr. Peter and wife.
Catrina of Hans Ulrich Peter and wife, bapt. Apr 23, 1749. Spon:
Heinrich Peter and Catrina Zimmer.
Maria Barbara of Hans Adam Wampler and wife, bapt. May 21, 1749.
Spon: Valentin Kueffer and wife.
Elisabetha of Benedick Brechbill and wife, bapt. May 21, 1749. Spon:
Michael Boltz and wife.
(The next entry was made by Rev. Mr. Runckel.)
Sabina of Jacob Küntzer and wife Anna, bapt. Feb 5, 1750. Spon:
Johannes Küstner and Sabina Bindnagel.
(Baptisims by John Conrad Tempelman, entered by himself.)
Johann Christoffel of Nicklaus Briech(?) and Anna Elisabetha, bapt.
May 28, 1751. Spon: Christoffel Zimmer and wife.
Ursula of Johannes Miller and wife, bapt. Aug 10, 1751. Spon:
Martin Imhoff and wife Ursula.
Maria Elisabetha of Johann Henrich Roellig and Anna Catrina, bapt.
Jan 8, 1752. Spon: Johannes Peter Lieb; Johann Jost Walter; and
wife Anna Elisabetha; Hermann Miller and Anna Maria.

Johannes of Henrich Meier and Barbara, bapt. Feb 26, 1752. Spon: Johannes Schotter and wife.

Catrina of Jacob Zimmer and Anna Margreta, bapt. Feb 30, 1752. Spon: Christoffel Zimmer and wife Catrina.

Anna Maria of Johannes Schotter and Anna Maria, bapt Jan 3, 1752. Spon: David Klemm and wife Anna Maria.

Johannes of Johannes Biechel and Barbara, bapt. May 30, 1752. Spon: Henrich Merk and wife Philippina.

Maria Barbara of Henrich Leidt and Anna Maria, bapt. Nov 28, 1752. Spon: Peter Brechbill and wife Maria Barbara.

Melchior of Melchior Leitterdt and Susanna, bapt. July 5, 1752. Spon: Henrich Dubs and Anna Mila (Emilia).

Elisabetha of Michael Wampler and Anna Elisabeta, bapt. Aug 12, 1752. Spon: Mathäs Bober and wife Magdalena; Jacob Brenneisen and wife.

Johann Henrich of Michael Umberger and Anna Maria, bapt. Dec 28, 1752. Spon: Henrich Merck and wife Philippina.

Anna Margreta of Johann Georg Huest and Elisabeta, bapt. Sep 3, 1753. Spon: Johannes Engel Enners; Anna Marg. Kitzmiller; Johan Henr. Röllig and wife Anna Catrina.

Johann Henrich of Johann Jost Walter and Anna Elisabet, bapt. Jun 14, 1753. Spon: Johann Henr. Röllig;, Johann Engel Weber; Appolonia, sister-in-law of Peter Wolf.

Catrina Elisabetha of Adam Schally and Elisabeta, bapt. Oct 16, 1755. Spon: Catrina Schallin and Michael Baltz.

Johannes Peter of Johann Peter Reisch and Maria Elisabeta, bapt. Sep 8, 1753. Spon: Johannes Geistweit; Joh. Peter Schaff; Juliana Maria Weber.

Anna Maria of Michael Umberger and Anna Maria, bapt. Mar 26, 1755. Spon: Adam Herber and wife Catrina.

Maria Lisbet of Valentin Stupfel and Anna Maria, bapt. Jun 15, 1755. Spon: Nicklaus Brechbill and Marilis Brechbill.

Anna Catrina of Henrich Seitz and Anna, bapt. Sep ---, 1755. Spon: Rudolf Hab and Catrina Heilmann.

Anna Catrina of Peter Kann(?) and Gert(rud), bapt. May 4, 1755. Spon: Jacob Killmer and Anna Catrina.

Johann Philip of Philip Bitteljan(?) and Anna Barbara, bapt. Sep 1, 1755. Spon: Joh. Phil. ---(?) and Elisabetha ---(?).

Barbara of Georg Heinr. Peter and Margareta, bapt. Mar 8, 1756. Spon: Jacob Wolf and Barbara Frentzler.

Philip Adam and Michael of Philip Graffert and Anna Maria, bapt. Feb 7, 1756. Spon: Casper Diller; Martin Henrich and wife; Michael Kleinit and Stoffel Zimmer and wife.

Johann Jacob of Rudolf Miller and Catrina, bapt. Mar 3, 1756. Spon: Jacob Miller and wife Esther.

Philippina of Nicklaus Hoff and wife, bapt. Jun 16, 1756. Spon: Henrich Merck.

(Baptisims of Conrad Tempelmann, Nov 1741- Jun 1756.)

Son of Michael Killinger and wife, b. Aug 15, 1759. Spon: Georg Killmeyer and wife.

Jacob of Michael Killinger and Anna Catrina, b. Aug 11, 1758; bapt. Sep 10, 1758. Spon: Jacob Killinger and wife.

Dau. of Valentin Stobelbein and Anna Maria, b. Jul 17, 1755. Spon: Nikolaus Brechbill and Elisabeth.

Maria Salome of Adam Hobeler and Maria Salome, b. Mar 28, 1759. Spon: Wendel Heyl and wife.

Son of Johannes Achenbach and wife, b. Mar 30, 1769. Spon: Peter Heilman and Salomonie.

(The following baptisms of the year 1760, were entered by the Rev. John Waldschmidt. This is evident from the same chrirography that is also found in his own records)

Magdalena of Abraham Heyd and Elisabet, b. Apr 26, 1760, bapt. May 15, 1760. Spon: Abraham Heid and Magdalena.

Johann Wilhelm of Johannes Rauch and Anna Kinkel, b. Apr 3, 1760, bapt.-------. Spon: Wilhelm Rauch and Barbara Merck.

Maria Margaret of Johannes Mueller and Elisabeth Ehl, b. May 15, 1760; bapt. Jun 9, 1760. Spon: Johannes Brechbill and Maria M. Fuchs.

Maria Magdalena of Valentin Ehrhart and Catharina, b. Jun 12, 1760; bapt. Aug 18, 1760. Spon: Antonius Kelker and wife Maria Magdalena.

Johannes of Balsar Schally and Barbara, b. Jul 12; bapt. Aug 18, 1760. Spon: Johannes Schally and Christina Schlosser.

Maria Margaretha of Michael Killinger and Catharina, b. Aug 15, 1760; bapt. Sep 14, 1760. Spon: Johannes Kriger and wife Margaret.

Dau. of Abraham Heit and wife, b. Apr 2, 1760; bapt. Apr 28, 1760. Spon: Johannes Friger (Criger) and wife.

Johannes of Philip Grünewald and Maria Margretha, b. Oct 17, 1760; bapt. Nov 9, 1760. Spon: Jonas Rub(Rupp) and wife Elisaeth.

Johann Jacob of Henrich Merck and Philippina, b. Sep 1, 1760; bapt. Nov 9, 1760. Spon: Jacob Baltz and wife Catrina.

Johan Adam of Johann Peter Schweickert and Anna Christina, b. Feb 9, 1760; bapt. Nov 22, 1760. Spon: Joh. Adam Wagener.

Andreas of Fridrich Nicodemus and Catharina, b. Nov 17, 1760; bapt. Dec 1, 1760. Spon: Andreas Weyel and wife Gertrud.

Johan Peter of Adam Schneider and Anna Catharina, b. Nov 6, 1760. Spon: Joh. Peter Schneider and Elisabeth Süss.

(This is the end of Waldschmidt's entries)

(Entered by Frederick Casimir Mueller from 1762 - 1766)

Dau. of Johannes Rauch and wife, bapt. May 9, 1762. Spon: Lehnhart Mueller and wife Martina.

Dau. of Andres Killinger and wife, b. Jun 1, 1762. Spon: Joh. Rieger and Anna Barbara Scherb.

Dau. of Michael Umberger and wife, bapt. Jun 1, 1762. Spon: Jacob Ralmer and Anna Margaretha.

Dau. of Michael Killinger and wife, bapt. Jul 28, 1762. Spon: Elisabetha Hallman and Joh. Weber and wife.

Son of Henrich Meister and wife, bapt. ---. Spon: Joh. Weber and wife.

Maria Barbara of Henrich Merck and Philipina, b. Mar 28, 1763; bapt May 12, 1763. Spon: Nicolaus Weiss.

Maria Barbara of Conrad Steinman and wife, bapt. Jun 5, 1763. Spon: Martin Kirchstetter.

Anna Cathrina of Abraham Heyd and wife, bapt. July 17, 1763. Spon: Adam Thony.

Son of --- Roth and wife, bapt. Aug 21, 1763. Spon: Joh. Rach.

Fronica (Veronica) of Jacob Boltz and wife,; bapt. Sep 14, 1763. Spon: Thomas Martin.

Dau. of Joh. Achenbach and wife, bapt. Oct 9, 1763, 1764. Spon: Elisabeth Heilman.

Dau. of Michael Killinger and wife, bapt.----6, 1764. Spon: Jacob Killinger and wife.

(The next seven baptisms were entred by an unknown hand.)

Son of Abraham Heit and Elisabet, b. Aug 7, 1766. Spon: Joh. Kriger and wife.

Son of Jonas Rupp and Elisabet, b. Mar 31, 1767. Spon: Johannes Umberger and wife.

Dau. of Johannes Steffen and Anna Mari, b. Jan 15, 1767. Spon: Michael Steffe and wife.

Son of Hendel Klein and Catrina, b. Apr 2, 1767. Spon: Jacob
Kitzmiller and wife.

Henrich of Antoni Kölliger and Madlena, b. Jun 20, 1767. Spon: Kilian
Märit.

Rudolf of Antoni Köliger and Madlena, b. Feb 2, 1768. Spon: Rudolf
Koliger and Margetha Merck.

Son of Michel Killinger and wife, bapt. Feb 2, 1766. Spon: Joh.
Krieger and wife.

*(This is the last baptisim recorded by Fred C. Mueller. He officiated
probably from Oct. 1761 to Feb 1766.)*

Dau. of Antoni Kelcker and wife, bapt. Apr 20, 1766. Spon: Jacob
Laubscher and Elisabeth Kelcker.

Son of Jacob Ziegler and wife, bapt. Mar 23, 1766. Spon: Georg
Maurer and Maria Magd. Heilman.

Dau. of Jacob Weber and Maria, b. Jun 11, 1767. Spon: Henrich
Schell and Maria Steib.

Dau. of Johannes Krieger and Margaret, b. Jun 25, 1767. Spon:
Abraham Heit and wife.

(The last three baptisms entered by unknown hand.
(There is a break in the record from 1767-1772.)

Hill Church

The following heads of the Lutheran families brought children to
Reve. John Caspaer Stoever to be baptized by him:

Heads of Lutheran Familes

Christoph Labengeirger, 1730
Francis Reynolds, 1732
David Fischer, 1733
Joh. Bindtnagel, 1733
Joh. Georg Ergebrecht, 1733
Martin Mayly, 1724
Joh. Martin Kirchstätter, 1734
Joh. Dietrich Kober, 1734
Peter Ruth, 1735
Joh. Diebi, 1735
Michael Barst, 1735
Peter Kucher, 1736

Christoph Meyer, 1736*
Michael Meyer, 1736
James Stuart, 1737
Heinr. Klein, 1737
James McCnees, 1738
Michael Boltz, 1738
Joh. Albercht Siechele, 1739
Anastasius Uhler, 1739
Peter Heylman, 1739*
Jacob Bentz, 1739
Georg Glassbrenner, 1739
Georg Meyer, 1740*
Adam Heylman, 1740*
Peter Baumbärtner, 1740
Georg Heinr. Peter, 1741*
Joh. Georg Maintzer, 1841
Carl Schally, 1742
Joh. Adam Kittring, 1741/2*
Jacob Frölich, 1742
Jonas Wolff, 1742
William Kally, 1742
Joh. Georg Hädderich, 1743
David Dreher, 1743
Michael Umberger, 1743
Jacob Rüger, 1743
Peter Hädderich, 1743
Joh. Adam Kreuel, 1743
Georg Caspar Rach, 1743
Wilhelm Huber, 1743
Peter Marcker, 1743.

*The names marked with an * are found also in the Reformed record.*

ZION EVANGELICAL LUTHERAN CHURCH, JONESTOWN

Martin of Nicholaus Biehl and Elisabetha, b. Nov 7, 1768; bapt. Dec 12, 1768. Spon: Martin Küffer and wife, Elizabtha.

Margret of Jacob Fisher and Sabine; bapt. May 4, 1784, 4 weeks old. Spon: Jacob Reuch and Gret.

Maria Elisabet of Joh Schwab and Catharine; bapt. May 4, 1783, 10 weeks old. Spon: J. George Goos and wife, M.E.

Johan Friedrich of Caspar Brensighofer, b. Aug 18, 1779; bapt. Aug 26, 1779. Spon: Georg Schaller and wife.

Maria Barbara of Jac. Böshar and Maria Barbara, b. Nov 28, 1780; bapt. Jan 1, 1781. Spon: Jacob Blank and wife Maria Magdalena.

Anna Maria of Henry Firnsler and Juliana, b. Mar 4, 1780; bapt. May 27, 1780. Spon: ----.

Eva Catharina of ----- Fuchs and Susann Margaretha, b. Mar 30, 1780 (?); bapt. May 14, 1780. Spon: Johan Philip Frank and Catharina.

Johan Friedrich of Jacob Kleman, b. Aug 17, 1779; bapt. Aug 18, 1779. Spon: Philip Frank and wife.

Anna Maria of Martin Küfer, b. February 26, 1758; bapt. Mar 4, 1758 [dead]. Spon: Heinrich Tugs (?) and wife.

Johann Friedrich of Martin Küfer, b. Oct 8, 1759; bapt. Oct 14, 1759. Spon: Johan Friedrich Küfer.

Johann Friedrich of Martin Küfer, b. Nov 17, 1763; bapt. Nov 26, 1763. Spon: Casper Hensaler and wife.

Elisabeth of Martin Küfer, b. Jan 6, 1764; bapt. Jan 16, 1764. Spon: Elisabeth Küfer.

Elisabeth of Martin Küfer, b. December 26, 1766; bapt. Jan 8, 1767. Spon: Nicolaus Bill and wife.

Maria Barbara of Martin Küfer, b. Aug 3, 1771; bapt. Aug 20, 1771. Spon: Heinrich Rubs and wife.

Eva Catharina of Martin Küfer, b. December 28, 1773; bapt. Jan 6, 1774. Spon: Kilian Bans (?) and wife.

Maria Catharina of Martin Küfer, b. December 30, 1776; bapt. Jan 10, 1777. Spon: Daniel Stroh and wife.

Johan Martin of Martin Küfer, b. December 13, 1778; bapt. December 26, 1778. Spon: Adam Wild and Elisabeth Tubsin.

Johan Peter of Martin Küfer, b. Jan 6, 1768; bapt. Jan 18, 1768 [dead]. Spon: Peter Küfer and wife.

Johannes of Martin Küfer, b. Jan 6, 1769; bapt. Jan 16, 1769 [dead]. Spon: Johannes Tubbs and wife.

Johan Jacob of Martin Küfer and Elisabeth, b. May 24, 1784; bapt.
Jun 20, 1785. Spon: Johann Gorian (?) and Barbara.
Maria Catharina of Jacob Naes and Maria Margaret, b. Nov 26, 1780;
bapt. Jan 1, 1781. Spon: Christian Selzer and Maria Catharina.
Sophia of Michael Stroh, b. Oct 25, 1779; bapt. Nov 28, 1779. Spon:
Johannes Bruner.
Baptised by Pastor Kurtz:
Annagretha of Herman Mäyer and Ottilia, b. Sep 27, 1786; bapt. May
27, 1787. Spon: Joh. Albrecht and Margretha.
Johan Georg of Peter Dittel and Anna Maria, b. Apr 15, 1787; bapt.
May 27, 1787. Spon: Georg Dittel and Anna Maria Seltzerin.
Michael of Michael Stroh and Eva, b. December 16, 1786; bapt. Jun
10, 1787. Spon: Michael Kreutzer and Barbara.
Catharina of Georg Weber Fröhne, b. Sep 27, 1787; bapt. Nov 4,
1787. Spon: Friedrich Gohna (?) and Sussanna.
Maria Elisabeth of Christian Schaufler and Barbara, b. Aug 20, 1787;
bapt. Nov 24, 1787. Spon: Heinrich Henkel and A. Maria.
Philip of Nicolaus Schäffer and Barbara, b. February 12, 1788; bapt.
Mar 24, 1788. Spon: Philip Schreiber and Maria.
Anna Maria of George Gassert and Christina, b. Mar 13, 1788; bapt.
Mar 24, 1788. Spon: George Gruber and Maria.
Margrethalis of Friedrich Kräutler and Catharinliss, b. Mar 10, 1788;
bapt. Mar 24, 1788. Spon: Johan Peter Weindelble and Gretha.
Abraham of Philip Stein and Susanna, b. Jan 28, 1788; bapt. Mar 30,
1788. Spon: Abraham Stein and Anna Maria.
Benjamin of George Böshar and Barbara, b. Apr 24, 1788; bapt. May
15, 1788. Spon: Jacob Blanck and Magdalena.
Philip Michael of Philip Finckle and Elisabeth, b. Oct 3, 1785; bapt.
Jun 10, 1788. Spon: Michael Stroh and Eva.
Catharina of Philip Finckle and Elisabeth, b. December 27, 1787;
bapt. Jun 10, 1788. Spon: Johannes Hautz and Catharina.
Juliana of Peter Brost and Magdalena, b. May 28, 1788; bapt. Jun 22,
1788. Spon: Juliana Schneiderin.
Sara of Daniel Wendel and Sara, b. May 22, 1788; bapt. Jul 6, 1788.
Spon: Michael Stroh and Eva.
Scharlottia of Abraham Deboi and Magdalena, b. Jul 15, 1788; bapt.
Aug 4, 1788. Spon: Heinrich Henckel and Maria.
Elisabeth Barbara of Ulrich Velten and Elisabeth, b. Jul 4, 1788;
bapt. Aug 4, 1788. Spon: Christian Schaufler and Barbara.
Maria Magdalena of Peter Zimmerman and Magdalena, b. Aug 2,

1788; bapt. Oct 26, 1788. Spon: Peter Böshar and Mar. Magdalena.

Samuel of Heinrich Stein and Elisabeth, b. Nov 15, 1788; bapt. Nov 23, 1788. Spon: George Heilman and A. Maria.

Heinrich of Paul Bien and Magdalena, b. Sep 29, 1788; bapt. December 21, 1788. Spon: Heinrich Jöckle and Barbara.

Margretha of Nicolaus Krähl and Catharina, b. February 8, 1789; bapt. Mar 1, 1789. Spon: Margretha Krählin, widow.

Jacob of George Heilman and A. Maria, b. February 20, 1786; bapt. Mar 26, 1786. Spon: Jacob Dups and Barbara.

Georg of Georg Heilman and A. Maria, b. February 24, 1789; bapt. Mar 29, 1789. Spon: Heinrich Henckel and A. Maria.

Gottfried of Peter Böshar and Magdalena, b. Mar 14, 1789; bapt. Apr 22, 1789. Spon: Gottfried Röhrer and Magdalena.

Maria of Conrad Gelen and wife, b. Mar 5, 1789; bapt. May 10, 1789. Spon: Maria Seidenstricker.

Johann David of Christian Seltzer and Elisabeth, b. May 3, 1789; bapt. May 31, 1789. Spon: Heinrich Henckel and Anna Maria.

Magdalena of Friedrich Böshar and Barbara; bapt. May 31, 1789. Spon: Jacob Clanck and Magdalena.

George of Heinrich Holtzberg and Elisabeth, b. Mar 7, 1789; bapt. Jun 14, 1789. Spon: Georg Roland and Maria.

Johannes of Johannes Schnebli and Catharina Sabina, b. Jan 20, 1789; bapt. Jul 5, 1789. Spon: Peter Fernsler and A. Margretha Gondrum.

Magdalena of Georg Brost and Elisabeth, b. Jun 8, 1789; bapt. Aug 2, 1789. Spon: Magdalena Heberlingin.

Georg of Heinrich Nees and Margretha, b. Jun 6, 1789; bapt. Aug 2, 1789. Spon: Jacob Blanck and Magdalena.

Elisabeth of Heinrich Hess and Elisabeth, b. Jun 23, 1789; bapt. Sep 27, 1789. Spon: Heinrich Zehring and Maria Elisabeth.

Catharina of Philip Stein and Sussanna, b. Oct 23, 1789; bapt. Nov 22, 1789. Spon: Jacob Wild and Catharina.

Catharina of Heinrich Dum(?) and Christina, b. Nov 2, 1789; bapt. Nov 22, 1789. Spon: Johannes Heil and Anna Catharine.

Georg Jacob of Georg Böshar and Barbara, b. Oct 27, 1789; bapt. December 6, 1789. Spon: Jacob Blanck and Magdalena.

Catharina of Christian Lehman and Rosina, b. Oct 19, 1789; bapt. Nov 22, 1789. Spon: Caspar Viehman and Catharina.

Michael of Jacob Cap and Elisabeth, b. Jan 20, 1790; bapt. February 28, 1790. Spon: Peter Böshar and Magdalena.

Johannes of Wilhelm Arentuch and Elisabeth, b. Jan 10, 1790; bapt. Aug 15, 1790. Spon: Valentin Schaufler and Magdalena.

Elisabeth of Heinrich Stein and Elisabeth, b. Aug 7, 1790; bapt. Aug 29, 1790. Spon: Heinrich Dups and Catharina.

Catharina of Jacob Jung and Magdalena, b. Oct 14, 1790; bapt. Mar 27, 1791. Spon: Caspar Vieman and Catharina.

Joh. Heinrich of Georg Heilman and Maria, b. February 21, 1791; bapt. Mar 27, 1791. Spon: Heinrich Henckel and Maria.

Elisabeth of Christian Seltzer and Elisabeth, b. February 25, 1791; bapt. Mar 27, 1791. Spon: Sophia Wildin.

Catharina of Daniel Wagner and Anna Maria, b. February 26, 1791; bapt. Apr 25, 1791. Spon: Caspar Wagener and Catharina Fischerin.

Johann Michael of Georg Brost and Elisabeth, b. Jun 10, 1791; bapt. Jul 17, 1791. Spon: Michael Schädt.

Catharina of Jacob Zimmerman and Magdalena, b. Jun 26, 1791; bapt. Jul 17, 1791. Spon: Jacob Fischer and Sabina.

Johann of Michael Ehler and M. Magdalena, b. Mar 20, 1791; bapt. Aug 12, 1791. Spon: Johann Petri and wife.

Anna Maria of Benjamin Herrnsen and Christina, b. Jun 7, 1791; bapt. Aug 14, 1791. Spon: Johannes Riet and Elisabeth Strohin.

Anna Elisabeth of Heinrich Holsberg and Elisabeth, b. Jun 7, 1791; bapt. Aug 14, 1791. Spon: Johannes Riet and Elisabeth Strohin.

Georg of Philip Stein and Sussanna, b. Aug 11, 1791; bapt. Oct 9, 1791. Spon: Georg Heilman and Anna Maria.

Anna Maria of Johannes Dellinger and Veronica, b. Oct 10, 1791; bapt. Nov 6, 1791. Spon: Anna Mar. Ditzlerin.

Maria Elisabeth of Adam Bart and Catharina, b. Nov 17, 1791; bapt. Apr 9, 1792. Spon: Heinrich Henkel and Anna Maria.

Elisabeth of Jacob Cap and Elisabeth, b. Nov 13, 1792; bapt. Jan 6, 1793. Spon: Gottfried Zimmerman and Anna Maria

Susanna of Philip Stein and Susanna, b. Jan 15, 1793; bapt. Mar 3, 1793. Spon: Jacob Jung and Magdalena.

Gertraut of Caspar Viehman and Catharine, b. Jan 1, 1793; bapt. Jan 21, 1793. Spon: Jacob Wild and Maria Catharina.

Joh. Jacob of Peter Beny and Maria, b. Jul 4, 1793; bapt. Oct 20, 1793. Spon: Joh. Lempel(?) and Magdalena.

Johannes of Henrich Weigand and Elisabeth, b. Jul 26, 1793; bapt. Jul 4, 1793. Spon: Johannes Bickel and Sabina.

Johannes of Jacob Wagner and Elisab, b. Sep 13, 1793; bapt. Nov 7, 1793. Spon: Joh. Vöbler and Elisabeth Theisin.

Martin of Matthes Hess and Rosina at the forge, b. February 4, 1793; bapt. Apr 9, 1793. Spon: Daniel Stroh and wife.

David of Moses Gallan and Cath., b. Oct 2, 1793; bapt. Apr 9, 1793. Spon: Daniel Stroh and wife.

Maria Elisabeth of Adam Barth and Catharina, b. Nov 17, 1792; bapt. Apr 9, 1793. Spon: Henrich Henckel and Anna Maria.

Michael of Lorentz Jaki and Catharina, b. Jan 23, 1793; bapt. Apr 9, 1793. Spon: Christina Meilin.

Salome of Jacob Miesch and Catharina, b. Jan 11, 1793; bapt. Apr 9, 1793. Spon: Joh. Bickel and Sabina.

Anna Maria Elisabet of Johannes Stroh and Susanna, b. February 20, 1793; bapt. Apr 9, 1793. Spon: Henrich Stein and wife.

Lydia of Philip Finckel, b. Jan 30, 1793; bapt. Apr 9, 1793. Spon: Jacob Winter and Magdalena.

Joh. Jacob of Jacob Wagner, b. Sep 12, 1792; bapt. Oct 7, 1792. Spon: Daniel Wagner and Agnes Maria.

Johannes of Matthes Hess and Rosina, b. Jan 26, 1793; bapt. Jul 28, 1793. Spon: Henrich Holtzberg and Elisabet.

Joh. Georg of Christian Schaufler and Barbara, b. Apr 13, 1793; bapt. Aug 11, 1793. Spon: Valentin Schaufler and Magdalena.

Johannes of George Brost and Elisabet, b. Jul 20, 1793; bapt. Aug 25, 1793. Spon: Philip Faber and Magdalena.

Johannes of Jacob Wendling and Anna Maria, b. Sep 22, 1793; bapt. Oct 6, 1793. Spon: Michel Seltzer.

Johannes of Jacob Wendling and Anna Maria, b. Sep 22, 1793; bapt. Oct 7, 1793. Spon: Michel Seltzer.

Susanna of Jacob Wendling and wife, b. Sep 22, 1793; bapt. Oct 7, 1793. Spon: Susanna Wendling.

Elisabet of Wilhelm Frickert; bapt. Oct 6, 1793, 4 weeks old last Tuesday. Spon: --- Helmin.

Jacob of Jacob Fessler; bapt. Oct 6, 1793,   13 weeks old last Tuesday. Spon: Jacob Wendling.

Maria Magdalena of Daniel Herman, b. Sep 29, 1793; bapt. Nov 17, 1793. Spon: Pet Spyker and wife.

Child of Joh. Herman; bapt. December 26, 1793. Spon: Parents.

Johannes of Jacob Zimmerman and Magdalena; bapt. Jan 12, 1794, 4 weeks old last Tuesday. Spon: Christoph Lerch and Anna Maria.

Peter of Johannes Stroh; bapt. Mar 9, 1794, 14 weeks old. Spon: Billy Wood.

Peter of Peter Achebach, b. February 23, 1794; bapt. Mar 20, 1794.

Spon: Henry Henkel and Anna Maria
Child of Henrich Miller and Eva Cath.; bapt. Apr 20, 1794. Spon: Joh.
Jacob Kapp.
Child of Jacob Dubbs; bapt. Apr 20, 1794. Spon: Henrich Hautz and
wife.
Joh. Valentin of Joh. Gärtner and Susanna, b. Jul 27, 1794; bapt. Aug
24, 1794. Spon: Valentin Schaufler and Magdalena.
Michel of Michel Stroh, Jr., b. Mar 7, 1794; bapt. May 31, 1794. Spon:
Parents.
Wilhelm of James McIntosh and Elisabet; bapt. ----, 6 weeks old.
Spon: Daniel Weitel and Sara.
Michel of Michel Schäd and Catharina, b. Aug 6, 1794; bapt. Sep 21,
1794. Spon: Valentin Schaufler and Magdalena.
Michel of Johannes Stähly and Eva, b. Jun 1, 1794; bapt. Sep 21,
1794. Spon: Michel Schäd and Catharine.
Elisabet of Georg Fosbig and Regina; bapt. Sep 21, 1794. Spon:
Catharina Petrin.
Joh. Jacob of Philip Stein and Susanna, b. Sep 18, 1794; bapt. Nov 9,
1794. Spon: Peter Frost and wife.
Joh. Henrich of Uhrich Velte and Elisabet, b. Oct 19, 1794; bapt.
December 25, 1794. Spon: A. Maria Velthin, widow.
Elisabet of Sebastian Velthe and Elisabet, b. Sep 12, 1794; bapt.
December 25, 1794. Spon: Jacob Jung.
Catharina of Daniel Weitel and Sara, b. Nov 26, 1794; bapt. Jan 4,
1795. Spon: Catharine Pickerin(?).
Child of Henrich Stein; bapt. Jan 25, 1795. Spon: Jacob Jung.
Stephan of Stephan Fitterer and Catharine, b. end of Jun, 1787;
bapt. February 19, 1795. Spon: Friedrich Stroh and wife.
Margreta of Stephan Fitterer and Cath., b. February 5, 1792; bapt.
February 19, 1795. Spon: Margret Wirtenberg.
Daniel of Daniel Lehme and Magdal, b. Jan 21, 1795; bapt. February
22, 1795. Spon: Chrisitan Schaufler and Barbara.
Margret of Friedr Homan and Susanna, b. Nov 20, 1794; bapt.
February 28, 1795. Spon: Philip Fösig and Elisabet.
Elisabet of Henry Hehs, b. May 28, 1794; bapt. Mar 8, 1795. Spon:
Martin Meilie and wife.
Elisabet of Matthes Hess and Rosina, b. Nov 1, 1794; bapt. Mar 24,
1795. Spon: Catharine Järling, the man's sister.
Johannes of Johannes Stroh and Susanna, b. Mar 18, 1795; bapt. Apr
30, 1795. Spon: Adam Stöver and wife.

Christoph of Jacob Seiler and Barbara, b. December 26, 1794; bapt. Apr 30, 1795. Spon: Christoph Seiler.

Margret of Georg Dollinger and Christina, b. Jan 9, 1795; bapt. Apr 30, 1795. Spon: Jacob Seiler and wife.

Joh. Georg of Joh. Gerberich and Catharina, b. Mar 21, 1795; bapt. May 3, 1795. Spon: Georg Gärtner and wife.

Jacob of Henrich Winter and Susan, b. Mar 1, 1795; bapt. May 14, 1795. Spon: Joh. Winter and Margret.

Johannes of Nicolaus Angst and Cath., b. Apr 3, 1795; bapt. May 17, 1795. Spon: Baltzer Stein and Elis.

Henrich of Henrich Fischer and Elisabet, b. May 21, 1795; bapt. Jun 14, 1795. Spon: Jacob Fischer and wife.

Johannes of Jacob Lehme, b. Jun 26, 1795; bapt. Jul 12, 1795. Spon: Christian Lehme and Regina.

Johannes of Israel Lang and Rachel, b. February 19, 1795; bapt. May 25, 1795. Spon: Joh. Bickel and Sabina.

Christoph of Catharine Leidich and Christoph Hassinger, b. February 28, 1793; bapt. Jun 14, 1795. Spon: Mother.

Wilhelm of Joh. Buchter and Anna, b. Oct 19, 1794; bapt. Jul 26, 1795. Spon: Daniel Herman and wife.

Maria Magdalena of Georg Böshaar and Magdalen, b. Apr 22, 1795; bapt. Aug 9, 1795. Spon: Barbara Böshaar, the man's sister.

Ana Maria of George Heilman and A. Maria, b. Jul 30, 1795; bapt. Sep 6, 1795. Spon: Heinrich Stein and Elisabet.

Anna Maria of Christian Seltzer and Elisabet, b. Jul 26, 1795; bapt. Sep 6, 1795. Spon: Georg Heilman and A. Maria.

Henrich of Georg Brost, b. Jun 30, 1795; bapt. Oct 4, 1795. Spon: Parents.

William of Peter Rank and Eva, b. Oct 19, 1795; bapt. Nov 1, 1795. Spon: -----

Catharina of Peter Achebach and Catharina, b. Oct 21, 1795; bapt. Nov 15, 1795. Spon: Peter ---.

Catharina of Jacob Titel, b. Oct 5, 1795; bapt. Nov 29, 1795. Spon: Jacob ---.

Joh. Geo. of George Fösig and Rosina, b. Aug 22, 1795; bapt. December 13, 1795. Spon: Petri--- and wife.

David of Jacob Wagner and Elisabeth, b. Oct 9, 1795; bapt. December 27, 1795. Spon: Henrich Titel and A.M.

J. Wilhelm of Christian Shaufler and Barb., b. Aug 13, 1795; bapt. December 27, 1795. Spon: Parents.

Child of Philip Fösig and Elisabet, b. Nov 27, 1795; bapt. February 7, 1796. Spon: Baltzer Stein and wife.

Rosina of Christian Lehme and Elisabet, b. December 14, 1795; bapt. February 7, 1796. Spon: Parents.

Johannes of Albert Uhl and Elisabet, b. December 17, 1795; bapt. February 21, 1796. Spon: Joh. Bickel and Sabina.

M. Magdalena of Michel Schäd and Catharina, b. December 27, 1795; bapt. Mar 20, 1796. Spon: Carl Schäd and wife.

Margret of Jacob Stähly and Margret, b. Jan 15, 1796; bapt. Mar 20, 1796. Spon: Michel Schäd and wife.

Johannes of Jacob Beltz; bapt. Mar 23, 1796, 6 weeks old at Benjamin Clark's place. Spon: Parents.

Child of --- Wendling; bapt. Mar 28, 1796. Spon: Michel Schäd and wife.

Elisabet of Jacob Fisher and Barbara; bapt. May 22, 1796. Spon: Parents.

Sally Sabina of Joh. Winter and Margret, b. May 5, 1796; bapt. Jul 10, 1796. Spon: Joh. Bickel and Sabina.

TRINITY EVANGELICAL LUTHERAN CHURCH
Colebrook, Londonderry Township

Johannes of Jacob Keisel and Anna Maria, b. Jun 30, 1778; bapt. Aug 2, 1778. Spon: Joh. Peter, single and Katharina Conradin.

Margareta of Adam Münchs and Anna Margareta, b. Sep 30, 1778; bapt. Oct 25, 1778. Spon: Mich. Zimmerman, single and Eva Münchin, single.

Johannes of Willhelm Treer and Catharina, b. December 5, 1778; bapt. December 26, 1778. Spon: Johannes Brez and wife Christina.

George Friedr. of Georg Keppert and Catharina, b. Jan 22, 1779; bapt. Mar 7, 1779. Spon: Wilhelm Schmidt and Anna.

Christina of Elias Conrad and Margaretha, b. Jan 13, 1776; bapt. February 13, 1776. Spon: Friedr. Kühner and Margaretha.

Sabina of Elias Conrad and Margaretha, b. Apr 22, 1778; bapt. May 22, 1778. Spon: Friedr. Kühner and Margaretha.

Johannes of Valentin Berger and Elisabeth, b. May 10, 1778; bapt. Jun 10, 1778. Spon: Elias Conrad and wife Margaretha.

Elisabeth of David Hild, Sr. and Elisabeth, b. December 10, 1773; bapt. Mar 28, 1779. Spon: Catharina Lattorin, Adam Bernhardt and wife Christina.

Jacob of David Hild, Sr. and Elisabeth, b. Jul 25, 1771; bapt. Apr 28, 1779. Spon: Catharine Lattorin, Adam Bernhard and Christina.

Benjamin of Ludwig Bender and Elisabeth, b. Apr 5, 1757; bapt. May 4, 1779. Spon: Joh. Brez and Jac. ---, Elders and Phil. Kühner and Mich--- Kopp, Deacons.

Magdalena of Michael Schilein and Magdalena, b. Apr 8, 1779; bapt. May 9, 1779. Spon: Elias Conrad and Margaretha.

Joh. Jacob of Andreas Schell and Sophia, b. Oct 4, 1779; bapt. Mar 19, 1780. Spon: Jac. Bert and wife, Sophia, wife of ---.

Maria Catharina of Abraham Edden and Catharina, b. Mar 4, 1780; bapt. Apr 16, 1780. Spon: David Eddin and Catharine.

Jacob of Val. Heith and Barbara, b. February 2, 1779; bapt. Apr 16, 1780. Spon: Parents.

Johannes of Jacob Miller and Susanna, b. Mar 23, 1780; bapt. Apr 17, 1780. Spon: Parents.

Conrad of Johannes Brez and Christina, b. Apr 16, 1780; bapt. May 14, 1780. Spon: Fried. Kühner and Margaretha.

Joh. George of Michael Schell and Maria, b. Apr 7, 1780; bapt. Jun 11, 1780. Spon: John Petr and Barbara.

Christina Magdalena of Joh. Bender and Dorothea, b. Apr 25, 1780; bapt. Jul 9, 1780. Spon: Christina Kräuserin.

Maria Susanna of Dan Fuhrmann and Christina, b. Sep 27, 1778; bapt. Jul 6, 1780. Spon: Johann Sieber and Mar. Susanna.

Elisabeth of Michl. Veldeberger and Elisabeth, b. Jul 25, 1780; bapt. Sep 3, 1780. Spon: Elias Conrad and Margaretha.

Elizabeth of Andreas Schell and Sophia, b. Jan 14, 1781; bapt. Mar 25, 1781. Spon: Parents.

Michael of Michael Schortz and Elisabeth, b. Jan 21, 1781; bapt. Mar 25, 1781. Spon: Michael Veldeberger and Elisabeth.

Joh. Jacob of Jac. Kuntz and Eva Cathr., b. Mar 14 (or 27), 1781; bapt. Apr 29, 1781. Spon: Henry Kuntz and Mar. Cathr.

Elizabeth of Antony Biehrly and An. Maria, b. Mar 22, 1781; bapt. Apr 29, 1781. Spon: Jacob Miller and Susannah.

Thomas of James Barret and Cathar., b. May 14, 1781; bapt. Jun 23, 1781. Spon: Mother.

Susannah Maria of Martin Weiss and Cathr., b. May 20, 1781; bapt. Jun 24, 1781. Spon: Georg Richter and Cathr.

Johannes of Abraham Ekert and Anna Maria, b. Jun 10, 1766; bapt. soon thereafter. Spon: Johann Deyer and Christina, Friedr. Fortenbacher and An. Maria.

Abraham of Abraham Ekert and Anna Maria, b. Sep 2, 1769; bapt. soon thereafter. Spon: Elisabeth Kühnerin, single.

Elisabeth of Abraham Ekert and Anna Maria, b. Jun 1, 1781; bapt. Jun 24, 1781. Spon: -----

Elias of Elias Conrad and Margaretha, b. Jun 9, 1781; bapt. Jul 15, 1781. Spon: George Keppfert and Catharina.

Jacob of Johannes Schaedel and Salome, b. Aug 1, 1781; bapt. Sep 16, 1781. Spon: Adam Bauer and Elizabeth.

Rosina Barbara of Val. Heith and Cathr., b. Aug 15, 1781; bapt. Sep 16, 1781. Spon: Parents.

Anna Catharine of Christph. Mäuseheldter and Elisabeth, b. Nov 3, 1781; bapt. December 26, 1781. Spon: Margaretha Kühnerin, grandmother.

Simon of John Gould and Marg., b. December 15, 1780; bapt. Jan 6, 1782. Spon: James Fields, single.

Mar. Elis. of Friedr. Gantz and Cathr. Elisabeth, b. December 14, 1780; bapt. Mar 12, 1782. Spon: Father.

George of Freidr. Gantz and Cathr. Elisabeth, b. Jan 29, 1782; bapt. Mar 12, 1782. Spon: Father.

Cathr. of Martin Beker and Cathr., b. February 3, 1782; bapt. Mar 13, 1782. Spon: Barbara Seidenstriker.

Johannes of --- Blak and Cathr., b. February 23, 1782; bapt. Mar 31, 1782. Spon: Martin Weiss.

Johannes of Willm. Crosser and Mary, b. Mar 13, 1782; bapt. Apr 21, 1782. Spon: Parents.

Anna Cathr. of George Kepffert and Cathr., b. Mar 10, 1782; bapt. Apr 21, 1782. Spon: Christoph Mäusehelder and Elisabeth.

Johannes of Benj. Bender and Anna, b. Mar 17, 1782; bapt. May 9, 1782. Spon: Mart. Weiss and Cathr.

Barbara of Andr. Schell and Sophia, b. Mar 13, 1782; bapt. May 9, 1782. Spon: Parents.

Maria of Batrik Kain and Elisabeth, Catholic, b. December 28, 1781; bapt. Jun 9, 1782. Spon: John Schaedel and Salome.

An. Barb. of Phil. Baum and Barbara, b. Apr 23, 1782; bapt. Aug 11, 1782. Spon: George Schank and Susannah.

Joh. Adam of Joh. Schaedel and Salome, b. February 3, 1782; bapt. Aug 11, 1782. Spon: Mar. Elis. Bäuerin, grandmother.

Joseph of Joh. Ruppert and Cathr., b. February 17, 1782; bapt. Aug 11, 1782. Spon: Thomas Connely and Magdl.

Maria Sara of Antony Bührly and Anna Maria, b. Aug 27, 1783; bapt. Sep 20, 1783. Spon: Jacob Müller and Susanna.

Barbara of Valentin Heidt and Catharina, b. Jan 7, 1783; bapt. Nov 2, 1783. Spon: Mother.

Peter of Joh.(?) Blasser and Margaretha, b. December 7, 1783; bapt. Jan 18, 1784. Spon: Johannes Appel.

Michael of Friedr. Gans and Catharina, b. Oct 13, 1783; bapt. May 8, 1784. Spon: Maria Kaisern.

Catharina of Diedrich Schulz and Ana, b. February 29, 1784; bapt. May 8, 1784. Spon: Adam Künert and Catharina.

Catharina of Johannes Appel and Magdalena, b. Apr 25, 1785; bapt. Jun 4, 1785. Spon: Jacob Scheÿer and wife.

Dorothea of Johann German and Barbara, b. Apr 26, 1785; bapt. -----. Spon: Georg German and his wife.

Margaretha of Georg Gepfert and Catharina, b. Jun 26, 1785; bapt. Jul 17, 1785. Spon: Jacob Künert and Margaretha.

Magdalena of Johannes Bretz and Christina, b. Jul 11, 1785; bapt. Aug 19, 1785. Spon: Parents.

David of Johannes Rubert and Catharina, b. Apr 12, 1785; bapt. Aug 19, 1785. Spon: Thomas Gonelÿ and Maria Magdalena.

Maria Margaretha of Friedrich Gans and Catharina, b. Aug 6, 1785; bapt. Sep 17, 1785. Spon: Philip Kaiser.

Heinrich of Heinrich Gepfert and Margaret, b. Aug 25, 1785; bapt. Sep 18, 1785. Spon: Parents.

Susanna of Philip Baum and Barbara, b. Oct 4, 1785; bapt. May 11, 1786. Spon: George Schank and Susanna.

Magdalena of Velte Heid and Catharine, b. Jan 4, 1786; bapt. Jun 24, 1786. Spon: Parents.

Maria Elisabeth of Philip Kaiser and Margaretha, b. May --, 1786; bapt. Jun 25, 1786. Spon: Maria Kaiser.

Esther Regina of Abraham Ittin and Catharine, b. Jul 4, 1786; bapt. -- - --, 1787. Spon: Parents.

Heinerig of Valentin Heid and wife, b. Jun 24, 1787; bapt. Oct 21, 1787. Spon: Parents.

Catherina of Johannes Bender and wife, b. Oct 29, 1786; bapt. Oct 21, 1787. Spon: Susana Millern.

Andton of Andton Bretz and wife, b. Aug 20, 1787; bapt. Nov 12, 1787. Spon: -----

Elisabeta of Heinrich Gödpferd and Margareda, b. December 3, 1787; bapt. December 16, 1787. Spon: -----

Michael of Christoph Meisenholtder and wife, b. February 18, 1788; bapt. Mar 9, 1788. Spon: -----

Maria of Heinrich Gepfert and wife, b. Jan 18, 1798; bapt. February 12, 1798. Spon: Parents.

Christoph of Christoffel Meisenhelder and Elisabeth, b. May 14, 1800; bapt. Jul 21, 1800. Spon: Henrich Rennstohn and wife.

Anna of Heinrich and wife, b. Apr 18, 1800; bapt. Jul 21, 1800. Spon: Christoffel Meisenhalder and wife.

Anna of Henerig Fundersal and wife, b. Apr 7, 1788; bapt. Jun 1, 1788. Spon: -----

Christina of Henerig Fundersal and wife, b. Apr 7, 1788; bapt. Jun 1, 1788. Spon: -----

Gottlieb of --- Meÿer, b. Nov 17, 1787; bapt. Jul 5, 1788. Spon: Wilhelm Meÿer.

Johannes of Abraham Ehtgen and Catharine, b. Jan 4, 1788; bapt. ---- -. Spon: Jacob Bordner.

Görg of Jui Blek and wife, b. Mar 23, 1788; bapt. Jul 6, 1788. Spon: Görg Meiling.

Heinerig of Abraham Göpferd and wife, b. Jun 3, 1788; bapt. Aug 24, 1788. Spon: -----

Friedrich of Friedrich Gans and Cathar. Elisabeth, b. December 22, 1788; bapt. May 24, 1789. Spon: Parents.

Elisabeth of Valentin Heidt and Cathar., b. February 25, 1789; bapt. May 24, 1789. Spon: Parents.

Maria Elisabeth of Johannes Schedel and Salome, b. Jul 7, 1788; bapt. Aug 14, 1789. Spon: Parents.

Maria Magdalena of Mich. Dochterman and Anna, b. Apr --, 1789; bapt. Aug 14, 1789. Spon: Jacob Scheÿer and Magdal.

Ana Maria of Elias Herber and wife, b. May 22, 1794; bapt. May 12, 1794. Spon: Samuel Detweiler and wife.

Maria Magdalena of Dietrich Schulz and Anna, b. Aug 2, 1790; bapt. Oct 19, 1790. Spon: Jacob Scheuer and Magdalena.

Michael of Jacob Scheuer and Magdalena, b. Aug 28, 1790; bapt. Oct 19, 1790. Spon: Dietrich Schulz and Anna.

Anna Maria of Johan Gebel and wife, b. -----; bapt. Oct 20, 1790. Spon: Anna Maria Marzahl, single.

Elizabet of Juÿ Blek and wife, b. May 4, 1794; bapt. Jun 12, 1794. Spon: Jacob Shayer and wife.

Johannes of Johannes Schwach and wife, b. Jan 3, 1794; bapt. Jun 12, 1794. Spon: Johann Sheÿdel and wife.

George of Christoffel Meisenhelder and Barra, b. Jul 1, 1794; bapt. Aug 10, 1794. Spon: George Gepfert and Catarine.

Elisabeth of Henrich Hefflebauer and Markreta, b. Jul 18, 1794; bapt. Aug 9, 1794. Spon: Parents.

Elisabeth of Sim Shreier?) and Maria, b. February 24, 1791; bapt. -----. Spon: -----

Barbara of Heinrich Wundersahl and Elisabeth, b. Mar 21, 1791; bapt. -----. Spon: -----

Philip of Friedrich Gantz and wife, b. Mar 18, 1791; bapt. -----. Spon: Philip Kaiser.

David of Christoffel Meisenhalder and wife, b. Jan 6, 1792; bapt. February 5, 1792. Spon: Henrich Gopffert and Markreta.

Son of Jacob Keiner and wife, b. Jan 7, 1792; bapt. February 5, 1792. Spon: Jacob Möngh and Barra.

Son of Georg Gepfert and Catharina, b. Mar 18, 1792; bapt. May 27, 1792. Spon: Johannes Münch and Christina.

Samuel of Jacob Ruhl and wife, b. --- --, 1793; bapt. Mar 17, 1793. Spon: Jacob Scheyer and wife.

Elisabeth of Friederich Gantz and Catharine, b. Jan 29, 1793; bapt. May 19, 1793. Spon: Adam Münch and Elisabeth.

Margaretha of Jacob Minnig and wife, b. Jul 20, 1793; bapt. Sep 1, 1793. Spon: Jacob Kühner and Margaretha.

Anna Maria of Johann Santer and wife, b. Aug 2, 1793; bapt. Sep 23, 1793. Spon: Adam Mennig and Elisabeth.

Abraham of Abraham Edion and wife, b. February 26, 1794; bapt. Mar 23, 1794. Spon: Jacob Bordner and Eva.

Esther of Heinrich Vendersal and wife, b. Jan 18, 1794; bapt. Mar 23, 1794. Spon: Parents.

Son of George Männig and Elisabeth, b. Sep 25, 1794; bapt. Nov 2, 1794. Spon: Jacob Männig and wife.

Maria of Samuel Bringens and wife, b. Nov 19, 1794; bapt. ------. Spon: Parents.

Petrus of Johannes Männig and Elisabeth, b. December 28, ----; bapt. --- 22, 1794. Spon: Peter Männig and Susana.

Johannes of Johannes Förry and wife, b. Mar 10, 1795; bapt. May 18, 1795. Spon: Johannes Garman and Veronica.

Susanna of George Scheier and wife, b. Nov 27, 1795; bapt. ------. Spon: Mother.

Philip of Christian Gruber and Catharina, b. Jan 1, 1795; bapt. ------. Spon: Johann Männig and Christina.

Anna of Johannes Flori and wife, b. Jan 14, 1795; bapt. ------. Spon: Peter Männig and Susanna.

Barbara of George Göpfert and Catharine, b. Jul 27, 1795; bapt. ------. Spon: Stoffel Meisenhelter and Barbara.

Johannes of Johannes Cenedy and Catharina, b. Mar 21, 1795; bapt. -----. Spon: Stoffel Schenck and Maria.

Catharina of Georg Männig and Elisabeth, b. Nov 11, 1795; bapt. Nov 28, 1795. Spon: Michael Männig and Barbara.

Johannes of Heinrich Göpfert and Margretha, b. Jan 19, 1796; bapt. -----. Spon: Parents.

Rosina of Stoffel Schenck and Maria, b. February 7, 1796; bapt. ------. Parents.

Elisabeth of Peter Männig and Susanna, b. Mar 21, 1796; bapt. May 16, 1796. Spon: Adam Männig and Elisabeth.

Maria of Valentin Heÿt and Catharina, b. Mar 13, 1796; bapt. May 16, 1796. Spon: Parents.

Johannes of Vallentin Bretz and Elisabeth, b. Jul 6, 1796; bapt. Aug 7, 1796. Spon: Johann Bretz and Christina Elisabeth.

Benjamin of Anthony Bretz and Magdalena, b. Jun 17, 1796; bapt. Aug 7, 1796. Spon: Parents.

Jacob of Jacob Kühner and Cathrina, b. Sep 14, 1796; bapt. Sep 30, 1796. Spon: Parents.

Jui of Jui Blek and wife, b. Oct 29, 1797; bapt. -----. Spon: -----

Elisabeth of Jacob Kühner and Catharina, b. Mar 24, 1799; bapt. Apr 25, 1799. Spon: Parents.

Jacob of Jacob Ruhl and wife, b. Nov 3, 1798; bapt. Apr 25, 1799. Spon: Parents.

Jacob of Frederick Gansz and wife, b. Sep 17, 1797; bapt. May 12, 1798. Spon: Parents.

Heinrich of Hannes Schatel and wife, b. Mar 24, 1798; bapt. -----. Spon: Parents.

Polly of Philip Henrich and wife, b. Mar 5, 1795; bapt. -----. Spon: George Grof and wife.

James of Philip Henrich and wife, b. February 19, 1798; bapt. -----. Spon: Hannes Schätel and wife.

Margaret of Heinrich Ramstohn and Anna Maria Schlauchin, b. Jul 8, 1798; bapt. -----. Hannes Schetel and wife.

Salome of George Grof and wife, b. Apr 19, 1799; bapt. Aug 4, 1799. Spon: Hannes Schetel.

Susanna of Peter Männig and Susanna, b. Oct 25, 1799; bapt. Jan 18, 1800. Spon: Peter Geberle and Susanna.

Samuel of Hannes Shetel and Salome, b. Oct 12, 1800; bapt. -----. Spon: Parents.

Anna of Joseph Wolf and Elizabeth Kaiserin, b. Apr 8, 1800; bapt. Apr 17, 1803. Spon: Maria Kaiserin, grandmother.

In the year 1779, May 27, the following were regularly confirmed after previous instruction, and on the 29th of the same went to confession and on the 30th of the same, on Trinity Sunday, were admitted to Holy Communion.

Grown or married persons, men:

Abraham Eddin, aged 24.
Benjamin Bender, aged 22, previously baptized.
Henry Keppfert, aged 20.

Single persons, men:

Johannes Münch, aged 16. Parent: Johannes Münch.
Jacob Miller, aged 15. Parent: Jacob Miller.
Anton Brez, aged 17. Parent: Johannes Brez.
Christian Kummrer, aged 14. Parent: Christian Kümmrer.
Christian Schreier, aged 14. Parent: Friedr. Schreier.
Jacob Groenau, aged 17. Parent: Andr. Groenau.

Grown or married persons, women:

Susanna Siebern
(A person, who already confirmed but without blessing was to
Communion and now, only account of the conscience, this allowed as
a poor sinner.)

Single persons, women:

Susanna Millerin, aged 18. Parent: Jacob.
Mar. Margar. Bresin, aged 15. Parent: Johannes.
Catharina Lenzin, aged 14. Parent: Jacob.
Christina Groffin, aged 14. Parent: Adam.
Elisabeth Kühnerin, aged 16. Parent: Friedr.
Anna Maria Benderin, aged 18. Parent: Johannes.

It was, therefore, a total of 16 persons who were confirmed and
   communed on the above dates
by Pastor Joh. Daniel Schröter, at that time Pastor loci.

In the year 1782, Jun 16, the 3rd Sunday after Trinity the following
persons were confirmed after previous instruction:

Names:Parents:
Catharina Elisabeth Ganzin, aged 22, Fr. Gantz's wife.
Abraham Kepfert, aged 19. Elisabeth Kepfertin.
Christian Schnepper, aged 16, George Schnepper from
Elisabethtown.
Jac. Münch, aged 17, Joh. Münch
Adam Miller, aged 16, Jac. Miller
Phill. Brez., aged 16, Joh. Brez

Marg. Schreierin, aged 15, Friedr. Schreier
Christine Küchlerin, aged 18, Jac. Küchler
Magd. Weissin, aged 16. Mart. Weiss
Elisabeth Fuhrmännin, aged 16, Dan. Fuhrmann
Eleonora Nikin, aged 14, David Niky
Marg. Lanzin, aged 15, Marg. Conradin, widow
Elisabeth Reierin, aged 16, Michl. Reier
Marg. Ewigin, aged 16, Marg. Ewigin, widow
Elis. Faberin, aged 14, Cath. Faberin, widow
Marg. Münchin, aged 16, Joh. Münch

Baptized by Pastor Joh. Daniel Schroter

ZOAR EVANGELICAL LUTHERAN CHURCH
Mount Zion, Bethel Township

Barbara of Johannes Blüek and Barbara, b. -----; bapt. Nov 16, 1794.
Spon: -----
Jacob of Johannes Mayer and Christina, b. Nov 13, 1794; bapt.
December 14, 1794. Spon: Christoph Mayer.
Joh Georg of Michael Wolfarth and Elisabeth, b. February 2, 1795;
bapt. February 22, 1795. Spon: Joh. Georg Lenz and Catharina.
Johan Jacob of Wilhelm Kriegbaum and Mar Catarina, b. Apr 5, 1795;
bapt. Apr 19, 1795. Spon: The parents.
Georg of Friedr Federhoff and Susanna, b. May 3, 1795; bapt. May
17, 1795. Spon: George Hochländer and Elisabeth.
Joh Georg of Peter Hammer and Catarina, b. Apr 25, 1795; bapt. Jun
14, 1795. Spon: Peter Dizler and wife.
Joh Georg of Andreas Weppert and wife, b. May 19, 1795; bapt. Jun
14, 1794. Spon: Melchior Weppert and wife.
Christian of Henr Spannhut and wife, b. Jun 22, 1795; bapt. Aug 9,
1795. Spon: Christian Uhrich.
Catharina of Henr Backstoe and wife, b. Jul 11, 1795; bapt. Aug 9,
1795. Spon: Catarina Riddelsin.
Elisabeth of Martin Walborn and wife, b. Jul 6, 1795; bapt. Aug 9,
1795. Spon: Madlena Deisin.
John of Daniel Duffy and Maria Barbara, b. Oct 17, 1794; bapt. Nov
1, 1795. Spon: Henrich Hautz and Michelsin.
Child of Johan Urich and wife, b. -----; bapt. December 25, 1795.
Spon: -----
Child of Jacob Riddel and wife, b. -----; bapt. December 25, 1795.
Spon: -----
Barbara of Jacob Reifein and Barbara, b. December 7, 1795; bapt.
Jan 24, 1796. Spon: Anna Elisa Reifeinin.
Anna Mar Magdalena of Arnold Hönelmann and Susanna, b. Mar 1,
1795; bapt. February 25, 1796. Spon: Anna Maria Budesin.
Johann Michael of Henrich Germann and wife, b. Jan 29, 1796; bapt.
February 25, 1796. Spon: Johann Michel German.
Elisabeth of Christian Bab and Elisab, b. February 14, 1796; bapt.
Mar 20, 1796. Spon: Christian Luz and wife.
Christian of Joh Geo Lenz and Catarina, b. Mar 8, 1796; bapt. Mar
20, 1796. Spon: Henr Riddel and Barbara.

Joh of Valentin Unger and Anna Mar, b. Mar 14, 1796; bapt. Apr 17, 1796. Spon: Michael Hörner and wife.

Jacob of Henr Häs and Dorothea, b. May 14, 1796; bapt. Jul 10, 1796. Spon: David Miller.

Johnnes of Franz Folz and Anna Mar, b. Jul 25, 1796; bapt. Aug 7, 1796. Spon: Jacob Schmidt.

Johnnes of Peter Ditzler and Maria Margr, b. Jul 19, 1796; bapt. Aug 7, 1796. Spon: Joh Jung.

Barbara of Christian Wolfe and Elizab, b. Jun 30, 1796; bapt. Aug 7, 1796. Spon: John Glüek and wife.

Jacob of Henr Backenstoe and Catar, b. Aug 10, 1796; bapt. Oct 2, 1796. Spon: Jacob Backenstoe.

Johnnes of Henr Riddel and Barbara, b. Sep 7, 1796; bapt. Oct 2, 1796. Spon: Abraham Wolf and wife.

Margretha of Patrick McCiver and Martha, b. February 30, 1796; bapt. Oct 30, 1796. Spon: Parents.

Maria Catarina of Tobias Stöver, Jr. and Mar Catarine, b. Sep 24, 1796; bapt. Nov 6, 1796. Spon: Georg Schäffer and Mar Catarina.

Johnnes of Andreas Weppert and Anna Maria, b. Nov 6, 1796; bapt. Nov 14, 1796. Spon: Michael Hörner, Jr. and Elisabeth Becklesin.

Child of Johannes Glück and Barbara, b. -----; bapt. Nov 27, 1796. Spon: Elisabeth Becklesin.

Susanna of Joh Moll and Susanna, b. December 11, 1796; bapt. Jan 22, 1797. Spon: Eva Walbornin.

Henrich of Martin Walborn and Elisab, b. December 5, 1796; bapt. Jan 22, 1797. Spon: Georg Walborn.

Johan Wendel of Johan Gerhardt and Christina, b. February 13, 1797; bapt. Mar 8, 1797. Spon: Wendel Harz and Catarina.

Johnnes of Johannes Wagner and Margret, b. February 14, 1797; bapt. Mar 19, 1797. Spon: Henr Mäs and Dorothea.

Christina of Henrich Spanhut and wife, b. Mar 29, 1797; bapt. Apr 16, 1797. Spon: Conrad Merkwart and wife.

Johan of Wilhelm Kriegbaum and wife, b. Apr 12, 1797; bapt. Apr 29, 1797. Spon: Parents.

Henrich of Casper Ditzler and wife, b. Apr 8, 1797; bapt. Apr 30, 1797. Spon: Henrich Hautz.

Child of Friederich Federhoff, b. -----; bapt. Apr 30, 1797. Spon: -----

Johannes of Michael Beck and wife, b. February 1, 1797; bapt. May 28, 1797. Spon: Friederich Federhoff and wife.

Catarina of Joh Georg Minjam and wife, b. May 1, 1797; bapt. Jul 23,

1797. Spon: Michael Zerber and wife.

Johnnes of Johannes Uhrich and wife, b. Aug 10, 1797; bapt. Sep 10, 1797. Spon: Christian Uhrich, single.

Peter of Johannes Hammer and wife, b. Jul 18, 1797; bapt. Oct --, 1797. Spon: Peter Bucher and wife.

Johnnes of Henrich German, b. Oct 11, 1797; bapt. Nov 3, 1797. Spon: Valentin Loser.

Child of ----- Weppert, b. -----; bapt. December 10, 1797. Spon: -----.

Mar Magdalena of Tobias Stöver, Jr. and wife, b. Nov 17, 1797; bapt. February 4, 1798. Spon: Peter Taub.

Henrich of Henr Backenstos and wife, b. December 25, 1797; bapt. February 4, 1798. Spon: Christian Walborn and Catharine Hörnerin.

Johnnes of Geo Walborn and wife, b. December 15, 1797; bapt. February 4, 1798. Spon: -----.

A girl of 5 years at Klopp's church baptized (Feb) 15.

Elizabeth of Geo Hochländer and wife, b. Jan 14, 1798; bapt. Apr 1, 1798. Spon: Parents.

Elizabeth of Joshua Swan and wife, b. May 9, 1798; bapt. Jun --, 1798. Spon: Joh Glüek and wife.

Elizabeth of Patrick McIver [McCiver?] and wife, b. May 8, 1798; bapt. Jun --, 1798. Spon: Parents.

Hanna of Christian Leman and wife, b. Jun 17, 1798; bapt. Jul 8, 1798. Spon: Jacob Leman and wife.

Johannes of Johannee Mayer and wife, b. Jun 25, 1798; bapt. Aug --, 1798. Spon: Abraham Diel and wife.

Catarina of Martin Walborn and wife, b. Jun 22, 1798; bapt. Aug --, 1798. Spon: Eva Walbornin.

Michael of Christian Wolf and wife, b. Jul 8, 1798; bapt. Aug --, 1798. Spon: Michael Hörner and Barbara Kilmer.

Barbara of Georg Lentz and wife, b. Aug 2, 1798; bapt. Sep --, 1798. Spon: Barbara Walborn.

Catarina of Wilhelm Arnpriester and wife, b. Aug 27, 1798; bapt. Sep 30, 1798. Spon: Peter Läutner and wife.

Henrich of Henrich Spanhut and wife, b. Aug 24, 1798; bapt. Sep 30, 1798. Spon: Johan Uhrich and wife.

Joh Jacob of Joh Jacob Reifein and wife, b. Sep 5, 1798; bapt. --- --, 1798. Spon: Johan Jacob Rauch and wife.

Child of Jacob Backenstos and wife, b. -----; bapt. February 3, 1799. Spon: Jacob Miller and Eva Miller.

Child of Joseph Thürwächter and wife, b. -----; bapt. --- --, 1799. Spon:

Michael Wolf and wife.

Anna Barbara of Valentine Unger and wife, b. Jan 1, 1799; bapt. February 19, 1799. Spon: Anna Barbara Ungerin.

Johannes of Friederich Hummeldorf and wife, b. February 19, 1799; bapt. Mar 3, 1799. Spon: Johannes Fehler.

Johan Henrich of Johannes Glück and wife, b. Jan 29, 1799; bapt. --- --, 1799. Spon: Friedrich Becklÿ.

Jacob of Peter Ditzler and wife, b. Mar 3, 1799; bapt. Apr 13, 1799. Spon: Jacob Konrad.

Madlena of Joh Hammer and wife, b. Mar 4, 1799; bapt. Apr 14, 1799. Spon: Christian Schuÿ.

Christina of Leonard Noll and wife, b. Mar 30, 1799; bapt. --- --, 1799. Spon: Johan Fehler and wife.

Anna Maria Michael Wolf and wife, b. February 21, 1799; bapt. May - -, 1799. Spon: Joseph Thürwächter and wife.

Jacob of Georg Walborn and wife, b. Apr 5, 1799; bapt. May --, 1799. Spon: Henr Backenstos and wife.

Anna Maria of Andreas Weppert and wife, b. Jul 27, 1799; bapt. Sep 1, 1799. Spon: Christina Hörnerin.

Cristina of Conrad Glück and wife, b. Aug 29, 1799; bapt. Oct --, 1799. Spon: Conrad Markwart and wife.

Johannes of Michael Hoffman and wife, Elizabeth, b. December 1, 1789; bapt. Nov 23, 1799. Spon: Parents.

Jacob of Michael Hoffman and wife, b. February 21, 1794; bapt. Nov 23, 1799. Spon: Parents.

Maria Madlena of Peter Leback and wife, b. -----; bapt. Nov 27, 1799. Spon: Mar Madlena Schallÿ, single.

Cristina of Henrich Backenstos and wife, b. Oct 27, 1799; bapt. December --, 1799. Spon: Catarina Hörnerin.

Elisabeth of Christian Wolf and wife, b. Nov 20, 1799; bapt. December --, 1799. Spon: Cristina Hörnerin.

Gottlieb of Jacob Riddel and wife, b. February 9, 1800; bapt. Apr 27, 1800. Spon: Michael Hörner.

Joh Jacob of Caspar Ditzler and wife, b. February 18, 1800; bapt. Apr 27, 1800. Spon: Joh Jacob Conrad and wife.

Anna Margreta of Christian Koch and wife, b. February 15, 1800; bapt. Apr 27, 1800. Spon: Elisabeth Noll.

Jonathan of Jacob Backenstos and wife, b. Apr 6, 1800; bapt. May --, 1800. Spon: Georg Lens and wife.

Maria Madlena of Martinues Walborn and wife, b. Apr 29, 1800; bapt.

Jun --, 1800. Spon: Barbara Walborn, single.

Eva of Henrich Riddel and wife, b. Aug 11, 1800; bapt. Sep 21, 1800. Spon: Michael Ramler and wife.

Catarina of Johannes Noll and wife, b. Sep 11, 1800; bapt. -----. Spon: Henr Backenstos and wife.

John George of Henry Spannhut and wife, b. Nov 17, 1800; bapt. --- --, 1800. Spon: Johann Georg Lenz and wife.

John Jacob of Henry Spannhut and wife, b. Nov 17, 1800; bapt. --- --, 1800. Spon: Joh Jac. Riddel and wife.

Joh Friederich of Friederich Stover, Jr. and wife, b. February 20, 1800; bapt. Apr 3, 1801. Spon: Tobias Stover, Jr. and wife.

Christian Bab's child, buried 1796.

Johannes of Valentin Unger and wife Anna Maria. Born Mar 14, 1796. Spon: Michael Hörner and wife. Sickness was a blood tumor on the cheek. Aged 16 weeks, 4 days. Buried Jul 10, 1796.

Henrich Hautz, b. 1745 in the month of Sep. Parents were Philip Hautz and Margareta. Baptized and confirmed in the Reform religion. In the year 1769 married Barbara, nee Dubsin, had 12 children, of whom 9 are still alive, 3 sons and 6 daughters. Sickness: coughing and asthma, but at the end a blood vessel burst, which put a sudden end to his life. In the morning healthy and at 10 o'clock forenoon dead on the field. 51 years old. Test Matthew 24, v. 42, Therefore be awake ... Buried Oct 2 at Klopp's Church.

Johannes, little son of Andreas Weppert and wife Ann Mar. born Nov. 6 this year. Baptismal sponsor was Elisab. Becklesin. Sickness: convulsions [Cichter]. 18 days old. Buried Nov 27.

Melchior Ditzler, b. 1726 in the month of Sep; bapt. in the Palatinate. Came to this land in his youthful years. Confirmed. Married first to Magdalena, nee Schaferin, in this marriage they had 2 sons and 1 daughter, who are still living; second he married widow Eva, nee Darbern, in 1763, they had together 5 sons and 6 daughters, of whom 2 sons are dead. Sickness: chill and fever. 70 years, 5 months and 8 days old. Text Ps. 90:9,10. Buried Mar 8, 1797.

Barbara of Joh. Gluck and wife Barbara, b. Oct 23, 1794. Baptismal sponsors Andreas Weppert and wife. Sickness: Asthma (hives). 3 years, 2 months, 10 days old. Phil. 1:21. Buried Jan 5, 1798.

Elisabeth of Andreas Weppert and wife Ann. Mar. born February 25, 1792. Spon: Philip Oberkersh. Sickness: swelling of the throat and asthma. 5 years, 11 months and 7 days old. Text was Hebrews 4:1. Buried Jan 20.

Henrich of Wilhelm Kriegbaum and wife Catarina, b. Apr 12, 1797. Baptismal sponsors were the parents. Sickness, same as the last one. 9 months, 15 days old. 2 Cor. 4:13, 14. Buried Jan 26.

Joh. Wilhelm of Wilhelm Kriegbaum and wife Catar. Sponsors, parents. Sickness, same as the last one, 8 days long. Born May 13, 1793. 4 years, 8 months and 17 days old. Buried February 1.

Jacob of the same. Born Apr 5, 1795. Spon: parents themselves. Sickness, same as the last. 2 years, 10 months and 5 days old. Buried February 12.

Peter of Joh. Hammer and wife. Born Jul 15, 1797; bapt.. 7 months less 5 days old. Buried February 15 at Klopp's Church.

Anna Reifeinin, widow of Adam Reifein, b. 1721 in the Odenwald in Oberkaisbach; bapt., confirmed in Lutheran religion. In 1748 she was married. Had 6 children. Sickness: asthma. 75 years old. Buried Mar 23.

Johannes of Christopher Loser and wife Ann Eva. Born February 10. Spon: Michael Braun and wife. 6 weeks, 3 days old. Buried Mar 29.

Daniel Mattern, b. 1733 in Bethel Township; bapt., confirmed in the Reformed religion, married Anna Elisabeth Krausin in the year 1760. 7 children, of whom only two are alive. Between 64 and 65 years old. Buried Apr 1.

Joh. Heinrich of Henr. Spanhut and wife, b. December 26, 1790. Baptismal Spon: Joh. Philippi. Sickness: Smallpox. 7 years, 4 months and 3 weeks old. Buried May.

Christina Graber, b. in Germany to parents Henrich Feyerbach and wife. Baptized. Came to this land in her sixth year. Confirmed in the Lutheran religion. She married Georg Hartman, had 7 children by him. Married Peter Bohny, had 2 children by him. Married Philip Graber. Sickness: Wasting away (Auzehrun). About 60 years old. Text Isaiah 45:10. Buried Jul 15.

Henrich of Henrich Backenstos and wife Catarina, b. December 25, 1797. Baptismal sponsors were Christian Walborn and Catarina Hornerin. Sickness: convulsions and swollen throat. 1 year, 8 months and 11 days old. Buried Sep 7.

Joh. Tobias of Tobias Stover and wife Catarina, b. May 20, 1794. Spon: the grandparents, Caspar Stover and wife. Sickness consisted of thick throat (mumps?). 5 years, 3 months, and 2 days old. Buried Sep 14.

Michael Wolf of Michael Wolfe and wife Catarina, b. Nov 1, 1783. Sponsors were Michael Horner and wife. Sickness consisted of a thick throat (mumps?). 15 years, 10 months, 2 weeks and 1 day. Buried Sep 17.

Anna Mar. Elisab. Ditzelerin of Johan Ditzler and wife Maria Margreta, b. Sep 5, 1785. Baptismal sponsors were Johannes Stoll and wife. Sickness was dysentery. 14 years and 12 days old. Buried Sep 17.

Margreta of Jacob Seiler and wife Barbara, b. Jul 27, 1796. Baptismal sponsor was Widow Gräbin. Sickness: thick throat (mumps?). 3 years, 3 months and 3 weeks old. Buried Nov 19.

Jacob of Michael Hoffman and wife, b. February 21, 1794. Baptized, parents were the sponsors. Sickness consisted of a thick throat (mumps?). 5 years, 9 months and 5 days old.

Johannes of Johannes Meÿer and wife Christina, b. Jun 13, 1798. Sponsors were Abraham Diel and wife Catarina. Sickness consisted of scarlet fever [Friesel]. Buried Apr 27, 1800.

BINDNAGEL EVANGELICAL LUTHERAN CHURCH

Michael Jr. of Michael Hitsch, Jr. and Elizabeth Franz, m. Jun 3, 1755, b. Oct 30, 1730; bapt. Dec 4, 1732. Spon: Michael Pfantz and wife.

Elizabeth of Michael Hitsch, Jr. and Elizabeth Franz, b. Nov 30, 1757; bapt. Dec --, 1757. Spon: George Wolf and Mary Bergner.

George Michael of Michael Hitsch, Jr. and Elizabeth Franz, b. Jul 7, 1760; bapt. Dec --, 1760. Spon: Michael Weiss and wife.

Catharine of Michael Hitsch, Jr. and Elizabeth Franz, b. Aug 14, 1764; bapt. Aug 19, 1764. Spon: George Wolf and wife Barbara.

John of Michael Hitsch, Jr. and Elizabeth Franz, b. Jan 19, 1767; bapt. Feb 2, 1767. Spon: John Erly and wife Regina.

John Jacob of Michael Hitsch, Jr. and Elizabeth Franz, b. Aug 13, 1769; bapt. Aug 27, 1769, died in infancy. Spon: John Oehrle and wife Regina.

Regina of Michael Hitsch, Jr. and Elizabeth Franz, b. Feb 26, 1772; bapt. Mar 1, 1772. Spon: John Oehrle and wife Regina.

Mary Barbara of Michael Hitsch, Jr. and Elizabeth Franz, b. Jan 8, 1777; bapt. Jan 26, 1777, died in infancy. Spon: John Schnock and wife Anna Mar.

Eve Catharine of George Henry Ziegler and wife Dorothea, b. Jan 17, 1767; bapt. Feb 7, 1767. Spon: John Schnug, Jr. and Hannah Zimmerman (both single).

George Henry of George Henry Ziegler and wife Dorothea, b. Dec 9, 1768; bapt. ----. Spon: John Schnug, Jr. and Hannah Zimmerman (both single).

John of George Henry Ziegler and wife Dorothea, b. Aug 6, 1770; bapt. ----. Spon: John Schnug, Jr. and Hannah Zimmerman (both single).

Christian of George Henry Ziegler and wife Dorothea, b. Dec 1, 1773; bapt. ----. Spon: John Schnug, Sr. and wife Catharine.

Magdalena of George Henry Ziegler and wife Dorothea, b. Jan 12, 1776; bapt. ----. Spon: Andrew Braun and wife Magdalen-.

Anna Christina of George Henry Ziegler and wife Dorothea, b. Nov 15, 1779; bapt. ----. Spon: John Schnug, Sr. and wife Catharine.

Anna Margaret of George Henry Ziegler and wife Dorothea, b. Sep 11, 1784; bapt. ----. Spon: John Schnug, Jr. and wife Anna Margaret.

Ernst Frederic Persoun, under his Royal Majesty in Prussia, b. Aug

12, 1726; bapt. Aug 20, 1726, m. Anna Heckeda on May 24, 1763: Jacob Emanuel of Ernst Frederic Persoun and Anna Heckeda , b. Mar 12, 1764; bapt. ----. Spon: Jacob Braun and wife.

Mary Barbara of Ernst Frederic Persoun and Anna Heckeda, b. Aug 9, 1766; bapt. ----. Spon: George Karmene and wife.

John of Martin Bindnagel and wife, b. Nov 6, 1778; bapt. Oct 31, 1779.

Hannah of Michael Zimmerman and wife Eva Hoenig, b. Jun 15, 1752; bapt. Jun 25, 1752. Spon: Wm. Stoever and wife Margaret.

John of Michael Zimmerman and wife Eva Hoenig, b. April 11, 1756; bapt. April 19, 1756. Spon: John Oehrle and wife Regina.

John Adam of Michael Zimmerman and wife Eva Hoenig, b. Dec 26, 1757; bapt. Dec 26, 1757. Spon: John Oehrle and wife Regina.

Eve Catharine of Michael Zimmerman and wife Eva Hoenig, b. May 9, 1761; bapt. May 20, 1761. Spon: John Oehrle and wife Regina.

Gottfried of Michael Zimmerman and wife Eva Hoenig, b. Dec 15, 1763; bapt. Dec 20, 1763. Spon: John Oehrle and wife Regina.

Mary Elizabeth of Michael Zimmerman and wife Eva Hoenig, b. Aug 11, 1767; bapt. Aug 16, 1767. Spon: Matthew Heess and wife Eva Cathar.

Christian of John Scheible and wife Eve, b. Feb 1, 1775; bapt. April 4, 1784. Spon: John Oehrle and wife Regina.

Conrad of John Scheible and wife Eve, b. Mar 1, 1779; bapt. April 4, 1784. Spon: Martin Binder and wife Mary Elizabeth.

Mary of Anthony Hemperly and wife Juliana, b. Jan 25, 1761; bapt. Feb 10, 1761. Spon: Anthony Blessing and wife.

Rosina of Anthony Hemperly and wife Juliana, b. May 3, 1764; bapt. May 15, 1764. Spon: Frederic Humbel and wife.

Eva of Anthony Hemperly and wife Juliana, b. Oct 2, 1765; bapt. Oct 15, 1764. Spon: Anthony Blessing and wife.

George of Anthony Hemperly and wife Juliana, b. Jul 15, 1767; bapt. Jul 19, 1767. Spon: George Wolf and wife.

Anthony of Anthony Hemperly and wife Juliana, b. Oct 20, 1768; bapt. Nov 1, 1768. Spon: Anthony Blessing and wife.

Catharine of Anthony Hemperly and wife Juliana, b. Mar 13, 1772; bapt. ----. Spon: John Cassel and wife.

Margaret of Theobald Schans and wife Margaret, b. Jun 20, 1782; bapt. Sep 29, 1782. Spon: Margaret Tielman and ---- Schank.

John of John Zimmerman and wife Anna Mary, b. Oct 17, 1767; bapt. Nov 8, 1767. Spon: John Weber and Hannah Zimmerman.

Catharine Elizabeth of John Neu and wife, b. Sep 23, 1782; bapt. Sep 29, 1782. Spon: Peter Neu and Rebecca Karmini (both single).

John George of John Simon and wife Anna Mary, b. Jul 29, 1783; bapt. Aug 13, 1783. Spon: George Walmer and wife.

Christian of Christian Schnug and wife, b. Aug 18, 1740; bapt. Aug 30, 1740. Spon: Christian Kreysfellow and Catharine Bergner.

Catharine of Christian Schnug and wife, b. Feb 1, 1765; bapt. Feb 2, 1765. Spon: Jacob Wolf and Susan Beyer.

Mary Elizabeth of Christian Schnug and wife, b. May 11, 1766; bapt. May 26, 1766. Spon: Frederic Fensler and Elizabeth Kuefer (Kiefer).

Eva Catharine of Christian Schnug and wife, b. Oct 10, 1767; bapt. Oct 11, 1767. Spon: John Schnug and wife Anna Cath.

Susan Margaret of Christian Schnug and wife, b. Jan 13, 1769; bapt. Jan 25, 1769. Spon: John Schnug and Susanna Margaret Bayer.

Anna Christina of Christian Schnug and wife, b. Aug 20, 1770; bapt. Sep 2, 1770. Spon: Christopher Fuchs and wife.

Christian of John Oehrle and wife Susanna, b. Jan 13, 1754. baptized ----. Spon: Eberhart Mathien and wife Jacobin.

John of John Oehrle and second wife Regina, b. Jul 31, 1757; bapt. ----. Spon: Albrecht Sichele and wife Eva. Eliz.

John William of John Oehrle and second wife Regina, b. Aug 10, 1763; bapt. ----. Spon: Michael Zimmerman and wife Eve.

Thomas of John Oehrle and second wife Regina, b. Nov 4, 1767; bapt. ----. Spon: Michael Reichs and wife Elizabeth.

Catharine of John Oehrle and second wife Regina, b. Jul 7, 1772; bapt. ----. Spon: George Peder (Peter) and wife Catharine.

Anna Margaret of John Oehrle and second wife Regina, b. Feb 28, 1779; bapt. ----. Spon: Christopher Ernst and wife Anna Margar.

Mary Barbara of William Neu and wife Julia, b. Jun 9, 1770; bapt. Jun 17, 1770. Spon: John Peter and wife Mary Barbara.

Catharine of William Neu and wife Julia, b. Mar 5, 1772; bapt. Mar 29, 1772. Spon: John Nicolaus and wife Eva Catharine.

Henry of William Neu and wife Julia, b. Nov 6, 1773; bapt. Nov 6, 1773. Spon: Daniel Biel and wife Barbara.

Mary Christina of William Neu and wife Julia, b. Aug 20, 1775; bapt. Sep 6, 1775. Spon: Michael Malfier and Mary Eliz. Neu.

Elizabeth of William Neu and wife Julia, b. May 13, 1777; bapt. May 17, 1777. Spon: John Neu and Catharine Fernsler.

John of William Neu and wife Julia, b. Oct 3, 1779; bapt. Oct 17,

1779. Spon: John Neu and Catharine Schuetz.

Anna Mary of William Neu and wife Julia, b. Dec 6, 1781; bapt. Jan 12, 1782. Spon: John Adam Neu and wife Veronica.

John Fred-- of William Neu and wife Julia, b. Nov 15, 1783; bapt. ----, 1783. Spon: ---- Virnsler and wife Juliana.

Anna Margaret of Joseph Karmene and wife Eva, b. May 15, 1759; bapt. Jun 17, 1759. Spon: Fred. Morell and wife Marg.

Juliana of Joseph Karmene and wife Eva, b. Dec 8, 1761; bapt. Dec 17, 1761. Spon: John Karmeni and wife Juliana.

Catharine Elizabeth of Joseph Karmene and wife Eva, b. Mar 28, 1765; bapt. April 16, 1765. Spon: Henry Dietzel and wife Catharine.

John of Joseph Karmene and wife Eva, b. Jul 2, 1768; bapt. Jul 10, 1768. Spon: Jacob Reisch and wife Margaret.

Susanna of Joseph Karmene and wife Eva, b. Oct 6, 1771; bapt. Oct 22, 1771. Spon: Conrad Reisch and wife Susanna.

Joseph of Joseph Karmene and wife Eva, b. Oct 8, 1773; bapt. Oct 12, 1773. Spon: John Oehrle and wife Regina.

Adam of Joseph Karmene and wife Eva, b. April 2, 1775; bapt. April 25, 1775. Spon: Adam Deininger and wife Rosina.

Jacob of Joseph Karmene and wife Eva, b. Jan 14, 1777; bapt. Jan 26, 1777. Spon: Jacob Reisch and wife.

George of Joseph Karmene and wife Eva, b. Jan 7, 1782; bapt. Jan 19, 1782. Spon: Jacob Kinzel and wife Eliz.

Anthony of Joseph Karmene and wife Eva, b. Dec 31, 1786; bapt. Feb 11, 1787. Spon: Anthony Hemberli and wife Julia.

Andrew of Andrew Vogel and wife Anna Mary, b. Jan 3, 1770; bapt. Jan 11, 1770. Spon: Martin Lange and Joanna Zimmer---, both single.

Elizabeth (born illegitimate after the father's death), b. Oct 20, 1772; bapt. Oct 27, 1772. Spon: Christian Bamberger and wife Eliz.

John of John Wolf Kisner and wife Sabina: John, b. Nov 6, 1778; bapt. Oct 31, 1779. Spon: Martin Bindnagel and wife Mary Eliz.

Eva Catharine of John Schaefer and wife Barbara, b. Oct 21, 1779; bapt. Oct 31, 1779. Spon: George Wolf and wife Barbara.

Mary Catharine of John --- Shereder and wife Anne Barbara, b. Nov 19, 1774; bapt. Dec 17, 1774. Spon: Jacob Bruner and wife.

John of John --- Shereder and wife Anne Barbara, b. Jan 1, 1776; bapt. Jan 29, 1776. Spon: Ad-- Weiss and wife.

John Jacob of John --- Shereder and wife Anne Barbara, b. Sep 24,
1777; bapt. Sep 27, 1777. Spon: Peter Brechbiel and wife.

John Daniel of John --- Shereder and wife Anne Barbara, b. Dec 30,
1779; bapt. Jan 2, 1780. Spon: Jacob Kramer and wife.

Isaac of John --- Shereder and wife Anne Barbara, b. Sep 3, 1782;
bapt. Sep 29, 1782. Spon: Jacob Bruner and wife.

Magdalena of John Oehrle and wife Margaret (Deininger), b. Feb 24,
1778; bapt. Mar 6, 1778. Spon: George Peter and wife.

John Jacob of John Oehrle and wife Margaret (Deininger), b. Dec 12,
1779; bapt. Jan 20, 1780. Spon: John Oehrle and wife Regina.

John William of John Oehrle and wife Margaret (Deininger), b. Mar
5, 1782; bapt. Mar 17, 1782. Spon: Michael Deininger and
Barbara Bindnagel, both single.

Daniel of John Oehrle and wife Margaret (Deininger), b. Feb 9, 1784;
bapt. Mar 7, 1784. Spon: Daniel Wunderly and Regina
Teinninger, both single.

Anna Christina of John Weber and wife Eva Margaretta, b. Feb 26,
1780; bapt. Mar 14, 1780. Spon: Andrew Braun and wife Anna
Christina.

John of John Weber and wife Eva Margaretta, b. April 6, 1781; bapt.
May 5, 1781. Spon: Christopher Braun and wife Anna Mary.

Andrew of John Weber and wife Eva Margaretta, b. Sep 16, 1782;
bapt. Sep 29, 1782. Spon: Andrew Braun and wife Anna
Christina.

Elizabeth of Martin Lange and wife Elizabeth, b. Jun 6, 1772; bapt.
Jun 16, 1772. Spon: Anthony Lange and Eva Catharine
Zimmerman, both single.

Eva Catharine of Martin Lange and wife Elizabeth, b. Oct 5, 1775;
bapt. Oct 20, 1775. Spon: Anthony Lange and Margaret Minnich,
both single.

Margaret of Martin Lange and wife Elizabeth, b. Oct 11, 1777; bapt.
Oct 24, 1777. Spon: Eva Mueller.

Juliana Barbara of Martin Lange and wife Elizabeth, b. Feb 2, 1780;
bapt. Mar 19, 1780. Spon: Anthony Hemperli and wife Juliana.

Christina of Martin Lange and wife Elizabeth, b. Nov 9, 1784; bapt.
Nov 28, 1784. Spon: Michael Botz and wife Veronica.

Jacob of Martin Lange and wife Elizabeth, b. Jul 17, 1791; bapt. at
birth. Spon: Jacob Botz and wife Elizabeth.

Eva Catharine of John Schnock and 1st wife, b. Mar 18, 1773; bapt.

Mar 26, 1773. Spon: John Henry Ziegler and wife Dorothea.
Christina of John Schnock and first wife, b. Dec 13, 1775; bapt. Dec
31, 1775. Spon: John Henry Ziegler and wife Dorothea.
Dorothea of John Schnock and first wife, b. Aug 14, 1776; bapt. Aug
24, 1776. Spon: John Henry Ziegler and wife Dorothea.
John of John Schnock and wife Anna Margaret, b. April 24, 1778;
bapt. ----. Spon: Michael Malvier and wife Mary Eliz. (Bohr).
John Henry of John Schnock and wife Anna Margaret, b. Feb 24,
1780; bapt. Mar 19, 1780. Spon: John Nicolas Bohr and
Catharine Botz, both single.
Anna Margaret of John Schnock and wife Anna Margaret, b. Mar 22,
1782; bapt. Mar 28, 1782. Spon: Peter Neu and Eliz. Bohr, both
single.
Mary Eliz. of John Schnock and wife Anna Margaret, b. Jun 19, 1784;
bapt. Aug 1, 1784. Spon: John Adam ---- and wife Eliz.
Anna Mary of John Fuchs and wife Mary Eliz., b. Feb 15, 1780; bapt.
Mar 26, 1780. Spon: Jacob ---- and wife Anna Ma.
John Jacob of Christopher Ernst and wife Anna Margaret: John
Jacob, b. Dec 5, 1779; bapt. --- 26, 1780. Spon: George Peter and
wife Catharine.
Catharine Eliz. of Jacob Kisner and wife Catharine, b. April 3, 1780;
bapt. May 7, 1780. Spon: Jacob Bauman and Eliz. Bindnagel,
both single.
John Henry of Jacob Kisner and wife Catharine, b. April 26, 1782;
bapt. May 11, 1782. Spon: Henry Kisner and Barbara Bindnagel,
both single.
John of Jacob Kisner and wife Catharine, b. Nov 7, 1785; bapt. Nov
27, 1785. Spon: Wm. Erle and Barbara Bindnagel, both single.
Eva Catharine of Jacob Kisner and wife Catharine, b. Dec 15, 1786;
bapt. Dec 26, 1786. Spon: George Sprecher and wife Eva
Catharine.
John Michael of Michael Botz and wife Fronica (Veronica), b. Jun 22,
1758; bapt. Jul 19, 1758. Spon: Andrew Fuchs and wife Barbara.
Jacob Frederic of Michael Botz and wife Fronica (Veronica), b. Mar 2,
1760; bapt. Mar 23, 1760. Spon: Jacob Botz and Catharine, both
single.
Cath. Sophia and Mary Barbara, twins of Michael Botz and wife
Fronica (Veronica), b. Oct 30, 1761; bapt. Nov 5, 1761. Spon:
Jacob Botz and Cath. Sophia, Michael Hohlender and Barbara
Botz.

John of Michael Botz and wife Fronica (Veronica), b. Nov 6, 1763; bapt. Dec 4, 1763. Spon: Jacob Neu and Cath. Sophia, both single.

George of Michael Botz and wife Fronica (Veronica), b. Nov 19, 1765; bapt. Dec 6, 1765. Spon: George Firnsler and Anna Sabina, both single.

John David of Michael Botz and wife Fronica (Veronica), b. Mar 12, 1768; bapt. Mar 26, 1768. Spon: Michael Botz and Barbara, both single.

John Frederic of Michael Botz and wife Fronica (Veronica), b. Nov 11, 1769; bapt. Nov 20, 1769. Spon: Michael Botz and Barbara, both single.

John Peter (died in infancy) of Michael Botz and wife Fronica (Veronica), b. Oct 18, 1771; bapt. Oct 28, 1771. Spon: John Zimmerman and Eliz. Miller, both single.

Cath. Eliz. of Michael Botz and wife Fronica (Veronica), b. Dec 21, 1772; bapt. Dec 24, 1772. Spon: Michael Hochlaender and wife Catharine.

John Peter of Michael Botz and wife Fronica (Veronica), b. Jan 29, 1775; bapt. Jul 16, 1775. Spon: Michael Hochlaender and wife Catharine.

John Peter of John Michael Botz and wife Eva, b. Dec 7, 1778; bapt. April 15, 1779. Spon: Michael Botz and wife Veronica.

John Jacob of John Michael Botz and wife Eva, b. Jun 23, 1780; bapt. Jul 8, 1780. Spon: Jacob Botz and Cath. Messerschmidt, both single.

Henry of John Michael Botz and wife Eva, b. April 24, 1782; bapt. May 11, 1782. Spon: Henry Mueller and Barbara Botz.

John Michael of John Michael Botz and wife Eva, b. Jul 17, 1783; bapt. Aug 13, 1783. Spon: Valentine Knoz (Knog) and wife.

John Jacob of Andrew Beyer and wife Margaret, b. April 3, 1780; bapt. Jun 4, 1780. Spon: Jacob Botz and Eliz. Wolf.

John Jacob of Andrew Beyer and wife Margaret, b. Feb 6, 1785; bapt. Jun 17, 1785. Spon: Jacob Botz and Eliz. Knoz.

Eva Elizabeth of John Stover (Stoever) and wife Barbara, b. Jun 5, 1780; bapt. Jun 25, 1780. Spon: John. Wm. Ehrli and Eva Wolf, both single.

George of John Stover (Stoever) and wife Barbara, b. Mar 14, 1783; bapt. April 18, 1783. Spon: George Sprecher and Cath. Wolf, both single.

Susanna Mary of John Flueger and wife Eliz., b. Jun 7, 1780; bapt.
Jun 25, 1780. Spon: George Wolf and wife Barbara.

Lewis (Ludwig) of John Flueger and wife Eliz., b. Feb 19, 1784; bapt.
April 16, 1784. Spon: Michael Ili and wife Mary Regina.

Anna Mary of John Flueger and wife Eliz., b. Mar 2, 1786; bapt. Mar
14, 1786. Spon: Michael Ili and wife Mary Regina.

Anna Mary and Magdalene, twins of George Wolf and wife Barbara,
b. Jul 29, 1780; bapt. Aug 17, 1780. Spon: Christina Stiegel,
Jacob Kisner and wife Catharine.

Mary Eve of Andrew Kiefer and wife Mary Eliz., b. Jul 26, 1780;
bapt. Aug 20, 1780. Spon: John Adam Weiss and wife Mary Eve.

Andrew of Andrew Kiefer and wife Mary Eliz., b. Jul 6, 1783; bapt.
Aug 3, 1783. Spon: Andrew Braun and wife.

John William of Andrew Kiefer and wife Mary Eliz., b. Aug 20, 1785;
bapt. Aug 25, 1785. Spon: John Wm. Oehrle and Barbara
Bindnagel, both single.

Susanna of Andrew Kiefer and wife Mary Eliz., b. Dec 7, 1788; bapt.
Jan 11, 1789. Spon: Jacob Sichly and wife.

Christina of Christian Oehrle and wife Eliz., b. Aug 23, 1780; bapt.
Sep 3, 1780. Spon: John Oehrle and wife Regina.

John of Christian Oehrle and wife Eliz., b. Feb 18, 1783; bapt. Mar
23, 1783. Spon: Jacob Sichele and wife.

Anna Catharine of Christian Oehrle and wife Eliz., b. May 13, 1784;
bapt. Jun 27, 1784. Spon: Michael Killinger and wife Cath.

John of Andrew Braun and wife Christina (second wife), b. Nov 5,
1780; bapt. Nov 12, 1780. Spon: John Weber and wife Eva
Margaret.

Andrew of Andrew Braun and wife Christina (second wife), b. ----,
1782; bapt. Mar 23, 1782. Spon: Frederick Lenert and wife.

Anna Margaret of John Nicholas Neu and wife Eva Catharine, b. May
12, 1772; bapt. May 26, 1772. Spon: John Nicholas Neu and wife
Anna Mar.

Christiana of John Nicholas Neu and wife Eva Catharine, b. Sep 22,
1773; bapt. Oct 2, 1773. Spon: Philip Baier and Mary Eliz. Neu,
single.

Mary Cath. of John Nicholas Neu and wife Eva Catharine, b. May 28,
1775; bapt. Jun 12, 1775. Spon: Philip Baier and Mary Eliz. Neu,
single.

John of John Nicholas Neu and wife Eva Catharine, b. Jul 9, 1776;
bapt. Jul 20, 1776. Spon: John Neu and Margaret Bohr.

Philip of John Nicholas Neu and wife Eva Catharine, b. Nov 2, 1778; bapt. Nov 16, 1778. Spon: John Neu and Cath. Schuntz.

Eva Cath. of John Nicholas Neu and wife Eva Catharine, b. Dec 25, 1780; bapt. Jan 7, 1781. Spon: John Neu and Cath. Schuntz.

Christina Barbara of John Nicholas Neu and wife Eva Catharine, b. Feb 1, 1783; bapt. Mar 1, 1783. Spon: Michael Malvier and Barbara Bi---.

John Henry of John Nicholas Neu and wife Eva Catharine, b. Dec 18, 1785; bapt. Feb 1, 1786. Spon: John Schnock and wife.

Anna Mary of John Christian Weisbach and wife Anna Sabina, b. Feb 14, 1781; bapt. Feb 25, 1781. Spon: Christian Vetter and wife Anna Mary.

Anna Cath. of John Christian Weisbach and wife Anna Sabina, b. Jan 11, 1782; bapt. Jul 7, 1782. Spon: Christian Vetter and wife Anna Mary.

John Michael of Adam Zimmerman and wife Eliz., b. Jan 15, 1781; bapt. Mar 25, 1781. Spon: Michael Braun and Eva Cath. Zimmerman.

Elizabeth of Andrew Kraemer and wife Eva Margaretta, b. Jul 10, 1774; bapt. Sep 11, 1774. Spon: Jacob Kiel and Rosina Kraemer.

John of Andrew Kraemer and wife Eva Margaretta, b. Mar 21, 1777; bapt. April 4, 1777. Spon: John Zimmerman and Mary Weber.

Christina of Andrew Kraemer and wife Eva Margaretta, b. Dec 14, 1778; bapt. Jan 20, 1779. Spon: Michael Botz and wife Veronica.

John Michael of Andrew Kraemer and wife Eva Margaretta, b. Oct 28, 1780; bapt. Jan 28, 1781. Spon: Michael Botz and wife Veronica.

Eva Catharine of Andrew Kraemer and wife Eva Margaretta, b. ----, 1782; bapt. Mar 23, 1782. Spon: Valentine Knoz and wife.

Anna Catharine of Daniel Mueller and wife Mary Catharine, b. Aug 8, 1781; bapt. Aug 26, 1781. Spon: Emanuel Shui and Anna Cath. Brunner.

Martin of Daniel Mueller and wife Mary Catharine, b. Jun 4, 1783; bapt. Jun 7, 1783. Spon: Martin Mueller and Eva Cath. Ziegler.

Balthasser of Nicholas Alberdahn (Alberthal) and wife Cath., b. Dec 7, 1781; bapt. Dec 30, 1781. Spon: John Weber and wife Eliz.

Jacob of John Adam Weiss and wife Eva, b. Dec 10, 1781; bapt. Dec 30, 1781. Spon: John Neu and wife Anna Mary.

Anna Cath. of George Michael Brunner and wife Eva Margaretta, b. Dec 18, 1781; bapt. Dec 30, 1781. Spon: Martin Meyer and

Catharine Brunner.

Simeon of Jacob Reisch and wife Margaret, b. Jan 5, 1781; bapt. Feb 29, 1781. Spon: Valentine Sterger and wife Mary Agn--.

John Jacob of Jacob Kinzel and wife Elizabeth, b. Feb 12, 1774; bapt. Feb 27, 1774. Spon: Jacob Hedderich and wife Anna Mar--.

Christian of Jacob Kinzel and wife Elizabeth, b. Nov 23, 1778; bapt. Nov 29, 1778. Spon: Michael Ili and wife Anna Mar--.

John of Jacob Kinzel and wife Elizabeth, b. Sep 13, 1781; bapt. Oct 7, 1781. Spon: Joseph Karmini and wife Eve.

John of Michael Meyer and wife Catharine, b. Jan 13, 1782; bapt. Feb 17, 1782. Spon: Adam Weiss and wife Eva.

Elizabeth of Michael Meyer and wife Catharine, b. ----, 1784; bapt. Jun 27, 1784. Spon: Conrad Meyer and wife Eliz.

Jacob of Jacob Stover (Stoever) and wife Eva, b. Oct 26, 1769; bapt. Nov 11, 1769. Spon: Matthias Hess and wife.

Anna Mary of Jacob Stover (Stoever) and wife Eva, b. Jun 28, 1771; bapt. Jul 10, 1771. Spon: John Schnug and Anna Mary Weber.

Adam of Jacob Stover (Stoever) and wife Eva, b. Jan 23, 1773; bapt. Feb 9, 1773. Spon: Adam Stover and Mary Weber.

Christina of Jacob Stover (Stoever) and wife Eva, b. Nov 26, 1774; bapt. Dec 13, 1774. Spon: John Stober and Christina Stobe-.

John of Jacob Stover (Stoever) and wife Eva, b. Sep 25, 1776; bapt. Oct 3, 1776. Spon: John Stober and Christina Stober.

Margaret of Jacob Stover (Stoever) and wife Eva, b. Nov 2, 1778; bapt. Nov 13, 1778. Spon: George Geistweid and Mary Geistweid.

Valentine of Jacob Stover (Stoever) and wife Eva1, b. April 16, 1780; bapt. May 14, 1780. Spon: George Adam and wife.

Michael of Jacob Stover (Stoever) and wife Eva, b. Mar 14, 1782. Spon: April 5, 1782. Spon: John Stober and wife.

Eva Catharine of John Gerberich and wife Catharine, b. Feb 10, 1782; bapt. Jun 7, 1782. Spon: Henry Schrieber and wife Eva Cat--.

Henry of John Gerberich and wife Catharine, b. Oct 22, 1783; bapt. Aug 1, 1784. Spon: Henry Schrieber and wife Eva Cat--.

Catharine of Jacob Bauman and wife Catharine, b. Jun 28, 1782; bapt. Jul 7, 1782. Spon: Adam Teinninger and Mary Hemperli.

John, b. Feb 6, 1784; bapt. April 3, 1784. Spon: Anthony Hemperli and wife Juliana.

John of Michael Ile and wife Mary Regina, b. Jul 8, 1773; bapt. Jul

24, 1773. Spon: Christian Hekedorn and Mary Weyrick.

Jacob of Michael Ile and wife Mary Regina, b. Mar 4, 1775; bapt. Mar 26, 1775. Spon: Jacob Weyrick and wife.

Elizabeth of Michael Ile and wife Mary Regina, b. Jul 23, 1776; bapt. Aug 12, 1776. Spon: Michael Daniel and wife.

Mary of Michael Ile and wife Mary Regina, b. Sep 6, 1778; bapt. Dec 26, 1778. Spon: Jacob Kitzel (Kinzel) and wife.

Mary Cath. of Michael Ile and wife Mary Regina, b. April 5, 1781; bapt. April 12, 1781. Spon: John Meyer and wife.

Mary Margaret of Michael Ile and wife Mary Regina, b. Jun 12, 1784; bapt. Jun 27, 1784. Spon: Elizabeth Betteliohn.

Christina of Michael Ile and wife Mary Regina, b. Mar 10, 1786; bapt. ----. Spon: John Oehrle and wife.

Twins daughters (no names) of Michael Ile and wife Mary Regina, b. Oct 17, 1787; bapt. Nov 4, 1787. Spon: George Ilinger and wife. John Held and wife.

Susanna of Michael Ili and wife Mary Regina, b. Sep 20, 1789; bapt. Sep 27, 1789. Spon: Jacob Lung and wife Elizabeth.

Michael, b.----; bapt. ----. Spon: Thomas Oehrle.

John George of Valentine Knoz (Knog) and wife Cath. Sophia, b. Oct 25, 1782; bapt. Jan 1, 1783. Spon: John George Knoz and Barbara Botz.

John David of Valentine Knoz (Knog) and wife Cath. Sophia, b. April 19, 1784; bapt. May 17, 1784. Spon: Michael Botz and wife Veronica.

John of John Zimmerman and wife Margaret, b. Jan 28, 1783; bapt. Mar 28, 1783. Spon: Henry Mueller and wife.

Elizabeth of John Zimmerman and wife Margaret, b. May 27, 1781; bapt. Jun 5, 1781. Spon: Henry Mueller and Eliz. Minnich.

Michael of John Zimmerman and wife Margaret, b. Dec 9, 1784; bapt. Jan 4, 1785. Spon: Jacob Sichele and wife Susanna.

Margaret of John Zimmerman and wife Margaret, b. Feb 8, 1788; bapt. Feb 16, 1788. Spon: Dan'l Hufnagel and wife Christina.

John Jacob of John Zimmerman and wife Margaret, b. Oct 19, 1790; bapt. Oct 31, 1790. Spon: Jacob Kraemer and wife Catharine.

Jonas of Jerome (Hiironimus) Hennig and wife Eliz., b. Mar 3, 1783; bapt. Mar 23, 1783. Spon: Jonas Voigt.

Mary Elia. of Jacob Jungman and wife Eliz., b. Nov 13, 1783; bapt. Mar 23, 1783. Spon: Christopher Maurer and wife.

Anna Margaret of George Ramberger and wife Margaret, b. Jan 29,

1782; bapt. Mar 23, 1783. Spon: Casper Stoever and wife.
Catharine of Peter Schmelzer and wife Catharine: John, b. Mar 16,
1783; bapt. Jun 12, 1783. Spon: John Reinhert and wife Eliz.
John Michael of Peter Killinger and wife Christina, b. Jul 1, 1783;
bapt. Jul 6, 1783. Spon: Andrew Killinger and wife Eliz.
Christina of Valentine Steger and wife Agnes, b. Jul 17, 1783; bapt.
Aug 6, 1783. Spon: Jacob Reist and wife.
Mary Christina of Adam Weber and wife Elizabeth, b. Sep 21, 1783;
bapt. Oct 17, 1783. Spon: Daniel Hufnagel and Christina
Minnich.
Jacob of Adam Weber and wife Elizabeth, b. Dec 25, 1785; bapt. Feb
19, 1786. Spon: Stoffel Miller and Rosina Muecnh.
Catharine of Michael Stucki and wife Elizabeth, b. Jan 13, 1781; bapt.
Jan 28, 1781. Spon: Peter Neu and Cath. Virnsler.
John Michael of Michael Stucki and wife Elizabeth, b. Sep 27, 1783;
bapt. Nov 16, 1783. Spon: George Sprecher and Cath. Huber.
John Jacob of Henry Hertzler and wife Barbara, b. Sep 30, 1783;
bapt. Nov 16, 1783. Spon: John Jacob Hertzler and Margaret
Sprecher.
John Michael of Gottlieb Neuman and wife Joanna Augusta, b. Nov
17, 1783; bapt. Dec 25, 1783. Spon: Michael and wife.
Barbara of Peter Neu and wife Rebecca, b. Oct 4, 1783; bapt. Oct 18,
1783. Spon: Barbara Neu.
John of Peter Neu and wife Rebecca, b. Jan 27, 1785; bapt. Mar 27,
1785. Spon: John Neu and wife Catharine.
John Weber of Peter Neu and wife Rebecca, b. Mar 27, 1787; bapt.
Nov 18, 1787. Spon: Michael Neu and Barbara Biclinson.
A son (name not given) of Peter Neu and wife Rebecca, b. ----, 1791;
bapt. ----. Spon: Adam Biele and wife.
Benjamin of Jacob Sichele and wife Susanna, b. Nov 22, 1777; bapt.
Mar 4, 1778. Spon: John Zimmerman and Margaret Minnic.
Catharine of Jacob Sichele and wife Susanna, b. Jun 28, 1779; bapt.
Jul 4, 1779. Spon: George Peter and wife.
Elizabeth of Jacob Sichele and wife Susanna, b. Oct 7, 1781; bapt.
Oct 20, 1781. Spon: Dan'l Wunderlig and wife.
Magdalena of Jacob Sichele and wife Susanna, b. Nov 6, 1783; bapt.
Dec 11, 1783. Spon: Catharine Minnich.
Catharine Eliz. of John Wolf and wife Elizabeth, b. Jan 6, 1784; bapt.
Jan 11, 1784. Spon: Andrew Braun and wife.
Anna Cath. of Michael Braun and wife Christina, b. Jan 21, 1784;

Anna Cath. of Michael Braun and wife Christina, b. Jan 21, 1784;
bapt. Mar 7, 1784. Spon: Michael Braun and wife.

Elizabeth of Jacob Botz and wife Elizabeth, b. Jan 14, 1784; bapt.
Mar 7, 1784. Spon: John Botz and Christina Virnsler.

John Frederic of Andrew Killinger and wife Eliz., b. Mar 27, 1784;
bapt. Sep 16, 1784. Spon: Frederic Bickel and wife Dorothea.

John Henry of Henry Schell and wife Dorothea, b. Mar 13, 1784;
bapt. May 17, 1784. Spon: Martin Bindnagel and wife Mary El--.

Mary Eliz. of Adam Wirth and wife Elizabeth., b. May 8, 1784; bapt.
May 29, 1784. Spon: John Schnug and wife Anna Margaret.

John of Jacob Jung and wife Magdalena, b. May 15, 1784; bapt. Aug
1, 1784. Spon: John Reinhert and wife Eliz.

Elizabeth of Michael Noulan and wife Peggi (Margaret), b. Aug 30,
1782; bapt. Sep 26, ----. Spon: The Parents.

Henry of Michael Noulan and wife Peggi (Margaret), b. Jun 11, 1784;
bapt. Sep 26, ----. Spon: John Oehrle and wife Eliz.

Jacob of Daniel Hufnagel and wife Christina, b. Nov 22, 1784; bapt.
Jan 8, 1785. Spon: John Adam Weber and Eliz. Minnich, single.

Mary Barbara of Peter Neu and wife Juliana, b. Jan 17, 1785; bapt.
Mar 13, 1785. Spon: Joseph Carmini and wife Eva.

John Jacob of Jacob Kraemer and wife Catharine, b. Mar 2, 1785;
bapt. Jun 12, 1785. Spon: John Zimmerman and wife Margaret.

Peter of Jacob Kraemer and wife Catharine, b. Jun 18, 1790; bapt.
Aug 29, 1790. Spon: Adam Weber and wife Eliz.

John George of Jacob Kraemer and wife Catharine, b. Nov 9, 1787;
bapt. Jun 8, 1788. Spon: John George Minnich and Gredless
(Margaret) Brechbiel.

John George of George Wolf and wife Barbara, b. Jan 26, 1785; bapt.
Sep 23, 1785. Spon: John Flueger and wife Eliz.

Christopher of Christopher Fuchs and wife Susanna Margaretta, May
30, 1785; bapt. Aug --, 1785. Spon: Jacob Kraemer and wife Anna
Cath.

Catharine of John Wolf and wife Elizabeth, b. Sep 13, 1785; bapt. Sep
25, 1785. Spon: Conrad Tielman and Catharine Wolf.

Christina of John Adam Deininger and wife Rosina, b. Feb 17, 1755;
bapt. ----. Spon: John Oehrli and wife Regina.

Margaret of John Adam Deininger and wife Rosina, b. Jan 1, 1758;
bapt. ----. Spon: Michael Keiner and wife Margar--.

John Adam Jr. of John Adam Deininger and wife Rosina, b. Oct 12,
1760; bapt. ----. (John Adam Sr. and John Adam Jr. known as

Michael of John Adam Deininger and wife Rosina, b. Nov 17, 1763; bapt. ----. Spon: Nicolas Brechbiel and wife Julian--.

Regina of John Adam Deininger and wife Rosina, b. Feb 26, 1766; bapt. ----. Spon: John Oehrli and wife Regina.

Susanna of John Adam Deininger and wife Rosina, b. Feb 5, 1769; bapt. ----. Spon: John Oehrli and wife Regina.

John of John Adam Deininger and wife Rosina, b. Jan 1, 1772; bapt. - ---. Spon: John Oehrli and wife Regina.

John of Nicholas Palm and wife Catharine, b. Mar 2, 17--; bapt. April 14, 17--. Spon: John Palm and wife Eliz.

George of Adam Berger and wife, b. Mar 5, 1790; bapt. Jun 27, 1790. Spon: George Sprecher and wife Catharine.

Magdalene of Adam Berger and wife, b. Jan 1, 1792; bapt. Jan 8, 1792. Spon: John Oehrli and wife Regina.

Magdalena of Christian Ramberger and wife Magdalena, b. Jun 12, 1769; bapt. Sep 28, 1769.

John of Christian Ramberger and wife Magdalena, b. Feb 26, 1772; bapt. Mar 3, 1772.

Christina of Christian Ramberger and wife Magdalena, b. Jan 8, 1774; bapt. Sep 24, 1774.

Michael of Christian Ramberger and wife Magdalena, b. Jan 1, 1776; bapt. Sep 30, 1776.

Anna of Christian Ramberger and wife Magdalena, b. Jan 2, 1778; bapt. Sep 2, 1778.

Catharine of Christian Ramberger and wife Magdalena, b. Mar 17, 1779; bapt. Sep 30, 1779.

William of Christian Ramberger and wife Magdalena, b. Feb 8, 1783; bapt. Sep 30, 1783.

Jacob of Philip Johannes (John) and wife, b. Sep 25, 1791; bapt. Oct 30, 1791. Spon: John Schui and wife.

Christina of Philip Johannes (John) and wife, b. Sep 27, 1793; bapt. Oct 27, 1793. Spon: Conrad Mayer and wife.

Margaret of George Sprecher and wife, b. Jan 26, 1791; bapt. Mar 6, 1791. Spon: Margaret Sprecher.

Elizabeth of Jacob Kamp and wife, b. Mar 20, 1795; bapt. May 3, 1795. Spon: Thomas Fernsler and ----.

John, Conrad Wolf and wife Eliz., 9 months old; bapt. May 3, 1795. Spon: John Wolfersberger and ----.

Frederic of Henry Goetz and wife, b. Feb 4, 1795; bapt. May 8, 1795. Spon: Frederic Wolfersberger and ----.

Spon: Frederic Wolfersberger and ----.

Adam of Jacob Bischof and wife Eliz., b. Feb 26, 1795; bapt. May 8, 1795. Spon: Peter Eisenhaur and Miss Molly Oehr--.

Jacob of Peter Faernsler and wife Susanna, b. April 12, 1795; bapt. May 3, 1795. Spon: Joseph Carmini.

Elizabeth of Peter Neu (Ney) and wife Rebecca, b. Jan 20, 1795; bapt. May 23, 1795. Spon: Christian Hawerter and wife.

Catharine of Jacob Hofnagel and wife, b. May 3, 1795; bapt. May 23, 1795. Spon: Jacob Kraemer and wife.

John of Ger. Munch and wife, b. Jan 13, 1795; bapt. May 23, 1795. Spon: Jacob Hofnagel and wife.

Eliz. of Frederic Faernsler and wife, 4 weeks old; bapt. May 23, 1795. Spon: Mrs. Christian ----.

George of Jacob Heims and wife Eliz., b. April 23, 1795; bapt. Jun 28, 1795. Spon: Jacob Bauman and wife Mary.

George of Martin Lang and wife Eliz., b. Nov 19, 1794; bapt. Nov 30, 1794. Spon: Gottfried Zimmerman and wife.

Daniel of John Pflueger and wife Eliz., b. Sep 20, 1794; bapt. Nov 30, 1794. Spon: Daniel Held and wife.

Christina of Christian Ehrly and wife Eliz., b. Jan 1, 1795; bapt. Feb 8, 1795. Spon: Conrad Meyer and wife.

John of Simon Gutman and wife Christina, b. Dec 21, 1794; bapt. Feb 8, 1795. Spon: John Jacob Sichely and wife.

Catharine of Leonard Doll and wife Catharine, b. Jan 11, 1795; bapt. Feb 8, 1795. Spon: Michael Zeller and wife.

George of Peter Killinger and wife Christina, b. ----; bapt. Feb 8, 1795. Spon: Thomas Ehrly and wife Sabina.

Sabina of Jacob Kissner and wife Catharine, b. Feb 11, 1795; bapt. April 6, 1795. Spon: John Oehrly and wife Margaret.

Magdalena of John Deininger and wife Christina, b. Mar 21, 1795; bapt. April 6, 1795. Spon: John Oehrly and wife Margaret.

Catharine of John Sander and wife Anna Mary, b. May 24, 1795; bapt. Jun 28, 1795. Spon: David Hufnagel and wife.

John of Gottfried Zimmerman and wife, b. Jun 5, 1795; bapt. Jun 28, 1795. Spon: Martin Carmini and wife Cath.

Margaret, illegitimate daughter of ---- Deitrich (mother), b. ----; bapt. Jun 28, 1795. Spon: Mrs. Ehrly (widow of John Sr.)

Catharine of Adam Graemer and wife Barbara, b. May 21, 1795; bapt. Jul 25, 1795. Spon: Mrs. Barbara Eile.

Peter of Joseph Hedrich and wife Cath., b. Dec 10, 1794; bapt. Aug 7,

1795. Spon: Mrs. Eliz. Bickel.

Catharine of Henry Baumgaertner and wife Eliz., b. Jul 6, 1795; bapt. Aug 23, 1795. Spon: Jacob Meyer and Mrs. Cath. Kraemer.

Salome of Matthew Bor and wife Eliz., b. Aug 21, 1795; bapt. Sep 20, 1795. Spon: John George Schneider and wife Cath.

John of George Walmer and wife Barbara, b. Dec 11, 1794; bapt. Nov 15, 1795. Spon: George Sprecher and wife.

Jacob of Jacob Lenz and wife Eliz., b. Oct 19, 1795; bapt. Oct 19, 1795. Spon: Thomas Oehrly and wife Sabina.

Elizabeth of Philip Maegtling and wife Cath., b. Aug 10, 1795; bapt. Dec 12, 1795. Spon: John Zering and wife Eliz.

Catharine of Peter Seyfret and wife, b. Nov 7, 1795; bapt. Dec 13, 1795. Spon: John Reinhart and wife.

Rosina of Michael Deininger and wife Anna Mary, b. Sep 30, 1795; bapt. Dec 27, 1795. Spon: John Killinger and wife.

Magdalene of Adam Schmelzer and wife Magdalene, b. Dec 22, 1795; bapt. Feb 7, 1796. Spon: Jacob Steinman.

Salome of John Deininger and wife Eliz., b. Dec 15, 1795; bapt. Mar 6, 1796. Spon: Michael Deininger and wife Mary.

Christina of Simon Gutman and wife Christina, b. Jan 23, 1795; bapt. Jan 23, 1795. Spon: Hury Peter and wife Christina.

Frederic of John Kl-ger and wife Margaret, b. Aug 2, 179-; bapt. ----. Spon: The Father.

John of Leonard Doll and wife Cath., b. Mar 22, 1796; bapt. Mar 28, 1796. Spon: Mrs. Regina Oehrle.

Anna Christina of Frederic Biely and wife Christina, b. Aug 25, 1795; bapt. Mar 28, 1796. Spon: Adam Biely and Eliz. Fernsler.

Susanna of Michael Leidig and wife, b. Jan 19, 1795 (?); bapt. Mar 28, 1796. Spon: Jacob Steinman and wife.

John of Christian Schulz and wife Sarah, b. Feb 29, 1796; bapt. May 1, 1796. Spon: George Berger and Magdalene (Lens or Sens).

John of Abram. Walter and wife Barbara, b. Mar 5, 1796; bapt. May 1, 1796. Spon: Adam Biel and Eliz. Fernsler.

John of John Carmini and wife Eliz., b. Feb 1, 1796; bapt. May 1, 1796. Spon: The Parents.

John of Thomas Lutin and wife Rebecca, b. Jan 28, 1796; bapt. May 1, 1796. Spon: Christian Selser and wife Barbara.

Catharine of John Maulfuer and wife Margaret, b. Nov 5, 1795; bapt. May 1, 1796. Spon: Jacob Frans and wife Cath.

John Martin of Philip Johannes and wife Cath., b. Mar 19, 1796;

bapt. May 1, 1796. Spon: George Walmer and wife.

George of Jacob Gutman and wife Cath., b. May 19, 1795; bapt. May 29, 1795. Spon: Francis Fuchs and Margaret Lang.

John Henry of John Albrecht and wife Margaret, b. May 13, 1795; bapt. Jun 26, 1795. Spon: Henry Ziegler and wife.

John of George Ramberger and wife Margaret, b. Jul 2, 1795; bapt. Jul 24, 1795. Spon: Casper Stoever and wife.

Mary Magdalene, illegitimate daughter of John Nimian and ---- Schmelzer, b. Jun 10, 1795; bapt. Jul 24, 1795. Spon: Magdalene Schmelzer.

Conrad of Jacob Steinman and wife Barbara, b. May 21, 1795; bapt. Aug 21, 1795. Spon: Conrad Meyer and wife Eliz.

Elizabeth of Jacob Bauman and wife Mary, b. Aug 7, 1795; bapt. Aug 21, 1795. Spon: Michael Zeller and Magdalene William.

Catharine of Adam Barth and wife Cath., b. Jun 18, 1796; bapt. Aug 21, 1796. Spon: Gottfried Zimmerman and wife Anna Mar.

George, illegitimate son of George Berger and Juliana Jung, b. Sep 14, 1796; bapt. Oct 18, 1796. Spon: Thomas Oehrly and wife.

Christina of John Zimmerman and wife Margaret, b. Sep 29, 1796; bapt. Nov 13, 1796. Spon: Christopher Miller and wife Rosina.

Elizabeth, illegitimate daughter of Catharine Baumgeartner, b. Jul 8, 1796; bapt. Jan 8, 1797. Spon: George Sprecher and wife Cath.

Anna Mary of Henry Miller and wife Cath., b. Nov 25, 1796; bapt. Feb 5, 1797. Spon: Tobias Stoever and wife Hannah.

Elizabeth of Henry Fuchs and wife Margaret, b. Dec 23, 1796; bapt. Feb 5, 1797. Spon: Martin Lang and wife.

John of John Maulfuer and wife Margaret, b. Dec 23, 1796; bapt. Mar 5, 1797. Spon: Conrad Meyer and ----.

Andrew of Andrew Palm and wife, b. Jan 25, 1797; bapt. Mar 5, 1797. Spon: Jacob Bauman and wife.

David of John Adam Deininger and Christina, b. Feb 18, 1797; bapt. Mar 5, 1797. Spon: The Parents.

Margaret of Adam Kraemer and wife Barbara, b. Dec 11, 1796; bapt. Jan --, 1797. Spon: Jacob Jung and wife.

Samuel of Nicholas Neu and wife Eva Cath., b. Feb 15, 1797; bapt. April 2, 1797. Spon: Martin Lang and wife.

Mary Margaret of John Pflueger and wife, b. Feb 7, 1797; bapt. April 2, 1797. Spon: Frederic Fernsler and wife.

Michael of Gottfried Zimmerman and wife, b. April 5, 1797; bapt. April 14, 1797. Spon: Adam Barth and wife.

Jacob of Valentine Hofnagel and wife Eve, b. Nov 30, 1796; bapt.
April 14, 1797. Spon: Jacob Backenstos and wife Barbara.

William of John Saunders and wife, b. Dec 21, 1796; bapt. April 14,
1797. Spon: John Gasser and wife.

John of Frederic Becker and wife, b. April 10, 1797; bapt. May 14,
1797. Spon: Jacob Hufnagel and wife.

Jacob of Christian Oehrly and wife, b. April 5, 1797; bapt. May 14,
1797. Spon: Conrad Mayer and wife.

Leonard of John Neu and wife, b. Mar 30, 1797; bapt. May 14, 1797.
Spon: Christian Howerter and wife.

John of George Sprecher and wife, b. May 15, 1797; bapt. Jul 9, 1797.
Spon: Michael Stucky and wife.

John Jacob of Jacob Kuper and wife, b. May 30, 1797; bapt. Jul 9,
1797. Spon: Conrad Mayer and wife.

Anna Mary of John Scheirich and wife, b. May 20, 1797; bapt. Jul 9,
1797. Spon: Christian Hepting and wife.

John George of John George Frey and wife, b. Jan 20, 1797; bapt. Jul
9, 1797. Spon: Thomas Oehrly and wife.

Regina of Peter Eisenhawer and wife, b. Aug 7, 1797; bapt. Aug 23,
1797. Spon: Regina Oehrly, widow.

John Henry of Peter Neu and wife, b. Jul 22, 1797; bapt. Sep 3, 1797.
Spon: John Schnock and wife.

Anna Magdalene of Abraham Walmer and wife, b. Jun 17, 1797; bapt.
Sep 3, 1797. Spon: Magdalene Fernsler, widow.

Eliz. of Ludwig (Louis) Gruber and wife, b. Mar 9, 1797; bapt. Oct 1,
1797. Spon: Peter Neu and wife.

John of Philip Mechlin and wife Magdalene, b. May 18, 1795; bapt.
Oct 1, 1795. Spon: John Nichol Alberthal and wife.

Eliz. of Michael Heissee (Heisse) and wife, b. Oct 5, 1797; bapt. Oct
29, 1797. Spon: John Adam Biele and wife.

Mary Eliz. of Philip Johannes and wife, b. Oct 29, 1797; bapt. Nov 26,
1797. Spon: Andrew Kiefer and wife.

Jacob of Jacob Hofnagel and wife, b. Sep 23, 1797; bapt. Nov 26,
1797. Spon: John Zimmerman. (Another one, may have been a
twin.)

Elizabeth of Adam Schally and wife, b. Oct 29, 1797; bapt. Dec 25,
1797. Spon: Frederic Gutman and wife.

John Michael of Michael Deininger and wife, b. Nov 25, 1797; bapt.
Dec 25, 1797. Spon: Michael Killinger and wife.

John of Jacob Gutman and wife, b. Jan 4, 1798; bapt. Jan 21, 1798.

Spon: Thomas Oehrly and wife.

Susanna of John Heob (Job) and wife, b. Jan --, 1798, bapt. Feb 18, 1798. Spon: Valentine Hufnagel and wife.

----, child of ----, b. --; bapt. --. Spon: John Neu and wife.

Catharine of William Reuter and wife, b. Feb 13, 1798; bapt. Mar --, 1798. Spon: Juliana Fortner.

John George of John Deininger and wife, b. Dec 30, 1797; bapt. April --, 1798. Spon: Conrad Mayer and wife.

Andre, illegitimate son of Andrew Killinger and Eve Cath. Schnock, b. Feb 18, 1798; bapt. April --, 1798. Spon: John Gutman and wife.

John Jacob of ---- Coral, 8 years of age; bapt. April 29, 1798. Spon: Conrad Meyer.

Max-- Eliphas, illegitimate son of Margaret Neu, b. Dec 7, 1797; bapt. ----, 1798. Spon: Eve Cath. Neu.

Jacob of Conrad Doll and wife, b. Jun 14, 1797; bapt. May 24, 1798. Spon: Jacob Bauman and wife.

Sabina of George Frey and wife, b. May 13, 1798; bapt. May 24, 1798. Spon: Thomas Ohrly and wife.

Rebecca of Daniel Schuy and wife, b. May 16, 1798; bapt. Jul --, 1798. Spon: John Schuy and wife.

Peter of Nicholas Alberthal and wife, b. Jun 22, 1798; bapt. Jul 29, 1798. Spon: Jacob Faehrling and wife.

Jacob of Frederic Duy and wife, b. Mar 1, 1798; bapt. Jul 29, 1798. Spon: Jacob Hofnagel and wife.

Charlotte of Ludwig Gruber and wife, b. April 23, 1798; bapt. Jul 23, 1798. Spon: Jacob Sichely and wife.

Christian, child of Wm. McElwee and wife, b. April 1, 1798; bapt. Jul 23, 1798. Spon: Thomas Oehrly and wife.

William of Jacob Lentz and wife, b. Jul 4, 1798; bapt. Aug --, 1798. Spon: Christian Oehrly and wife.

David of John Ernst and wife, b. Jul 1, 1798; bapt. Aug --, 1798. Spon: Thomas Oehrly and wife.

Jacob of Henry Miller and wife, b. Aug 8, 1798; bapt. Aug --, 1798. Spon: Jacob Kapp and wife.

Henry of Joseph Hetrich and wife, b. Jul 8, 1798; bapt. Aug --, 1798. Spon: Franz Boehler and wife.

Jacob of Jacob Ellinger and wife, b. Feb 1, 1798; bapt. Oct 28, 1798. Spon: John Roessly and wife.

Susanna of Michael Lenich and wife, b. Sep 26, 1798; bapt. Oct 14, 1798. Spon: Henry Leman and wife.

Anna Margaret of John Albrecht and wife, b. Aug 11, 1798; bapt. Oct 14, 1798. Spon: Barbara Alberthal.

Jacob of Peter Kunz and wife, b. Oct 24, 1798; bapt. Nov 10, 1798. Spon: Jacob Kitzmiller and wife.

John of Henry Baumgartner and wife, b. Aug 25, 1798; bapt. Nov 10, 1798. Spon: George Sprecher and wife.

John George of George Miller and wife, b. ----, Dec 26, 1798. Spon: John Adam Miller and wife.

Jacob of Gottfried Zimmerman and wife, b. Nov 12, 1798; bapt. Dec 26, 1798. Spon: Jacob Kapp.

David of Valentine Bolten and wife, b. Nov 6, 1798; bapt. Dec 26, 1798. Spon: Henry Ziegler.

John of Jacob Rauch and wife, b. Oct 20, 1798; bapt. Jan 28, 1799. Spon: John Zering.

Thomas of Jacob Bauman and wife, b. Jan 15, 1799; bapt. Jan 28, 1799. Spon: Thomas Oehrly.

Charles of Thomas Luthin and wife (in Roman letters), b. ----; bapt. Jan 28, 1799. Spon: Frederic Biely.

Catharine of Franz Fuchs and wife, b. Dec 3, 1798; bapt. Feb 17, 1799. Spon: George Miller and wife.

Catharine of Peter Killinger and wife, b. Jan 17, 1799; bapt. Feb 17, 1799. Spon: George Sprecher and wife.

Thomas of Jacob Braun and wife, b. Dec 21, 1798; bapt. Feb 17, 1799. Spon: John Adam Biely and wife.

Catharine Eliz. of Abraham Walter and wife, b. Dec 25, 1798; bapt. Mar 16, 1799. Spon: John Neu and wife.

Regina of Christian Oehrly and wife, b. Feb 18, 1799; bapt. Mar 31, 1799. Spon: Jacob Lenz and wife.

Elizabeth of John Maulfuer and wife, b. Sep 14, 1798; bapt. Mar 31, 1799. Spon: George Ziegler and wife.

Mary Margaret of Valentine Hufnagel and wife, b. Jan 10, 1799; bapt. Jun 9, 1799. Spon: David Hufnagel and wife.

Mary Cath. of Michael Leidig and wife, b. Mar 19, 1799; bapt. Jun 23, 1799. Spon: Nicholas Alberthal and wife.

Anna Mary of George Haerter and wife, b. Mar 28, 1798; bapt. Jun --, 1798. Spon: Adam Barth and wife.

George of Henry Zeigler, Jr. and wife, b. Sep --, 1796; bapt. ----. Spon: Henry Zeigler, Sr. and wife.

Catharine of Simon Schell and wife, b. Nov 13, 1797; bapt. ----. Spon: John Reinhert and wife.

Christina of John Rauch and wife, b. Dec 11, 1797; bapt. ----. Spon: Philip Johannes and wife.

Catharine of John Rauch and wife, b. Mar 3, 1799; bapt. ----. Spon: Simon Schell and wife.

Michael of Michael Mayer and wife, b. Mar 13, 1799; bapt. ---, 1799. Spon: John Maulfuer and wife.

John Jacob of John Jacob Meyer and wife, b. Jan 18, 1795; bapt. ----, 1795. Spon: George Walmer and wife.

John of John Jacob Meyer and wife, b. Sep 20, 1797; bapt. ----, 1797. Spon: John Hauk and wife.

John of Adam Schmelzer and wife, b. May 27, 1799; bapt. Jul 21, 1799. Spon: John Zimmerman and wife.

Mary Cath. of Philip Michling and wife, b. April 7, 1799; bapt. Jul 21, 1799. Spon: Barbara Alberthal.

Christian, child of Peter Ober and wife, b. May 30, 1799; bapt. Aug 18, 1799. Spon: Christian Gillman and wife.

Jacob of John Hauk and wife, b. Jul 30, 1799; bapt. Aug 18, 1799. Spon: Conrad Meyer and wife.

Elizabeth of John Adam Baumgardner and wife, b. Jun 26, 1799; bapt. Sep 15, 1799. Spon: Susanna Wagner.

Barbara of John Neu and wife, b. May 23, 1799; bapt. Sep 15, 1799. Spon: Henry Peters and wife Christina.

John of Daniel Schuy and wife, b. Jul 18, 1799; bapt. Jul 18, 1799. Spon: Conrad Meyer and wife.

William of William Reuter and wife, b. Sep 30, 1799; bapt. Nov 10, 1799. Spon: Henry Zeigler and wife.

John George of Jacob Kupper (Cooper or Kiefer) and wife, b. Sep 26, 1799; bapt. Nov 10, 1799. Spon: John Zimmerman and wife.

Cath. Eliz. of Peter Karschnitz and wife, b. Sep 29, 1799; bapt. Dec 7, 1799. Spon: Cathrine Lenz.

John of Jacob Ellinger and wife, b. Oct 23, 1799; bapt. Dec 8, 1799. Spon: Daniel Nilson (Nelson) and Cath. Kissinger.

Thomas of Peter Eisenhaur and wife, b. Jan 1, 1800; bapt. Jan 19, 1800. Spon: Thomas Oehrle and wife.

Elizabeth of George Kuefer and wife, b. Dec 12, 1799; bapt. Mar 16, 1800. Spon: John Baumgardner and wife.

Margaret of Jacob Bauman and wife, b. Mar 11, 1800; bapt. Mar 16, 1800. Spon: Widow Oehrle.

Barbara of Jacob Wagner and wife, b. Oct 27, 1799; bapt. Mar 16, 1800. Spon: Barbara Alberthal.

Sarah of Adam Deininger and wife, b. Nov 2, 1799; bapt. ----, 1800.
Spon: The Parents
Susanna of Jacob Rauch and wife, b. Jan 26, 1800; bapt. April 13,
1800. Spon: Henry Rauch and wife.
John of John Deininger and wife, b. Feb 1, 1800; bapt. April 13, 1800.
Spon: John Hauk and wife.
John of John Zehring and wife, b. Feb 22, 1800; bapt. May 11, 1800.
Spon: Philip Michlin and wife.
Elizabeth of George Franz and wife, b. Dec 6, 1799; bapt. May 11,
1800. Spon: John Zehring.
Jacob of Jacob Gutman and wife, b. Mar 29, 1800; bapt. May 11,
1800. Spon: Martin Lang and wife.
Elizabeth of Jacob Meyer and wife, b. Dec 21, 1799; bapt. May 11,
1799. Spon: Conrad Meyer and wife.
Elizabeth of Henry Baumgardner and wife, b. Mar 27, 1800; bapt. Jul
--, 1800. Spon: Conrad Meyer and wife.
Catharine of Adam Biely and wife, b. ----; bapt. ----. Spon: Barbara
Biely, widow.
Henry of John Bolden (Bolton) and wife, b. May 6, 1800; bapt. Jul 6,
1800. Spon: George Walmer and wife.
Michael of Jacob Heims and wife, b. May 21, 1800; bapt. Jul 6, 1800.
Spon: Jacob Lentz and wife.
Elizabeth of Edward McWik (McQuigg) and wife, b. Sep 18, 1799;
bapt. Jul 6, 1800. Spon: William Biele and wife.
Mary of Louis Gruber and wife, b. April 3, 1800; bapt. Jul 6, 1800.
Spon: Thomas Oehrle and wife.
Eve of Edward McWik and wife, b. Sep 18, 1797; bapt. Jul 6, 1800.
Spon: The Mother.
Rosina of Leonard Doll and wife, b. Jul 1, 1800; bapt. Aug 3, 1800.
Spon: Jacob Lentz and wife.
John George of George Haertter and wife, b. Jul 6, 1800; bapt. Aug
3, 1800. Spon: Thomas Oehrle and wife.
Elizabeth of William McWain (McIlwain) and wife, b. ---; bapt. Oct 26,
1800. Spon: Thomas Oehrle and wife.
Eliz. Nancy, illegitimate daughter of Catharine Burnet, b. May 23,
1800; bapt. Aug --, 1800. Spon: Thomas Oehrle and wife.
Henry of Gottfried Zimmerman and wife, b. Aug 15, 1800; bapt. Sep -
-, 1800. Spon: John Zeigler and wife.
Catharine of Adam Biely and wife, b. Mar 15, 1800; bapt. Sep --,
1800. Spon: Widow Biely.

Mary of George Kuns and wife, b. Oct 21, 1800; bapt. Nov 23, 1800. Spon: Jacob Sichele and wife.

Elisabeth of John Gutman and wife, b. ---- 1800; bapt. Jan --, 1801. Spon: Jacob Lenz and wife.

John of Michael Deininger and wife, b. Sep 23, 1800; bapt. ----. Spon: Michael Killinger and wife.

John Jacob of John Maulfair and wife, b. Dec 21, 1800; bapt. Mar 15, 1801. Spon: Michael Maeyer and wife.

Rosina of Michael Palm and wife, b. Dec 25, 1800; bapt. Mar 29, 1801. Spon: Thomas Oehrle and wife.

Elizabeth of John Buchter and wife, b. Aug 10, 1800; bapt. May 25, 1801. Spon: Philip Michael and wife.

Rebecca of Isaac Williams and wife Elizabeth, b. Jun 12, 1781; bapt. Oct 21, 1801. Spon: ----.

William of Jacob Ellet and wife, b. Jun 23, 1800; bapt. Oct 24, 1801. Spon: The Mother.

Samuel of George Hatz (Hotz or Hartz or Hots) and wife, b. Jan 17, 1800; bapt. May --, 1802. Spon: The Parents.

John of Michael Palm and wife, b. Jul 12, 1768; bapt. May --, 1803. Spon: The Parents.

George of Michael Palm and wife, b. Aug 3, 1790; bapt. May --, 1803. Spon: The Parents.

Barbara of Michael Palm and wife, b. Jun 17, 1792; bapt. May --, 1803. Spon: The Parents.

Anna of Michael Palm and wife, b. April 7, 1794; bapt. May --, 1803. Spon: The Parents.

Michael of Michael Palm and wife, b. Nov 13, 1796; bapt. May --, 1803. Spon: The Parents.

MARRIAGES

Christian Weissbach m. Anna Sabina Vetter on April 9, 1780.

Peter Eisenhauer m. Anna Oehrle on Aug 24, 1795. Witnesses: The Parents, Thomas Oehrle and wife Cath.

James Raddick m. ---- on Aug 24, 1795.

Andrew Albrecht (single) m. Catharine Steiner (widow) on Dec --, 1795. Witnesses: Henry Ost and wife Rebecca.

Anthony Hemperly m. Catharine Vogt on Dec --, 1795. Witnesses: George Hewperly and Jacob Kitzmiller.

Jacob Meyer m. Susanna Zent on Dec --, 1795. Witnesses: Jacob

Valentine Bolten m. Magdalene Ziegler on Mar 5, 1796. Witnesses: Henry Ziegler and Gottfried Zimmerman.

John Job m. Elizabeth Rudy on Mar 7, 1796. Witnesses: Jacob Rudy, the father, and Catharine Rudy.

Benoni Pew (Pugh) m. Margaret Harstig on Feb 18, 1798. Witnesses: Thomas Oehrle and others.

John Baumgartner m. Eliz. Kiefer on Feb 20, 1798. Witnesses: The Parents and Friends.

Martin (?) Goetz m. Salome Neydig on April 17, 1798. Witnesses: Christian Oehrly and Daniel Miller, etc.

Michael Kitsch m. Elizabeth Franz on Jun 3, 1755.

Ernst Frederic Persoun m. Anna Mary Heckeda on May 24, 1763.
"From biographical sketches:"
John Michael Zimmerman m. Eve Koenig on May 15, 1750. Witnesses: Baden Durlach, stepdaughter of J. George Berger.

John George Ziegler m. Anna Eliz. on Jan 3, 1736.

John Leonard Lang (widower) m. Mrs. Ann Eliz. Ziegler on Dec 3, 1743.

Christian Ramberger (widower) m. Mrs. Ann Elizabeth Lang on ----, 1759.

John Frederic Bickel m. Cath. Dorothea Mueller in 1742 or 1743. Witnesses: Massenbach.

John Frederic Bickel (widower) m. Mrs. Elizabeth Berger on Nov --, 1788.

Philip Hauck (widower) m. Barbara Fessler on Feb --, 1773. Place: Earl Township on Conestoga (---Co.)

John Palm (came to America in 1749, Kloster, Heilbron, apparently came to this country a widower) and m. Miss Salome Fenger, 1750 - 1752. Died 1764, mother of 8 children.

John Palm (widower) m. Mrs. Eliz. Klein, 1766 - 1768.

Michael Palm (widower) m. Miss Rosina Hemperly in 1787.

Nicholas Neu (from Germany) m. ---- in 1770.

John Ziegler m. Miss Eve Catharine Felter on Jun 1, 1800.

Henry Rauch m. Miss Mary Schumacher in 1783 or 1784.

Anthony Barto m. Miss Mary Rauch in 1792 or 1793.

John Fuchs m. Mrs. Susanna Vollmer in 1793.

Leonard Doll m. Miss Catharine Hemperly on Mar 7, 1789.

Adam Kraemer m. Mrs. Barbara Biele in 1793.

John Nicholas Geotz m. Mrs. Barbara Nechlin in Mar 1775.

Christian Oehrly m. Miss Elizabeth Killinger in 1779.

Christian Oehrly m. Miss Elizabeth Killinger in 1779.

Jacob Lautermilch m. Miss Anna Mary Neff (Steff) (Muehlbach, Germany) in 1764.

Jacob Kuefer (widower) (Gersdorf, Alsace) m. Miss Catharine Alt--- in 1754.

Peter Fernsler m. Miss Susanna Carmene (also spelled Carmenis) in Dec 1791.

Peter Mechlin m. Miss Anna Barbara Kohr in 1759 or 1760.

William Neu m. Miss Juliana Fernsler on April 18, 1769.

Joh. Adam Deininger (Wuertemburg, Germany, came to America in 10th year and married in his 26th year) m. Miss Rosina Diller (Dieler) in 1747.

Joh. Adam Deininger (widower) m. Mrs. Elizabeth Neff about 1782.

William Blecher m. Miss Dorothea Schalle (Palantine/Pfalz) in 1747.

Jacob Sprecher m. Mrs. Dorothea Blecher in 1759.

Jacob Bauman m. Miss Juliana Gassele (Baden Durlach), 1750-1755.

Anthony Hemperly m. Mrs. Juliana Bauman in 1760.

Joseph Carmene m. Miss Eve Frey (Wuertemberg) in 1758 or 1759.

Michael Deininger m. Miss Anna Mary Killinger (died Oct 1802) on April 21, 1789.

John Oehrle m. Miss Susanna Brumbach or Brumshear (died 1754) on April 10, 1753.

John Oehrle m. Regina Sichele on Mar 11(?), 1755.

John Oehrle, Jr. m. Miss Margaret Deininger on Sep 4, 1777. Londonderry Township, Leb., fron J.C. Stoever's records.

John Adam Deininger, Jr.m. Miss Christina Fernsler on Feb 1, 1785.

BURIALS

Anna Eliz. Ramberger, buried Sep 13, 1794. Daughter of John Leonard Ziegler and wife Margaret, b. May 19, 174 in Bergwangen. Sponsors: John Michael Werner and wife Regina. Married John George Ziegler on Jan 3, 1736, had two children, one son yet living. Married John Leonard Lang on Dec 3, 1743, had eight children. Married Christian Ramberger in 1759, had one son, still living. Lived to see 23 grandchildren, 3 great-grandchildren. Died Sep 11 at age 80 years 3 months 24 days.

John Welsch, buried Oct 29, 1794. Son of John Welsch and wife Christina; bapt. Oct 2, 1792. Sponsors: John Gontram and wife. Disease - dysentery, sick 11 days. Age 2 years 3 weeks 3 days.

Elizabeth Neu, buried Jul 15, 1795. Daughter of John Nicholas Neu and wife Eva Catharine, b. Aug 13, 1793. Sponsors: John Adam Biel and Mary Elizabeth Fernsler. Disease - fever and ----. Age 1 year ---- 1 day.

Joh. Frederic Bickel, buried Aug 12, 1795. Son of Joh. George Bickel and wife Anna Mary, b. Oct 5, 1723 in M---bach. Sponsors: John Michael Mueller and Mary Margaret Raucher. Confirmed and admitted to communion. Married (1) Cath. Dorothea Mueller in Nov 1788, had 7 children. Married (2) Mrs. Eliz. Berger, no children. Disease - ???. Age 71 years 10 months, ----.

Catharine Graemer, buried Oct 18, 1795. Daughter of Adam Graemer and wife Barbara, b. May 31, 1795. Sponsors: Barbara Biele. Age 4 months 2 weeks 4 days.

John Oehrly, buried Oct 21, 1795. Son of Thomas Oehrly and wife Margaret, b. Jan 9, 1724 at Jesmgen, Wuertemberg. Sponsors: Geroge Spitz and Anna Cath. Algayer. Confirmed. Came to America in 1750. Married (1) Susanna Brumbach in 1752, had one child, still living. Married (2) Regina (relict of whom not said), nee Sichele, in 1755, had 9 children, 5 still living - 3 sons and 2 daughters. Disease - asthma and feebleness of years. Died Monday 8 p.m. Age 72 years 8 months 10 days.

Barbara Hauck, buried Oct 21, 1796. Daughter of Leonard Fesle and wife Margaret, b. Jun 26, 1745 in Earl Township on Conestoga; bapt. and confirmed in the Lutheran faith. Married Philip Hauck in Feb 1773, had 7 children, 5 still living - 4 sons, 1 daughter. Died Saturday, Oct 19th at 9 p.m. Age 51 years 5 months less 7 days.

Elizabeth Fernsler, buried Mar 10, 1797. Daughter of Peter Fernsler and wife Susanna; bapt.. Sponsors: The Parents. Sickness - convulsions. Age 8 weeks, 3 days.

John Sichely, buried Aug 23, 1797. Son of Jacob Sichely and wife Susanna, b. Jun 18, 1793. Sponsors: Christian Oehrly and wife Eliz. Dysentery. Age 4 years 2 months 4 days.

Charlotte Gruber, buried Sep 12, 1797. Daughter of Ludwig Gruber and wife Eliz., b. Jun 5, 1795. Dysentery. Age 2 years, 3 months, 5 days.

Rosina Wilhelm, buried Mar 17, 1798. Daughter of Abraham Wilhelm and wife Mary, b. Oct 17, 1785. Smallpox. Age 12 years, 5 months.

Margaret Sprecher, buried April 14, 1798. Daughter of George

Sprecher and wife Catharine, b. Jan 26, 1791. Sponsors:
Margaret Sprecher. Smallpox. Age 7 years 2 months 17 days.

Henry Neu, buried April 17, 1798. Son of Peter Neu and wife
Rebecca, b. Jul 22, 1797. Sponsors: John Sch--- and wife.
Smallpox. Age 8 months, 25 days.

George Deininger, buried April 25, 1798. Son of Adam Deininger and
wife Christina, b. Nov 1, 1790. Sponsors: Michael Deininger and
wife. Smallpox. Age 7 years, 5 months, 24 days.

David Deininger, buried May 2, 1798. Son of Adam Deininger and
wife. Sponsors: The Parents. Smallpox. Age 1 year, 2 months,
15 days.

Eliz. Bauman, buried May 14, 1798. Daughter of Jacob Bauman and
wife Mary Cath., b. Aug 7, 1796. Sponsors: Michael Zeller and
Anna Mary Wilhelm. Smallpox. Age 1 year, 9 months, 7 days.

George Killinger, buried May 14, 1798. Son of Peter Killinger and
wife Christina, b. Dec 2, 1794. Sponsors: Thomas Oehrly and
wife. Burned to death. Age 4 years, 4 months, 3 days.

John Palm, buried April 1799. Native of Kloster Heilbraun, b. Jul 25,
1713; bapt. and confirmed in the Lutheran faith. Married (1) in
Germany, had one son. Came to this country in 1749. Married
(2) Salome Fenger, had 8 children, she died in 1784. Married (3)
Mrs. Eliz. Klein (widow), had one child. Age 85 years, 9 months.

Rosina Palm, buried Jun 1799. Nee Hemperly, b. May 3, 1764; bapt.
and confirmed in the Lutheran faith. Married Michael Palm in
178-, he is still living, had 7 children, of whom 5 survive. Died in
confinement. Age 35 years, 1 month, 7 days.

Barbara Deininger, buried 1800. Daughter of Leonard Deininger and
wife, b. in 1723 at Aichhols, close by Schwaebis Hallé. Came to
this country in her 8th year. Confirmed in the Lutheran faith.
Never married. Age 76 years 7 months.

John Hicks, buried Aug 18, 1800. Son of George Hicks, b. Aug 13,
1799. Sponsors: John Romich. Age 11 months 5 days.

Frederic Biely, buried Mar 1800. Son of Frederic Biely, b. Jan 1800.
Died of spasm. Age 10 weeks.

Catharine Biely, buried Sep 2, 1800. Daughter of Adam Biely and
wife, b. Mar 15, 1800. Sponsors: Mrs. Biely (widow). Age 5
months 2 weeks 3 days.

Nicholas Neu, buried Nov 8, 1800. b. in Germany on Jun 6, 1742;
bapt., came to this country in his 8th year with his parents.
Confirmed in 1770. Married.

Eva (Rudasil), buried 1800. Married 30 years, had 12 children, of whom 9 survive. Age 58 years 4 months 28 days.

John Malvier, buried Nov --, 1800. Son of John Malvier and wife, Margaret, b. Dec 23, 1796. Sponsors: Conrad Meyer and wife Eliz. Age 3 years 11 months 25 days.

Eve Catharine Ziegler, buried ----, 1800. Daughter of Peter Fetter and wife Anna Margaret, b. Aug 1, 1781. Sponsors: Adam Stoever. Confirmed in the Lutheran faith. Married John Ziegler Jun 1, 1800, lived with him 1 day less than 5 months. Cause of death - premature confinement. Age 19 years, 2 months, 20 days.

Mary Barto, buried Dec --, 1800. Daughter of Jacob Schumacher and wife, wife of Anthony Barto. b. Aug 1763; bapt. and confirmed. Married Henry Rauch, had 4 children. Married Anthony Barto, no children. Age 37 years, 2 months, 8 days.

Jacob Hemperly. b. Dec 6, 1800, died Oct 17, 1859. Age 58 years, 10 months, 11 days.

George Keim. b. Mar 25, 1792, died Jul 23, 1862. Age 70 years, 3 months, 28 days.

Catharine Zehring, wife of George Keim. b. Aug 7, 1799, died April 22, 1873. Age 73 years, 8 months, 15 days.

Mariah Cath. Reed, wife of Samuel Gutman. b. Nov 1, 1797, died Jul 8, 1872. Age 74 years, 8 months, 7 days.

George Lang. b. Nov 19, 1794, died April 21, 1876. Age 81 years, 5 months, 2 days.

Eve Catharine, wife of George Lang. b. Sep 12, 1800, died Nov 25, 1870. Age 70 years, 2 months, 13 days.

Michael Zimmerman. b. April 5, 1797, died Dec 25, 1868. Age 71 years, 8 months, 20 days.

Henry Lautermilch. b. Oct 16, 1800, died April 11, 1870. Age 69 years, 5 months, 15 days.

Maria Cath. Dullenbone. b. Jan 6, 1748 in Germany, died Jul 25, 1822. Age 74 years, 6 months, 19 days.

Elizabeth Moury. b. Sep 5, 1787, died Jan 9, 1761. Age 73 years, 4 months, 4 days.

George Keller. b. Oct 19, 1793, died Oct 30, 1861. Age 68 years, 11 days.

Andreas Loy. b. Feb 16, 1795, died Oct 27, 1863. Age 68 years, 8 months, 11 days.

Christina Kreider, wife of Wm. Oehrle. b. Sep 11, 1784, died Sep 28, 1868. Age 84, years, 17 days.

Christina, wife of Daniel Franz. b. Jun 16, 1795, died Feb 21, 1873.
Age 77 years, 8 months, 5 days.

Anna, wife of John Farhling. b. Mar 12, 1794, died Mar 18, 1871.
Age 80 years, 6 days.

SELECTED PASTORAL RECORDS OF JOHN CASPER STOEVER
of baptisms and marriages performed in and around Lebanon County

Children of William Trotter, Swatara:
James, b. Aug 31, 1735; bapt. Oct 7, 1735. Evidences, James Trotter,
Jos. Reynolds and Hannah M. Carey.
Mary, b. Feb 19, 1737; bapt. May 19, 1737. Evidences, Jos. Reynolds,
Anna Trotter and Elizabeth Trotter.

Mary of Thomas Anderson of Swatara and his wife Mary, b. Oct 1717;
bapt. Oct 7, 1735. Evidences: Peter Von Beber and wife Anna and
Sarah Reynolds.
Thomas Hui of Swatara, b. Oct 1714; bapt. Oct 17, 1738. Evidences,
Joseph Von Beber and Joseph Reynolds.
Isaac of James McChees, Lebanon, b. Jul, 1737; bapt. Feb 7, 1735.
Testes, Peter Kucher and wife Anna Barbara.

Children of Anastasius Uhler, Lebanon:
Christopher, Lebanon, b. Feb 2, 1741; bapt. Mar 25, 1741. Spon:
Balthasar Ort and his wife Barbara.
Anna Barbara, b. Mar 20, 1743; bapt. Mar 27, 1743. Spon: Balthasar
Ort and his wife Barbara.
John Martin, b. Sep 24, 1744; bapt. Oct 28, 1744. Spon: Martin
Kirstaetter and his wife.
Michael, b. Apr 23, 1743; bapt. May 25, 1746. Spon: Michael Wagener
and Margaretha Zoth.

Children of Peter Heylmann, Lebanon:
Anna Maria, b. Nov 14, 1739; bapt. Dec 6, 1739. Spon: Martin
Kirstaetter and his wife Maria Dorothea.
John Adam, b. Nov 4, 1740; bapt. Mar 25, 1741. Spon: John Adam
Heymann and wife.
Anastasius, b. Mar 3, 1742; bapt. Apr 15, 1742. Spon: Anastasius Uhler
and wife.
John Peter, b. May 16, 1743; bapt. May 23, 1743. Spon: Superiores.
Maria Magdalena, b. May 1, 1746; bapt. Jun 24, 1746. Spon:
Superiores.

Children of Jacob Bentz, Swatara:
John Jacob, b. Feb 3, 1739; bapt. Apr 15, 1739. Spon: Peter Rousch

and wife.
Maria Barbara, b. Oct 29, 1740; bapt. Mar 26, 1741. Spon: Maria
Elizabetha Borst.
John George, b. Apr 9, 1743; bapt. May 23, 1743. Spon: John George
Kuntz and wife.

Rosina of Peter Kucher, Lebanon, b. Mar 20, 1741; bapt. Mar 28, 1741.
Spon: Christopher Meyer and wife Rosina.
Maria Christiana Margaretha of George Glassbrenner, Lebanon, b. Feb
28, 1741; bapt. Mar 25, 1741. Spon: Andreas Weltz and wife and
Margaretha Glassbrenner.

Children of Michael Kleber, Swatara:
George Ludwig, b. Jul 4, 1736; bapt. Sep 12, 1736. Spon: George
Ludwig Friedle and wife.
Anna Maria, b. Sep 4, 1738; bapt. Jan 30, 1739. Spon: Heinrich Klein
and wife.
Michael, b. Mar 1, 1740; bapt. Mar 26, 1741. Spon: Heinrich Klein and
wife Anna Maria.
Barbara, b. Feb 25, 1744; bapt. Mar 18, 1744. Spon: Ottmar Schnabele
and wife Barbara.
Susanna, b. Feb 19, 1749; bapt. Mar 19, 1749. Spon: Martin Speck and
wife Susanna.

Children of Martin Kirstaetter, Lebanon:
John, b. Sep 3, 1739; bapt. Nov 5, 1739. Spon: John Schmeltzer and his
wife.
Julianna, b. Jan 25, 1741; bapt. Mar 25, 1741. Spon: Julianna
Umberger.

Children of Andreas Kraemer, Swatara:
Andreas, b. Feb 8, 1741; bapt. Mar 26, 1741. Spon: Martin Kappler and
wife Margaretha.
John George, b. Feb 12, 1746; bapt. Mar 16, 1746. Spon: John George
Einert and wife.

Christoph of Heinrich Meyer, Lebanon, b. Oct 20, 1736; bapt. Nov 19,
1736. Spon: Christoph Meyer and wife Anna Rosina.

Children of John Schmeltzer, Swatara:

John Peter, b. Dec 8, 1738; bapt. Jan 30, 1739. Spon: Peter Kucher
and his wife.
Johannes, b. Apr 11, 1741; bapt. Jun 2, 1741. Spon: Peter Kucher and
his wife Barbara.
Sabina, b. Sep 2, 1746; bapt. Sep 14, 1746. Spon: Thomas Kreugel and
his wife Margaretha.

Elizabetha of Michael Boltz, Quitapahilla, b. May 10, 1741; bapt. Oct 9,
1741. Spon: George Berger and his wife.
Catarina of George Heinrich Peter, Quitapahilla, b. Jun, 1741; bapt.
Oct 4, 1741. Spon: George Berger and his wife.
Maria Sabina of Heinrich Dups, Swatara, b. Sep 2, 1741; bapt. Oct 4,
1741. Spon: Ludwig Bors and Margaretha Kappler.
George Jacob of John George Kuenig, Swatara, b. Aug 28, 1741; bapt.
Oct 4, 1741. Spon: Sebastian Naess and Barbara Kuefer.
Maria Elisabetha of John George Veltin, Swatara, b. Sep 4, 1741; bapt.
Oct 4, 1741. Spon: Valentin Kuefer and his wife.
Maria Catarina of Lampert Bubar, Swatara, b. Jul, 1740; bapt. Oct 4,
1741. Spon: Daniel Schui and his wife.
Maria Barbara, of Andreas Bort, b. Jul 20, 1741; bapt. Nov 28, 1741.
Spon: Frantz Seip and Catarina Barbara Spaller.

Children of Jacob Birckel, Swatara:
John Jacob, b. Jan 7, 1734; bapt. Apr 28, 1734. Spon: Peter Gaertner
and his wife.
Michael Leonhardt, b. Aug 20, 1736; bapt. Nov 9, 1736. Spon:
Leonhardt Billmeyer and spouse Ana Bart.
Anna Eva, b. May 8, 1739; bapt. Jun 12, 1739. Spon: Adam Vollmar
and his wife.
Maria Dorothea, b. Nov 27, 1741; bapt. Jan 2, 1742. Spon: Frederich
Haehle and wife Margaretha.

Children of John Dietrich Kober, Lebanon:
Anna Elisabetha, b. May 12, 1734; bapt. Jul 21, 1734. Spon: John
Adam Heyl and his wife.
John Egidius, b. Dec 18, 1738; bapt. Dec 24, 1738. Spon: Egidius
Hoffmann.
George, b. Jan 27, 1741; bapt. Feb 22, 1741. Spon: John Egidius
Hoffmann and his wife.
Anna Margaretha, b. May 13, 1743; bapt. May 23, 1743. Spon:

Thomas Krevel and his wife.
John Michael, b. Nov 30, 1748; bapt. Nov 27, 1749. Spon: David
Fischer and his wife.

Children of Martin Kappler, Swatara:
John Jacob, b. Sep 20, 1734; bapt. Nov 10, 1734. Spon: Sebastian Ruhi
and Elisabetha Kaiser.
Catarina Barbara, b. Jun 19, 1736; bapt. Sep 12, 1736. Spon: Cunradt
Lang and his wife.

Children of John George Meyer, Swatara:
Anna Barbara, b. Oct 6, 1734; bapt. Jan 1, 1735. Spon: Anna Barbara
Teufersbiss.
Veronica, b. Feb 28, 1737; bapt. Oct 10, 1737. Spon: John Schmeltz
and his wife.
Elisabetha, b. Apr 7, 1739; bapt. Jun 12, 1739. Spon: Philip
Schnaetterle and wife Sabina.
Anna Sabina, b. Jun 3, 1745; bapt. 1745. Spon: Philip Schnaetterle and
his wife.

Children of Peter Kucher, Lebanon:
John Frantz, b. Jul 13, 1736; bapt. Aug 1, 1736. Spon: John Frantz
Fuchs and his wife.
Anna Catarina, b. Jul 12, 1738; bapt. Feb 7, 1738. Spon: John George
Graff, junior, and Catarina Kopfenhoefer.
Christoph, b. Mar 19, 1739; bapt. Apr 22, 1739. Spon: Christoph Meyer
and his wife.
Rosina, b. Mar 20, 1741; bapt. Mar 25, 1741. Spon: Christoph Meyer
and his wife.
John Peter, b. Feb 12, 1743; bapt. Mar 27, 1743. Spon: Albrecht
Siechele and his wife.

Children of Dorst Breckbiel, Swatara:
Elizabetha, b. Jun 3, 1739; bapt. 1739. Spon: George Hauck and his
wife.
John Peter, b. Nov, 1750; bapt. Apr 5, 1751. Spon: Johannes Bindnagel
and his wife Regina.
Johannes, b. Sep 21, 1741; bapt. Jan 1, 1742. Spon: Frederick Kuehner
and his wife.
Isaac of Abraham Williams, Swatara, b. Nov 7, 1741; bapt. Jan 1, 1742.

Spon: Frederick Deabi and his wife.

Children of Benjamin Clark, Swatara:
Jane, b. Apr 17, 1739; bapt. Jun 12, 1739.
Mary, b. Apr 12, 1741; bapt. Jan 1, 1742. Spon: Abraham and Christian
Williams.
Thomas, b. Dec 7, 1746; bapt. Apr 26, 1747. Spon: Thomas Kreuel and
his wife Margaretha.

Catarina of Frederick Deebi, Swatara, b. Nov 6, 1741; bapt. Jan 1742.
Spon: John Tittle and wife.
John Peter of Carl Schally, Lebanon, b. Sep 29, 1741; bapt. Jan 3,
1742. Spon: John Peter Kucher and his wife.

Children of Peter Ruth, Lebanon:
Anna Catarina, b. Jan 29, 1735; bapt. Jun 29, 1735. Spon: Susanna
Barbara Teuss.
Maria Catarina, b. Oct 27, 1741; bapt. Jan 3, 1742. Spon: Michael Myer
and his wife.
Barbara, b. Nov 25, 1742; bapt. Dec 20, 1742. Spon: John Immel.

Children of John Adam Kittring, Lebanon:
George Michael, b. Dec 11, 1741; bapt. Jan 3, 1742. Spon: Michael
Boltz and his wife Maria Barbara.
Maria Margaretha, b. Aug 4, 1743; bapt. Nov 15, 1743. Spon: Michael
Boltz and his wife Maria Barbara.
Rosina Barbara, b. Mar 18, 1745; bapt. Apr. 28, 1745. Spon: Michael
Boltz and his wife Maria Barbara.

Children of George Adam Vollmar, Swatara:
Anna Maria, b. Jan 6, 1739; bapt. Jun 3, 1739. Spon: Jacob Birckel and
his wife Dorothea.
Maria Magdalena, b. Sep 19, 1743; bapt. Oct 23, 1743. Spon: Maria
Magdalena Kraemer.

Children of Jacob Herman, Swatara:
Anna Maria, b. Aug 29, 1737; bapt. Nov 5, 1739. Spon: George
Bernhardt Mann and his wife.
Maria Elisabeth, b. Oct 22, 1742; bapt. Dec 21, 1742. Spon: George
Bernhardt Mann and his wife.

Children of Adam Heylmann, Lebanon:
Catarina, b. Apr 7, 1740; bapt. May 26, 1740. Spon: Anastasius Uhler and his wife.
Anna Elizabeth, b. Mar 2, 1743; bapt. Apr 15, 1742.

Children of Philip Schnatterle, Swatara:
Sabina, b. Jul 13, 1735; bapt. Oct 7, 1735. Spon: Heinrich Dubs and the child's mother.
Heinrich, b. Dec 23, 1738; bapt. Jan 30, 1739. Spon: Heinrich Kline and his wife Anna Maria.
John Michael, b. Mar 12, 1740; bapt. May 26, 1740. Spon: John Seigmund Haehnle and his wife.
Martin, b. Sep 31, 1741; bapt. Jan 1, 1742. Spon: Heinrich Klein and his wife.
John Jacob, b. Feb 22, 1744; bapt. Mar 2, 1744. Spon: Heinrich Klein and his wife.
John George, b. Sep 17, 1745; bapt. Oct 26, 1745. Spon: George Meyer and his wife.
Adam, b. Apr 4, 1747; bapt. Apr 26, 1747. Spon: Adam Faber and wife of George Meyers.

Children of Peter Baumgaertner, Swatara:
Johannes, b. May 13, 1740; bapt. May 26, 1740. Spon: John Brechbiel and his wife.
John Dorst, b. May 9, 1742; bapt. Jul 18, 1742. Spon: Dorst Brachtbill, Anna Barbara Brechbille, John Brechbill's wife.

Children of George Meyer, Lebanon:
Anna Catarina, b. Jul 11, 1740; bapt. Aug 10, 1740. Spon: Peter Roth and his wife, Catarine.
John Heinrich, b. Dec 19, 1741; bapt. Apr 2, 1742. Spon: Heinrich Beyer and his wife.
Michael, b. Oct 19, 1744; bapt. Apr 28, 1745. Spon: Peter Marcker, Ulrich Peter and Elizabeth Latz.
John Jacob, b. Aug 28, 1746; bapt. Nov 9, 1746. Spon: John Jacob Schlaub and wife, Ursula Elisabetha.

Children of John Michael Boltz, Lebanon:
Anna Dorothea, b. Feb 18, 1738; bapt. Mar 30, 1738. Spon: Balthasar Ort and his wife.

Catarina Barbara, b. Jun 23, 1745; bapt. Aug 24, 1745. Spon: George Buerger and his wife.

Children of Isaac William, Swatara:
Isaac, b. Nov 3, 1746; bapt. Apr. 26, 1741. Spon: Philipp Schnatterle and his wife.
Jacob, b. Mar 23, 1753; bapt. Jun 17, 1753. Spon: Valentine Gerhard and Mary Rosenbaum.
Mary Elisabetha, b. Jan 27, 1755; bapt. Jun 8, 1755. Spon: Veronica Meyer.
George, born in 1757; bapt. Sep 3, 1757. Spon: Anastasius Uhler and wife.

Children of George Ludtwig Friedtel, Swatara:
John George, b. Mar 31, 1737 (?); bapt. Aug 14, 1737 (?). Spon: John George Houck and his wife.
Maria Magdalena, b. Apr 28, 1739; bapt. Jun 11, 1739. Spon: Johannes Hohmann and his wife Maria Magdalena.

Christina Regina of John Albrecht Schell, Swatara, b. Dec 22, 1737; bapt. Feb 6, 1738. Spon: John Bindtnagel and his wife Regina.

Children of Johannes Dirbi, Lebanon:
John George, b. Nov 6, 1734; bapt. Jul 29, 1735. Spon: John George Steitz.
Maria Catharine, b. Sep, 1737; bapt. Feb 6, 1738. Spon: Maria Catharine and Johanna Catharine Blum.

Children of Michael Borst, Lebanon:
Maria Elizabetha, b. Mar 9, 1735; bapt. Aug 29, 1735. Spon: Martin Kirstaetter and his wife.
Susanna, b. Dec 8, 1736; bapt. Sep 11, 1737. Spon: Dorothea Kirstaetter.
Anna Dorothea, b. Dec 25, 1738; bapt. Jan 29, 1739. Spon: Anastasius Uhler and wife Dorothea.

Children of Peter Marcker, Swatara:
Maria Elizabetha, b. Apr 21, 1743; bapt. May 23, 1743. Spon: Christoph Zimmer and his wife.
Julianna, b. Feb 3, 1746; bapt. Mar 3, 1746. Spon: Adam Ulrich and his

wife Juliana.
Catarina, b. Feb 4, 1751; bapt. Mar 17, 1751. Spon: George Mueller
and his wife.

Peter of John Tittle, dec'd., Swatara, b. Sep 20, 1742; bapt. Apr 27,
1747. Spon: George Meyer and his wife.

Children of Jonas Wolf, Lebanon:
John Jacob, b. Jan 4, 1742; bapt. Apr 15, 1742. Spon: John Jacob
Kaemmerling and his wife.
John Herman, b. Aug 5, 1743; bapt. Aug 28, 1743. Spon: Herman Trott
and his wife.
Anna Maria, b. Jan 7, 1745; bapt. Jan 19, 1745. Spon: Herman Trott
and his wife.
Simon, b. Oct 28, 1746; bapt. Dec 7, 1746. Spon: George Wagner and
wife Anna Elizabetha.

Children of John Albrecht Siechele, Lebanon:
John Peter, b. Mar 7, 1741; bapt. Apr 15, 1742. Spon: Peter Kucher
and his wife.
Eva Barbara, b. Oct 2, 1744; bapt. Oct 28, 1744. Spon: Peter Kucher
and his wife.

Anna Catarina of Jacob Froelich, Lebanon, b. Oct, 1741; bapt. Apr 15,
1742. Spon: Buerger and his wife.
Sarah of William Kally, Lebanon, b. Apr 6, 1742; bapt. Apr 15, 1742.
Spon: Andreas Wolf and his wife.

Children of Heinrich Wilhelm, Swatara:
Maria, b. Dec 4, 1741; bapt. Apr 16, 1742. Spon: Magdalena Homann.
John Philipp, b. Jan 28, 1743; bapt. Jul 19, 1743. Spon: Philipp Lorentz
Houtz and wife.

Children of Martin Speck, Swatara:
Anna Maria, b. Jan 15, 1741; bapt. Apr 16, 1742. Spon: Sigmund
Haehnle, Jr., and Anna Maria Becker.
Maria Catarina, b. Aug 28, 1748; bapt. Sep 4, 1748. Spon: Sigmund
Haehnle and his wife.
Johannes, b. Sep 18, 1754; bapt. Oct 7, 1754. Spon: Jacob Loresch and
his wife.

Children of Friederich Haehnle, Swatara:
Jacob Friederich, b. Mar 12, 1742; bapt. Apr 16, 1742. Spon: Jacob
Birckel and his wife.
John Michael, b. Oct 12, 1743; bapt. Oct 23, 1743. Spon: George
Frederich and his wife.
Anna Margaretha, b. Dec 30, 1745; bapt. Mar 12, 1746. Spon: Wendel
Heyl and wife Anna.
Maria Eva, b. Mar 5, 1747; bapt. Mar 29, 1747. Spon: Wendel Heyl and
wife Anna.
Elizabetha, b. Dec 18, 1748; bapt. Dec 25, 1748. Spon: Wendel Heyl
and wife Anna.
Eva Catarina, b. Jan 6, 1751; bapt. Jan 21, 1751. Spon: Veit Kapf and
wife Gertraudt.
Anna Barbara, b. Jan 14, 1753; bapt. Feb 25, 1753. Spon: Wendel Heyl
and wife Anna.

Children of John Brown, Swatara:
Maria Regina, b. Feb 26, 1742; bapt. Apr 16, 1742. Spon: John
Bindtnagle and wife.
Jacob, b. Mar 27, 1746; bapt. Apr 27, 1746. Spon: John Bindtnagle and
wife.
Anna Barbara, b. Apr 6, 1755; bapt. Jun 15, 1755. Sponsors not given.

Children of Antonius Rosenbaum, Swatara:
Susanna, b. May 3, 1739; bapt. Apr 16, 1742. Spon: Martin Speck and
his wife.
Salome, b. Mar, 1741; bapt. Apr 16, 1742. Spon: Philip Dubs and his
wife.

Children of Christoph Meyer, Lebanon:
John George, B. Dec 4, 1735; bapt. Apr. 18, 1736. Spon: John George
Klein and his wife Anna.
Maria Barbara, b. Aug 12, 1738; bapt. May 21, 1738. Spon: John Peter
Kucher and wife Maria Barbara.
Anna Maria, b. Jun 16, 1742; bapt. Jul 18, 1742. Spon: Thomas
Koppenhoefer and wife Anna Maria.

Children of Michael Lauer, Swatara:
John Michael, b. Jun 29, 1742; bapt. Jul 18, 1742. Spon: Michael
Spengel and his wife.

Catharine Barbara, b. Mar 11, 1744; bapt. Apr 15, 1744. Spon: Valentine Kuefer and wife Anna Barbara.

James of James McNeess, Lebanon, b. Sep 4, 1741; bapt. Jul 18, 1742. Spon: Anastasius Uhler and his wife Dorothea.

Anna Sara of John Joakles, Swatara, b. Feb, 1742; bapt. Jul 18, 1742. Spon: John Deeby and his wife.

John Jacob of John Wendel Heyl, Swatara, b. Jun 13, 1742; bapt. Jul 18, 1742. Spon: John Jacob Dubs and Barbara Kappler.

Children of John Reynolds, Swatara:

Bridgitte, b. Nov 20, 1742; bapt. Dec 21, 1742. Spon: Francis Reynolds, Patrick and Sarah McKue.

Elisabetha, b. Mar 23, 1744; bapt. Apr 15, 1744. Spon: Thomas and Elisabetha McKay, also Joseph Reynolds and Rebecca Reynolds.

John, b. 1746; bapt. 1746.

Joseph, b. Nov 10, 1747; bapt. Nov 24, 1747. Spon: Joseph Reynolds, Sarah McKue and Sarah Reynolds.

Children of Christoph Labengeiyer, Swatara:

Maria Catarina, b. May 18, 1730; bapt. Sep 29, 1730. Spon: Anna Maria Meyer.

John Jacob, b. Apr 8, 1734; bapt. Apr 21, 1734. Spon: John Jacob Beyer and his wife Margaretha.

Anna Barbara, b. Jun 14, 1736; bapt. Jul 18, 1736. Spon: Michael Ranek and his wife Anna Barbara.

Christoph, with his second wife, b. in Oct, 1741; bapt. Apr 15, 1742. Spon: Christoph Meyer and his wife.

Children of John Bindtnagel, Swatara:

Anna Sabina, b. Sep 11, 1733; bapt. Sep 17, 1733. Spon: John Martin Meyle and his wife Anna Sabina.

Johannes, b. Feb 7, 1735; bapt. Mar 23, 1735. Spon: Melchior Heuter.

John Martin, b. Sep 7, 1736; bapt. Oct 3, 1736. Spon: John Martin Meyle.

Children of John George Ergebrecht, Lebanon:

Catarina, b. Mar 26, 1733; bapt. Sep 17. 1733. Spon: Anna Catarina Mast.

Anna Elisabetha, b. Feb 20, 1735; bapt. Apr 27, 1735. Spon: Jacob Mast and his wife.

Children of Michael Bauer, Swatara:
John Valentin, b. Sep 17, 1739; bapt. Oct 21, 1739. Spon: John
Valentin Stober and his wife Eva.
John Martin, b. Dec 27, 1741; bapt. Jan 1, 1742. Spon: Valentin Kuefer
and Anna Maria Frederich.
Anna Eva, b. Jul 28, 1746; bapt. Aug 17, 1746. Spon: Michael Spiegel
and wife Anna Eva.
Anna Maria, with second wife, b. Jan 12, 1749; bapt. Mar 19, 1749.
Spon: Sigmund Haehnle and his wife.

Children of Heinrich Klein, Lebanon:
Anna, b. Feb 26, 1737; bapt. Mar 27, 1737. Spon: George Klein and his
wife Anna.
Sabina, b. Oct 1, 1738; bapt. Jan 30, 1739. Spon: Philipp Schnatterle
and his wife Sabina.
Maria Barbara, b. Apr 6, 1740; bapt. May 26, 1740. Spon: John
Braechbil and his wife Maria Barbara.
John George, b. Mar 2, 1742; bapt. Apr 16, 1742. Spon: Philipp
Schnatterle and his wife.

Children of John Martin Meyle, Lebanon:
Elisabetha, b. Nov 7, 1733; bapt. Apr 28, 1734. Spon: Michael Baettle
and his wife.
Johannes, b. Jan 26, 1735; bapt. May 25, 1735. Spon: John Bindtnagel
and his wife.
John Martin, b. Jul 25, 1737; bapt. Dec 25, 1737. Spon: Michael Baettle
and his wife.
Heinrich, b. Jan 16, 1742; bapt. Apr 15, 1742. Spon: Heinrich Klein and
his wife.

Children of Bernhardt Friedel, Swatara:
Susanna, b. May 16, 1743; bapt. May 23, 1743. Spon: Martin Speck and
his wife.
Jacob, b. Apr. 15, 1745; bapt. Oct 26, 1745. Spon: Jacob Preschinger
and his wife.
John Martin, b. Jun 25, 1747; bapt. Aug 16, 1747. Spon: Martin
Kappler and his wife.
John Bernhardt, b. Dec 27, 1749; bapt. Mar 18, 1750. Spon: Martin
Kappler and his wife.
Elisabetha, b. Dec 20, 1757; bapt. Mar 23, 1758. Spon: Adam Brecht

and wife.

Rosina of John George Haedderich, Lebanon, b. Jan 15, 1743; bapt. Mar 27, 1743. Spon: Christoph Meyer and his wife Rosina.

Children of David Dreher, Lebanon:
John Heinrich, b. Mar 29, 1743; bapt. May 23, 1743. Spon: John Heinrich Marcket and wife.
Daniel, b. Mar 11, 1752; bapt. Apr 12, 1752. Spon: Daniel Born and Margaretha Speck.
Maria Barbara, b. Dec 26, 1755; bapt. Jan 25, 1756. Spon: Leonhardt Kneuget and his wife.

John Leonhardt of Michael Umberger, Lebanon, b. Aug 28, 1743; bapt Sep 25, 1743. Spon: Leonhardt Ramler and wife.
Maria Barbara of Heinrich Merck, Swatara, b. Sep 9, 1743; bapt. Sep 25, 1743. Spon: Michael Lauer and his wife.

Children of Thomas Kreuel, Swatara:
John Adam, b. Sep 9, 1743; bapt. Sep 26, 1743. Spon: John Adam Kreuel and his wife.
Johannes, b. May 14, 1747; bapt. Jun 21, 1747. Spon: Johannes Schmeltzer and his wife.
Anna Catarina, b. May 5, 1750; bapt. Jun 20, 1750. Spon: Anna Catarina Zimmer.
Ana Maria, b. 1752; bapt. Jan 1, 1753. Spon: Christoph Zimmer and Ana Maria Meyer.

John Jacob of Jacob Reuger, Lebanon, b. Aug 18, 1743; bapt. Oct 23, 1743. Spon: Heinrich Klein and his wife.
John George of Peter Haedderich, Lebanon, b. Sep 12, 1743; bapt. Oct 23, 1743. Spon: John George Huber and his wife.
John Heinrich of Hans Adam Mueller, Swatara, b. Sep 23, 1743; bapt. Nov 15, 1743. Spon: Heinrich Weschenbach and his wife Elisabetha.
Maria Margaretha of John Adam Kreuel, Lebanon, b. Oct 17, 1743; bapt. Nov 15, 1743. Spon: Thomas Kreuel and his wife.

Children of Christian Schmidt, Swatara:
Christian, b. Nov 27, 1743; bapt. Nov 20, 1743. Spon: Christian Mueller and Margar. Creutzberger.

George Heinrich, b. Dec 27, 1744; bapt. Jan 20, 1745. Spon: Heinrich Bruender and wife Ana Catarina.

Children of Wendel Heyl, Swatara:
Margaretha, b. Dec 19, 1743; bapt. Feb 2, 1744. Spon: Frederich Haehnle and his wife Margaretha.
Anna Barbara, b. Oct 27, 1745; bapt. Nov 30, 1745. Spon: Frederich Haehnle and his wife Margaretha.
Elizabetha, b. Nov 24, 1747; bapt. Jan 6, 1748. Spon:Frederich Haehnle and his wife Margaretha.
Christina, b. Nov 23, 1751; bapt. Dec 2, 1751. Spon: Frederich Haehnle and his wife Margaretha.
Anna, b. Feb 19, 1754; bapt. Mar 24, 1754. Spon: Andreas Murr and Catarina Roenninger.
Johannes, b. Mar 26, 1756; bapt. Apr 15, 1756. Spon: Andreas Murr and his wife.
Jacob, b. Jun 6, 1742; no bapt. date given. Spon: Jacob Dubbs.

Anna Maria of George Zeh, Swatara, b. Dec 20, 1743; bapt. Feb 2, 1744. Spon: Heinrich Dubbs and his wife.
John Frederich of John George Mohr, Swatara, b. Jan 22, 1744; bapt. Feb 2, 1744. Spon: John Friederich Rathfang and his wife Maria Elisabetha.
Valentin of Vincens Kuefer, Lebanon, b. Mar 5, 1745; bapt. Mar 31, 1745. Spon: Valentin Kuefer and his wife Barbara.
Elizabeth of James Williams, Swatara, b. Nov 1, 1743; bapt. Mar 21, 1744. Spon: John Blum and wife Elizabeth.

Children of Johannes Pontius, Swatara:
John Heinrich, b. Feb 24, 1744; bapt. Apr 1, 1744. Spon: John Heinrich Zoeller and his wife.
John Peter, b. Oct 22, 1747; bapt. Oct 25, 1747. Spon: Peter Hoffman and his wife.
Johannes, b. Aug 16, 1751; bapt. Aug 18, 1751. Spon: Johannes Schnaebel and his wife.

Children of Abraham Williams, Swatara:
Margaretha, b. Mar 14, 1744; bapt. Apr 15, 1744. Spon: John Tittle and wife Elisabetha.
Abraham, b. Mar, 1748; bapt. Apr 17, 1748. Spon: James Williams and

wife.

Children of George Veit Kapp, Swatara:
Margaretha, b. Mar 24, 1744; bapt. Apr 15, 1744. Spon: George
Frederich and his wife.
Anna Catarina, b. Apr 17, 1746; bapt. Apr 27, 1746. Spon: Philipp
Maurer and his wife.
Maria Magdalena, b. Jul 20, 1747; bapt. Aug 2, 1747. Spon: Frederich
Haehnle and wife Margaretha.
Eva, b. Apr 18, 1749; bapt. May 1, 1749. Spon: Peter Beettel and wife
Eva.
Margaretha Elisabetha, b. Jul 16, 1751; bapt. Jul 21, 1751. Spon:
Frederich Haehnle and his wife.
Anna Barbara, b. Nov 6, 1753; bapt. Dec 2, 1753. Spon: Peter
Heckman and his wife.

Ludwig Heinrich of Michael Katz, Swatara, b. Apr 4, 1744; bapt. Apr
15, 1744. Spon: Ludwig Heinrich Schui and Cat. Eliz. Goldman.

Children of Michael Speck, Swatara:
Anna Maria, b. Jan 15, 1741; bapt. Apr 16, 1742. Spon: Siegesmund
Haehnle and his wife and Anna Maria Becker.
Martin, b. Mar 23, 1744; bapt. Apr 15, 1744. Spon: Frederick Haehnle
and his wife.
Eleanora, b. Mar 30, 1746; bapt. Apr 27, 1746. Spon: Bernhardt Friedle
and his wife.
John Michael, b. Dec 29, 1750; bapt. Jan 21, 1751. Spon: Michael
Kleber and wife Elizabetha.
John Jacob, b. Apr 29, 1753; bapt. May 20, 1753. Spon: Michael Kleber
and Elisabetha.

Children of Stephen Cunradt, Swatara:
John George, b. Mar 21, 1744; bapt. Apr 29, 1744. Spon: Lorentz
Hautz.
John Peter, b. Jul 27, 1745; bapt. Sep 1, 1745. Spon: George Peter
Batdorf and Eva Elisabetha Ried.
Anna Elizabetha, b. Feb 13, 1747; bapt. Mar 15, 1747. Spon: Eva
Elizabeth Ried.
John Stephen, b. Feb 26, 1749; bapt. Mar 5, 1749. Spon: John Jacob
Loewengut.

Anna Margaretha, b. Feb 2, 1751; bapt. Mar 3, 1751. Spon: George Lechner and wife.
George Philipp, b. Nov 21, 1752; bapt. Dec 17, 1752. Spon: George Lechner and Anna Margar Lay.
John Nicolaus, b. Jan 16, 1755; bapt. Jan 20, 1755. Spon: John Nicolaus Gebhardt and wife.

Children of Philipp Maurer, Swatara:
Catarina Margaretha, b. May 30, 1744; bapt. Jun 10, 1744. Spon: Leonhardt Ramler and wife.
John Philipp, b. Nov 15, 1746; bapt. Nov 23, 1746. Spon: John Veith Kapp and his wife.
John Jacob, b. Jun 9, 1748; bapt. Jul 10, 1748. Spon: John Jacob Ramler and wife Margaretha.
Eva Margaretha, b. Oct 30, 1749; bapt. Nov 20, 1749. Spon: Jacob Ramler and wife.
John George, b. Apr 23, 1751; bapt. May 26, 1751. Spon: George Schaefer and wife.
Maria Elisabetha, b. Jul 25, 1754; bapt. Aug 11, 1754. Spon: George Schumacher and wife Maria Eva.
George Michael, b. Jan 13, 1756; bapt. Jan 25, 1756. Spon: the above.

Anna Regina of Jacob Degan, Swatara, b. Sep 22, 1744; bapt. Oct 12, 1744. Spon: Christian Battorf and Anna Regina Carstnitz.
Margaretha of Frantz Seibert, Swatara, b. Oct 12, 1744; bapt. Nov 25, 1744. Spon: Philip Schnatterle and wife.
Maria Barbara of Ottmar Schnaebele, Swatara, b. Oct 17, 1744; bapt. Nov 25, 1744. Spon: Casper Schnaebele and wife Barbara.
Maria Barbara of Philip Holinger, Lebanon, b. Nov 2, 1744; bapt. Nov 30, 1744. Spon: Leonardt Umberger and wife.

Children of Antonius Hemperle, Lebanon:
Anna Maria, b. Dec 15, 1744; bapt. Jan 6, 1745. Spon: John Bindnagle and wife.
Martin, b. 1747; bapt. Jun 21, 1747. Spon: the above.

Margaretha of George Friederich, Swatara, b. Dec 21, 1744; bapt. Jan 15, 1745. Spon: Freiderich Haehnle and wife.

Children of Jacob Zieger, Lebanon:

Anna Maria, b. Dec 3, 1744; bapt. Mar 3, 1745. Spon: Jacob Schober and Anna Barbara Uhler.

George Heinrich and Anna Maria Elisabeth, (Twins), b. Jan 13, 1765; bapt. Jan 25, 1765. Spon: George Heinrich Reinoehl and wife, Christoph Meyer and wife Catarina.

Children of George Casper Rasch, Lebanon:
Elizabetha, b. Jan 29, 1745; bapt. May 1, 1745. Spon: Catarina Ort.
Anna Magdalena, b. Jan 4, 1747; bapt. Mar 29, 1747. Spon: Anna Maria Ergebrecht.
Johannes, b. Jul 27, 1757; bapt. Sep 25, 1757. Spon: John Eberhard Kress and Barbara Stuck.
Anna Barbara, b. May 23, 1760; bapt. Jun 15, 1760. Spon: Peter Shaaf and wife.

Elizabetha Barbara of George Hatz, Lebanon, b. Jul 2, 1745; bapt. Aug 18, 1745. Spon: John Adam Hambrecht and wife.

Children of Michael Spiegel, Swatara:
Gottfried, b. Oct 16, 1745; bapt. Oct 26, 1745. Spon: Michael Bauer and wife.
Eva Christina, b. Sep 19, 1747; bapt. Oct 11, 1747. Spon: Michael Bauer and Joseph Heller's wife.

Children of Adam Faber, Swatara:
Barbara, b. Sep 29, 1745; bapt. Oct 26, 1745. Spon: Philip Schnatterle and his wife.
Philipp, b. Feb 18, 1747; bapt. Mar 29, 1747. Spon: the above.
Johannes, b. Feb 7, 1750; bapt. Mar 18, 1750. Spon: Bernhardt Faber and his wife.

Children of Martin Kappler, Swatara:
Susanna, b. Oct 22, 1745; bapt. Nov 30, 1745. Spon: Bernhardt Friedle and wife Dorothea.
Christina Magdalena, b. Apr 5, 1735, bap. Jun 17, 1753. Spon: Philipp Jacob and Magdalena Roof.

Children of Peter Eisenhauer, Swatara:
Petrus, b. Sep 6, 1745; bapt. Oct 13, 1745. Spon: Valentine Kuefer and wife.

Maria Barbara, b. Aug 22, 1747; bapt. Jan 6, 1748. Spon: Michael
Bauer and Maria Barbara Graefin.
John Nicolaus, b. May 6, 1749; bapt. May 14, 1749. Spon: John
Nicolaus Eisenhauer and wife.
George Michael, b. Aug 4, 1751; bapt. Sep1, 1751. Spon: Michael Graf
and Magdalena Eisenhauer.
John Frederich, b. Oct 6, 1753; bapt. Oct 7, 1753. Spon: John Nicolaus
Eisenhauer and wife.
Maria Magdalena, b. Mar 7, 1756; bapt. Mar 21, 1756. Spon: John
Lohmueller and Maria Magdal. Eisenhauer.
Anna Maria Elisabetha, b. Apr 25, 1759; bapt. Jun 10, 1759.
Samuel, b. Nov 25, 1763; bapt. Sep 6, 1764 (?). Spon: Michael Graf and
his wife.
John Jacob, b. Apr 13, 1777; bapt. Aug 24, 1777. Spon: John Jacob
Neff and wife.

John Thomas of George Andreas Ziegler, Lebanon, b. Dec 15, 1745;
bapt. Feb 2, 1746. Spon: John Thomas Madern and his wife.

Children of Johann Casper Stoever, Lebanon:
Maria Catarina, b. May 6, 1734; bapt. May 12, 1734. Spon: John Jacob
Kitzmueller and wife Anna Maria, also Ludwig Stein and wife Maria
Catarina.
John Caspar, b. Mar 10, 1736; bapt. Mar 14, 1736. Spon: Michael
Beyerle and wife, also Peter Ensminger and wife.
Anna Margaretha, b. Aug 21, 1738; bapt. Sep 10, 1738. Spon: George
Klein and wife Anna, Martin Weidtmann and wife Margaretha.
Anna Christina, b. Nov 24, 1740; bapt. Dec 2, 1740. Spon: Michael
Oberle and wife Christina Barbara and Anna Frantzina Merckling.
Sophia Magdalena, b. Apr 26, 1743; bapt. May 12, 1743. Spon: Adam
Lesch and wife Sophia, also Peter Anspach and wife Magdalena.
Anna Maria, b. Jan 27, 1746; bapt. Feb 2, 1746. Spon: John Jacob
Kitzmueller and wife Anna Maria, also Friederich Kraemer and wife
Anna Maria.
John Adam, b. Jun 18, 1748. bap. Jul 19, 1748. Spon: Johannes
Bischoff and wife and Adam Simon Kuhn and wife.
Tobias, b. Feb 11, 1751; bapt. Feb 17, 1751. Spon: Tobias Wagner,
Evangelical Lutheran minister and his wife, also Elisabetha
Templemann.
Johannes, b. Jul 5, 1753; bapt. Jul 15, 1753. Spon: Johannes Schwab
and wife Eva Margaretha.

John Frederich, b. Dec 16, 1755; bapt. Dec 18, 1755. Spon: Johann
George Sprecher and wife Eva Margaretha, also Freiderich Kraemer
and wife (absent).
John Frederich, b. Sep 20, 1759; bapt. Sep 30, 1759. Spon: Christoph
Freiderich Webman and wife Anna Maria.

Children of John Nicolaus Gebhardt, Swatara:
John Jacob, b. Dec 25, 1745; bapt. Feb 26, 1746. Spon: John Jacob
Kitzmueller and wife Anna Maria.
John Phillip, b. Jun 27, 1748; bapt. Jul 10, 1748. Spon: Philipp Hautz
and his wife.
Anna Catarina, b. Dec 16, 1750; bapt. Jan 6, 1751. Spon: Sebastian
Stein and wife Anna Catarina.
Anna Barbara, b. Jul 12, 1753; bapt. Jul 29, 1753. Spon: Philipp
Gerhart and his wife.
Johannes, b. Jan 6, 1756; bapt. Jan 11, 1756. Spon: Johannes Gebhart
and ---- Korr.

Children of Andrew Kochdorfer, Swatara:
Geo. Philipp, b. Apr 8, 1746; bapt. May 8, 1746. Spon: Geo. Philip Ruhl
and Anna Margaret Roth.
John Christoph, b. Aug 11, 1750; bapt. Sep 16, 1750. Spon: Christoph
Kaysser.

Children of Philipp Beyer, Lebanon:
Catarina, b. Jul 15, 1744; bapt. Aug 12, 1744. Spon: Adam Ulrich and
Catarina Buerger.
Eva, b. Jul 18, 1746; bapt. Jul 20, 1746. Spon: Jacob Dietz and Eva
Buerger.

Children of James Williams:
Benjamin, b. Feb, 1746; bapt. Aug 17, 1746. Spon: Benjamin Clark and
wife.
Christiana, Jan, 1749; bapt. May 14, 1749. Spon: Philipp Kolb and
Christina Kolb.
Johannes, b. Jul 4, 1762; bapt. Sep 5, 1762. Spon: Johannes Dietz and
wife, Elisabetha.

Children of George Veltey, Swatara:
Johannes, b. Jul 1, 1746; bapt. Aug 17, 1746. Spon: Valentine Kuefer

and his wife.

John Cunradt, b. Apr 8, 1749; bapt. May 1, 1749. Spon: Cunradt Goer and his wife.

Maria Barbara, b. Jun 15, 1750; bapt. Aug 5, 1750. Spon: Michael Boltz and wife.

John Heinrich, b. Jan, 1755; bapt. Feb 22, 1755. Spon: Ulrich Jeckel and wife.

Juliana, b. Feb 28, 1757; bapt. Mar 19, 1757. Spon: Adam Ulrich and wife.

John Ulrich, b. Nov, 3, 1759; bapt. Dec 23, 1759. Spon: Ulrich Jeckel and wife.

Sebastian, b. Sep, 1762; bapt. Oct 17, 1762. Spon: Ulrich Jeckel and wife.

Anna Barbara, b. Sep, 1766; bapt. Oct 26, 1766. Spon: George Obermeyer and wife Anna Barbara.

John George of Philipp Firfnszler, Lebanon, b. Mar 27, 1746; bapt. Jul 20, 1746. Spon: Michael Boltz and his wife.

Martinus of Peter Bucher, Swatara, b. Aug 1, 1746; bapt. Aug 17, 1746. Spon: George Meyer and wife.

George Ernst of Peter Schlosser, Lebanon, b. Aug 8, 1746; bapt. Sep 4, 1746. Spon: George Steitz and his sister-in-law Margaretha.

Christoph Ulrich of Adam Ulrich, Lebanon, b. Aug 22, 1746; bapt. Sep 9, 1746. Spon: Martin Schreiner and wife Margaretha.

John Michael of Christoph Widder, Lebanon, b. Aug 1, 1746; bapt. Sep 14, 1746. Spon: Adam Ulrich and wife Juliana.

Margaretha of Johannes Wollenweber, Swatara, b. Sep 17, 1746; bapt. Oct 12, 1746. Spon: Frederich Haehnly and wife.

Walther of Jacob Kintzer, Lebanon, b. Sep 21, 1746; bapt. Nov 9, 1746. Spon: Seideler Newman and Sabina Bindtnagel.

Children of Michael Kleber, Swatara:

George Ludwig, b. Jul 4, 1736; bapt. Sep 12, 1736. Spon: George Ludwig Friedel and wife.

Anna Maria, b. Sep 9, 1738; bapt. Jan 30, 1739. Spon: Heinrich Kline and wife Anna Maria.

Michael, b. Mar 1, 1740; bapt. Mar 26, 1741. Spon: Heinrich Klein and wife Anna Maria.

Barbara, b. Feb 28, 1744; bapt. Mar 18, 1744. Spon: Ottmar Schnaebele and wife Barbara.

John Bernhardt, b. Jan 17, 1747; bapt. Feb 1, 1747. Spon: Bernhardt
Friedel and wife.
Susanna, b. Feb 19, 1749; bapt. Mar 19, 1749. Spon: Martin Speck and
wife Susanna.
John Martin, b. Aug 15, 1751; bapt. Sep 1, 1751. Spon: the above.
Heinrich, b. Apr 18, 1754; bapt. May 19, 1754. Spon: Heinrich Sauter
and wife Sabina.

Anna Catarina of Albrecht Siechele, Lebanon, b. Mar 1, 1747; bapt.
Mar 29, 1747. Spon: Anna Catarina Baseler and Maria Catarina
Stoever.

Children of George Schirman:
Simon, b. Jan 22, 1743; bapt. Jan 23, 1743. Spon: Simon Schirman and
wife.
Anna Maria, b. Oct 3, 1744; bapt. Oct 14, 1744. Spon: Philipp Adam
Schirman and Adelheit Pfostberger.
Joh. Simon, b. Oct 19, 1746; bapt. Oct 26, 1746. Spon: Johannes Riegel
and wife.

Abraham of Peter Heydt, Lebanon, b. Mar 15, 1747; bapt. Apr 4, 1747.
Spon: Abraham Heydt and his wife Magdalena, Casper Low and his
wife Anna Margaretha.

Children of Charles Konnoway, Lebanon:
Catarina, b. Feb 19, 1747; bapt. Apr 4, 1747. Spon: Jacob and Barbara
Schilling.
Arthur, b. Nov 3, 1745; bapt. Feb 11, 1746. Spon: Abraham Heydt and
his wife.

Children of Robert Jones, deceased, Swatara:
John, b. Jun 27, 1744; bapt. Oct 11, 1747. Spon: Wendel Heyl and wife
Anna.
Margaretha, b. May 12, 1746; bapt. Oct 11, 1747. Spon: James Clark
and wife Margaretha.

Children of Frederich Troester, Swatara:
John Heinrich, b. Nov 2, 1747; bapt. Nov 22, 1747. Spon: John
Heinrich Roetelstein and wife.
John Jacob, b. Feb 3, 1751; bapt. Mar 13, 1751. Spon: John Jacob
Spiess and Elisab. Catarina Simon.

Children of Johann George Kastnitz, Swatara:
George Noah, b. Dec 13, 1747; bapt. Jan 24, 1748. Spon: Noah
Friederich and Elisabetha Kastnitz.
Christina Johannetta, b. Apr 26, 1749; bapt. May 14, 1749. Spon: Noah
Friederich and Johannetta Mueller.
Catarina Elisabetha, b. 1752; bapt. Jul 5, 1752. Spon: Wendel Ronning
and wife.

Margaretha of Michael Schwartz, deceased, Swatara, b. Jan 16, 1748;
bapt. Jan 29, 1748. Spon: Frederich Haehnle and wife Margaretha.

Children of Jacob Rammler and wife Eva Margaretha:
Eva Margaretha, b. Jan 13, 1748; bapt. Feb 6, 1748. Spon: Michael
Koppenhoefer and wife Eva Margar.
John Michael, b. Dec 4, 1750; bapt. Dec 23, 1750. Spon: Michael
Koppenhoefer and wife Eva Margar.
Martin, b. Jun 23, 1753; bapt. Jul 2, 1753. Spon: Martin Kappler and
wife.

John George of George Reed, Dorum's son-in-law, Swatara
b. Feb 20, 1748; bapt. Feb 6, 1749. Spon: Peter Brosius and Catarina
Dor.

Children of Jacob Reess, Swatara:
John George, b. Jan 23, 1748; bapt. Apr 3, 1748. Spon: John George
Emmert and wife.
John Nicolaus David, b. May, 1746; bapt. May 1, 1748. Spon: John
Nicolaus Deck and wife. *Illegitimate son of Mrs. Reess before
marriage.

Children of Jacob Kitzmueller, Swatara:
John Caspar, b. Mar 25, 1746; bapt. Apr 1, 1746. Spon: John Caspar
Stoever and wife Maria Catarina.
Maria Catarina, b. Mar 26, 1748; bapt. Apr 5, 1748. Spon: John Caspar
Stoever and wife Maria Catarina.
Andreas, b. Nov 14, 1733. Spon: Andreas Kraft and wife.
Anna Maria, b. May 28, 1735. Spon: Anna Maria Meivel.
John Jacob, b. Aug 22, 1736. Spon: John Kitzmueller, Sr.
Anna Margaretha, b. May 7, 1738. Spon: John Keller and wife.
Maria Catarina, b. May 9, 1749. (Died.)

Johannes, b. May 14, 1742. Spon: Jacob Kintzer and wife.
George Adam, b. Jan 22, 1744. Spon: Geo. Thomas Suter and wife.

John Jacob of David Fischer, Swatara, b. Apr 8, 1748; bapt. Apr 17, 1748. Spon: John Jacob Weyman and Margaretha Kober.

Children of Johannes Hollenbach, Lebanon:
Maria, b. Feb 9, 1748; bapt. Jun 12, 1748. Spon: Bernhardt Friedel and wife Dorothea.
Jinny Maria, b. 1751; bapt. May 12, 1751. Spon: Adam Ulrich and wife.
John Mattheis, b. 1753; bapt. bap. Apr 23, 1753. Spon: John Adam Herbert.
Anna Maria, b. 1761; bapt. Aug 2, 1761. Spon: John Kissner and wife Sabina.

Children of Mattheis Boesshaar, Swatara:
John Peter, b. Nov 29, 1748; bapt. Dec 25, 1748. Spon: Melchior Huengerer and wife Elizabetha.
John George, b. Jul 3, 1751; bapt. Aug 4, 1751. Spon: John George Huengerer and Sabina Schnatterle.

Children of Johannes Schmeltzer, Swatara:
Jacobina, b. Apr 13, 1749; bapt. May 1, 1749. Spon: Jacob Haeckert and wife.
John Jacob, b. 1752; bapt. Jul 5, 1752. Spon: Jacob Haeckert and wife.

Anna Barbara of Adam Klein, Swatara, b. Apr, 1749; bapt. May 1, 1749. Spon: Casper Korr and wife.
John Christoph of Philip Kolb, Swatara, b. Dec 1, 1748; bapt. May 1, 1749. Spon: Carl Veit and wife.
Christina of Jacob Moser, Swatara, b. Mar 20, 1749; bapt. May 14, 1749. Spon: Heinrich Bachman and wife.
Anna Maria of Casper Jost, Swatara, b. Apr 13, 1749; bapt. May 14, 1749. Spon: Peter Hedderich and his wife.
John Leonhardt of George Schuetz, Swatara, b. Oct 16, 1749; bapt. Jan 3, 1750. Spon: Leonhardt Mueller.
Maria Eva of Peter Goettel, Swatara, b. May 11, 1750; bapt. Jun 10, 1750. Spon: Veit Kapp and wife Gertraud.
Jacob of Jacob Riess, Swatara, b. Aug 9, 1750; bapt. Aug 19, 1750.

Spon: Thomas Bauer and wife.

Children of Thomas Bauer, Bethel:
John Jacob, b. Oct 3, 1750; bapt. Oct 28, 1750. Spon: Michael Spiegel and wife.
Eva, b. Feb 22, 1753; bapt. Mar 11, 1753. Spon: Michael Mooser and wife.

John of Clemens Gillighan, Swatara, b. Oct 21, 1750; bapt. Jan 21, 1751. Spon: John Eisenhauer and sister.
John Philipp of George Schaeffer ("Across the Large Swatara."), b. Nov 27, 1750; bapt. Apr 14, 1751. Spon: Philipp Maurer and wife.

Children of George Riedt, Swatara:
Andreas, b. Apr 6, 1751; bapt. Apr 28, 1751. Spon: Andreas Schmidt and wife.
Anna Susanna, b. Jan 28, 1753; bapt. Feb 11, 1753. Spon: Michael Hartman and Susanna Thorum.

Children of Peter Heckman, Swatara:
Ana Maria, b. 1751; bapt. Apr 28, 1751. Spon: George Friederich and wife.
Elizabetha Margaretha, b. Apr 1, 1753; bapt. Apr 22, 1753. Spon: George Friederich and wife.
John Peter, b. Sept, 1754; bapt. Oct 20, 1754. Spon: Veit Kapp and wife Gertraudt.

Anna Margaretha of Peter Sumi, Swarta, b. Apr 9, 1751; bapt. Jun 23, 1751. Spon: John Adam Stein and wife.
Anna Margaretha of Michael Sumi, Swatara, b. Mar 29, 1751; bapt. Jun 23, 1751. Spon: Ana Margaretha Guschwa.

Children of Bernhardt Faber, Swatara:
Maria Barbara, b. Aug 7, 1751; bapt. Aug 17, 1751. Spon: Adam Faber and wife.
Margaretha, b. May 20, 1755; bapt. Jun 8, 1755. Spon: Adam Faber and wife Anna Maria.

Children of Nicolaus Wolf, Bethel:
Carolus, b. Oct 20, 1751; bapt. Oct 27, 1753. Spon: Carl Scheidt and

wife.

Maria Margaretha, b. Sep 22, 1753; bapt. Oct 7, 1753. Spon: Cunradt Rounner and sister Margaretha.

John Jacob of Gottfried Baumgaertner, Bethel, b. Dec 7, 1751; bapt. Dec 22, 1751. Spon: Wendel Heyl and wife Anna.

John Gottlieb of Adam Klein, Bethel, b. Dec 9, 1751; bapt. Dec 22, 1751. Spon: John Gottlieb Thurm and Jacob Vornwalt and wife.

Children of Casper Weber, Swatara:

John Adam, b. Jan 2, 1752; bapt. Jan 7, 1752. Spon: Wendel Heyl and wife Anna.

Maria Catarina, b. Nov 25, 1759; bapt. Dec 23, 1759. Spon: Peter Felten and wife.

Children of Wendel Roenninger, Swatara:

Maria Margar. Barbara, b. Dec 24, 1751; bapt. Jan 7, 1752. Spon: Martin Eisenhauer and wife Barbara.

Maria Salome, b. May 27, 1756; bapt. Jun 13, 1756. Spon: Friederich Haehnle and wife.

Margaretha of Johannes Haeffele, Swatara, b. Feb 1, 1752; bapt. Feb 17, 1752. Spon: Cunradt Roenninger and Margaretha Speck.

John Frantz of Andreas Kastnitz, Swatara, b. Jan 28, 1752; bapt. May 30, 1752. Spon: John Frantz Fuchs and wife.

Maria Elizabetha of Peter Becker, Swatara, b. Feb 2, 1752; bapt. Mar 30, 1752. Spon: Dorst Brechbiel and wife.

Maria Salome of John Peter Spat, Swatara, b. Mar 27, 1752; bapt. Mar 30, 1752. Spon: John Michael Huber and wife.

Children of Martin Eisenhaur, Swatara:

Johannes, b. Jun, 1752; bapt. Jul 5, 1752. Sponsors not given.

George Martin, b. Mar, 1754; bapt. Apr 7, 1754. Spon: George Graff and wife.

John Peter, b. Mar 17, 1756; bapt. Mar 21, 1756. Spon: Peter Schuy and Anna Margaretha Eisenhauer.

John Valentin, b. 1759; bapt. 1759. Spon: Valentine Keller.

Maria Margaretha of George Gordon, Bethel, b. Sep 6, 1752; bapt. Nov 6, 1752. Spon: Wendel Heyl and Elizabetha Gray.

Johannes Jacob of John Lehn, Bethel, b. Sep 24, 1752; bapt. Nov 19, 1752. Spon: John Jacob Thani and his wife.

Anna Margaretha of John Eisenhauer, Bethel, b. Feb 14, 1753; bapt. Mar 26, 1753. Spon: John Nicolaus Eisenhauer and wife.

Children of Carl Schmidt, Bethel:
Eva, b. Dec 17, 1752; bapt. Feb 25, 1753. Spon: Lorentz Hautz and wife.
Susanna, b. Oct 27, 1754; bapt. Nov 3, 1754. Spon: Peter Klein and Susanna Grossmann.

Elizabetha of Serenius Schaefer, Bethel , b. Feb 10, 1753; bapt. Mar 26, 1753. Spon: John Schmetter and wife.

Children of Jacob Loresch, Bethel:
Margaretha, b. Apr 8, 1753; bapt. Apr 22, 1753. Spon: Frederich Haehnle and wife.
Maria Barbara, b. Mar 21, 1755; bapt. Apr 13, 1755. Spon: N. N.

Children of Antonius Nagel, Bethel:
Maria Barbara, b. Apr 9, 1753; bapt. Apr 22, 1753. Spon: Balthaser Noll and Barbara Nagle.
Maria Dorothea, b. Dec 20, 1754; bapt. Jan 19, 1754. Spon: John Elder and wife Dorothea.
Eva Catarina, b. Mar 9, 1756; bapt. Mar 21, 1756. Spon: Martin Oberlin and wife.

Maria Elisabetha of Adam Brecht, Bethel, b. Jun 15, 1753; bapt. Aug 12, 1753. Spon: Jacob Eprecht and wife.
Anna Margaretha of George Maess, Bethel, b. Jun 10, 1753; bapt. Aug 12, 1753. Spon: Herman Eckel and wife.

Children of Gottlieb Thuerner, Bethel:
Agnes Magdalenea, b. Oct 1753, bap. Nov 5, 1753. Spon: Jacob Haecker and wife.
John Wilhelm, b. Feb, 1757; bapt. Mar 13, 1757. Spon: John Popp and also Barbara Haecker.

Children of George Dielmann, Bethel:
Andreas, b. Dec 27, 1753; bapt. Jan 27, 1754. Spon: Michael Weber and

Eva Goettel.

Anna Margaretha, b. Sep 13, 1758; bapt. Sep 24, 1758. Spon: Michael Braun and wife Anna Juliana.

Susanna Rosina, b. Aug 1763; bapt. Aug 31, 1763. Spon: Heinrich Mueller and Susanna Rosina Heinrich.

Cunradt, b. Oct 25, 1765; bapt. Nov 1, 1765. Spon: Cunradt Weber.

Catarina Elisabetha of Johannes Haffner, Bethel, b. Apr 18, 1754; bapt. May 19, 1754. Spon: Gottfried Stempel and wife.

George of Philipp Eisenhauer, Bethel, b. Dec 19, 1754; bapt. Jan 13, 1755. Spon: George Philipp Schnattele.

Susanna Margar. of Cunradt Roenninger, Bethel, b. Jan 26, 1755; bapt. Feb 23, 1755. Spon: Michael Haehnle and wife.

Margaretha Elisabetha of Jacob Breh, Bethel, b. Feb 9, 1755; bapt. Feb 16, 1755. Spon: Robert Grain and wife.

Anna Maria of Philipp Metzger, Bethel, b. Aug 13, 1755; bapt. Sep 7, 1755. Spon: Herman Degreif and wife.

Children of Adam Brecht, Bethel:

Christian, b. Sep 8, 1755; bapt. Oct 5, 1755. Spon: Christian Kaufman and wife Magdalena.

Maria Margaretha, b. Jan 8, 1758; bapt. Mar 11, 1758. Spon: Bernhardt Friedel and wife Margaretha.

Catarina Elisabetha of Bernhardt Mann, Bethel, b. Aug 18, 1755; bapt. Oct 5, 1755. Spon: Phillip Schnatterle and Catarina Elisabetha Eissenhauer.

Children of Christian Kaufman, Bethel:

Anna Maria, b. Oct 22, 1755; bapt. Nov 30, 1755. Spon: Adam Mosser and Anna Maria Dub.

Veronica, b. May 7, 1762; bapt. May 30, 1762. Spon: John Eisenhauer and wife Veronica.

Children of Andreas Morr and wife Catarina, Bethel:

Anna Catarina, b. Feb 3, 1756; bapt. Feb 23, 1756. Spon: Wendell Heyl and wife Anna.

Christina, b. Aug 4, 1757; bapt. Aug 28, 1757. Spon: Michael Weber and wife.

Children of Caspar Schnaebele (Anabaptist) and wife, (Lutheran), Bethel:

Sophia Sabina, b. Jan 21, 1756; bapt. Feb 23, 1756. Spon: Sabina Sauter.

John Jacob, b. Nov 27, 1758; bapt. Apr 15, 1759. Spon: Anastasius Uhler and wife Dorothea.

Maria Barbara of Peter Niesz, Bethel, b. Mar 17, 1756; bapt. Mar 21, 1756. Spon: John Caspar Stoever, Jr., and Maria Barbara Nagel.

Children of Jacob Wentz, Lebanon, Kruppen:
Maria Catarina, b. May 27, 1756; bapt. Jun 6, 1756. Spon: David Herbster and wife.
John Jacob, b. Jan, 1758; bapt. Feb 12, 1758. Spon: the above.

Susanna of John Gambil, Lebanon, b. Jun 5, 1756; bapt. Jun 14, 1756. Spon: Ralph Whiteside and wife Sarah Wilson.
Johannes of Johannes Schuy, Bethel, Lancaster Co., b. Jan 9, 1757; bapt. Mar 13, 1757. Spon : John Lohmueller and Barbara Hautz.

Children of Simon Espert, Lebanon:
John George, b. Aug 20, 1767; bapt. Sep 25, 1757. Spon: George Schumacker and wife.
Anna Elizabetha, b. Apr, 1765; bapt. May 12, 1765. Spon: Arnold Scherertz and wife.

John Jacob of Friederich Kramer, Bethel, b. Apr 10, 1757; bapt. May 8, 1757. Spon: Jacob Eprecht and wife.
John George of Noah Friederich, Bethel, b. Mar 27, 1757; bapt. May 8, 1757. Spon: George Friederich and wife.
Johannes of Johannes Kuemmerling, deceased, b. Dec, 1756; bapt. May 8, 1757. Spon: Johannes Dieb, Jr., and wife.
Cunradt of Jacob Wagner, Bethel, b. Sep 15, 1757; bapt. Sep 26, 1757. Spon: Wilhelm Hardt and wife.

Children of John Casper Stoever, Jr., Bethel:
Anna Margaretha, b. Jan 24, 1758; bapt. Feb 12, 1758. Spon: Heinrich Bickel and Anna Margaretha Stoever, both single.
Maria Catarina, b. Aug 4, 1759; bapt. Aug 25, 1759. Spon: Maria Catarina Stoever, Sr.
Anna Christina, b. Aug 2, 1761; bapt. Aug 9, 1761. Spon: Anna Christina Stoever.

Anna Maria, b. Nov 3, 1763; bapt. Dec 11, 1763. Spon: Anna Maria
Stoever.

John Casper, b. Feb 27, 1765; bapt. Mar 24, 1765. Spon: John Casper
Stoever, Sr., and his wife Maria Catarina.

John Adam, b. May 29, 1767; bapt. May 31, 1767. Spon: John Adam
Stoever.

Anna Christina, b. Aug 15, 1769; bapt. Aug 20, 1769. Spon: Johannes
Fehler and wife Catarina.

Tobias. Spon: Tobias Stoever.

Anna Eva. Spon: Philipp Firnssler and wife Anna Christina.

John Frederick, b. Aug 1, 1776; bapt. Aug 25, 1776. Spon: John Casper
Stoever and wife Catarina.

Children of John Martin Kuefer and wife, Elisabetha, Bethel:

Anna Maria, b. Feb 26, 1758; bapt. Mar 11, 1758. Spon: Heinrich Dupp
and wife.

John Frederich, b. Nov 17, 1762; bapt. Dec 5, 1762. Spon: Casper
Heussler and wife.

Elizabetha, b. Jan 5, 1765; bapt. Mar 10, 1765. Spon: Cunradt
Gerhardt and Maria Elizabetha Kuefer.

Maria Elizabetha, b. Dec 3, 1766; bapt. Mar 15, 1767. Spon: Nicolaus
Biel and wife Maria Elizabetha.

Maria Barbara of Jacob Schnaebele, Bethel, b. Jan 29, 1758; bapt. Mar
11, 1758. Spon: Ottmar Schnaebele and wife.

Maria Catarina of Valentin Gerhardt, Bethel, b. Sep 11, 1758; bapt.
Sep 24, 1758. Spon: Heinrich Schnatterle and Anna Catarina Uhler.

Anna Sabina of Hans George Dumm, Lebanon, b. Mar, 1759; bapt. Apr
15, 1759. Spon: John Wolf Kissner and wife, Anna Sabina.

John George of Martin Schmidt, Swatara, b. Oct 4, 1758. bap. Oct 22,
1758. Spon: George Glassbrenner and wife.

Children of Gottfried Steupel, Lebanon:

Rosina, b. Jun 1, 1759; bapt. Jun 24, 1759. Spon: David Herbster and
wife Rosina.

John David, b. Feb, 1763; bapt. Feb 20, 1763. Spon: David Herbster
and second wife Anna Maria.

Eva Catarina, b. Jan, 1760; bapt. Feb 26, 1766. Spon: George Mueller
and wife.

Children of Peter Fischer, Lebanon:
Johannes, b. Oct 14, 1759; bapt. Nov 11, 1759. Spon: John Dups and
Margaretha Boecklin.
Barbara, b. Jul 13, 1765; bapt. Jul 14, 1765. Spon: Heinrich Boeckle
and wife Anna Maria.
John Jacob, b. Nov 5, 1765; bapt. Nov 16, 1766. Spon: Jacob Engel and
wife Margaretha.

Anna Margaretha of Andreas Bartruff, Lebanon, b. Feb 11, 1759; bapt.
Mar 11, 1759. Spon: John Wilhelm Klein and Anna Margar. Schuetz.
Anna Sabina of Martin Meyly, Jr., Lebanon, b. Apr 17, 1760; bapt. May
25, 1760. Spon: Jacob Weber and Anna Sabina Meyly.
Maria Magdalena of Casper Hiszler and wife, Rosina, Bethel, b. Sep 24,
1760; bapt. Oct 5, 1760. Spon: George Sydebueger and wife.

Children of Sebastian Nagel and wife, Maria Magdalena, Bethel:
John Christian, b. Oct 24, 1760; bapt. Nov 30, 1760. Spon: John
Christian Koch and wife.
Anna Maria Barbara, b. Feb 17, 1762; bapt. Feb 21, 1762. Spon: John
Caspar Stoever and wife.
Johannes, b. Sep 2, 1763; bapt. Sep 18, 1763. Spon: Johann Christian
Lauer.

Children of George Sedelmeyer (Seidelmeyer) and wife, Magdal.,
Bethel:
Anna Rosina, b. Mar 3, 1761; bapt. Mar 19, 1761. Spon: Casper
Heussler and wife Rosina.
John Caspar, b. Mar 17, 1762; bapt. Apr 4, 1762. Spon: Caspar Roeder
and Regina Gerhard.
Maria Elisabetha, b. Jun, 1767; bapt. Jul 12, 1767. Spon: Ulrich Joeckel
and wife.
Heinrich, b. Oct 9, 1774; bapt. Oct 18, 1774. Spon: Heinrich
Schnatterle and wife Barbara.
Children of John Daniel Madern and wife, Elisabetha, Bethel:
Maria Eva Rosina, b. Apr 19, 1761; bapt. May 17, 1761. Spon: Maria
Eva Strauss.
John Thomas, b. 1762; bapt. Oct 31, 1762. Spon: John Thomas Madern
and wife Veronica.
Michael, b. Oct, 1766; bapt. Oct 26, 1766. Spon: John Thomas Madern
and wife Vernica.

Sabina Elisabetha of Philipp Schnatterle, Bethel, b. Jun 25, 1761; bapt. Oct 18, 1761. Spon: Sabina Schnatterle.

John Bernardt of Heinrich Mueller and wife, Jacobina, Bethel, b. Sep, 1761; bapt. Oct 18, 1761. Spon: John Boesshaar and wife.

Children of Christoph Wittmyer, Bethel:
Maria Barbara, b. Nov 2, 1761; bapt. Nov 16, 1761. Spon: Ottmar Schnaebele and wife Barbara.
Anna Maria, b. Dec 19, 1763; bapt. Jan 6, 1764. Spon: John Adam Kern and wife Anna Maria and widow Anna Maria Fischer.

Children of Wendel Keller, Lebanon:
Jacobina Rosina, b. Nov 14, 1761; bapt. Nov 29, 1761. Spon: Michael Laurie and wife.
George Wendel, b. Jul, 1764; bapt. Jul 24, 1764. Spon: Michael Balmer and wife.

Children of Matthias Heesze and wife Eva Catarina, Swatara:
Johannes, b. Dec, 1761; bapt. Dec 20, 1761. Spon: Michael Zimmerman and wife Eva.
John Michael, b. Feb, 1765; bapt. Mar 3, 1765. Spon: the above.
Eva Catarina, b. Oct, 1767; bapt. Nov 8, 1767. Spon: --- Weber and Catarina Zimmerman.

Chidren of George Meyer and wife, Anna Barbara, Bethel:
Maria Elisabetha, b. Oct 22, 1762; bapt. Nov 14, 1762. Spon: Philipp Jacob Bortner and wife Elisabetha.
Anna Maria, b. Dec, 1766; bapt. Jan 18, 1767. Spon: George Felty and wife Anna Maria.

Children of Philipp Jacob Bortner and wife Maria Elisabetha, Bethel:
Heinrich, b. Apr 24, 1761; bapt. May, 1761. Spon: Heinrich Mueller and wife Jacobina.
John George, b. Feb 1, 1763; bapt. Apr 1, 1763. Spon: George Velten and wife Anna Maria.
Johannes, b. Jun 3, 1765; bapt. Jun 16, 1765. Spon: Johannes Felten and wife.
Jonathan of David Jones, b. Mar 27, 1761; bapt. Aug 31, 1763. Spon: Henry Sowder and wife Sabina.

Children of Michael Krehl, Bethel:
John Michael, b. Oct 20, 1763; bapt. Nov 20, 1763. Spon: Nicolaus Wolf
and wife.
Carolus, b. Jul, 1766; bapt. Aug 3, 1766. Spon: Carl Schedt and wife.

Anna Margaretha of Leonhardt Herger, Bethel, b. Oct 30, 1763; bapt.
Jan 6, 1764. Spon: Cunradt Schmidt and wife Anna Margaretha.
John Peter of Peter Albert, Bethel, b. Mar 30, 1764; bapt. May 13,
1764. Spon: Martin Hess and wife.
Maria Margaretha of Philip Gruenenwaldt, Lebanon, b. Jul 18, 1765;
bapt. Jul 18, 1765. Spon: Christoph Embisch and wife.
John Friederich of George Federhoff and wife Anna Elizabetha,
(Lebanon Township.), b. Aug 6, 1765; bapt. Aug 11, 1765. Spon:
Friederich Jensel and wife Maria Agnes.

Children of Christoph Embisch and wife, Lebanon:
Johannes, b. Sep 5, 1765; bapt. Sep 8, 1765. Spon: Phillip Gruenenwalt
and wife.
John Friederich, b. Feb 22, 1767; bapt. Mar 8, 1767. Spon: Philipp
Marstaller and wife.

John Heinrich of Andreas Hoerauf and wife, Swatara, b. Sep, 1765;
bapt. Sep 15, 1765. Spon: Johannes Oehrle and wife Regina.
Maria Magdalena of Adam Schneider and wife, Bethel, b.
Oct 26, 1764; bapt. Sep 29, 1765. Spon: Heinrich Naess and Maria
Magdalena Haehnle.
John Peter of George Schill and wife, Bethel, b. Oct 11, 1765; bapt.
Oct 27, 1765. Spon: Nicolaus Biel and Barbara Kuefer.
Margaretha of Carl Schedt and wife, Williamsborough, b. Dec, 1766;
bapt. Jan 19, 1766. Spon: Michael Grehl and wife Margaretha.
Johannes of Johannes Schwartz and wife, Esther, Lebanon Town.
Spon: George Sprecher and wife Margaretha.
Maria Catarina of Jacob Weber and wife Anna Maria, Lebanon, b. Dec
26, 1766; bapt. Jan 11, 1767. Spon: Heinrich Boeckle and wife.
Johannes of James Williams and wife, now dead, (Bethel.), b. Jan 10,
1767; bapt. Jan 18, 1767. Spon: Johannes Diebin and Margar.
Haehnlin.
John Freiderich of John Nicolaus Biel and wife Maria Elisab., Bethel, b.
Feb 8, 1767; bapt. Mar 15, 1767. Spon: Martin Kuefer and wife Maria
Elisabetha.

John Jacob of Johannes Huber and wife Elisab., Lebanon, b. Jul 27, 1767; bapt. Aug 2, 1767. Spon: Jacob Stieb and wife.

Philip Jacob of Jacob Ziegler, Jr. and wife Judith, Lebanon, b. Jul, 1767; bapt. Aug 2, 1767. Spon: Philipp Brenner and wife.

Christoph Freiderich of Martin Kuemmerling and wife Anna Magar., Bethel, b. Aug 22; bapt. Sep 6, 1767. Spon: Christoph Frederich Weyman and wife Eva Maria.

Christian of George Glass and wife, Eva Elizabeth, b. Dec 25, 1768; bapt. Jan 29, 1769. Spon: Jost Schwetzel and wife Susanna.

John Adam of Peter Kraemer and wife Margaretha, Lebanon b. Feb 19, 1767; bapt. Mar 22, 1767. Spon: John Adam Waible and wife Anna.

Children of Christoph Ziebold and wife Barbara, Lebanon:

Catarina, b. Jul 19, 1769; bapt. Jul 24, 1769. Spon: Conradt Braun, Sr., and wife Agnes.

Anna Maria, b. Jul 19, 1769; bapt. Jul 24, 1769. Spon: Michael Rieder and wife Anna Maria.

Catarina of John Nicolaus Bopp and wife Catar. Margar. (Swatara.), b. Jan 28, 1776; bapt. Feb 11, 1776. Spon: Peter Felt and wife Catarina.

Johannes of Johannes Gassert and wife Anna Maria, (Bethel.), b. Jun 28, 1776; bapt. Aug 25, 1776. Spon: Martin Kuefer and wife Elisabetha.

John Heinrich of Jacob Neff and his wife, Williamsborough, b. Feb 20, 1778; bapt. Apr 5, 1778. Spon: Carl Schedt and wife Eva.

John Heinrich of Mattheis Braunwell and wife, Kruppen Land., b. Oct 11, 1778; bapt. Dec 6, 1778. Spon: Martin Weitz and wife.

John Adam of David Riehl, Heidelberg, b. Aug 12, 1751; bapt. Aug 18, 1751. Spon: Jacob Sensebach and wife.

Anna Maria of Michael Schaurer, Heidelberg, b. Nov 19, 1730; bapt. Dec 13, 1730. Spon: Heinrich Zeller and wife.

Sebastian of Michael Burger, Heidelberg, b. May 11, 1751; bapt. Aug 18, 1751. Spon: Sebastian Obold and his wife.

Children of Jacob Dreisch, Heidelberg, and wife Susanna:

George Leonhardt, b. Feb 1757; bapt. Apr 23, 1759. Spon: John Leonhardt Dreisch.

John Reichardt, b. Dec 25, 1758; bapt. Apr 23, 1759. Spon: John Leonhardt Dreisch.

Rosina, b. Dec 25, 1760; bapt Mar 19, 1761. Spon: Jacob Wentz and wife.

These entries were made after the death of John Casper Stoever in 1779.

Children of Johann Frederick Stoever and wife Margaretha nee Daenscherlz:

Maria Catarina, b. Jan 9, 1781; bapt. Jan 18, 1781. Spon: Catarina Stoever, widow.

Maria Catarina, b. 1782; bapt. Oct 9, 1782. Spon: Catarina Stoever, widow.

John Frederich, b. Apr 15, 1785; bapt. May, 1785. Spon: Samuel Mery and wife Catarina.

John Jacob, b. Jun 10, 1787; bapt. Jul, 1787. Spon: John Caspar Stoever and wife Barbara.

Johannes, b. Nov 29, 1789; bapt. Jul. Spon: John Stoever and his wife.

William, b. Aug 21, 1792; bapt. Nov, 28, 1792. Spon: Johannes Stoever (son of Adam) and Catarina Franck, both single.

John Philipp, b. Apr 8, 1795; bapt. Apr, 1795. Spon: John Philipp Fernsler.

Cattarina, b. Oct 13, 1798; bapt. Nov 4, 1798. Spon: Johann Gloninger and wife Catarina.

MARRIAGES

1731
Feb 25 Francis Reynolds and Catarina Steitz, Quittapahila.

1734
Dec 18 Christoph Meyer and Anna Rosina Kopfenhoefer, Lebanon.

1735
Oct 6 John Peter Kucher and Anna Bar. Koephenhoefer, Lebanon.

1738
Feb 6 John Welsh and Elizabeth Whitside, Quittapahilla.
Aug 2 Mattheis Schierisser and Catarina Koppenhoefer, Lebanon.
Dec 12 Francis Reynolds and Elenore Thistle, Quittapahilla.

1739
Jan 29 Peter Heylman and Salome Frey, Lebanon.
Jun 12 Peter Stout and Margaretha Cypher, Swatara.

Jun 12 James Russell and Jane Russell, Lebanon.
Nov 30 Matthew Clark and Elisabetha Ingerham, Lebanon.

1741

Jan 23 John Heinrich Wilhelm and Catarina Haermaennin, Swatara.
Nov 21 James Tennin and Elisabeth Adams, of Swatara.

1742

Jan 3 Nicolaus Kintzer and Anna Catara. Hoester, Quittapahilla.
Mar 22 John Abraham Leppo and Anna Margaretha Schueler, Swatara.
May 16 John Gilbert and Elizabetha Pannel, Swatara.
May 16 John Kuehny and Elizabetha Cars, Swatara.
Jun 9 John Welsh and Anna Sharp, Lebanon.
Oct 29 Casper Loewe and Margaret Esskuch, Lebanon.

1743

Jan 6 Andreas Keterle and Catarina Barbara Becher, Lebanon.
Jul 31 Heinrich Meyly and Veronica Spitaler, Bethel.
Aug 23 Heinrich Wilhelm and Elizabetha Scherb, Bethel township.
Sep 26 John Peter Wampler and Anna Barbara Brenneiss, Swatara.
Oct 23 John Herman Eckel and Anna Margaretha Ohrendurf, Lebanon.

1744

Jan 21 John Tomson and Susannah Hammon, Lebanon.
Jan 31 John Tomson and Susannah Margaretha Vollmar, Bethel.
Feb 2 John Philipp Holinger and Juliana Umberger, Lebanon.
May 22 John Friederich Zeh and Maria Ottilia Stempel, Swatara.
Jun 19. John Martin Kirstaetter and Magdalena Huckenborger,
    Lebanon.
Jul 8 Christian Bienen and Maria Sara Maennerin, Swatara.
Oct 2 William Leadsoorth and Elizabeth Loodenton, Bethel.
Nov 12 John George Kastnitz and Anna Maria Gottliebin Dupss,
Bethel.

1745

Jan 15 George Andreas Ziegeler and Anna Margaretha Madern,
    Swatara.
Sep 24 John Cunradt Tempelmann and Maria Elisab. Buechin,
Lebanon.

1746
Jan 7 Mattheis Boger and Anna Magdalena Wampsler, Lebanon.
Feb 11 Michael Ackermann and Anna Barbara Albert, Lebanon.
Apr 27 Leonhardt Kern and Anna Margaretha Schmidt, Swatara.
May 11 Jacob Kanterrmann and Catarina Mueller, Swatara.
May 15 James Clarck and Margaretha Tratter, Lebanon.
May 25 Johannes Kuehny and Margaretha Schneider, Swatara.
Dec 3 Dennis Druggon and Johanna Conner, Lebanon.
Dec 15 William Packwood and Sarah Hough, Bethel.

1747
Jan 13 Jacob Brenneiser and Anna Veronica Wampsler, Lebanon.
Oct 12 Jacob Reess and Rachel Dyx, servants at Henry Schmidt's,
  Bethel.
Dec 29 Valentin Herchelrodt and Elisabetha Meusser, Lebanon.
Dec 29 Jacob Schober and Maria Dorothea Zimmerman.

1748
May 2 Peter Goettel and Eva Friederich, Bethel.
May 10 Moses Moor and Jane Gillighin, Lebanon.
Jun 15 Abraham Richardson and Mary Margaretha Mintz, Lebanon.
Jun 21 Adam Schneider and Anna Maria Bort, Lebanon.
Jun 21 George Michael Bronner and Barbara Tempelmann, Lebanon.
Jun 21 George Michael Bronner and Barbara Templemann, Lebanon.
Jul 14 Samuel Jones and Rachael Tittle, Bethel.
Sep 24 John Carr and Margaretha Ross, Lebanon.
Oct 13 Peter Tittle and Mary Hough, Lebanon.
Oct 25 John Michael Wagner and Elisabetha Madern, Swatara.
Oct 30 Leonhardt Faber and Catarina Barbara Roesser, Swatara.
Dec 21 Johann Jacob Dietz and Catarina Holtzwart, Lebanon.

1749
Jan 8 George Borden and Anna Catarina Umbehaur, Lebanon.
Jan 12 Robert Ellit and Elisabetha Aar, Lebanon.
Feb 9 William Wilson and Sarah Allen, Lebanon.
Mar 2 Samuel Packwood and Mary Pannel, Bethel.
Mar 3 William Gibson and Anna Paxtang, Bethel.
May 1 William Morris and Rebecca Oliphants, Lebanon.
Jun 1 David Pitts and Welsh Lewis, Lebanon.
Oct 24 George Velty and Anna Maria Meyer, Bethel.

1750

Jan 30 Samuel Welsh and Sarah Reynolds, Bethel.
Apr 26 Adam Buerger and Maria Barbara Meyer, Lebanon.
May 10 Michael Zimmerman and Eva Kuenig, Swatara.
May 28 Gottfried Baumgartner and Anna Catarina Kueffer, Lebanon.
Jun 25 John Henderson and Anna Simple, Lebanon.
Aug 14 John Mattheis Bohr and Maria Elizabeth Neu, Lebanon.
Sep 25 George Naess and Anna Maria Kreuber, Bethel.
Oct 9 Jacob Wagner and Magdalena Gehrhardt, Lebanon.
Oct 9 Johann Wolf Kissner and Anna Sabina Bindtnagel, Lebanon.

1751

Jan 8 Noah Frederich and Margaretha Becker, Bethel.
Jan 8 Peter Gutman and Anna Maria Hauck, Bethel.
Jan 10 Johannes Becker and Catarina Umberger, Lebanon.
Jan 10 Thomas Davies and Nels Read, Lebanon.
Jan 21 John Brennesen and Christina Minier, Bethel.
Feb 5 Johann Peter Falter and Maria Catarina Neu, Lebanon.
Feb 19 Hanzs Martin Ergebrecht and Susanna Forr, Lebanon.
May 16 Joseph Zieffle and Maria Catarina Guenthuer, Lebanon.
Jun 11 Sebastian Kirstaetter and Magdalena Derver, Lebanon.
Jun 18 John George Eichelberger and Christina Dorothea Best, Lebanon.
Jun 18 Melchior Winckelmann and Barbara Sigrist, Lebanon.
Oct 8 Frantz Caspar Wagner and Margar. Kirstaetter, Lebanon.
Dec 17 Joseph Stout and Catarina Meylie, Bethel.
Dec 17 James Rafler and Barbara Meylie.

1752

Jan 2 Peter Kraemer and Magdalena Leidyn, Lebanon.
Jan 7 George Michael Graff and Maria Margar. Meyer, Bethel.
Jan 7 Johannes Eisenhardt and Veronica Meyer, Bethel.
Mar 31 Leonhardt Mueller and Anna Maria Raetelsperger, Lebanon.
Jul 5 Adam Brecht and Margaretha Battesteld, Bethel.
Nov 14 Philipp Weigandt and Magdalena Baur, Lebanon.

1753

Jan 23 Jacob Schnaebele and Susanna Hurter, Bethel.
Jan 30 John Adam Barth and Elisabetha Weisenkind, Lebanon.
Feb 26 Michael Kally and Mary Kuhny, Bethel.

Feb 27 Henry Cowen and Jane Varner, Lebanon.
May 6 Johannes Huber and Maria Elisab. Ritscher, Lebanon.
Jun 5 Johan Michael Kirstaetter and Maria Dorothea Dietz, Lebanon.
Aug 14 Heinrich Hortle and Catarina Firnssler, Lebanon.
Dec 18 George Wendel Keller and Barbara Straup, Bethel.
1754
May 23 Robert Gibson and Els. Davies, Lebanon.
Jun 3 Johann George Obermeyer and Maria Magdl. Rosenbach, Bethel.
Jun 25 Caspar Heussler and Rosina Schrellbecker, Lebanon.
Aug 5 George Hansz Dietrich and Veronica Meyer, Lebanon.
Aug 25 Johannes Kuemmerly and Catarina Margaretha Dieb, Bethel.
Aug 27 Simon Burckard and Catarina Brandes, Lebanon.
Nov 3 Ludwig Weidner and Maria Engel Gerst, Heidelberg and Bethel.
Nov 28 William Williams and Rebecca McCaddoms, Bethel.
Dec 2 Michael Bunert and Barbara Schnelb, Bethel.

1755
Jan 13 Andreas Morr and Catarina Roenninger, Bethel.
Jan 13 Christian Kaufman and Magdalena Schnaebele, Bethel.
Apr 9 Adam Riesz and Anna Margaretha Seemahr, Bethel.
May 28 George Sprecher and Eva Margaretha Schwab, Lebanon.
Jul 21 Johann Adam Bohr and Anna Barbara Labengeiger, Lebanon.
Jul 21 Johann Peter Pannekuchen and Catarina Dietz, Lebanon.
Aug 3 Johann Adam Wirth and Eva Elizabetha Schnug, Lebanon.
Aug 26 John George Roessler and Elizabetha Catarina Aras, Lebanon.
Sep 23 Jacob Dobler and Anna Hough, Bethel.
Sep 23 Samuel Stout and Mary Elizabeth Thomas, Bethel.
Sep 23 Lorentz Fischer and Catarina Boner, Bethel.
Oct 5 Lorentz Kurtz and Maria Elizabetha Saur, Lebanon.
Nov 18 Johann Adam Stoehr and Eva Catarina Ietter, Lebanon.

1756
Feb 10 George Rein and Anna Maria Meyer, Lebanon.
Mar 8 Johannes Werner and Christina Grossmann, Bethel.
Mar 23 Abraham Clark and Jane Clark, Lebanon.
Mar 25 Michael Malfir and Anna Eva Schnug, Lebanon.
Mar 30 Iost Iotter and Eva Catarina Hubeler, Lebanon.
Apr 20 Peter Maurer and Catarina Elizabetha Kniesz, Bethel.
Jun 1 Johann Martin Kirstaetter and Elizabetha Bickel, Lebanon.

Jun 13 Melchior Webert and Elizabetha Biener, Bethel.
Jun 15 George Hansz Dietrich and Dorothea Boltz, Lebanon.
Jul 4 Wendel Keller and Elizabetha Fuchs, Bethel.
Jul 6 John Michael Pfrang and Anna Catarina Gring, Lebanon.
Jul 11 John George Kupper and Elizabetha Zimmerman, Lebanon.
Aug 26 Joseph Scot and Anna Kalliah, Lebanon.

1757

Feb 15 John Peter Ritscher and Anna Margaretha Kirber, Lebanon.
Mar 1 Michael Fischer and Maria Magdalena Eisenhauer, Bethel.
Mar 2 Matheis Schmutz and Regina Zwerontzor, Lebanon.
Mar 14 John Lerkin and Margaretha Thompson, Lebanon.
Mar 15 Andreas Kochendoerfer and Elizabetha Nagel, Bethel.
Mar 22 John Jacob Boltz and Catarina Madern, Lebanon.
Mar 29 Johannes Krueger and Anna Margaretha Heydt, Lebanon.
Apr 13 Jacob Zimpfer and Anna Maria Lorentz, Lebanon.
Apr 19 Johann Martin Kuefer and Elizabetha Meyer, Bethel.
Apr 26 Johann Casper Stoever, Jr., and Anna Maria Barbara Nagel,
   Lebanon.
May 31 Johannes Kuemmerling and Anna Maria Pfrang, Lebanon.
May 31 George Hatz and Anna Margaretha Dieb, Lebanon.
Aug 7 Martin Schmidt and Catarina Fischer, Lebanon.
Sep 4 Hansz Ulrich Huber and Elizabeth Firnsler, Lebanon.
Oct 18 Peter Kraemer and Anna Margaretha Ernst, Lebanon.
Oct 25 John Adam Neu and Veronica Barbara Koemmet, Lebanon.
Nov 22 John Heinrich Hertle and Catarina Kuehn, Lebanon and
   Bethel.
Nov 24 John Nicolaus Brechtbiel and Juliana Diller, Lebanon.
Nov 24 Sebastian Nagel and Maria Magdal. Diller, Bethel.
Dec 20 Adam Stephan and Maria Agnes Pfrang, Lebanon.

1758

Jan 3 George Fischer and Anna Elisabeth Knopf, Lebanon.
Feb 14 John Jacob Bickel and Eva Margaretha Ietter, Lebanon.
Feb 14 Antonius Ditzler and Anna Magdalena Mader, Bethel.
Feb 27 Antionius Karmenie and Anna Christina Hetzler, Lebanon.
Mar 29 Andreas Bartruff and Christina Sophia Klein, Lebanon.
Apr 2 Johannes Hebberling and Maria Elisab. Pressler, Lebanon.
Apr 4 John Martin Kuemmerling and Elisabetha Kirstetter, Lebanon.
Apr 24 Abraham Heydt and Elisabetha Sieg, Lebanon.

Jun 15 Robert Rogers and Anna Christina Ramberg, Lebanon.
Jul 2 Peter Fischer and Catarina Bockle, Lebanon.
Nov 14 Johann Schweickhardt Imboden and Eleanora Diller, Lebanon.

1759
Jan 29 Johannes Stohler and Anna Maria Glassbrenner, Heidelberg
 and Lebanon.
Mar 5 Jacob Sprecher and Dorothea Blecher, Lebanon.
Jul 9 Heinrich Berhardt and Catarina Bendter, Lebanon.
Aug 21 Peter Brechbiel and Maria Catarina Franck, Lebanon.
Aug 21. Jacob Strauss and Elizabetha Brecht.
Aug 30 Thomas Clark and Margaretha Heydt, Lebanon.
Sep 18 Martin Herman and Anna Dorothea Borst, Lebanon.
Oct 28 Philipp Baasz and Anna Weimer, Lebanon.
Oct 28 John Ernst Curt and Margaretha Riedt, Lebanon.
Nov 4 Matthias Hess and Eva Catarina Stober, Warwick.
Nov 11 John Leonhardt Fischer and Barbara Gerhardt, Bethel.
Dec 13 James Huens and Maria Sabina Felleberger, Lebanon.

1760
Jan 21 Jacob Ziegeler and Juliana Kirstetter, Lebanon.
Jan 21 Abraham Schaeffer and Maria Barbara Sirer, Lebanon.
Jan 22 Adam Dumm and Catarina Heydt, Lebanon.
Feb 19 David Herbster and Anna Maria Barbara Hacker, Lebanon.
Feb 26 Frantz Caspar Wagner (widower), and Elizabetha Wirtz,
 Lebanon and Cocalico.
May. 6 John George Seidelmeyer and Magdalena Wagner, Bethel.
May 20 Wendel Hautz and Catarina Elizaba. Riegel, Bethel, Lebanon
 Co., and Tulpehocken.
Jun 9 Peter McCarthy and Nancy Thompson, Lebanon.
Jun 9 Laurence Rack and Brigitta Strattel, Lebanon.
Jun 26 Michael Kirber and Anna Maria Schlatter, Lebanon.
Jul 6 Adam Bayer and Maria Sara Ritschor, Lebanon.
Aug 19 Philipp Jacob Bortner and Maria Elizabetha Velt, Bethel.
Aug 31 Abraham Kroh and Maria Schaeffer, Bethel, Lebanon Co.
Sep 2 John Christoph Friederich and Ana Maria Wagner, Lebanon.
Sep 16 John Brown and Anna Maria Moser, Bethel.
Sep 16 Christian Mueller and Elizabeth Ried, Lebanon.
Sep 29 Edward Steans and Mary Martin, Lebanon.
Oct 14 Peter Benedict and Maria Elizabetha Lauckster, Lebanon.

Oct 28 Matthies Staub and Sophia Fischer, Lebanon.
Nov 18 George Ulrich and Elizabeth Naess, Lebanon and Cocalico.
Nov 18 James Atkinson and Anne Carnill or Camell Lebanon and York county.
Nov 25 John Friederich Kuefer and Sabina Vollmar, Derry and Bethel.
Nov 25 Heinrich Mueller and Jacobina Wagner, Bethel.
Dec 2 Matthies Schwertzel and Catarina Barbara Laey, Lebanon.
Dec 30 John Christian Demmen, or Dennam, and Margar. Magdal. Mueller, Lebanon.

1761
Jan 27 Johann Wendel Weber and Elizab. Magdalena Eichelberger, Lebanon.
Feb 3 John George Held and Maria Magdalena Wolf, Lebanon.
Feb 5 John Collins and Catarina Finley, Lebanon.
Feb 17 Thomas Kintzel and Ana Maria Holderbaum, Lebanon.
Mar 19 Thomas Atkinson and Elizabeth Williams, Lebanon.
Apr 7 Johann Ludwig Kleber and Anna Magdalena Ellinger, Lebanon.
Apr 30 Johann Friederich Kuhbauch and Anna Catarina Felt, Lebanon and Bethel.
Apr 30 George Meyer and Barbara Felt, Lebanon and Bethel.
May 11 Christian Goellnitz and Maria Elisab. Steg, Lebanon.
May 19 Peter Kuefer and Anna Waibel, Bethel and Lebanon.
Jun 16 John Daniel Stroh and Catarina Barbara Uhler, Lebanon.
Jun 16 Heinrich Schnatterle and Anna Barbara Uhler, Lebanon.
Oct 6 Jno. Jacob Kitzmueller and Catarina Peter, Lebanon.

1762
Apr 18 Johann Philipp Firnssler and Anna Christina Stoever, Lebanon.
Apr 27 Owen Davies and Anna Maria Weber, Lebanon.
May 17 John Robinson and Mary Beset, Lebanon.
May 18 Benjamin Davies and Lyddia Cloward, Lebanon.
Jun 7 William Bear and Sarah Boile, Lebanon.
Jul 22 Thomas Kees and Rebecca Shmidt, Midletown and Paxtang.
Aug 24 George Fischer and Elisabeth Cunradt, Bethel and Lebanon.
Sep 2 Laurence Clark and Susanna Clark, by license, Lebanon.
Sep 7 Jacob Egler (?) and Catarina Biliams (?), Lebanon and Lancaster.
Sep 28 John Michael Fischer and Anna Magdalena Fischer, Bethel.
Nov 22 Jacob Looser and Margaretha Schmidt, Bethel and Heidelberg.

1763

May 21 Caspar Roeder and Regina Gerhardt, Bethel.
Jul 24 Johannes Fihler and Eva Catarina Raup, Bethel.
Oct 23 Jacob Scheretz and Elisabetha Rausch, Lebanon.
Dec 13 Nicolaus Kihmer and Elisabetha Teiss, Lebanon.

1764

Mar 6 Jacob Firnssler and Magdalena Peter, Lebanon.
Mar 7 Philpp Lorentz Hautz and Anna Maria Mueller, Lebanon.
Mar 20 George Balmer and Barbara Olinger, Lebanon.
Apr 5 George Dumm and Anna Maria Geiger, Derry and Lebanon.
Apr 10 Christian Schnug and Catarina Boyer, Lebanon.
Apr 5 Johannes Peter and Barbara Firnszler, Lebanon.
May 30 William Whitside and Elenore McNees, Bethel.
Jul 23 Christoph Friederich Wegman and Maria Eva Pfrang, Lebanon.
Aug 7 Jno. Atkinson and Catarina Dieb, Bethel.
Oct 9 Peter Kober and Margaretha Stroher, Lebanon.
Oct 16 Heinrich Meyer and Juliana Emrich, Bethel.
Oct 16 Johannes Seydelmeyer and Rosina Layblin, Bethel.
Oct 28 George Federhoff and Anna Elisabetha Schnaebelin, Lebanon.
Nov 20 Adam Solomon and Dinah Backer, Lebanon.
Dec 11 Carl Buerger and Anna Elisabetha Henninger, Bethel.

1765

Mar 5 John Adam Maennig and Anna Margaretha Holtz, Rapho and
Lebanon.
Mar 5 Christian Michael and Maria Barbara Eisenhauer, Bethel.
Mar 19. Andreas Kastnitz and Elisabetha Gockel, Lebanon.
Apr 15 George Ellinger and Anna Maria Catarina Weyhrich, Lebanon.
Apr 23 Heinrich Boebel and Anna Maria Ellinger, Lebanon.
May 7 Peter Eisenhauer and Anna Maria Fischer, Bethel.
Jun 24 Jno. George Schock and Anna Catarina Maurer, Lebanon and
Heidelberg.
Sep 29 Christian Frendling and Anna Wolf, Lebanon.
Oct 8 John Jacob Wolf and Anna Margar. Schnug, Lebanon.
Nov 26 Philipp Rauh and Anna Maria Regina Braun, Bethel.
Dec 10 James Williams and Magdalena Haehnlin, Bethel.

1766

Feb 6 Johannes Stein and Eva Barbara Kucher, Lebanon.

Mar 4 Jacob Bickel and Maria Catarina Braun, Lebanon.
Mar 4 John Nicolaus Bohr and Maria Margaretha Kobnar (Kolmar), Lebanon.
Mar 4 John Martin Kolmar and Anna Magdalena Hetzler, Lebanon.
Apr 1 Peter Schumacher and Anna Dorothea Schaaf, Lebanon.
Apr 8 Jno. Martin Kuemmerling and Anna Margar. Edelmann, Bethel
Apr 8 Anastasius Heylmann and Rosina Barbara Maurer, Lebanon an Heidelberg.
Apr 8 Geo. Maurer and Magdalena Heylmann, Lebanon.
Apr 14 Caspar Elias Diller and Eva Magdalena Meyer, Lebanon.
Apr 15 George Heinrich Ziegler and Dorothea Schnug, Lebanon.
May 27 John Nicolaus Biohl and Elisabetha Kuefer, Bethel.
May 27 John Adam Balmer and Barbara Schauffler, Lebanon.
Jun 4 John Schnug, widower, and Catarina Duliban, Lebanon.
Jun 17 Antonius Hauer and Barbara Kueffer, Bethel.
Jul 29 John Hicks and Elisabetha Holderbaum, Lebanon.
Aug 4 John Adam Weiss and Maria Eva Meyer, Lebanon.
Sep 9 Heinrich Bickel and Catarina Gerhardt, Bethel.
Sep 23 Andreas Patz and Catarina Stuck, Bethel and Lebanon.
Sep 30 Conrad Hornberger and Catarina Maag, Bethel.
Oct 28 Martin Koch and Elisabetha Schantz, Lebanon.
Nov 18 Andreas Karg and Anna Maria Heinrich, Lebanon.
Nov 18 Daniel Jungblut and Anna Maria Elizabeth Heinrich, Lebanon.
Nov 25 John Leonhardt Kirstaetter and Anna Elisabetha Zehrung, Lebanon.
Dec 9 John Christoph Uhler and Margar. Barbara Spicker, Lebanon.

1767
Jan 26 Johann Wendel Wolf and Anna Dorothea Endress, Lebanon.
Mar 10 Christoph Ulrich and Juliana Umberger, Lebanon.
Mar 17 John Nicolaus Fehler and Barbara Leonhardt, Bethel.
Apr 21 George Meyer and Maria Elisabetha Stoehr, Rapho and Lebanon.
May 1 John Thome and Anna Maria Reiss, Lebanon.
May 18 John George Dollinger and Margaretha Jones, Williamsborough.
Aug 11 Samuel Zerfass and Sabina Baltz, Cocalico and Lebanon.
Sep 1 Johannes Petry and Catarina Oehler, Williamsburg and Lancaster.
Oct 12 Johannes Scharf and Susanna Michael, Bethel.

Oct 18 Jacob Oberholtzer and Barbara Faber, Bethel.
Oct 20 Johannes Reyer and Maria Elisabetha Neu, Warwick and Lebanon.
Oct 25 Heinrich Keim and Catarina Reiber, Bethel.
Oct 27 Andreas Kueffer and Elisabetha Bickel, Lebanon.

1768
Jan 5 Lucas Schally and Maria Elisabetha Boger, Lebanon.
Jan 19 Christoph Meyer and Anna Margaretha Ilin, Lebanon.
Mar 4 John George Feltin and Catarina Elisabetha Burckhardt, Bethel.
Mar 15 John Martin Uhler and Ana Elisabetha Stroh, Lebanon Town.
Mar 22 Rudolph Koellicker and Anna Maria Weidman, Lebanon Town.
Apr 17 Jacob Fischer and Sabina Rauch, Bethel.
May 30 George Thany and Margaretha Elisabetha Truckemueller, Bethel.
Jun 21 George Volck and Catarina Germann, Lebanon.
Jul 5 John Cunradt Bingeman and Catarina Barbara Feuerbach, Bethel.
Jul 5 Johannes Herman and Catarina Herman, Lebanon.
Aug 16 Leonhardt Albrecht and Anna Catarina Stroher, Lebanon.
Aug 21 Johannes Wagner and Maria Elisabeth Gur, Conestoga and Bethel.
Nov 14. Heinrich Naess and Christina Heyl, Bethel.
Nov 14 Jacob Fischer and Anna Maria Steinmann, Bethel and Lancaster.
Nov 22 John Frantz Helm and Anna Maria Koch, Lebanon.
Nov 29 Johannes Mohr and Margaretha Gallmeyer, Lebanon.
Dec 12 Andreas Endress and Anna Maria Gingrich, Lebanon.

1769
Jan 2 John Peter Fischer and Anna Elizabetha Heylman, Lebanon.
Feb 7 Balthaser Laber and Rosina Wentz, Lebanon.
Feb 12 Anastasius Ellinger and Catarina Ollinger, Lebanon.
Mar 16 Michael Bosch and Elizabetha Koch, Lebanon.
Mar 28 Gottlieb Roth and Anna Elizabetha Brecht, Bethel.
Apr 10 Conradt Braun and Agnes Schneider, Lebanon.
Apr 10 John Wilhelm Neu and Juliana Firnssler, Derry and Lebanon.
Apr 25 Daniel Scherertz and Maria Catarina Meyer, Lebanon.
Apr 25 Robert Hunter and Isabel Waters, Lebanon.

May 2 Adam Bach, Jr., and Barbara Flohr, Lebanon and Rapho.
May 9 John Melchior Abmeyer and Anna Maria Kuemmerling, Lebanon.
May 23 Johann Heinrich Frey and Anna Maria Boger, Lebanon.
Jun 20 John Heinrich Rheinoehl and Juliana Gebhardt, Lebanon.
Aug 22 Caspar Jungblut and Catarina Felleberger, Lebanon.
Nov 28 John Bigham and Catarina Watson, Lebanon.
Dec 12 Michael Kleber and Catarina Holderbau, Lebanon.
Dec 12 Peter Neuschwanger and Agnes Mueller, Codorus and Bethel.

1770
Mar 6 Peter Deissinger and Margaretha Roth, Bethel.
Mar 27 Johann Ulrich Ohlinger and Catarina Roeszlin, Lebanon.
Apr 16 Friederich Boeszhaar and Barbara Heyl, Bethel.
Apr 24 Michael Hoerner and Margaretha Loesch, Bethel.
Apr 24 John Adam Stoever and Catarina Elizabetha Heylman, Lebanon.
May 8 Thomas Atkinson and Magdalena Kintzel, Lebanon.
Aug 21 Andreas Lay and Hannah Dinniss, Lebanon.
Aug 21 Johannes Heckendorn and Maria Catarina Hammann, Lebanon.
Aug 21 Peter Eisenhauer and Maria Elizabetha Schmidt, Bethel.
Aug 28 Isaac William and Maria Elizabetha Falck, Bethel.
Nov 13 Johannes Schirck and Catarina Schnaebelin, Bethel.
Nov 20 Christoph Friederich Seiler and Maria Elizabetha Kintzel, Lebanon.

1771
Jan 15 Johannes Wepner and Catarina Bauman, Lebanon and Bethel.
Feb 3 Jacob Roth and Maria Elizabetha Stoltz, Bethel.
Feb 19 Martin Ulrich and Regina Feltin, Lebanon and Bethel.
Feb 26 Joseph McLyntie and Margaretha McQuien, Lebanon and Londonderry.
Mar 26 John Nicolaus Neu and Eva Catarina Rudiesiehl, Derr and Lebanon.
May 28 Andreas Beistel and Christina Pflantz, Lebanon.
May 28 Jacob Suter and Philippina Beistel, Lebanon.
Aug 27 Johannes Bickel and Maria Feltin, Bethel.
Oct 1 John Martin Lang and Elizabetha Huber, Lebanon.
Oct 19 Thomas Owens and Dorothea Zieger, Lebanon.
Nov 14 Daniel Leng and Maria Barbara Koerner, Bethel.

Dec 8 Nicolaus Gebhardt and Anna Appolonia Kornmann, Lebanon.

1772
Jan 5 Christian Meyer and Margaretha Eisenhauer, Bethel.
Jan 7 Daniel Brians and Elizabetha Reush, Lebanon.
Apr 21 Tobias Stoever and Hannah Zimmerman, Lebanon.
May 19 Johannes Schnug and Anna Christina Heylmann, Lebanon.
May 31 Stephan Huck and Christina Decker, Lebanon.
Jun 16 Johannes Schmidt and Christina Nunnenmacher, Lebanon.
Jun 21 Michael Karmenie and Catarina Meyer, Lebanon.
Jun 21 Andreas Heckman and Susanna Gerhardt, Bethel.
Sep 18 Martin Guntrum and Maria Catarina Boesshaar, Bethel.
Nov 17 Michael Haehnle and Catarina Looser, Bethel.
Dec 15 Peter Koch and Juliana Heinrich, Lebanon.

1773
Feb 9 John Michael Neu and Justina Bart, Lebanon.
Apr 18 Johann Frantz Boehler and Catarina Breit, Lebanon.
Apr 20 John Michael Uhler and Anna Maria Elizabetha Stroh,
       Lebanon.
Jun 6 Christian Fremdling and Susanna Maria Glasser, Lebanon.
Jun 29 John Martin Wagner and Charlotta Kintzel, Lebanon.
Sep 26 David Mueller and Elizabetha Catarina Wild, Bethel.
Sep 28 Johannes Meyer and Anna Maria Rehwald, Lebanon.

1774
Jan 25 John Michael Conradt and Margaretha Eschbach, Bethel.
Feb 22 John Adam Fischer and Maria Elizabetha Becker, Lebanon.
May 24 Johannes Stoever and Anna Engel Kissecker, Lebanon.
May 31 Martin George Leonhardt and Maria Barbara Eschelbach,
       Bethel.
May 31 James Miley and Margaretha Brown, Williamsborough.
Jul 17 John Philipp New and Elizabetha Preiss, Lebanon.
Jul 26 Heinrich Diettel and Margaretha Pilgrum, Bethel.
Aug 30 John Christoph Franck and Anna Margaretha Maurer,
       Lebanon.
Nov 22 Johannes Philipp Loeffler and Catarina Riedt, Bethel.

1775
Mar 21 Mattheis Stroeher and Anna Barbara Brechtbiel, Lebanon.

May 12 Michael Meck and Margaretha Motz, Muehlbach.
Sep 5 George Adam Eckhardt and Maria Margaretha Kraemer, Lebanon.

1776
Jan 18 Daniel Clarck and Anna Maria Bilgeram, Bethel.
Jan 18 Michael Haehnle and Anna Maria Boltz, Bethel.
Mar 19 William Cunningham and Nancy Glascow, Lebanon.
Mar 26 Heinrich Peter and Anna Christian Imbode, Lebanon.
Apr 30 Theoboldt Wildt and Anna Maria Achebach, Bethel and Lebanon.
Oct 13 Jno. Cunradt Kachel and Margaretha Schwab, Lebanon.
Nov 28 Jno. Jacob Bickel and Christina Schindel, Lebanon.

1777
Feb 18 Jacob Eprecht and Elizabetha Weitzel, Lebanon.
Mar 30 John George Glassbrenner and Catarina Rudy, Lebanon.
Apr 8 John Peter Neu and Mary Regina Reusch, Lebanon and Londonderry.
Apr 14 Andreas Eckert and Sabina Sauter, Bethel.
May 4 Johannes Schultz and Barbara Korr, Bethel.
Jun 17 Jacob Wolandie and Catarina Bickel, Bethel.
Dec 23 Mattheis Boyer, Jr., and Barbara Foerster, Lebanon.

1778
Mar 18 Johannes Staehly and Eva Maria Schedt, Bethel.
Mar 21 Valentin Schauffler and Catarina Heyl, Bethel.
Mar 31 Michael Leutz and Anna Elisabetha Uhrich, Bethel.
Jun 30 Thomas Gordon and Susannah McLinty, Lebanon.
Aug 23 Heinrich Meyly and Magdalena Kroh, Bethel.
Sep 22 Johannes Peter and Salome Bender, Lebanon.
Oct 27 Johannes Beltz and Maria Heyer, Lebanon.
Dec 1 Duncan McGregor and Anne Kezey, Elizabeth.

1779
Feb 16 John Peter Neu and Juliana Karmenie, Lebanon and Londonderry.
Feb 23 Nicolaus Heinrich and Catara. Elisaba. Becker, Lebanon.
Mar 7 Jost Knaegy and Anna Schirck, Bethel.
Apr 19 John Wilhelm Bohr and Ana Magdal. Boger, Lebanon.

May 2 Rudolph Doerr and Sabina Sauter, Williamsborough.

"The following marriage was after the death of J. C. Stoever: "May 29 Heinrich Schwab and Elisabetha Stelbzer.
By the Herrn Pfarrer Mindbohner (Melsheimer?).
Nov 9 Johann Friederich Stoever, Lebanon, and Anna Margaretha Daenschaerez, Hendelberg (Heidleberg?).

April 26, 1742. John George Emmert and Eva Maria Graff. Heidelberg.
August 30, 1743. Heinrich Frey and Catarina Schauer. Heidelberg.
February 16, 1747. John Von Huss and Hannah Cheeck. Heidelberg.
September 24, 1752. Heinrich Fryman and Anna Catarina Gesell. Heidelberg.
November 3, 1754. Ludwig Weidner and Maria Engel Gerst, Heidelberg and Bethel.
February 13, 1755. John Dieben and Anna Margaretha Ramler, Hanover and Heidelberg.
November 9, 1755. Balthaser Hetzler and Anna Barbara Dohm. Heidelberg.
July 6, 1756. John Walker and Jane Wilson, Derry and Heidelberg.
August 23, 1756. Bartholomaeus Heck and Margaretha Aulenbach. Heidelberg.
February 28, 1758. Johannes Berger and Anna Barbara Hoerchelrodt. Heidelberg.
April 10, 1758. Jacob Schmidt and Elisabetha Hoerchelrodt, Heidelberg.
July 16, 1758. Johannes Busch and Anna Maria Huber, Heidelberg.
September 22, 1758. Benedict Ledig and Maria Juliana Boehmer, Heidelberg.
Jun 17, 1760. Michael Lindenmuth and Maria Eve Noecker, Heidelberg.
Oct 23, 1760. Peter Hedderich, Jr. and Margar. Hoerchelradt, Heidelberg and Hanover.
Dec 16, 1765. Heinrich Muench and Catarina Ried, Heidelberg and Tulpehocken.
Sepember 15, 1767. Michael Stroh and Eva Barbara Goettel, Heidelberg and Hanover.
December 13, 1768. Christoph Neiss and Barbara Stober, Heidelberg and Hanover.
November 9, 1779. Johann Friederich Stoever, Lebanon and Anna Margaretha Daenschaerez, Hendelberg (Heidelberg?)

INDEX

301; John Henry, 298;
Leonard, 245; Leonhardt,
353; Margaret, 298;
Margareta, 259; Martin, 54;
Sophia, 54
ALEXANDER, Elias., 33;
Elisabeth, 33; Gottfried, 33
ALGAYER, Anna Cath., 307
ALLEN, James, 218; Margaret,
242; Sarah, 345
ALLSTATT, Elisabeth, 44;
Johann Georg, 44; Johannes,
44
ALSTADT, Elisabeth, 40, 43;
Johannes, 40, 43; William, 43
ALT, Adam, 218, 249;
Catharine, 306; Elizabeth,
218; John, 218; Mary, 218;
Sarah, 218
ANDERSON, Elizabeth, 113;
Mary, 311; Thomas, 311
ANDREAS, Hannah, 17; Peter,
17
ANDRES, Peter, 28
ANGST, Cath., 264; Daniel, 62,
63, 124, 181, 209, 234, 245;
Johannes, 264; John Daniel,
181; John Michael, 181;
Juliana, 62; Magdalene, 234;
Maria Elisabetha, 62, 63;
Nicolaus, 264; Susanna
Elizabeth, 181
ANNIAS, Catharine, 119;
Christian, 119; Dewalt, 119
ANSPACH, Jacob, 112; John,
204; John Peter, 85, 87, 168;
Magdalena, 327; Magdalene,
168; Mary Magdalene, 85, 87;
Peter, 87, 327
APFFEL, Maria Margaret, 165;

William, 165
APPEL, Catharina, 268;
Johannes, 268; Magdalena,
268
ARAS, Elizabetha Catarina, 347
ARDNT, Carl, 24; Jacob, 24;
Margaretha, 24
ARENTUCH, Elisabeth, 261;
Johannes, 261; Wilhelm, 261
ARMASCHON, Barbara, 56;
Mathias, 56; Sarah, 56
ARMISCHONG, Catharine, 55;
Gertrude, 55; Margaret, 55;
Mathias, 55
ARND, Anna, 26, 32, 38; Carl,
1; Carolus, 32; David, 32
ARNDT, Anna, 45; Anna Maria,
45; Barbara, 4; Carl, 4;
Jacob, 45; Susanna, 45
ARNOLD, Anna Maria, 101,
167; Catharina, 18;
Catharine, 101; Henrich, 18;
John Adam, 167; Lorentz,
48, 167; William, 101
ARNOLDT, Georg Jacob, 103;
Magdalene, 103; William, 103
ARNPRIESTER, Catarina, 277;
Wilhelm, 277
ARNT, Anna Catharina, 26;
Carl, 26
ARTZT, Anna Maria, 68, 70;
John, 68, 70, 113; Margaret,
68
ASTON, Elisabeth, 46; Georg,
46; Sarah, 46
ATDORFER, Barbara, 250;
Henrich, 250; Ursula, 250
ATHERN, Anna Margaret, 115
ATKINSON, Anna Barbara, 4,
7; Cathrina, 11; Eleonora, 11;

53
BAHNERT, Elizabeth, 51;
Margaret, 51; Nicholas, 51
BAHR, Johannes, 158;
Magdalena, 159; Margaret,
158, 159; Samuel, 158, 159
BAIER, Andrew, 56; Anna
Margaret, 56; David, 56;
Elizabeth, 56; Philip, 289
BALD, Adam, 7; Anna Maria, 7;
Christina, 7
BALDT, Adam, 124; Catharine
Margaret, 124; Chistine, 124
BALMER, Adam, 50, 186; Anna
Elizabeth, 186; Barbara, 50,
186; Christina, 184; Eva
Elizabeth, 186; Geo. Mich.,
186; George, 244, 351;
George Michael, 186; Joh.
Adam, 186, 245; John Adam,
352; Michael, 340; Philip
Adam, 184, 185, 209
BALMUS, Anna Mary, 244
BALSLE, John, 53, 91;
Margaret, 53; Michael, 53
BALSLEY, Joh., 11; Joh. Jacob,
11; Margaretha, 11
BALSLY, John, 53; Margaret,
53
BALTZ, Catrina, 255; Jacob,
136, 255; Michael, 253;
Sabina, 352
BAMBERGER, Charles, 109;
Christian, 285; Christina,
228; Eliz., 285; John, 115;
Magdalene, 236; Michael, 220
BANNER, Henry, 98; John
Nicholas, 98; Maria
Margaret, 98
BANS, Kilian, 258

BAR, Samuel, 157
BARBARA, John, 205
BARD, Johannes, 40
BARDO, Dorothea, 146; Martin,
146
BARDT, Adam, 202, 237, 239;
Anna Mary, 204, 218;
Catharine, 190; Elizabeth,
204, 237; Elizabeth B., 239;
Eve, 218; Jacob, 239; Joh.
Adam, 237; Joh. Nichl., 237;
John, 218, 226; John Adam,
190, 204, 248; Justina, 203,
207; Mary, 237
BARNET, James, 241
BARR, Elizabetha, 6; Johannes,
6; John, 6
BARRET, Cathar., 267; James,
267; Thomas, 267
BARRY, Bartholomew, 21;
Bridget, 21; Christine, 55;
Deborah, 21; John, 55;
Rebecca, 55
BARST, Michael, 256
BART, Adam, 261; Catharina,
261; John Adam, 203;
Justina, 355, 246; Maria
Elisabeth, 261
BARTH, Adam, 184, 185, 195,
197, 214, 227, 233, 236, 248,
262, 298, 301; Ann Barbara,
185; Cath., 298; Catharina,
262; Catharine, 233, 298;
Christina, 248; Elizabeth,
195, 197, 214, 233, 236; Joh.
Adam, 185; John, 218, 225,
226; John Adam, 346;
Justina, 184; Mar.
Magdalene, 218; Maria
Elisabeth, 262; Mary

Martin, 321; John Valentin, 321; M. Barbara, 149; Marie Eva, 149; Maurice, 184; Michael, 321, 326; Moritz, 184; Thomas, 333

BAUERIN, Mar. Elis., 268

BAUM, An. Barb., 268; Barbara, 269; Phil., 268; Philip, 269; Susanna, 269

BAUMAN, Anna, 45; Barbara, 6; Catarina, 354; Catharina, 45; Catharine, 291; Eliz., 308; Elizabeth, 9, 298; Georg, 45; Heinrich, 6; Henrich, 1; Henry, 185; Jacob, 45, 287, 291, 296, 298, 300, 301, 302, 306, 308; Joh. George, 185; Joh. Heinrich, 9; Joh. Jacob, 6; Johannes, 9; Juliana, 306; Margaret, 185, 302; Mary, 296, 298; Mary Cath., 308; Salome, 45; Sarah, 45; Thomas, 301

BAUMANN, Anna, 42; Barbara, 7; Catharina, 42; Christina, 42; Georg, 42; Heinrich, 7; Johannes, 44; Joseph, 44; Phillippus, 44; Rebecca, 44

BAUMBARTNER, Peter, 257

BAUMBERGER, Carl, 169

BAUMGAERTNER, Anna Catharine, 242; Catharine, 124, 297; Eliz., 297; Gottfried, 184, 241, 334; Henry, 124, 297; Joh. Dorst, 182; Joh. Jacob, 184; Johannes, 316; John, 124, 182; John Dorst, 316; John Henry, 124; John Jacob, 334; Peter, 182, 316; Rosina, 124

BAUMGARDNER, Elizabeth, 302, 303; Henry, 303; John, 302; John Adam, 302

BAUMGARTNER, Adam, 130, 131; Balthasar, 127, 129, 131, 132, 134; Elizabeth, 129, 130, 131; Gottfried, 346; Henry, 301; Joh. Adam, 218; John, 127, 131, 218, 301, 305; John Adam, 129, 132; John George, 218; Magdalene, 127, 131, 132, 134; Maria Barbara, 129; Maria Catharine, 130; Mary Magdalene, 129; Philip, 127, 134, 135

BAUMGEARTNER, Catharine, 298; Elizabeth, 298

BAUMGERTNER, Elisabeth, 34; Elisabeth Augustin, 34; Georg Augustus, 34; Philip, 136; Samuel, 34

BAUR, Eva, 50; Magdalena, 346; Magdalene, 242

BAURMANN, Elizabeth, 50; George, 50; John Leonard, 50

BAYER, Abraham, 104; Adam, 243, 349; Anna Maria, 53, 79; Anna Mary, 225; Barbara, 104, 166, 218; Catharine, 175, 176, 182, 244; Christina, 182, 218; Christopher, 175, 176; David, 218; Elizabeth, 208; Elizabeth Catharine, 182, 246; Esther, 176; Eva, 182; Frederic, 218; George, 53; George Peter, 176; Henry, 175; Jacob, 113; Joh. Adam, 182; Joh. Frederic,

268
BELCHER, Anna, 111; Eliza,
111; Henry, 111; Jost, 10;
Mar. Elizabeth, 10
BELER, Catharine, 167; John,
167; John George, 167
BELISTEIN, Abraham, 31
BELLEMANN, Catharine, 114
BELTZ, Jacob, 265; Johannes,
265, 356; John, 247
BELZ, Abraham, 132; Thomas,
132
BENDE, Adam, 153; Christina,
153
BENDER, Adam, 145, 146, 151;
Anna, 268; Barbara, 109;
Benj., 268; Benjamin, 266,
272; Cath. Elisabeth, 146;
Catharina, 269; Christina,
145; Christina Magdalena,
267; Christine, 145, 146;
Dorothea, 267; Elisabeth,
266; Eva, 107, 109; George
Valentin, 145; J. Adam, 153;
Jacob, 190; Joh., 267;
Johannes, 151, 268, 269;
John C., 206; Ludwig, 266;
M. Christina, 151; Margaret
Elizabeth, 116; Maria Magd.,
60; Maria Magdalene, 107;
Marie Magd., 151; Salome,
247, 356; Valentine, 107, 109,
145
BENDERIN, Anna Maria, 273;
Johannes, 273
BENDTER, Catarina, 349
BENE, Anna Maria, 91, 93, 94,
95, 109, 112; Anna Maria
Thiel, 97; Barbara, 94; David,
109; Henry, 112; Jacob, 91,

93, 94, 95; Margaret, 97;
Peter, 97, 109, 112
BENEDICT, Peter, 243, 349
BENI, Barbara, 149; Melchoir,
149; Peter, 149
BENJAMIN, Alex., 17;
Alexander, 13, 16; Anna
Elisabeth, 16; Anna
Elisabetha, 13; Anna Maria,
13; Elisabeth, 17; Godfried,
17; Jacob, 16
BENNER, Barbara, 158; Carl,
78, 80; Carl Philip, 7, 72;
Carolus, 80; Charles, 219;
Elisabeth, 21; Elisabetha, 10,
38; Elizabeth, 72, 77, 78, 80;
Jacob, 158; Joh., 10; Joh.
Martin, 14; Johannes, 38;
John, 77, 78; John Christian,
72; John George, 78; John
Philip, 80; M. Magdalena,
158; Martin, 21, 77, 114;
Matthew, 78; Susanna, 38
BENNY, Jacob, 57
BENS, Elizabeth, 114; Mary
Magdalene, 111
BENSON, Alexander, 237
BENTER, Anna Elizabeth, 76;
Barbara, 248; Carl Philip, 76;
Elisabeth, 76; Elizabeth, 248;
John, 76, 248; Ludwig, 16;
Mar. Elisabeth, 16; Salome,
16
BENTZ, Jacob, 257, 311; John
George, 312; John Jacob,
311; Maria Barbara, 312
BENY, Barbara, 155, 157;
Catharine, 155; Fischer, 162;
George, 162; Jacob, 157; Joh.
Jacob, 261; M. Margaret,

John Nicholas, 72;
Magdalene, 114; Margaret,
288; Margaretha, 320; Mary
Catharine, 197; Michael, 14;
Philip, 181, 209; Philipp, 328;
Susan, 284
BEYERLE, Michael, 327
BIBEL, Anna Catharina, 36;
Johannes, 35; Margaretha,
35
BIBELL, Dan, 3; Maria
Margaret, 3
BICHER, Catharina, 37; Jacob,
37, 43; Maria Catharina, 43
BICKEL, Anna Barbara, 135;
Anna Catharine, 127; Anna
Maria, 138; Anna Mary, 307;
Barbara, 129, 131; Catarina,
356; Catharine, 137, 142,
247; Catharine Barbara, 129;
David, 158; Dorothea, 184,
294; Elisabetha, 353; Eliz.,
297; Elizabeth, 142, 242, 245;
Elizabetha, 347; Eva, 105;
Frederic, 184, 294; Heinrich,
337, 352; Henrich, 146, 151,
152, 153, 158; Henry, 66,
129, 133, 134; Herman, 210;
J. Henrich, 153; Jacob, 1,
133, 135, 137, 138, 352, 356;
Joh., 262, 264, 265; Joh.
Frederic, 307; Joh. George,
307; Joh. Jacob, 245;
Johannes, 151, 261, 354;
John, 124, 127, 130, 133,
135, 136, 137, 139, 142; John
Frederic, 305; John Jacob,
137, 243, 247, 348;
Magdalena, 66, 146, 151, 152,
153, 158; Magdalene, 129,

134; Margaret, 133, 153;
Maria, 137; Mary, 135;
Rudolf, 142; Sabina, 127,
130, 133, 139, 142, 151, 261,
262, 264, 265; Susanna, 138;
Tobias, 59, 66
BICLINSON, Barbara, 293
BIEBER, Joh. Dietrich, 218,
219; Peter, 163
BIECHEL, Barbara, 253;
Johannes, 253
BIEDER, Anna Mary, 190
BIEGELT, David, 73; Maria
Catharine, 73; Maria
Christine, 73
BIEHL, Elisabetha, 258; Martin,
258; Nicholaus, 258
BIEL, Adam, 297; Barbara, 284;
Christina, 248; Daniel, 284;
John Adam, 307; John
Freiderich, 341; John
Nicolaus, 341; Maria Elisab.,
341; Maria Elizabetha, 338;
Nicolaus, 338, 341
BIELE, Adam, 293; Barbara,
305, 307; John Adam, 299;
William, 303
BIELY, Adam, 297, 303, 308;
Anna Christina, 297;
Barbara, 303; Catharine, 303,
308; Christina, 297; Frederic,
297, 301, 308; John Adam,
301; Mrs., 308; Widow, 303
BIEN, Heinrich, 260;
Magdalena, 260; Paul, 260
BIENER, Elizabetha, 348
BIGHAM, John, 354
BIGLER, Carl, 251; David, 251
BILGERAM, Anna Maria, 356
BILIAMS, Catarina, 350

Joseph, 239; Jost, 10, 13, 17,
165, 166; Jost William, 165;
Magdalene, 165, 166;
Margaret, 101, 109; Maria
Catharine, 166; Maria
Elisabeth, 10, 13; Maria
Magdalena, 24; Maria
Margaret, 106, 109; William,
109, 164, 165, 173, 175, 306
BLECHMAN, Maria Barbara,
110
BLECKER, Anna Mary, 239
BLEISTEIN, Catharina, 39
BLEK, Elizabet, 270; Gorg, 269;
Jui, 269, 272; Juy, 270
BLESSING, Anthony, 185, 283;
Antonius, 185; Philip Adam,
185
BLESSLE, Antonius, 198; Mary
Salome, 198
BLEYSTEIN, Abraham, 18, 28,
30, 127; Christina, 18; Eva
Elisabeth, 18; Johannes, 28;
John, 127; Louisa, 127
BLOSS, Jacob, 80; John Henry,
80
BLUBACHER, John, 166
BLUEK, Barbara, 275;
Johannes, 275
BLUM, Christine, 173;
Elizabeth, 323; Joanna Cath.,
187; Johanna Catharine, 317;
John, 173, 323; Maria
Catharine, 317; Mary
Catharine, 187
BOBER, Magdalena, 253;
Mathas, 253
BOBY, Daniel, 101; Salome, 101
BOCK, John, 248
BOCKLE, Catarina, 349

BOCKLIN, Maria Ursina, 8
BOEBEL, Heinrich, 351
BOECKL, Catharine, 243
BOECKLE, Anna Maria, 339;
Catharine, 243; Heinrich,
339, 341; Henry, 244
BOECKLIN, Margaretha, 339
BOEHLER, Francis, 218; Franz,
300; Heinrich, 14; Johann
Frantz, 355; John Frantz,
246; John Simeon, 232; Mar.
Margretha, 5; Simon, 5
BOEHMER, Maria Juliana, 357
BOEHN, Anna, 247
BOEKLIN, Elisabetha, 8; Eva
Margartha, 8; Ulrich, 8
BOESHAAR, Anna Maria, 126,
131; Apollonia, 126; Barbara,
125, 131; Catharine, 130,
131; Catharine Barbara, 131;
Christine, 128; Elizabeth,
131, 139, 140, 141;
Frederick, 125, 131, 139;
George, 130, 131; Jacob, 128,
131; John, 126, 131, 136,
138, 140, 141; John Adam,
136; John Peter, 126;
Magdalene, 137, 141;
Margaret, 139; Maria
Apollonia, 129; Matthias,
126, 129; Ottilia, 131; Peter,
137, 141; Rosina, 141
BOESHAHR, Adam, 100; John
Michael, 100; Margaret, 100
BOESHAR, Anna Maria, 122,
129, 138, 139; Anna Maria
Margaret, 129; Cathar.
Barbara, 186; Catharine
Barbara, 186; John, 122, 139,
186; John George, 122; John

Anna Catharine, 177; Anna
Maria, 100, 177, 178, 179;
Catharine, 99, 114;
Elizabeth, 99, 166; Eva, 179;
Frederick, 106, 108; Joh.
Friederich, 20; John, 99, 100,
167, 177, 178, 179; John
Adam, 166; Magdalene, 166;
Nicholas, 180; Susanna, 20,
106, 108
BOLLMANN, Abraham, 171;
Adam, 169, 170, 171;
Elizabeth, 164, 169, 171;
John Adam, 164; Mary
Christine, 169; Mary Eliza,
171; Mary Elizabeth, 170
BOLMAN, ---, 1; Frederick, 98;
Susanna, 98
BOLS, Anna Maria, 45;
Catharina, 45; Henrich, 45
BOLTEN, David, 301;
Valentine, 301, 305
BOLTON, Henry, 303; John,
303
BOLTZ, Adam, 219; Anna
Dorothea, 181, 242, 316;
Anna Maria, 356; Anna
Mary, 185; Anna Sabina,
181; Catarina Barbara, 317;
Catharine, 185, 213, 214;
Catharine Barbara, 181, 187;
Catharine Sophia, 186;
Dorothea, 202, 348;
Elizabeth, 181, 219, 249;
Elizabetha, 313; Fronica,
255; George, 186, 219; Jacob,
137, 141, 185, 214, 219, 255;
Joh. Jacob, 242; Joh.
Michael, 185; John Jacob,
348; John Michael, 316;

Margaret, 141; Maria
Barbara, 315; Maria
Elisabeth, 26; Mary Barbara,
186, 194; Mary Catharine,
185; Mary Magaret, 194;
Mcihael, 215; Michael, 26,
181, 186, 194, 209, 210, 213,
252, 257, 313, 315, 329;
Rudolph, 141; Sabina, 186;
Susanna, 219; Veronica, 186,
255
BOLZ, Anna Marg., 228;
Catharine, 228; Henry, 249;
Jacob, 199, 228
BONER, Catarina, 347
BONNER, Anna Catharine, 72;
Carl Philip, 72; Elizabeth, 72
BONYN, A. Marie, 149
BOOSHAAR, Anna Maria, 132;
Benjamin, 132; John, 132;
Maria Apollonia, 132;
Matthais, 132
BOPP, Catar. Margar., 342;
Catarina, 342; John Nicholas,
247; John Nicolaus, 342
BOR, Anna Mary, 241; Eliz.,
297; Joh. Nich., 219;
Matthew, 297; Salome, 297
BORDEN, George, 345
BORDNER, Anna Maria, 67;
Daniel, 67; Eva, 271; Eva
Maria, 67; Jacob, 67, 269,
271; John, 67; Peter, 67;
Susanna, 67
BORGENER, Peter, 45
BORGER, Anna Elizabeth, 79;
Catharina, 22; Catharine, 79;
Peter, 22
BORGERT, Anna Eva, 49;
Maria Elizabeth, 49; Michael,

Maria, 94, 95; Anna Maria
Bickel, 97; Henry, 94, 95, 97;
John, 94
BRINGENS, Maria, 271;
Samuel, 271
BRITON, Anabella, 5; James, 5;
Mary, 5
BRITZIUS, Jacob, 175;
Magdalene, 175
BROGNER, Christian, 75
BRONNER, George Michael,
345; Geroge Michael, 241
BROSIUS, Catarina Dor., 331;
Jacob, 176; Margaret, 176;
Peter, 331
BROSS, Elizabeth, 140; George,
140; Jacob, 135; Magdalene,
135; Peter, 135
BROSSMAN, Barbara, 178;
Francis, 87; John, 178; Maria
Salome, 87
BROST, Elisabet, 262;
Elisabeth, 260, 261; Georg,
260, 261, 264; George, 262;
Henrich, 264; Johann
Michael, 261; Johannes, 262;
Juliana, 259; Magdalena, 259,
260; Peter, 259
BROWN, A. Barbara, 147; Anna
Barbara, 319; Eva Mary, 182;
Jacob, 319; Joh. Valentine,
182; John, 182, 319, 349;
Margaretha, 355; Maria
Regina, 319; Marie, 147
BRUBATCHER, John, 219
BRUCKER, Jacob, 50; Susanna
Magdalene, 112; Veronica,
112
BRUENDER, Ana Catarina,
323; Heinrich, 323

BRUG, Johannes, 45
BRUMBACH, Susanna, 306,
307
BRUMSHEAR, Susanna, 306
BRUN, Susanna, 25
BRUNER, Anna Margaret, 118;
Anna Maria, 118; Jacob, 285,
286; Johannes, 259; John,
118; John Peter, 118
BRUNNER, Anna Cath., 290;
Anna Catharine, 123; Anna
Margaret, 128, 131; Anna
Maria, 127, 128; Barbara,
148, 150, 154; Catharine,
128, 132, 148, 149, 154, 291;
Christine, 111, 174; Daniel,
130; Elisabeth, 149; Eva
Margaretta, 290; George
Michael, 164, 290; Henry, 57,
113, 128, 132, 174, 175, 176;
J. Jacob, 148; Jacob, 123,
125, 127; John, 119, 128,
129, 131, 176; John Jacob,
127; John Peter, 128; M.
Barbara, 150; Margaret, 119,
129; Maria Barbara, 125;
Maria Margaret, 123, 125;
Ottilia, 130; Peter, 128, 148,
150, 154; Sophia, 52;
Susanna, 174, 175, 176;
Veronica, 57
BUBAR, Lampert, 313; Maria
Catarina, 313
BUBIKOFER, Anna Maria, 86;
John Henry, 86; Joseph, 86
BUCH, Dorothy, 89; Henry, 89;
Johannes, 28; Mary
Elizabeth, 241; Peter, 28
BUCHER, A. Barbara, 145; A.
M., 155; A. Maria, 152; A.

Michael, 342; Sebastian, 342
BURKERT, Andrew, 49;
Bastian, 49; Elisabeth, 145;
Michel, 145
BURKHARD, Catharine, 64;
Maria Catharine, 64; Martin,
64
BURKSTHALER, Mrs., 81
BURNET, Catharine, 303; Eliz.
Nancy, 303
BUSCH, Anna Cathrine, 219;
Anna Eva, 13; Anna Maria,
165; Anna Mary, 186, 191,
214, 218, 248; Catharine,
185; Cathrina, 6; Christian,
181; Elisabeth, 6; Elisabetha,
9; J. Nicklaus, 13; Johannes,
357; John, 219; John
Andrew, 165; John Nic., 181;
John William, 165; Juliana,
186; Margaret, 181;
Margretha, 13; Maria
Barbara, 9; Martin, 185, 186,
191, 214, 219, 222, 234;
Mary, 234; Michael, 6, 9
BUSCHELMACHER, Holb, 82
BUSCHONG, Elisabeth, 44;
Jacob, 44; Philippus, 44
BUSCHUNG, Elisabeth, 43;
Jacob, 43; Leah, 43
BUSH, Barbara, 12; Michel, 2
BUSHER, Conrad, 2
BUTLER, Isabel, 104; Sarah,
104; Thomas, 104

-C-

CAECHOG, Catharina, 66; Eva
Christina, 66; John, 66
CAFFEROTH, Eva Fredericka,
50; Gerhard, 50; John

Henry, 58; Juliana, 50; Mary
Magdalene, 50; William, 50,
58
CAMILL, Anna, 243
CAMPBELL, Anna, 243;
Johann, 160; Joseph, 16;
Magdalena, 160
CAMPER, Elisabeth, 69;
Elizabeth, 160; Frederick, 69;
Friederich, 160; John
George, 69; Peter, 69
CAMPLE, Joseph, 16
CANNOWAY, Arthur, 186;
Catharine, 187; Charles, 186,
187; James, 187
CANTZ, Jacob, 213; Joh. Jacob,
208
CAP, Elisabeth, 261; Elisabth,
260; Jacob, 260, 261;
Michael, 260
CAPLER, Anna Margaret, 118;
Catharine, 117; John Henry,
117; Leonard, 118; Margaret,
117; Martin, 117, 118
CAPP, Gertrude, 83; Veitt, 83
CAREY, Hannah M., 311
CARMELL, Anne, 350
CARMEME, Christine, 239
CARMENE, Barbara, 219; John,
219; Joseph, 306; Susanna,
306
CARMENIS, Susanna, 306
CARMENY, Catharine, 2;
Michael, 2
CARMINI, Anna, 219; Anna
Christina, 193; Anna Mary,
220, 233; Anthony, 219, 224,
230, 235; Anton, 193;
Barbara, 199, 233; Cath.,
296; Christina, 230; Eliz.,

COHREN, Anna, 67; John
Jacob, 67
COLLINS, John, 350
CONNELY, Magdl., 268;
Thomas, 268
CONNER, Joanna, 241;
Johanna, 345
CONRAD, A. Marie, 149;
Andrew, 57; Anna Barbara,
18; Christina, 266; Daniel,
18; Elias, 266, 267; Elizabeth,
74; George Magnus, 57;
Jacob, 74; Joh Jacob, 278;
Magnus, 51; Marg. Eliz., 113;
Margaret, 51, 116, 149;
Margaretha, 266, 267;
Nichlas, 149; Peter, 18;
Sabina, 266
CONRADIN, Catharina, 266;
Marg., 274
CONRADT, John Michael, 355
CONRATH, Anna Maria, 38;
Georg, 38; Margaretha, 38;
Maria, 113
CONTERMAN, Jacob, 75; John,
75
COOPER, Jacob, 302; John
George, 302
COR, Barbara, 126; Michael,
126
CORAL, John Jacob, 300
CORNMAN, Anna Elisabeth, 18;
Anna Maria, 14, 15;
Cathrina, 6, 12, 19; Elis.
Margr., 17; Elisabeth, 8, 9,
13, 17, 18; Elisabeth
Margaret, 14, 15; Elisabetha
Margaret, 18; Felton, 6, 9,
12, 13, 17, 18; Heinrich, 13;
Joh., 13, 17, 18; Joh. Jacob,

17; Joh. Philip, 9; Johann, 8;
Johannes, 9; Margaretha, 6,
9, 13; Peter, 19; Valentin, 14,
15
CORNMANN, Eva Margaret, 4;
Felton, 4; Margaret, 4
CORROSER, Anna, 11; Mary,
11; William, 11
COUNTY, Joseph, 4;
Magdalena, 4; Maria
Margaret, 4
COWEN, Henry, 347
CRAMER, Christian, 12;
Elisabetha, 12; Maria, 12;
Martin, 118
CREMER, Catharine, 117;
Frederick, 117; Maria
Barbara, 117
CREUTZBERGER, Margar., 322
CROB, Casper, 118
CROSSER, Johannes, 268;
Mary, 268; Willm., 268
CRUM, Cathrina, 13, 16;
Johann Georg, 13; Phil, 16;
Philip, 13; Sybilla, 16
CRUMBEIN, ---, 1
CUNDRATH, Elizabeth, 244
CUNNINGHAM, William, 356
CUNRADT, Anna Elizabetha,
324; Anna Margaretha, 325;
Elisabeth, 350; George
Philipp, 324; John George,
324; John Nicolaus, 324;
John Peter, 324; John
Stephen, 324; Stephen, 324
CURT, Joh. Ernst, 243; John
Ernst, 349
CUSCHWA, Anna Catharine,
59; Anna Christina, 59;
Isaiah, 59

296, 298, 308; David, 298,
308; Eliz., 297; George, 308;
Joh. Aam, 306; Joh. Adam,
306; John, 295, 296, 303,
304; John Adam, 294, 295,
298, 306; John Michael, 299;
Leonard, 308; Magdalena,
296; Margaret, 294, 306;
Michael, 286, 295, 297, 299,
304, 306, 308; Regina, 295;
Rosina, 285, 294, 295, 297;
Salome, 297; Sarah, 303;
Susanna, 295
DEININGR, John, 300; John
George, 300
DEISIN, Madlena, 275
DEISINGER, Cath. Dorothea,
148; J. Jacob, 146, 149; J.
Peter, 145; Johannes, 154;
Margaret, 144, 145, 146, 148,
149, 153; Peter, 144, 145,
146, 148, 149, 153, 154;
Susanna Maria, 144
DEISS, Anna Margaret, 87;
Anna Maria, 33; Catharina,
24; Catharine Elizabeth, 87;
David, 2, 22, 24, 27, 33;
Elisabeth, 24; Elisabetha, 22,
29; Eva Elisabetha, 37;
George, 87; Jacob, 29, 33, 37;
Johann Jacob, 27;
Magdalena, 33, 37; Maria
Eliz., 87
DEISSINGER, Peter, 354
DEITRICH, Margaret, 296
DELLINGER, Anna Maria, 261;
Johannes, 261; Veronica, 261
DEMMAN, John Christian, 350
DEMMEN, Joh. Christian, 243;
John Christian, 350

DENEY, Jacob, 5
DENIUS, A. Maria, 16; Anna
Dorothea, 7; Anna Maria, 5,
7, 8, 10, 14, 15; Barbara, 10;
Catharina, 21; Cathrina, 7;
Dorothea, 8, 10, 14, 15; Elis.,
18; Elisabeth, 14, 15; Joh., 7,
10, 14, 15; Joh. Henrich, 9;
Joh. Jacob, 18; Joh. Philip,
10; Johannes, 8; Magdalena,
10, 24; Nicklaus, 9, 14, 15,
18; Nicolaus, 21; Phil., 24;
Philip, 10; Regina, 9, 14, 15,
18, 21; Wilhelm, 5, 7, 14, 15;
William, 8, 10
DENNY, J. George, 146; Jacob,
144; Margaret, 144, 146;
Susanna, 144
DERING, Maria Catharina, 38
DERKER, Caspar, 157; Marie
Catharine, 157; Sara, 157
DERRY, Jacob, 197
DERSCHT, Elizabeth, 104; John
Jacob, 104; Peter, 104
DERST, Elizabeth, 100; John,
100; Peter, 100
DERVER, Magdalena, 346
DESCH, A. Elis., 159; A.
Elisabeth, 158; A. Elizabeth,
159; A. Margaret, 159;
Catharine, 158; Christina,
159; Elisabeth, 156, 158;
Elizabeth, 160, 162; J. Philip,
145; Johannes, 151, 152, 154,
156, 158, 159, 160, 162;
Magdalena, 156, 159;
Margaret, 145, 147, 152, 159,
162; Philip, 145, 147, 162
DESTER, Anna Barbara, 76;
Barbara, 73, 78; Eva

DOSH, Ann Lisb., 156;
Johannes, 156
DOWNEY, Charles, 233
DRAUTMAN, George, 168
DREDENBACH, Maria
Elizabeth, 85
DREHER, Daniel, 322; David,
187, 257, 322; Joh. Henry,
187; John Heinrich, 322;
Maria Barbara, 322
DREISCH, George Leonhardt,
342; Jacob, 342; John
Leonhardt, 342; John
Reichardt, 342; Rosina, 342;
Susanna, 342
DRIAN, Elizabeth, 170; Michael,
170
DRIANN, Mary Elizabeth, 169;
Michael, 169
DRICKI, Dorothy, 131; George,
131; John, 131
DRION, Catharina, 39;
Catharina Elisabeth, 30;
Johann Georg, 30, 31, 39;
Sarah, 39
DRUGGAN, Dennis, 241
DRUGGON, Dennis, 345
DRUMME, Adam, 243
DRYON, Barbara, 177; John
Frederick, 177; John Georg,
32; John George, 177
DSCHOB, Anna, 60; Barbara,
60; Caspar, 60; Casper, 112;
Jacob, 60
DUB, Anna Maria, 336
DUBBS, Anna Maria, 125, 127,
129; Barbara, 130;
Catharina, 24; Catharine,
124, 125, 156; Cathrina, 14,
15; Christine, 126; Heinrich,

323; Henrich, 156, 161;
Henry, 129; Jacob, 126, 129,
263, 323; Johannes, 24; John,
14, 15, 124, 125, 129, 130;
John Henry, 125, 127; John
Jacob, 129; John Michael,
124; Maria Magdalena, 14,
15; Susanna, 126, 128, 129
DUBEL, Anna Barbara, 118;
Moritz, 118
DUBEN, Catharine, 129
DUBOI, Abraham, 132;
Magdalene, 132
DUBOY, Abraham, 12, 16, 133,
135; Anna Catharina, 23;
Anna Maria, 12; Christina,
13; Elisabeth, 11, 16;
Elisabetha, 21; Elizabeth,
132; Henrich, 21; Joseph, 13;
Magdalena, 12, 16;
Magdalene, 132, 133; Mary
Magdalene, 133; Philip, 16,
21, 23; Philip Jacob, 11
DUBS, A. Marie, 148; Anna,
122; Anna Barbara, 122;
Anna Maria, 68, 117, 118,
119, 120, 121; Anna Mila,
120, 253; Barbara, 63, 118,
120, 122, 123, 140, 142, 147;
Catharina, 24, 43; Catharine,
123, 130, 133, 134, 137, 158;
Cathrina, 19; Christine, 132;
Elizabeth, 120, 134, 138;
Emilia, 253; Heinrich, 316;
Henrich, 147, 148, 158, 253;
Henry, 117, 118, 119, 120,
121, 122, 123, 130, 132, 133,
134; Jacob, 122, 136, 137,
138, 140, 142; Joh., 24;
Johannes, 19; John, 63, 118,

334; Martin, 334; Peter, 296,
302; Thomas, 302
EISENHAUSER, Elisabeth, 66
EISENHAWER, Peter, 299;
Regina, 299
EISENHUT, Anna Maria, 75;
John Bernard, 75
EISENHUTH, Bernard, 133;
Elizabeth, 133; Magdalene,
133
EISENMENGER, Catharine,
176; Henry, 176; John
Henry, 172, 173; Susanna,
173; Susanna Catharine, 172
EISSAUER, Anna Maria, 114
EISSEN, Anna Elizabeth, 183;
Jacob, 183; Joh. Jacob, 183;
Joh. Michael, 183; Vernoica,
183
EISSENHAUER, Catarina
Elisabetha, 336; Nicholas,
188
EKERT, Abraham, 267; Anna
Maria, 267; Elisabeth, 267;
Johannes, 267
ELDER, Dorothea, 335; John,
335
ELI, Catharina, 40; Cathr., 40;
Peter, 40
ELKLER, Rosina, 152
ELLER, Henry, 188; Mary
Elizabeth, 188
ELLES, Agnes, 34; Angnes, 34;
Eckes, 34; Georg, 41;
Thomas, 34, 41
ELLET, Jacob, 304; William,
304
ELLINGER, Anastasius, 245,
353; Anna Magadalene, 244;
Anna Magdalena, 350; Anna

Maria, 6, 19, 351; Anna
Mary, 244; Catharina, 30, 38,
41; Elisabetha, 41; Elizabeth,
6; Georg, 6, 8, 14, 19, 30, 31,
38; George, 244, 351; Jacob,
38, 41, 300, 302; Joh. Jacob,
19; John, 302; Mar. Cathrina,
14; Maria Catharina, 36;
Maria Cathrina, 8; Michael, 8
ELLIT, Robert, 345
ELY, Anna Margaret, 245;
Jacob, 29, 31; Magdalena, 29;
Michael, 31; Peter, 29, 31;
Susanna, 31
EMANUEL, Jacob, 283
EMBICH, Anna Maria, 35;
Bernhart, 36; Catharina, 39;
Christoffel, 35; Christoph,
21, 24; Georg, 39; Joseph,
36; Magdalena, 21; Maria, 24
EMBIG, Friedrich, 46;
Margaretha, 46
EMBISCH, Christoph, 341;
Johannes, 341; John
Friederich, 341
EMERICH, Anna Gertrude,
233; Elisabeth, 146; Johan,
146; Johannes, 146; John,
233; Margaret, 147
EMICH, Christoph, 22;
Elisabeth, 153; Johann, 153
EMMERT, Benajmin, 60;
Catharine, 60; George, 61,
147; George Leonard, 60,
112; John George, 331, 357;
Maria Eva, 61
EMPICH, Jacob, 39
EMPTICH, Cathrina, 6; Joh.
Jacob, 7
EMRICH, Andreas, 150; Andres,

John, 189, 287, 305; John
Frantz, 194, 314, 334; John
George, 135; M. Catharine,
162; Margaret, 194, 298;
Maria Margaret, 124; Mary
Eliz., 287; Susan Catharine,
233; Susann Margaretha,
258; Susanna Margaretta,
294
FUEHMAN, Adam, 99;
Catharine, 99; Susanna, 99
FUETTER, Jacob, 220
FUETTERER, Elizabeth, 236;
Jacob, 236; Susan, 235
FUHRMAN, Anna, 40; Juliana,
40; Peter, 40
FUHRMANN, Christina, 267;
Dan, 267; Maria Susanna,
267
FUHRMANNIN, Dan., 274;
Elisabeth, 274
FUNCK, Marg., 24; Michael, 24
FUNDERSAL, Anna, 269;
Christina, 269; Henerig, 269
FURER, Elisabeth, 149
FUSCHS, Anna Margaret, 196;
Frantz, 196

-G-

GAEHY, Magdalene Dorothea,
50; Maria Dorothea, 50;
Samuel, 50
GAENTZLER, Mary Barbara,
188; Peter, 188
GAERTNER, Peter, 313
GALL, Elizabeth, 88; George, 88
GALLAN, Cath., 262; David,
262; Moses, 262
GALLMEYER, Margaretha, 353
GALLY, Catharine, 53; John,
53; Peter, 53
GAMBER, Elisabeth, 149
GAMBIL, John, 337; Susanna,
337
GAMER, Elizabeth, 145
GANS, Catharina, 268, 269;
Cathr. Elisabeth, 270;
Friedr., 268; Friedrich, 269,
270; Maria Margaretha, 269;
Michael, 268
GANSZ, Frederick, 272; Jacob,
272
GANTZ, Catharine, 270; Cathr.
Elisabeth, 267; Elisabeth,
270; Fr., 273; Friederich,
270; Friedr., 267; Friedrich,
270; George, 267; Mar. Elis.,
267; Philip, 270
GANZIN, Catharina Elisabeth,
273
GARDEN, John, 109; Mary
Magdalene, 109; Nancy, 115;
William, 109
GARREWEL, Dorothy, 32;
Johann Henrich, 32; Michael,
32
GARTE, Jacob, 52; Maria
Elizabeth, 52
GARTNER, Georg, 264; Joh.,
263; Joh. Valentin, 263;
Susanna, 263
GASHERT, Jacob, 147
GASSEL, Anna Mary, 205;
Elizabeth, 130; John Adam,
130; Michael, 205
GASSELE, Juliana, 306
GASSER, Adam, 106, 109, 114;
Anna, 65; Anna Maria, 130,
131, 132, 135, 137; Baltzer,
42; Catharine, 106, 109, 111;

GELEN, Conrad, 260; Maria,
  260
GEMBERLING, Anna
  Elizabeth, 50; Catharine, 50,
  53; Elizabeth, 50; Jacob, 50,
  53; John Philip, 47; Mary
  Magdalene, 53; Paul, 47, 50
GEMPEL, Cath. Elisabeth, 150;
  Johan, 150; M. Magdalena,
  150
GENGRICH, Christian, 140;
  Eva, 140; Jacob, 140
GENSEMER, Barbara, 91;
  Christine, 173; Georg, 91;
  George, 173; Margaret, 91,
  173
GENTZEMAR, George Daniel,
  165; M. Catharine, 165
GEORG, Johannes, 37; John
  Jacob, 77; Maria, 37; Schims,
  37
GEORGE, Ernst Leonard, 216;
  Mary Susanna, 216
GEOTZ, John Nicholas, 305
GEPFERT, Catarine, 270;
  Catharina, 268, 270; Georg,
  268, 270; George, 270;
  Heinrich, 269; Margaret, 269;
  Margaretha, 268; Maria, 269
GEPHART, Juliana, 238
GERBERICH, Andrew, 129,
  130, 143, 207; Anna Barbara,
  130; Anna Maria, 142;
  Barbara, 129, 143; Catharina,
  264; Catharine, 141, 291;
  Christine, 142; Elizabeth,
  128; Eva Catharine, 291;
  George John, 128; Henry,
  141, 291; Joh., 264; Joh.
  Georg, 264; John, 128, 131,

141, 291; Philip, 142
GERHARD, Anna Maria, 125;
  Catharine, 121; Christina, 70;
  Conrad, 125; Frederick, 70;
  Regina, 339; Susanna, 70;
  Valentine, 119, 121, 317
GERHARDT, Anna Elizabeth,
  131; Anna Maria, 129, 131;
  Anna Regina, 131; Barbara,
  349; Catarina, 352; Conrad,
  129, 131; Cunradt, 338;
  Jacob, 115; Johan, 276;
  Magdalena, 241; Maria, 133;
  Maria Catarina, 338; Regina,
  351; Susanna, 355; Valentin,
  338; Valentine, 215
GERHART, Catharine, 122;
  Cathr., 39; Christina, 70;
  Conrath, 39; Georg, 39;
  Johann Conrad, 250, 251;
  Johann Conradt, 251; John,
  70, 114; John Adam, 122;
  Philipp, 328; Regina, 123;
  Susanna, 70; Valentine, 122,
  123
GERLI, Catharina, 38
GERMAN, ---, 96; Adam, 34, 78;
  Anna, 22, 23; Anna
  Catharine, 190; Anna Mary,
  190; Barbara, 268; Cath.
  Elizabeth, 8; Catharine, 77;
  Dorothea, 8, 268; Elisabeth,
  18, 151; Elizabeth, 78, 217;
  Georg, 8, 268; Henrich, 277;
  Jacob, 8, 22, 23, 74, 77, 78,
  144; Joh., 18; Johann, 268;
  Johannes, 151, 271; John, 78,
  190, 217, 248; John Jacob,
  78; Johnnes, 277; Maria
  Catharine, 78; Maria

Henry, 108; John, 108
GLASBRENNER, John George, 247
GLASCOW, Nancy, 356
GLASS, Eva Elizabeth, 342; George, 342
GLASSBRENER, Georg, 36
GLASSBRENNER, Anna Eizabeth, 6; Anna Maria, 349; Anna Mary, 243; Elisabetha, 22; Georg, 22, 257; George, 312, 338; Joh. Georg, 6; John George, 240, 356; Margaretha, 312; Maria Christiana, 312
GLASSER, Susanna Maria, 355
GLEBER, Michael, 121
GLONINGER, Anna Maria, 40; Catarina, 343; Catharina, 27, 38; Cathrina, 40; Elisabeth, 46; Elisabetha, 32; Georg, 23, 32, 38, 40; Johann, 343; Johannes, 23, 27, 38, 40; Maria, 23, 40; Peter, 46; Philip, 27, 32; Wilhelm, 46
GLUCK, Barbara, 276, 279; Conrad, 278; Cristina, 278; Elizabeth, 131; Jacob, 131; Joh., 279; Johan Henrich, 278; Johannes, 276, 278
GLUECK, John, 80
GLUEK, Joh, 277; John, 276
GOBRECHT, Christopher, 93
GOBRETCH, Christoph, 91
GOCKEL, Elisabetha, 351
GODPFERD, Elisabeta, 269; Heinrich, 269; Margareda, 269
GOEBEL, Nicholas, 182, 189
GOECKEL, Anna Mary, 190;

Jacob, 190; Joh. George, 190; Joh. Jacob, 190
GOELLNITZ, Christian, 350; Joh. Christian, 244
GOER, Cunradt, 329
GOETTEL, Eva, 336; Eva Barbara, 357; Jacob, 135, 137; Magdalene, 135; Maria Eva, 332; Peter, 332, 345; Sarah, 135
GOETZ, Barbara, 142; Frederic, 295; Henry, 295; John Nicholas, 142; Martin, 305
GOHNA, Friedrich, 259; Susanna, 259
GOLDMAN, Cat. Eliz., 324; Conrad, 83, 86, 87; E. Barbara, 154; Eva, 87; Hannah, 86, 87; Jacob, 110, 111, 154; John, 86; M. Magdalena, 154; Magdalene, 87, 111; Mary Magdalene, 110
GOLDMANN, Catharina Barbara, 30; Christian, 40; Jacob, 30; Mary Magdalena, 30
GONDRUM, A. Margaretha, 260
GONELY, Maria Magdalena, 268; Thomas, 268
GONTERMANN, Catharina, 43; Jacob, 43; Johannes, 43; Michael, 43
GONTRAM, John, 306
GOOD, J. I., 54
GOOS, J. George, 258; M. E., 258
GOPFERD, Abraham, 269; Heinerig, 269

GRINEWALT, Philip, 250
GRING, Anna Catarina, 348;
Elizabeth, 168, 173; Henry,
168, 173; John Henry, 168
GROB, Elisabeth, 38; Elizabeth,
56; Jacob, 56
GROENAU, Andr., 273; Jacob,
273
GROF, George, 272; Salome,
272
GROFF, Jacob, 32
GROFFIN, Adam, 273;
Christina, 273
GROH, Susanna, 112
GROO, Barbara, 88
GROS, John, 113
GROSBART, Adam, 155;
Johannes, 155; Sibylla, 155
GROSSMAN, Christina, 347;
Susanna, 335
GRUBER, Catharina, 271;
Catharine, 231; Charlotte,
300, 307; Christian, 221, 231,
271; Eliz., 299, 307;
Elizabeth, 221; George, 259;
Louis, 299, 303; Ludwig, 299,
300, 307; Maria, 259; Mary,
303; Philip, 271; Susan, 231;
Susanna, 221
GRUENENWALDT, Maria
Margaretha, 341; Philip, 341
GRUENENWALT, Philip, 341
GRUENEWALD, Philip, 1
GRUENEWALDT, Margaret,
189; Philip, 189
GRUMM, Catharine, 130
GRUN, Catrina Elis., 251;
Cornelius, 26; Johann Georg,
26
GRUNDRUH, George, 114

GRUNDRUM, Anna Barbara,
133; John, 133; Susanna, 133
GRUNEWALD, Anna Maria, 29;
Barbara, 37, 40, 41;
Catharina, 22, 25, 40;
Christian, 31; David, 35;
Elisa. Gretha, 31; Elisabetha,
39; Joh. Leonhard, 14;
Johann, 29; Johann Carl, 42;
Johann Nicolaus, 25; Johann
Philip, 25, 27, 40; Johannes,
25, 34, 39, 41; Margaret, 4;
Margareth, 25; Margaretha,
9, 14; Margretha, 6; Maria
Margaretha, 14; Matheis, 37,
41; Matthaus, 30; Mattheis,
40; Michael, 22; Nicolaus, 22;
Phiip, 35; Philip, 4, 6, 9, 14,
26, 28, 30, 31, 34, 37, 39, 40,
42; Rebecca, 41; Regina, 41;
William, 37
GRUNEWALT, Philip, 1
GRUNZWEIG, Elizabeth, 161;
Jonathan, 161
GRUPENSCH, Elisabeth, 12;
Elizabeth, 5; Geo., 12; Georg,
5; Joh. Godried, 12; Johann
Philip, 5
GRUPPENSCH, Catharine, 4;
Elizabeth, 4; Georg, 4
GRUSE, Catharine, 52;
Elizabeth, 52; Philip, 52
GRUSIUS, Catharine, 100
GUDTMANN, Adam, 126; John
Jacob, 126; Regina, 126
GUENTHER, Mary Catharine,
241; Rebecca, 198
GUENTHUER, Maria Catarina,
346
GUEST, Susanna Catharine,

96, 99, 101, 103, 107, 110;
Christian, 110; Dorothy, 165;
Elizabeth, 107, 111; Eva
Margaret, 178; George, 179;
Henry, 91, 111, 115; John,
165, 179; John George, 165;
Magdalene, 99, 178; Maria
Catharine, 96; Micahel, 99;
Michael, 90, 91, 92, 101, 109,
111, 178, 179; Nicholas, 96,
101, 103, 107, 110; Sabina,
90, 91, 92, 109; Salome, 179;
William, 103
HAAG, Barbara, 97; Catharine
Rudi, 97; Michael, 97, 98
HAARK, Maria Catharine, 47;
Michael, 47
HAAS, Anna Barbara, 180;
Anna Catharine, 180; George
Ludwig, 180; Ludwig, 180;
Margaret Elisabeth, 173;
Margaret Eliza., 86
HAB, Rudolf, 253
HABERLAND, Catharine
Dorothea, 242
HABERLING, John, 67;
Margaret, 67; Peter, 67
HACHENBACH, Krafft, 112
HACK, Elizabeth, 109; Henry,
109; Jack, 90; John Jacob,
90; Michael, 90; Sabina, 90
HACKER, Anna Maria Barbara,
349
HADDERICH, Joh. Georg, 257;
Peter, 257
HAECKER, Agnes, 191; Anna
Mary Barbara, 243; Barbara,
335; Jacob, 191, 335
HAECKERT, Jacob, 332
HAEDDEICH, Joh. George,

190; Rosina, 190
HAEDDERICH, Joh. George,
190; John George, 322; Mary
Barbara, 190; Peter, 190,
322; Rosina, 322
HAEFFELE, Johannes, 334;
Margaretha, 334
HAEHLE, Frederich, 313;
Margaretha, 313
HAEHN, Anna Margaret, 110;
Daniel, 116; John, 110;
Maria, 116
HAEHNLE, Anna Barbara, 319;
Anna Margaretha, 319; Anna
Maria, 117; Elizabetha, 319;
Elyizabeth, 244; Eva
Catarina, 319; Frederich,
323, 324, 331, 335;
Frederick, 324; Freiderich,
325; Friederich, 319, 334;
Jacob, 319; John Michael,
319; John Seigmund, 316;
John Sigmund, 117;
Margaretha, 323, 324, 331;
Maria Eva, 319; Maria
Magdalena, 341; Michael,
336, 355, 356; Siegesmund,
324; Sigmund, 318, 321
HAEHNLIN, Magdalena, 351;
Margar., 341
HAEHNLY, Frederich, 329
HAERMAENNIN, Catarina, 344
HAERTER, Andrew, 221; Anna
Mary, 301; Elizabeth, 221;
George, 301; John, 221;
Salome, 221
HAERTTER, George, 303; John
George, 303
HAFFNER, Catarina Elisabetha,
336; Elizabeth, 112;

Jacob, 77; Maria Margaret, 77

HATZ, Elisabetha Barbara, 326; Elizabeth, 190, 200, 202; Eva Catharine, 190; George, 190, 202, 242, 304, 326, 348; Joh. George, 205; John George, 123; Samuel, 304; Wendel, 250

HAUCK, Anna Maria, 346; Barbara, 307; Elizabeth, 120; George, 314; Philip, 305, 307; Rudolph, 120

HAUENSTEIN, Christina, 16

HAUER, A. Barbara, 147; A. Margaret, 147; A. Marie, 147, 162; Anthon, 145, 147; Antonius, 352; Bernd., 146, 148, 150, 151, 157; Bernhardt, 146, 148; Catharine, 148, 150, 151, 154, 157, 158; Catherine, 146; Elisabeth, 153; Gret, 156; Jacob, 144, 145, 146, 147, 149, 153, 156; Johannes, 150, 156; Magdalena, 149; Magdalene, 240; Margaret, 144, 145, 146, 149, 153, 156; Margret, 157; Maria Barbara, 145; Marie Catharine, 145, 157; Marie Catherine, 146; Marie Elisabeth, 146

HAUK, Jacob, 302; John, 302, 303

HAUPT, Anna Mary, 238; Fredr., 236; John, 238; John Fredr., 239; Susan, 239

HAUSER, Barbara Brecht, 53; Catharine, 53; Elizabeth, 51; Jacob, 57; John Michael, 57;

Ludwig, 51; Peter, 53

HAUTZ, Anna, 65, 79; Anna Catharine, 77; Anna Christine, 79; Anna Eva, 65; Anna Margaret, 117, 118, 120; Anna Maria, 59, 60, 61, 63, 94, 119; Balthasar, 65; Barbara, 59, 60, 61, 62, 63, 64, 65, 66, 67, 68, 134, 337; Catharina, 259; Catharine, 59, 61, 70, 126, 152, 173; Christian, 59, 60, 61, 62; Christina, 70; Christine, 108; Elisabeth, 62, 64, 65, 66, 70, 150; Eva, 60, 62, 64, 119; George, 64, 66, 150; Henrich, 263, 275, 276, 279; Henry, 59, 60, 61, 62, 63, 64, 65, 66, 67, 68, 70, 75, 93, 108, 134; Johannes, 259; John, 60, 64, 70; John Christian, 117; John Christopher, 120; John Wendel, 125; Lawrence, 60, 62, 64, 65; Lorentz, 324, 335; Magdalena, 66; Margareta, 279; Maria Barbara, 59, 93, 112; Maria Eva, 61; Maria Magdalena, 68; Martin, 67; Michelsin, 275; Philip, 117, 118, 120, 279; Philip Henry, 59; Philip Lawrence, 61; Philip Lorentz, 59, 77, 79, 117, 119, 173, 244; Philip Peter, 152; Philipp, 328; Philipp Lorentz, 351; Sarah, 68; Susanna, 68; Wendel, 65, 68, 113, 151, 349

HAUZ, Anna Cathrina, 14, 15; Laurenz, 14, 15; Mar. Cathrina, 14, 15

HEFFELGINGER, A. Maria, 96; Martin, 96
HEFFER, Andrew, 58; John, 58
HEFFLEBAUER, Elisabeth, 270; Henrich, 270; Markreta, 270
HEFFLER, Anna Barbara, 59; John, 59
HEFFNER, Catharine, 92
HEGY, Christina, 11; Jacob, 11
HEHS, Elisabet, 263; Henry, 263
HEID, Abraham, 250, 252; Catharine, 269; Elisabetha, 250; Heinerig, 269; Magdalena, 269; Valentin, 269; Velte, 269
HEIDLER, Georg David, 21; Magdalena, 21; Wilhelm, 21
HEIDT, Barbara, 268; Cathar., 270; Catharina, 268; Elisabeth, 270; Valentin, 268
HEIL, Anna Catharine, 260; Johannes, 260
HEILL, Anna Maria, 169; Henry, 169
HEILMAN, A. Maria, 260, 264; Adam, 112, 238; Ana Maria, 264; Anastasius, 236, 237; Anna Cath., 239; Anna M. H., 238; Anna Maria, 261; Cath., 237; Cath. Elizabeth, 238, 239; Elisabeth, 255; Georg, 260, 261; George, 260, 264; Jacob, 260; Joh. Adam, 236; Joh. Heinrich, 261; John, 238; Maria, 261; Maria Magd., 256; Peter, 251; Philip H., 237; Rachel, 238; Salome, 237

HEILMANN, Adam, 43, 252; Anna Maria, 252; Cathr., 43; Catrina, 253; George, 150; Marie, 150; Marie Cath., 150
HEIMS, Eliz., 296; George, 296; Jacob, 296, 303; Michael, 303
HEINRICH, Anna Maria, 352; Anna Maria Elizabeth, 352; Anna Mary Elizabeth, 245; Juliana, 193, 246, 355; Martin, 197; Mary Elizabeth, 197; Nicholas, 247; Nicolaus, 356; Susan Mary, 245; Susanna Rosina, 336
HEISSE, Eliz., 299; Michael, 299
HEISSEE, Eliz., 299; Michael, 299
HEIT, Abraham, 255, 256; Elisabet, 255
HEITH, Barbara, 266; Cathr., 267; Jacob, 266; Rosina Barbara, 267; Val., 266, 267
HEKEDORN, Christian, 292
HELD, Daniel, 29, 296; John, 292; John George, 350
HELDT, John George, 244
HELFFRICH, John Henry, 53
HELLER, Isaac, 112; Joseph, 326
HELM, Barbara, 142; Conrad, 75, 142; John Frantz, 353; Margaret, 75
HELMIN, ---, 262
HEMBERLI, Anthony, 285; Julia, 285
HEMMERLING, Johannes, 28
HEMMING, Elisabeth, 4; Elisabetha, 3; Johannes, 3, 4
HEMPERLE, Anna Maria, 325;

HERCHELRODT, Elizabeth,
188; Lawrence, 188;
Valentin, 241, 345
HERCHELROTH, Anna
Elizabeth, 165; Barbara, 85;
Catharine, 51; Christine, 51;
Christine Momma, 53; Eva
Christine, 53; Henry, 51, 53;
John Henry, 84; Mrs., 82;
Valentine, 85
HERCKERT, Anna Maria, 85;
Elizabeth, 85; John, 85
HERGEHEIMER, Michael, 121
HERGELRATH, Lorentz, 49
HERGELROTH, Christine, 53;
Henry, 53
HERGER, Anna Margaretha,
341; Leonhardt, 341
HERMAN, Anna Maria, 315;
Catarina, 353; Daniel, 262,
264; Dorothea, 211; George
Michel, 149; Henrich, 149,
154; Jacob, 233, 315; Joh.,
262; Johann, 161; Johannes,
163, 353; John, 161;
Madlene, 149; Maria
Elisabeth, 315; Maria
Magdalena, 262; Martin, 211,
243, 349; Sara, 161
HERMANN, Catharine, 245;
John, 245
HERPER, Adam, 126; Anna
Catharine, 128; Anna Maria,
126; Catharine, 126
HERRAUF, Catharine, 136;
Peter, 136
HERRNSEN, Anna Maria, 261;
Benjamin, 261; Christina,
261
HERSCHBERGER, Abraham,
142; Christian, 136;
Elizabeth, 142; Samuel, 142;
Veronica, 142
HERTER, Anna Mary, 248;
Elizabeth, 248
HERTLE, Henry, 242; Joh.
Henry, 242; John Heinrich,
348
HERTZLER, Anna Magdalena,
245; Barbara, 293; Henry,
293; John Jacob, 293
HESS, Catharine, 131; Elisabet,
263; Elisabeth, 260; Georg,
36; Heinrich, 260; Jacob, 36;
Johannes, 262; Martin, 262,
341; Matthes, 262, 263;
Matthias, 291, 349; Rosina,
262, 263
HESSLER, Casper, 242
HETRICH, Anna Delila, 118;
Henry, 300; Joseph, 300;
Peter, 118
HETTERICH, Anna Maria, 78;
Jacob, 78; John Philip, 78;
Peter, 190
HETTERICHT, Joh. George,
194
HETTINGER, Anna Margaret,
109; Maria Catharine, 109;
Peter, 109
HETTRICH, John, 235; Peter,
235
HETZEL, Eva, 116; Eva
Elizabeth, 186; Peter, 186
HETZLER, Anna Christina, 243,
348; Anna Magdalena, 352;
Balthaser, 357; George, 58;
Maria Barbara, 58
HEU, Albert, 96; Barbara, 123;
Carl, 124; Eva, 124; Eva

John, 192
HEYMANN, Barbara, 192;
　Peter, 192
HEYR, Mary, 247
HEYSER, Jacob, 47
HEYT, Catharina, 271; Maria,
　271; Valentin, 271
HIBSCHMANN, Maria, 114
HICKS, George, 221, 308; John,
　221, 245, 308, 352
HIESTER, Johannes, 44; Maria,
　44, 103; Wilhelm, 44;
　William, 44, 80, 103
HIIRONIMUS, Eliz., 292;
　Jerome, 292; Jonas, 292
HILD, David, 266; Elisabeth,
　266; Jacob, 266
HILLER, Barbara, 140; George,
　140
HILTENBEITEL, Adam, 168,
　170; John Adam, 168; John
　Jacob, 170; Maria Elizabeth,
　168; Maria Ursula, 168;
　Ursula, 168, 170
HIMMELBERGER, Susanna,
　115
HIPPENSTIEL, Catharine, 112
HIRCHBERGER, Catharine,
　133; Christian, 133; Maria
　Catharine, 133
HIRSCHBERGER, Abraham,
　221, 223; Christian, 135;
　David, 135; John, 221
HISZLER, Casper, 339; Maria
　Magdalena, 339; Rosina, 339
HITSCH, Catharine, 282;
　Elizabeth, 282; Elizabeth
　Franz, 282; George Michael,
　282; John, 282; John Jacob,
　282; Mary Barbara, 282;

Michael, 282; Regina, 282
HIX, Anna Christina, 192;
　Elizabeth, 192; Henry, 115;
　Jacob, 192; John, 192
HOCH, Sarah, 223
HOCHLAENDER, ---, 295;
　Catharine, 288; Michael, 288
HOCHLANDER, Elisabeth, 275;
　Elizabeth, 277; Geo, 277;
　George, 275
HOEFELFINGER, Anna Maria,
　93; Maria Barbara, 93;
　Martin, 93
HOEFFELFINGER, Anna
　Margaret, 88; John, 88;
　Judith, 88
HOEFFER, Anna Catharine,
　240
HOERAUF, Andreas, 341; John
　Heinrich, 341
HOERCHELDRADT, Margar.,
　357
HOERCHELRODT, Anna
　Barbara, 357; Elisabetha, 357
HOERNER, John Casper, 217;
　Michael, 354
HOESTER, Anna Catara., 344;
　Anna Catharine, 240
HOF, Elisabeth, 46
HOF(MANN), John Jost, 164
HOFER, Catharine, 175;
　Ludwig, 175
HOFF, Benedict, 168; Jacob,
　113; Magdalene, 168; Mary
　Catharine, 169
HOFFELFINGER, Anna Maria,
　50; J. Jacob, 50; Martin, 50
HOFFER, Catharine, 240
HOFFMAN, Adam, 47, 92; Anna
　Elizabeth, 180; Catharine,

HOLTZMAN, Anna Maria, 60;
Henry, 60, 64; Maria
Magdalena, 64
HOLTZWART, Catarina, 345
HOMAN, Friedr, 263; Margret,
263; Susanna, 263
HONELMANN, Anna Mar.
Magdalena, 275; Arnold, 275;
Susanna, 275
HOOCH, Margaret, 126
HOOK, Hannah, 4; Maria, 4;
Samuel, 4
HORNBERGER, Catharine
Elizabeth, 191; Conrad, 352;
Jacob, 191
HORNEFIUS, Christophel, 42;
Elisabeth, 42, 43, 46; Georg,
46; Jacob, 35, 42, 46; Johann
Jacob, 43; Johann Philip, 35
HORNER, Margaret, 148;
Michael, 276, 277, 278, 280;
Michel, 148
HORNERIN, Catarina, 278, 280;
Catharine, 277; Christina,
278; Cristina, 278
HORSCHESHEIMER, Michel,
122
HORTLE, Heinrich, 347
HOSLBERG, Anna Elisabeth,
261; Elisabeth, 261; Heinrich,
261
HOSTER, ---, 82; Anna
Elizabeth, 85, 86, 87, 88;
Catharine, 98, 101, 240;
Christian, 98, 101, 144;
Christine, 112; Conrad, 77,
95; Elizabeth, 94, 98; Eva
Catharine, 102; Eva
Christine, 81; Joanna, 83;
John Conrad, 83; John

William, 83, 84, 85;
Margaret, 77; Maria
Elizabeth, 87, 101; Maria
Elizabeth Schwartz, 95;
Mary Catharine, 102;
Susanna Elizabeth, 85; W.,
81; William, 86, 87, 88, 94,
101, 102
HOTLZWART, Catharine, 241
HOTS, George, 304; Samuel,
304
HOTZ, George, 304; Samuel,
304
HOUCK, John George, 317
HOUGH, Anna, 347; Mary, 345;
Sarah, 345
HOUTZ, Philipp Lorentz, 318
HOWART, Mary, 16
HOWERDER, Christian, 43;
Juli, 43
HOWERTER, Christian, 221,
226, 248, 299; Elizabeth, 221;
George, 221; Jacob, 221;
Juliana, 221; Samuel, 221
HUBELE, Anna Maria, 37, 40;
Elisabeth, 37; Friedrich, 37,
40
HUBELER, Eva Catarina, 347;
Eva Mary, 241
HUBER, ---, 82; A. Maria
Magdalena, 7; Andreas, 26,
30; Anna Maria, 40, 137, 357;
Anna Oteliana, 190; Cath.,
293; Catharine, 113, 129,
140, 152, 156; Cathrina, 9;
Christian, 141; Daniel, 152;
David, 26; Elisab., 342;
Elisab. Marg., 151; Elisabeth,
40; Elizabeth, 124, 161, 189,
191, 246, 247; Elizabetha,

HYDT, Catharine, 243

-I-

IBA, Barbara, 56; Henry, 56
ICKEL, John Herman, 240
IETTER, Eva Catarina, 347;
    Eva Margaretha, 348
IHLY, A. Maria, 17; Mich., 17
ILE, Christina, 292; Elizabeth,
    292; Jacob, 292; John, 291;
    Mary, 292; Mary Cath., 292;
    Mary Margaret, 292; Mary
    Regina, 291, 292; Michael,
    291, 292; Susanna, 292
ILI, Anna Mar--, 291; Anna
    Margaret, 245; Mary Regina,
    289; Michael, 289, 291
ILLICK, Eva Maria, 168;
    Leonard, 172; Maria
    Catharine, 168; Maria
    Dorothea, 172
ILLIN, Anna Margaretha, 353
ILLINGER, George, 292
IM(HOFF), Michael, 87
IMBODE, Anna Christian, 356
IMBODEN, Adam, 221, 222,
    225; Anna Christina, 193,
    247; Anna Mary, 221;
    Catharine, 188; Christina,
    193, 221; Diel, 237; Elenora,
    221; Eleonora, 193, 198, 222,
    231, 236, 237; Elisabeth, 41;
    Elizabeth, 221, 237; George,
    248; Henry, 221; Jacob, 193,
    239; Joh. George, 193; Joh.
    Philip, 193; Joh. Schw., 222,
    223, 231, 237, 239; Joh.
    Shweick, 221; Joh.
    Sweichert, 231; Johann
    Schweickhardt, 349; John,

188, 193, 248; John Adam,
    193; John Schw., 221; John
    Schweickard, 221; John
    Schweickhard, 193; John
    Schweickhardt, 243; John
    Schweigert, 237; John
    Schweighard, 198; Juliana,
    199, 238, 248; Leonora, 221;
    Magdalene, 221; Margaret,
    221; Mary, 221; Philip, 41,
    221, 235, 248; Schweikart,
    221; Solomon, 193, 231
IMHOFF, Anna Maria, 13, 72;
    Barbara, 9, 10, 17, 23;
    Christina, 41; Frederick, 177;
    Henrich, 37, 41; Joh. Jacob,
    17; Johann Henrich, 251;
    Johann Martin, 9; Johannes,
    5, 41; Joseph, 37; Maria, 7;
    Maria Barbara, 5, 13; Martin,
    5, 9, 10, 13, 17, 23, 72, 251,
    252; Mary Magdalene, 177;
    Philippina, 23; Ursula, 72,
    252
IMMEL, Barbara, 205; John,
    205, 215, 315
INGERHAM, Elisabetha, 344;
    Elizabeth, 240
IOTTER, Iost, 347
ISCHLER, Apollonia, 10;
    Barbara, 231, 238; Bernhard,
    10; Catharine, 220;
    Elisabetha, 41; Georg, 41;
    George, 224; Ludwig, 10;
    Susan, 41; Susanna, 224
ISED, Jacob, 49; Maria
    Elizabeth, 49
ISLER, Christian, 248
ISTLER, Apollonia, 3, 7;
    Appollonia, 2; Barbara, 2;

KAPF, Gertraudt, 319; Veit, 319
KAPLER, Christine, 119; John
    Bernard, 119; Martin, 119
KAPP, Anna Barbara, 324;
    Anna Catarina, 324;
    Christina, 147; Elisabeth,
    147; Elizabeth, 111; Eva,
    101, 324; George Veit, 324;
    Gertraud, 332; Gertraudt,
    333; Jacob, 300, 301; Joh.
    Jacob, 263; John, 111, 115;
    John Veith, 325; Magdalene,
    111; Margaretha, 324;
    Margaretha Elisabetha, 324;
    Maria Magdalena, 324;
    Peter, 147; Veit, 332; Viet,
    333
KAPPLER, Barbara, 320;
    Catarina Barbara, 314;
    Christina Magdalena, 326;
    John Jacob, 314;
    Margaretha, 312, 313;
    Martin, 312, 314, 321, 326,
    331; Susanna, 326
KARG, Andreas, 352; Andrew,
    197, 245; Susanna, 197
KARMENE, Adam, 285; Anna
    Margaret, 285; Anthony, 285;
    Catharine Elizabeth, 285;
    Eva, 285; George, 283, 285;
    Jacob, 285; John, 285;
    Joseph, 285; Juliana, 285;
    Susanna, 285
KARMENI, Anna Christian,
    197; Antonius, 197; Juliana,
    247
KARMENIE, Ann Christina,
    198; Anna, 199; Anna
    Christina, 198; Anna Mary,
    199; Anthony, 243;

Antionius, 348; Antonius,
    198; Catharine, 199;
    Catharine Elizabeth, 198;
    Christina, 198; George
    Adam, 198; Joh. George, 199;
    Joh. Philip, 198; John, 198,
    199; John David, 199; John
    George, 198; John Martin,
    198; John Philip, 198;
    Juliana, 198, 199, 356; Mary
    Barbara, 198; Michael, 198,
    246, 355; Philip, 199;
    Rebecca, 198
KARMINI, Anna, 199, 203;
    Anthony, 202, 248;
    Catharine, 204; Christina,
    202; Eve, 291; George, 248;
    John Philip, 248; Joseph,
    291; Philip, 199, 203;
    Rebecca, 284
KARSCHNITZ, Andrew, 235;
    Cath. Eliz., 302; Peter, 302
KARSTNITZ, Catharine, 90;
    Christian, 90
KARSTSCHNITZ, Andrew, 225
KARTSCHNITZ, Catharine, 248
KASSEL, Catharine Elizabeth,
    85; Elizabeth, 85; Jacob, 159;
    John Adam, 85; Magdalena,
    159; Salome, 62
KAST, Martin, 169
KASTER, Jacob, 157
KASTNITZ, Andreas, 334, 351;
    Andrew, 244; Catarina
    Elisabetha, 331; Christina
    Johannetta, 331; Elisabeth,
    331; George Noah, 331;
    Johann George, 331; John
    Frantz, 334; John George,
    344

KIRKPATRICK, Maria, 106;
Thomas, 106
KIRSCHBAUM, Gertrude, 63;
William, 63
KIRSCHSTATTER, Joh.
Martin, 256
KIRSCHSTETTER, Martin, 255
KIRSH, Baltzer Ober, 154
KIRST, Magdalena, 154
KIRSTAETTER, Anna
Catharine, 196; Anna
Margaret, 196; Dorothea,
181, 187, 216, 317; Elizabeth,
243; Joh., 196; Joh. Adam,
196; Joh. Leonard, 196; Joh.
Martin, 196, 214, 241, 242;
Joh. Michael, 242; Johann
Martin, 347; John, 196, 312;
John Leonhardt, 352; John
Martin, 344; Juliana, 243,
312; Magdalena, 196;
Magdalene, 216; Margar.,
346; Margaret, 241; Maria
Dorothea, 311; Martin, 181,
187, 213, 215, 311, 312, 317;
Mary Elizabeth, 196;
Michael, 187, 196, 216; Sarah
Elizabeth, 196; Sebastian,
196, 216, 241, 346; Veronica,
196
KIRSTAETTR, Johan Michael,
347
KIRSTETTER, Elisabetha, 348;
Elizabeth, 4; Juliana, 349;
Martin, 4
KISELER, Margaret, 64;
Nicholas, 64
KISNER, Catharine, 287, 289;
Catharine Eliz., 287; Eva
Catharine, 287; Jacob, 287,

289; John, 285, 287; John
Henry, 287; John Wolf, 285;
Sabina, 285
KISSECKER, Anna Engel, 246,
355
KISSINGER, Andrew, 183;
Cath., 302; Susanna, 183
KISSNER, Anna Sabina, 338;
Catharine, 296; Daniel, 195;
Jacob, 296; Joh., 208; Joh.
Michael, 195; Joh. Wolff,
181; Johann Wolf, 346; John,
195, 207, 215, 332; John
Wolf, 338; John Wolff, 195,
241; Mary Barbara, 195;
Mary Eve, 195; Mary Regina,
195; Sabina, 195, 207, 208,
215, 296
KISSNES, Joh., 202; Sabina,
202
KISTER, Margaret, 127; Philip,
127
KITSCH, Michael, 305
KITTRING, George Michael,
194, 315; Joh. Adam, 257;
Joh. Valentine, 191, 208;
John Adam, 194, 315; Maria
Margaretha, 315; Rosina
Barbara, 315
KITZEL, Jacob, 292
KITZMILLER, A. M., 151; A.
Marie, 153; Anna Marg., 253;
Anna Mary, 235; Casper, 13;
Catharine, 215; Christina,
222; Jacob, 153, 215, 219,
222, 235, 256, 301, 304;
Johann, 153; Johannes, 151;
Juliana, 13; Maria Rebecca,
13; Sabina, 151
KITZMOLLER, Barbara, 89;

202
KLEVER, Anna Dorothea, 222;
John, 222
KLIEN, Andrew, 211; J. Albert,
160
KLIENFELDER, Ann Elisabeth,
156; Johannes, 156;
Magdalena, 156
KLINE, Anna Maria, 316, 329;
Heinrich, 316, 329
KLINGER, A. Marie, 158; Carl,
145, 148, 150, 152, 154, 156,
158, 159; Charles, 145;
Christina Regina, 145;
Elisabeth, 154; Eva Barbara,
152; Frane, 150; Frany, 145,
152, 154, 158; Frenie, 148; J.
Friedrich, 145; J. Heinrich,
148; Jacob, 150; Joseph, 159;
Magdalena, 156; Rosina, 156;
Veronica, 145, 159
KLOLINGER, Johannes, 30
KLOPP, Peter, 86, 116;
Werrine, 86
KLOSS, Anna Susanna, 81; P.,
81
KLUNK, Andreas, 144;
Magdalene, 144
KNABEL, A. M., 151;
Christoph, 151; Eva, 151
KNAUER, Adam, 172;
Catharine, 172; Margaret,
172
KNEAGY, Jost, 356
KNEB, A. M., 151; Christoph,
151; Eva, 151
KNEBEL, Herman, 63; Jacob,
63; Margaret, 63; Maria
Magdalena, 63; Maria
Salome, 63

KNEUGET, Leonhardt, 322
KNIES, Elisabeth, 144; John,
144; Marie Barb., 145
KNIESEL, Thomas, 232
KNIESLY, Thomas, 228
KNIESZ, Elizabetha, 347
KNIS, Elisabeth, 62; John, 62
KNIS, Anna Margaret, 61;
Elisabeth, 61; John, 61
KNISS, Catharine, 124;
Catharine Elizabeth, 83;
John, 83, 124; Maria
Barbara, 83
KNOBEL, Elisabeth, 151
KNOCHEN, Anna Margaret,
222; Anna Mary, 222;
Barbara, 223; John, 222, 223
KNOG, Cath. Sophia, 292; John
David, 292; Knoz, 288;
Valentine, 288, 292
KNOPF, Anna Elisabeth, 348;
Elizabeth, 243
KNOX, Catharine, 106; Henry,
106
KNOZ, Cath. Sophia, 292; John
David, 292; Valentine, 290,
292
KOB, Anna Catahrine, 197;
Elizabeth, 197; Frederick,
180; George, 197; Joh.
George, 196; Joh. Valentine,
197; Valentin, 36
KOBB, Catharine, 122; Dorothy,
122; Philip, 122
KOBEHEBER, Catharine, 142;
Maria, 142; Thomas, 142
KOBEL, Catharine, 93; John,
93; Susanna, 93
KOBER, Anna Elisabetha, 313;
Anna Elizabeth, 194, 197;

KUHBAUCH, Johann
Friederich, 350
KUHN, Adam Simon, 327;
Barbara, 78; John, 76, 78
KUHNER, Adam, 22; Catharina,
22; Cathrina, 272; Elisabeth,
272; Fried., 266; Friedr., 266;
Jacob, 271, 272; Joh. Jacob,
22; Margaretha, 266, 271;
Phil., 266
KUHNERIN, Elisabeth, 267,
273; Friedr., 273;
Margaretha, 267
KUHNS, Catharine, 78; Jacob,
78; John, 78
KUHNY, Mary, 346
KUMLER, Hannah, 56; Henry,
56; Susanna, 56
KUMMEL, Elisabetha, 42;
Samuel, 42
KUMMRER, Christian, 273
KUNCKEL, Anna Catharine,
81; Catharine, 105, 179;
Daniel, 179; Jacob, 107;
John, 81, 82; Michael, 179;
Susanna, 107
KUNERT, Adam, 268;
Catharina, 268; Jacob, 268;
Margaretha, 268
KUNIGIN, Eva, 251
KUNKEL, Catharine, 59, 67;
John, 59; Michael, 67; Philip,
67
KUNKELIN, A. Marie, 148
KUNS, George, 304; Mary, 304
KUNSELE, Catharine, 97;
Christian, 97; Rudolph, 97
KUNSELMAN, Maria Barbara,
125; Philip, 125
KUNSLE, Catharine, 92, 96;

Rudolph, 92, 96
KUNTERMAN, Catharine, 72;
Jacob, 72; Simon, 72
KUNTZ, Anna Elizabeth, 127;
Barbara, 124; Catharine, 67;
Eliz. Catharine, 85;
Elizabeth, 124, 126; Eva
Catharine, 66, 68; Eva
Cathr., 267; George, 124,
127; Henry, 267; Jac., 267;
Jacob, 66, 67, 68; Joh. Jacob,
267; John George, 126, 312;
John Henry, 126; John
Philip, 68; Mar. Cathr., 267;
Margaret, 66; Peter, 85
KUNTZER, Anna, 252; Jacob,
252; Sabina, 252
KUNTZLE, Catharine, 95; John
Jacob, 95; Rudolph, 95
KUNZ, Anna Mary, 223;
George, 223; Jacob, 223, 301;
Peter, 301; Philip, 223
KUNZELMAN, Barbara, 152,
153; Henrich, 152; Philip,
152, 153
KUPER, Jacob, 299; John
Jacob, 299
KUPP, Jacob, 248; John, 248
KUPPER, Elizabeth, 197; Jacob,
197, 302; Joh. Adam, 197;
Joh. George, 197; John
George, 302, 348
KURTZ, Lawrence, 242;
Leonard, 50; Lorentz, 242,
347; Mr., 82; Pastor, 259;
Ursula, 50
KURZ, Henry, 229
KUSTER, Catharine, 76, 92;
Dorothy, 91; John, 76, 92;
Peter, 91

LANZIN, Marg., 274
LATSCHER, Abraham, 132;
    Catharine, 132
LATTORIN, Catharina, 266
LATZ, Elizabeth, 316
LAUBER, Baltasar, 9; Cathrina,
    9
LAUBSCHER, Jacob, 10, 256;
    Juliana, 10, 39; Mary Eve,
    240
LAUCK, Catharina, 23;
    Elizabeth, 142; John, 142;
    Simon, 23
LAUCKSTER, Maria
    Elizabetha, 349; Mary
    Elizaeth, 243
LAUER, Catharine Barbara,
    320; Christian, 83, 96, 112;
    Christine, 96; Elisabetha, 37;
    Elizabeth, 115; Eva
    Elizabeth, 106; Johann
    Christian, 339; John, 199;
    John Michael, 319; Michael,
    199, 319
LAUREI, Michael, 340
LAURER, Anna Eliz., 96;
    Michael, 322
LAURI, Jacobina, 6; Joh. Georg,
    6; Michael, 6
LAURY, James, 30; Maria, 16;
    Mary, 7, 11, 16; Robert, 7,
    11, 16, 30; Schems, 30;
    William, 7
LAUTERMILCH, Anna
    Catharine, 172; Anna
    Margaret, 164; Anna Maria,
    55, 178; Catharine, 172, 173,
    175; Christina, 41; Gottfried,
    164; Henry, 309; Jacob, 306;
    Johannes, 41; John, 213;

John Adam, 164; John Geo.,
    172; Magdalene, 167; Maria
    Elizabeth, 172; Melchior, 49,
    58, 172, 173, 175
LAUTNER, Peter, 277
LAUX, Casper, 114
LAWLER, Anna Maria, 129;
    James, 129; Susanna
    Catharine, 129
LAY, Andreas, 354; Andrew,
    246; Anna Margar, 325;
    Anna Maria, 45; Johann
    Henrich, 45
LAYBLIN, Rosina, 351
LE FEBRE, David, 112
LE ROUCHE, Anna Bar.
    Elizabeth, 84; Elizabeth, 84;
    Jonas, 84
LE ROY, Anna Maria, 90, 95
LEADSOORTH, William, 344
LEB, Anna Engel, 165; Anna
    Margaret, 165; Casper, 165
LEBACK, Maria Madlena, 278;
    Peter, 278
LEBBO, Abraham, 83, 86; Anna
    Margaret, 86; Catharine, 91,
    110; Henry, 91; John Adam,
    83; John Jacob, 86
LEBENGUT, Anna Catharine,
    120; Jacob, 120
LEBO, Christopher, 116; Henry,
    114; Margaret, 176; Peter,
    175, 176
LECHNER, George, 325;
    Margaret, 95, 99
LEDIG, Benedict, 357
LEG, Magdalene, 76; Michael,
    76
LEHMAN, Catharina, 260;
    Christian, 260; Elisabeth, 69;

Elizabeth, 297; Philip, 297
MAEINTZER, Anna Catharine,
202; Elizabeth Catharine,
202; Geoerge Christopher,
202; Joh. George, 202; Mary
Elizabeth, 202
MAENNERIN, Maria Sara, 344
MAENNIG, Joh. Adam, 244
MAENNING, John Adam, 351
MAENZINGER, Jacob Conrad,
231
MAERCKE, Barbara, 88; John,
88
MAES, Anna Christine, 78;
Catharine, 53; Elizabeth, 52,
53, 78; George, 52, 53; Jacob,
53; John, 78; John Adam, 78;
John Jacob, 53; John
Nicholas, 50; Susanna, 50
MAESS, Anna Margaretha, 335;
Benjamin, 52; Elizabeth, 77;
George, 335; John, 77; John
William, 77; Nicholas, 52;
Susanna, 52
MAEYER, Michael, 304
MAGOLLOCH, Catharine, 55;
Jim, 55; Susanna, 55
MAHS, Elisabetha, 14; Joh.
Jacob, 14; Johannes, 14
MAIER, Elizabeth, 167; John,
79, 167; Michael, 79
MAINTZER, Joh. Georg, 257
MALFIER, Michael, 284
MALFIR, Magdalene, 247;
Michael, 203, 242, 347
MALVIER, John, 309;
Margaret, 309; Mary Eliz.
Bohr, 287; Michael, 287, 290
MALVIR, Joh. Michael, 189
MANCHEN, Heinrich, 10; Maria

Cathrina, 10
MANN, Bernhardt, 336;
Catarina Elisabetha, 336;
George Bernhardt, 315
MANNIG, Adam, 271; Barbara,
271; Catharina, 271;
Christina, 271; Elisabeth,
271; George, 271; Jacob, 271;
Johannes, 271; Michael, 271;
Peter, 271, 272; Petrus, 271;
Susana, 271; Susanna, 272
MARCKER, Catarina, 318;
Catharine, 200; Juliana, 200;
Julianna, 317; Maria
Elizabetha, 317; Mary
Elizabeth, 200; Peter, 200,
257, 316, 317
MARCKET, John Heinrich, 322
MARCKY, Anna Maria, 89;
Diederich, 89
MARDER, Jacob, 199
MARIT, Kilian, 256
MARKWART, Conrad, 278
MARSCHALL, David, 44;
Elisabeth, 44; Elisabetha, 44;
Johannes, 44
MARSTALLER, Philipp, 341
MARSTELLER, Joh. Philip,
212; John Henry, 83;
Magdalene, 172, 212; Philip,
172, 216
MARTE, Catharine, 151;
Friederich Walter, 150; J.
Friederich, 150; M. Christina,
151; Susanna, 150
MARTHER, Johannes, 29
MARTIN, Catharine, 151; Fred
W., 163; Henry, 200, 225;
Juliana, 200; M. Christina,
151; Mary, 349; Regina, 251;

George, 171; John Michael, 180; Magdalene, 170; Mary Elizabeth, 170; Michael, 180
MAY, Catharina, 65; George, 65
MAYER, A. Rosine, 145; Angelica, 53, 176; Angelina, 175; Anna, 166; Anna Angelica, 176; Anna Barbara, 26, 52, 169, 175; Anna Cath., 61; Anna Margaret, 84; Anna Maria, 64, 65, 66, 116; Annagretha, 259; Barbara, 90, 166, 175, 177; Catharine, 52, 66, 94, 97, 102, 103, 104, 105, 106, 108, 110, 116, 170, 172, 174, 175, 178, 179; Catharine Elisabeth, 69; Cathrina, 28; Christian, 144, 163; Christina, 161, 275; Christine, 101, 102, 104, 110, 177; Christoph, 275; Christopher, 170, 172; Conrad, 90, 295, 299, 300; Daniel, 101, 102, 104, 110, 115; Dorothea, 61; Elisabeth, 65; Elizabeth, 90, 104, 108, 113, 141, 161, 172, 174, 175, 176; Eva, 30, 102, 116; Gertraud, 150; Hannah, 239; Henrich, 32, 147, 148, 150, 152; Henry, 53, 62, 145, 166, 170, 172, 175, 176, 177; Herman, 259; Jacob, 178, 275, 297; Johann, 161; Johann Peter, 29; Johannee, 277; Johannes, 28, 29, 30, 163, 275, 277; John, 52, 54, 102, 103, 106, 108, 166, 169, 170, 174, 175, 176, 177; John George, 52, 172, 178, 179;

John Henry, 53, 86, 166; John Jacob, 102; Juliana, 62, 145, 147, 150, 152; Magalene, 104; Magdalena, 32, 61; Margaret, 60, 61; Maria Catharine, 84, 177; Maria Salome, 101; Marie Magdalena, 148; Martin, 65, 66, 69; Michael, 108, 114, 172, 174, 175, 176, 302; Ottilia, 259; Peter, 60, 61, 64, 66, 84, 116; Philip, 66, 69, 97, 106; Salome, 104; Theobald, 176; Valentine, 102, 104; Wilhelm, 163; William, 103
MAYLY, Martin, 256
MAYSER, George, 177
MEAS, Barbara, 2; Catharine, 2; Charlotte, 2, 3; Christian, 2, 3
MEASS, Cathrina, 11; Jacob, 11
MEBEN, Mary, 241
MECHLIN, John, 299; Magdalene, 299; Peter, 306; Philip, 299
MECK, Michael, 356
MECKGUNDEL, Catharina, 45; Johann Georg, 45; Johannes, 45
MECKLING, Johannes, 38; Robert, 38; Simon, 38
MECKMOLLEN, Berthin, 41; Daniel, 41, 42; Elisabetha, 42; Rebecca, 41, 42
MECKMORE, Elisabeth, 39; Elisabetha, 39; Joseph, 39; Sarah, 39; Thomas, 39
MECUL, Catharina, 33; Elisa., 30; Joseph, 30, 33

MEE, Anna Maria, 57
MEES, Barbara, 19; Caspar, 19;
Catharina, 37; Catharine, 53,
54; Cathrina, 9, 14, 19;
Dorothy, 139; Elizabeth, 78;
George Henry, 139;
Johannes, 19; John, 73, 78;
Mar. Cathr., 19; Michael, 29,
37, 53, 54; Philip, 9, 14, 19;
Sophia Barbara, 54; Wilhelm,
37
MEESE, Georg, 6; Michael, 33
MEESS, Anna Barbara, 74;
Catharine Elizabeth, 74;
Cathrina, 10; Charlotte, 3;
Christian, 3; Elisabeth, 11;
Elizabeth, 6; Eva Elizabeth,
74; Georg, 11; George
Matheys, 11; J. Philip, 10;
Joh. Philip, 10; Johannes, 3,
6, 11; John, 74; Maria
Elisabeth, 11; Michael, 79;
Philip, 11
MEGELOCH, Juy, 27; Susanna,
27
MEGOLOCH, Juy, 30; William,
30
MEGONDEL, Catharina, 38;
Georg, 32; Johannes, 32, 38;
Magdalena, 32; Susanna, 32,
38
MEGONTEL, Alexander, 35;
Georg, 35; Susanna, 35
MEGUNDEL, Jacob, 29;
Johannes, 29
MEHR, Elizabeth, 180; George,
180
MEIER, Barbara, 76, 251, 253;
Elizabeth, 52, 120; Henrich,
253; Henry, 52; Johann

Valentin, 251; Johannes, 253;
John, 49; John Henry, 52;
Jorg, 251; Marcia, 72
MEILE, Anna Maria, 30;
Cortius, 33; Curtius, 33;
Elisabetha, 33; Georg, 33;
Samuel, 33; Simon, 30
MEILI, Christine, 139, 140;
Martin, 139, 140
MEILIE, Martin, 263
MEILIN, Eliz. Cathrina, 9;
Emmanuel, 9; George, 9;
Maria Catharina, 9; Martin,
9; Rachel, 9
MEILING, Gorg, 269
MEILY, Cath., 145; Catharine,
148, 155, 159
MEILYN, Cath., 144
MEINZINGER, Conrad, 238
MEINZINGR, Barbara, 238
MEIR, George, 72; Verena, 72
MEIRY, Barbara, 72
MEISENHALDER, Christoffel,
269, 270; David, 270
MEISENHELDER, Barra, 270;
Christoffel, 269, 270;
Elizabeth, 269; George, 270
MEISENHELTER, Barbara,
271; Stoffel, 271
MEISENHOLTDER, Christoph,
269; Michael, 269
MEISER, Anna, 168, 172; Anna
Barbara, 170; Anna
Catharine, 176; Anna Maria,
174; Anna Mary, 171;
Catharine, 114, 168, 169,
174, 175, 176, 177; George,
174, 175, 176; George
Michael, 168; Geroge, 172;
Henry, 171, 174; John, 57,

168, 169, 175, 176, 177; John
George, 174, 175; John
Michael, 57, 170, 171; Maria
Catharine, 175, 176; Michael,
170
MEISSER, Anna, 166, 167;
Henry, 47; John, 57, 166;
John George, 166, 167; John
Henry, 167; John Philip, 47
MEISTER, Henrich, 255
MEIUN, Cath., 145
MEIVEL, Anna Maria, 331
MELI, Anna, 121
MELIE, Hannah, 27; Jorg, 27
MELIN, Christina, 262
MELIUN, Cath., 145
MELL, Adam, 112
MELLINGER, Barbara, 35, 40;
Benedict, 23; David, 35;
Jacob, 23, 25, 35, 40;
Margaretha, 23; Samuel, 40
MELLINGR, Barbara, 23;
Jacob, 23
MELSCHEIMER, Frederick,
247
MELSHEIMER, Charles
Theodore, 202; Frederic
Ernst, 202; Frederic
Theodore, 202; Herrn
Pfarrer, 357; John Frederic,
202
MENGES, Adam, 77; Margaret,
77; Maria Catharine, 88;
Peter, 88
MENNIG, Adam, 271;
Elisabeth, 271
MENZINGER, Barbara, 2, 14,
15; Conrad, 2, 14, 15
MERCK, Abraham, 125; Adam,
132, 136, 142; Anna, 140;

Anna Catharine, 126; Anna
Maria, 125; Catharina, 3, 32;
Catharine, 127; Christine,
142; Conrad, 35, 125;
Conradt, 23, 25; Conrath, 27,
31, 39, 42; David, 138, 141;
Eisabetha, 35; Elisbetha, 42;
Georg, 31; George, 140;
Geroge, 224; Gertrude, 141;
Heinrich, 252, 322; Henrich,
255; Henry, 125, 187, 199;
Jacob, 20, 32, 138, 224;
Johann Georg, 39; Johann
Jacob, 255; Johannes, 31;
John, 126; John Williams,
224; Killian, 125, 127;
Magdalena, 27, 133;
Magdalene, 136; Margaret,
25, 142; Margaretha, 23, 25,
42; Margetha, 256; Maria
Barbara, 255, 322; Philipina,
255; Philippina, 23, 128, 199,
255; Phillippina, 125; Regina,
57, 252; Rudy, 158; Samuel,
224; Susanna, 23
MERCKE, Barbara, 90, 91;
John, 90, 91
MERCKLE, Catharine, 57, 58;
Elizabeth, 57; Peter, 58
MERCKLING, Anna Frantzina,
327
MERCKLY, Elizabeth, 110;
John, 110
MERCKY, Elizabeth, 104; John,
104
MERK, Anna, 139; Cathr., 16;
George, 139; George Henry,
139; Henrich, 253; Jacob, 18;
Kilian, 16; Philippina, 253
MERKLING, Christian, 228;

Charles, 201; Joh. Heinrich,
10, 17; Joh. Jacob, 6, 14, 15,
200; Johann Heinrich, 251;
Johanna, 17; Johannes, 10,
14, 15, 281, 355; John, 49,
54, 107, 165, 166, 167, 169,
201, 292; John George, 168,
314, 319; John Heinrich, 316;
John Jacob, 108, 127, 165,
302, 316; John Michael, 201;
John. Henry, 200;
Magdalena, 10, 21; Mar.
Magdalena, 14, 15; Margaret,
144; Margaretha, 4; Maria
Barbara, 166, 319, 346;
Maria Catarina, 353; Maria
Catharine, 47; Maria
Elisabetha, 340; Maria
Elizabeth, 129; Maria Eva,
352; Maria Magdalena, 5;
Maria Margar., 346; Maria
Margretha, 5; Martin, 106,
290; Mary Barbara, 200, 241;
Mary Catharine, 201, 216,
245; Mary Eve, 245; Michael,
49, 54, 70, 116, 200, 201,
205, 257, 291, 316; Michel,
251; Mrs., 166; Nicholas, 108;
Philip, 70; Rosina, 190, 194,
312, 322; Susanna, 166, 168,
169; Veronica, 314, 317, 346,
347; Wilhelm, 269
MEYLE, Elizabeth, 200;
Elizabetha, 321; George, 200;
Heinrich, 321; Henry, 200;
Joh. Martin, 200, 205;
Johannes, 321; John, 200;
John Martin, 200, 320, 321;
Sabina, 200; Smauel, 30
MEYLI, Cathr., 18; Cathrina,

18; Georg, 18; Heinrich, 18;
Rahel, 18; Samuel, 18
MEYLIE, Barbara, 346;
Catarina, 346
MEYLIN, Catharine, 3; Johan
David, 3; Martin, 3; Rosina,
113
MEYLY, Anna Sabina, 339;
Catharine, 3; Catherine, 5;
Cathrina, 14, 15, 16, 18;
Elisabeth, 16; Elisabeth
Cathr., 18; Georg, 16;
Heinrich, 5, 14, 15, 344, 356;
Joh. Martin, 14, 15, 181;
Martin, 14, 181, 339; Rachel,
16; Sam., 16; Samuel, 3, 5,
18
MEYSER, Anna Barbara, 167;
John George, 167
MICHAEL, ---, 85; Anna Maria,
85; Catharine, 170; Christian,
351; Elisabeth, 66; Jacob, 66,
221; Ludwig, 86, 170; Maria,
66; Philip, 304; Susanna, 352
MICHEL, Anna Catharine, 88;
Catharine Elisabeth, 64;
Christian, 65; Eva Maria, 64;
Jacob, 62, 64, 65; John
Eberth, 88; Ludwig, 48, 73;
Margaret, 65; Maria, 62;
Regina, 62, 116
MICHLIN, Philip, 303
MICHLING, Mary Cath., 302;
Philip, 302
MIELLER, Catharine, 51;
Frederick, 51; Jacob, 55;
Magdalene, 55; Margaret, 55
MIES, Barbara, 23; Casper, 23;
Catharina, 24; Elisabetha,
23; Philip, 24

MILLERN, Susana, 269
MIMMIAN, Elisabeth, 70; John
George, 70
MINDBOHNER, Herrn Pfarrer,
357
MINIER, Christina, 346
MINJAM, Catarina, 276; Joh
Georg, 276
MINNIC, Margaret, 293
MINNICH, Catharine, 293;
Christina, 293; Eliz., 292,
294; John George, 294;
Margaret, 286
MINNIG, Jacob, 271;
Margaretha, 271
MINTZ, Mary Margaret, 241;
Mary Margaretha, 345
MISCH, Anna marai, 74; Anna
Margaret, 74; Anna Maria,
74; Cath., 239; Elizabeth, 74;
Jacob, 74; John, 74
MISS, Anna Barbara, 26;
Casper, 26
MOCK, Catharine, 51;
Catherine, 51
MOENCH, Christopher, 98;
Maria Sarah, 98
MOGG, Catharine, 53; Eva, 53;
Henry, 53
MOHR, Anna Catharine, 99;
Anna Margaret, 14;
Benjamin, 37, 39, 40;
Catharine, 175; Conrath, 37;
Elisabeth, 37; Elizabeth, 99,
174, 175, 176, 177, 178;
George, 177; Jacob, 175;
Johannes, 37, 353; John, 99,
113, 165, 166, 167, 171, 172,
174, 176, 177, 178; John
Frederich, 323; John George,

323; John Michael, 175;
Magdalena, 37, 39, 40;
Margaret, 208; Margaretha,
26; Maria Magdalena, 39;
Maria Susanna, 166, 167;
Mary Susanna, 172; Michael,
116; Philip, 178; Regina, 115;
Sarah, 37; Susanna, 165,
167, 171, 174, 176
MOLL, John, 276; Susanna, 276
MOLLER, Anna Margaret, 89;
Anna Maria, 89; Daniel, 57;
Dewald, 57; Elizabeth, 124;
Frederick, 57; Jacob, 89;
John, 124; John Nicholas, 89;
Margaret Elizabeth, 89;
Michael, 89; Nicholas, 89
MONGH, Barra, 270; Jacob, 270
MOOR, Adam, 178; Barbara,
178; E., 81; Elizabeth, 178;
John, 178; Moses, 241, 345
MOOSER, Michael, 333
MORDIG, Catharine, 110; Maria
Catharine, 110; Robert, 110,
115
MORELL, Fred., 285; Marg.,
285
MORGAN, Anna, 203; Nancy,
19; Thomas, 19, 203; William,
203
MORR, Andreas, 336, 347; Anna
Catarina, 336; Catarina, 336;
Christina, 336; Margaret, 208
MORREL, Dietrich, 199; Joh.
Nic., 191
MORRELL, Dietrich, 199;
Margaret, 199
MORRIS, William, 345
MORRISON, Robert, 224, 233;
William, 224, 233

Margaret Magdalena, 243;
Maria Catharine, 83, 142;
Maria Elizabeth, 83, 85, 105;
Martin, 290; Martina, 255;
Mary Catharine, 290; Mary
Margaret, 202; Mary Regina,
202; Nicholas, 82; Peter, 83;
Regina, 133, 135; Rosina,
142; Rudolph, 202; Susanna,
193; Valentine, 95, 105, 109
MUENCH, Heinrich, 357;
Stoffel, 293; Susanna, 247
MUENZGER, John, 223
MUENZINGER, Barbara, 224;
Catharine, 224; Conrad, 224
MULLER, Anan Maria, 75;
Anna Maria, 90, 167, 175,
177, 179; Barbara, 35, 41;
Benjamin, 168, 176, 177;
Carl, 1; Carolus, 31;
Catharine, 55, 166, 177, 178,
179; Catherine, 117;
Cathrine, 117; Christian,
112; Christine, 55; Christoph
Frederick, 75; Christopher,
83; Daniel, 90; Elisabetha,
44; Elizabeth, 90, 166, 167;
Eva, 178, 179; Felix, 1;
Frederick, 55, 178; Fridrich
C., 1; Georg, 2; George, 115,
164, 165, 175, 179; Hanna
Maria, 118; Hannes, 35;
Henrich, 44; Henry, 75, 90,
177; Herman, 117; Jacob, 26,
55, 177, 268; Johann
Henrich, 41; Johannes, 26,
41; John, 178; John George,
167, 179; John Herman, 117;
John Nicholas, 167;
Magdalena, 1; Magdalene, 55,

179; Margaret, 178, 179;
Margaret Stump, 53; Maria,
114; Maria Barbara, 83;
Maria Catharine, 164, 165,
166, 175; Maria Elizabeth,
167, 173, 174; Maria
Elziabeth, 168; Martin, 177;
Mary Magdalene, 53;
Michael, 53, 167, 168, 174,
178, 179; Michel, 167;
Nicholas, 175; Rudolf, 29;
Salome, 41; Samuel, 31;
Sarah, 178, 179; Susanna, 1,
29, 90, 268; Valentine, 55
MUNCH, Adam, 270; Catharina,
10; Catharine, 174; Charles,
56; Christina, 270; Christine,
176, 177; Elisabeth, 270;
Ger., 296; Henry, 174; Jac.,
273; Joh., 273; Joh. Heinrich,
10; Johannes, 270, 273; John,
296; Jonathan, 176; Mar.
Cathrina, 10; Margaret, 56;
Michael, 176, 177; Philip,
174; William, 56
MUNCHE, Cathrina, 14;
Christina, 14; Henry, 14
MUNCHIN, Eva, 266; Joh., 274;
Marg., 274
MUNCHS, Adam, 266; Anna
Margareta, 266; Margareta,
266
MUNICH, Benjamin, 176;
Catharine, 173; Catharine
Margaret, 129; Christine,
174, 176; George, 174;
Henry, 173; Maria Elizabeth,
173; Michael, 174, 176
MURR, Andreas, 323
MUTH, John Frederick, 115

PANNEKUCHEN, Catharine, 205; Joh. George, 205; Joh. Peter, 205; Joh. Valentine, 205; Johann Peter, 347; Mary Catahrine, 205; Peter, 205

PANNEKUHEN, John Peter, 242

PANNEL, Elisabetha, 344; Mary, 345

PARSONS, Barnabas, 112

PATTON, Abraham, 12; Elisabeth, 12, 18; Mary, 241; Robert, 18

PATZ, Andreas, 352; Barbara, 155

PAULUS, Jacob, 174; Margaret, 174; Maria Elizabeth, 174

PAWTER, Anna Mary, 207; George, 207

PAXTANG, Anna, 345

PEDER, Catharine, 284; George, 284

PEIER, A. Maria, 14; Michael, 14

PEIFER, Elizabeth, 163; Peter, 163

PEIFFER, Anna Maria, 111; Catharine, 113; Henry, 111; Michael, 111

PEISCHLEIN, Elsa Rosina, 165; John Andrew, 165

PENTER, John, 205; Magdalene, 205; Mary Elizabeth, 205

PERSOHN, Mary Barbara, 205; William Ernst, 205

PERSON, Catharine, 179; George, 177, 179

PERSOUN, Anna Heckeda, 283; Ernst Frederic, 282, 283, 305; Mary Barbara, 283

PESCH, Anna Maria, 165; John Andrew, 165; John William, 165

PETER, Ann Christina, 8; Anna, 225; Anna Catharine, 235; Anna Maria, 26; Barbara, 60, 61, 231, 253; Catarina, 313, 350; Catharina, 26; Catharine, 204, 205, 234, 284, 287; Catharine Regina, 205; Cathrina, 20; Cathrina Elisabeth, 19; Catrina, 252; Christina, 42, 219, 221, 297; Christoph, 61; Christopher, 60; David, 42; Elisabeth, 252; Georg, 36; Georg Heinr., 253, 257; George, 205, 234, 235, 284, 286, 287, 293; George Heinrich, 313; George Henry, 196, 204; Hans Ulrich, 252; Heinrich, 252, 356; Henrich, 42; Henry, 189, 193, 219, 221, 224, 227, 229, 247; Hury, 297; Jacob, 20; Joh., 19, 266; Joh. Conrad, 20; Joh. Henry, 186; Johann, 251; Johann Heinrich, 251; Johann Jacob, 251; Johannes, 8, 351, 356; John, 231, 244, 247, 284; John George, 224; Jorg, 251; Jorg Heinr., 251, 252; Magdalena, 351; Magdalene, 244; Margaret, 189; Margareta, 253; Maria Barbara, 251; Mary Barbara, 284; Mary Christina, 193; Philip, 26; Rudolf, 251, 252;

167; John Adam, 166;
Magdalene, 166; Mary
Christine, 169; Mary
Elizabeth, 170
PONTIUS, Johannes, 323; John
George, 116; John Heinrich,
323; John Peter, 323
PONZIUS, Nicholas, 62
POPELE, Adam, 176;
Catharine, 176
POPP, John, 335
~POPPEL, Magdalene, 85; Peter,
85
PRACHT, John Adam, 102;
Margaret, 102
PREESE, William, 241
PREIS, Barbara, 93; Christine,
93; Georg, 93
PREISS, Elizabeth, 111, 246;
Elizabetha, 355; John Georg,
111; Mary, 246
PRESCHINGER, Jacob, 321
PRESSLER, Maria Elisab., 348
PUGH, Benoni, 305

-Q-
QUARREL, Joseph, 16; Robert,
16; Susanna, 16

-R-
RAAB, Anna Maria, 50; John
George, 50
RAAM, Catharine, 50; Conrad,
50
RACH, Georg Caspar, 257; Joh.,
255
RACK, Laurence, 349
RADDICK, James, 304
RADENBACH, Catharine, 98;
Peter, 98

RADMANN, Salome, 98
RAETELSPERGER, Anna
Maria, 346; Anna Mary, 242
RAFLER, James, 346
RAIER, George, 163
RALLY, Charles, 206
RALMER, Anna Margaretha,
255; Jacob, 255
RAM, Melchior, 17; Melchoir,
11; Rebecca, 11, 17
RAMBERG, Anna Christina,
243, 349
RAMBERGER, Adam, 224;
Anna, 295; Anna Eliz., 306;
Anna Margaret, 292;
Bartholomew, 232;
Catharine, 295; Christian,
207, 295, 305, 306; Christina,
295; Daniel, 224; Elizabeth,
207, 224; George, 207, 224,
292, 298; John, 295, 298;
Magdalene, 295; Margaret,
292, 298; Michael, 295;
William, 295
RAMLER, Barbara, 178, 213;
Eva Eliz., 6; Eva Margaret,
83; Jacob, 83; John, 209, 213;
John Jacob, 325; Leonhardt,
322, 325; Margaretha, 357;
Margretha, 325; Michael, 279
RAMMEL, Barbara, 86; John,
86
RAMMELER, Barbara, 88;
John, 88
RAMMLER, Anna Maria, 102;
Anna Mary, 240; Barbara,
95; Catharine, 99; Christian,
99; Eva, 92; Eva Margaretha,
331; Hoster, 99; Jacob, 92,
93, 331; John, 95, 99; John

309
REES, Jacob, 241
REESE, Jacob, 331; John
    George, 331; John Nicolaus
    David, 331
REESS, Jacob, 345; Mrs., 331
REGEL, Abraham, 224, 226;
    Sarah, 224
REGUEL, Abraham, 224
REHOE, Catharina, 66; Eva
    Christina, 66; John, 66
REHRIG, Carl, 145; Margaret,
    145
REHWALD, Abraham, 10; Anna
    Maria, 3, 10, 17, 18, 23, 355;
    Catharine, 3; Heinr., 18;
    Heinrich, 3, 10, 17; Henrich,
    21, 23; Joh. Christian, 3; Joh.
    Heinrich, 18; Maria, 21
REIBER, Catarina, 353
REICH, Barbara, 173; Matthew,
    173
REICHARD, Carl, 113;
    Catharine, 113; Christopher,
    90; John Michael, 90
REICHART, Barbara, 207;
    Catharine, 207; Charles, 207;
    Dorothea, 207; Elizabeth,
    207; Henry, 207; John
    Henry, 207
REICHERT, Adam, 225, 229,
    230; Elizabeth, 229; Frederic,
    229
REICHS, Elizabeth, 284;
    Michael, 284
REIDEL, Barbara, 56; Christine,
    56; John, 56; Margaret, 56;
    Maria Catharine, 56; Peter,
    56
REIER, Catharine, 120;

Christopher, 120
REIERIN, Elisabeth, 274;
    Michl., 274
REIFEIN, Adam, 280; Barbara,
    275; Jacob, 275; Joh Jacob,
    277
REIFEININ, Anna, 280; Anna
    Elisa, 275
REIFWEIN, Anna Elizbeth, 79;
    Catharine, 75; John Adam,
    74; John Jacob, 74
REIHER, Christian, 207;
    Elizabeth, 207; John, 207
REILY, Anna Susanna, 98;
    Elizabeth, 94, 98; Isaac
    Mayer, 94; John, 94, 98
REIN, Abraham, 49; Anna
    Barbara, 206; George, 242,
    347; Hannah Justina, 206;
    Joh. Charles, 206; Joh.
    Christian, 206; Joh. George,
    206; Joh. Martin, 206; Joh.
    Michael, 206; Valentine, 206
REINHARD, Bernhard, 19;
    Bernhardt, 24; Cathr., 18;
    Elisabetha, 24; Mar. Cathr.,
    11; Maria Cathrina, 7; Maria
    Elizabeth, 7; Math., 18;
    Matheys, 11; Mattheys, 7;
    Veronica, 24
REINHARDT, Bernhardt, 25;
    Elisabeth, 25; Marilisabeth,
    25
REINHART, Bernhart, 28, 31,
    40, 44; Elisabeth, 40, 44;
    Israel, 44; John, 297; Joseph,
    31; Samuel, 40; Susanna
    Cathrina, 28
REINHERT, Eliz., 293, 294;
    John, 293, 294, 301

ROESZLIN, Catarina, 354
ROETELSTEIN, John Heinrich,
330
ROGERS, Martha, 241; Robert,
243, 349
ROHLAND, Abraham, 1
ROHRER, Anna, 65; Anna
Barbara, 6; Anna Maria, 27;
Barbara, 2, 5, 6, 10, 12, 18,
188; Catharina, 30; David, 2,
45; Elisabeth, 45; Elisabetha,
42; Gottfried, 260; Heinrich,
18; Jacob, 12, 65, 188; Joh.,
6, 10, 12; Johann, 5;
Johannes, 27, 30, 33, 42, 44,
45; John, 2, 18; Magdalena,
260; Salome, 42
ROHRIG, Carl, 147, 148;
Christina, 147; Margaret, 147
ROLAND, Abraham, 4, 9;
Elisabeth, 6; Georg, 260;
George, 136, 137; Johann
Philip, 9; John, 136; Maria,
137, 260; Maria Elis., 7;
Maria Eva, 4, 9; Samuel, 114
ROLLIG, Anna Catrina, 253;
Johan Henr., 253
ROMICH, John, 221; Susan, 248
ROMMEL, George, 84
RONNING, Wendel, 331
RONTEL, Elizabeth, 121; John,
121
ROOF, Magdalena, 326; Philip
Jacob, 326
RORIG, A. Margaret, 146; Anna
Margaret, 145; Carl, 145,
146, 149, 152; Cath.
Elisabeth, 145; Christina,
152; Gret, 152; Johannes,
149; Margaret, 145, 149

ROSENBACH, Maria Magdl.,
347
ROSENBAUM, Antonius, 319;
Salome, 319; Susanna, 319;
Valentine, 317
ROSENBERG, Erasmus, 128;
Regina, 128; Rudolph, 128
ROSENBERGER, Anna
Barbara, 206; Anna
Catharine, 206, 207;
Erasmus, 206, 207, 242;
John, 207; John Frederic,
206
ROSS, John, 114; Margaretha,
345
ROSSEL, Jacob, 84, 87; John
Jacob, 84; Margaret, 87;
Maria Margaret, 84; Maria
Salome, 87
ROSSLY, John, 16; Susanna, 16
ROST, Anna Maria, 91; George
Henry, 91; Henry, 91
ROSWEILER, Maria Catharine,
49
ROTH, ---, 255; A. Elisabeth,
146; A. M., 151; Anna
Margaret, 328; Anna Maria,
99, 114; Barbara, 89, 90, 92,
173; Catarine, 316; Cath.
Dorothea, 146; Christina,
147; Elisabeth, 144, 151;
Elizabeth, 126; Georg, 99;
Gottlieb, 144, 146, 151, 153,
353; Gottlieg, 149; Hanna,
149, 153; Jacob, 126, 149,
354; John, 50, 89, 90, 92,
144, 173; John Georg, 103;
John Jacob, 99; John Philip,
126; Margaret, 213;
Margaretha, 354; Maria, 103;

RUPP, Anna Cath., 239; Anna
Mary, 239; Elisabet, 255;
John, 236, 240; Jonas, 135,
255
RUPPERT, Cathr., 268; Joh.,
268; Joseph, 268
RUSSEL, Arthur, 116
RUSSELL, James, 240, 344;
Jane, 240, 344
RUSSLIN, Georg, 3; Susanna, 3
RUTE, Frederick, 74
RUTH, Anna Catarina, 315;
Anna Catharine, 205; Anna
Maria, 77; Barbara, 200, 315;
Catharine, 96; Elizabeth,
178; Frederick, 72; John,
178; Magdalene, 115; Maria
Catarina, 315; Martin, 77;
Mary Barbara, 205; Mary
Catharine, 205; Michael, 96;
Peter, 172, 200, 205, 256,
315
RUTHI, Elizabeth, 97, 98;
Francis, 97; Hieronymus, 98
RUTTER, Benjami, 114
RUY, Elizabeth, 72; Frederick,
72; Jonas, 72

-S-
SAENGER, Anna Gertrude, 86;
Michael, 86
SALLSBERRY, Magdalena, 45;
Sarah, 45; William, 45
SALSMANN, Catharine
Elizabeth, 120; Maria
Catharine, 120; William, 120
SALTZBERGER, Henrich, 40;
Juliana, 40; Maria, 40
SALTZBERRY, Henrich, 42;
Juliana, 42; Margaretha, 42

SALTZEGEBER, Eva, 172;
Henry, 172; John George,
172
SALTZER, Anna Maria, 70;
Catharine, 70, 105; Jacob,
49; John, 70, 105; Maria
Catharine, 49; Samuel, 105
SALTZGEBER, Andrew, 85,
164; Anna Maria, 85, 164;
Catharine, 174, 175, 176;
Eva, 174; Henry, 168, 174;
John, 174, 175, 176
SALTZGERBER, Andrew, 89;
Anna Maria, 89
SALZGEBER, Andrew, 84
SANDER, Anna Mary, 296;
Catharine, 296; John, 296
SANDERS, Salome, 249
SANDERSON, Anna, 230;
Joseph, 230
SANTER, Anna Maria, 271;
Johann, 271
SARG, A. Catharine, 161;
Andres, 161
SARTER, John Henry, 77
SASSAMAN, Joh., 11
SATTELZAN, Adam, 123; Anna
Maria, 123
SATTELZAUM, Adam, 161;
Elizabeth, 139, 161; Jacob,
139; Magdalene, 139
SATTETZAUM, A. Marie, 147;
John Adam, 147
SATTEZAHN, Jacob, 140;
Magdalene, 140; Susanna,
140
SATTEZAUM, A. M., 151; A.
Maria, 144; A. Marie, 153,
157; Adam, 144, 151, 153,
157; Anna Margaret, 144;

Anna Maria, 59, 116;
Catharine, 59, 115, 154, 207;
Elizabeth, 219, 232; George,
154, 333; Henry, 103, 113;
John, 59, 183; John Philipp,
333; Magdalene, 120;
Margaret, 103; Maria, 349;
Mary, 243; Mary Engel, 120;
Michael, 114; Nicholas, 120;
Peter, 154
SCHAERDEL, Bernard, 114
SCHAERTEL, Bernard, 111;
Elizabeth, 111; Mary
Magdalene, 111; Philip, 115
SCHAFER, Alexander, 51; Anna
Eliza, 164; Anna Eva, 51;
Anna Maria, 51, 164;
Catharine, 51, 64, 65;
Christina, 61; Eva, 54;
George, 164; Henry, 54;
John, 51, 64, 65; John Jacob,
164; Maria Magdalena, 64;
Paulus, 164; Sabina, 54;
Susanna, 51, 54; Veronica, 65
SCHAFERIN, Magdalena, 279
SCHAFF, Joh. Peter, 253
SCHAFFER, Abraham, 173,
174; Alexander, 47; Anna
Elisabetha, 6; Anna
Margaretha, 8; Anna
Margreth, 6; Anna
Margretha, 6; Barbara, 259;
Catharine, 61, 173, 174;
David, 14, 15; Elisabeth, 14,
15; Eva, 8; Georg, 276;
Heinrich, 6, 8; Henry, 91;
Jacob, 8; Johannes, 6; John,
61, 168, 171; John Henry,
173; Ludwig, 6; Mar
Catarina, 276; Maria

Margaret, 174; Nicholas, 259;
Philip, 259
SCHAFFNER, Anna Christina,
29; Anna Maria, 21, 40;
Christina, 21, 24, 25, 31, 40;
Eva, 6, 9, 12; Henrich, 21,
24, 25, 26, 29, 31, 34, 36, 40;
Jacob, 6, 9, 12; Martin, 43;
Philip, 6, 26; Sarah, 31;
Veronica, 43
SCHALL, Anna Mary, 186, 195,
210; Cath. Elizabeth, 204;
Catharine Elizabeth, 202;
Elisabetha, 36; Elizabeth,
195; Mary Elizabeth, 204
SCHALLE, Balthasar, 76;
Barbara, 36, 76, 223;
Catharina, 41, 44; Catharine
Elizabeth, 202; Dorothea,
306; Elisabetha, 36;
Johannes, 36, 40, 41; Lucas,
36, 41, 44, 222; Magdalena,
44; Margaret, 76;
Margaretha, 36, 40; Mary
Elizabeth, 222; Mary
Magdalene, 76
SCHALLEN, Anna Maria, 4
SCHALLER, Barbara, 135;
Georg, 258; George, 135
SCHALLEY, Charles, 208; Joh.
Peter, 208; Joh. Valentine,
208; John, 206
SCHALLIE, Johannes, 151
SCHALLIN, Cartrina, 253;
Magdalena, 44
SCHALLY, Adam, 2, 5, 9, 12,
252, 253, 299; Anna Maria, 4,
195; Anna Mary, 195, 210;
Baltasar, 13; Baltaser, 4;
Baltsar, 9; Barbara, 4, 9, 13,

Magdalena, 152; Marie, 158; Micahel, 342; Peter, 144, 145, 146, 147, 148, 152, 153, 154, 158, 160; Philip, 225, 231; Regina, 225, 231; Samuel, 225, 231; Siegmund, 203; Sigmund, 148

SCHAUFFLER, Barbara, 245, 352; Magdalene, 141; Rosina, 131; Valentin, 356; Valentine, 136, 141

SCHAUFLER, Barbara, 259, 262, 263; Christian, 259, 262, 263; Joh. Georg, 262; Magdalena, 261, 262, 263; Maria Elisabeth, 259; Valentin, 261, 262, 263

SCHEDEL, Daniel, 41; Johannes, 41, 270; Maria Elisabeth, 270; Salome, 41, 270

SCHEDT, Carl, 341, 342; Eva, 342; Eva Maria, 356; Margaretha, 341

SCHEFER, Catharine, 68

SCHEFFER, Anna Maria, 121; George, 121

SCHEIB, Martin, 114

SCHEIBLE, Christian, 283; Conrad, 283; Eve, 283; John, 283

SCHEIDT, Carl, 333

SCHEIER, George, 271; Susanna, 271

SCHEIRICH, Anna Mary, 299; John, 299

SCHELL, Andr., 268; Andreas, 266, 267; Anna Catharine, 89; Barbara, 107, 109, 111, 268; Catharine, 87, 91, 301;

Catharine Elizabeth, 89; Christina Regina, 208, 317; Dorothea, 294; Elisabeth, 12; Elizabeth, 267; Heinr., 12; Heinrich, 14, 15; Henrich, 256; Henry, 109, 294; J. Albrecht, 208; Joh. George, 266; Joh. Jacob, 266; John Albrecht, 317; John Henry, 294; John Peter, 87, 89; Margaretha, 12; Maria, 266; Maria Catharine, 118; Maria Margaretha, 14, 15; Martin, 87, 89, 91; Michael, 266; Mr., 81; Peter, 89, 90, 107, 109, 111, 114, 118; Regina, 14, 15; Simon, 301, 302; Sophia, 266, 267, 268; Susan Barbara, 107; Susanna Margaret, 89, 90

SCHENCK, Jacob, 246; John Philip, 167; Maria, 271; Maria Elizabeth, 167; Philip Carl, 167; Rosina, 271; Stoffel, 271

SCHENCKEL, Carl, 174; Maria Elizabeth, 174

SCHENEIDER, Christoph(er), 156; George, 220; Gret, 156; J. Adam, 156

SCHERB, Anna Barbara, 255; Elizabetha, 344

SCHERBLIN, Barbara, 127; Brisilla, 132; Jacob, 132; John Jacob, 132; Priscilla, 132

SCHERCK, Andrew, 131; Anna Maria, 131; David, 20, 21; Elizabeth, 131; Mar. Cathrina, 20; Susanna, 20,

41

SENS, Magdalene, 297
SENSEBACH, Jacob, 342
SENTZEL, John Frederick, 169;
    Wilhelmina, 169
SERGEANT, Jacob, 225; John,
    225; Joseph, 225, 248
SEUBERT, Francis, 56; John,
    56; Mrs., 81; Susanna, 56;
    William, 56
SEYBERT, William, 114
SEYDELMEYER, Johannes, 351
SEYFRET, Catharine, 297;
    Peter, 297
SEYLER, Anna Margaret, 137;
    Anna Maria, 68; Barbara, 5,
    137; Christoph, 19;
    Elisabeth, 19; Elizabeth, 137;
    Eva Cathrina, 10, 13;
    Heinrich, 10, 13; Johannes,
    5; John, 131, 137; John
    Jacob, 133; Maria, 5, 133;
    Peter, 137; Valentin, 68
SHAAF, Peter, 326
SHAEFFER, David, 198
SHAFER, Eva Schneitzer, 54;
    Henry, 51
SHAFFNER, Christina, 19;
    Heinr., 19; Margareth, 19
SHALLY, Adam, 9; Elisabeth, 9
SHANER, Catharine, 152;
    Johannes, 152
SHAQUE, Adam, 12; Barbara,
    12; Cathr. Elisabeth, 12;
    Elis., 12; Elisabeth, 8; J.
    Nicklaus, 18; Jacob, 8; Joh.
    Georg, 8; M. Eis, 18
SHARP, Anna, 240, 344; J.
    Adam, 17
SHAUFLER, Barb., 264;

Christian, 264; J. Wilhelm,
    264
SHAYER, Jacob, 270
SHEREDER, Anne Barbara,
    285, 286; Isaac, 286; John,
    285, 286; John Daniel, 286;
    John Jacob, 286; Mary
    Catharine, 285
SHETEL, Hannes, 272; Salome,
    272; Samuel, 272
SHEYDEL, Johann, 270
SHICK, Eva, 148; Samuel, 148
SHIELIN, Cathrina, 10;
    Lambert, 10; Susanna, 10
SHILLING, Barbara, 187;
    Jacob, 187
SHREIER, Elisabeth, 270;
    Maria, 270; Sim, 270
SHUI, Emanuel, 290
SHUMACHER, Jacob, 309
SHWACH, Johannes, 270
SICHELE, Albrecht, 284;
    Benjamin, 293; Catharine,
    293; Elizabeth, 293; Eva.
    Eliz., 284; J. Albrecht, 208;
    Jacob, 216, 289, 292, 293,
    304; Magdalena, 293; Mary
    Regina, 208; Regina, 210,
    306, 307; Susanna, 216, 292,
    293
SICHELY, Anna Catharine, 235;
    Jacob, 234, 300, 307; John,
    307; John Jacob, 296
SICHER, Eva Catharine, 113
SICHLY, Jacob, 289
SIEBER, Adam, 23; Anna
    Elisabetha, 23; Elisabetha,
    23; Johann, 267; Mar.
    Susanna, 267
SIEBERN, Susanna, 273

SOWDER, Henry, 340; Sabina, 340
SPAETH, Anna Maria, 17; Georg, 17; Susanna, 17
SPALLER, Catarina Barbara, 313
SPANG, Jacob, 114
SPANHUT, Christina, 276; Henr., 280; Henrich, 276, 277; Joh. Heinrich, 280
SPANNHUT, Christian, 275; Henr, 275; Henry, 279; John George, 279; John Jacob, 279
SPANSEILER, Jacob, 202
SPAT, John Peter, 334; Maria Salome, 334
SPECK, Anna Maria, 318, 324; Dorothea, 246; Eleanora, 324; Johannes, 318; John Jacob, 324; John Michael, 324; Margaretha, 322, 334; Maria Catarina, 318; Martin, 312, 318, 319, 321, 324, 330; Michael, 324; Susanna, 312, 330
SPEIGEL, Michael, 333
SPENGEL, Michael, 319
SPENGELER, John, 68; Maria Salome, 68
SPENGLER, Adam, 92, 94, 95; Anna, 179; Anna Maria, 54, 102, 106, 109, 111; Barbara, 97, 102, 111; Catharine, 52, 54, 109, 161; Catharine Christine, 96; Christine, 99, 100, 102, 107, 110; Christine Riegel, 97; Elizabeth, 52, 87, 91, 92, 94, 96, 99, 100, 103; Elizabeth Margaret, 83, 87; Eva, 92, 94; Georg, 97, 102, 111; George, 76; Henry, 111, 115, 179; Jacob, 49, 50, 88, 89, 91, 92, 93, 96, 175; John, 49, 98, 100, 104, 106; John Adam, 111; John George, 76; John Martin, 83; John Peter, 81, 101; Lydia, 102; Magdalene, 76, 92, 104; Margaret, 87; Maria, 100, 101, 103, 107, 110; Maria Catharine, 88, 97, 98; Maria Elizabeth, 49, 50, 88, 89, 93, 103, 175; Maria Margaret, 91; Martin, 97, 99, 100, 102, 106, 109, 111, 114; Mary Magdalene, 98; Michael, 76, 81, 83, 87, 98; Mrs., 89; Peter, 52, 54, 87, 93, 100, 101, 102, 103, 107, 110
SPEYER, Frederick, 52; Margaret, 52
SPICKER, Anna Maria, 21; Benjamin, 21, 23; Catharina, 21, 23; Catharine, 139, 141; Elisabetha, 21; Johanna Regina, 21; Margar. Barbara, 352; Peter, 21, 112, 139, 141; Regina, 21
SPICKERT, John, 73; Regina, 73
SPIEGEL, Anna Eva, 321; Eva Christina, 326; Gottfried, 326; Michael, 321, 326
SPIESS, Anna Margaret, 14; Herman, 14; John Jacob, 330
SPIKER, Anna Maria, 11, 14, 16, 20; Benj., 16, 18; Cathr., 16; Cathrina, 18; Joh. Jacob, 20; Joh. Peter, 16; Johannes, 11; Peter, 11, 14, 16, 20

Matthias, 243
STAUCH, Elizabeth, 113
STAUDT, Maria, 116
STAUFFER, Christian, 234;
 Daniel, 228; Elizabeth, 226;
 Eve, 228; Eve Elizabeth, 234;
 John, 226; Margaret, 226
STAUT, Margaret, 97; Maria
 Sarah, 97; Philip, 97
STAUTT, George, 51; Margaret,
 51
STEANS, Edward, 349
STECHEER, Anna Maria, 32;
 Barbara, 32; Henrich, 32
STECHER, Barbara, 37;
 Elisabeth, 38; Elisabetha, 37;
 Friedrich, 38; Henrich, 37,
 43; Johannes, 43; Peter, 33,
 37; Philip, 43; Regina, 43
STECKBECK, Barbara, 45, 147;
 David, 36; Michael, 36, 45;
 Veronica, 42
STEEGER, Catharine, 112
STEEL, Margaret, 113;
 Rebecca, 114
STEER, Anna Maria, 29; James,
 27; Maria, 28; Moses, 27;
 Schims, 27, 28
STEFFE, Michael, 255
STEFFEN, Anna Mari, 255;
 Johannes, 255
STEG, Maria Elisab., 350; Mary
 Elizabeth, 244
STEGER, Adam, 26; Agnes,
 293; Anna Marg., 7; Anna
 Maria, 35; Baltasar, 4;
 Barbara, 30, 42, 45; Cath.
 Eliz., 4; Catharina, 30;
 Cathrina, 14, 15; Catr.
 Elizabetha, 4; Christina, 293;

Elisabeth, 4, 19, 25, 34, 45;
 Elisabetha, 14, 15, 25, 42;
 Friedrich, 27; Hannes, 29;
 Henrich, 26, 30, 42; Jacob,
 14, 15, 25, 29, 30, 34; Joh.,
 14, 15, 19; Johann Jacob, 30;
 Johann Peter, 26; Johannes,
 19, 25, 26, 34, 45; John, 80;
 Johyann Peter, 29; Peter, 35,
 45; Valentine, 293
STEHER, Elizabeth, 238;
 George, 238
STEHLI, Barbara, 134
STEHR, Johannes, 30, 32
STEIB, Maria, 256
STEIN, Abraham, 133, 135, 136,
 259; Adam, 8, 70, 82, 88, 89,
 131, 141; Anna Catrina, 328;
 Anna Margaret, 82, 85, 88;
 Anna Margaretha, 7; Anna
 Maria, 20, 84, 133, 259;
 Baltzer, 264, 265; Barbara, 7,
 12, 14, 15, 20, 22; Catharina,
 260; Catharine, 88, 172;
 Daniel, 172; Elis, 264;
 Elisabet, 264; Elisabeth, 14,
 15, 152, 260, 261; Elizabeth,
 84, 115, 119, 138; Georg, 7,
 14, 15, 19, 20, 261; George,
 12; Heinrich, 260, 261, 264;
 Henrich, 159, 262, 263;
 Henry, 137, 138, 139; J.
 Adam, 131; Joh., 7, 14, 15,
 20; Joh. Adam, 3, 4; Joh.
 Georg, 4; Joh. Jacob, 263;
 Johannes, 8, 12, 22, 152, 351;
 John, 82, 85, 87, 116, 245;
 John Adam, 82, 83, 84, 85,
 87, 88, 89, 125, 127, 128,
 333; John George, 84, 125;

TAUD, Margaret, 127
TAUNEN, Johannes, 34
TEBEN, Catharine, 124; John, 124
TEE, Georg, 11; Margaret, 11; Thomas, 11
TEINNINGER, Regina, 286
TEISS, Elisabetha, 351; Elizabeth, 244
TEMPELMAN, John Conrad, 252
TEMPELMANN, Barbara, 345; John Cunradt, 344
TEMPLEMAN, Joh. Conrad, 241
TEMPLEMANN, Anna Maria, 251; Barbara, 241, 345; Conrad, 72, 117, 120; Elisabetha, 327; Johannes, 251; Maria, 250; Michel, 251
TENNIN, James, 344
TESCHLER, Barbara, 76; Peter, 76
TESTER, Eva, 14; Peter, 75
TEUFERSBISS, Anna Barbara, 314
TEUSS, Susanna Barbara, 205, 315
THANI, John Jacob, 335
THANY, George, 353
THEIS, Barbara, 103, 106; David, 103, 106; Elizabeth, 106; Michael, 106
THEISIN, Elisabeth, 261
THEISS, Barbar, 112; Barbara, 100; Christian, 177; David, 100; Elizabeth, 73, 76; John, 100; John Michael, 75; Margaret, 91; Maria Elizabeth Bollinger, 177;

Michael, 72, 73, 76; Philip, 76, 114; Regina, 114
THEISSINGER, Nicholas, 113
THEYS, Anna Margaretha, 10; Anna Margretha, 14; Barbara, 5; David, 5, 9, 10, 14, 18; Elisabeth, 14, 18; Elisabetha, 5, 10; Elizabetha, 9; Johannes, 9; Mar. Barbara, 18; Regina, 9
THIEL, Christian, 57
THIESS, Eva Elizabeth, 106; Henry, 106; Magdalene, 106
THISTLE, Elenore, 343; Eleonore, 240
THOM, Anna Maria, 3, 7, 14; David, 14, 224; John, 3, 7, 14; Maria, 3
THOMA, Anna, 52; Anna Wolfersberger, 57; Barbara, 57; Jacob, 169; John, 52, 57; John Jacob, 169; Margaret, 52; Maria Margaret, 169; Martin, 166
THOMAH, Ursula, 4
THOMAS, Anna, 56; Anna Maria, 68, 69, 75; Christian, 69; Elisabetha, 33; Friedrich, 33; Gottfied, 69; Gottfried, 68; Jacob, 4; John, 166; Maria, 68; Maria Elisabeth, 69; Mary Elizabeth, 347; Peter, 114; Susanna, 57
THOME, Anna, 51; Anna Barbara, 60; Anna Mary, 216; Caspar, 60; Jacob, 51; John, 51, 216, 245, 352
THOMEN, Durst, 47; Regina, 47
THOMPSON, Margaret, 242;

TREADY, Nargareth, 13; Sarah,
13; William, 13
TREER, Catharina, 266;
Johannes, 266; Willhelm, 266
TRION, Michael, 175, 176
TROESTER, Frederich, 330;
John Heinrich, 330; John
Jacob, 330
TROMB, Cathrina, 36;
Elisabetha, 37; Georg, 36, 37;
Philip, 37
TROTT, Herman, 215, 318
TROTTER, Anna, 311;
Elizabeth, 311; James, 311;
Margaret, 241; Mary, 311;
Richard, 187; William, 311
TROXEL, John, 226
TRUCKEMUELLER,
Margaretha Elisabetha, 353
TRUMP, Elizabeth, 234
TRUMPF, Elizabeth, 248
TRYON, Eliza., 174; Elizabeth,
173; Mary Elizabeth, 169;
Michael, 169, 173, 174
TSCHOB, Anna Barbara, 64;
Caspar, 64
TSCHOFFT, Hannah, 120;
Jacob, 120; John, 120
TSCHOP, Anna Christine, 78;
Anna Maria, 78; Barbara, 14,
75, 76; Caspar, 14; Casper,
75, 76; Christian, 75; Eva,
14; Jacob, 78; John Peter, 76
TSCHOPP, Anna, 12; Anna
Barbara, 77; Catharine
Barbara, 77; Hans, 48; Jacob,
12; John, 47; John Casper,
77; John Jacob, 48;
Magdalene Stoler, 48;
Regina, 47

TUBBS, Johannes, 258
TUBEN, Amelia, 125
TUBS, Barbara, 33; Henrich,
27, 31, 33; Johann Henrich,
33; Johannes, 31; Maria, 27
TUBSIN, Elisabeth, 258
TUEBEN, Anna Amelia, 126;
Anna Catharine, 128; Anna
Maria, 130; Catharine, 126,
131; Dorothy, 130; Elizabeth,
140, 141; John, 126, 128,
130, 131, 140, 141; John
Jacob, 126; Sabina, 132;
Samuel, 141
TUEBIN, Amelia, 125; Anna
Maria Elizabeth, 128;
Catharine, 128; Jacob, 128
TUGS, Heinrich, 258
TUNGES, Elisabeth, 28;
Hannah, 28, 33; Hannes, 28;
Nicholaus, 28; Nicolaus, 33;
Philip, 32
TUNNINGER, Adam, 291

-U-

UHL, Albert, 265; Elisabet, 265;
Johannes, 265
UHLER, Anastaisus, 211;
Anastasius, 181, 182, 188,
189, 190, 200, 209, 213, 240,
257, 311, 316, 317, 320, 337;
Ann Barbara, 217; Anna
Barbara, 213, 244, 311, 326,
350; Anna Catharine, 196,
338; Barbara, 3, 11, 185;
Catarina Barbara, 350;
Catharine, 205, 209, 214,
239; Catharine Barbara, 213,
244; Christina, 226;
Christoffel, 39; Christoph,

Leonardt, 325; Leonhard, 13; Margaretha, 6, 9; Maria, 13; Maria Barbara, 251; Michael, 184, 213, 240, 251, 253, 255, 257, 322; Philip, 227; Phillippus, 45

UMHOLTZ, Anna Margaret, 126; Bernard, 126; Henry, 124, 125, 126; Jacob, 125; John, 125; Margaret, 125

UNCKSCHEN, Juliana, 113

UNGER, Anna Barbara, 278; Anna Mar, 276; Anna Maria, 279; Eva, 50; George, 136; Johannes, 279; John, 50, 276; Valentin, 276, 279; Valentine, 278

UNGERIN, Anna Barbara, 278

URICH, Catharine, 161; Christian, 89, 161; Elizabeth, 89, 94, 100, 161; Henrich, 161, 163; Johan, 275; Johann, 161, 163; Johannes, 163; John, 100; Susanna, 100; Valentine, 100

-V-

VAN BEBE, Anna, 205

VAN DER SCHLEUSS, Catharine, 105; George, 105; John, 105

VARNER, Jane, 347

VEIT, Carl, 332

VELDE, Henry, 113

VELDEBERGER, Elisabeth, 267; Michael, 267; Michl., 267

VELT, Maria Elizabetha, 349

VELTE, Elisabet, 263; Joh. Henrich, 263; Uhrich, 263

VELTEN, Anna Maria, 340; Elisabeth, 259; Elisabeth Barbara, 259; George, 340; Johannes, 340; Michael, 129; Ulrich, 259

VELTEY, Anna Barbara, 329; George, 328; Johannes, 328; John Cunradt, 329; John Heinrich, 329; John Ulrich, 329; Juliana, 329; Maria Barbara, 329; Sebastian, 329

VELTHE, Elisabet, 263; Sebastian, 263

VELTHIN, A. Maria, 263

VELTIN, John George, 313; Juliana, 131; Maria Elisabetha, 313

VELTY, George, 195, 241, 345; Peter, 209

VENDERSAL, Esther, 271; Heinrich, 271

VETTER, Anna Mary, 290; Anna Sabina, 304; Christian, 290

VETTERHAFE, Baltzer, 150; J. George, 154; M. Elisabeth, 154; Marie, 150; Mathias, 154

VETZEBERGER, Cathr., 23; Daniel, 23

VICMAN, Caspar, 154

VIEHMAN, Adam, 52; Caspar, 50, 260, 261; Casper, 133; Catharina, 260; Catharine, 133, 261; Elisabeth, 71; Eva, 71; Eva Christine, 50; Gertraut, 261; Jacob, 52; Leonard, 71; Susanna, 52; Susanna Margaret, 50; Susanna Sophia, 50;

George, 90, 91; George
Michael, 131; Henry, 186,
216, 244; J. Martin, 18;
Jacob, 39, 45, 178, 290; Joh.
Adam, 193, 245; Joh.
Henrich, 7; Joh. Nicolaus, 10;
Johannes, 18; John, 178;
John Adam, 290, 352; M.
Cathrina, 19; Magdal., 19;
Mar. Elisabetha, 11;
Margaretha, 39, 45; Maria,
178; Mart., 268; Martin, 19,
50, 267, 268; Mary
Catharine, 216; Mary Eva,
216; Michael, 53, 282;
Nicholas, 74, 79; Nicholaus,
255; Nicklaus, 3, 5, 10, 14,
15; Nicolaus, 39, 255;
Susannah Maria, 267
WEISSBACH, Christian, 304
WEISSIN, Magd., 274; Mart.,
274
WEITEL, Catharina, 263;
Daniel, 263; Sara, 263
WEITZ, Martin, 342
WEITZEL, Elias, 218; Elizabeth,
247; Elizabetha, 356
WEIZEL, A. Maria, 14, 15, 19;
Elias, 224; Maria Catharina,
19; Martin, 14, 15, 19
WELS, Elisbeth, 153
WELSCH, Christina, 306; John,
306
WELSH, Anna, 16; Dorothea,
19; Georg, 16, 19; John, 240,
343, 344; Maria Dorothea,
16; Samuel, 346; Sarah, 19
WELSHORN, Daniel, 17; Maria
Elisabeth, 17; Maria
Magdalena, 17

WELTER, Elizabeth, 108; Eva,
107; Magdalene, 107; Peter,
107
WELTZ, Adam, 194; Andreas,
312; Andrew, 217
WENDEL, Christina, 276;
Daniel, 259; Johan, 276;
Madlena, 162; Peter, 115;
Sara, 259
WENDLING, ---, 265; Adam,
136, 138; Anna Maria, 138,
140, 141, 262; Elisabetha, 35;
Elizabeth, 138; Jacob, 140,
141, 262; Johannes, 262;
John Henry, 136; Mary, 236;
Mary Magdalene, 138; Peter,
35, 226; Susanna, 262
WENGERT, ---, 112; Barbara,
160; Catharine, 104;
Elizabeth, 104; John Georg,
104; Joseph, 160
WENNER, A. Catharine, 156;
Jacob, 70, 155, 156, 159, 160;
M. Magdalena, 155, 156;
Magdalena, 70, 156, 159;
Philip, 70
WENRICH, Catharine, 110;
Elizabeth, 173; Esther, 85;
Francis, 85; Jacob, 115;
John, 110; Margaret, 115;
Michael, 173
WENTZ, Jacob, 337, 342; John
Jacob, 337; Maria Catarina,
337; Rosina, 245, 353
WENTZEL, Anna Maria, 63;
Christina, 63, 65, 66; Geo.
Nicholas, 66; George
Nicholas, 63; John Adam, 65;
Nicholas, 65
WEPNER, Johannes, 354

Heritage Books by F. Edward Wright:

*18th Century Records of the German Lutheran Church at Philadelphia, Pennsylvania
(St. Michael's and Zion): Volume 1, Baptisms, 1745–1769*
Robert L. Hess and F. Edward Wright

*18th Century Records of the German Lutheran Church at Philadelphia, Pennsylvania
(St. Michael's and Zion): Volume 2, Baptisms, 1770–1786*
Translated by Robert L. Hess, Ph.D. Edited by F. Edward Wright

*18th Century Records of the German Lutheran Church of Philadelphia, Pennsylvania
(St. Michael's and Zion): Volume 3, Baptisms, 1787–1800*
Translated by Robert L. Hess, Ph.D. Edited by F. Edward Wright

*18th Century Records of the German Lutheran Church at Philadelphia, Pennsylvania
(St. Michael's and Zion): Volume 4, Marriages and Confirmations*
Robert L. Hess and F. Edward Wright

*18th Century Records of the German Lutheran Church at Philadelphia, Pennsylvania
(St. Michael's and Zion): Volume 5, Burials*
Robert L. Hess and F. Edward Wright

Abstracts of Bucks County, Pennsylvania, Wills, 1685–1785

Abstracts of Cumberland County, Pennsylvania, Wills, 1750–1785

Abstracts of Cumberland County, Pennsylvania, Wills, 1785–1825

*Abstracts of Philadelphia County, Pennsylvania, Wills:
Volumes: 1682–1726; 1726–1747; 1748–1763; 1763–1784; 1777–1790;
1790–1802; 1802–1809; 1810–1815; 1815–1819; and 1820–1825*

Abstracts of South Central Pennsylvania, Newspapers, Volume 1, 1785–1790

Abstracts of South Central Pennsylvania, Newspapers, Volume 3, 1796–1800

Abstracts of the Newspapers of Georgetown and the Federal City, 1789–99

Abstracts of York County, Pennsylvania, Wills, 1749–1819

Adams County [Pennsylvania] Church Records of the 18th Century

Baltimore Directory of 1807

Berks County, Pennsylvania, Church Records of the 18th Century, Volumes 1–4

Bible Records of Washington County, Maryland

*Bucks County, Pennsylvania, Church Records of the 17th and 18th Centuries,
Volume 1: German Church Records*

*Bucks County, Pennsylvania, Church Records of the 17th and 18th Centuries,
Volume 2: Quaker Records: Falls and Middletown Monthly Meetings*
Anna Miller Watring and F. Edward Wright

*Bucks County, Pennsylvania, Church Records of the 17th and 18th Centuries,
Volume 4*

Caroline County, Maryland, Marriages, Births and Deaths, 1850–1880

Citizens of the Eastern Shore of Maryland, 1659–1750

Colonial Families of Cape May County, New Jersey, Revised 2nd Edition

*Colonial Families of Delaware:
Volumes: Volume 1; Volume 2: Kent and Sussex Counties;
Volume 3 (2nd Edition): Kent and Sussex Counties;
Volume 4: Sussex County; Volume 5: New Castle; Volume 6: Kent*

Middlesex County Virginia, Marriage References and Family Relationships, 1673–1800

Middlesex County, New Jersey, Records of the 17th and 18th Centuries

*New Castle County, Delaware, Marriage References
and Family Relationships, 1680–1800*

Newspaper Abstracts of Allegany and Washington Counties [Maryland], 1811–1815

Newspaper Abstracts of Cecil and Harford Counties [Maryland], 1822–1830

Newspaper Abstracts of Frederick County [Maryland], 1811–1815

Newspaper Abstracts of Frederick County [Maryland], 1816–1819

*Northampton County, Virginia, Marriage References
and Family Relationships, 1634–1800*

*Northumberland County, Virginia, Marriage References
and Family Relationships, 1645–1800*

Orphans' Court Proceedings of New Castle County, Delaware, 1742–1761

Quaker Minutes of the Eastern Shore of Maryland: 1676–1779

*Quaker Records of Henrico Monthly Meeting and Other Church Records
of Henrico, New Kent and Charles City Counties, Virginia*

Quaker Records of South River Monthly Meeting, 1756–1800

Richmond County, Virginia, Marriage References and Family Relationships, 1692–1800

Sketches of Maryland Eastern Shoremen

St. Mary's County, Maryland, Marriage References and Family Relationships, 1634–1800

Stafford County, Virginia, Marriage References and Family Relationships, 1661–1800

Supplement to Maryland Eastern Shore Vital Records, Books 1–3

Sussex County, Delaware, Marriage References, 1648–1800

Sussex County, Delaware, Wills: 1800–1813

Tax List of Chester County, Pennsylvania, 1768

Tax List of York County, Pennsylvania, 1779

The Maryland Militia in the Revolutionary War
S. Eugene Clements and F. Edward Wright

Vital Records of Kent and Sussex Counties, Delaware, 1686–1800

Washington County [Maryland] Church Records of the 18th Century, 1768–1800

Western Maryland Newspaper Abstracts, Volume 1: 1786–1798

Western Maryland Newspaper Abstracts, Volume 2: 1799–1805

Western Maryland Newspaper Abstracts, Volume 3: 1806–1810

Wills of Chester County, Pennsylvania, 1766–1778

York County, Pennsylvania, Church Records of the 18th Century, Volume 1
Marlene S. Bates and F. Edward Wright

York County, Pennsylvania, Church Records of the 18th Century, Volume 2
Marlene Strawser Bates and F. Edward Wright

York County, Pennsylvania, Church Records of the 18th Century, Volume 3

York County, Virginia, Marriage References and Family Relationships, 1636–1800

York County, Virginia, Wills Inventories and Accounts, 1760–1783

www.ingramcontent.com/pod-product-compliance
Lightning Source LLC
Chambersburg PA
CBHW071352290326
41932CB00045B/1429